THE RALPH GLASSER OMNIBUS

Ralph Glasser spent his childhood and adolescence in the Old Gorbals of Glasgow. Taken from school at fourteen he became a barber's soap boy and a presser in a garment factory. After years of night study he won a scholarship to Oxford.

A psychologist and economist, he was concerned for many years with development problems, mainly in the Third World, campaigning against the destruction of traditional communities.

THE
RALPH GLASSER
OMNIBUS

RALPH GLASSER

BLACK & WHITE PUBLISHING

This omnibus edition first published 2006 by
Black & White Publishing Ltd
99 Giles Street, Edinburgh EH6 6BZ

ISBN 13 978 1 84502 082 8

ISBN 10 1 84502 082 0

Growing Up In The Gorbals was first published in 1986
by Chatto & Windus Ltd

Gorbals Boy at Oxford was first published in 1988
by Chatto & Windus Ltd

Gorbals Voices, Siren Songs was first published in 1990
by Chatto & Windus Ltd

A CIP catalogue record for this book is available
from the British Library.

Printed and bound by
Nørhaven Paperback A/S

Contents

GROWING UP IN THE GORBALS

GORBALS BOY AT OXFORD

GORBALS VOICES, SIREN SONGS

GROWING UP IN THE GORBALS

I

Charlie Disappears to Russia

Charlie Varnett said: 'We're all going back to Russia soon.'

'Going back?' I said, stupidly. 'But you've never been there?'

'I mean, my dad wrote to Russia asking to let us – the family I mean – go back and they've said "yes" and so we're going.'

Charlie's parents were immigrants from the old Russia, or rather from its dominion Lithuania, where the family name had been Varnaitis; they had 'Englified' it, as they put it, into Varnett. Their children had been born here.

We were eight years old.

As Charlie's announcement struck fully home, the cobbled pavement cracked apart at my feet. Charlie had been a solid foundation in my world, my close friend, my *alter ego*. *Had* been – for these words of his, crisply uttered but with an underlying thrill of excitement, had changed everything. That relationship now belonged to another time, already distant, no longer to be reached out for with the ease and simple confidence of other days, but remembered for what it had been, a constant understanding, an unquestioning acceptance, a support that never failed, which I would forever recall as a magical gleam in the dark forest of the past, and wonder at it through my tears.

The words now hung in the air between us, containing an unknowable power that pushed us apart. He was still physically with me, and yet – the most puzzling thing to my childhood heart – part of him was not there, or rather had changed; the emotional linkage between us was now mixed with another, bitter quality. He was not as he had been. He had already begun to move away, and belonged, inexplicably, frighteningly, to a different world. The distance dividing us was a raw wound whose edges, hard as steel, rasped and cut and stung – and could never heal.

So life was taking him away from me for ever. For ever? What was that? It was something people said, meaning, I supposed, a long time. 'She's gone away for ever!' was what they had said when mother died two years ago. The word cancer, which I had also heard at the time, meant nothing. The words 'gone away' suggested a commonplace departure on a journey. So people could just 'go' for ever? *Never* was a thought impossible to grasp. And yet mother had *not* come back from that journey. I *did* know, somewhere in my heart, yet feared the knowledge, what 'for ever' meant. And Charlie too would go *for ever*. That was what death meant. Now I knew. Mother and now Charlie. And that was how life would go on, from one death to the next.

Under the grey autumn sky a steely wind had been blowing in from the Clyde, and we had pushed against it with hunched shoulders as we walked, halting sometimes to put cupped hands over our mouths to warm them with out breath. The wind blew straight through me.

Charlie was slightly built, with abnormally high shoulders, the result of some spinal deformity which had also rounded out his chest so that he looked barrel-shaped. Malnutrition was rife in the Gorbals, exacerbating any abnormalities from birth. Rickets was common. Many children had bone and joint deformities, bow legs, knock knees, limbs of unequal length. Some clanked along with a leg enclosed in iron struts from ankle to knee, or thumped the ground with an iron frame attached to the sole of a boot, a device to make a short or bowed leg function as though it were of equal length with the other. These were everyday sights.

Charlie always looked steadily at the world with his wide grey eyes, marching straight ahead, confidently meeting life as it came. Never, for instance, did he get drawn into a fight, an immunity foreign to life in the Gorbals. Not that he did anything especially to avoid a fight. Some rare quality reached out to people like an invisible ray of peace and drained their aggression away.

Fights often had themes, each with its own season. In spring, mysteriously, the constant obsession with Catholic and Protestant feuding erupted in battles between two factions – the Billies and the

4

Dans. The Billies were identified with the Protestant interest, and the Dans with the Catholic. What Billy? Why Dan? The Billies, I speculated when older, no doubt took their sobriquet from William III and the Battle of the Boyne – echoes of Ireland were strong in Glasgow – but why 'Dan' should mean Catholic remained a mystery. One day in the Abbotsford School playground, a windy expanse of concrete with a rain gutter sloping down the middle of it from the smog-darkened sandstone Victorian buildings, enclosed by high cast-iron railings with a knobbed bar along the top, a gang of boys had rushed at us shouting a challenge:

'Wha' are yese – Billy or a Dan? Billy or a Dan?' Fists up, they were going to beat us to pulp if we gave the wrong answer.

This was the first time either of us had heard of 'Billy' or 'Dan'. And we had no idea which faction *they* belonged to. This was war and no mistake. You had to answer the challenge one way or the other even if you had no means of knowing, as in this case, what the words meant – and answer *quickly*, or you got a beating willy nilly. So we stood a fifty-fifty chance of getting that beating whether we answered 'Billy' or 'Dan'.

Charlie's deeply sunken chin moved up a fraction. Undisturbed, he studied the gang one by one as they crowded round us. Red-faced, their excitement crackling electrically in the air, they hurled the challenge at us over and over again.

In a quiet, enquiring voice, he asked: 'Whit's a Billy? An' whit's a Dan?'

They were shocked into silence. Then from their midst came a thin, plaintive cry: 'Och don't yese know then?'

'No.'

The leader, a heavily built, shock-headed boy whose red hair almost matched the high colour of his wind-reddened face, pushed up close to us and seemed about to explain. And then, as if something snapped in the air around us, all the dynamism of the moment faded. To explain to us a cause whose meaning they themselves almost certainly did not understand, was suddenly too heavy a burden. They had never enquired into it, sanctified by battle as it was. Charlie's question came to them as sacrilege, and yet his stillness of the spirit, his solid innocence, left them nothing to oppose, nothing to do battle about. Some primitive sense of justice may have played its part too, which would be violated it they were to fight without a cause to defend. The gang shuffled and muttered, and in a moment streamed away to find some other target, and we were left alone.

When Charlie made his calm announcement about going to Russia, we were passing the gates of Dixon's Blazes, the blast furnace near our school on the southern fringe of the Gorbals. Outside the twenty-foot high gates were clustered a couple of dozen men in cloth caps, fustian jackets and mufflers, heavy black trousers tied with string below the knees. Lantern-jawed, saturnine, faces glazed with cold, collars turned up under their ears and heads bowed, they stood huddled in upon themselves, sheltering within their own bodies, as sheep do on a storm-swept hillside. Now and then they stamped their feet against the cold. A few others trudged back and forth along the pavement under Dixon's high brick boundary wall with its covering of poster hoardings, then returned to their vigil at the gates. Here and there a man would light up a Woodbine from a paper packet of five and take a long slow draw, expanding his chest and holding in the smoke, and blow it out between narrowed lips. A few moments later he would take another; and then, bending over the cigarette with wistful care as he held it with finger and thumb close to the lighted end, flick the red tip cleanly away with his thumb nail, and slide the shortened cigarette back again into the flimsy packet.

Oh that magical tracery of wild honeysuckle on those packets of green and gold! Child of this industrial city, I had never set eyes on honeysuckle, and yet this image on the packet wove a powerful spell. I kept a number of these little paper packets and marvelled at the perfect repetition, time after time, of those stylised tendrils and blooms, instigators of dreams.

Woodbines were tuppence for five, fourpence for ten. If a man could afford to buy ten cigarettes at one time, the packet would not be of paper but of stiffish paste board. A twenty-packet was made of ever more substantial card, no doubt because it had to last much longer. You did not often see one; a man had to be flush, maybe have backed a winner with the street bookie, or had a birthday, to possess *twenty* Woodbines.

Between puffs the man would hold the cigarette with the lighted tip facing inwards into his cupped hands so as to get the fullest comfort from the little point of warmth.

When, by these restrained instalments, the cigarette was smoked down to a 'dout' too short to hold between finger tips and smoke on its own, the man would store it away in an empty Woodbine packet he kept for the purpose. When he had saved up enough 'douts' he would carefully pick away the remnants of cigarette paper that clung to them, tease out the little balls and shreds of tobacco, darkened from burning and from saliva, and rub them together between the palms to form a cylinder of 'makings'; then, using a leaf of Rizla cigarette paper, roll a cigarette. If he could not afford a packet of those pre-gummed papers he would use a piece of newspaper as a wrapping for the 'new' cigarette and stick the edge down with gummed paper torn from the flap of an old envelope or, failing that, with his own spittle. The result, bulky and irregular in shape, could contain twice – or thrice – smoked tobacco, and gave out such a pungent smell that old soldiers said it reminded them of burning camel dung.

These men waited for a stroke of luck, a call for extra hands. It could come at any moment, or you could wait for weeks; and you had to be there and ready for it. Often enough this good fortune came because ill-luck had befallen someone else, an accident inside the works. A man might stumble too near a flow of molten metal. With luck he might suffer nothing worse than a bad burn. More seriously he could be hit by material falling from an overhead gantry crane. If he were unlucky? We would hear the men outside the gates exchange grim anecdotes, of terrible things – of men crippled for life, or killed outright. The concluding words of one of these tales gave men nightmares for a long time: 'There was nothing left of the poor bugger but his feet!'

When an accident took a man out of a work gang, his absence could jeopardise an entire chain of processes and result in considerable financial loss, and sometimes additional danger to other workers; an immediate replacement had to be found. And so, at the very moment that a victim was being carried away, a call would go to the gates for a man to take his place. As the ambulance drove away with the injured man, those waiting would follow it with narrowed eyes, and turn to each other and mutter: 'Aye. Tha' yin had 'is number on it!' – a piece of fatalism brought back from the trenches in France.

To us eight-year-olds the sight of men waiting there day in and day out, in rain and sleet and snow, aroused no special feelings; it was a natural feature of the living world. With the fleeting curiosity of children we did sometimes ask: 'Why are these men not working?' The word unemployment meant little to us, but we did know, again a familiar phenomenon, that people who were not working went 'on the Broo' – the Unemployment Bureau, a great room crowded with shabbily dressed cloth-capped men standing about in straggly lines. Along one wall were high counters like a defensive barrier, behind which were clerks with card index boxes before them. They took cards out, wrote something on them and put them back in the boxes again. When a man got to the head of his queue he would answer cryptic questions posed by the clerk and sign a card; then he would go to another counter where a clerk would give him a few shillings to jingle in his pocket.

If a man could not go on the Broo, for some reason we did not grasp at the time – usually because he did not have enough stamps on his employment card or had run out of 'benefit' through long unemployment – he went 'on the parish', Public Assistance, to get food, boots and clothing for himself and his family, and blankets and coal in winter. Inexplicably, the grown-ups thought that being 'on the parish' was shameful.

One thing was certain about the Varnett family's decision to return to Russia: unemployment was not the cause. Charlie's father, an experienced foundryman in Dixon's Blazes, was always in work. Probably, looking back on it, the Russian authorities had allowed him to return because they needed skilled men for their build-up of heavy industry. Mr Varnett's impulse to go arose from an upsurge of political hope. The Russia he said he was going to was the

Utopia he and so many other visionaries had dreamed would one day come to pass. It was a changed land, and not the one he had left; it was a new world in which the workers ruled, not the old despots who had ground the faces of the poor.

The Bolshevik Revolution was only about ten years old. We had heard so much about it and understood so little. The grown-ups talked endlessly about it – exalted, wistful, wondering, eager. In that strongly immigrant milieu the intellectual influence of the Enlightenment was strong, with all its Continental rigour and emotional intensity, Romantic in its belief in the perfectibility of man, and in its high-flown evangelical language. The heady atmosphere would have been familiar and congenial to Herzen and Bakunin.

At the Workers' Circle, over a bakery in Oxford Street near Gorbals Cross, at almost any hour, in clouds of throat-catching cigarette smoke, men sat and reshaped society, as children tirelessly experimented with plasticine or clay. The Circle was a social and political club, union supported, a gathering place for immigrant Jews. It had three rooms and a little kitchen. Two small rooms were for quiet study, committee meetings, English classes, cards; the large room, starkly white-washed, served as drawing room and open debating chamber, an indoor version of the piazza or village square. It was furnished with a few brown stained tables whose tops had the grain picked out in a lighter shade, long wooden benches against the walls, a scatter of old brown bentwood chairs. In bookshelves fixed to one wall were rows of revered source books – Mill, Spencer, Marx, Engels, Keir Hardie, Lenin, Kropotkin, de Leon, Kautsky. Heaps of socialist and anarchist papers and pamphlets, dog-eared and tea-stained, lay on a table nearby. On the walls, in frames of slender gilt, hung faded sepia pictures of Kropotkin, Marx, and Proudhon, and one of frock-coated men brandishing guns and sabers at a Paris Commune barricade. On a small round table at the rear, near a grimy window that overlooked the baker's yard, a shiny brass samovar bubbled and hissed. In the middle of the room stood a bulbous grey charcoal stove, the wide black flue of which went straight up to the ceiling and then across to an outlet near the window.

Sometimes, drawn to the warmth there, Charlie and I wandered up the reverberating wooden staircase and stood staring in at the doorway, thumb in mouth. Perhaps, with a child's fresh insight, I understood, more profoundly than they did themselves, why these men congregated there: that they found consolation, a spiritual refuge from the struggle with the day-to-day world, a place to recharge their dreams.

They sustained themselves with milkless tea and sometimes with black bread from the bakery. They talked with the certainty and passion of people who saw a bright deliverance within reach, convinced that they were in the van of those who would secure it. Listening to their throaty talk, so often punctuated by tubercular coughs and spitting, voices often raised in impatience with one another, it was possible to believe that at any moment they would compel the world to realise their dreams. Restless exiles, making a hard life in an alien environment, they nourished their souls by fixing their gaze on the far horizon, obstinately proclaiming the innocence of man and his necessary unity with all his kind. Theirs was a desperate optimism. Like storm-lost navigators they fed their hopes with signs and portents. For many of them the Bolshevik coup in Russia was 'the new dawn of human betterment'. Soon the whole of mankind would be delivered from the burdens of poverty, class, despotism, religious prejudice – for Jewish socialists the crucial evil of the old order. Life would be bright and rewarding. Man's nature would become a hundred per cent good once something called capitalism had been everywhere destroyed as it had now been in Russia.

Some of the families in our tenement building pooled resources to give the Varnetts a farewell tea. The Victorian building, in red sandstone blackened by smoke from Dixon's Blazes, was in decay. Splintered and broken floor boards sometimes gave way under your feet. The minimal plumbing hovered on the verge of collapse. Interior walls carried patches of stain from a long succession of burst pipes or ill-mended leaks. Rats and mice moved about freely, seeming to share the accommodation with us grudgingly, as if *we* were the intruders and they the rightful occupiers. Although every family set traps night after night, and dozens of marauding cats, some half-wild, maintained bloody patrols, the rodent population did not noticeably diminish. On the common staircases, six or eight flats shared two lavatories, each tucked into a tiny intermediate landing between two floors. You had to hold its decrepit door shut with your foot or wedge it with a lump of wood. And when the flush system did not work or the soil pipe was blocked, which was often, the floor was soon awash and the overflow spread freely down the main staircase. Going to the lavatory, we had to remember to carry a supply of newspaper, not only for use as toilet paper but also to clean the soles of our boots of excrement and urine before going back into the flat.

For this special day every possible surface on our staircase, inside and outside the flats, had been scrubbed with carbolic soap. Above all, in the festive room itself unfamiliar luxury had been produced. There was a real linen tablecloth of dazzling white, stiff as cardboard, with hard ridges where it had been folded and put away after its use long ago at some other great occasion, a 'briss' – circumcision – perhaps, or a wedding. It may well have lain in the pawnbroker's shop round the corner, been redeemed for this one occasion, and would go back there tomorrow. There were big flowered teapots with wicker handles topped with silver knobs, and best china cups and saucers and plates; and little dishes piled with lumps of sugar, for many of the grown-ups preferred to drink tea in what we understood to be the Russian style, a lump of sugar held between the teeth and the tea sucked through it with a loud indrawing of breath. There were great dishes of sliced pickled herring, and plates heaped with home-baked sponge cake.

All this was set out in the parlour of one of the larger flats, which was crowded elbow tight to the walls; and overflow filled the little hallway. The place seemed to be heaving as people struggled to pass the tea and the plates of food from hand to hand, with everyone shouting across to one another or to catch the ear of Mr Varnett or his wife at their place of honour at the head of the table. It seemed as if the whole street was there, all talking at once.

We children were given especially big helpings of cake as a treat.

But my sadness enclosed me totally, and I could eat nothing. My piece of cake was soon drenched with tears.

Mr Varnett gave out an address, a foundry on the Lithuanian border. He would write to us and tell us about the new workers' paradise. The grown-ups talked excitedly about it. Most of the Jews present struggled with bitter memories. Was it true that in this new dispensation, with Jews in positions of power, oppression of Jews was ended? Had the workers in Russia, regardless of race or creed, entered upon their birthright at last? Oh brave new world!

How wistfully they talked – but with a mixed happiness. Certainly some of those present envied the Varnetts as well as being pleased for them. Other faces were shadowed, not so much by the sadness of parting but by something I would understand only when much older: an unidentifiable foreboding.

On a dark December day a large group from the street walked with the Varnetts to the station to see them off on the train to Leith where the Russian boat would be waiting. A cold mist rose like grey steam from the brown water of the Clyde as we went across the Victoria Bridge from Gorbals Street. My ribs felt frozen and separate from the rest of me, confirming a sense of unreality and isolation. Moisture from half-melted snow on the pavements seeped through the carboard I had put in my boots to cover the holes in the soles. Some of the children had nothing on their feet at all, so I was lucky. But the cold was really within me. I still could not take hold of the thought that someone so close to me should go so far away, a whole world away.

Charlie wore a heavy grey jacket, made from one of his father's, black trousers of thick cloth, 'polisman's cloth' we called it, and heavy tackety boots. His two sisters also wore their 'other' clothes, as best clothes were called, made of stiff fustian, to which home-knitted scarves of thick rope-like wool added some colour. Charlie held his mother's hand and stared straight in front of him; he held his shoulders higher than usual. We did not accompany them on to the platform: we could not afford the pennies for platform tickets. At the gate Charlie turned and looked at me with his usual steadiness but this time with something added. He seemed to want to transmit to me, as a parting gift, a beam of confidence; and also to draw the moment into his mind and store it carefully away. A gentle smile flickered over his face. He sensed that this parting hurt me more than it did him. Charlie was one of life's accepters. Not in any meek sense; he opened himself fully to what the moment had to offer and then fashioned it into something of his own. Yet he did care about what was happening now, to us, to him and to me, and wanted to show me that he did, so that the thought would give me some comfort. He gripped my hand, and I could see he was trying very hard to think of exactly the right thing to say to me. Later, much later, I would understand how far beyond our eight-year-old emotional understanding and strength the demands of that moment were.

At last he spoke: 'I wonder,' he said gravely, 'when we shall be seeing each other?'

All I wanted to do was to stop him going. I was filled with fury at my helplessness, a new and frightening feeling, at the thought that I was held fast by time and age and the mystifying ways of the grown-up world. A torrent of words rushed through my mind but I choked them all back as useless.

Mr Varnett took his hand and led him away. My eyes were so full of tears that I could see Charlie only dimly through them, and all I properly sensed was the thudding of his tackety boots on the stone platform, growing fainter as the little group trudged away from us.

I stayed pressed against the iron trellis gates, and stared and stared, and poured tears on to the cold metal. I heard the engine whistle. Charlie and his father and mother and sisters, huddled at a carriage window, leaned out and waved, their faces reddened and moist. And then, once more, came the engine's imperious whistle, the last farewell. The couplings clanked rat-at-tat all along the train as the whole long line jerked into motion; and then the chuff-chuffing engine dragged it all away out of sight. I shut my eyes, for I could not bear to watch it go. And then, when all sound of it had died away, I opened my eyes and dully contemplated the empty platform, a still-life of forlorn wheelbarrows and dead leaves of newspaper scattered by the freezing wind that stretched grey into the distance to where, beyond the station canopy, the dark winter sky pressed down upon the world.

A piece of ice was stuck fast within me. I fought against the knowledge that Charlie had walked away out of my life. How could something like that be for ever?

Months went by. No letter came; not from Charlie nor from Mr Varnett nor from any of them. Not a single family heard from them. I wrote to Charlie, many times. Other families wrote to the Varnetts. Whether our letters reached them no one ever found out. In daydreams I saw the train that had taken them away, fixed in that moment, and it seemed to me that perhaps it was still journeying, that it would journey on for ever, out there somewhere in a cold desert of time.

We children, naturally monitoring the conversation of the grow-ups, picked up their perplexity at the fact that no word had come, no sign, not even a rumour. We sensed a nagging disquiet too, and recalled the shadow on the faces of some of the guests at the farewell party.

One evening in the following spring, I was loitering at the street door that gave on to the staircase that led up to the Workers' Circle. A few steps away was the door of Feinstein's bakery, a favourite place to linger. I loved to be near the baker's sweet and magical warmth that made the air come alive, and the feeling – which I could put into words only much later – that the bakers were working with the living stuff of life, continuing in that hot chamber the life-giving work of the sun and the rain in the fields, and that I shared the magic by being close to them.

On a lucky day one of the men might throw me the burnt end of a loaf, hot from the oven; or even, as an additional treat, let me stand near the ovens and watch them unload the trays and pile the hot bread into deep baskets, my head filled with the powerful yeasty aroma and my heart full of the mystery of it all.

Mottel Bialystoker, a burly man wearing a flat baker's cap and flour-white shirt and trousers, stood at the door taking the air, floury forearms folded, watching people hurrying home from work, greeting acquaintances with a nod, exchanging a word here and there. Pyotr Lavinsky, a cabinet maker who lived in the next tenement on our street, came along. Short and stocky, his hair nearly white, he walked with a stoop, said to be a mark of his trade; but I had also heard that it was due to bad eyesight, worsened by peering at poorly printed political pamphlets through six-penny Woolworth's spectacles. A dirty white apron showed below a ragged jacket. About to enter the adjacent doorway that led to the stairs up to the Workers' Circle, he turned to the baker:

'Motelleh, tell me – have *you* heard anything? From Leibel Varnett yet?'

'No, Pyotel, nothing – nothing at all!' Mottel shook his head frowning, 'And no one else has either. I don't know what to think.'

They spoke Yiddish, the common language, as I explain later, of Jews of eastern Europe and large areas of Russia. First heard at his mother's breast, every Jewish child understood it.

The two men stood facing one another in a communion of sad silence. Pyotr rubbed his unshaven chin and expelled his breath in a loud sigh:

'Ech! How can we know what to think, eh? An accident perhaps? But then an accident, God forbid, wouldn't happen to every single one in the family? *Somebody* would be left to send news to their friends and tell us how they are! It is not much to ask it? Leib Varnett is not the man to turn his back on his old friends like this!'

'Maybe,' the baker began in a low voice, glancing about him cautiously. Seeing me he hesitated, then shrugged and went on, 'Maybe – who knows – could it be that things have not turned out so well for them? And Leibel is ashamed to write back and tell us? He was always a proud man, no?'

Pyotr became excited. 'No, no, Motteleh! How could that be? Look at the pamphlets from Russia we have up there!' – he gestured up at the windows of the Workers' Circle rooms – 'Look at the marvellous pictures! Happy people! Smiling and healthy children! Everything is good for the workers there! Great new factories! No one goes hungry or without shoes for his children if he is willing to work; and if he cannot work then it is all right also, for it is the dictatorship of the proletariat, remember! The workers are in charge, and they'll look after you! It is all there in black and white! You should come up and see for yourself.'

Mottel shook his head. 'No. All that anarchism and bolshevism's not for me. Live and let live! That's what I say. I don't believe all the things they write down in those revolutionary papers of yours. It's all propaganda – "Come the revolution and everybody is changed into an angel!" No. Everyone's out for himself – and why should it be different over there in Russia? It's human nature! Always has been and always will be.'

Pyotr moved his shoulders impatiently. This was obviously an old, long-continued argument: 'Anyway, Motteleh, we disagree! We agree to disagree – no? But still,' again he sighed, 'it does worry me that no word has come.'

They stood in silence, as if sharing a prayer.

'Maybe,' the baker said meditatively, 'Maybe, after all, the truth is that life there is harder than anybody knows?'

The other seemed about to reject this hotly but thought better of it.

Beginning to turn away, he spoke a little over his shoulder: 'No, but one day, you wait! We will know the truth.'

Some time after that I wandered into the Gorbals public library and went up to the counter.

'Please, Miss,' I asked the young woman assistant, 'Could you tell me the address of the high heid yins in Russia?'

She seemed a kindly woman. She had large round spectacles, and wore a floppy grey blouse fastened at the neck, oddly I thought, with a man's black tie. She looked at me in astonishment and then leaned far over towards me, flattening her blouse on the counter.

'And what d'ye mean, my little man?' she asked in a humouring voice.

'I want to write tae the high heid yins of Russia about my friend Charlie Varnett that went there a long time ago. And they said they'd write and nothing's come. And we've written an' written tae them and got nae answer! That's why.'

She looked at me carefully for a time. I stood my ground. Then I thought her eyes became wet, for she took off her glasses and dabbed her eyes with a little lace-trimmed handkerchief. Then she opened a door in the counter and said, 'Come on in here. Ye're a brave little man. You come in and sit here beside me for a minute.'

I went in behind the counter and sat down beside her desk and she gave me a sweet.

I put it in my mouth and then a worrying thought struck me. Was she trying to put me off? I tucked the boiled sweet into a corner of my mouth and said firmly: 'But, Miss, I do want to write to Russia!'

'Aye, I know ye do,' she said seriously, but with a gentle smile, 'And I think I might be able to help you. You just sit there a minute while I go and look up something in a big book. And then we'll see.'

She came back holding a writing pad: 'Now, little man, I have written down here the address of the Russian Embassy in London. An embassy is a kind of big house the governments of other countries have in this country. Now then, have you got the address of your friend in Russia?'

'Aye, I have it here.' I held out the crumpled piece of paper. 'His feyther gave i' oot just before they all went.'

'Wait a minute,' she said.

She sat down and took a sheet of paper and wrote:

To whom it my concern, Embassy of the Soviet Union, London:
I am writing this on behalf of a brave little boy of eight whose close friend, another little boy of eight, went to live in your country some months ago with his parents, Mr and Mrs Varnett, giving the following address for letters. ... As he has written many times without receiving an answer, it is possible that there has been some mishap in the post or a mistake in writing down the address. Since your government's records will show where the Varnett family are living, I am sure that this little boy would be made very happy, and that he would be very, very grateful, if you could be so kind as to arrange for his letter, enclosed herewith, to be forwarded to his friend? I do hope that this can be done. Thanking you in anticipation ...

She took a large envelope, and wrote on it the address of the Russian Embassy.

'Now,' she said to me, 'You run off home and write your letter to your friend, put it in an envelope with his name on it and the address you were given, but don't stick it down. And, mind, don't forget to write your own address very clearly, in block capitals, on the back of the envelope to show who it is from. Bring it back here to me and I'll put it into this big envelope together with this little note that I've written asking them to send your letter on. And maybe they'll be very kind and do that! And then let's hope you get an answer from your friend Charlie. It's worth trying anyway.'

I came back the next day with my letter, and watched her put it with her note into the big envelope.

'Here,' she said, 'I've got a book of stamps in my handbag. Because you're a brave little man I will put a stamp on it for you. And now you take it and post it.'

Before I could say anything to stop her she had licked the stamp and pressed it down on the envelope.

'Oh Miss,' I said, crying a little, 'I've go' a stamp here ready.'

'Never mind. Use it next time, I'm giving it to you as a little present because I like what you've done! Run along then and post it, and come back and tell me when you get an answer.'

A few weeks later my letter came back stamped: 'Communication not permitted.'

Not many years later, with the Moscow show trials, I would see the true face of that world that had swallowed up Charlie Varnett, and which thought it dangerous for him to be in touch with me. Meanwhile, in lingering emotional shock, sadly daydreaming, I threw questions into the silence. *Why* did the great ones in Russia not want Charlie to write to me – or his father or mother or sisters – and tell us what it was like there? What sort of people would stop a letter from Charlie getting through to me? How could it possibly matter to them? Was this what those people in the Workers' Circle hailed as the glorious new dawn?

2

'Laugh as the Wheel Turns'

If there had been anyone at home with whom to talk out my
sorrow I might have broken free of the sense of a capricious, implacably evil force always lying in wait, of a world deaf to the
pleadings of simple humanity, as a child always sees its logic to be.
Home was a lonely place. Father had always been a solitary and
distant figure, but after mother's death it seemed – though I could
not have put the feeling into words – that his course veered ever
further from us. I shall explain that later. More crucially, my two
sisters were too distant in age for me to reach them, or for them, it
seemed, to want to reach me. Mary was fifteen and beginning to
look outwards, and Lilian at twenty-eight was totally absorbed in
a hectic, Machiavellian business and private life. Where I craved
warmth and certainty their egoism gave me disappointment and
perplexity. To have seen my desolation and drawn near me to understand and help was presumably beyond them. And from them
two blows would come. In a year or so Lilian would leave home, in
a manner that would wound father and me deeply; and Mary
would follow a couple of years after that.

We lived in a mid-Victorian tenement of blackened sandstone in
Warwick Street, near the Clyde, in the heart of the Gorbals, a
bustling district of small workshops and factories, a great many
pawnshops and pubs and little shops, grocers, bakers, fish-sellers
and butchers and drysalters, tiny 'granny shops' – where at almost
any hour of the day or night you could buy two ounces of tea, a
needle, *Pig's Paper* and *Answer*, a cake of pipeclay, a hank of mending wool – public baths and a wash-house, many churches and several synagogues. The streets were slippery with refuse and often
with drunken vomit. It was a place of grime and poverty, or rather
various levels of poverty and, in retrospect, an incongruous cling-

ing to gentility, Dickensian social attitudes and prejudices.

In the late Nineties and the early years of the present century the Gorbals was a staging post for the westward surge of emigrants, mainly Jewish, from the Russian and Austrian Empires to the United States. For Jews the motive was escape from oppression, and economic only because of the hope that almost anything found in the west must be better. Poignant anecdotes from *der heim* – the ghetto of origin – constantly overheard, seared into the brain: of casual pogroms with their cold, Dantesque brutality, routine rapes, floggings, merciless discriminations, extortion both financial and sexual.

Many of the exiles went no further. Those who prospered moved as soon as they could from the Gorbals to what were considered more refined districts like Langside, Kelvingrove and Hillhead. For the rest the Gorbals was a social and economic sump from which they could hope to escape only vicariously, through sons and daughters.

The older generation read *Die Zeit*, a large format newspaper in Yiddish, printed in Hebrew characters, whose contents, in tone not unlike *The Times* of those days, you would hear chewed over, in the heavy accents of Eastern Europe, by little groups in the street of a summer evening, or at the Workers' Circle on a Sunday morning.

Yiddish, a dialect mixture with a basis in archaic Low German, was spoken by Jews in a wide area of Eastern Europe. The immigrants came to the Gorbals mainly from small towns and villages in their lands of origin – Lithuania, Poland, Hungary, Bohemia – and Yiddish was a life-line on their first landfall, helping them to find their feet in the new place, and to trace relatives or friends; or if destitute – victims of officials or other villains on their journey – to appeal for a crust of black bread and perhaps some barley broth, before being passed on to the Jewish Board of Guardians. Thereafter the 'Mammaloshen', mother tongue, remained an easy means of converse with other exiles, a rest from the struggle with English, a way of retaining links with the more wholesome features of the common past. For many years it was the language of daily life; the younger ones knew it well enough too, for their parents spoke to them in Yiddish and they replied in English. In the syna-gogue the Rabbi spoke Yiddish from the pulpit.

They wrote in Yiddish to their families left behind, for parents and grandparents – tired, frail, feeling too old to put down new roots – did not often join them.

With its rich written and oral tradition, Yiddish provided a but-tress for identity, its colloquial warmth a comfort in retailing mem-ories of ghetto life stripped by time of its unpleasanter associations. A Yiddish Theatre flourished up to the late Thirties, not in the Gorbals itself but across the Clyde in Stockwell Street; visits to it from the Gorbals, with sixpences saved over many months, were special treats.

The new arrival was quickly spotted. A man with a week's growth of beard, eyes bleary from wakefulness on his long journey, would shuffle wearily through Gorbals Street with his *peckel*, his belongings strapped in a misshapen suitcase, listening for the famil-iar tones of this lingua-Judaica from the East European Marches, and approach such a group with the sureness of a questing blood-hound. He would fumble in the pocket of a shapeless coat and show them a much-thumbed envelope:

'Lansmann! Sogmer, wo treffich dos?' ('Fellow-countryman! Tell me. Where can I find this address/person?'). 'Lansmann', literally, meant someone from the same language area or the same ghetto, but it was often used loosely as 'mate' or 'man', a friendly way of hailing a stranger. From his pronunciation his hearers usually knew his origins instantly. Often, his coming would have been expected, from gossip in workshop or street, or at the Workers' Circle – though far from accurately, for delays in obtaining permits and other documentation, usually the result of failure to bribe the right official, or by the right amount, might detain him for weeks or even months.

Sometimes the group consisted of men not yet assimilated enough to be able to read the address on the envelope. One of them would call out to a child playing on the pavement near them: 'Shmoolka! Koomaherr! Lezmir dos!' ('Sammy! Come here. Read this for me!').

Father never learnt to write English; he could sign his name in beautiful copperplate, no more. However, he taught himself to read English almost perfectly. Mother somehow taught herself enough English to get the gist of the contents of English newspapers. Father, oddly, refused to read the English papers; I fancy he thought more highly of books. I dimly remember evenings, before mother became very ill, when she sat with him at the kitchen table while he ate his dinner, and with obvious delight read an English paper to him. She also of course read *Die Zeit*, and letters in Yiddish from relatives left behind in Lithuania; these came more and more infrequently and finally died away. I suppose she never had time to read anything else; as a rule, especially in her last year or so, when she did sit down in the evening it was to work at her treadle sewing machine in the kitchen.

Often the group did contain a true 'Lansmann', and the stranger was beset with questions about relatives, conditions in 'der heim', their common place of origin – who was married, who else had left, who had died, when is so-and-so coming? Then someone awoke the group to the newcomer's need:

'Genugshen! Sterber yetzt! Feerten zu.' ('That'll do now! He's all in! Let's get him there.') And one of the group, or the nearest roving child who could be trusted, would show him the way to the tenement address he clutched in his hand.

I pictured father arriving in this fashion, wretched after the days spent huddled with other living cargo in the steerage on a timber ship from Riga. That must have been in about 1902, when he was in his early twenties. Mother, as was the custom, was left behind while father got his bearings, found work, and – as the saying went – made a place for her, and for Lilian their first child, born in mother's birthplace, Liebenyang, near Marienpol in Lithuania, then under the Czar. Father came from the same district.

Lilian never acquired British nationality, which would have been simple, having come to Britain a babe in arms. Asked why, she was evasive – 'Oh I can't be bothered!' I think, being the oldest in the family and therefore closest to father and mother, she had absorbed the well-founded fear of officialdom they had brought with them from the ghetto, and could never shake it off.

Mother was small in build, with broad brow, wide eyes, fine straight nose, small mouth, and jet black hair. She dressed neatly in black skirt and black blouse fastened high under the chin, and a white apron that always seemed freshly ironed. The small tight mouth and the drawn features, recalled from early memory, must have already shown the work of the cancer that would shortly kill her; as well as the pain of protecting the family from the effects of father's struggles with himself.

Father was the son of a rabbi. In Yiddish, as in the demotic tongues of other cultures, there are plenty of sardonic jokes and pithy comments about traditional figures. In this vast oral stock, the rabbi of course is a convenient target. One, about the rabbi's son, goes like this: 'If you go to the farthest and most uncivilised place in the world and pick up the roughest stone, you will find that it is the rabbi's son!' Father must often have brooded on it. Paradoxically, great as were his deviations and conflicts, in his heart he kept a core of faith inviolate. There, perhaps, lay his tragedy – the unavailing, self-punishing, and in its way naïve struggle to marry purity with worldly compromise, and the stubborn postponement of movement until it should succeed.

He was of medium height, strongly built, with ginger hair and moustache, and grey-blue eyes whose liquid appearance could give his stare a frightening ambiguity. Essentially solitary, laconic in speech, he veered unpredictably between aloofness and tenderness; he could be brilliantly wide-ranging, imaginative in story-telling and in anecdotes of life in the ghetto, tireless in applying himself to a child's small interests. Once, in the season for spinning tops in the street, he used his early training in wood turning to make me a whip with a beautifully finished handle and a leather thong magically inlaid into the wood, the envy of all the other children. These times were rare. For the rest he would try to show interest and then I would feel a chill, a tiredness spreading out from his soul. Perhaps I had arrived in the world too late for him to give me of his best.

One terrible event he recounted stuck in my mind. Later I would wonder whether it had contributed the tincture of poison that tortured his heart. He had a cousin, Aaron, to whom he was closely attached. One night Aaron's wife, heavily pregnant, longed for fish. It was winter and fish was scarce. Aaron lovingly told her he would go out and bring her fish. And so on a bitter Baltic night he went alone on to a frozen lake and knocked a hole in the ice; a freak gust of wind, it was said, made him overbalance, and he fell through and was drowned. 'It was said!' Father uttered the words again in ironic dismissal. 'So somebody did see him fall down – maybe pushed him, who knows? It wouldn't have been the first time that happened to a Jew! But in any case it was only a Jew on the ice – who cared what happened to him?'

He told me the story not long after mother died; I was about six or seven, and we were walking back from the synagogue in South Portland Street on a Friday evening. After a long silence he said, 'The wrong people die.'

Then he added, trying to pull himself up: 'Basherrt! ('It was fated!') Your mother always said: "Lach zum draydl" ('Laugh as the wheel turns'). That's hard to do – but you've got to try.'

The flow of Jewish immigrants, stopped by the Great War, became a trickle after it, and in the early Twenties, with tighter Bolshevik controls, stopped altogether. By that time, too, the Gorbals itself was a flux, as earlier immigrants moved away, or onwards to the Golden Land. The word community, often used to describe these collections of exiles, would not have been appropriate. Perhaps the strongest bond was created by loneliness and poverty, and anti-semitism's poisonous proximity. Despite the roseate vignettes often painted, the Jewish religion, far from being a wholesome unifying influence, was identified with the oppression from which they had fled. The bitter-sweet picture of the semi-rural ghetto left behind, the subject of sickly sentiment many decades later – in *Fiddler on the Roof* for example – would have been angrily rejected. For many exiles, and even more so for their children, the best solution for the Jewish problem was to cease to be Jews. The Balfour Declaration of recent memory, that flight of British *realpolitik* in 1917, the crucial year of the Great War, pledging Britain to work for the establishment of a Jewish National Home, was often talked about at the Workers' Circle, but with fading hope, as pointing the way to ultimate escape, not to preserve the religion, but to close the door firmly on the past.

Few tenements were occupied solely by Jews – a situation that was probably avoided for good protective reasons, since a mixed tenement was less likely to attract the impulsive anti-semitic attack. Where the immigrants lived, Jewish or Irish, was determined by their level of poverty. To be fair, until the advent of Mosley's Blackshirts, there was little organised molestation of Jews in the Gorbals; there is reason to attribute some of this moderation to the quiet influence of Christian clergy.

At school, however, persecution was relentless, though patchy. When I was about nine, I challenged a boy who was kicking me in class; we would fight in the playground after school. I was short-sighted and wore glasses, and soon, in the gathering gloom of the winter afternoon, with the tight circle of boys – none of them Jews – around us, I was getting steadily beaten up. I went on slugging it out, or tried to, for my opponent was stronger and a much better boxer. After a time my glasses fell off and my nose bled.

'Are ye gointae gie' up?' he shouted.

Something made me shout back: 'Not till ye say ye're sorry!'

He stopped in amazement: 'Whit for?'

'For callin' me a Sheeny.'

'But ye *are* a Sheeny, aren't ye?'

We started fighting again. A few moments later, when I thought I could not stand up much longer, an older boy shouted from the crowd: 'Hey, it's no' fair, he's gettin' beat. Come on. Stop it.'

The crowd filtered away. Someone had picked up my glasses and now gave them to me and wandered off.

I was never attacked again. That perhaps proves nothing. But it must be remembered that part of the prejudice of that time was that the Jew triumphed over the guileless Christian by art and sub-terfuge, that he was somehow slippery, hard to pin down, a coward. I had stood and fought, and though I had lost the battle, I had done something to weaken the myth.

When I got home, father spoke more in sadness than to chide me:

'Don't get into trouble again. Always remember, if a Jew gets into trouble he's always blamed more than the Goy. It's the way the world is.'

Keep your head down. Don't be noticed. He handed down to me the lesson of the Pale.

Another exile population with a special identity were of Irish origin, almost exclusively Roman Catholic; they held themselves distinct, in some ways defiantly so, partly for religious but perhaps more for political reasons. Although when drunk – and often when sober – many were as ready as Protestants to shout 'Sheeny' and 'Ikey-mo' or 'fuckin' Jesus killer' and worse at Jews on their way to synagogue on Friday nights, their relationship with the Jewish exiles seemed slightly easier than with the 'Prods', the indigenous Protestants. One reason may have been that their perception of the Jew, a blind expression of lurid emotional prejudice, was uncomplicated by any political animus, such as that which was directed against the Protestant ascendancy in Ireland and transferred to the local Prods – and seen at its most savage in the bloodletting between Prods and Papists on the annual Orange Walk. Another reason may have been economic. Most Jewish families put aside a few pence each week to enable them to employ a Christian neighbour – more often than not, as it happened, a Catholic – as a 'Shabbos Goy' to light the gas or the fire on the Sabbath or do some other task that the strict Hallachah, the Jewish ritual code, forbade.

Even at that early age the practice mystified me, and shocked me too. If certain deeds on the Sabbath constituted offences against the Almighty, surely He would *know* that you were getting someone else to do them for you and be just as angry as if you did them yourself! The Torah said that the preservation of your life took precedence over ritual; ergo, if to preserve your life and that of your family our needed to light a fire for warmth or the gas to cook food, why did it make you feel holier to get a Shabbos Goy to do the lighting for you? And the same had to be said for all other actions, classified as 'work', that were forbidden on the Sabbath. Surely it was monstrously sinful to try to deceive God?

I must have managed to express these thoughts to father, for I remember him trying to answer them somewhat as follows: 'You see, the rules were made many hundreds of years ago for rough and simple people, to protect them from their own ignorance! If you told one of them it's all right to light a fire to cook food with, he might say to himself, well a fire is a fire! I am a baker, I will make the fire a little bigger and bake bread with it for the whole village! Or if you said to him, you must not do work but it is all right to carry a little flour for your family – well, he might say to himself, I am strong, what is the difference between carrying a small sack and a big sack? I will carry a big sack so that I can bring back a whole load of flour from the mill! And if to carry one sack is all right, why not another – and then another one, and another, and so on, and soon he will be *working* as hard as on a normal day! So to prevent that the Rabbis said: you must carry nothing – not a single thing. You must light not even a small fire! That is the reason.'

'But father, why is it better to get a Shabbos Goy to light the fire for you than to do it yourself? Surely he's got a soul just as well as we have?'

He nodded as if to say he had often asked himself that question. He looked away and tugged at his moustache: 'When you grow up, please God, you may have the wisdom to answer that for yourself. I don't know the answer.'

George Gideon's father tried to be a latter-day exemplar, in theory at least, of the total observance demanded of those primitive People of the Book all those centuries ago. He would spend a year or so doing no work at all while his family worked hard to support him, and devote his entire time to prayer and total obedience to the Hallachah. Every day was fully taken up; he devoted the early morning to 'lay tefillin' – binding leather straps, with little leather boxes at intervals along them containing sacred scrolls, on forehead, elbow and wrist and finger, saying prescribed prayers the while – and set aside the rest of the day to attending synagogue for four devotional sessions each of about two hours, and to 'learning', the study of the Torah and the Commentaries. For him, observance of every jot and tittle of the Hallachah was a 'Mitzvah' – an absolute good, a holy deed – and earned blessedness not only for himself but for all in contact with him. To this end he solved the Sabbath problem of 'carrying' a handkerchief by binding it round his waist and pretending it was a belt to keep his trousers up, though like most men in those days he wore braces. When he unwound the handkerchief to blow his nose he gripped the waistband of his trousers and pretended to be holding them up till he could replace the handkerchief.

This conduct frightened me. I must be missing an important truth. God could not be deceived! Surely He must be furious? Were we not told at our religion school, the Talmud Torah in Turriff Street, that the heart of the Jewish faith, its very core and basis, was right behaviour – summed up by the sage Hillel as 'Do not do unto others what is hateful to you'. What had tying your handkerchief round your waist got to do with that?

Hillel, challenged by the proselyte Shamai to condense the Jewish faith into a few words, stood on one foot and did so: 'Do not do unto other ...' He added, significantly, 'The rest is commentary' – meaning, 'Go and learn what adherence to the Hallachah is intended to do to you as a person!'

Disappointed as I was that father had not given me a ready answer, I must have seen, with a child's clarity and wonder, that he had searched for one over the years and, failing, some sense of rightness had made him reject the unthinking observance and self-deception of the Mr Gideons of the world. I respected him for that, but I would not understand my feelings about it till I was much older.

On Saturday mornings the dimly-lit synagogue with its rows of battered wooden benches was packed, the men on the ground floor in blue serge suits and skull caps, the more prosperous in homburg hats; the women, many of them wearing the *sheitel*, the ritual wig of the married woman, were segregated, as orthodoxy demanded, in the gallery that ran round three sides of the chamber. Many of the smaller Jewish businesses and workshops closed on Saturdays but were open, braving intermittent Christian objections, on Sundays. The rabbi, his long white beard brushing the outer edge of the lectern, stretched his arms wide under the faded, parchment-hued Tallis – prayer shawl – and thundered at the congregation, as I imagined Moses did when he came down from the mountain. With detailed examples he examined their misdeeds: neglect of the spiritual, leading to inconsiderate conduct between husband and wife, children and parents, brother and sisters, neighbours, friends, and fellow-workers; sins of the market place; and, I assume in retrospect – for I was too young to catch all the inference – sins of the flesh as well. And he warned them of the retribution they had earned, *now*, in this life: 'Gott will ihr stroffen!' – 'God will punish you! There is no escape from His wrath.'

His words frightened me, but when I looked round they appeared to frighten no one else. In later years I would realise that such occasions, this outwardly dutiful assembly, that minatory voice, were ghosts of a once-effective past, when thunder from the pulpit did have some restraining hold. Or perhaps that was wrong too? Perhaps that lonely, sad, despairing rabbi up there did have some effect on the baser instincts? Without his lamentations and homilies and exhortations would life have been infinitely worse?

Even so, in later years I would wonder how different my life might have been if a few people, those closest to me, *had* been frightened – just a little.

3

Barber's Soap Boy

We lived on the top, third floor of our tenement. At night, when everyone was asleep, I often crept to the window and stared out and saw visions.

To the right the sky was tinged orange by the perpetual flame above Dixon's Blazes. But to the east and north on clear nights I could see the stars hanging like distant snowflakes on a vast curtain of dark blue velvet stretched across the world, and I imagined that I pushed my way through the window and stood on the ledge outside and floated away into the sky and journeyed through it deeper and deeper, through limitless space and time. And in that silent flight I would sometimes turn and look back at the earth and see it as a ball bounced by some all-encompassing hand long long ago, and still continuing to soar through stars that fell around it like white blossom scattered before the wind. And so it would soar and sail on and on. Where, when, would its flight end?

In dreams I wrested with the question of how to encompass the mystery of the heavens, and how to draw them into a pattern; that, and so much more. What pattern? That I did not know. Why a pattern at all? Some search for order, in a world where my infant mind could observe none but longed for it, must have driven me. Perhaps the stars and the heavens stood for many other things.

One day, when I was about seven, I woke up and I knew that I had found something apocalyptic. I was so sure of it that I had to tell it to someone who would understand. I would tell my sister Mary. She was then about fifteen, slim, mercurial, a darting sprite whose long brown hair, stretching to below her waist and done in two pigtails, flew behind her. She, surely, would understand me.

'Listen. Just imagine you could travel through the sky, on and on and on, and suppose you came tae a sort o' finish tae it, like a wall, yes?'

She looked fearful, impatient, wanting to move away: 'Oh ah wish ye would-nae talk nonsense! It makes me frightened to hear ye talk like tha'. Ge' along wi' ye now.'

'No, wait!' I had to tell her. It was desperately important. 'Wait, listen a minute. Jist try an' imagine i'? So, you'd get to a wall or something like tha' – wid ye no' think?'

'Ye-es. I suppose so.'

'Well' – I was triumphant – 'Wid ye no' say tae yoursel': "There must be somethin' on the *other* side o' tha' wall," wouldn't ye? Come on now, wouldn't ye?'

'Oh leave me alone. Anyway, ye shouldnae worry yer little head aboot such things. I'm goin' …'

'No!' I caught her hand, my excitement barely overcoming my tears. 'Please, oh please listen. Just this once. Now wouldn't ye say tha'? Wouldn't ye say: "Whit's behind tha' wall?" '

'All right then. Yes.'

'Right ye are then! And just think. Ye'd climb over tha' wall and ye'd travel on and on again, an' ye'd come tae another wall. An' ye'd say the same thing: "Whit's on the other side o' it?" And another, and another?'

'Ye-es.'

'There ye are! We say tha' because oor minds cannae think o' something that just *ends* – wi' nothing comin' after i'. There *must* be something the ither side o' the wall! An' tha's got tae go on and on and on, forever. Tha's called infinity! It means there cannae *be* an end to the universe, a wall wi' *nothing the other side of it*. That's proof of the existence of infinity, don't ye see? But because oor minds cannae imagine infinity, that proves tha' God really does exist! Because only He could have created infinity. What d'ye think o' tha'? Isn't tha' wonderful?'

Her dark brown eyes opened wide and she stared into me, and she held out her arms and took me close to her and hugged me and rocked back and forth, and I leaned into her, glad that she was pleased with me. And then I felt her cheeks were wet against mine and I was afraid, not knowing how my wonderful thought could have made her unhappy.

'Oh ye mustnae think these things,' she moaned, 'Ye'll have such nightmares. D'ye hear? Now yew run along down tae the back court an' play an' forget all about i'. Go on then.'

Who else could I talk to? Father showed a passing interest, and I did feel, for one glorious instant, that he understood and was pleased with me. He picked me up in his strong arms and put me on his knee and said softly: 'These are thoughts too big for a little boy. Keep them for when you grow up, please God.'

He sat in shirt sleeves in our cold kitchen, dirty dishes beside him on the oil cloth table cover. His calloused hand felt rough on my knee. The liquid blue green eyes were fixed somewhere far away. The fire in the grate had gone out. My skin felt cold, but that was nothing out of the ordinary; this time, however, I knew that it was for a different reason, not then understood. A signal from the waiting future.

He added: 'I do not need proof that God's there. I know He is. Only too well sometimes.'

That too meant nothing to me then. Later I would understand his sense of being punished for mother's death, and for his gambling. But now all I wanted was someone to see what I had seen. The symmetry I had found was joy in itself. The music of the spheres rang in my head.

Alas, such visions, fitting into no language, a poetry of the soundless ether, I could communicate to no one.

Indirectly, that private play with ideas and relationship, a euphoric marshalling of thoughts whose amplitude I would understand only much later, brought suffering. At school, in one of the annual examinations, I was the only pupil ever to get a hundred per cent in mathematics. For weeks afterwards, everyone else in school seemed united in hatred and envy of me, wreaking vengeance. I was not only frightened but innocently amazed. Why should I be hated for getting good marks? I had done nobody any harm!

Looking back, it is plain that the teachers were either too indifferent or too over-worked – we had classes of over forty children – to think of coming to me to offer comfort, much less advice on how to conduct myself in the face of all this venom; nor did they intervene and stop it. And no one at home bothered about such things. So, desperately, I must have decided on my own self-wounding method; at every subsequent examination I got low marks in mathematics.

Privately I still listened to the music of the spheres, contemplated the heavens, wondered and dreamed. At what age I first heard of Einstein I cannot recall, but increasingly over the years the name rang in my head like a golden bell. I spent hours, days, in the great Reading Room of the Mitchell Library. Young as I was, in my ragged shorts, frayed jersey and ill-fitting jacket, incongruous among the sleek, well-nourished university students, I became so familiar to the staff that they dubbed me, in kindly fashion, 'the young professor'. One day, perhaps as a piece of sympathetic magic, I looked up Einstein's massive entry in *Who's Who* and copied it out word for word, his universities, degrees, honorary doctorates, publications. I kept that transcript pasted into an exercise book, a talisman.

By the age of about thirteen I had some grasp, or thought I did, of the theory of relativity. A few weeks before my fourteenth birthday I read that Einstein was coming to Glasgow to address the university, and made up my mind to go and listen to him. How I gained admittance to the great hall at Gilmorehill I have no idea. I sat on one of the back benches. All around me were people arrayed in what to me was the majesty of full academic dress, with draperies of crimson, gold, purple, vermilion, green.

On the raised platform far away at the other end of the hall, it seemed to me the length of a football pitch away, a figure in brocaded long sleeved robe and silver trimmed and tasseled mortar board ushered in the great man – small, stooped, brown faced, with a little walrus moustache. How could such a giant be so insignificant? He read his address in a soft, clipped voice, slurring certain passages in a casual, dismissive manner: '... as I explained in my special theory of relativity,' as if these immense strides in thought were to him mere tip-toes.

I thought I understood a good deal of what he said, and with that I was exalted – a feeling I can only liken to the glory, years later, when I breasted the last ridge of mountain in the Haute Savoie and breathed the needle-sharp air, and saw in the tumbled masses of sun-glinting snow and ice far off the outline of Mont Blanc, dubbed locally 'tête de Napoleon'. But another euphoria, over-stepping this, was the sense of being near him, in some way part of that world where, one day, I dreamed of joining him. As he sat down, my mood of communion was shattered when two men in the row in front of me, gowned with crimson hoods, turned to each other. One said, in comic despair: 'Well, I suppose you understood all of that, eh?' And the other replied with a grin: 'As much as you did I imagine!'

Well, I thought, if these great people had not understood much, there was hope for me.

When I got home that day, ecstatic, full of power and confidence, I told father where I had been; and foolishly blurted out that I meant to study hard and go to university and be a physicist like Einstein.

Father was standing in his shirt sleeves washing dishes at the long shallow sink. Without turning, he said: 'You'll be fourteen in two weeks' time and that means you can leave school. I can't keep you at school. You'll have to go to work. You've got to have a trade in your hands.'

I turned away so that he should not see the tears that flooded down my face. But he had seen them.

In later years I would understand that his rages were fuelled by guilt. I may even have sensed as much at that moment. From as far back as I could remember I had known that gambling had him by the throat, but the wider significance of that knowledge, if dimly seen, had been shrugged off. And even now, it was hard to relate it to his decision. He had always been a giant to me, clever, resourceful; he could do anything if he made up his mind. If he did not, it was because he did not really want to. In my black and white logic at that moment there was no sympathy to lessen my misery. Whatever else, father was neither stupid nor insensitive, even though he often behaved as if he were both. He knew what my dreams meant to me. To pretend he did not was his way of making his actions tolerable to himself.

He repeated, parrot fashion, a piece of conventional wisdom of the slums: 'You must have a trade in your hands. With a trade you can go anywhere!'

A trade lifted you above the common labourer.

Two weeks later, on my last day at school, the headmaster said to me: 'Pity. You should go to university. You would do well there, but still … understand.'

He knew there was no chance, and probably knew why too. Not that the specific reason mattered. Of the boys I knew, none remained at school after fourteen.

And then my father took me to a barber shop in Gorbals Street, and I started being a soap boy. The ritual was simple but strict. You ushered the customer to the wooden armchair, clicked its ratchet-held neck rest to the correct height, spread a white sheet over him and tucked its top edge into his shirt collar, and then spread a small towel like a bib under his chin. Then you applied shaving soap to his face with a bushy bristle brush, spread the soap and lathered it into the skin with a massaging action of the fingers and hand. The barber then stropped his cut-throat razor with brisk back and forth strokes on a length of leather that hung from the back of the chair and, to the accompaniment of breezy chatter, shaved the customer. 'Soap boy!' he would call, 'Ready now!'

You applied hot towels and cleaned up all the flakes of soap round the edge of the shaved area of the face, combed the man's hair, smartly whipped away the towel and the sheet, and turned and called the next customer.

I felt miserable having to touch these beery, bristly faces, but I tried to be stoical. One day, somehow, I would escape.

Perhaps father sensed my feelings. Perhaps he wanted to test me further. One evening, after only a few days at the barber shop, he said:

'An intelligent boy like you should learn the trade in no time. Come, I'll sit here and you can practise shaving me.'

He pulled one of the battered wooden chairs away from the kitchen table and sat in it and put a towel round his neck and I soaped his face. Then he stropped his open razor and handed it to me, the concave hollow ground blade shining like bright silver. I took the razor, held it as I had seen the barber do so, between thumb and forefinger on the haft of the blade, the other fingers steadying it by resting on the little curved tail that projected behind the guard, and drew back the loose skin under his chin to make the first, grazing, upward stroke. I hesitated.

'Come on!' he barked. 'Don't just stand there like that. It's easy!'

Tears came again, and I could hardly see. Quickly I put the razor down on the kitchen table. 'I can't do it, father. I – I am afraid I – I'll cut you!'

I count not bring myself to say why I had to put the razor down quickly. But I could see that *he* knew. I was afraid I would cut his throat.

I knew I could not do that. I also knew that with that scalpel-sharp blade in my shaking hand the risk was there, and I dare not take it. Forces worked within me, shaking me with their battle against filial discipline and moral restraint, in furious rebellion against what he had done to me. Knowing that he had fought in vain against his destiny, I felt an enervating fear that I too might fail, indeed that he was bequeathing a similar destiny to me, insisting that I too should not rise above it.

He did not meet my eyes. Without saying a word he took the towel from under his chin, stood up, turned the chair round and tucked it once again under the flap of the kitchen table, took the razor, a fine German one and a prized possession, and carefully cleaned it in his own special fashion. He spread a handkerchief across his left hand and held it taut across the cushion of flesh at the base of the thumb, held the rounded butt edge of the hollow blade on it and slid the blade over it from butt side to the hair-thin edge, then swivelled it over on to its other face and slid it back again across the fabric; back and froth, back and forth, in a smooth, rhythmic hypnotic motion, intent, absorbed, almost tender, as if he caressed a loved one. Then he held it up to the light and twisted it back and forth, inspecting it for specks of dust on the fine edge, and the blade glittered with a vibrant mirrorlike sheen, as if it answered him in a private communion, as the magic sword Durendal might silently have spoken to its heroic master. Then he folded the blade into its ivory guard and placed it gently in the shaped blue velvet cushion in its slender leather case and closed it.

At last he turned to me, the jaws tight, and spoke with a softness that I knew meant suppressed anger: 'All right. You won't go back to that barber's tomorrow. You'll come with me and learn to be a presser. You won't have to be afraid you'll cut someone's throat *that* way.'

The next day I started as an under-presser at Bompert's garment factory in Stockwell Street. The work was simple. Soon I could stand all day in a hermetic kingdom of my own, while I pressed seams open, edges and stitched canvas fronts and collars into shape, working fast and pushing the work pieces through to keep pace with the other workers. The hard part was to swing and manoeuvre the iron, an eighteen-pound block of metal with a high twisted bar as a handle. I got used to that and soon forgot the strains, but they must have taken their toll on my still-growing body, and led to the agonies of back trouble that would hit me years later.

I counted my blessings. I was free to dream, to think, to wonder, the long day through – sixteen hours in the busy time – and wait for the blessed moment in the evening when I could bang the iron down for the last time that day, and walk across town and sit at my accustomed desk at the Mitchell Library, my only true home.

In the years before I was taken from school – from about eleven – I think I read to fuel dreams as well as from curiosity; I dreamt of a magic stairway to a kind of Olympus where the great ones held a rarefied converse in which I might one day join. At about that time I started to write a book about a group of people setting out to cross a wilderness; but the further I got into the story the more discouraged I became at my lack of knowledge about the world and about the way people thought, their passions, the triggers of action. I decided that I must put it aside till I knew more. Years later I looked for those two red-covered exercise books with their close lines of copperplate writing. In the course of many flittings they had been lost. Perhaps I have been trying to complete that book ever since.

After I left school, the Olympian dream shattered, the Mitchell became if possible even more important. I read widely, indiscriminately: the lives of the great philosophers and scientists, history and ideas, particularly of the Renaissance and the Enlightenment, logic. It was a halting progress, for at every step I had to make up for lack of background, of facts, of definitions, of words, and buried my nose in dictionaries and the *Encyclopaedia Britannica*, which led of course to more and more sideways reading. At about sixteen, timidly, I started going to Extension Courses at the University, in Logic, English Literature, Philosophy.

Father was well read politics and in the nineteenth-century novelists, Dickens and Trollope being his favourites. But his reading nourished the sour scepticism that deeply possessed him. One day, when I was about fifteen, he said to me sharply, a shade enviously I afterwards thought, 'Why d'you waste your time with all this reading? It won't get you anywhere!'

'I don't know,' I answered. 'I can't help it.'

4

Messiah at Gorbals Cross

While still in his teens, first in the Gorbals, then in all Clydeside, Bernard had been acclaimed as a demagogue, Messianic revolutionary, coming man in the forces of radical changes. At Gorbals Cross of an evening, among the vociferous groups on the pavements, people spoke of him almost in the same breath with Harry McShane and Willie Gallacher, living legends of Red Clydeside.

Bernard was a cutter's assistant in our factory, about five years older than me. His friendship had in some ways filled the void Charlie had left. Perhaps because he was older, the relationship had a sense of proper separateness, being based more on a sharing of curiosity about the world than of emotional attitudes. Stocky, deep chested, he had the brilliantly ruddy complexion of some dark-haired people, sparkling dark eyes and full lips. He was a mercurial character: striding forcefully along, in a brown tweed jacket the pockets of which bulged with pamphlets, and baggy fustian trousers, he radiated electricity, the force of his chosen role as saviour of the people.

Gorbals Cross was a large open space, roughly circular, a little way along Gorbals Street to the south of the River Clyde, where Norfolk Street came in at right angles from the west and became Ballater Street to the east of the crossing. Gorbals Street stretched about a third of a mile, from within sight of Dixon's Blazes at its southern end up to the Clyde at the Victoria Bridge. Gorbals Cross was also the name of the square granite monument in the middle of the open space. At each corner of its central block a plinth jutted out, supporting a Doric column from the capital of which a scrolled buttress curved inwards to where, high on one face of the main block, were the city's arms; above was a little four-sided stepped pyramid with a decorated cross of wrought iron at its peak. The embrasures between the plinths had stone ledges or benches, little open air drawing rooms where in fine weather men in cloth caps and mufflers smoked and talked. In one of them, stone steps led up to a bronze drinking fountain with two iron beakers hanging on heavy chains on either side of its basin.

The space occupied by the monument and the broad pavement surrounding it was some twenty-five feet in diameter. At the outer perimeter of the crossing, like an enclosing wall, rose black tenement buildings in the handsome classical style favoured in their epoch, the middle years of the nineteenth century.

Tram rails set into the smooth grey cobbles took a wide curve round the monument. As the tall glass-sided vehicles moved sedately in their circuit their wheels grated on the metal with a sonorous, brassy note that reverberated from the walls of the close ring of tenements, and rang in the mind like the sustained call of a horn in a far valley. In the quiet hours late at night and in the early morning you could imagine that the call came from a lonely oracle sending a message to the world. As it faded, taken up perhaps in another valley, and another, you felt its continuing power even in the ensuing silence. One day its meaning would come plainly through the mists. Long years afterwards, wherever you were in the world, you had only to think back to that time, and the poignant and questioning call vibrated in your head once again.

The day would come when the trams stopped. The rails would be dug up from the cobbles. But the horn note in the far valley would still sound in one's heart.

As long as motor vehicles shard the streets with many horse drawn carts and vans, till about 1930, traffic was not heavy, and moved with convenient slowness. People walked unhurriedly over to the Cross from the periphery, took a drink of water from the fountain, stood and stared, passed the time of day with friends. They took one of the large iron beakers, pitted and dented from years of rough use, and pressed its rim against a button under the spout to release a jet of sparkling water, crisply refreshing, that came from Loch Katrine in the Trossachs, some forty miles to the north of Glasgow.

I had never seen Loch Katrine, but the name had magical power. It conjured up steel engravings of *The Lady of the Lake*, remembered from English lessons at school, gothic scenes of wild crags and dark groves full of mystery, and figures on the Silver Strand moving in their romantic destinies – thoughts of earth spirits. In dour contrast was the inscription, in gold letters beneath the coat of arms, that met your eye as you drank from the beaker: 'Let Glasgow flourish', a shortened version of the City's motto: 'Lord let Glasgow flourish through the preaching of thy Word and praising thy Name'.

Did they want us to believe that religion was good for business? Did they themselves believe it? They. Them. The people who had mastery over the likes of us.

Children played on the uneven paving surrounding the monument. Grown-ups lingered there and talked and watched the passing scene, or called to friends on the far perimeter; and the latter might thread their way through the traffic to join them. As the years went by and motor traffic filled the streets more and more, there were demands to have the Cross removed – from business interests arguing for faster transport, and do-gooders, mainly from the better-off parts of the city, who felt that the Gorbals should be shorn of its old ways and appearance. In 1932 the City Fathers did have it taken away – not for any of these reasons, it was said, but because it led to accidents by tempting people to wander over to it across the path of the now faster-moving vehicles.

For a long time Gorbals folk behaved as if this had not happened. They returned again and again, halted at the periphery of the crossing and started with unbelief at the empty place in the centre; turned and paced about restlessly, deprived of a mysterious comfort, vital but indefinable. The monument had been the focus of many emotions and many associations of ideas, a source of answers to myriad unspoken questions; it had drawn them close, the hub of a moving wheel, its magic acknowledged, or rather felt, only in retrospect, after it had gone.

No one could put the loss fittingly into words. Few were inclined to dwell on it. It strengthened the conviction that the world, 'they', cared not a scrap for the feelings of people without power.

When I first saw the patch of concrete where the monument had been, I was transported back to the moment when Charlie Varnett went away. I saw the empty station platform again, cold and wounding as on the day itself long ago. 'Is this what life will always do to you? Are there no enduring links?'

For Bernard it was simply the fault of the system. Under the dictatorship of the proletariat, 'they' *would* care.

The time would come, in the decades after the last war, when a new generation of City Fathers went vastly further. The whole of the Gorbals was wiped off the map, all the tenements for nearly a mile around the spot where the old Cross had stood, the little workshops and family businesses that had given the Gorbals bread and work and life, the ancient street plan obliterated entirely, leaving a desert that stretched from the Clyde to where Dixon's Blazes used to be. In it they erected a few twenty-four-storey tower blocks, sombre monoliths presiding over windswept vistas of sparse, muddy, littered turf, all the old landmarks gone.

One day, years after I had left, I walked through that desert and could not decide where Gorbals Cross had been. Here and there in the devastation stood a bit of broken masonry, a jagged piece of railway arch, a gable with only the sky behind it. What had it belonged to? What street had it been in? Pacing the emptiness between the Cyclopean monoliths, memory was not enough. At the Mitchell Library, hardly changed from when it had been my special home, I found an old street plan in the Glasgow Room. Even with its help the new wilderness defied efforts to place Warwick Street, where my first-remembered home had been and where mother had died, or where Oxford Street and the Workers' Circle rooms had stood, and Mottel Bialystoker's bakery, or Norfolk Street where Aunt Rachel and Uncle Salman had lived and worked and died. I wandered to the south, to where Dixon's Blazes had flown its yellow plume of flame and sent out its angry furnace roar, where I had stood with Charlie Varnett when he had made the shocking announcement of his going. The site was silent; the great chimney no more. Near it, all points of reference gone, I threaded my way among great piles of fallen stone, builders' debris, isolated lumps of blackened masonry.

Why had they erased the old Gorbals? Class guilt about its sordid slums, its poverty? A fear of folk memories, in the new days of discontent, if its identity was encouraged to survive?

Something in this dismal wreckage prodded my memory. I stood before a broken railway arch whose black rusticated blocks framed high curved double doors, only emptiness behind, a rusty padlock still joining the two arms of a retaining bar. I stepped closer. On the door, in lettering nearly washed away by time and weather, I read 'A. G. Emet – Master Upholsterer and Cabinet Maker.' A ghost walked over my grave. Cold sweat made me shiver. Phil Emet, one of our group at the swimming baths long ago, had taken over this workshop from his father! Phil, clever and fiercely worldly, careless architect of tragedy for Annie Dalrymple, fallen star of my adolescence – of whom more presently. After the war, when he had left this place behind on his way to bigger things, no one had bothered to erase the name.

There was not a soul about, and I went over to the archway and stood in it. I touched the rotting wood of the doors, a physical link across time, the only one I had found, and thought of Annie's fight with the new life in her and with death; and Phil's indifference, and his brilliance, the dark and the light; and of Meyer Melek, crushed when he opposed the debt-collectors' terror in our street. The perplexities of us all.

I trudged on among the misshapen standing stones, disdained when the bulldozers passed by. I emerged into another cleared space, rounded another fragment of a broken gable, and there before me, unbelievably, stood a piece of the past completely intact, the first school I had ever been to, Abbotsford Primary School, named after the then adjacent Abbotsford Place, now erased. With the eyes of a child of four or five I had never seen it in its wholeness, or so I thought, but I must have done so for I recognised it instantly – a beautiful building, strongly classical, the upper windows grouped and recessed within moulded frames and divided by Doric pilasters. Above the rusticated main entrance, where I had first climbed what seemed at the age of four to be high stone steps, and been given a whole penny to calm my fears and tears, were stone heads of John Knox and David Livingstone, appropriate attendant spirits when it was opened in 1879. It had survived, pristine it seemed, as a listed building, still carrying out its original function. I went in, and there was the wide central double stairway divided down the middle by an iron railing; little boys and girls must not mix while ascending or descending. Outside, near the entrance, was the stone for sharpening our slate pencils.

Here at last was a piece of my past still living, comforting if poignant, for the rest now crowded in upon me. This desert was peopled again: all the tenements sprang up once more, and the past reasserted its hold upon the present.

On Sunday mornings on Glasgow Green, the park on the northern bank of the Clyde opposite the Gorbals, at the speakers' pitch on the park's edge facing the High Court, Bernard set up his wooden rostrum in the crescent-shaped space in front of the gates, helped by a group of the faithful from the party rooms in Hospital Street across the river. They had carried the rostrum for him, and a stock of literature to sell during his meeting, including the *Daily Worker* – renamed *The Morning Star* a generation later – and party pamphlets.

The speakers' pitch was bounded by a line of poplars, between whose slender sentinel trunks the eye was drawn past the Doric portico of the High Court to a structure in the middle distance that dominated the scene not so much by its bulk as by the attitudes it proclaimed. A massive red sandstone railway bridge was planted in the river like a great squat gate, with bulging rusticated piers and crenellated towers, disclaiming refinement. It blasted forth a forceful counterpoint to the political discussions taking place, lustily affirming the heroic materialism of the later Victorian age. Here was a historic dialogue, two attitudes to life irreconcilably apart but in some fundamentals at one; a belief in material values, for example, was basic to both.

Bernard claimed to take his stand on Reason alone, but his message reeked of faith, not logic; faith, especially, in the instinctual sureness and purity of Man in the mass. Destroy capitalism, and Man will regain the innocence, the clear and certain vision he had possessed in the state of Nature.

The bridge held to faith too, in the glory and enrichment to be found in Man's exercise of power and free-ranging creativity. Certainly compassion for the weak and the unfortunate was often lacking, but this dark side of life would always be with us, needing constant vigilance and charity. Any other view of human affairs was a delusion.

Cynically one thought of the stock image of the bloated capitalist, silk-hatted, perched on the back of the honest son of toil. Even so, some instinct told me that its rough approach was more firmly rooted in life's realities than Bernard's, with his gospel of root and branch destruction and starting Man's pilgrimage afresh. How many old and warm and valued things would he willingly destroy in saving Mankind?

The party shared the speakers' pitch with other evangelistic groups – the Anti-Parliamentarian Workers' Republican Party, the Independent Labour Party, the Social Democratic Federation, and a few individuals who spoke for themselves alone, each with a recipe for saving the world. One, nicknamed the Clincher – no one seemed to remember his name – tall and cadaverous with a voice like a bass drum, whose long steel-grey hair furled itself round his head in the keen river breeze like a worn battle flag, was fond of brandishing a piece of paper, evidently his discharge from a mental hospital, as a telling piece of theatre:

'There ye are ma friends,' he boomed, 'they gave it tae me in black and white! And now ah'm askin' yese – ah'm givin' yese this challenge! Is there anybody here that can hold up black and white proof that *he's* in his right mind?'

From beneath tufted grey brows he glared at his semi-circle of listeners, poised to discredit a rival claim. They acknowledged the familiar gambit with friendly sympathy, smiling and nodding to each other, knowing what would follow.

'Aye, ah thocht as much!' he roared in triumph, 'No' a soul among yese can match the proof ah have here.' He waved the paper again. 'So now yese can listen tae me! Ah'm goin' tae tell yese how tae make this wurrld a better place.'

An eclectic prescription, compounded of theism, Rabbie Burns's individualism and tolerance, and goodwill towards human diversity. Where did it stand with Bernard's destruction and rebirth? Or the bridge's reliance on Man's free-ranging assertiveness – get on with what you want to do and the Devil take the hindmost? And the faith Bernard and the bridge shared, that people would always behave well to each other given a completely free choice; completely free meaning a choice that did not conflict with self-interest! The Clincher was more honest, or more clear-sighted; selfishness was the great evil. 'Live and let live!' The key was to give free rein to Man's 'better nature', another name for his primordial purity.

Could it be true, I wondered, that each of us came into the world with a lodestone that would guide us truly if we allowed it to? If so, why was it so hard to know what course to follow? Why did life contain so much conflict, selfishness, deceit, hatred, domination, cruelty?

Like most radicals of the day, Bernard at this time was under the spell of the naïve behaviourism that marked the New Enlightenment of the early years of the century. With the right conditioning everyone could be, *would be*, benevolent. Ethics were simple commonsense, requiring no state power, and no religion either, to instil and maintain. Even with its reluctant curbs on its own savagery, and the enlistment of charity – itself an insult to Man's dignity – to heal the wounds it inflicted, Capitalism red in tooth and claw was so rotten as to be beyond redemption. To destroy it was the prerequisite for curing the ills of men and women. *Anything* you put in its place must be an improvement. Oh the childhood dream of destruction and renewal, the world reborn fresh and clean! Power of the thought and the word:

> To make, then break,
> the springtime fancy ...

46

5

Zeitgeist at the Baths

One blustery winter evening when I was about eighteen, Bernard and I were making our way to a meeting at the Workers' Circle. Walking in Bedford Street, which ran west to east, in the lee of buildings on its northern side, we were sheltered a little from the cold rain sheeting across the Clyde on the hard north wind. At the corner when we turned left into Gorbals Street and went towards the river, we lowered our heads to shield our faces and pulled our coat collars higher. Rain bounced off the flagstoned pavement. Trouser legs were soon soaked. My boots let the wet straight in, as if I walked in bare feet. Never mind, in the Workers' Circle rooms it would be warm, steamy in fact. We would go to the big stove in the middle of the main room and drape our socks on the hot casing to dry. Their smell would soon be lost in the fug of tobacco, coal smoke, and the accumulated expiration of sweat in the crowded room.

The Lipchinskys lived round the corner from us in Bedford Street, in a tenement that backed on to the Gorbals Baths. The Baths was an important building, as magnetic and significant, though less obviously spiritual, as Gorbals Cross. Its late Victorian façade was encrusted with corbels and scrolls; its interior walls were clad with coloured and moulded tiling, and wherever stained glass could be used, in doors, windows, transoms, skylights, were panels depicting flowers, foliage, urns and garlands, scenes of Arcadia. In its display of romantic sentiment, classical culture, condescending commitment to the uplift and care of the lower orders, and above all its display of industrial virtuosity, it spoke for its epoch.

One of its departments was a wash-house, aptly known as the Steamy, a long barn-like room kept in perpetual twilight by clouds of steam rising from washing boiled in rows of coppers, a miasma in whose crepuscular depths one dimly saw figures in kerchiefs, long fustian skirts and dark cotton blouses, sleeves rolled up above the elbows, hauling and lifting, scrubbing and banging and carrying, moving with the heavy measure of fatigue, enchained in punishing ritual. In a clangour of boiler doors, iron buckets and chains, rumble of slack gears in the mangles, scrape and clatter of metal-lined scrubbing boards, and counterpoint of shrill voices calling, they heaved bundles of clothing and bed linen and blankets about, banged press irons, turned the drive wheel of a mangle with rhythmic push of straight arm and shoulder on the handle projecting from the rim, and then a pull back with the whole upper body, while the other hand fed layers of wet washing, like lumpy slabs of glistening clay, between the thick wooden rollers.

Now and then one of the vaguely seen figures became distinct as she emerged from the grey cloud and hastened over to a bench against a wall at the entrance, beneath high begrimed windows that supplied the only natural light; a number of babies lay there in a row, wrapped in stained and tattered blanket, sucking on dummies, with here and there a barefoot child of three or four standing in patient attendance. She snatched up her baby, comforted it with a cuddle and a rock in her arms or sat down and, unbuttoning her blouse with flying fingers, impatiently gave it the breast, then laid it down again and moved heavily back into the rank half-light.

In the streets their leaning outlines were familiar as they trudged to the Steamy or homewards from it, backs bent under sagging bundles of washing, often 'taken in' to earn a few shillings – staring down at the pavement, lustreless hair drawn tightly away from the face in a bun or a thick plait, the washing wrapped in a sheet with its four corners knotted together and held under strain with a two-handed grip at the shoulder, long skirt swaying at thickened ankles, grey stockings wrinkled over battered black shoes. Here and there one of them also carried a living bundle in front. The baby lay diagonally across her bosom with its head resting on her free shoulder, cocooned in a shawl wrapped tightly round her upper body and secured at her waist with a long safety pin.

Another department of the Baths had the genteel title 'Slipper Baths for Ladies and Gentlemen' – rows of narrow cells each with a glazed stoneware tub, a duckboard on the cement floor, and a wooden stool. The bath's timber casing was a pale tan streaked with silver from years of scrubbings, its broad-headed brass screws burnished to shine like old gold. Such signs of elbow grease, and a strong smell of carbolic, reminded ex-servicemen of barrack room days, as did the smell of bodies and sweat and old, worn clothes. A burly attendant, arms covered with tattoos of mermaids and anchors and flowers, showed you into a cell, with rough courtesy if you had tipped him, brusquely if you had not. Tuppence, one-third of the entrance fee, was an adequate tip.

Having cleaned the tub after the previous occupant, at least in theory, he ran a bath for you. On the tiled wall at the head of the bath, instead of handles marked Hot and Cold, were two bolt heads needing the attendant's spanner to turn them. Presumably the idea was to prevent you dispensing free baths to members of your family or friends smuggled into your cell. Implied, too, were Poor Law attitudes to the lower orders. Your use of these baths proved you belonged to the lower orders and were therefore not to be trusted to make prudent use of the amenities here 'given' you.

On brass chains bolted to the wall hung a long-handled back brush and a hand brush, bristles almost as hard as the tufted wire of horse brushes, with 'Corporation of Glasgow' burned into their wooden backs. Most clients brought their own soap and towel. If you were flush you could hire these, but we never heard of anyone who did. Twenty minutes' occupancy cost sixpence, expensive for the likes of us. So the clients were mainly our parents' generation. People of our age sometimes went there in preparation for an important function, a wedding or Bar Mitzvah, that warranted the expense of a long soak in hot water.

The swimming pool cost only threepence. Bernard and I went two or three times a week after work, less often when the factory was slack, before Christmas and in the spring, when we were on the Broo drawing fifteen shillings a week dole money. Among the pool's attractions, apart from physical uplift as we entered into full possession of ourselves after ten or twelve hours' heavy work, was the luxury of standing and talking under the hot showers. Unlike the slipper bath, you could stay virtually as long as you liked for your money.

Under the showers a group of us debated the world – or thought we did, for it was more of a debate each one with himself. How should you confront the world? What should you try to do with life? We shouted to be heard above the noise of pumps and the hiss of water and the cries of the swimmers, thrown back thunderously from hard surfaces of tiles and stained glass. We shouted to quell the tumult within us.

For Bernard's family, living more or less on top of the Baths was a blessing in winter. The boiler room, which heated water for the pool and its showers, the slipper baths, and the Steamy, was below their windows; its hot flue ran up the wall of their tenement and heated their flat so well that they hardly ever had to light a fire, and the coal cooking range in the kitchen was damped down for most of each day, whereas most other people kept theirs going all day for warmth. But in summer the money saved by using fewer sacks of coal was paid for in extreme discomfort, for the boiler flue made the heat in their flat almost tropical; and even with many sticky fly-papers hanging from the ceiling, there was no escape from the swarms of great black flies that bred in the open rubbish dump – the ash-pit – in the unpaved yard below.

I lived only a hundred yards away in Warwick Street, which ran for most of its length parallel to Gorbals Street, from the Clyde southwards to Cumberland Street where it was crossed by a railway bridge; and where Pollokshaws Road, a continuation of Gorbals Street, veered west to meet it. Arches under the bridge housed little workshops – furniture makers and repairers, carpenters, jobbing engineers, repair shops of various kinds, many of them serving the large engineering works, factories and shipyards along the Clyde.

Our street was a backwater, mainly of three-storey tenements, of red sandstone blackened by smoke, interspersed with older buildings, one-storey stable blocks and sheds, and a fine building by

Charles O'Neill in the Italian Renaissance style, St John's Catholic School. A few stables still housed horses, great Clydesdales used for general cartage and coal lorries. Often at evening, passing the tall wooden gates, one heard a stamping of hooves muffled by straw; one of these strong and patient and beautiful animals heard our step and banged down a great fringed hoof in greeting. A black-smith, one of the last in the locality, worked in one of the sheds; as well as shoeing horses he repaired broken ironwork on carts and vans or made new parts. He also did household jobs like making brackets to keep a broken table or chair in service, mending an iron bedstead or welding a new hinge plate on the door of a cooking range. Other sheds were workshops. A few had been divided; the front part made into a small shop, and the back a combined living room, bedroom and kitchen for the family running it. In this style our street had a cobbler, draper and dressmaker, grocer, dairy, tailor.

The tailor earned his living mainly from 'altering and making-over', making second-hand garments fit the new owner; or altering clothes handed down to growing children so that they could go about 'respectably'. This work usually came from the better-off Gorbals family, for in most Gorbals homes the mother did it. If pre-vented by illness or disability, and if she had no daughter at home able to do so, whenever she could she put a penny in a special tea caddy on the high shelf above the kitchen cooking range against the day when she would ask the tailor, or a skilled neighbour – for that was cheaper – to make over a pair of trousers or a jacket for a child. It must not be too obvious that her family wore reach-me-downs, for that was not respectable.

'Respectable' was an important word. Certain ways of behaving, using bad language, a girl wearing a blouse or dress too close-fit-ting or in other ways too revealing or suggestive, staying out after ten at night, were not respectable. When a mother was getting chil-dren off to school of a morning, she would make sure that each had some pieces of newspaper stuffed into a pocket for nose blowing, because to do so on your sleeve was not respectable.

For your underwear to be respectable could be more important than life and limb, especially for a woman. Seeing a teenage or grown-up daughter putting on a torn under-garment, or one that too obviously needed washing, the mother would cry out in alarm: 'What if you met with an accident in the street and had to be taken to hospital, and they saw your underclothes in that state! What are they going to *think*?' That was usually enough to bring a lazy or forgetful girl to heel.

One of the neighbourhood's many pawn shops was at the corner of Warwick Street where it crossed Bedford Street. The three golden balls hung from a wrought iron bracket, with a motif of slender leaves like willow fronds, that jutted out from the angle of the building and could be seen from either street, a life saving beacon, a reminder of failed hope washed up on a barren shore. In the window a notice said 'Unredeemed Pledges for Sale', adding, with unconscious irony, 'Good Quality!' Eternity rings, wedding rings, gold watches engraved with twenty-first birthday wishes, used blankets and bed-linen, carefully laundered shirts, china teapots, dinner plates, soup tureens, cutlery, a linen tablecloth embroidered with the words: 'To our beloved daughter Bunty on her wedding day. May The Good Lord bless and keep her.'

As I relate later on, mother knew it well. When father came home skint from gambling on pay day, there she would hurry, a prized silk blouse or linen tablecloth wrapped in newspaper tucked under her shawl, and bring back a few paper bags of food.

After our swim and the talk under the hot showers, we dashed home to hang up swimming briefs and towels to dry above the coal range in the kitchen, swallow a 'tea' of bread and margarine or fried bread, and then sally out to meet again at the corner ten minutes later. The Workers' Circle was about three hundred yards to the north, past the Cross towards the river.

Bernard had always seemed to march ahead with total confidence, fully armed with maturity, values, a comprehensive world view, a certainty I envied, though I knew that his road was not for me – the only certainty I had.

There was a thrill in sharing, in the shower room group, the mood of the time – unfocused discontent, resentment at having been cozened into believing in the solidity of a world that consisted of façades, stages sets sustained by, and sustaining, make-believe. People said the Great War had destroyed them, but they still stood. The make-believe was weaker, that was all.

We hungered for a world whose values were true and dependable, though how we would know it when we found it we had no idea. How could we know that we never would? And that in the world we were entering we would find even les solid ground than in the one we knew?

We longed to reject the world view that the preceding generation seemed to be passing on to us, attitudes of submission, of 'make do', of finding comfort in old saws and signs and portents, in thrift, prudence, automatic religious observance with little faith, in survival one day at a time.

Examples were dinned in our ears: 'Life is a see-saw. So smile when you're up, and smile when you're down!' or: 'Expect nothing and you will never be disappointed!' Such profound resignation, pitiful and frightening to young sensibilities, repelled us. Did they want us to abandon hope before we had even started? Yet theirs were the only values we knew. Reject them and we faced an icy wilderness, with no signposts, no goals, no belief in anything or anybody. We swung between revulsion at received values and fear of living without them.

Perplexity was worsened by the suspicion that the world view of our elders did have fixity and pattern and certainty, of a sort. Deeply hidden beneath phlegmatic humour and resignation we sensed an obstinate faith in the ultimate triumph of good over evil. The world was not as bad as it seemed, or as it might be. Beneath the appearance of confusion a striving for order and decency did somehow sustain itself. We must help it to hold its own. But we must not expect too much from it.

Some of us were aware that the elders' code was beginning to be attacked in literature and the theatre, and timidly in the press, as at best self-deception, at worst an elaborate hypocrisy generated by an arrogant and opportunist élite. Faith and trust and honour and integrity were the corner stones of society. Hard work, and pride in work, were worthy ends in themselves. Respectful and courteous behaviour would always be reciprocated. Life conducted on those principles acquired a fulfilling grace. As a world view it had certainly had its charm. But it had been pounded into the mud at Passchendaele and the Somme.

Of that we were reminded many times a day. Survivors dragged themselves about in tenement and street, some on crutches with an empty trouser leg, or a sleeve crudely sewn up and swinging in the wind. Seeing them we felt guilty that our bodies were still whole. With a cold shiver we marvelled that the glorious image of God could be shattered like this – and being so, could live. In rags they confronted us at the factory door on pay day, begging for pennies. Young men, or rather young in years, their was a world beyond all time. Not our world. From within the prison of their broken bodies they stared at us with eyes frozen in disbelief, silently crying out to God: 'Why? What for?' We echoed that, but not in their presence, for we had not suffered as they had.

Sometimes the thoughts boiled over. One Armistice Day morning the signal sounded for the eleven o'clock silence, and in the streets people stopped in their tracks in living stillness like the arrested figures of Delvaux or Magritte. A group of youths at the Broo violated the silence by stamping back and forth along the pavement, filling the air with the ugly staccato of tackety boots slamming down, saying nothing. People in the street all round them, held fast in the silence, glared in shock and fury. Then came the long eerie moan of the siren terminating the two minutes of reverence. The stilled figures exploded in roars of indignation and abuse: 'You fuckin' traitors!' 'Cowardly scum!' 'Insultin' the men who laid down their lives for yese!' 'Have ye no' go' any feelings at a'?' 'Have ye nae pity?' 'Rats like you don't deserve such a sacrifice. Ye should pu' up against a wall and shot!'

The youths stared back in confusion, vainly blustering. They had meant no disrespect for the dead or their sacrifice. They knew no other way of saying that the outpouring of a generation's goodness of spirit had achieved no sensible purpose. They thought they expressed a general revulsion at the influences that had made it happen, or failed to prevent it, or stop it when it had begun.

No one asked a different question: what 'gain' could ever justify putting millions of people through a titanic slaughter machine? Doubtless many who abused the youths secretly shared their anger and sorrow and frustration. The young fellows' mistake had been to force these emotions into the open.

In their innocence – most of them were about the age of the men who had marched away to that slaughter – they had expected their gesture of rejection and disquiet to be received at least with understanding if not sympathy. How, they asked, could that past continue to be honoured by the generation that had lived through it? Too young perhaps, they could spare no sympathy for that generation, nor see that it must cling to what remained of its faith, including belief in the sacrifice, or be left with nothing. Instead, they felt resentment, and disgust for its seeming weakness of vision and of will. It had brought its sorrow upon itself. It had no right to pass them on, much less to expect sympathy. They refused to accept the elders' pain as the inheritance that each generation had to accept from the one that had gone before.

A moody despair gripped the mind. Or was it divine discontent? Virtuous, in a sense, it certainly was, or rather virginal. Some of us tried, for a time, to reject all action as tainted. We knew this position to be untenable, for apart from anything else it made us feel inadequate. Action flowed from certainty, and lack of certainty showed lack of manhood. Guilt accumulated as we waited for certainty, like Grace, to flood over us. We drew uncashable cheques on the bank of experience. We hoped for hope.

Most of these questions were screens for other, deeper perplexities, about relationships and the movement of the personality. Delicate materials – how did you *work* them? Most of us were not deeply self-regarding. To formulate one's concerns clearly, let alone decide what would cure them, was beyond us. Instead we dealt in image. In our group under the hot showers someone mentioned a folk hero – Benny Lynch the boxer, Johnny Weissmuller, Olympic swimming champion and screen Tarzan, Ronald Colman. 'Don't you think he was great when he...?' – mentioning an attribute he wanted to copy, hoping for the others' approval so that he would have the confidence to attempt it. There would follow a discussion in minute detail, on whether the hero's behaviour had been admirable or not, which facets of his personality it expressed, and what we each would have done in his place. At the same time, secretly, we chewed over our private doubts.

Bernard put himself above all this shadow boxing, and insisted on bringing us back to 'objective reality', a favourite bit of party jargon. He would move away from the showers, dart to the line of hooks on the one dry wall, take his towel and drape it over one shoulder, Roman toga fashion, assume a declamatory pose, gasping from the steam in the air, and shout out to silence us:

'Hey! You're wasting your time! It doesn't matter how much you try to change yourself. You're in the hands of the System. It will frustrate any plans you make. The *basics* – that's what you should worry about! The fact that the control of the means of production and exchange is concentrated in too few hands. That's what we have to change ...'

The rest listened politely for a minute or two, then someone would say with a tolerant chuckle: 'Och Bernard, come off yer platform! Ye can't expect us to talk politics all the time!'

And then, brushing the hot water from faces and eyes, they resumed the talk about Jack Dempsey or Gene Tunney, or whoever had been the heroes focused on that day – golden images of maturity.

I asked him one day, 'Why d'you always turn away from discussing life, people, how they should behave to each other, what sort of people we should try to be? It's as if you thought all those things weren't important?'

'Life? Did you say life?' A teasing smile spread over the ruddy cheeks. 'Who says this is life we're living?'

'Come off it!'

'All right, then,' he sighed. 'But we've been through all this many times. No, of course I see what you mean. But we shouldn't be wasting time on all that introspective stuff. It's no good pretending we can escape from the immediate task, which is to achieve the

Revolution. That's the only goal. Nothing must distract us from it – nothing! – if we really want people to have a better life. That's all there is to it!'

I said, 'That's just running away from life! It has to be lived *now*, at this minute. You can't wait till you've made your "System" exactly as you want it! Life doesn't wait for you! You can see so much else, so why can't you see that?'

'First things first!' he said irascibly 'This self-questioning, yours and the others', is escapism! I'm doing something *about* things. You're marking time.'

We were all living on borrowed time as it turned out, but not in the sense he meant. Perhaps he was right but for a different reason altogether. Maybe most people did not question life as we did, lived for the moment as best they could? How lucky they were! That evening as we butted against the drenching north wind, I voiced the thought.

'There must be plenty of people who accept without question whatever life sends them, who go on working, eating, sleeping – day after day! It must be fine to be like that?'

'I don't think it's fine at all! They don't understand what they're doing. They're nothing but' – his lip curled – 'lumpen proletarians! The slave mentality! He halted and seemed to ponder what he had said, looked at me warily, and added with a faint smile, 'I'd never say that in public of course. But I get fucking well fed up with such people. If only they would wake up and help us a bit! The Revolution would be that much nearer.'

'I won't tell on you!' I said.

He disapproved of me as one of life's dreamers. 'Be practical!' he pleaded. Practical and objective were favourite words of his then. To dream was an excuse for staying out of the 'objective' world, the world of action, meaning action of the only kind that mattered, aimed at destroyed the System. Life, the party line said, had no other terms of reference.

Most of us were dreams to some degree. Visions of escape, like mirages indistinct yet irresistible, turned the energy inwards in day dreams, leaving just enough free to do the day's work and push the day itself away. Dreams of power, acclaim, virginal conquest. Above all release from the treadmill of thrift. How wonderful not to have to scheme and calculate about pennies and ha'pennies!

A few in the shower room group, in some matters as rebellious as the rest, followed the old standards in their own way.

George Gideon, bull-necked physical culture devotee with an arcane language of calories, proteins, muscle balance and muscle tone, wanted to be a professional racing cyclist, and reach out for fame and money that way. Meyer Melek, dark and sleek and heavy-shouldered, with the boxer's measuring eye and poised step, had already won a few professional bouts as a lightweight. He was going to join the army when the next slack season came round.

'Join the army and see the world!' said the recruiting posters outside the Baths and at the Broo.

'No sense in hanging around here,' he said in his clipped, careful way. 'They give you plenty of facilities for training in the army. And that is worth a lot. I will serve out my time and save hard; and with that and gratuity, whichever way my fights go in the meantime, I'll start something when I get out, maybe a gym and sports equipment business.'

Meyer was careful of his diction. He wanted to be accepted into 'refayned' society. In the determined way that he prepared for his fights he was in strict training to lose the Gorbals twang. On his early morning run, when only a few carts rattled over the cobble stones in the empty streets, he would repeat to himself, in rhythm with his pace, his 'words of the day': I, I, I – for 'ah'; or my, my, my for 'mah'=, 'matter' and 'bottle' without the glottal stop – 'ma'er', 'bo'lle'. Sometimes his diction slipped back: 'When ah was oo' on ma run this mornin' ah saw a lo' o' bo'lles fallin' aff the back o' a larry, an' ...' He endured our good-humoured laughter calmly. Like most serious minded fighters he reserved his aggression for the ring.

Phil Emet cared nothing for diction. He would use worldly power to compel refayned society to accept him, Gorbals twang or no. A powerful back and shoulders attested to his hard work in the upholstery workshop, pulling tight the jute and sisal belting and the covering fabrics, and manhandling finished pieces of furniture. Black wavy hair grew low on his forehead; his dark eyes were watchful and darting. A long nose, slightly acquiline, gave his sallow features a narrow, pointed appearance, almost timid, at variance with the strength radiating from him. Fast-talking, nimble-witted, we called him a 'chancer', local slang for a schemer you should deal with carefully – not unkindly, but in the way members of a family tolerantly refer to one of their number.

Phil prepared himself in his own way for an attack on the world. He worked long hours at his upholstery apprenticeship and in helping in his father's small furniture-making and repair workshop under the Cumberland Street railway bridge. Wherever he went he carried an old school satchel containing a dozen red-covered exercise books, his detailed dossier on the furniture business, one book for each topic. With the black triangular-shaped marking pencil he used at work, he filled the pages in the rounded copperplate handwriting we were taught at school, with figures, diagrams, cuttings from trade journals, about production methods, materials, costings, suppliers, design trends, and changes in market demand such as the furniture and equipment needs of the new housing schemes rising up in the suburbs.

'When ma apprenticeship's oo' o' the way,' he said, 'ah'm goin' tae take over ma feyther's workshop. Ah'll ge' tha' wurrkin' a damn sight be'er! An' then ah'll move intae mass production.'

He went on: 'That's the way furrniture's got tae go, mass production for the mass market! The day o' the craftsman like ma feyther's over an' done wi'. You just wait and see! Ah'll have ma hoose up at Newton Mearns, wi' a big garden an' a car, afore ah'm thurrty!'

Newton Mearns, on high ground about ten miles south of Glasgow, showed crucially how the world was moving from patterns that had seemed set for all time. When I first went up to the Mearns I saw a tranquil rural world of fields and cows and hayricks, copses and burns and flowering hedgerows, with here and there a little hamlet and a church: a secret, ancient design. On a hot summer day some of us would make a foray up there, to a foreign land, the country. Timidly we looked at a life we had known of only in the abstract, from hearsay, from old people speaking of childhood in the country, from fairy tales or the scant Nature instruction at school, or the penny matinée at the cinema on Saturday afternoon. We saw the people of the Mearns as a different race, purposeful, endowed with quiet certainty, unhurried, at ease in their mystery, their dealings with the earth and with beasts, plants, wind and rain and the great sky, who walked erect in the world. They looked at us as if *we* were the foreigners.

We got up there by tram and then by bus, or on bikes. You could hire a bike for sixpence a day: to buy one cost four or five pounds. Buying for cash was beyond any of us. George Gideon and one or two others were buying bikes on the never-never at sevenpence-ha'penny a week.

We carried bread and hard-boiled eggs in our pockets and picnicked on the bank of a burn. We lay prone and leaned out over the shallow stream where it sprang over broad flat stones streaked with reds and yellows and slate greys, to catch the cold, tangy water, flashing with rainbow light, in mid-air between our lips. Then we turned on to our backs and gazed up through waving traceries of leaves at the great openness of the sky, listened to blackbird and lark and the gentle murmurings of the earth and the multitude of creatures sensed moving on it. And life floated on the scent of freshly-cut hay and the mingled smells of many growing things. It was hard to take it all in, and we knew in our bones, sadly, resentfully, that we never could, because our roots were not there. We were exhilarated and disquieted, strangers in Arcady.

That first vision was only a year or two earlier. Perhaps, knowing so little of rural life, we had not noticed the changes already begun. Now they were plain. Fields and boscage and hedgerows were being eaten away. The mysterious race of country folk was in retreat. Villas had sprung up, others were building, red and raw, in discord with the gentle greys and browns and greens of the old settlements. Prosperous Glasgow people moved out to live in the Mearns in the country but not of it, proud of this step up in life.

Why was living in the country a step up? It had not always been. Many Gorbals dwellers were no more than a generation or so away from it. Their forebears had seen 'the country', whether in the Highlands and Islands, Ireland, Italy or Eastern Europe, as a place like any other where you worked hard for a living. To go and live there from choice, or to visit it for pleasure or for one's health – the latter often a Calvinistic cloak for the former – was an urban invention filtering down to us from the lower middle class. Moving to the country following material success often amounted to ostentatious expenditure, as in later years would be an expensive car or a winter suntan, which other people blindly strove to copy.

Helping to form this new attitude to the country among the lower orders was the propaganda put out by groups of do-gooders promoting schemes to take poor city children on country or seaside holidays at subsidised prices or, in 'deserving' cases, gratis. 'Fresh Air Fortnights', one of them was called. Intentionally or not, their message implied that country air was a cure for deprivation.

Bernard and the party detested the charity element in such schemes. The aim, they thundered, was to gull the workers into believing that charity was the proper answer to social ills and injustice, and to deflect them from insisting that the system itself should be replaced with a better one. Such 'benefits' should be available as of right. Acceptance of charity blunted the lower orders' discontent and quenched their militancy.

Shrewdly, the party stopped short of advocating boycott for that might alienate support, especially among women. In this they implicitly acknowledged that among the poor it was the women, more the men, who carried the burden of life, in unceasing toil in the home and Steamy, and in heartache for their families when money was more than usually short of food, fuel, clothing, blankets, medicine. For many women in the tenements, charity could be in the truth a life saver. And in these Fresh Air Holidays schemes they saw a heaven-sent way of getting children off their hands for a while and giving themselves a spell of lessened work and worry, a holiday for them too. If children benefited, as the propaganda said, so much the better! Competition for places was intense, short of money as most of the schemes were. Some mothers had to be content to go on a waiting list for possible cancellations later in the year or, failing that, for places the following year.

Up there in Newton Mearns the new immigrants from the city could boast of having fresh air all the time.

In the villa settlements, lanes and landmarks kept their rural names – Rick Lane, Smiddy Crossing, Lang Byre Brig – but the ways of life they signalled were gone, leaving only echoes and symbols, a few oases of greenery, glimpses of distant fields; enough, however, to charm the new arrivals. But a decade or so later most of these residues would disappear under a further wave of building and transformation, in effect the creation of new *urbs* – shops, garages, workshops, offices. The true 'country' gone for ever.

For the present, however, Newton Mearns was the Shangri-la on which many Gorbalians focused their hopes, and some would one day attain. And to own a car! No one we knew owned one. On top of your achievement in moving to Newton Mearns, the sight of you in your car would proclaim to the world day in and day out, especially to the Gorbals slum-dwellers you had left behind, that you really were on your way up.

'Traitors to their class!' Bernard said angrily, 'Using their abilities to perpetuate the system. They don't see that. *Will* not is more to the point! But they will one day. By God they will!'

There was menace in his words, sad to hear from this warm-hearted soul. There was bitterness too. Phil and the others were determined on joining the ranks of the class enemy, the capitalists. When the day of confrontation came, they would be on the wrong side of the barricades.

Part of him, I suspected, saw his political dedication as self-denial on their behalf. He too could have chosen the golden road. He must often have asked himself whether his sacrifice was no more than masochism. So Moses raged at those who knelt before the Golden Calf.

Of late I had sensed a less secure note in his affirmation of faith, and attributed it to the compassion central to his character. Did he say to himself sometimes: 'Let them enjoy worldly achievement while they may. Why must it be jam tomorrow and never today? Alas, how sure am I that it *will* be jam?'

The hounds of doubt paced close behind.

No wonder the menace in his words sounded overdone. If you fear that you have not enough cold commitment to see you through, you fall back on passion.

'You talk,' I said, 'as if the Revolution will answer all life's questions. That's impossible. Life is about *the individual*, the sort of person you want to be, not people in the mass as when you speak about the system, this system or that system.'

'How can you be anything but a wage slave when the System keeps you chained in that position?'

'Come on!' I said, 'The word "slave" makes it sound worse but it doesn't change anything. We'll still have to work for wages whatever the system! You can still be a person of a special kind, with feelings about life special to you, even if you *are* earning wages. You talk about people as if they had no faces, as if they all had exactly the same feelings, or none at all – the people this, and the people that! The individual does matter, what he is and what he wants to be.'

He gritted his teeth: 'For Christ's sake it doesn't matter a damn what you or anyone else *wants* to be! The system doesn't allow you to be anything else than a cog in a machine making profits for the capitalists. Only after the Revolution, when everyone will have equal rights to the fruits of production, will people be able to develop their talents the way they want to. "From each according to his abilities, to each according to his needs." That's the only possible way to look at it.'

Stock repetition of the creed was his way of turning a deaf ear. I wanted to share with him the thought I was wrestling with: the person you are, or are trying to be, is your own work of art to refine and change through life, a burden no one escapes. Substitute another System for this one and that burden will still be yours alone. Even Bernard, tougher-minded than the rest, resisted ideas that came too close for comfort.

I was learning a depressing lesson – the truer the insight the greater the peril in revealing it, what Mephistopheles had in mind when advising Faust:

> Das beste, was du wissen kannst,
> Darfst du den Buben doch nicht sagen.

('The most precious knowledge you can attain, you must not tell to boys.')

I said: 'It's something hard to explain. I'm trying to talk about the questions life puts to you as a person, *inside yourself*. They must be the same whether you're living in comfort in a house with hot and cold running water and a bathroom and wearing a bespoke suit, or in a Rose Street tenement and getting free clothes off the parish!' Rose Street was a byword for the lowest of the low in slums, even by Gorbals standards.

He shook the rain off his head like a dog, and seemed to chew over what I said. This was new too. His mercurial mind was always so quick to answer.

I went on: 'And another thing. You talk as if revolutions are made by angels! It's all about people hungry for power! They'll murder and torture to get it and hold on to it. Look what the "high heid yins" in Russia are doing to people, even to their own old comrades who risked their lives for the Revolution! When it comes to villainy there doesn't seem much to choose between the new bosses there and the old ones they got rid of!'

On the public platform, Bernard dutifully echoed the self-righteous Russian communiqués on the Moscow trials and purges: the great new socialist state, in self-defence, was meting out well-deserved retribution to its enemies.

Honest soul, the party line had to be the truth or he could not live with it. But the revelations coming out of Russia worried him, the partiality of its legal procedures, the cruelty to those of inconvenient opinions, the Machiavellian misuse of words like democracy, the treatment of people as units of conformity. More crucially he was troubled by the cynical and manipulative elements in the Comintern's *realpolitik*.

Tough-minded politician though he had become, the sensitivity that had drawn him to the cause ruled him still. Suffering moved him even if the creed condemned the victims. Later I would understand why his anger boiled over now. He had made up his mind to join the International Brigade in Spain, and in a few weeks he would go.

These were days of strange faiths and nostrums, of innocence still hungry for a cause to follow. The day of the heroic and exemplary act was not past. Belief and action could gloriously coincide. The Spanish War was a holy war for liberty and democracy, for good against evil. But Bernard, surely, was not fitted to the Quixotic role! Dapper speech-maker with the intellectual's stoop, what was he thinking of, going off to shoulder a rifle in Spain?

How wrong I was. He was to prove himself as tough as the rest. Tougher in fact, luckily for him. But he would not find the cause he had gone to fight for.

Was he going to Spain to put himself through a test of suffering and danger, as some ascetics scourged themselves to strengthen their faith, feeling the hounds of doubt? My questioning of his creed that day, innocent then as it had always been, must have given him particular pain. His anger came as a shock:

'It's *you* that's closing your eyes to the truth!' He spat the words from the side of his mouth, blowing the rain away. 'These are the growing pains of the Revolution. Only fifteen years ago this country, and other imperialists had troops in Russia fighting a war of intervention. They financed the White armies of Denikin and Kolchak and the rest, trying to kill the Revolution and restore the Czarist oppression! And they still dream of doing it. They'll use *any* means, including getting discontented comrades to sabotage the Revolution.'

'I will give you this much,' he went on, 'I suppose it is just possible some comrades in Russia disagreed with the party line on how to build socialism, disobeyed the rule that the Central Committee's decisions must not be opposed, and fell foul of the authorities from honest conviction. I admit that's worrying. But this is too dangerous a time to be soft with such people.'

He wiped the rain from his face with the back of his hand and said quietly, 'It's hard to judge what's going on in Russia from where we are standing.' Frowning, he fell silent again.

A few months ago the hint of weakened belief would not have slipped out. He hurried on as if to blot it out: 'What I mean is, you can't afford to go on giving deviationists the benefit of the doubt. Whether you call them traitors or misguided people is not the point. If you're convinced that what they're doing is endangering the Revolution then they've got to be stopped.' Awesome words spoken with tight lips and a dying fall.

The echoes of his doubt continued in the air between us: 'It's hard to judge ...'

Press reports from Russia had an unreal quality, suggesting that observers did not dare believe the horror thinly concealed in what they saw. Enough filtered through. The Old Bolsheviks at their show trials moving and talking like sleep walkers, the standard wording of their confessions, and other signs, pointed to the truth, or rather a minute degree of the full horror. We shrank from believing that such things could happen in a civilised country in the enlightened twentieth century. Soon, equally unbelievable truths of Nazi barbarism would be revealed. In both cases the most chilling characteristics was that such things were done by 'ordinary' people, the sort you would pass in the street or in a bus queue without a second glance.

After Hitler's War I met an aristocratic German ex-officer in Italy, and Eichmann's name cropped up. Count M. had come across him during the war, in circumstances left unclear. 'That little Scrooge!' he exclaimed with contempt, meaning an insignificant, ordinary little man. But his laugh as he said it told me that he dismissed as of no importance, also, what Eichmann and his like had done.

Count M., too, was in his way ordinary, a man of his class and time. Observing this hardened but well cared-for middle-aged gentleman with the ramrod back, bearer of one of the most distinguished names in the Almanach de Gotha, one saw what he once had been, the athletic and debonair young nobleman much like many another, of easy cosmopolitan manner, not given to deep thought but shrewd enough, pursuing the patterned life of his landed class in the inter-war days, schooled to hold the reins, heading smoothly towards hierarchical and business influence.

His mind was serene. Nothing that anyone had done in Germany, during the war or before it, was worth a second thought. Split milk, errors of judgement, that was all: 'My dear chap, politics! What can you expect? All I know about politics, which isn't much, is that it's about power, and the power game is a kind of war! It's tough. Oh yes! People make mistakes and behave badly, stupidly.' He grimaced, putting aside the thought. 'All part of the tough game of life, one might say!' He laughed again, 'Preferably tougher for the other fellow than for me, of course! It's the way the cards fall. What else can one say?'

An understandable attitude, remembering that the very existence of the old aristocracy exemplified the principle of 'Anything goes and Devil take the hindmost.'

Those were the words, too, of that bridge across the Clyde.

6

The Frighteners

I said that Meyer Melek confined his aggression to the ring. Only
once did I see him break that rule – a traumatic experience for him,
both in itself and in its denouement. For me, sorrowing for him and
for all of us, it was an awesome visitation of demonic powers.

We grew up with violence. It simmered and bubbled and boiled
over in street and close, outside the pubs, at the dance halls in
Bedford Street and Ballater Street and Crown Street, sometimes in
gang raids from adjacent slum areas, Kinning Park,
Hutchesontown, Govanhill, Kingston. Seldom did such attacks
find the defenders unprepared. Like the raiders they would be
armed, with bicycle chains, knuckle-dusters, chisels, open razors,
or the fearsome Razor Cap – razor blades embedded in the peak of
a cloth cap with their cutting edges projecting, and swung in a
scything motion across an enemy's face and neck.

More often, violence settled private accounts, transgression of
codes, the spilling over of grievance or spleen. It was so closely in-
tertwined with everyday life, its inescapable rough edge, logical,
cathartic, that its occurrence, like rain and cold and frequent shortage of food, was recognised with equal fatalism. That it could also
be an instrument of cool business calculation never occurred to me,
until one day in the slack summer season a ruthless enactment in
our street brought a harsh awakening. I saw that the smooth face
of successful business could conceal a use of violence and terror as
merciless, as detached and as passionless as anything in the annals
of the Borgia or the Medici. I shared Meyer's misery, the hurt to his
sense of manliness, his pride, his simple view of right and wrong. It
darkened the sun more cruelly than anything since Charlie went
away. It was a reminder from the Furies.

With two older brothers Meyer worked in his father's joinery workshop, part of old stables in a lane behind Warwick Street, a few minutes from our tenement. With its cobbled floor and high blackened rafters, it was a place of saturnine gloom, in which a half-light was provided by three gas mantles on long thin pipes projecting from high up on the dun-coloured walls; ankle deep in sawdust and curly shavings, one could barely move for planks leaning tall against the walls, work-benches, partly assembled shelving and shop counters and wall fixtures. The business was probably too small for four adults to earn a living from it, and in better times one of the brothers, probably Meyer as the youngest, would have gone to work somewhere else. As it was they worked hard for what they did wring out of it. I often saw Mrs Melek – small, stooped, plaited black hair wound in a tight roll on top of her head, sallow features deeply lined at the mouth – hurrying towards the workshop carrying an earthenware jug of soup covered with a towel to keep its contents warm, and half a loaf of black bread wrapped in a handkerchief. Though their house was so near, they dared not spare the time to go home to eat.

Early one evening I went there to collect Meyer on my way to the Baths. As we rounded the corner into our street we heard shouting from a little group on the pavement outside Meyer's close a few doors away from mine.

'Fuckin' hell!' Meyer ran ahead. Two heavily built young men were scuffling with an older man in shirt sleeves who, as we came near, fell to his knees on the wet pavement. Blood from his nose and lips had made dark streaks on his collarless shirt. Like a penitent before inquisitors he held up his hands in supplication. It was Mr Fredericks – middle-aged (old to us), white hair thinning, narrow-chested, afflicted with the almost universal bronchial cough. With his wife and consumptive daughter he lived on Meyer's staircase. Like many of us in the garment trade, he was out of work in this off-season.

'It's the fuckin' menodge men,' Meyer muttered.

The street was unnaturally quiet. Here and there a face peeped out from shop doorway or close mouth. This was a time, the code said, when it was safer to see nothing. To be known to have watched could be interpreted as participation, support for one of the contestants, and retribution might follow. It was a time not to be involved.

The words 'menodge men' carried terror for the tenements – more than 'the factor' or rent collector, and perhaps comparable to the black shadow that hovered round the sheriff's men who came to distrain on property for non-payment of rent or, since there was seldom anything worth distraining, to put you out on to the street.

A menodge – a local word, probably from the French 'ménage' – was in its origins a thrift system. It became for a great many people the only way to buy clothes, bedding, household equipment, furniture, on credit. You began by making payments, usually through a neighbourhood collector working on commission, of perhaps sixpence a week to a 'warehouse', in effect a retailer selling at a high mark-up to people lacking the ready money to buy at a normal shop. When your 'menodge book' showed a stipulated credit balance you went to the warehouse and chose goods to that value. In the interim the money held in your name was of course at the interest-free disposal of the warehouse. If you undertook to continue weekly payments of a stated figure you could become a credit customer and take away goods up to a certain 'loan' value. Concealed in the price of the goods was a high interest rate on that loan. From then on, as in the 'loan shark' system exploited by the Mafia in America, you were encouraged to be in dept for evermore.

Since you would not be in the menodge at all if you could afford to buy elsewhere for cash, you were a captive customer in every sense. One-and-three-ha'pence a week was a common loan repayment figure, high for most people even when in work, impossibly so when they were on the dole and bringing home fifteen shillings a week.

Almost by definition menodge customers had no reserves, so when life hit them hard, through illness or unemployment, and the one-and-three-ha'pence could not be found, they could do nothing but hope, miserably, that the menodge men, 'the frighteners', would not come to their door and make a public example of them.

There was a dreadful irony in that. People became menodge customers from a desire to remain respectable, to pay their way and avoid the great indignity, 'going on the parish', the pauper's way. And so the others, those who *were* on the parish, showed little sympathy for them when the frighteners did come. They stood back and watched, not with satisfaction but allowing themselves a breath of comfort, as if they said to themselves: 'There but for the grace of God – or our better judgement – go we! They shouldn't have been so stuck up – they should've gone on the parish like the rest of us.'

The label Rachmanism had not been invented then but the form of customer discipline was familiar and, from a narrow point of view, effective. For the menodge or credit warehouse the purpose was twofold – so to terrorise the defaulter that he could put his debt before every other need, even food and coal, and to send a terrible warning to everyone else. For the latter reason the defaulter must be attacked and humiliated publicly.

These frighteners, we would hear, were acting for Great Universal Stores in Cathedral Street, a forbidding factory-like building of blackened sandstone with broad, flat-arched windows, beside the railway lines at the back of Queen Street Station. Seeing it I always thought of 'the dark Satanic mills'.

As we ran up, Mrs Fredericks was standing at the close mouth, shaking with distress, wiping away her tears with a soiled black apron. Then she too held out her hands in appeal. The men stood over her husband's crumpled form, dour messengers from the Inferno, seemingly pondering what further suffering to inflict.

'For God's sake have pity on us! We're at our wits' end! Please give us time – till he's in work again. It's not our fault. We *want* to pay but we can't!'

One of the men kicked Mr Fredericks in the ribs and he howled in pain and toppled on his left side and lay groaning and gasping for breath. With a cry she tried to push past, reaching out to him. The other man put out a foot and she fell heavily to the ground.

I had seen Meyer in the ring, a figure of poised, scientific intensity, showing no emotion. In these few seconds it seemed that his whole frame shook as with a fever. His face had gone dead white. I was afraid for him.

'Fuckin' bastards!' He leapt between them and with a shoulder lunge and a trip kick, toppled the one on his left. The other, turning, slow to react, accustomed perhaps to meek submission, had time only a few snarled words, the beginnings of an automatic response: 'Fuck off! This is none o' yewr ...'

Meyer, swivelling like a dancer, chin tucked in, shot out a left to the solar plexus and, as the man grunted and bent forward, hurled his weight behind a straight right to the jaw that toppled him like a falling log. The back of his head hit the pavement with a sullen, bony thud and he lay still.

Turning as the first one got to his feet, Meyer ducked a wild swing and delivered a straight left to the jaw; and as the other rocked back, followed with a lightning right hook to the head and another straight left to the chin, his whole frame lunging behind it like a battering ram. The man's knees sagged and he subsided vertically like a collapsing building and lay inert.

I glanced round. Every furtive face had disappeared. We stood in an icy desert.

We helped the couple to their feet and led them to their house.

'It's no good,' Mrs Fredericks muttered through sobs, 'They'll come back. They never give up.'

'I don't understand,' Meyer said. 'They can't get money out of you if you haven't got it.'

We both knew that that was not the point. The supreme purpose of sending in the frighteners was *pour encourager les autres*.

In our simplicity we felt their hurt as our own. We raged for them within, all the more because we felt so powerless to help them. In truth we could do nothing. We went downstairs.

We feared, primitively, the contagion of their defeat. We raged again, this time for ourselves. If we could have raised swords and struck hard at the world and made it weep too, how golden that moment would have been. But where *was* that world? Who? What? And in what gruesome way were we ourselves accomplices in it?

We lingered in the close mouth. Where the frighteners had lain the pavement was empty. Meyer contemplated the blood on his cut knuckles.

We had crossed a dangerous frontier.

I think we knew that the hardest lessons of this episode were still to come, added to other tremors in the ground beneath our feet. And that the chain of effect would be understood only much later – perhaps too late.

'It's no good,' Mrs Fredericks had wailed. 'They'll be back.'

We were too full of it to say much as we walked the hundred yards or so to the Baths. Meyer, I knew, would suffer most, at least immediately. He had attacked the menodge's front line troops. Who could tell what would happen now? Perhaps *all* the menodges would close ranks and bear down on us, a massive show of strength to snuff out any thought of further challenge? Who could prevent them? We knew nothing about the law, how to appeal to the mighty in the land to protect us. For us the menodges *were* the mighty – part of the big battalions of the boss class. Who could challenge them on level terms? Who, for that matter, would care?

We reached the Baths about twenty minutes after the fight, but plainly news of it had flown ahead. The shower room group showed muted sympathy, ashamedly uncomfortable that, in self-protection, they could do no more. Few families felt immune. In any case, what had happened to the Fredericks, and what was almost certainly in store for Meyer, were simply variations in the common round of life's hard knocks. A fear of a quite different kind was that the menodges might blacklist any family seen to be linked with Meyer's revolt – a penalty far worse, in most people's short-term reasoning, that the chance of a visit from the frighteners in the future.

No one paused to think that the menodges needed all of us just as much as we might need them. The immediate truth was that the menodges struck hard when and where it chose, and with impunity. It was wise to stand clear.

Two evenings later I again went to collect Meyer at the workshop. As we walked along Bedford Street towards the Baths a large black car drove slowly past us and stopped at the kerb a few yards ahead. Private cars were a rare sight in the Gorbals then, especially large and expensive-looking ones. We looked at it with interest.

There were five men in it, two in front and three in the back; the one in the front passenger seat was expensively dressed – it must have been the first time I had ever seen cuff-links worn – and that might have been enough to give him an air of authority. In his eyes there was an expectation of obedience, but above all a cold, implacable will. He beckoned to us. As we came up to the car the other four, in a well-drilled movement, got out and surrounded us – large, silent, menacing. At a signal from the leader, two of them pinioned my arms and lifted me like a sack and set me down again a few feet away. Then the four of them closed in on Meyer and pushed him close to the open passenger window so that he stood before the leader like a prisoner awaiting sentence.

The hard eyes held him fast. Fingers drummed on the car window frame. At last he spoke in a flat, soft, menacing voice:

'You were a bit rough with my lads the other evening. You're interfering in business and we don't allow that. You'd better get that into your head before you get hurt. Understand?'

Meyer had obviously tried to prepare himself for something like this. Strong as he was, finely tuned physically, he was young in the world, and could hardly have foreseen the pitiless force he would face.

He said as through clenched teeth: 'How can you go around knocking harmless old people about like that? It's a crying disgrace. Why don't you go and make a living some other way?'

The man tapped his fingers again, studied Meyer stonily: 'You've got spirit, I'll say that for you. But there's a lot you don't understand. One thing's for sure. I can't afford to have any more of this.' He stared hard again. 'Tell you what I'll do. I could use a lad like you who can look after himself. I'll give you a tenner a week plus expenses. You do what I tell you and ask no questions, that's all. And don't worry, I look after my lads when there's any trouble.'

'You mean dirty work like the other night?'

There was a snort of impatience: 'I said I look after my lads didn't I? What do *you* care? You've only got to ask yourself one question; could you pull in that sort of money anywhere else?'

He pointed to Meyer's cut knuckles: 'You ought to look after those hands. You could get them hurt bad. That's right lads, isn't it?' He looked up at his cohorts, who by a slight movement of the heavy shoulders signified agreement. 'You could get your fingers jammed in a car door maybe, or someone might accidentally smash your knuckles with a sledgehammer. A great pity. Happened to one or two promising young boxers, I seem to remember.'

As if in reflex action, Meyer stuffed his hands in his trouser pockets. Reddening, he removed them.

'That's right,' said the man. 'I advise you to be careful of those hands.'

Meyer's features paled and flushed, and paled again. In the smooth face before him he saw the savage world for the first time. He could find no answer.

The other said: 'Listen, I'm a busy man. I've no time to waste. I'm a man of my word and that means I don't make idle promises, and I don't make idle threats either. You've got till tomorrow to make up *your* mind.'

He signed to the driver, who stepped quickly round the front of the car, got in and started the engine.

Turning back to Meyer he said: 'Tell you what. I'll make it fifteen, there you are! We'll be back tomorrow. Don't get any more foolish ideas. It's my last word. You just think about those hands!'

He signalled to the others. They piled into the car and it moved softly away.

As on that other evening, we stood in an apparently deserted street. Not a single face looked out. Of course everyone had seen, and understood.

The car turned the corner and was gone. As if on cue the street was full again. Shop door bells tinkled. People came and went. Children were let out of closes to play. No one looked us in the face. There must be no connexion with us till our fate was decided.

Meyer was taking the brunt of it and I was sad for him. One generous impulse, one quixotic moment, and what cataclysmic forces he had summoned up?

Yet I too had felt the chill of that basilisk stare. I too had been warned.

For him nothing could be undone. They would never let him be. They dared not, or their power would be at an end.

He might have been echoing my thoughts, for he half-turned as if to retrace his steps to the workshop, then faced me again. No, his look said, there's no way back.

The street swirled about us. Did any of these hurrying people guess the revelation that had come to us, that we saw this world, at last, in all its invincible savagery? Perhaps some of them did, reflecting that this initiation had better come to us now then later? The wound would grow its protective scar. It always did.

Slowly, in silence, we continued on to the Baths. There, at least, we were in our own world. No, that was wrong: there was no such place, not any more.

Once again the news had preceded us. Amazingly, they even knew about the offer of employment. Perhaps, with the threat of retribution, it had been deliberately put about, for if Meyer accepted he would be diminished, and if he did not, the lesson would still be driven home: opposition was futile.

No one spoke of it till we had done our stint of lengths and were in the shower room.

Phil said: 'Ye could do wurrse. It's no' yewr fault if people buy stuff they cannae pay for. Business is business efter a'!'

Meyer shrugged, tight-lipped.

Bernard, unusually, remained silent till we were about to leave: 'You can't do that!'

'But there's the money!' Meyer muttered unhappily. 'We don't make that in a month! Anyway, father could do with taking it easier now. And what chance have I got if I don't?'

'You couldn't do it. I know you couldn't.'

'I wish I could. God help me if only I could!'

'Listen, you were going to go into the army? You father's going to have to manage without you sooner or later. Maybe this'll turn out for the best. Your slack time's coming on. Now's your chance.'

'I have been thinking about that.'

Meyer's eyes were moist. This was not the way he had wanted it to be. Early next morning he went out to Maryhill Barracks.

7

Annie

For me the hints and rumours coming out of Russia were evidence enough. The later flood of anecdote and reportage would simply add detail.

Not everyone had been troubled. The Gorbals was not a place of political sophistication. Few people, apart from soldiers and sailors and merchant seamen, knew other countries. Not many had travelled more than fifty miles from Glasgow. When, later, Chamberlain would speak of Czechoslovakia as 'a little country far away that we know little of', it would be true for everyone we knew.

Ruled by folk lore and simple stereotypes, how innocent and prejudiced we were. Italians were dagoes or wops. Germans all had duelling scars on their faces. The French? Incomprehensible and wicked: had they not invented the French letter, the French kiss, French knickers?

Soldiers' tales. Black and white visions brought back from the mud. Tommy Atkins' fugitive pleasures:

> Mademoiselle from Armentières,
> Parlez-vous?

And who were we? Some of those from exile families sought certainty in stock images of the host culture. We belong to a great country! Nobody tries anything with us or we give them what for! We send in the Navy and that's that. The Empire on which the sun never sets, that's us and we're proud of it. And Glasgow's its Second City. And we're the workshop of the world!

Seafaring men confirmed them: 'Aye, ye go ashore a' any place ye like tae name, Rangoon or Shanghai, Valparaiso or Fiji, anywhere, an' walk over tae a crane on the dockside, or look a' a generator or a boiler or a pump or some other bit o' machinery, an' there's the plate on it with the name of a British company – Carron, or Braby's, or Babcox and so on – frae Clydeside, Birmingham, Manchester, some place in this country. The same on the pilot boat or some other craft. An' the locals there'll tell ye: "If it comes frae Britain we know it's the best!" '

Sunset visions. How could we know the sunset had begun some fifty years before? With unexplained foreboding some of us wondered if these stereotypes did belong to the past, as the light of the stars we could see was not of the present but of a time far off in the past. If they did belong to today, why did the great leaders in London put up with the hooligan behaviour of Hitler and Mussolini?

What rights and wrongs from long ago, what unpaid debts, now clamoured for settlement?

Had people always walked in shadow, oppressed by uncertain identity, belief, direction? We knew we needed loyalties, though we couldn't have said why. Where should ours be?

With the workers, was Bernard's answer. 'The workers owe loyalty to no country, only to each other! That's why we must be loyal to the Spanish workers. Their cause is ours too.'

'When Joey Morri's father went bankrupt,' I said, 'and had to close his factory and go and work for somebody else, did he stop being evil because he wasn't an employer any more? Did he become a good person overnight because he was working for somebody else for wages?'

He disdained to reply. Talk was over, and the time for action had come. Though neither of us could know it, this particular difference between us would soon be over for ever. Spain was about to write *finis* to a page of his life.

Some of us were sure that Spain was a curtain-raiser for another Great War. Would that war – could it – be any different, less horrible, less disillusioning?

We sensed in the older men around us – old to us, but some only turned forty or so – a continuing shock from the Great War. They remained in the grip of a timeless ordeal for which nothing had prepared them, continuing to struggle with an enigma to which there was no key: how to fit the cataclysmic scale of the slaughter, and especially its impersonal character, to the world of human warmth and meaning they had grown up to believe in. The individual had been overwhelmed in man's first production line war, in which millions of able-bodied men were executed as a terminal stage in the manufacture of killing machines and their delivery to an appointed place. It was not merely organised slaughter; in a sense it was *mutually agreed slaughter*, a shocking negation of a tradition, instinct with honour and nobility, they could not bear to see pass away, in which war was *personal*, the enemy an identifiable individual, whose cause you could at least understand if not accept, whose aggression you could respond to with passion of your own, muscle with muscle, skill with skill, steel with steel.

The survivors had brought back only fragments of the picture. It was an unbelievable one, but believed it had to be. Many could not bear to speak of it at all. Others told what they knew again and again, possessed by a grim wonder, of remote machines raising higher and higher the mounds of dead in front of the trench fire step, and still knew no face to fix their fury upon. Even the word enemy had lost its old meaning. Death, like life, had to have an aim, a purpose. In these dunes of putrefying flesh there was none. From life too a needed rationale had gone. The old one, for all its faults, had served them and their forebears well enough. Who could read the broken message of life in these piled-up fragments?

We also sensed among them a feeling that what they had given an affirmation for which all life had prepared them, had failed of its purpose. They had given everything but not enough.

Would *anything* more, even if they had had it to give, have led to anything worthwhile? What, after all this, did worthwhile mean?

It could mean righting wrongs, one supposed. Old men remembered 'wrongs' that politicians, as proxies for the people, had fulminated about: the Kaiser and the Ems telegram, the Fashoda incident, the murder at Sarajevo. Were *we* in the Gorbals today better off because these wrongs had been 'righted' – and who could say they had been? And now, though causes had different labels, Danzig, the Sudetenland, as abstract to us as earlier ones must have been to the common folk, it seemed that a profound essence of feeling, the springs of passion and action, remained unchanged. Was the 'cause' irrelevant?

How could the Spanish War be different?

Not long ago we had been to an anti-war exhibition – horrifying photographs of mutilation, death, destruction in the Great War. It had been mounted by the party, in the interests of the current Comintern strategy active in the disarmament and anti-war movement, to project its desired image as the only genuine worker for peace.

One photograph imprinted itself especially on my mind – a huge enlargement in grainy black and white, more than six feet high, of a man's face with one side blown off by a shell. In place of half his mouth and one cheek was a yawning cave of flesh kept open with metal struts so that food and breath could pass. There were others.

Disturbing in a different fashion was a section devoted to the arms industry, telling of a factory on the border between France and Germany that during the Great War had supplied munitions to both sides.

Bernard snorted: 'That only happens in a capitalist war! Spain is a working-class war. The first one!'

We would soon learn that worse things were happening in the Spanish War.

The tidal wave of anti-war and disarmament movements, the first of our time, displayed an innocence now hard to understand, until we think of the Flower Children of the Sixties – an appeal to the softer side of human nature, faith in the power of gentleness and the will to peace. 'If only people and nations would let themselves be swayed by kindness! If only "they", the people who fear us and insist on arming against us, would believe we are innocent and that we only wish for good to prevail – and not attack us first!'

One was the Peace Pledge Union, its name a native throwback to the campaign in the early years of the century of for 'signing the pledge' against the demon drink, instinct with the belief that if you but had the *will*, everything was possible. So the will to peace, the mind suppressing the brutish passions, was all that was needed to 'outlaw' war. Many peace propagandists declared, and some still do, that for a nation to be armed at all was to provoke aggression. If only *one* nation would disarm it would exert an irresistible moral pressure on all the others to do the same.

Many of the disarmament and peace groups were party front organisations; in others, party underground members formed cells, and by their dynamism and through constitutional manoeuvres moved into positions of control. The party steered money into them, and boosted their efforts with opportunist propaganda. In these ways it created a Fifth Column to fulfil Russia's designs, one of which was the military weakness of its 'host' country.

In spite of our inexperience, or perhaps because of it, our sympathy made us feel the trauma of Great War survivors as our own, so that the peace movements' plea spoke to us powerfully. It joined together two fears: that the Western powers' war plans would steer us into mass slaughter again and another lost generation, and that in the process a ray of hope for a humaner society, the image of Russia that so many people wanted to believe in, would be extinguished. War plans? How could we know that Britain and France were militarily at their weakest for twenty years? Party branches were ordered to monitor the movements of trains and ships carrying munitions and chemicals and military units, and send the information to King Street, whence of course it went to Moscow. Some of it, one must assume form later events, was filtered by Moscow onwards to German Intelligence.

Groping for some sense, a clear view, trying to provoke Bernard out of his stonewalling, something made me say: 'All right, about this worker solidarity you talk about, if I go and fight in Spain, will the workers here make up my dole money to more than fifteen shillings a week when I get back? Better still, will the union fight to get me a decent job all the year round?'

I was ashamed the moment I had spoken. It was a silly way of expressing futility.

His forbearance snapped. Angrily he halted, tugged at my sleeve to stop me in my tracks, and pointed past me at something:

'Just you look at that!' He was hoarse with fury. 'For Christ's sake stop bellyaching and take first things first! Do you want to live like *that* all your life – you and everybody else round here? Do you! Look, man! Look!'

I turned to see what he was pointing at. We were at the mouth of a close, the narrow slit in a tenement façade entered directly from the street, giving on to a stone-paved corridor barely wide enough for two people abreast, about five yards long, leading to stone stairs up to flats on three storeys above. At the foot of the stairs the corridor angled itself sharply past them and continued, narrower still, in darkness untouched by the feeble yellow light of the gas mentle projecting from a slender pipe on the wall above the stair-foot, to a little unpaved back yard with its ash-pits – rubbish dumps – and posts for clothes lines.

I took a few steps into the close and he followed. At first glance it could have been any one of hundreds in the Gorbals, sights and smells so familiar that I had long ago ceased to be aware of them. Looked at carefully as we stood between the nudging walls in the dim light, this one was worse than most, the one where I lived in Warwick Street for instance, but it required an effort to remember and compare. Nearly all the stone steps in the first flight up to the half-landing were broken, with jagged edges where bits of tread had fallen away. Some had almost no tread left. Plaster had come away from the walls from ceiling to floor, and along the lower part the bared cement, originally grey, was stained yellow and smelt of urine. On a patch where the rough surface of brickwork was exposed, someone had vomited, probably a passing drunk whose sense of propriety, demanding privacy, had deterred him from being sick in the street; or a returning resident who could not wait to climb the few steps to the communal toilet on the first half-landing. The detritus had stuck to the pitted surface in a wide streaky band as it slid lumpily from chest height to the floor. Judging by the strength of its smell, a mixture of beer and fish and chips, the vomit was recent. Another powerful smell, of decaying rubbish, came mainly from the ash-pits at the far end of the corridor, but also from a deposit scattered over the floor. Despite the cold wet wind blowing in hard from the street, the cloud of mephitic vapours lingered stupefyingly about our heads.

No one could afford to throw away food leavings that had any good left in them. They used up what they could in broths and soups and pies. But a final residue, potato peelings, fish heads or meat bones from which repeated boiling had extracted all nourishment, or food that had gone off – refrigerators were for the rich – was thrown on the ash-pits, whence it was scavenged by rats and stray cats. At dead of night, sometimes even in daytime, one heard their furious scrabblings there, resulting in a scatter of rubbish all over the close, so that one picked one's way among little heaps so far gone in putrefaction as to be rejected by even these ravening beasts. Here at our feet, great holes among the broken flag stones overflowed with such rotting material, foul bits of paper, excrement, mud, broken glass.

I realised I was looking at a close, really looking, for the first time. Perhaps the sickly yellow gloom, all the light the tiny gas mantle produced, worsened the impact. A revulsion hit me like a heavy punch to the head. In the fleeting dizziness I had a nightmare vision. I stood among gigantic glistening boils that had burst and the pus spattered on me and oozed down, like the vomit on the wall, in a foul stream to the floor.

How could I not have seen all this before, surrounding me as it did everywhere I went? Of course I had seen it. I had shut it out, tolerated it, accepted it as the given. We all had. Expect Phil and his like. Traitors to their class!

Yes, it could be any close.

Bernard stood at my side, silently insisting on an answer. It was now his turn to blow the flame of inner crisis within me, as I had done to him. He wanted me to come away from the sidelines, stop my inner war of uncertain aims, resentments and thwarted will, and harness the wasted energy at last. And become, presumably, as committed as he?

Why should I be so disturbed? What external spark had I been awaiting? I knew only one thing for certain. Not only Bernard would shift: I would too. How, and in what direction, I had no idea.

In provoking him I had sapped at my own position too. Nothing made any sense – though what did 'sense' mean?

I told myself that my dismay and sadness and self-accusation were simply the shock of looking upon these lower depths and seeing them truly at last, that I recoiled not from these visible truths alone but from all the questions in life they stood for, and from what its recognition would demand of me. I had tried, amazingly, to forget that I myself was part of this horror.

And yet I made excuses. This was only part of life after all. You didn't look at life layer by layer, like Peer Gynt with the onion. You looked at the whole. At relationships as they were and as they could be. Yes, that was the heart of the matter. How could you make 'sense' out of fine gradations between one face of suffering and another?

I heard myself say, and wondered afterwards at how inadequate the words were: 'It could do with a bit of titivating, couldn't it, like a lot of other things?'

'A bit!' he shouted. 'My God! Are you blind! Look at the shite flowing out of that lavatory, and that broken tap up there with all the water pouring away and taking the shite down the stairs with it …' This close, like a great many others, had a shared water tap, as well as a shared lavatory, on a little half-landing at the turn of the stairs between floors. '… and the ash-pits stinking out the whole street! And the shite and the piss and the vomit and God knows what else! We're *standing* in it! And how do you like *this*? No wonder there's disease everywhere!'

He pointed down to fresh rat droppings on the flag stones.

A shout startled us. It came from the far end of the corridor at the opening to the back yard, in the dark angle of wall beneath the stairs that the weak gas light could not reach:

'Aw, fuck aff an' gie us a bi' o' peace wull ye!' – a young man's voice, breathless, grumpy.

There was a rustling sound in the darkness and a girl's loud whisper: 'Wheesht, dear, wheesht!'

The man growled: 'Aw, hen, ah hadnae time tae ge' intae ye!'

The girl giggled and whispered audibly again: 'Maybe that's just as well dear! Ah tellt ye ah never minded when tha' happened!'

'Bu ah *do*!' came the furious reply.

In her throaty whisper she said soothingly: 'Anyway, dear ah'll ge' ma monthlies all right this way, won't ah?'

The man grunted non-committally. Her thoughts of pregnancy – calculation or fear? – were evidently of no interest to him.

'Wait now,' he muttered. 'Ah'll be ready again soon enough.'

More whisperings, now subdued.

> The natural vigour in the venial sin,
> Is the way in which our lives begin ...

Oh Venus of the ash-pits! How many virgins have you bled here? How many seeds of life implanted?

A private place, in effect the only one, where lovers expected to be left undisturbed, where exploration began, love's fruit set.

Parental approval of 'walking out' seldom extended to canoodling, petting, at home. In theory, canoodling did not take place. Apart from moral prohibitions, most houses, as tenement flats were called, were full to bursting, and privacy was out of the question. A spare room was a rare luxury, possessed by a few better-off families, better off by Gorbals standards – clergymen, skilled artisans – who might live behind Renaissance façades in the tenements in Abbotsford Place on the southern edge of the Gorbals near Eglinton Toll, where Victoria Road and Pollokshaws Road took you to the lower middle class districts of Langside, Shawlands, and on to Newton Mearns.

In most of the houses we knew every foot of space was taken up by beds, mattresses on the floor, a few bare wooden chairs, a battered kitchen table. One or even two of the younger children commonly shared the parental bed, usually a mattress on planks resting on trestles in a curtained alcove in the kitchen.

To enable a coupling to take place in a semblance of privacy behind the curtain, the woman would step out in her shift, snatch a blanket off the bed and wrap the child in it and lay him on the floor boards near enough to the cooking range for him to get some radiated warmth from its banked-up fire. Afterwards she parted the curtains and came out naked to lift the unsleeping, finely aware child back into bed, to lie between her and the man lying open mouthed in post-coital sleep. And then mother and child might lie awake for a while, locked in unique perplexities. She, her body prompting her still, with no finality in her, turned her world over and over again in her mind's restless fingers. The child, possessed by wonder and nameless hauntings, tried to join together the heavings and creakings and groans and gasps and little cries he had heard as he lay on the floor, his mother's disturbed concentration now, his father's stillness as if felled, and the sticky warmth in which he lay between them, something more than the sweat that was there before, a substance he divined as elemental, mysterious, newly decanted, that touched his flesh and his senses with profound, unattainable meaning.

If there had been two children in the bed, the other, a toddler, also put out on the floor, might well have slept through it all. His turn for nocturnal wonderment would come.

For an unmarried girl to live away from home on her own was unthinkable. Even if special circumstances, such as the death of parents, led to her living under someone else's roof as a lodger, she would not be allowed men visitors in her room. As for the few unmarried men who could afford to live on their own in single ends, one-room tenement flats, no respectable, girl, or married woman for that matter, would want to be seen visiting one of them unchaperoned.

That corner of a close beside the ash-pits was a place outside time. Because the celebration did not take place under anyone's roof, moral responsibility could be kept at a distance if need be.

The place of that shrine of Venus in the life of the locality was understood by everyone. Fathers knew where to look for daughters out too late.

A girl impatient to escape from home might go there with her 'feller' and let him 'stamp her card' – get her with child. And then, with luck, persuade him to accept paternity and marry her: a common enough route to matrimony.

No one approved. Few openly disapproved. Fatalistically, all connived.

Residents making their way through the close to the ash-pits or the clothes lines in the back yard, sensing a couple's presence, retreated discreetly and returned later. Lovers seeking a vacant shrine wandered on to the next close, and the next. Some, driven and impatient, gave up the search and stood together in a lavatory on one of the half-landings. But that infringed the code and nearly always led to trouble. In theory each lavatory was shared by people from two floors, about six flats, but in practice by many more. Almost invariably the other lavatory in the close, or some in closes nearby, would be out of action because of blocked pipes or damaged cisterns or flush mechanisms, so there was seldom a moment during the day and well into the night when every functioning lavatory in a tenement was not in heavy demand, often with a queue stamping their feet waiting to get in. If a couple were making love in one, the anxious souls waiting on the cold stone steps made their feelings plain, firmly but usually not unkindly: 'Och come on! Go an' find yersels a place o' yer ain doon the stairs tae do yer canoodlin' in! Ah'm tellin' ye, if ah don't ge' in there in a minute ah'm gonnae shi' ma troosers!'

Most people entering a close, especially in the evening, would have half-expected that dark corner by the ash-pits to be occupied, and not lingered talking. Forgetfully, we had infringed the code, and being shouted at was only to be expected, and nothing to be disturbed about. But I had recognised the girl's voice, and a ghost had walked over my grave.

I had a surreal feeling of being outside everything, the present moment cancelled, the future already joined to the past.

Annie! That voice, that whisper. Annie, Annie!

Annie was a sewing machinist in the garment factory where Bernard and I worked. That was where it had begun, nearly two years ago.

Our sewing machines were in three double banks of twelve, each of two lines of six facing one another, the whole powered by a master motor from which transmission belting ran on pass wheels slung from the ceiling, with a transfer wheel and a separate belt taking power down to each bank. Separating the facing lines of machines in a bank was a smooth wooden trough; when a machinist finished seaming up a section of garment she tossed it into the trough and pushed it towards her neighbour in the line to do the next operation. At the end of the trough a passer – inspector – quickly checked the work, and if satisfactory threw it into a bin to which the pressers came to replenish their supply of work at the long pressing table, about thirty feet long and six wide, a few paces away. All of us, on piece work, depended for the level of our wages on the speed of those in the previous work stage, as well as on our own of course. With everyone increasing the pressure on everyone else, stress was high. The sewing machinists in particular showed it, with their heads down and their hands frenziedly pushing the work under the drumming sewing heads as if to urge the power needles, moving so fast as to be blurred, to sew faster still. And all the while the throaty hum and thump of power, the slap-slap-slap of drive belts, the bang and hammer of the press irons and the hiss of steam, the clang of metal as the irons were slung through narrow slots in the cast-iron chambers behind each presser where gas jets re-heated them, filled the head to bursting, drove out all sense. The only escape was to numb the mind.

And accidents happened.

The commonest injury at the sewing machines was a needle through a finger tip. The trade joke was that you were not a proper machinist till that had happened to you. But it was far from a joke when it did. In the immediate agony the victim instinctively pulled her impaled finger away and the needle broke, leaving part of itself embedded under the nail. Blood-poisoning, and sometimes amputation, could follow.

One day Annie's hair caught in the sewing foot of her machine. Some was actually drawn down to the shuttle and sewn into the seam she was working on, and her head was pulled down and banged hard against the fast moving vertical piston of the sewing head. No great injury was done, but she sustained a nasty bruising on the forehead and some blood was shed. Her cry was heard, as might the high-pitched mew of a kitten, through the general clamour and roar. Her bank of machines was the nearest to where I stood at the pressers' table and I got to her first, seized a pair of shears and cut her hair free, and then ran and got the first aid box from the boss's office and dabbed iodine on the cuts on her forehead. She wept a little but set her lips together and tried to push me away so that she could turn back to her work. Fearfully she glanced round at the other machine hands pushing pieces of garments along the wooden trough towards her work place and then at the passer who was getting worried because of the blockage of work beginning to grow at this point. For when an accident happened, unless it was a serious one, as when Jack Nimms dropped a press iron and burnt and tore the flesh all down his leg and broke the shin bone and some bones in his foot, never to walk properly again, the pace of work did not slacken. So now the machinists to Annie's right continued to push their completed pieces along the trough to her, and the two on her left were sitting waiting for work, losing working time, and money. Until she did *her* seaming up on these pieces, they could not do their part on them. If the hold up lasted much longer we would all be losing money. Even as I put a bandage round her forehead she reached under the sewing machine to remove the shuttle and began to clear it of shreds of her hair preparatory to re-threading.

Her voice shaky with the pain she said: 'Ye'd be'er le' me go! Thanks all the same. Ah've got tae ge' on wi' ma pieces now!'

'Can ye that?' I asked, for she was white as chalk.

'Ah'll have tae!' She gave me a quick taut smile and bent her head to re-thread the needle.

And so we drew close.

Annie had fiery red hair, greenish eyes, dimpled, laughing features, creamy skin, and a lovely, taut, sinuous figure. She did not walk so much as strut, swinging her body on flexed muscles in a way that shocked some of the older folk.

'There's that Annie Dalrymple flaunting herself! The brazen girl!'

I did not think the word brazen fitted her. With me she was innocent. She had, however, a hungry awareness, an impatience for experience, that might have been misunderstood. Or perhaps it was I who misunderstood?

89

She seemed to look far into me, eyes wide in wonder, face aglow; and her body sweat, a hot vapour sweeping up from the depths of her, overwhelmed me like a potent drug. That first experience of mingling chemistry was like a magical discovery long imagined, and claimed at last.

We sought to know everything about one another at one breath, one glance. Miraculously that did seem to happen as we walked the pavements at night hand in hand, or stood on the Suspension Bridge over the Clyde, feeling it vibrate with passing footsteps, and watched the lights along the river bank reflected in the dark oily waters; or sat in silence in the front seat of the upper deck of a tram and let our dream worlds flow together. We played the game of telepathic sympathy, comparing what we had each thought at a certain hour when we had been apart and taking delight in finding that we had been closely in tune.

Sometimes we bought a tuppenny bag of chips to eat together as we walked, and after a time would be amazed to find that we had forgotten to eat them, and that the greasy chips were stone cold.

One day, some weeks after we had first gone out together, we wandered in silence to some long grass in the park, and lay down and looked up at the sky, and after a while timidly turned to each other. Innocents, we learnt from each other intuitively, slowly. After a few months we went for the first of many hiking weekends to the Socialist Camp at Carbeth, a few miles north of Glasgow.

Before we set off she whispered shyly: 'Will ye put somethin' on yersel' when – when we're taegither?'

'Aye, ah've bought some.'

Our sublime unity continued for about a year. Then one evening I waited for her as usual at the factory door. I heard her step clicking down the stone stairs, and she was close beside me, speaking fast, in an unfamiliar monotone: 'Ah'm no' goin' oot wi' ye again. Ah cannae explain. An' don't try to come after me.' She walked briskly away.

Pride prevented me following. In shock I stumbled away to the refuge of the Mitchell Library. A light had died.

That was centuries ago. And the 'I' that had become entwined with her, body and soul I had thought, was lost in the past. No, not lost, not entirely. That was what the savage resurgence of sadness and hurt now told me. Why, after being dormant so long, should these feelings hit me so hard now?

The full meaning of her presence here in the back close struck home.

I had hardly spoken to her for a year. When girls and fellows stopped going out they treated one another with a remoteness we did not think of as unfriendly, rather as a decent correctness.

For a time Annie was one of the few politically conscious girls of the neighbourhood. 'Politically conscious' was a fine new jargon term, meaning that you were one of an élite who knew what was wrong with the world and would devote a few days or months to curing its ills before you sorted out your own life. They were far more impatient for *change*, far less tolerant than most of us fellows. Any action would do, so long as it upset the conventions that restrained them.

Apart from the common discontents, they were fired by resentments special to them, puzzling to the rest of us; long battened down beneath a pretence of conformity, now coming into the open. Unread as most of them were, they had somehow picked up the mutterings of the female soul, like unheard voices in the air, part of the *zeitgeist*.

They seldom attempted to express these feelings, perhaps could not; understood later, they are obvious enough. Women, in so many ways treated as less eligible both privately and publicly – paid lower wages than men, for instance – were owed a heavy debt by society for past and present injustice, and the time had come to set the account to rights. And so they strove to tear themselves away from their roots, reach out for freedoms only dimly perceived. Many were drawn to the party, beguiled by its pretence that all the unfairness in thought and deed was the fault of the System and only awaited the Revolution to be put right.

Meanwhile they snatched at ways of acting unconventionally, sympathetic magic to conjure that indistinct identity they hungered for, 'turn the wheel on which you turn'.

Innocently they transmitted their confusion to the fellows they went with, who, blindly following the masculine convention that girls should be treated as 'good for only one thing', at first refused to believe in their unfeminine rejection of submissiveness and dismissed them as prick-teasers. Or, pretending to meet the girl on her own terms but unwilling – or unable – to resonate with her questing spirit, retreated in ill-tempered perplexity.

For each of these girls a time of private reckoning would come. Rebellious behaviour had failed to move their world. Time was passing. Resignedly they resorted to precisely that 'only one thing', a valuation of themselves previously dismissed as soulless, the base metal and not the gold. They too, in their turn, would assume the conventional strategy for fitting themselves into the world as it was.

The New Woman dream was not abandoned: it had to be put aside as a luxury.

In going composedly to the shrine at the ash-pits to get their card stamped, they were content – or so they pretended – to confirm the masculine prejudices.

And soon the exultantly physical girl ripened into the burdened mater-familias, reddened arms folded beneath sagging bosom, worriedly gossiping on stair landing or in close mouth, or trudging along the street with an infant cocooned in a shawl and another on the way, withdrawn in a frowsty female freemasonry, tired drudges of the Steamy.

Whether a girl was the conventional sort, or rebellious and polit-ically conscious, if she was well into her twenties and still unmar-ried, time became the whipper-in. She must move fast if she was not to drift away into isolation, lose links hitherto dismissed as old-fashioned and valueless, now seen to have worth, retain the warmth of a shared outlook with mother and grandmothers, and friends already settled.

And now, shockingly, Annie too was following the same ritual.

Annie was about nineteen now, surely too young to be driven by that fear. How could I know what other conflicts drove her now? Regret about *us*? Hardly. She had never once given me the slightest sign of that. If only she had! Or simply impatience to be free of home? That and something else perhaps, much worse, a shift of the spirit altogether. The ripening seed in the belly freed a girl simply by leaving her no time to remake the world – to remake anything, herself least of all.

In a delayed reaction, it struck me that I knew the man's voice too. Phil Emet. And that, to my surprise when I later thought about it, did not immediately make me jealous, or any more unhappy for *myself*, but rather for her. It explained her behaviour in a completely different way – money and status, a seemingly clear escape from all this.

On the face of it, Phil was a sensible choice for an ambitious girl. He was marked out to make money. He would reach the Shangri-la of Newton Mearns.

But if she thought he would take her with him she was vastly mistaken.

If she followed the usual pattern, once she knew her card was stamped, she would noise it about that he was the father of the child she carried. And he, if he behaved with conventional masculine arrogance, would already have abetted her plan by boasting of the conquest.

The form modern, the sense ancient.

> I entered the sacred wood;
> I made her heave in joy!

I thought of the ritualistic scene enacted many a time in our shower room group.

The girl's name would be mentioned by one of the group with pretended casualness. Of course they all knew! They were feeding lines to the proud conqueror: 'Aw, man!' he would respond, voice guttural and compressed, right first clenched as the forearm rose up perpendicular under the impact of the left first in the crook of the right elbow. 'Aw that was a marvellous lumber!' Dreamily, eyes half-closed, a soft smile on the lips, his voice stretched out the remembered ecstasy and the triumph: 'An' ag-ain and ag-ain and ag-ain!'

'An' ye're no' carin' if ye've stamped her caird or no'?'

'Widdy ah care? Them hairies know whit tae do don't they?'

Perhaps a shadow of a care did flit across the face. And then a shrug, as if to say: 'Well, if ye're goin' tae be caught – ye're caught! It's got tae happen sooner or later!'

Social pressure, tradition, tribal force of habit, or more respectably convention, usually fulfilled the girl's plan.

This must be a recent conquest for Phil, or we would have heard of it. Who was going out with whom was quickly known. But Phil would not be caught that way. He would defy the tribe and turn his back on a stamped card. He would follow his own star no matter who he left by the wayside. That was Phil.

Who could tell Annie this with any hope of her believing it?

Filled with these thoughts, lacerated by bitterness at what she was doing a few yards away, I retreated to the close mouth. Bernard joined me and we stood there in silence. I stamped my feet to get the circulation going again, and wriggled frozen toes in the soaked cardboard padding in my boots. The pain of numbed feet returning to life brought me sharply back.

To my surprise I saw intense disapproval of Bernard's face. The shrine at the ash-pits was as familiar an institution to him as it was to all of us. But then, I recalled, the thought of it always had disturbed him much more than any other feature of Gorbals life, an odd puritanism when one thought of the party's inclusion of free love in its revolutionary ethic. In practice, however, its support for sexual freedom, and other personal emancipations like that of women from the kitchen stove, were minor themes, stated conditionally, with care, so as not to upset too many sensibilities. Privately, the party mandarins were strait-laced. They explained away this inconsistency by arguing that promiscuity's consequences – unwanted pregnancies, illegitimacies, forced and sordid marriages, venereal disease – like other over-indulgences such as drunkenness, only more so, deflected comrades' energies from the basics. Apostles must not waste their energies in wild living. Remaining pure they were better fighters for the cause.

He looked up at the sky. The rain had stopped. A watery moon, waning, appeared fitfully between banks of black cloud, gale-driven across a steel grey sky. A bleak night on which to look for renewal of hope, or faith. Reverting to the Spanish War he sighed:

'It's part of a bigger war – a war to destroy the System. The symptoms of its evils are all around us.'

He gestured behind us, in a manner that succeeded in including not only the squalor of the close but the now silent lovers: 'What a place to start your life together, the stinking ash-pits! Isn't that enough to poison life for evermore? So this war in Spain is vital whichever way you look at it. We had to start somewhere.'

'Tell me,' I said, 'what's Russia doing to help in this holy war?'

He frowned. 'They've sent a few military experts and technical advisers and so on, and some food and arms.' He shook his head. 'They're fully stretched building upon the Revolution. We can't expect them to do any more, like sending troops, to weaken themselves to the extent that the imperialists can go in and destroy the Revolution! After all, their Revolution is really *ours*, and we must help them to keep it strong.'

He turned to face me. His shoulders drooped, an exhausted runner. Quietly he said: 'Let's leave all this for now?'

Let me be! I must keep going the way I am or I'm lost.

In all the years we had been friends I had never seen him so unhappy. And I was unhappy for his sake now.

A thought struck me that I knew was important but understood fully only much later. Being unhappy for other people's sakes was a way of holding the world at arm's length. Bernard had been doing that too. How much longer could he continue? Should I hope, for his sake, that he could do so for ever? That would be cruel. Self-denial dried up the soul.

I saw too that being sorry for others was a kind of condescension, in the end self-wounding. Sometime, somehow, I would find a way of striking a blow for myself.

In silence we stepped out of the close and went on to the Workers' Circle.

8

A Taste of Freedom

'Annie Dalrymple came here, 21st June 1936.'

Incised on a block of ironstone in the remnant of Roman wall, her proclamation, in the stealthy dawn of a summer day long ago, her dawn, and mine. Through the long slow measures of the constellations, forgotten but preserved, waiting in the shadows to be rediscovered, as Destiny had preserved that flint axe-head in the earth, debris of a skirmish at a Roman outpost, of her to snatch it up, as from the banks of Phlegethon, and set her exultation in stone.

> Moment of light and fusion.
> Beginning and end of youth.

I think, as she did so, as in a warning intuition I foresaw that I would return and find it again, long after she herself had become a ghost. I saw that future day in something very like its eventual detail. Both visions have their place here.

What Destiny ordained, wandering near that place probing for the past, that I turn a corner in a street of peeling bungalows and discover these words, her shout of joy and triumph, poignant as a distant cry at evening, fixed here in shadow as it had waited deep in memory, in this forgotten patch of rank undergrowth, all that remained of the wilderness of stunted oak and wild blackberries and acrid bracken that we had ranged in freedom, Carbeth Muir?

Her memorial to herself. Skull beneath the skin.

Her moment had outlived her. So it would continue through time and chance, as had the embrasure in the wall long before.

Carbeth Muir, a great stretch to moorland north of Glasgow that had separated the city from a region of arable and dairy farmland beyond Milngavie, now lay buried beneath a scabby dormitory sprawl in decline, suburban twilight.

On the far edge of the Muir had been the Socialist Camp. Tuppenceha'penny on the tram to the terminus at Milngavie, and then a tramp across the hummocky wasteland on a Friday night after work – if we were not wanted in the factory on the Saturday – tired but drunk with freedom. Dreams could soar. With every step we were renewed. The track across it led *out* in every sense.

On it you met habitués of the Socialist Camp, or hikers aiming further afield, sometimes singly, meditatively whistling or playing a mouth organ while striding along, or in little voluble groups whose voices came to you long before as a murmur on the wind. Or you came upon them in the shelter of an embrasure in an old wall or beside a massive oak felled by lightning, having a 'drum-up' – a halt to fill a gap with tea and bread and jam, and perhaps a fry-up of bacon and bread – at a fire of fallen branches. You saw the red glow as a spark in the far darkness well in advance of the scent of wood smoke wafting to you. You could count on a welcome at a fire, even from strangers. Hikers were still few, the enlightened who were joined in a mystic affinity. There would be a shout from the little group seated on boulders round it:

'Come on an' have a drum-up?'

You stopped and unshouldered your pack and dumped it on the ground and unhooked your enamelled tin mug from one of its buckles. A space was made for you, and someone with spare tea in a billy can would pour you some, to refresh you while you brewed up your own, to be shared in its turn, and you moved into the flow of talk as if you had been there all the time.

Talk was of politics, of jobs and apprenticeships and what to do next with one's life, of sex and conquest, except when there were girls in the party, when there would be a strong admixture of gossip and mild sexual banter. There would be talk of the outdoors and its freedoms and what it did for you, 'the road', of good places of sleep out and drum up – urban dwellers picking up scraps of intelligence about the country, learning from each other as guerrillas learn how to survive in alien territory; except that with us the mystic affinity made us protective towards it. An enlightened self-interest, a shared ceremony of thanksgiving for what we breathed and dreamed on the road, for the expansion of the soul we found there.

And then the people who had called out to you to join them might stretch and look up at the sky. Thoughts of the waning hours, the moments of freedom drifting by. Time to stow food and plates in packs, hang mugs on buckles, stand up and shrug the shoulders snugly into the broad webbing straps. Time to move on. Turning away to rejoin the track, they called out the customary parting:

'See you on the road then!'

A benediction.

And you gave an equal reply: 'Aye. See you on the road!'

Staying and tending the fire while you finished your own drum-up, you might hear other footfalls approach, and you in turn would hail a pack-laden figure or little group to join you at the fire. When they did, the flow of talk continued as if there had been no interruption. And then, moving on yourself, you handed over the fire to their care. If no one else came along by the time you wanted to move, you would follow the rule of the mystic affinity. You stamped out the fire and piled stones over the embers, after burning combustible left-overs, and buried empty cans or bottles.

Encountering someone at a crossing of paths on the Muir, you might be told: 'There's a fire about a mile back there.'

So pilgrims long ago, meeting in the wilderness, passed on news of comfort to be found along the ways they had come.

Sometimes, when hailed by people sitting at a fire, you might not be in the mood to join a group, or in a hurry to catch up with someone further along the track. You shouted back: 'Och, no' the noo, thanks. See yese on the road!'

'Aye, see ye on the road then,' came the answering murmur, and they turned again to the comfort of the flames and the talk.

Most of us carried old army webbing packs, some brought back home by survivors of the trenches and handed down within families, but mostly bought for a shilling at the government surplus stores. Some of the 'surplus' packs had never been used, to judge from the stiffness of the heavy cotton, nearly as thick as the belting that powered the sewing machines in the factory. Others showed signs of many treatments of army blanco. Here and there a dark stain would send a shiver down the spine. Thoughts of shot and shell, of blood.

These square packs were just big enough to hold a spare shirt – often army surplus khaki – and pants and socks, towel and soap, a loaf of bread, a few small tins of baked beans, slices of sausage loaf wrapped in greased paper, tin plate, knife and fork and spoon, old tobacco tins for tea and sugar, salt and pepper in little twists of paper. The pack fitted so closely on the back that, even with this light load, after half-an-hour of walking your jacket and shirt and vest were soaked in sweat; and sometimes the skin got painfully blistered. We looked with envy at the superior equipment of some of the people we met, from the better-off parts of Glasgow like Kelvinside or Hillhead, near the University – the Bergen rucksack for example, one of the first with a frame to keep an air space between your back and the pack, preventing painful friction and the accumulation of sweat; and breeches and long stockings or puttees, and boots with tricouni nails round the edges of the soles. Our boots were the single pair we possessed, perhaps with an extra sole hammered on at home. To buy special hiking clothes was totally beyond us.

The Socialist Camp, high on a stony hillside, was approached by an old farm track that meandered a mile or so up from the road that went north to Drymen and the Trossachs. Large ridge tents, pitched to form a square, stood on wooden platforms, some with two or three broad plank steps at the entrance to offset the slope. It was a place of traditional socialist earnestness and uplift. The grassy space within the square was used for community singing in the evenings round a log fire, and lectures and Socialist Sunday School meetings.

As you turned off the road, and just before you began the stiff pull up a cart track lined with blackberry bushes leading to the Camp, you passed an old single-decker bus body standing alone beneath the spreading branches of a venerable oak. Crammed with shelving, fitted with a sliding widow in its side like that in a railway booking office, with a corrugated iron canopy over it to shelter customers in rainy weather, it had been ingeniously converted into a rural general store. In a tiny compartment at one end of it were sleeping quarters; and a lean-to at the back, made from old doors and tarred felt, contained a primitive kitchen and chemical toilet. Here, running a business with many mysterious ramifications, Jimmy Robinson dreamed and preached.

It was hard to tell his age, for his tall and lean figure looked strong and he moved lightly and with vigour, but the close cropped hair was silvery, the leathery face deeply lined. He could have been in his late fifties or older. He went about in a frayed khaki shirt, perhaps the same one, and old khaki trousers with flat brass buttons on the waistband, anchorages for elasticated red and white striped braces, heavily stained.

He studied you from between narrowed lids, seeming to stare through you to some distant horizon and place you in context with it: the hard, measuring gaze of the wanderer. We envied what we saw in him, the free spirit *par excellence*, new in our experience, who had been to the far places of the world and brought back a cargo of wisdom. It had come, he proclaimed, from privation, from wounds inflicted by the harsh edges of the world, the forces of nature and of man, in coal mines and timber camps, in the ruthless tempo of New World factories, the Dantesque realities of the Chicago stock yards. We did not pause to think that the Gorbals had suffered as much, if differently, and if that were the sole test we were as fitted as he to pass on to us the lessons of living. The magic of far places, the sound and scent of battles under strange banners, gave him a stronger claim. We sat at his feet.

Those summer nights at his door were not really endless and totally wonderful but they seemed to be. Dark outlines of hedgerows and trees, and tall bracken dimly seen and merging. Prussian blue velvet sky spangled with silver. Whispers of the earth. Life itself whispering, nudging us. Wonders waiting in the wings.

We drank strong tea from mugs dipped into the blackened skilly can never absent from a brazier made out of a holed oil drum, that stood under a sheet of corrugated iron he had rigged as a canopy under an overhanging branch at his back door; in its shelter we sat round him on empty packing cases or logs stood on end. We listened to his memories of bumming across America, of working with the Wobblies, the International workers of the World, and groups of anarcho-syndicalists – 'the Movement' of O'Neill's *The Iceman Cometh* – who would destroy the System with bomb and gun and bring purity to the world. Preachers of beneficial death, curative killing; early urban guerrillas.

Shades of Sacco and Vanzetti. Fighters under the black flag. Honoured martyrs. Purity of vision excuses any act. They must not have died in vain.

It was never clear whether he had been an active member of the Movement or a fellow-traveller, literally and metaphorically, experimenting with its underground life while riding the rails across America and sleeping in the 'jungles', shanty camps to be found at railroad junctions on the way. If he had been a member, he was certainly among the more successful of those it left behind as the dream of world dominion by a brotherhood of the horny-handed sons of toil faded away, as the Movement was broken by bloody industrial battles, internal feuding, betrayals, armed clashes with the law.

Hunted down in America, disillusioned remnants scattered far and wide to nurse their dreams and wait for their day; and hand on, as he did, the torch of faith and hope.

Some survived less well than others. Like Larry Slade and Hugo Kalman in *The Iceman Cometh*, they chose to sink to the bottom of society rather than compromise with the System. Or perhaps they did not know how to compromise and remain pure? Jimmy, perhaps harder or shrewder, more worldly and detached than he presented himself to be, plainly did know. At Carbeth he lived in gypsy style, but there were hints of a large house in Edinburgh and unspecified business deals that took him away for a few days now and then. During such absences someone from the Camp would look after the little shop for him.

There was always someone there to do the odd job. It sheltered what amounted to a little colony of drop-outs, a sturdy *maquis* living in the shadowy purlieus of the System or, as Jimmy grandly put it, 'a brotherhood at the bottom of the heap'. In those doldrums of unemployment, especially during the long summer emptiness, to stay at the Camp was as good a method of pushing time away as hanging round street corners or at the Broo. If you were resourceful, you could exist there without any money in your pocket at all. You did simple maintenance jobs at the Camp, or some fetching and carrying for Jimmy, in return for basic rations, the odd can of beans, loaf, portion of sausage meat, a few eggs, some milk. At night you might go out and lift some potatoes or other produce in the surrounding farmland. Taking food 'within reason' wasn't really stealing! In this manner a few hardy fellows even survived at the Camp the whole of the winter.

Sometimes they tried to lord it over us wage slaves. They were beating the System, they arrogantly affirmed; doing that you raised yourself above it. They were not beating the System, and I sometimes wondered whether the assertion was no more than a comforting pretence. Jimmy, a merchant, apart from his other enterprises, was part of it, indeed exemplified it, and doing jobs for him was to stay within it too. And as for 'lifting' produce from the fields, they did not like to be reminded that someone had worked hard to plant and cultivate it. 'So much the worse for them,' they would retort, 'for working to maintain the System!' In a small way they were predators, speciously justified according to their lights but predators none the less. Indeed, I argued, at one remove they preyed on *us*. But that was too strong medicine for them.

All the same there was something attractive in their seeming independence, a romantic, picaresque quality.

'But what happens,' I asked one of them, 'if things get really hard, and you can't make ends meet out here?'

He was amazed at the naïve question. 'Ah jist thumb a lift back tae Rose Street an' move in wi' the family again!'

I felt like saying: 'So your family, the wage slaves, bail you out? So that's what your high talk about independence and not compromising with the System amounts to?' But what was the point?

Wage slave or no, the job at the factory was a life-line, a thin one, but I was lucky to have it at all.

Sometimes we arranged with the boss to work late on a Friday instead of going in on the Saturday; that meant we could leave for Carbeth straight from the factory that night, giving us two clear days of escape. But it could mean that it was midnight or even later when we made our way across the Muir. No matter how late, even in the small hours, from far off we saw the yellow glimmer of Jimmy's oil lamp. We kept it in view, dipping and rising and veering as we followed the windings and undulations of the familiar track. Up on the hill the Camp was asleep. All around us to the invisible horizon no farmhouse showed a light. His never dimmed. Whatever the hour we could knock on his window if we needed a can of condensed milk, a pan loaf, a small tin of beans. Out he would come in trousers and the torn khaki shirt.

'Come on and join me! Take the weight off yer feet. I'll blow up the fire. There's tea in the skilly. Help yourselves.'

When was there not tea in the skilly?

Those arrivals in the night were uniquely wonderful, filled with a sense of homecoming, to a place where your lungs lustily drew in new air that was your very own. And the darkness emphasised the sense of personal mystery. On our way across the brooding wilderness we trod the earth in a kind of dedication, celebrants straining towards a secret shrine of the spirit. Hearts newly freed from the hammering of the factory, we felt wrapped round and comforted by the silence, the touch of air that carried freedom on light wings, caressed by the scents and little sounds of the sleeping land, rush and ripple of burns and flowing ditches, sudden flap of a disturbed bird, distant hoot of barn owl, rustle of a small animal in the bushes.

He seemed to need company then more than in the day. I pictured him sitting up into the night fiercely wishing to hear the sound of plodding footsteps, the rattle of billy-cans in rucksacks.

Not only talk but disciples. The individualist creed must spread, the doors of freedom must be opened, violence the only key. A latter-day Bakunin. How certain he was that he would see the awakening of the world's workers, and the mass slaughter of the privileged! Yes, *mass* slaughter. *They* did not deserve the luxury of the private tumbril! The Great Day of the barricades. This time the Communards would be vindicated. Their spirit would triumph the world over.

'The Great Day will come! Oh yes it'll come all right, when we storm the armouries and arm the people and mount the machine guns opposite the Stock Exchanges and the banks and mow down the exploiters, every man jack of them. Then we'll be free of them for good an' all.'

After such a pronouncement he would lean back on a bedraggled car seat wedged against the back door of the old coach and regard us proudly, a warlord after a harangue to the faithful, but also quizzically, testing us. Perhaps, through us, he searched for weaknesses in the testimony? The yellow rays of a storm lantern that hung from a hook over the door above his head illuminated a narrow patch of beaten earth where the brazier stood, and touched a branch and a nearby bush; and the downward rays picked out his lined features in a bronze radiance, an oracular chiaroscuro. He lifted to his lips a carved meerschaum pipe with a thick silver ring round the flared bowl, and a silver strap about the stem inset with little glittering stones. Catching my interested glance one night, as the stones flashed in the light, he said:

'Sure, diamonds me lad! It came out of a raid by some o' the Movement boys, out near Houston I remember. To get money for ammunition and explosives, an' – yes, an' livin' expenses. This thing was too identifiable. Nobody wanted to risk tryin' to sell it! I "found" it, ye might say!' He showed blackened teeth in a hard grin. 'Stashed it away till I got back here. We called the raids "reappropriations", like Lenin called the bank raid at Tiflis and other places. What we take from the boss class is simply takin' back what they stole from *us*, see?'

Stories of riding the rails across America, of meeting Robert Service and Daniel de Leon. America the golden land, the melting pot, where the System was at its most savage. And perhaps, being new, at its most vulnerable. Days of turmoil and hope, of blows struck and groups scattering, to lie low and come together again and plan the next blow, or the next reappropriation. The present was only a hiatus. The movement bided its time, its spirit nourished so long as here and there in the wilderness disciples tended the flame – of righteousness, liberty, and nemesis for the exploiters.

Innocents, we were uplifted by this gospel of the victory of benevolence. Probably none of us took his talk of the need for bloodshed seriously. It was an abstraction, rhetorical emphasis.

Bernard would not have taken it seriously either, but for different reasons, had he ever come with us, but he never did; for him the Camp itself was not serious. It was for 'milk and water socialists', for drifters and dreamers, for ineffectual drop-outs.

But for Jimmy the drop-out – the 'bum', as we called him – was the virtuous standard-bearer, the independent spirit fearlessly following a glorious star. Plainly he saw himself as one, side-stepping the fact that he had become a prosperous entrepreneur. That incongruity certainly occurred to us, but in youthful excitement at touching new ideas we did not linger on it; or perhaps we shrank from being tactless enough to question him about it.

As we sat round his brazier in the dark hours, mugs of tea in hand, we sang softly with him:

> Hallelujah I'm a bum!
> Hallelujah bum again!
> Hallelujah give us a handout,
> To revive us again…

Fellowship of the night; a time for innocents.

The track across the Muir passed a stretch of old Roman wall, said to be Agricola's – to the casual glance simply a hummock covered with scrub, bracken, thicket of bramble and hedgerow flowers. At one point, where a shallow declivity had been bridged by deeper courses of massive stone, hidden by stunted oak, was an embrasure roofed by slabs of granite, originally perhaps part of a storage chamber in the fortifications. Presumably it had been uncovered, many years before, in an archaeological dig that had run out of funding. In it on fine summer nights, if we were more than usually late on the road, probably having done sixteen hours that day in the factory, and felt too tired to go the remaining three miles or so to the Camp, we often slept.

Visions of those times reappeared, hovered heavy with regrets unappeased, as I walked again over that ground, or where it had been, many years later, a whole world away. Now there was nothing recognisable. Where were the vistas of rolling moorland freely mingling in yellow and brown and green, trees leaning under the west wind, ranks of bracken standing stiffly, and the golden scented broom waving, long neglected dry stone walls dipping and winding, a wild-running demesne owing discipline to no one? All erased. Choked now beneath a labyrinth of villas, semi-detached houses, military lines of council houses, one-storey shopping parades, the standard arrays of off-licence, newsagent-cum-sweet shop, self-service grocer, dry cleaner, launderette, garage. In the withdrawn mood induced by pacing between endlessly similar suburban walls, from whose peeling stucco and marl and brick the hard sunlight struck back and pounded the mind, I turned a corner and stopped abruptly in a cul-de-sac that ended in a high bank of sun glazed foliage and brilliant wild flowers.

I knew.

Compelled as in a dream I parted a clump of giant sunflowers. Deep in the green shadows, sun-dappled, I saw the venerable greys and browns and slatey greens of sleeping stonework. Behind splintered fencing and bits of old cars was the Roman storage chamber, our cave. I had stepped into the past. On one of the blocks marks were visible. Elbowing further through the rank greenery, I picked out the incised words, tracing each mark upwards and downwards as my lips formed them. And once again, as in my mind's eye I had done so many times over the years, I saw her knuckles tighten as she gripped the sharp flint she had picked up, her tumbled fiery hair falling over her face and sweeping the paleness of a slender pointed shoulder, and with parted lips entered her name and her moment in this record of history and slow time.

For her a beginning, and an end.

'Annie Dalrymple came here, 21st June 1936.'

I stared at the word 'came'. Discovery and self-discovery! Had she ever returned? Stood before that block of stone, and reflected, as I did now, on our broken history?

9

A Letter from Oxford

For many months after I had overheard Annie and Phil at the ash-pits at the back of that close, at unguarded moments of the day and night, her loud whisper echoed in my mind: 'Ah tellt ye ah never minded when tha' happened!'

The combination of intimacy and calculation in her voice burnt like acid. This was not the Annie I had known. For her sake, for both our sakes, I mourned a many-stranded tragedy. The road she had chosen spoke out loudly, like a Greek chorus lamenting the future – mine, hers, the destinies of all of us.

Especially poignant was her implied verdict on me and on my worldly prospects. She had chosen Newton Mearns – not Phil, but the prizes his road would bring her. An old, old pattern. Her forecast for me was probably right. I was not the stuff that captains of industry were made of, even if I had had Phil's advantage of a family business to start from. But where now were the principles we had once shared – as I had thought – when we swore to each other that we were important for what we were and not for what we possessed? Now it was Newton Mearns and to hell with what you were as a person.

Had my faith been so hopelessly astray? Or was it simply that for her, at last, the pull of the world, the corruption Bernard inveighed against, was too strong?

One day these thoughts were driven totally from my mind. A letter arrived that I had not expected, or rather that I had told myself not to expect. It was from Oxford:

I am pleased to inform you that you have been appointed to a Special Category Open Scholarship on your performance in this year's Essay Competition. Please inform me as soon as possible

whether you are willing to accept the appointment. If you are,
would you also confirm that you will take up residence in College
on the first day of Michaelmas Term next?

That morning I had left home for the factory at five, long before
the post came. I found the letter when I got home about seven in the
evening. While I read it I bolted my tea as usual. Then I read it
again, a message from a distant planet, with its strange, sonorous,
processional language. 'Willing to come into residence ...': you
didn't go and stay, you went into *residence*!

I tried to think clearly. What could I possibly have to do with
Oxford, or Oxford with me? I had to stand away from the idea to
see it at all. Could it be a hoax? Me, of all people? Oxford! Oh, yes,
I *had* written that essay. I *had* sent it off, an arrow shot at a venture;
best forgotten.

But the Fates had decreed that I would never forget that essay, or
rather its theme, which must have touched profound sensibilities
within me; in diverse disguises it would be a *leitmotiv*, especially in
my writing, in all the years to come: 'Has Science Increased Human
Happiness?' In the essay my answer was 'no', as it would continue
to be.

I felt breathless; there seemed precious little air in this kitchen of
ours, steamy and yet cold too, smelling of stale fat, decay, damp.

I shoved the letter into my pocket, snatched towel and swimming
briefs, and hurried out to the Baths. In the street I threaded automatically through the evening bustle, seeing no one. Thoughts
whirled and rocketed about, would not be controlled; it was like
being drunk for the first time. The world was upside down. How
do you start thinking about a bombshell like this, that breaks
through everything you're used to, asks you to decide something
you've no precedents for? A stupid question hammered away in my
mind: 'Do I dare tell anyone?' It would be a long time to keep it to
myself. What they called Michaelmas was nearly a year away.

I turned out of Bedford Street and went along Gorbals Street,
and as I came near the Baths entrance I was remotely aware that
Annie was standing there, apparently studying the notice beside the
arched doorway that gave the times of opening of the various

departments and prices of admission. In my indrawn and bewildered state I idly noted her presence, nothing more, felt no special
response. As I came near, she turned and seemed to notice me with
surprise. Suddenly she stood in my path.

I suppose my mind was too full to wonder about this coincidence. Later I did, and reminded myself that most people who
knew our group could easily discover that we now met at the Baths
on three nights a week, on Monday, Wednesday and Friday. This
was Wednesday.

At the factory I had seen her only from a distance. I may have noticed her more often of late. Yes, I must have done. I had caught
myself looking at her, bent over the drumming sewing head of her
machine, hands and arms in feverish motion as she steered the
edges of cloth or lining material under the whirring needle, hair
curtaining pale cheek, half-shielding her eyes. Pools of green fire I
had known so well. Memory unnerved me again and again, till I reminded myself how it had ended, abruptly, like a light switched off,
which was how it felt; but with lingering pain, made worse by the
sense that on her part it had been a decision coolly reached.

In the last few days I had sometimes caught her glancing in my
direction in a puzzling, equivocal manner, but it had not occurred
to me that she might be trying to catch my eye. There was no reason why she should. So I had let the glance slide past me. We had
not spoken.

Now, coming near, she greeted me with her old welcoming smile:

'Wha' a coincidence! Ah was just thinkin' aboo' ye! What d'ye
think o' that?' Turning her face half away and tossing her head,
looking at me from the corners of her eyes, she added: 'All that long
time ago? Remember?'

She came close, and her green eyes gazed luminously into mine.

The letter in my pocket held my thoughts. Her words barely registered. I heard myself reply woodenly:

'Aye, Annie, a long time ago!'

'Too long!' She went rushing on, 'For too long! Aye, ah've been
thinkin' a lot aboo' us – and that time, ye know?'

'What d'ye mean?' I asked dumbly.

She turned to stand at my side, put her arm through mine, and to my surprise pressed close. A cloud of scent enveloped me. That was new. She never wore scent when we went about together. Beneath it, surging through to me compellingly, came her familiar sweat, touching my senses and my mind with the soft magic of her flesh, so sweet in memory, which I would conjure up as long as I lived whenever that fiery spirit of hers called to me across the years.

She spoke in my ear to compete with the rattle and bustle of the street, the voice hot and urgent: 'Ah've go' so much tae say tae ye! Oh please listen tae me! Ah've been meanin' tae talk tae ye like this for long enough! Oh ah'm sorry, real sorry for wha' ah did! Ah'm beggin' ye tae forgive me. Ah must have been mad tae leave ye! Ah've loved ye a' the time, an' ah didnae know it till – till – well ah know it now right enough! Ah really mean it, dear. Come wi' me! Come up tae oor hoose. They've a' gone tae ma Granny's. We'll have the place tae oorsels an' we can talk? Ah want tae make i' up tae ye. Ah *know* we'll be happy taegither. We'll be happy for ever. Happier than we ever were. Ah promise. Ah really and truly promise. Oh come wi' me now?'

The heat of her body as her loins pressed upon me as if she would enwrap me in her flesh, those secret fumes pulsing up into my head, were near to sweeping away all sense.

Then some perversity interposed itself. That personal vapour of her, once irresistible, awoke the past and revived the hurt of rejection. The letter in my pocket reasserted its hold on my mind, and everything here became distant. Close to me as she now stood, I saw her on the far side of a barrier, and I had no room in my mind for what lay beyond it. I wanted desperately to think about what that letter would do to me. Nothing else.

Only part of me stood here on the cold pavement in the Gorbals that was the only world I knew, suddenly aware that my time here was being foreclosed. The rest of me stood apart and read the letter again and again, incredulously seeing myself in a perspective that stretched away to a wider world I knew only from hearsay, that I had never seriously thought I could enter, apart from the freakish impulse that had made me shoot that arrow into the blue months ago, and had now brought me the letter. That world was the preserve of people not of my kind, who I must meet on their ground, not mine. Far, far away. Another life. Distant trumpets! Stuff of new dreams, new fears.

Now that that unattainable mirage had become beckoning destiny, I had the dizzying feeling that time itself had accelerated and was whirling me away from everything I had known here, too fast for me to think about. Too fast for me to hold in check. And then the next moment it seemed that it was this world of the Gorbals that was being pulled away from *me*, as the quay recedes from one who stands at the rail of the departing ship.

In this state of separateness the power and feeling and urgency in her words were like the sound, overheard from a distance, of someone knocking on the door of an empty house, a summons addressed to someone else, no concern of mine. Above all I did not *want* it to be my concern. Even though her flesh sang to me, dizzied me. I had no room in my mind to rehearse the past. An urgent voice told me that I must move away from her. I searched for the right words.

A few minutes ago I had resolved to keep quiet about the scholarship in the coming weeks and months, the instinctive impulse to avoid ill-humoured murmuring: 'He's giving himself airs isn't he?' No doubt my uncertainty nudged me too. What if I simply couldn't take up the scholarship in the end? Best not to talk about it till I was good and sure.

But I was flustered and off guard. I blurted it out:

'It's too late, anyway. I'm going away from here. I've won a scholarship to Oxford.'

She entwined herself tighter still, searched my face with the intentness of unbelief – and fear.

'Too late?' Colour faded from her face. She mouthed the words again as if the meaning would change if she did so. 'Too late did ye say! Oh don't say that! Please, dear, it cannae be too late. Oh it mustn't be! Ah'll do anything tae make things good for ye! Anything. I promise. Please!'

Amidst the turmoil in my mind the command to move away

from her became insistent: 'Leave this alone! Get away from it! It's dangerous!'

Gently I loosened her arms from about me. 'I'm going away. My time here's over. Something very important's just happened to me.'

I was tempted to be less definite, temporise. But that would be cruel, weak – and false. The truth was that I distrusted my feelings. Yet that inner voice told me to say an unequivocal 'No'. What my doubts were I did not know. But I knew in my bones that I must draw away from her. I said weakly, repeating myself:

'Something very important's just happened tae me. Let me go now. We'll speak together again. Yes, afterwards, in a little while.'

She would not let go.

'Aw come wi' me now! This minute! If we don't it might be …' She turned her head away. Then, correcting her course, she faced me again, brows puckered in supplication: 'Please. Ah can't bear it!'

'Not now. Not now!' I clung to the words as to a lifeline. Then added desperately: 'Listen. If it's waited two years it can wait a bit longer. The most important thing that's ever happened to me, maybe that ever will happen to me, has just happened. And I've got to look at my life all over again. Let go now.'

The terror in her eyes puzzled me, but I dared not pause to speculate about it. Stupidly searching for something considerate to say I muddled on: 'You mustn't think I don't – I mean …' How to finish the thought was beyond me. Lamely I said: 'We can wait. We – I mean – I *must* wait and – and see what happens to me.'

What on earth was I saying? What did I mean: '… see what happens to me'?

'Oh but ah cannae wait –' She bit off her words, hung her head, began to sob. She no longer pressed herself against me. She leaned for support. Tears streamed down her blotched cheeks and soaked into the lapel of my coat.

No one took special notice of the sad tableau we must have presented there on the edge of a circle of yellow gas light from a street lamp. Women came past from the Steamy bent low under their loads. Men returning from work trudged heavily by, huddled into old army greatcoats or other cast-offs, dirt-encrusted boots thud-ding on the pavement flag stones, lunch cans dangling at the wrist. Others, coming out for the evening having rested and eaten, strode past aiming for one of the dozen or so pubs near the Cross. A women weeping on a man's shoulder was a common enough sight, the causes common too – drink, debts, infidelity, children's delin-quency, general despair, the wear and tear of living. Best not to show interest. There might be a fight, families and allies taking sides. That was how neighbourhood battles started.

She raised her head, seeing defeat but not quite accepting it. In a low voice, throaty and broken, she said: 'Ye might be askin' me tae wait too long. The way ah feel now ah cannae wait at a'!'

I put my hand in my pocket to touch the letter again. For one mad moment I wanted to give it to her to read. I felt I ought to prove that I was not being carelessly unfeeling. My life *had* changed.

No, that would not do. It would draw her into my affairs at a moment when I was pushing her away. And then it struck me that the letter was irrelevant. Why? I had no idea. But I was sure it was.

Her voice broke into my thoughts, but so softly that I missed the first words: '…that ah love ye. Ah always have. Ah see that now. I want ye tae know that.'

She pushed herself from me, turned away and went quickly along the pavement in a pale shadow of the old hip-swinging, proud and preening gait. I would recall that moment again and again, as well as the thought that pierced for an instant into the tur-bulence within me: 'How tired she looks.'

10

Lost Illusions

Sometimes the factory was a refuge from the world. The noise that battered you on every side could also protect you. Normal talk was impossible. Communication needed a tremendous effort and some ingenuity. You had to pitch your voice high, condense your message to the barest minimum, supplement shouted words with gestures. A question. A request. A warning perhaps. First you alerted the person, shouted to make him look up: 'Hey Alec!', or Ian or Jimmie, and if he remained oblivious you might even throw something, preferably soft like a piece of cloth, to land on the table in front of him. Looking up at you and studying the gestures and expression with which you supplemented your words, he would decode what you said, only partly heard if at all: 'Hey! Throw me that bundle of facings!' or 'Here's that iron-holder you wanted – catch!'

Apart from such signalling you were enclosed in the noise as effectively as a hermit in his cell.

Since our encounter outside the Baths I had not consciously avoided Annie at the factory. It was the busy winter season and we were hard at it for sixteen hours a day producing garments for the spring trade. You came to work in the dark of early morning, walking half asleep past bakeries just finishing the night shift, where white-clad figures stood in the doorways having a drag before going home, the sweet smell of warm dough and yeast and new-baked bread wafting round your head in the keen night air and uplifting the heart; and stables where the big Clydesdales stamped and clattered as the hands began to groom them and clean out stalls and yard and get the carts ready for the day's haulage. Wet cobbled streets were empty, pools of yellow gaslight disturbed only by a few other lonely figures hurrying to work, or a prowling cat drawing its tapering shadow along a wall. When we left work in the evening, numb with fatigue, feet and ankles stiff from standing, it was dark again, the streets crowded with office and factory and shop workers heading home, shoppers, theatre goers, in a roar and clatter of buses and trams and horse-drawn vehicles. By chance or design Annie's arrivals and departures did not coincide with mine. An encounter could easily have been brought about if one of us had decided to linger, choosing the time, by the factory door on the Broomielaw, the quay on the north side of the Clyde at the Victoria Bridge opposite the Gorbals, or on the stone staircase leading up to our long workroom. But that did not happen.

I had replied to the letter. Yes, I would 'come into residence' on the first day of Michaelmas Term next year.

That certainly was hostage to fortune, for I had no idea how I was going to get together all the things needed to present myself there – money, clothes, books and, perhaps most uncertain of all, myself. Still, there was nothing for it but to pretend that I *was* certain and do my damnedest to get ready.

Obsessively I wrestled with the practicalities, most of them only dimly understood. I worried about the things you needed in order to be a student at Oxford. In answer to my letter of acceptance, I was sent daunting information, including lists of clothing I ought to bring with me. I had practically nothing but what I stood up in. With amazement I learnt that I ought to have at least three suits of pyjamas. I had none at all. How strange to put on special clothes to sleep in? I had no suitcase, for I had never travelled anywhere. There was a long list of books to be read. I had no books at all. I had done all my reading in the Mitchell Library, a fair distance from both the factory and our house. And being so busy at work now, there was not much of the evening left in which to get there and do any solid reading. Somehow I must find the money to buy some books and get some reading done at home. For this and all rest I could not possibly save anything like enough money in the time. Soon, when this busy season came to an end just before Christmas, there would be a slack time for about six weeks until we started another hectic busy season producing for the summer trade. I could manage, just about, if I could borrow a few shillings here and there on the strength of the scholarship money to come.

In secret I sought out Aunt Rachel. It had to be secret, for father, angry because she had helped my sister Mary to leave home, and taken her into her own house to live, had forbidden all contact with her. I showed her the letter that had told me I had won the scholarship.

Aunt Rachel, mother's younger sister, little and wiry, was round-shouldered from years of bending short-sightedly at her sewing in Uncle Salman's tiny clothing repair workshop in Norfolk Street. Within herself, however, she was strong and upright. Brown hair, gathered to a tight bun near the crown of her head, framed fresh rounded features and a high forehead. She spoke sparingly, always after clear thought. Her attitude to life was summed up in a favourite saying of hers that stuck in my memory from early childhood: 'Speech is silver. Thought is gold!'

With her shiny black apron she cleaned her Woolworth's spectacles, thick lenses in metal frames with wire side pieces, and read the letter, screwing up her eyes.

I said, 'I don't know if you can manage it, but do you think you could lend me a little money to get a few things I need? Clothes and books? I'll pay you back as soon as I get the scholarship money.'

She looked up into my face with great intensity, then bent her head and read through the letter again. She tugged the spectacles off her nose and went to a tall dresser and stood on tip-toe to see into the top drawer, took out a folded handkerchief and held it by a corner and shook it out. She kept her back turned, but I had seen the tears.

She dried her eyes, blew her nose, refolded the handkerchief and tucked it away in a pocket in her black skirt, and studied me again, many feelings revealed in her changing aspect – pleasure, pride, wistfulness, concern at yet another demand in a burdened life. 'You're a good boy, and it's a credit to you, what you've done. An Oxford student! Who would have thought it could happen? You deserve it. We'll do what we can. But it'll be only a few shillings, mind!'

'Thank you, Auntie. It'll be a godsend. You'll definitely get it back as soon as I get the money from the college.'

She shook her head, and looked away, fumbled for the handkerchief again. Her voice was unsteady now: 'I wasn't thinking of that. If only your mother could have been spared to see you turn out like this? Her beautiful baby boy she had to leave so soon! Still. I must not say that. It was God's will.'

Tactfully she did not ask what father was doing to help. She knew how badly things stood.

Apart from the things to be bought, I worried about the adjustments I had to make within myself – outlook, prejudices, ways of thinking and conducting myself; what was needed I could only guess.

And the letter burned in my pocket, a secret, magical flame. I carried it wherever I went. A talisman. Proof that I was not the victim of a powerful delusion. It became so tattered, coming apart at the folds, that I pasted it on to a piece of the stiff paper the cutters in the factory used for marking out patterns. All thought turned inward.

As for Annie, a shadow must have remained at the back of my mind. Now and then, idly looking round as I stood at my pressing board – the 'donkey' – I saw her raise her head from her work and turn in my direction, but in the steam and dust and dim light I was never sure whether the look had any important meaning for me. If it did, I probably did not want to see it, for reasons I preferred not to examine. In retrospect a signal there must have been. Getting no response, she did not come near.

I kept the world at a distance. Not much of it was real to me. The letter had raised a dust storm within me in which all things became indistinct, even these I knew so well, the work I did like an automaton – seams opened and pressed flat, edges and shoulders and shapes manipulated and fixed in place with accustomed care and skill – the daily routine of factory, food, and sleep, and the Baths, the visits now shorter to make more reading time, familiar streets and tenement stairs and closes, all experienced and seen, but not seen.

And always Oxford hung perplexingly on the horizon. Alien

territory. Preserve of the boss class!

Standing at my pressing board one Monday morning, I was roused by a commotion over by the sewing machines. I caught only one word, but it was one that always sounded a note of profound alarm among us: 'Hospital'. I may have caught that word because, unawares, I had been expecting it. Something important must have happened for hands to leave their piece work in such agitation: a shocking bit of news.

At his work place on the opposite side of the pressing table Alec Birrell was mouthing words at me in the exaggerated manner we employed to help each other lip-read through the noise. This time I failed. I shouted as him:

'Hospital? Who? Who is it?'

He had just spread a damp rag over a piece of work, the long front edge of a coat. Lined with soaped canvas, that edge needed plenty of steam followed by heat to fix canvas and cloth together and make the edge hang straight and clean; the damp rag was a large sheet of cotton soaked and wrung out in a water bucket that we shared at the end of our table. As I shouted he was in the act of banging down upon it a newly heated iron. A cloud of steam sizzled up round him and hid his face. Head inclined, manoeuvring the big iron with his right hand, he swung his left arm to the side at shoulder height and pointed to the nearest bank of sewing machines. I saw an empty place there. Annie's.

I put down my iron on its metal rest beside the donkey and went round to his side of the table. The story, in essentials, was nothing out of the ordinary. Yesterday, Sunday, Annie had drunk a whole bottle of patent medicine, a specific for clearing the bowels. Some time later, seized with violent vomiting, and probably delirious, she had dragged herself out of the house and staggered down the spiral stairs in her close making for the lavatory tucked into the concave wall, lost her footing on the overflow of excrement and hurtled down a whole flight of the jagged stone steps.

Our shower room group, in the scabrous and cruel musings of the young and green, feeding sexual fantasies, had often dwelt upon the ironies of a woman locked in contradictory battle with her flesh, on the crude antitheses of desire and the grim prudence that life demanded, on pleasure and its capricious consequences. We would never have admitted to being puritanical, but in an ambivalence of open glee and private censure we gloated over sin with imagery that glistened with the sweat and heat and lubricity of primordial passion, as in Somerset Maugham's 'Rain' the missionary, Davidson, was perversely obsessed with Sadie's flesh. Unlike Davidson, however, we knew, being very young, that we need not fear sin. Youth is invulnerable, immortal. In imagination *we* could play with fire, with sin, safely. But deeply hidden in his dream talk was a disturbing mixture of envy and fear of woman, the unattainable, unknowable, dark magic that dwelt in her. Her power to conjure life.

'Funny! Whit it must be like for a hairy when she's been reamed oot wi' a big prick! Wonderin' if she'll ge' 'er monthlies next time, eh? An' then she doesnae ge' them, and starts prayin' tae God it's a mistake! An' then she doesnae ge' them the second time, oh Christ is she in a panic! Nothin' for it bu' a bliddy great dose o' strong clearin' oot medicine or somethin' drastic like that tae gie her insides a bashin' an' ge' 'er wurrks started again! Some o' them get sae desperate they try a fall doon the stairs. Sometimes the shock does the trick ye see? Or she has a go wi' the auld knittin' needle! Or if she can ge' a few shillins taegither she goes tae Maggie O'Reilly in Rose Street to dae it for her. Aye, an' then in a wee while there she is in the back close, red hot in her hole tae ge' reamed oo' again! Aye, there's allus plenty mair where the last yin came frae.'

The ambulance had taken Annie to the Royal Infirmary. Some of the girls from her bank of machines would go in and see her there this evening after work.

Stupidly unaware still, I stood there staring at him. For one chill moment, fool that I was, it crossed my mind that she might have attempted suicide because I had rejected her plea. Yet it was not such a stupid thought. The romantic Annie I had known, or felt I did, would have been capable of it.

'Christ! What came over her to do a thing like that?'

He studied me wonderingly, then broke into a sarcastic grin: 'Ye cannae be serious!'

'What d'ye mean?'

'Whit's the ma'er wi' ye?' he asked despairingly. 'Hiv ye no' wakened up this mornin' yit? It's as plain as plain as plain! That lassie had 'er caird stamped good an' proper!' He shrugged. 'An she drank up tha' stuff tryin' tae bring on 'er monthlies! The auld, auld story! Some jaunty lad refused tae feyther the wean in 'er belly!'

He nodded knowingly. He knew who the jaunty lad was, and assumed I did too.

And then it hit me hard, the truth of what she had done to me, or tried to do and failed. Not trusting myself to speak, I turned away so that he should not read my face. I went back to my pressing board and lifted the iron, which now seemed to weigh much more than its eighteen pounds, and blindly carried on working, hardly knowing what I did. The sweat felt cold on my back.

Had my mind not been so full of that letter – and innocence – surely I would have put the pieces together? How could I have failed to be alerted by at least a grain of suspicion when she waylaid me at the Baths and coolly – I saw it now – tried to make me go home with her?

With these thoughts came such a surge of fury that my head seemed ready to burst. Oh to destroy something, anything, shatter, rend and tear and batter into dust! If Annie had stood in front of me at that instant? God help me, what might I have done! I slammed the iron down on its steel rest, dug my nails into my palms to keep control.

I thought of my father and his frightening rages. Was this what they felt like? Were they my inheritance too? And the misery that provoked them?

Some control returned. I looked round to see if anyone had noticed. The weak electric bulb hanging before me, under its dusty green shade like an up-turned soup plate, cast a patch of miserly light on the donkey, but the spot where I stood was in shadow, deepened by the clouds of concealing steam about the pressing table. In any case everyone had his head down working away for dear life.

And then, to my surprise, I felt sorry for her. I remembered how pale she had become when I said 'Too late,' with no idea of the other meaning those words had for her.

No wonder Alec was amazed at my stupidity. Phil Emet had turned his back on the stamped card. That was obvious. In panic she had resorted to me. Had I gone with her that evening, how transparent her plan was now. At her home emptied of her family, in a bogus reconciliation, her contrived euphoria would have swept aside any thought of being careful. French letters were not cheap. Some fellows carried them around all the time or claimed they did. I didn't. And then some days later she would have come to me, in desperation then totally understandable, to place paternity at my door and demand, sweetly but determinedly, immediate marriage.

Premature births were common among women of the tenements.

As Alec had said: 'An auld, auld story.'

At the Baths that evening Phil remarked with detachment: 'Aye it's a real shame about her. She shouldnae've panicked like tha'! *They* know whit tae do, don't they? Plenty gurrls've gone tae Maggie O'Reilly in Rose Street hiven't they? An' been none the wurrse!'

Tactfully the talk was deflected. Phil knew as well as we did that girls had died after a visit to Rose Street. And some were left permanent invalids. No one wanted to dwell on such thoughts. Behind the bragging and the coarse jests, the shadow remained. One day, any day, their turn might come. Would they, like Phil, have the nerve to shrug and walk away?

Annie had fractured her skull, cracked a vertebra at the top of her spine, broken her jaw and her left arm. She was lucky, they said, not to have broken her neck. As for the stomach and bowel damage from what she had drunk, she would suffer from it for the rest of her life.

Nothing was heard of a pregnancy, so in that respect she had succeeded.

I could not bring myself to visit her in hospital, or send her any message. Over and over again I wished I could blot out what she tried to do to me, and think of her again as she once had been. And then the shock would return and resentment burn again as I thought of how close I had been to the snapping of that trap, forced to turn my back on the door that had been opened by that letter from Oxford.

The enigma of the female. No wonder the Sphinx was a woman, and all who failed to divine her riddle paid with their lives.

Behind the shower group's gallows humour was a frightened huddling together before that Sphinx, her secret feebly guessed at in the callow terms in which they saw life. Repelled as I often was by their savage simplicity, they seemed to me to speak for the received view, and when I was with them my insecurity was temporarily stilled – though in calmer moments I knew that they were as insecure as I was. How profoundly separate was the woman's vision, doomed in the end to be mortally opposed to ours! The ripening seed in the womb – *or the unthought desire for it* – imposed its own laws, its own expedient calculations, its egoistical assumptions about right and wrong, refracted all vision, changed all perspectives. To use the man, or failing the one chosen, *any* man, to fulfil her destiny was simply to implement a natural law, ruthlessly if necessary, carelessly to invoke the life force!

But these primitive sophistries cloaked apocalyptic ironies and I wanted to reject them all. For me the truth was simple, and nothing could excuse it. A sense of right, of trust, had been violated. What harm had I done her? None whatever. It was she who had rejected *me* – suddenly, without warning, from one day to the next. Was it simply caprice? Or some inadequacy in me unexpected discovered? In some ways either reason would have been bearable, or at least accepted as honourable. The truth hurt because it was shabby, and because it meant that judgement, faith, vows, had been worthless.

Yes, the truth was simple and in its way understandable, the compulsion of a higher fancy she could follow only with someone else. Very well. That was her business, not mine. Desperate she may have been when Phil turned away, but how cruel to try to gull *me*, struggling so hard to do the best I could with my life, into becoming a victim of *her* miscalculation?

It did not occur to me till much later that I too could have turned my back on a stamped card. Why not? It happened often enough, which was how Maggie O'Reilly got most of her clients! That, in its way, was part of the received view too. No, I couldn't have done that. I was not Phil Emet and that was that. It was an aspect of me that Annie knew she could depend on. Her judgement of me had been accurate – unlike mine of *her*.

Alec Birrell remarked thoughtfully: 'If we could tell how many couples got wed this way, aye, an' went on tae live guid lives taegither efterwards, ah guarantee we'd be very suprised! Efter a', who are we tae judge?'

The auld, auld story. Did it really matter that much? Yes it did. I was sure of that. These were deep waters, too deep for me. Alec was paraphrasing an old saw: 'The heart is not troubled by what it does not know!' Maybe. But *she* would have known it! And knowing that I did not, she would have betrayed me every day of her life. And who knew what intuition might plant the dark thought in my heart, unknowable and unprovable, to haunt me through the years?

How could I ever have forgiven her if that had happened? And how could I forgive her now having attempted it? She had tried to exploit my trust. And my love. Alas, love would remain. I would never escape from that. She knew it. And for her to have acted on that knowledge, if nothing else, made her deed unforgiveable.

11

Bernard, Spain, Disenchantment

In Spain Bernard was wounded, a bullet in the side of the neck, luckily in the muscles at the join of the shoulder. When he was out of hospital he was given a 'political guidance' job. He went from unit to unit in the shifting fronts, up and down through the command organisation to get 'appreciations' and provide political briefings, attending high-level policy meetings to adjust his political tuning to shifts in the party line and changes in directives to its cells in the military and governmental structure. Subtly, his role change from the revolutionary sage giving political perspectives, to the inquisitor searching for deficiencies in faith. It shocked and oppressed him to discover that, like the inquisitors of old, he carried the power to invoke death.

He saw the purity of the cause as diluted. Too often he found himself compelled to defend a party policy or, worse, the behaviours of highly-placed comrades or groups, that betrayed the faith he had come to Spain to fight for. In his travels, physically across the war-riven country, mentally up and down the shaky political and military levels, from the fighting men on the ground living hard, to the well turned-out politicians meetings in gilded salons, he saw most of the game.

He was to tell me of Russian generals living high, who in the intervals between orgies critically influenced strategy and the movement of supplies – sometimes, he suspected, their stoppage – and the fate of leaders, in the interests of a remote *realpolitik*. He spoke of doctrinally divergent groups fighting one another, the strife taking precedence over the efficient prosecution of war, doing Franco's work for him. They behaved like states within the state, leaders strutting like war lords, bargaining for supplies, for politically advantageous positions in strategic plans, sometimes at gun point.

They executed comrades on flimsy excuse, not only as supposed dangers to the cause but as possible rivals in the power struggle within it. To kill people of your own side in order to promote your brand of salvation became commonplace, and to dispose of anyone who shrank from doing so an accepted necessity. Dark statecraft hung menacingly over everybody.

With a hardening clarity that turned him into a dangerous man, Bernard was coming to the conclusion that if it ever had been the workers' war for freedom and justice, with capitalism the sole enemy, it was that no longer.

He asked himself whether his role really had changed, or whether he had been too innocent to see it earlier for what it truly was. Presented to him at first as one of helping to strengthen morale in the International Brigade, in the hectic climate of fighting a war with amateur soldiers and a rickety organisation pitted against a professional army, in an atmosphere of make-do-and-mend and uncertain unity, he had reluctantly begun to see his role partly as secret surveillance, partly as that of a 'mind policeman', marking out the politically unreliable – 'deviationist' became the dread label – whose 'removal' would favour the party's potency in the internecine strife. Such men would end up on rubbish heaps or in ditches, a bullet hole in the back of the head. Like the French Revolution, the cause had turned sour on itself and was destroying its own. He had become one of the destroyers.

'Would you believe it?' he chuckled humourlessly, 'Yours truly going round with a forty-five in a shoulder holster?'

He could stomach no more and was on the knife-edge of deciding to leave it all, when something happened that made the decision for him.

He told me about it on another grey winter's day not long after he had reappeared from Spain. We had halted on the pavement in Castle Street, a steep hill that climbed towards the mound on which stood cheek-by-jowl two bastions of life and death – or vice-versa depending on your point of view – the Royal Infirmary and the Necropolis, surrounded by an assembly of churches and religious institutions of many shades of doctrine, gospel halls, mission halls, evangelical rooms, Band of Hope meeting halls, supporting troops. A wag once remarked that the party must have been 'guided' to site its headquarters, which sheltered behind its bookshop in Castle Street, in the midst of these strong points of faith, in order to hedge its bets. 'Aye! Maybe we should call it the Karl Marx Band of Hope Rooms!'

The hill became dangerously slippery under frozen snow and slush. People broke bones, in the elderly the injuries could be fatal, and the Royal Infirmary, only a couple of hundred yards up the hill, was conveniently near.

Horses fell, and as often as not were shot on the spot.

The Necropolis, filled with elaborate Victorian tombs and funerary statuary, was now in the main a civic monument, but up there on the crest of the hill adjoining the Infirmary grounds, with the grim visage of John Knox on his column dominating the whole *mise-en-scène*, it jolted the minds of people visiting patients in the Infirmary with thoughts of death and damnation.

'Did *you* have to do any of that dirty work?' I asked him. 'I mean kill people like that yourself?'

'More of that some other time,' he said. 'I'll only tell you this just now. Because – well, I have to talk about it to somebody, and there's no one else I can tell it to – not yet. How it all came to an end for me there.'

He had acquired a tight-lipped manner, wary, laconic. The once full face was now lean, almost lantern-jawed, the ruddy features leaden. The wound have left him with a permanent tilt of the head into the left shoulder. The battlefield surgeon had cut deep.

The most noticeable change of all was that the old ebullience of the street demagogue was no more; he had retreated into himself. He had aged twenty years. The once cheerful black eyes were stilled and watched, the face concealing expression, spontaneity suppressed. A sad man.

Before he continued he looked about him as if searching for something that should be there, or which he feared was there, with an expression as chilling as the air about us.

'Sometimes I can hardly believe it myself,' he said, his lip curling in an attempt at a smile. 'Anyway, this is the way it happened. I had just got to a small town on the northern coast on a job. I had a few hours to wait for a meeting that night, and I had the desperate feeling that I must get away from people for a bit. There was never any end to people and meetings. Watching points every moment of the day, analysing this or that statement or action or even mannerism, signs of motives or attitudes that needed looking into. I was hardly ever on my own. My head was full to bursting. I needed to think things out.

'So I went out of the town. The shoreline was deserted. Not a soul about. The sea empty. I walked along for about a mile. The day was hot and the gun felt especially heavy and the holster strap was hurting like hell, cutting into me at the place where they had dug out the bullet. I found a shady spot down by the water, under an overhang of the cliff. I tucked myself well down among some rocks. It was second nature to pick yourself a good defensive position wherever you stopped. And I sat there staring at the water. Thinking what to do. From force of habit I cleaned and oiled the gun. In the life I was leading you did that regularly. It wasn't healthy to be slow in getting off a shot.

'The things life can do to you! If anyone had told me the day would come when I would go around with a pistol under my coat, watching my back, ready at any moment to draw and get a shot in first, I would never have believed it.' He nodded thoughtfully: 'Yes. And sleep with the gun ready to hand.'

I said nothing. I felt I knew what was coming and was sickened in advance, responding perhaps to the residual shock I sensed in him.

'As a matter of fact,' he said, 'I discovered I was a naturally good shot with a pistol.'

He shrugged. 'So I re-loaded, and went on sitting there with the gun in my hand, thinking through everything, my political position, how things had moved from what I had expected, and from what they had been when I came to Spain. I kept on coming back to the same point. What had happened to the principle I had come to Spain to fight for? I certainly hadn't come to kill my own comrades simply because some top party men didn't like their opinions, or their faces. Some of our lads would never get back across that water because of me. I'd been manipulated into doing terrible things. I wasn't the only one, but that didn't help. So far I'd been lucky. All I'd got was a nick from a Fascist bullet. But now it was a fair bet that I'd get one in the back from somebody on my own side. After all, directly or indirectly that was what I was doing to others. That was the life I was leading. Sooner or later my luck would run out.

'I thought of many things. What hope was there now? Was there any way forward? Could all this confusion, this fighting and killing inside our ranks, this corruption of a great cause, be stopped in time? And by whom? Individuals like me wouldn't have a chance in hell if we tried to stand out against the people pulling the strings at the top. And not just in Spain but far away behind the scenes in Moscow. We'd be got rid of – no question of it. I should know: who better? That's what they were using people like *me* for. So what was I going to do? Every line of thought brought me back to the same dead end. And over and over again the question hammered at me: "What good was I doing?" '

He pushed his lower lip up, and seemed to contemplate the evening crowds hurrying home from work, hunched up against the wind. He was looking far beyond them.

'I must have sat like that for hours. The scar was aching. It does that at night sometimes. I thought that was what had roused me. But I wasn't sure. The light was fading. The sea and the sky had turned grey. It was time to go to the meeting. From force of habit I checked in all directions before I moved. It was a much as your life was worth not to do that. All I saw was the line of cliffs and the narrow pebbly foreshore stretching away to the dark smudge of the town in the distance. Not even any birds. I waited another minute or so. Nothing moved. Not a sound. Feeling a bit stiff from all that time I'd been sitting, I began slowly to stand up. I caught a little clinking sound, like a pebble falling against another, and by instinct I ducked down again. And if I hadn't done that I wouldn't be standing here talking to you now. I heard the shot and felt the wind of it going past my head. The round ricocheted off the rock next to me and on into the water a few feet away. He fired another three rounds rapid, which gave me his position exactly. He had crept up to about twenty-five yards of me, and was in a crack in the cliff face to the left of me. He was between me and my way back into the town.'

He drew his breath in quickly with a small whistling sound, eyes narrowed like a hunter's.

'His gun must have jammed. Trying to clear the action in that tricky half-light he must have bent his head forward. Just for a second I saw the dark curve of it outlined against the pale cliff face. And I got off two rounds and saw him go down. It was an instinctive reflex. You don't *think* when you're under attack. You just act. I think I dropped him with my first shot.'

He shook his head slowly.

'I went over to him lying there. I recognised him. Curiously enough that didn't surprise me. Can you understand that? As if I had been expecting it. But it shocked me all the same. We'd drunk a glass of red wine together many a time. A decent fellow. From South Wales. A miner. Doing much the same job as me in the group I had been sent to purge. Yes, purge: that was the word we used. What d'you think of that?'

I didn't say anything. I knew he didn't expect me to.

'And why were they after *me*? God knows. Maybe the leadership in that group had got nervous about my visit and decided to get me first, and so send a warning to the central committee to leave them alone. Or maybe the group had been given the word by the central committee to get rid of *me*, and I had been sent there like a lamb to the slaughter. That's how it was done sometimes. That was the kind of scheming and double-dealing that went on all the time. You had to watch your step. You had to be very, *very* careful, like living in a spider's web. I though I had kept my doubts to myself, but maybe I hadn't been careful enough.'

He laughed with teeth clenched. 'Now I knew what it was like to live in Russia! Anyway, I never found out why he had been sent to kill me, or by whom. I was too busy *running*, believe you me!'

He did not tell me how he had got out of Spain and made his way back home.

'One day I will,' he said, 'when it's safe to talk freely. I mean,' he added quickly, 'don't take this the wrong way. It's not that I don't trust you. It's only that you may let something out without meaning to.'

He had left the party. Officially, he was described as expelled, for no one was allowed to resign. He got his job back in the factory, and we saw his idealism turn in another direction, working hard in our trade union branch. Then, after a few months, the union gave him a job as organiser for the West of Scotland. That was a step up in the world. Now he was a brief-case man in a bespoke blue serge suit and smart snap brim hat, and he wore a clean white shirt every day – the kind with the newly fashionable attached semi-stiff collar – and a tie: an ambition of many a Gorbals man with calloused hands.

He commented on that shift in status one day. 'Between ourselves, I did feel a bit guilty, moving up from the standard of living of many of my members. But here's something else Spain taught me. Self-abasement can be a kind of hypocrisy, cynical window dressing, almost a kind of arrogance, like Peter Kerrigan wearing that open-necked grey shirt in the dead of winter.'

Kerrigan was party leader in Glasgow and British representative on the Comintern, a hard-liner who dutifully defended Stalin's murder of comrades. Bernard was not the only one who saw that open-necked shirt as a carefully selected symbol of unity with the proletariat.

'You might as well live decently,' Bernard went on, 'not in luxury but decently, in the way you'd like everyone else to live in fact, so that you can think clearly and give of your best.'

'You don't have to explain yourself to me!' I wanted to say, but plainly he felt he did. What he expressed was more than a political feeling. It was innocence; in seeming to distance himself from the people he cared about, he might unwittingly betray them. I would understand how he felt, but for different reasons, one day soon. But that was hidden from me.

He moved away from the Gorbals with his family, to one of the more respectable tenements near Charing Cross at the western end of Sauchiehall Street, at the back of the Mitchell Library, on the fringe of the University area.

The Mitchell Library! My private temple. My Aladdin's Cave. There and at the Socialist Camp at Carbeth I was more at home than at the house in Warwick Street. The Library drew me like a magnet, after work of an evening in the busy time, and for whole days in the slack season. I could have found my way there with my eyes shut. Even now the feel of those hard mahogany chairs in its great arched reading room returns instantly, all the hours and days I sat in them; as well as my envy of the students sauntering in and out without a care, who treated it as a social club, a place for assignations, or to sprawl away a waiting hour in tennis flannels on a summer afternoon. What an irony, I used to think, that they did their stint at these reading desks by *force majeure* as I did at the factory, thinking of it as hardship. What did they know of hardship?

Bernard, fortuitously, remained in remote contact with the party. Union work took him to meetings of the Trades Council, on which the party, through 'underground' members, sat in strength. Council committees sometimes met in a mission hall a few doors away from the party bookshop. One day I arranged to meet him after one of his meetings and we had our first long talk since his return. Absorbed, we paused on the pavement a few paces from the shop.

In its tall narrow bowed windows, with small panes set in rounded wooden glazing bars, were tall jars of sticky Russian sweets, red and yellow and green, standing like lonely glass towers amid pamphlets bearing the faces of Lenin, Harry Pollitt, Bernard Shaw, copies of *Ten Days that Shook the World*, and the innocently named *Labour Monthly*, the party's ideological journal edited by the glacier-minded Rajani Palme Dutt. He it was who dismissed Stalin's purges and mass slaughter as 'a spot on the sun'.

In a back room the Agitprop Committee met, the party's key operations group for Scotland. Agitational propaganda stood for destabilisation, Machiavellianism from below, the selection, or creation, of 'issues' on which to agitate for wrongs to be righted, whereby the party would be seen in shining armour, the only true champion of the underdog. Issues chosen, self-evidently worthy like bad housing, were tools to win support, no more. Until his 'expulsion' from the party Bernard had been a member of the Agitprop Committee.

Perhaps he had never stopped to question the cynicism of Agitprop, but had lived with it only for the sake of his higher dream. The end justifies the means. When, in Spain, he had finally questioned that principle, feeling, inescapably, that the human price was too high, it had nearly cost him his life.

Yet when I thought about the tenements, one water tap for six families or more, lavatories overflowing yellow and brown down shattered stone steps, rats in full possession, and people skimping and scraping to be allowed to live in such places, why should one be disturbed at the party's Machiavellian motives? Surely Agitprop must do some good even if the party did use it, and us, for its own purposes of power?

We stood without speaking, stamped our feet and blew breath into cupped hands against the cold. Clydesdale draught horses, white hair hanging over their broad feet like dainty aprons, slithered on rounded wet cobbles as they tried to slow the long cart of coal or cement on the steep hill, massive legs quivering with veined muscle, flared nostrils blowing jets of steamy breath, while the driver held the brake lever hard back and the steel-rimmed wheels squealed and held and squealed again, scattering sparks. Wonderful, noble, patient beasts. What a shame they could not change their condition.

That was the truth for all of us.

And so Bernard searched for another faith. And I was moving too. From where, towards what? I was not looking for anything as grand as a faith, but for confidence in *something*.

He might have been listening to my thoughts. He bared his teeth in that humourless laugh: 'Are you saying that is what we both want? Have faith and forget the truth, just like the old religions.'

I said: 'In a way you were happy then.'

The thought echoed between us, and faded away.

He chewed his lip, and watched another team of struggling horses go past.

He said: 'You were right in a lot of things. Remember that night in the close near the Workers' Circle, when the fellow in the back with his girl told us to fuck off? The last time we talked hard about things before I went to Spain? And you trying to pin me down with my own doubts? That worried you at the time, and maybe still does. Don't worry! You probably did me a lot of good and might have saved me ... Well, what's the point of saying "If only"? If only I'd listened. I didn't want to believe what I'm sure I knew already, or suspected. Or maybe I did believe it but thought – no that's wrong, I didn't *think*, not properly. I was blinded by feeling. Impatience. Desperation. Christ, how naïve I was! I didn't bargain for the callous and clever and dangerous men who would be operating when the chips were down. What sickens me most of all is the corruption of the *will for good*. And I can see no way out of it.'

Softly he said, unbelievingly, as of a miracle: 'And I nearly didn't live to tell the tale.'

As if startled by the words 'tell the tale', he looked quickly up and down the pavement. Astonished and dismayed, I saw that he feared to be overheard.

It began to sleet. Passers by turned up coat collars and pulled caps lower down over their faces and quickened their steps. We retreated from the edge of the pavement and hurried for shelter to the nearest close mouth; as it happened it was next door to the bookshop.

It occurred to me that this might be too near for him. But the sleet was heavy, and my coat thin. He was wearing a fine new heavy trench coat with a wool lining and a smart trilby and was well protected. He made no objection. We might not have to shelter here long.

Incongruously, I thought about his reference to Annie and Phil by the ash-pits. Had he identified the voices? It was strange that he should have taken note of their presence then, at a moment when uppermost in his mind was the challenge of Spain and battle. And of all things to speak of it again now? I wondered if he had known about me and Annie in the past. We had talked confidentially on many things over the years, but for some reason I had kept Annie – winning her and losing her – to myself.

He said: 'And I'll tell you this. These fine gentlemen next door here, the party apparatchiks, they wouldn't hesitate to serve you the same as they did me in Spain if they ever got power in this country. And to think that I used to sit in that back room with them! God help me, I'd have to do the same if I were still one of them. What am I saying? I *did* do the same, in Spain.'

He brought up his right hand, and flexed the fingers once, and looked hard at the palm.

The power and fury of the gun. Death had been the only sure victor in that holy battle.

'Yes, I do feel guilty for some of the things I had to do in Spain. No, "had to" is wrong! I didn't *have* to. I did them willingly, at first anyway, even with a sense of doing the right thing for the cause I had gone there to fight for. I believed they were necessary. I must have done! I feel a bit empty now.'

Suddenly he moved, in a light springy step that had menace in it, like a hunter delicately placing himself in killing range, to the very edge of the close mouth and glanced quickly to the right, at the glass door of the shop. This time there was no mistaking the reason. He drew back and turned to face me again, and a dark cloud of fear moved over the strained features. The street was full of the clatter and rumble of carts and lorries, the clang and jingle of harness, the shouting of drivers, the hubbub of loading and unloading at a warehouse at the corner, the bustle of people, a mad syncopation bouncing back and forth between the facing tenements. No one could possibly have heard his words, least of all in the bookshop. He managed an apologetic smile. But that fear had been real enough. Momentarily, for his sake, I shared it, or tried to. Spain had wounded him more deeply than the bullet in the neck. It had found his heart.

I would probably never feel disillusion with the sharp edge that he did. In a sense I had foretold it, but that gave me no satisfaction.

He at least had tried to do something, bravely, with a good heart. He had put himself into the hazard. If he had not done that, how would he know?

I too felt an emptiness. If there were no answers to be found, any-where, what should we do? What should anyone do? Did it matter?

That was the most depressing question of all.

12

The Devil you Know

Alec Birrell was tall and lean, ginger haired, with long bony features and a jutting lower jaw. He had a natural elegance even in his working garb of fustian coat and trousers and off-white woollen muffler. And an easy charm. He gave the impression of uncaringly letting the current of life carry him where it would.

But he had his share of worry. Nearly every shilling he earned went to the care of his ailing, widowed mother, and a half-crippled sister, who hobbled about lop-sidedly because of a defective hip, victim of rickets; a sweet and kindly girl, her chances of marriage were small.

He was not a deep thinker in any formal sense. For him the world had been set on a certain course for better or worse, and whatever balance it had, having been set through uncounted ages, had better be left undisturbed; any alternative, untried by time, was certain to be even worse. You learned to live with that balance, whatever trials it brought you, made yourself familiar with its idiosyncrasies, for life to be possible at all.

And yet in his fashion he did ruminate on the ways of the world, the fitness of things, manners, choices.

His relaxed exterior could be dangerously deceptive, for within he was hard as steel. Not easily roused, his fury could be white hot. One day Jimmy Gillan from the far end of our pressing table, a beetle-browed and surly fellow in his thirties, started teasing him about sticking to his Roman Catholic faith. Jimmy, a lapsed Catholic, was already set on the familiar road of blotting out life with drink, a negative soul who found Alec's accepting and pragmatic personality profoundly irritating. Religion was a risky subject to joke about. Jimmy had been at the factory longer than any of us and should have known who he was dealing with. If he had not been drinking at the lunch break he might have had the wit not to provoke Alec, or having done so, known when to stop. He stood at Alec's elbow as he worked, and sneeringly, with the foulest of language, persisted in the attack.

The rest of us read Alec's face and saw the danger signs. Superficially, he appeared unperturbed. He kept his head bent to his work, banged the bulky iron down on the damp rag, ran it back and forth to steam the cloth all over, lifted the iron and ripped the rag away from the garment, then turned the iron upside down in the air and touched its silk smooth dark foot swiftly with the palm of his free hand to make sure it would not burn the cloth, then swung it down and moved it back and forth briskly to dry the coat, skimming its surface with the lightest possible contact to avoid creating a sheen that would take the bloom off the cloth.

Failing to get a rise out of him, Jimmy fell into a frenzy of frustration and began to lard his curses with obscene blasphemy, forgetting that even though people might pretend to be indifferent to religion they usually drew the line, superstitiously maybe, at insults to the Holy Family.

After some minutes Alec looked up, slowly turned to face Jimmy, jaw thrust out, and shouted: 'That's *enough*! Ah'm tellin' ye!'

Fearing a fight, some of us moved round the table towards them, ready to separate them. Not that we cared that they might knock each other about – they could do that outside after work if they wanted to – but a fight in the factory interrupted the flow of work and lost us piece work pay; we might have to work extra hours to push through enough work to recoup the losses.

Apart from Alec's now evident fury, the sight of us closing in should have warned Jimmy that he was going too far, but he ignored us and went on: 'Why don't ye go an' tell that priest tae shove it up 'is Holy Mother fuckin' arse! Like *ah* tellt 'im masel?'

Alec put his iron down carefully on the metal rest beside the donkey, folded his damp rag, hung up the garment he had been working on, turned to him again, his face pale as death:

'Listen you! Ah'm here tae knock oot a livin' an' that's a'! Ah'm no' here tae listen tae *your* fuckin' nonsense. This is ma last warnin'! Jist yew let me alone. Understand?'

He turned his back on the other, reached for another coat from the pile at the end of the table between his workplace and mine, threw it flat on the donkey and draped collar and shoulders on its rounded end ready for pressing.

Jimmy did not understand. He backed away a pace or two, eyes glazed, a face with a numbed brain behind it, and yelled a retort: 'Yew go an' fuck yersel' ye great big Holy Mary fucker!'

Alec was not, to use his own words, 'much of a religion hand'. He hardly ever went to Mass. But foul language about religion upset him. He turned and stood rigidly facing Jimmy, who was now giggling tipsily, and spoke slowly: 'Don't say ah didnae warn ye.'

Bony jaw held tight, Alec turned his back on him again, and carried on working quietly for the rest of the day.

Jimmy lurched back to his work place at the far end of the long table, the grin somewhat forced now, trying to catch our eyes for support as he passed by. We all bent our heads to our work. We knew this was not the end of it. No one knew what to expect, though some had their suspicions. Better not to appear to take sides – yet. If at all.

The next day Jimmy did not come in to work. The word went swiftly round. The previous evening he had been set upon in his close and beaten up. We never learnt who his assailants were. These attacks, normal events, were seldom random; they represented rough justice according to *someone's* lights, the working out of long-running feuds, passing quarrels, drunken sessions of insult like this one. The culture fed on its primitive passions.

Jimmy was off work for three days.

He had a wife and two young children. Three days off was too short a time for one to qualify for sickness benefit, and the loss of half-a-week's wages could be catastrophic. Alec went to the parish priest, we heard later, and begged him to help; and Father Millan made a collection among his flock and gave the few shillings to Jimmy's wife to buy food and coal while he was off work.

More important was the danger to Jimmy's job. We were in one of the busy seasons and the boss might reasonably have taken on another presser in Jimmy's place, concerned as he naturally was about meeting delivery dates, and therefore anxious to avoid hold-ups in the flow of intermediate processes – machining and button-holing, for instance, that required phased pressing – and bad feeling among the piece workers. Alec, with his quiet charm, per-suaded him to take on a temporary presser for the few days and have Jimmy back.

When Jimmy did come back the following Monday, Alec be-haved as if the incident had never happened. The matter was never mentioned again.

Alec was *l'homme moyen raisonnable*. 'Ye mus'nae ask too many questions o' life. There's never enough time tae wait for the answers!'

Hidden in the near future, he was to be proved right. He did have too little time. In the D-Day landing, ashore in one of the first waves, he silenced a German pill-box whose accurate fire was working havoc on the crowded shingle. According to the citation, 'Corporal Birrell on his own initiative, and with great coolness and total disregard for his own safety, went ahead on all fours till he was below the gun's level of fire, then ran to the emplacement wall and stood up and lobbed a grenade into the firing slit.' Then he fell dead. In the hurricane of cross-fire, death could have come from friend or foe.

He was content enough to work hard at the pressing, 'ge' a lassie in the back close' whenever chance offered, play billiards, and look after his mother and sister as best he could. Grinning, lips drawn away from big white teeth, he would say: 'Ye live a bit, eat a bit, fuck a bit, an' sleep an' wake up the next morning'! Whit else can ye ask for?'

One evening a few weeks after Annie had gone into the Royal Infirmary, we were doing the usual clearing up in the factory after working late; we each dried our damp rag and the cloth cover of the pressing donkey with a hot iron, sorted the work tickets for the garments worked on that day, made up the piece work tally and handed in the counterfoils to his cousin Bunty in the little glass-partitioned office, turned off the gas in the ovens that heated the press irons, swept up round the work place. Looking round I saw that Alec had finished and was sitting on the edge of the pressing table waiting for me. We went down the stone stairs together into the evening crowds.

Hands deep in trouser pockets, he whistled softly as we picked our way along the pavements littered with debris from fish and fruit and vegetable stalls, made the more slippery by recent rain. I waited for what he must have on his mind.

He began cautiously: 'Ye willnae' mind me talkin' a wee bit *personal*, will ye now? Ah mean it for the best. Ah've heard aboot ye goin' away tae Oxford. Ah've been thinkin' a lo' aboo' tha'. Ah'm wonderin' if ye're daein' the right thing? Efter a' ye've go' a guid trade here in yer hand! Whit guid's it goin' tae dae ye bein' a student? How're ye gonnae ge' back intae a job efter? These are bad times ah don't need tae tell ye! Wi' a' the unemployment. Ah know it's an honour yew winnin' a scholarship tae Oxford. All credit's due tae ye! Ah jist a bit fearful ye might be *very* disappointed in the end.

'Apart frae anythin' else,' he went on meditatively, 'it's a gey different wurrld ye'll be goin' intae. Well-to-do fellers frae hames where naebody ever wanted fer anythin'! Wi' different ways an'ideas. Yew're no' goin' tae understand *them* an' they're no' goin' tae understand *yew*!

'Or I should say,' he added, 'won't go out of their way tae understand ye!'

My thoughts had swung away. How did he know about the scholarship? I had told only my father and Aunt Rachel, and sworn them to secrecy, for there were a great many things to settle before I could be sure that I could go at all; and I was superstitious enough to take nothing for granted. In any case, even if they had let the news slip out, their links were totally different from Alec's and it was inconceivable that he could have learned of it by that route. And then I remembered that I had blurted it out to Annie.

It was easy to see how it might then have leaked out further. Desperate when she had staged that meeting with me outside the Baths, my news, if it had touched her mind at all, would have been pushed aside as irrelevant. Later, after the accident on the stairs, lying in the Royal Infirmary ward and slowly resuming awareness, I could imagine that resilient will of hers collecting itself again, turning her fate over and over and wondering what had gone wrong with her plan to entrap me, passing in review every possibility, running the film back and forth again and again. And then there must have come back to her, like an unheeded murmur of the Fates, the words I had let slip: 'I've won a scholarship to Oxford!' and understood at last. The unforeseeable factor!

Unburdening afterwards to one of the girls visiting her – by chance it could even have been one of Alec's lasses – she could well have mentioned it, the cruel stumbling stone! And that friend had passed it on, an interesting piece of gossip. For someone to win an Oxford scholarship, after all, was an unheard of thing to happen in the Gorbals.

How many days had Alec meditated on it, standing there opposite me on the far side of our work table, studying me, before deciding to speak? And now, gently, stepping carefully, he was bringing into the open the very unknowns that worried me. Or most of them. Oddly enough, fear that I might not get a job was not among them. Something quite different, much more crucial and personal, returned again and again to nag at my mind. He had put it delicately: 'it's a gey different wurrld ye'll be goin' intae.' Not one question mark but many. Would I fit in? Could I stand the pace in that foreign culture, among people who had come straight from public schools and grammar schools at eighteen, my schooling having been chopped off at fourteen? How isolated, how inadequate, would I feel?

So his intuition was accurate. More astonishing, and touching, was that he should show concern at all. We were not exactly friends. We knew each other only from the factory. Out of it, our paths diverged. Except on pay day sometimes, when after work a few of us had a game of billiards at the saloon a few doors away. Threepence per head for an hour at the table. I had given this up in recent months, for though I enjoyed the game the others preferred to play for money – sixpence a corner – and I never would. To tell them why would have been to betray father's gambling addition.

Alec in kindly fashion had tried to reason me out of my 'scunner' against playing for money:

'Ye've nae call tae be afeart ye know? Yew play a guid game! Look how many times ye've beat me?'

Praise indeed, for he was a fine, thoughtful player. Sometimes, humouring me, they agreed to play without the corner bets, but I could see that this spoiled their pleasure, and I found excuses not to join them.

He went on: 'Ye see, ye could fin' yersel' very unhappy there. Ye'll have thrown away the wurrld ye know. Och we know things are bad here in the Gorbals, but at least *yew* know where ye stand here. Ye can make real relationships here – well, yes, good and bad, I know, ye don't have tae tell me! – but ye make 'em wi' yer ain kind. There ye'll be a freak! A brainy freak, they'll see ye're brainy right enough – aye, an' maybe hate ye for it – but it'll no' make ye one o' *them*. Never. They'll make sure o' that. An' that'll hit ye hard because yew're no' the kind tae tell 'em tae go an' fuck 'emsels! So ye'll be caught in no man's land. An' as fer ye "goin' native" – I mean *joinin'* them an' beatin' them on their home ground – well!' He gave a sad laugh and shook his head, Because ye're no' callous enough! Ah'm no' sayin' tha' for any discredit tae ye mind. It's a guid thing in some ways. So long as ye never let the other side get tae know!'

Here was an unsuspected depth to Alec, so down to earth, reflecting on all this with such care, speaking out for my sake. Here was a sample of the warmth he was talking about. Perhaps he guessed that he posed a question I did not want to ask myself. Was I really following my star? Or a will o' the wisp?

He said: 'I hope ye don't mind ma sayin' these things? Ah've seen a lo' o' lads who couldnae ge' away frae the Gorbals quick enough, an' then they found the wurrld ootside wis *wurrse*! But it wis wurrse in a way they could never understand. It wis sae cauld an' everybody kept ye at a distance. An' then, thinkin' back, they see tha' some things here are be'er – sma' things, the way ye talk tae people, whit they think o' the wurrld, things ye never notice when ye *are* here – an' that's jist 'cos ye *know the score here*! But then, if they try tae come back here, in a way it's too late. 'Cos this wurrld, the one they knew here, wull've changed as well! An' the things they missed an' came back tae find again willnae be the same any mair. Och, ah don't know if ah'm talkin' sense! Or if it's ony use? But that's why ah'm sayin' it anyway.'

There may have been another motive, hidden even from himself. When someone goes away, those who remain are forced, uncomfortably sometimes, to re-examine where *they* stand.

As if he had overheard my thoughts he added: 'Here ye know where *yew* stand. Oot there ye'll know none o' these things. An' yew're the kind that needs warmth.'

How much did he know about Annie and me? If he was right that I would not make relationships easily 'out there', it might not be for the logical reasons he advanced, but because I would cling too long to the emotional debris of the past.

I said: 'I don't know where to begin. One thing I do know, I appreciate you saying all this. I didn't expect it. You're right, it'll be a different world. Apart from everything else I'll be lying far back in the race. All the same I can't see how I can *not* go. It's like Fate taking a hand. I never expected anything like this to happen. I just went in for it saying to myself: "Well, why not? Who knows, it could just happen!" And now that it has, I can't turn my back on it. I've got to chance my arm.'

13

Priestess of the Night

Now that he had moved north of the Clyde, Bernard never came to the Baths; in fact he was seen in the Gorbals rarely, when union business brought him, as when he attended inter-union meetings at the Workers' Circle that had a bearing on the garment industry, or met union members from the few small garment workshops south of the River. The latter discussions were usually held after the workshop closed for the day, on the pavement outside it or in a nearby close, occasionally at the Workers' Circle. The days of doing union business in the boss's time and on his premises were in the future. When this work was done he never lingered. I had not seen him for some weeks, since before the letter from Oxford.

I never asked him directly why he seemed to shun the Gorbals. Thinking about it later it was obvious. For him the place rang with a voice he had abandoned, that of the confident evangelist of Red Revolution. Spiritual wounds were still raw.

New traits showed in him, one of them a self-mocking irony, as when he remarked: 'Maybe it's better to work from the ground up as I'm doing now, dealing with 'issues' of hours and conditions, Trade Board regulations, proper lighting at the work place, washing facilities and lavatories and toilet paper! Nothing grander than that. Instead of from the top *down*, taking the God-like view, as I used to think I could. It was easy *then*, get the big questions settled and the little ones will take care of themselves!'

Thus he confided his sadness. Where was the old exaltation? 'Give me one fixed point and I will move the world!' Remaking the world is a job for giants. I too can walk among them. I too can see to the far horizons of time.

Not for him the long littleness of life, the bread and dripping of ordinary things. He listens to the music of the sibylline winds. He

carries their message to the groundlings. Oh to breathe that rarefied air once more!

Gradually he strengthened his new self in the course of dealing
with the 'day to day realities' as he called them, in contrast to 'the
basics' he used to take his stand upon.

'Maybe,' I said, 'there really is nothing else?'

With the stooped stance his wound had left him with, he had to
make a special effort to raise his head and look at you, so that his
regard seemed more intense than before, conveying the feeling that
everything one said needed profound probing before an answering
word could be let slip. That was another important change. Where
was the old mercurial talent, the swift scalpel swoop of the mind?
All that had surely not vanished altogether, only gone underground.

Unbelievably, the word 'humble' came into my mind for this new
Bernard, modest, practical, attentive to mundane detail, who now
placed supreme value on personal feelings and relationships, sensitive to the subtleties, who did not rush his thoughts at you like battering rams as he once did. I preferred to think of this time as an
interlude in which he digested Spain, tempered his soul in his own
internal fires, and that a new spirit, feeling and responsive, willing
to speak his heart with power, was arising within, grooming itself
to emerge.

In what avatar?

He was seldom at his desk. Recruiting, interceding with employ-
ers in the dozens of garment factories in the Glasgow area, going to
meetings all over the city, he was always on the move. Sometimes,
late in the evenings, he might be found at the union's district offices
in the Saltmarket not far from our factory; but to do so without
prior arrangement meant hanging round their dingy entrance after
work on the chance of catching him.

And that, with the mind turbulent and the flesh hot, could be a
disturbing experience.

The Saltmarket and the little streets running off it, on the north
bank of the Clyde near the Albert Bridge, constituted a distinct
quarter, of fish and vegetable and meat and grain merchants, ware-

houses and workshops and small traders. People mentioning the Saltmarket often meant the quarter as such, rather than solely the street of that name. Strewn with refuse, rotting produce, horse droppings, the quarter stank high in summer and mouldered foully in winter. But rents were low on the upper floors of the warehouse buildings.

Alec propounded a different reason for the union offices being there. Close to the main business area, its ill-lit side streets deserted in the late evenings, loading bays and adjacent railway arches providing shelter and many dark corners for privacy, the quarter was a favoured place for street prostitutes to get and serve clients.

'Ye mean tae tell me the union heid yins didnae know tha'?' His long bony face half-serious, he elaborated with relish: 'Aye, never any shortage o' cunt *there!* Dozens o' them. Jist yew imagine a' them skirts swingin' free, knickers stuffed intae their handbags, ready an' waitin' fer ye! Hiv ye no' seen them hingin' roon the door at night when we come oo' o' the branch meetin'? That's real *serrvice* fer ye! Nae wonder them meetin's are well attended!'

> Keepers of the sacred labyrinth,
> Priestesses of the stream of life,
> And of the night.

We were walking home from the factory late one night, about ten o'clock, the streets stilled. Something in his mood suggested he wanted a cue to talk.

I said: 'Have you ever had one of them?'

'Aye, a few times,' he replied in assumed indifference, 'when ah've been hard up for ma hole. That wis where ah had ma first hoor, when ah was aboo' fifteen. Ah wis jist this minute thinkin' aboo' 'er! In fact she comes tae mind many a time. She wis ma first proper fuck!' He fell silent. 'But that's no' the reason. She wis, ah don't know how tae put i'. She wis warm an' understandin' an', well, she was genuine. She wanted me tae be happy! She made me feel ah wisnae jist *anybody*. Ah'll never ferrget it. Never. A wee thin-faced lassie wi' red hair, verry pale, shiverin' in the cauld wi' a thin coat an' skirt on. A guid bi' older than me she was, aboo' twenty-five. An' wi' a weddin' ring on.'

He pushed his lips out: 'It wis one payday, an' it wis snowin' an' cauld, an' ah wis comin' away frae the workshop late at night dog tired an' for some reason ah don't remember an wis gaun hame through the Saltmarket an' no' thinkin' aboo' anythin'. An' suddenly there was this lassie beside me an' she caught haud o' ma hand sayin': "C'mon ah'll show ye somethin' wonderful!" An' she pulled me intae a big dark archway an' before ah knew anythin' she'd put ma haun' up 'er skirt – Jesus ah can feel it this minute – an' she'd got haud o' me an' a couldnae stop masel'! Christ wis ah ashamed! Bu' she said, quiet an' soft: "Never yew mind. Ah'll wait. An' ye'll be fine wi' me in a wee while." And she held me tight, an' kissed me as if she really meant i'. An' efter a minute she shivered and said: "Ah'm sae cauld! Ah'm tha' hungry. Will ye gie me a sixpenny piece an' ah'll go an' ge' a bag o' fish an' chips?" '

He snorted, 'If a hoor said that tae me the noo ah widnae trust her tae come back! Bu' ah wis only a boy. An' she'd been sae warm and gentle wi' me. She looked sae peaked ah wanted 'er tae have somethin' tae eat. Ah gave 'er a whole shillin'. Ah'd have tae tell ma mither ah'd lost it on ma way hame. In a way that wis true! She took tha' shillin' in baith 'er hauns it could've been a gold sovereign! An' she said: "Yew jist wait here an' rest yersel'. Ah'll be back in a wee minute." '

'An' ah wis left standin' there all flustered an' lonely an' wonderin' whit was happenin' tae me. Ah felt ah wis seein' this wurrld fer the verry furrst time. Aye, seein' a lo' o' things fer the furrst time. Ah thought of 'er walkin' aboo' hungry in tha' God forsaken place, through the piles o' rubbish an' horse shit dirrty white wi' the snow left lyin'. A' the emptiness an' loneliness. And the bitter cauld that had driven a' the ither hoors hame. An' her sae desperate. Grabbin' hold of a boy tae ge' a shillin' aff of, for a bag o' fish an' chips an' pennies fer the gas an' the price o' a pint o' milk! An' *her* bein' nothin' tae me, an' *me* bein' nothin' tae her. An' the next minute ah thought: "No. That's wrong! I' *is* somethin'! If it wis nothin' ah wouldnae be carin' at a'! It's *got* tae mean somethin'!"

'Ah started shiverin', standin' there under the arch, the freezin' cauld creepin' up ma legs frae the pavement. Ah wanted tae feel 'er warm body pressin' against me again, an' 'er gentleness sayin' nothin', jist *bein'* there wi' me. An' then ah started wonderin' if it wid be different fuckin' her than blockin' ma sister.'

I should not have been shocked but I was, and I must have shown it, or at least that I was surprised, perhaps by the slightest shift in my step or a questioning turn of the head, for he looked at me in astonishment. 'Yours've done it wi' yew surely?'

I shook my head, not sure what words would fit.

'Come on!' he said, disbelieving, 'Yewr sisters must've shown ye whit's what? Ah'll lay ye odds o' a hundred tae one ye'll no' fine a feller, who's go' an older sister, who's no' been intae 'er – aye many times, sleepin' in the same bed night efter night! Hiv ye really no' done i'? Ah'll no' tell on ye mind!'

'No. It really is true.' I searched for a bland excuse. 'Maybe it was because they were so much older than me.'

Most Gorbals parents, trying to instil the standard prohibitions, fought against impossible odds. Girls and boys were not even supposed to undress in each other's presence after a certain age, but in most families they had to share bedrooms and as often as not beds, and so the rules were dead letters. In our house they were of little relevance for a different reason; when Mary started having periods I must have been only about three or four. By the time I was old enough for sexual experiment, she was adult, her interests outside the house. In the tiny room I shared with her, hardly bigger than a bathroom in a present day council house, father rigged up a dividing screen that folded away during the day; on one side of it she slept in a chair bed – a wooden armchair that opened out into a single bed, its three cushions of velveteen cord laid end to end as a mattress – and on the other I lay on a narrow flock palliasse on the floor.

I have a dim memory of Mary, every few weeks, sleeping with mother for several nights in the alcove bed in the kitchen, and father occupying the chair bed. After mother died, Mary still went for those few nights to sleep in the kitchen. I never got a satisfactory answer to questions about this monthly shift of sleeping arrangements.

Father said: 'Girls get a bit unwell once a month.'

He called it 'the change'. He was not especially prudish for his generations; he felt, probably, that it was a waste of time explaining such things to a child, that I would learn about it all when I was ready.

How could I ever begin to explain all that?

Alec paused for only a moment: 'Aye, ah see whit ye mean. Maybe that's it.' He dismissed it. 'Anyway, *ma* sister went at i' wi me fer years. She used tae play wi' ma prick in oor bed even before ah'd go' any hair on me; an' after ah grew ma bush an' started comin', she go' me tae take 'er maidenhied.'

The memory jolted him: 'Christ tha' wis a night an' a half! Wonderin' whit tae do aboot the big bloodstain in the bed. Though at first when she saw it she was sae overjoyed – no, ah mean light-hieded like she wis drunk. Ah couldnae understand.'

He thought about it: 'What *do* ye understand at tha' age? Ah wis only thirteen or fourteen ah suppose. She's no' married yet, an' maybe never wull be, crippled like tha'. An' maybe – God help her – somethin' tellt 'er she'd better ge' a' the blockin' she could frae me?' He sighed. 'Well, anyway, in the end we decided she'd pretend she'd had a freak early monthly! An' ah'm no sure tae this day if ma mither believed 'er! Still an' a', nothin' wis said. Efter tha' she go' me tae block 'er over an' over again, nearly every night sometimes! But it wis never a proper fuck 'cos she never let me come inside 'er. She always knew when ah wis goin' tae come an' pulled me oo' jist before. Well, she stopped a' tha' when ah was aboo' sixteen. Ah've go' an idea tha' Father Millan, seein' ah was gettin' tae be a big lad, had a quiet word wi' er only day in Confession, an' tellt 'er it was bad for her immortal soul! An' mine too. How 'e knew, well, ye can guess. Them priests! Aye, them priests. They're on tae everythin' that's goin' on. Too bliddy much.'

I wondered if he was about too branch off into that familiar pastime, scurrilous talk about priests and female parishioners. Not this time. The encounter in the Saltmarket long ago, shining within him over all the years, needed to have its say.

'Anyway, as ah wis sayin', ah stood there under the arch freezin'. It wis snowin' again. There wisnae a soul aboo'. Every single hoor must a' given i' up that night. An' ah did begin tae wonder if she'd come back. An' then ah heard the quick steps muffled in the snow, an' ah smelt the chips an' vinegar, an' the next minute she was pressin' against me there in the dark. Shiverin' an' movin' against me tae ge' the warmth. An' d'ye know? She'd waited till she was back wi' me afore she started to eat any! Ah could tell she wis real hungry 'cos she ate them fish an' chips as if she hadnae had anythin' tae eat fer days. Ah hadnae the herrt tae take a chip frae the bag. Bu' after she'd had most of i', she stood there leanin' close an' put chips in ma mooth one a' a time till the bag was finished.'

We walked on for several minutes in silence and I thought he would reveal no more. He needed to, but couldn't.

At last he did, quietly, somberly: 'Well, as she'd said, ah' wis fine wi' her in the end. She showed me many things. Aye, many things. An' then she came! She really did. A lo' o' hoors jist pretend tae come so's tae make ye feel great. Aye an' tae make ye think they're enterin' intae the spirit o' things an' no' jist standin' there thinkin' aboo' the gas meter! Anyway ah'd never felt anythin' like i'. I' made me feel – ah don't know how tae say it – i' made ma herrt feel full tae burstin'. An' then she went very quiet an' hung on tae me all limp an' said: "Haud me up dear ah cannae stand." '

It had all been said sadly, far from the bragging manner of the shower group. He might have been pouring out his heart for a long lost love. His silence could have been of mourning, and reverence, for the lost bounty of innocence and revelation.

I had never been with a whore. In all the shower room anecdotes about them there had been nothing to compare with the enrichment he had spoken of. I thought of Annie. Would I, ten years from now, still cherish that experience as he did this one, and see all else as dross?

'No, it was a' different,' he said at last. 'It wasnae like wi' ma sister at a'! Ah suppose an should've known tha' anyway! It was – it meant more. Somethin' important. I mean important for the baith o' us. It's hard tae explain.'

'Did you see her again?' I asked.

'Whit did ye say?'

He had fallen into reverie once more.

'Did you ever see that hoor again?'

'See her? Ah wish ah could've stayed wi' er for ever!' The word rushed out. He stopped an looked at me, in wonder at himself.

He turned away and we walked on. When he spoke the emotion had gone underground again. The tone was different. He had moved away from re-living the experience, perhaps in flight from it, from regret at how far away it was, the simple closeness, with its freeing of emotions so precious but so beyond his power to comprehend and hold.

'Ah never fucked 'er again if that's whit ye mean. Bu' ah've seen 'er plenty o' times. She's lived a' the time in the next close tae us! Married wi' two kids. Her man's on the booze, an' knocks 'er aboo' regular. He's given 'er tha' many black eyes she cannae see tae wurrk. She used tae be a button hole hand. *They* always ge' bad sight, bu' getting' a' them black eyes as well must've buggered up 'er sight good an' proper! She cannae see tae thread the needle any more. Come tae think of i', if 'er eyes'd been be'er she'd 'ave recognised me in the dark that night afore she'd got hold o' me. An' maybe left me alane? Anyway, bein' hungry an' cauld, whit can ye say? She needed that shillin'.'

And now, to free himself from the attachment, attempting to denigrate the quality of the experience, he feebly essayed to kill the emotion, ordained to be out of time, a taste of something that would remain out of reach for ever, an antidote to bitterness.

The truth was in the words he had spoken before: 'If it wis nothin' ah wouldnae feel anythin' aboo' 'er at a'!'

A lost love. Or rather a love that might have been, if the dissonances of age and circumstance had not put it out of reach. Her continued presence in the next close kept the emotion fresh, and the pain too. She must now be a worn shadow of what she had been, but still able to sustain the memory of the tender, caring, courageous soul who had come towards him and awakened him long ago. That was the image, glowing in its indefinable sympathy, that would remain inviolate in his heart.

'Somethin' important. It's harrd tae explain.'

14

Feuds

Since so much of Bernard's work was done out of the union offices, and out of office hours – in the evenings and at weekends when union members could attend meetings – there had to be a way of reaching him at home. And so he became the first person I knew to have a private telephone, and it was in trying to reach him, not long after the letter from Oxford, that I used a phone for the first time. I needed to hear his reaction to my news. I had brooded on it alone long enough. Knowing more of me than Alec did, and with the crucible of Spain so recent, Bernard might have a different, more courageous view.

A telephone kiosk had recently been erected near the monument at Gorbals Cross, resembling the ticket collector's wooden hut at the boating lake in the park. Walking past it every day on my way to and from the factory I never saw anyone actually using the instrument. Sometimes a meths drinker went in and subsided on the floor, knees up to his chin, and slept away a morning, that is if he was not evicted by a passing bobby. Luckily the kiosk was placed next to the steps leading down to the public lavatory, and it was only occasionally used as a toilet.

One evening I got two pennies ready and went to the Cross, and gingerly pulled open the green painted door. The interior smelt so strongly of a recent cleaning with carbolic that my eyes smarted, and I kept the door open an inch or two with my foot to dilute the vapour with fresher air. I lifted the long black receiver from its sprung hook at the side of the little brown wooden box on the wall, and was startled when a girl's voice sounded in my ear, amazingly fresh and close. I asked for the number at his new home about a mile-and-a-half away across the river.

There came a distant 'Burr-burr', like an other worldly rat-a-tat on the door of their house, then the girl said briskly: 'Press Button A please!'

I did so and two pennies clattered down into the recesses of the long black box. Bernard's mother said: 'Yes? What do you want? My son is not here.'

She was in her fifties, small and dark and energetic, with an oval face and bright, inquiring, blackberry eyes – houseproud, thrifty, always neatly dressed in a shiny black blouse and skirt and a newly pressed white apron, busy at her sewing machine when she was not looking after the house. Her husband, a skilled cutter in one of the high-class men's bespoke tailoring workshops, was slim and distinguished looking, with finely chiselled features and sensitive mouth. Cutters were the élite of the tailoring craft. A dignified figure in clerical grey suit and wing collar, he typified, too, the working-class intellectual. For years he had been much in demand as a lecturer on Kropotkin's life and work, as well as on his own brand of 'gentle nihilism'. But these appearances had become fewer, for of late his consumptive condition had worsened. Whenever I saw him he seemed thinner, walked in a stooped posture and with effort, and coughed with a deep rumble of phlegm.

Bernard, now able to support his parents, wanted him to give up work, but hesitated to press him.

'He says he would die quicker if he gave up work than if he stayed at it. He may be right. I don't like trying to force him in case it does him harm. And mother would never go against anything he felt so strongly about. It's hard to know what to do for the best. It breaks my heart to see him dragging himself about like that, coughing his lungs out, back and forth to the workshop. It makes you wonder what life's for.'

Mrs Lipchinsky shouted down the phone at me as if she were leaning out of the tenement window to address me in the street below: 'What are you doing out there? You must come 'ere and knock at the door, like you used to! Tell me, 'ow is your father keeping? And 'ow are you keeping? We never see anybody after we move here. It is all strangers 'ere. It feels so far away!'

'Please, Mrs Lipchinsky, it's hard to go visiting after working late, with you living there now. Yes I will come soon, with Bernard. Please give him this message; I need to talk to him about something important. Can he meet me tomorrow evening after I finish work if I come to the union office, say about half-nine? Tell him to leave a message for me at the factory.'

'All right. I tell 'im. And you be sure to come with him here! It is not good to be wandering about the streets, you hear?'

'Yes, I hear.'

'An' tell your father good 'ealth from me! You hear?'

'Yes, I hear.'

There had been a tremor in her voice. I knew why, and she knew I did. It was something we had never talked of openly, and probably never would. In the years when I was growing out of childhood, shedding its egocentricity and looking outward, piecing together adult utterances overheard, I had been saddened to feel that some people blamed father's gambling, his manic melancholy, his lacerating rages, for hastening mother's death – if not actually causing it. To accept this opinion was unthinkable; a Gorgon's head that must not be contemplated. However wounding our quarrels, no matter how much I longed to grow up fast to be free of them, I needed to honour him.

For all I knew it was he who merited sympathy, caught in a maze of wrong vision and wrong action. I longed to help him escape, but had no idea how, and even if he had brought himself to air his problems to me, as a child they would have meant nothing, and when I reached my teens too much had happened. And he was too far off course. So I grew up in conflict.

Mrs Lipchinsky's undeviating respect and sympathy for him always uplifted my heart. Though she and mother had been close friends, she never accepted that simplistic verdict on father, indicating, without actually saying so, that mother's personality must be brought into the account too, *her* method of dealing with life, her responses to his longings and dreams, action and reaction, all understood in their wholeness together; it was wrong to see their life together as one-way traffic, from him to her but not the reverse. And so it was unjust to see his behaviour as wilfully evil or determinedly egoistical, but rather as a response, inadequate or mistaken though it might have been but sincere, to life as he perceived it.

Integrity, she maintained, was his outstanding feature. He might have been happier had he been a better opportunist, less open with people, readier to dissemble and manipulate them. The apportionment of blame was not for us. Life's purpose remained an enigma. We must contend with it for ever.

She permitted herself one explicit judgement. Life had given him too many knocks. 'To be left a widower with a family! What can he do?' she had exclaimed more than once. 'What a pity it is.'

Her view of him, balanced and detached as far as I could tell, was important to me. She could surely not be alone in it? Many others must see light in him too.

People spoke of his charm. Did that explain some of the sympathy? I could never see it. Perhaps he let it flow freely only for outsiders, and when so minded? But alas not enough!

Father had started his working life in the craft of bone and wood turning at a time when gentlemen sported walking sticks with turned and carved handles in bone and ivory and fine woods. That market was in decline. Replacing it was an increasing demand, extending down the social scale to the better-off workers, for umbrellas. With two brothers, he opened a shop in Dalmarnock Road to sell and repair them. At first the business prospered. Then came quarrels. Father, I learnt much later, suspected his brothers of swindling him, and scheming to squeeze him out. They accused *him* of neglecting the business and borrowing its cash for gambling.

One evening, I must have been about five, I was in the shop when a fight started between the three of them, two against one, my father alone. The savagery of it, and the awesome sense of sacrilege, as even my child's mind saw it, of brothers raising their hands against one another, would return again and again through the years in all the furious movement and thunder of those few volcanic, terrifying minutes. In panic I hid behind the counter near the street door with its glass panes black against the night, furthest away from their hurtling bodies. I had often seen drunks fighting outside the pubs and taken little notice. But the sight of my father and his brothers hurting each other broke my world to fragments. It was unbelievable, yet there it was happening, the sickening crunch of blows, blood streaming from faces and hands, their great frames falling with a noise like thunder and rising again, the leaping to the attack, wild eyes willing destruction. Counters and showcases were smashed and stock scattered all over the floor, much of it reduced to bundles of broken umbrella frames and torn fabric, amidst splintered wood and shattered glass. My cries of terror reached them at last, for suddenly they stood still, like huge puppets arrested, and turned and stared at me. Perhaps they felt a moment's shame at what they had shown me of their adult world? They bent over me, gasping for breath, looming black giants dripping blood onto my face, united now in guilt.

I sensed the continuing rage burning with them, and that was as frightening as the fighting had been. My uncles seemed to be condescending to father, insulting him. Why, oh why was it happening? Tears flooded down my face, fear for myself, for father, for the whole world, the only appeal I knew. Words sparked between them like fireworks, the meaning going over my head but plainly loaded with fury and hate. Father at last turned his back on them with a contemptuous shrug of his broad shoulders, lifted me up in his arms, held me strongly, comfortingly, his bruised hands oozing blood onto me, and carried me out of the shop into a dark rainy night.

When I was old enough to think sensibly about it I could never be sure, in the tangle of family anecdote, what were the true facts. By that time my two uncles had emigrated to America with their families, taking with them, according to father, money from the shop that was rightfully his. The trail had gone cold. In any case the sadness of the past as I remembered it was enough; I had little desire to probe for more detail. But anger and shame and pity for father's sake never left me.

He had forbidden all contact with the brothers or their families; and when they went to America no correspondence was allowed. On a small child the latter prohibition had no impact, but as a result, by the time I was grown up, the links of kinship that *might* have been re-forged, at least between the younger members of the families, were lost. In my twenties, turning my back on the past, that was of no consequence. In any case the business of living crowded out any thought of seeking them out; abstract, possibly interesting, but luxury one could ill afford. In later years the sense of isolation grew, and I regretted letting that happen. Whether the regret was well-founded, except on the principle that family ties are self-justifying, there is no means of knowing. I often said to myself: 'If there was so much poison between the brothers, could their children have escaped infection?'

That fight finished the shop. From then on mother seemed to recede from life, as if she knew her course was set and how little time was left to her, sad only that she must abandon her children, mourning our fate in advance. Apart from that I am sure she did not sorrow to go. Her face, remembered as beautiful and full of dignity, vigour and blithe courage, bright with intelligence and humour, became drawn and fixed; and gradually turned yellow.

One day she came back from hospital accompanied by a woman neighbour who brought with her a brightly polished brass jam-making pan. I overheard her tell mother:

'Aye, the doctor says if ah could lend ye a brass pan like this, polished up, an' ge' ye tae look intae it often, tae use i' as a mirror, it'll make ye ge' be'er quicker, ye see? So don't yew ferget tae dae tha'. Ye mustnae use an' ordinary mirror at a'. It's nae guid fer tha'. Yew use this a' the time, see?'

Little as I was I wondered about that. In my teens the truth burst upon me with a terrible poignancy. If mother saw her reflection only in that brass pan she would not know how yellow her face was becoming, and this ignorance might slow her decline. Or, delaying awareness of it, comfort, her.

Cloud of unknowing.

I doubt if mother was deceived. I never saw her use the pan as a mirror.

Father and mother were proud souls, he mercurial, impatient, explosive, she with greater control turning the pain of life inwards.

He too must have begun to go downhill then. There were other business ventures, dry-cleaning, electrical goods, local delivery, all ephemeral, whether because of ill-chance or bad management I never knew. Luckily, with his natural understanding of mechanical things, and his skill with tools, father could turn his hand to most practical tasks. For many years, in the fallow periods between these attempts to become – as he put it – independent, he made good money doing maintenance work in the garment factories. Each problem differing from the one before, he enjoyed the challenge. His care for quality of workmanship, imprinted during his days as a high-class craftsman in the walking stick trade, was well-known and he was in constant demand.

But always he would be drawn like a somnambulist to the faro table at the gambling club in St Vincent Place, in the heart of the business area near the Royal Exchange, and there, too often, he left his wages.

I never heard them quarrel, even when he came home skint and there was not a scrap of food in the house. In our cramped flat we would have heard any words of anger or reproach, but there were none. Was it simply the self-discipline born of their pride? Or was it love, more powerful than misfortune, weakness, foolishness? Often in adult years I told myself that that is what it must have been; I did so wistfully because I should have liked to have understood it while they both lived, and been old enough to express my tribute to their love.

That must have been the vision of them that Bernard's mother had, and timidly tried to convey.

They loved profoundly simply, unquestioningly, acceptingly and, in their own fashion, with integrity.

One day of calamity, on which the only item of food left was some cocoa in the bottom of a tin – no milk, no sugar, no bread, nothing – must have stuck in my memory because with a little child's single-minded discontent I blamed Mary, who was alone with me in the house, and kicked her hard on the shin for it. She must have been about thirteen, in puberty consumed with perplexities she could not possibly have shared with me, and therefore more forlorn than I was. Certainly she must have been every bit as hungry and frightened. Her pale round face, beneath its plaited corona of dark auburn hair, twisted in pain as she doubled up clutching her leg. She picked up a long bread knife and held it out, the handle towards me, saying through her tears: 'Go on then! Kill me if you like.'

I thought she meant it. She probably did, the way she felt. And now fear and horror at the imagined deed – I couldn't have done it but it *seemed* that I could – drove away the pangs of hunger. Drove everything away, except dread and despair in our isolation and powerlessness. What if no one came back? We sat in oppressed silence and, as the day waned, in darkness, for there were no pennies for the gas meter and no candles; and in increasing cold, for there was no coal left. We climbed into the alcove bed in the kitchen and huddled together for warmth under the blankets. At last, well into the evening, father came in with a few little parcels of food wrapped in newspaper, and a small bag of coal. Mother must have been at the hospital. Lilian was out late as usual.

In moody silence he busied himself getting a fire going in the kitchen range. Gradually the wintry dampness thawed out of the air. He put a few pennies in the gas meter and soon the little gas mantle on its thin metal bracket high above the fireplace spread its meagre yellow light upon us, its hoarse guttering competing with the crackle of the sticks in the grate and the coal on top of them spitting and sparking as the red and orange and blue flames licked and danced. For me, if not for Mary, it was his capable presence as he went methodically about the kitchen, more than his care in bringing food and warmth for us, that made the world come alive again. He peeled some potatoes and put them in the gas to boil, cleaned a few herrings and laid them out to cook on a griddle over the fire. Soon, with hunks of black rye bread, we ate and were comforted and felt delivered. My infant soul ardently focused on the single moment, I soon forgot my hunger and despair, or thought I did, but Mary put each morsel of food into her mouth with an air of doing so under duress, with a kind of defiance, as in her emergent womanliness she essayed to judge him as a man, and made her verdict plain. Forgive him she never did. Years later she would tell me that she blamed him, not me, for that kick on the shin.

In her implacable nursing of wrongs she was very like him. Alas she knew it. And in other ways too. She was torn between her love for him and her hatred of his defects that were hers too.

Father often did save the day by forcing himself to leave the faro table while he still had a few shillings in his pocket. Had mother been at home he would have handed over the money to her, and *she* would have gone out to buy some basic food and a little coal. A silent message would have passed between them as he handed over the few coins. I often wished that I could have read his thoughts at such a time. Did he not see that this recurrent struggle on the frontier of survival was his own creation?

With his high earnings we would have lived comfortably by the standards of the time, not in the slums of the Gorbals, or in the Gorbals at all. Did he really feel, as he appeared to sometimes, condemned to lift the heavens single-handed, bemoaning a cruel fate like lonely Atlas? Not that he ever complained aloud; I could only guess. And now, standing at the sink there in shirt sleeves and braces scraping the scales off the herrings, with the eyes of two starving children boring into his back, what *did* he think of himself? Capable of great sensitivity, a compassionate and good-hearted man, how could he not read Mary's face, pale with fury and disdain and contradictory love? How could he not see that I sat there in fear, aware of a brooding despair in the air, racked with perplexity for I was aware – and feared the knowledge – that this was too heavy a burden, wondering what I *should* be making of it, knowing that whatever it was I had no power to change a jot of it?

When he came home not partially skint as on this occasion but totally so, and stood ashen-faced in front of mother in the kitchen, she stretched out a hand to his cheek in brief comfort, no word spoken, no sign of disappointment or reproach, then turned away and moved slowly, short of breath, to the curtains of the alcove bed, leaned on the wall and lowered herself carefully to her knees. With little gasps she reached under the bed and drew out a battered brown tin trunk, opened it with a key from her purse, and took out a beautifully embroidered tablecloth, treasured from her dowry, a silk blouse, or some other pawnable item from this emergency reserve. Dark head bent, breath coming hard, she closed the trunk and locked it and pushed it with obvious difficulty, nearly empty though it was, back under the trestle bed. Then, clutching the front timber of the bed, with a little groan she pulled herself up on to her feet again, spread the item on the bed cover and scrutinised every part of it to make sure it was in good condition, for if not its 'pledge value' would be diminished. If it needed ironing, that would be a worry, for as there was no money for the gas meter there was no way of heating the iron, unless a neighbour could be persuaded to put it on their gas stove for us. With such a crisis always threatening, mother must have regularly examined the trunk's contents to make sure that damp and mildew, or insect pests, had done no damage.

Ah that little key from her purse! Years later I came across it and put it on my key ring. It fitted nothing, for the old tin trunk had disappeared long ago, but it touched my heart strings with memory, brought vignettes of their strange, deep flowing, abiding love, of the ways in which she strove to save him from himself. Whispers on the wind. Oh how well she knew him! She kept that trunk locked as an iron control over the last reserve of pawnable items, lest in his despair one day he raided it to feed not us but the faro table.

The day would come when I would wish I had followed that example.

The trunk's contents did not long survive her death.

During this ritual of dragging it from under the bed and deciding what could be pawned, father stood apart, not because he would not assist her – he was always attentive to her in the home – but because a certain nicety restrained him from seeming eager to join in the plunder of treasured things to rescue us from his folly. Mary and I stood huddled, wide-eyed with wonder and fear; somehow we must have known that this enactment was at the very edge of existence, the commitment of our only reserves to the battle.

While Lilian lived at home such total crises were few. Father must have been less sunk in melancholy, and therefore less enslaved by the faro table, or luckier. I think it was the former. Even so she must often have got us out of trouble by contributing extra money for food when father came home skint.

As time went by another reason may have deepened his depression and tightened gambling's grip on him. After Lilian began to practise as an accountant, her income must have risen far above what he earned. While her success must have pleased him it must also have added to his conflicts, for he must have seen it as underlining his failure.

Lilian's going hit him hard – a judgement upon him, a desertion. A betrayal of *mother* he called it, though this was about three years after her death. I suppose he was too proud, or in his heart too clear-sighted, to call it a betrayal of *him*. He was also implying, unintentionally I am sure, that even in death mother was in some way still the linchpin of the family as she had been fully in life, and that he could not take over from her alone. How much lower could he cast himself down?

I never knew how much money Lilian contributed to the home. When she left he forbade all contact with her. Did he not guess that Mary and I could not go against our feelings, the attachment of blood come what may, and that his prohibition, apart from being futile, would distort our lives with anxiety and guilt? He even announced that he would never accept money from her; the pathos of that came fully home to me only when I was grown up, when I found out that for years after leaving home she often gave him money in secret to buy us clothes.

Why in secret? Even after so many years that thought could bring tears, that even in her continuing fury with him some tenderness made her protective of his pride.

Perhaps, too, she needed to protect her own? She could not bear to be thought soft. I once heard her tell Mary, after a furious row with him, 'When I leave home I'm not going to work my eyes out any more to pay for his gambling!'

Like many strong-willed people who think that they have fought their way through only by suppressing sentiment, she affected to despise it.

For Mary and me as children, torn by awareness of father's torment, the reasons for it remained a mystery. Mary may at this time have begun to understand what gambling was, and perhaps what it could do to people. I had no idea. I hardly knew what money was, except that it consisted of round bits of metal, silvery or brown, that you handed over the counter to the shopkeeper; and, on paydays, bits of paper that father and mother handled reverently. Certainly neither of us understood the emotions that enchained people to gambling. We sorrowed for him, Mary less and less as she became a woman, or rather as her conflict about him, the tug-of-war between contempt and love, increased. But I wished and wished that I would wake up one morning to find that I had discovered the magic spell to cure his unhappiness.

Lilian justified her leaving us as an act of self-preservation. When I was about eight I overheard her tell Mary:

'If he thinks I've slaved all these years, night and day, to get qualified as a professional woman, and then let him drag me down like mother, then he's making a big mistake!'

While working as a typist and later as bookkeeper in Hieger's cloth warehouse, Lilian had become one of the first women in Scotland to qualify as an accountant.

I had no idea what 'drag me down' meant, but the corrosive vehemence in her voice sent a shudder through me. Father must have done something terrible if she could speak of him like that.

Not long after, one bitter winter evening, she packed up to leave.

Since mother's death the place had had the air of life held in suspense, of little love, of stony coming and going, of grimly holding on. Lilian went to work about eight in the morning and returned late, sometimes around midnight. Father left a little after, usually accompanying Mary and me to school before going on to one of his maintenance jobs. Mary brought me back from school at four. That homecoming was the most depressing part of the daily round. Ill though mother had been for almost as long as I could remember, her simple presence when we came in from school radiated warmth even when the kitchen grate had no fire in it. These days the place was always cold. Each piece of our meagre furniture fixed me with a hostile eye as we came in, the kitchen range sullen in its neglected covering of ash and splashed fat, the only signs of life the glistening cockroaches scurrying in the shadows, and a scratching under the floorboards as mice hurried away at the sound of our footsteps.

Because Lilian was so much older, in fact had been a grown-up all my life, she appeared to my child's vision as a kind of parent; and so her going was in some way of the same nature as mother's, different only in the manner of it.

When mother died I remember standing in the darkened kitchen, not allowed to be near her lying in the alcove bed. Grown-ups towered closely round me, a forest of giants, seeming to wait for some signal from afar. Mother was making little murmuring sounds. And then there was a long hard deep sigh from her, followed by total silence. When I was a little older I understood that the murmuring sounds had been her struggles to breathe; the silence meant that the fight was over. The giants turned to each other and shook their heads as if puzzled. Women held each other and wept loudly. A few caught hold of me and keened over me and I wanted to push them away for they were disturbing my wonder at what was going on. 'Why,' I asked myself, 'are they making such a fuss? Mother is asleep, that's what they said would happen. She would fall asleep for a long time! That's what they said.'

Lilian's going was quite different. For one thing no one pretended. She was leaving us and I would not see her each day as before. But the most profound emotional difference, not fully understood till later but sensed, was that Lilian could decide *not* to go: Mother couldn't.

Though Lilian had been physically at home so little in each day, I saw her departure as the loss of one of the two remaining buttresses of our little family, a piece of adult strength I feared to be without.

The evening of her leaving the tension was almost palpable. Father sat at the kitchen table, shirt sleeves rolled up, bare elbows resting on the oil-cloth cover, and stared stonily at the range in its high black arch that filled most of one wall. The fire had gone out, and cold ash had spilled through the bars of the fire-cage and on to the hearth stone. While mother lived, the brass kerb had always shone like gold but it had probably not often been polished since her death, and was now a dull bronze flecked with droppings of fat.

Lilian called me from the little cubby hole she slept in next to the one I shared with Mary. Dressed in hat and coat ready to go, she stood tapping a foot, expressing the inflated self-justification that supports a violent act. Behind her on the wall the gas mantle at the end of its thin upturned pipe wheezed and sputtered, its tiny yellow incandescent shell throwing an enlarged silhouette of her on the faded white-washed wall a few feet away.

On the narrow iron bedstead lay an open suitcase, a large expanding one in brown fibre that was new to me, heaped with clothes, shoes, books, papers. Beside it lay a little pile of new, stiff-looking shirts and vests and pants and socks. She snatched it up and muttered through clenched teeth: 'Take these to father!'

She placed the bundle across my outstretched arms. The aseptic, impersonal smell of new clothes somehow called to mind that last huge sigh of mother's, presaging silence. Now I was sure, if I had not been before, that she really was going. Distant though she had always been I longed to reach out and cling to her, do anything she wanted, if only she would stay. Tears ran down my face and fell like rain on to the garments pressed against my chin.

'Oh come on now!' she hissed impatiently, 'You'll be all right. Go and do what I say.'

From her doorway across the tiny lobby to the kitchen was only a yard or so. She could almost have stretched across and handed them to him herself. But I knew that would not satisfy her. There had to be a go-between.

That realisation darkened everything. Something must have happened too terrible to be revealed.

I saw that in making me deliver this strange Parthian shot on her behalf – a shot it was, that much I understood – she dragged me into the crossfire of an incomprehensible adult battle. And this feeling that I was being thrown about by uncaring and savage forces far beyond my power to withstand cut deeply into me, a wound that would sting for many years. I would ask myself: 'Didn't she stop to think that I had feelings too? My own sister! What had I done to deserve it? Her quarrel with father was *her* affair, their affair, not mine!'

The fight in the shop would come back to me. If brothers could behave like that to each other, egoism obliterating the sympathy and compassion that close kinship was supposed to nourish, why should I be astonished at Lilian's cruelty to me? My feelings were irrelevant to her purpose and deserved no consideration. Where had I learnt that women were naturally kind, with a divine gift of sensitivity that made them tender and caring? Perhaps, like 'blood is thicker that water', that was an artful fiction too?

Something of these thoughts, or rather feelings, surged through me even then and fought to emerge, and because I could not properly grasp let alone formulate them, battered me inside. I turned away from her and went to father, and stood before him with the clothes lying across my arms as she had placed them there. That smell of new garments, so rarely experienced in our house, in spite of the deathly significance it now had, stirred a timid excitement. The child snatched at a morsel of comfort. We were to have new things to wear! How wonderful that was going to be! Then I felt the chill of father's stare, blank as of a face in marble, and my tears flooded out again.

I had the frightening sense of great forces fighting within him, and knew that he struggled to stop them roaring out in flame. Only in later years, turning over the experience again and again, would I identify them. Not so much anger as a rage with himself and with his fate, and disgust at her defection. And something else – fear. I smelt it. That *he*, my giant of a father, should be afraid tore the ground from under me.

Lilian had been the apple of his eye, brainy, articulate, lucent, confident, incarnation perhaps of the soul trapped inside himself, and secretly depended on to fight by his side, and with youthful dash and brilliance help him to realise the visions he had nursed from the days of his own youth. And now, with her going, a last hope would go too.

A premonition must have cast its shadow over me, to be under-stood years later. From this moment he would no longer confront life, only continue an unwinnable fight with himself.

Seeing me weeping as I held that apocalyptic gift out to him, he must have made a tremendous effort of control. He tried to smile:

'Listen to me,' he said, intending I knew to be warm and reassur-ing, but his words sounded hollow as from a tomb, 'what's happen-ing isn't your fault. Don't cry. She shouldn't have sent you with this. She shouldn't have sent it at all! It's a guilt offering. You won't understand that now but you will when you get older. It's an insult as well if it comes to that. I mustn't lower myself to take it back to her. I mustn't even touch it. *You* must take it back. Don't say any-thing. Put it down in front of her and come back and sit on my knee. Everything will be all right, I promise you.'

How closed in they both were, unaware, or only partly aware? Defeated in a sense they both were, and both knew it, and yet they could display a regal pride and treat with one another as from within turreted citadels.

I stifled my sobbing and did as he said. If only I didn't have to!

She stared at me with something like the mixture of emotions I had seen in father's face. Yes, they were very like one another, ruled by a perverse, misleading, destructive pride.

Then she fixed her eyes on the bundle I had brought back. Terrified and desolate though I felt, hurled about in my whirlpool of emotions, I had a kind of pity for her – shattering for a child to feel about a grown-up – seeing the pathos and perplexity on her plump face, and the dampness glinting on her eyelids behind the thick rimless spectacles.

Her lips tightened and opened and tightened again as if she struggled to speak and no sound would come, in disbelief that what she had done could rebound upon her like this. She had misread him, as he had so often misread her. No doubt she felt diminished. A hard blow to that haughty spirit – as he had intended.

To his way of thinking, no matter how hard life was under the parental roof, a daughter must not leave it as long as she was un-married. Duty to home, parents, sister, brother, was absolute. A professional woman must not live in a Gorbals slum tenement? That was no reason to leave home. Let her take the family with her! Where the family home was, there she must be.

Whether he knew of, or suspected, any of the intrigue that lay behind her going I never discovered.

Lilian was torn; like Mary, between profound love for him, as elemental as the wind and the rain, and contempt because he had wasted his talents – a cardinal sin to her, who gloried in the exercise of her own – and because he had stamped his failure upon mother's life, and probably shortened it. The latter thought oppressed her perhaps more than any other, for she feared that a similar fate awaited her too. An added reason, irrational and doubtless unconscious, to distance herself from him.

Her fear would prove will-founded. She too could not change her destiny. Leaving him would make no difference.

Perhaps her business ambition did have something to do with her leaving home, but not for the reasons she gave. Oddly for someone of her brains she blindly imitated the thinking and values of the rough and thrusting business people of the world in which she was making her way; and especially their superstitions. They had no time for the loser. He was to be shunned like the leper for fear you caught his infection, or lest other people imagined you had caught it and shunned *you*.

But these were minor influences. Years later, Mary would tell me of the crucial ones, sinister, cruel, destructive, in some of which she herself played a part.

Was father truly a loser? What *was* a loser? The tragic clown who could not accept that a course of action simply would not work despite failure after failure, and persisted in it? Or the man born under the wrong star, whose implacable destiny consigned him to ineluctable disappointment? Both descriptions turned on the observer's view of the desirable life. All they told you about the 'loser' was that he suffered.

Father was too complex a spirit, finely turned, sensitive, to be judged simplistically. For him certain standards of his own were decisive, and if they could not be met he would settle for nothing else.

This was brought home to me with dramatic force when I was about five. I was with him in the Synagogue in Turriff Street near Eglinton Toll, at the point in the High Holy Day observances when the Cohanim, members of the hereditary priestly tribe, were about to ascend the dais and stand before the Ark of the Law, cover their heads and faces with their prayer shawls, and perform their ancient duty of conveying to the congregation the blessing of the Almighty. As a number of men rose to their feet from the wooden benches and began to make their way towards the dais, he took me by the hand and whispered urgently:

'Quick. We must go out now.'

We had been sitting at the end of one of the rows of benches only a few steps from the swing doors, and were able to slip out quietly. I wondered whether he had chosen to sit there with that in mind. Out in the draughty vestibule he turned up the collar of his coat and glanced back at the doors, apprehensively I thought, towards the worshippers we had left behind.

He said: 'We will wait here till they've finished that part.'

I studied his sombre face far above me: 'Father, why did we have to go out?'

His face assumed the distant look I knew well, when he sought to put subtleties into language I would understand, something he did with charm and ingenuity, and I loved him for that alone. 'Those men you saw going up there to the bimah [the dais on which the Ark stood] are Cohanim, and we're Cohanim too, inheritors of the duty of priest, and they are going up there to give God's blessing to the people. As a Cohan myself I must not be in there when they do that.'

'Why?'

'Because I must either be up there with them blessing the people or be outside. And I can't go up there because I don't feel holy enough to bless the people on behalf of God.'

'Does that mean,' I persisted, with the cruel logic of a child, 'that all these other men going up to the bimah think they're holy?'

He stroked my face with a calloused hand and gave me a smile, partly of approval, partly of sadness. To try to explain might expose too much. And how could he, if he tried to answer the question truthfully, share with a little child the infinitely varied chiaroscuro of life?

'You ask hard questions my son. You don't know how hard! You'll have to wait till you're older – I'm sorry I'm always telling you that! And then you'll have to answer that question for yourself. Maybe they don't think they're holy. Maybe they're just pretending. Maybe they don't even think about it. Maybe they don't care. But I do care. And that's why I cannot go up there with them today. Maybe next year I will, only God knows that.'

A moral judgement on himself, the fruit of painful knowledge. Painful, too, to put it into words for his little son. Never mind what others did, *he* would not pretend that his soul was clean when he felt it was not, even if he suffered by the admission. Answerable, inescapably, to himself, and to God.

A child learns much by overhearing things. An innate shrewdness tells him to note in particular the unconsidered remark, and to discount much of what grown-ups deliberately say. In time he will learn to decode the prepared statements they use to conceal their thoughts.

'I made my own way,' I often overheard Lilian tell Mary, 'I worked late into the nights to pass my exams. Ruined my eyes to do it! He never paid a penny to help me. It was the other way round. It was me that came to mother's rescue many a time, to *his* rescue really! Who is he to tell *me* what my duty is?

'As for mother? He says I'm betraying her! How can I betray her when she's dead? What can anybody do for her now? If I don't get on with my professional career now, after all these years of bashing a typewriter and doing Hieger's books at night and studying all night to get qualified, it won't help *her*! She should've left him when she still had her health. But she was brought up in the old ways: "No matter what your man does, you stick by him!" Women are not thinking like that any more. But it's too late for her. And it'll be too late for *me* if I don't get away from him soon.'

Father dismissed such talk as a cloak for selfishness. Loyalty was all. A man's luck, good or bad, was not his alone but belonged to his wife and children as well. The good times were shared. So must the bad. You were all in it together. The Captain Scott dilemma: should the stronger members of a stricken group go on alone and save themselves, if there was no hope for their companions whether they stayed or not? Or remain and perish with them?

From what father from time to time let slip, he too had been tempted, long ago, to break away and go on alone. Had it been his own fierce principle – 'You go on together or perish together' – that held him back? Or, in a secret corner of his heart had he in truth mistrusted himself? And had that doubt blunted his will? Better the Devil you know …

Perhaps only part of him had stayed, while another part looked back over his shoulder at what might have been?

Wait for Destiny to speak.

Lilian's answer was different. She would go forward alone and save herself. Or so she thought.

Standing trembling before her with the bundle of clothes resting on my outstretched arms, I could not know what thoughts fought with each other behind those round flushed cheeks. Thinking of it with the knowledge of later years I fancy she too examined her standards, as father had just done; and like him, seeing that life refused to conform to them, could not or would not act differently. Her pride dictated an angry and blinkered response.

'All right!' she snapped, 'I'll take them back to the warehouse and get my money back. Does he think I care, throwing things back in may face? He's done that once too often, you tell him that. Go on!'

She seized the bundle from me, bent down to the suitcase, and with jerky movements, range spilling over, began to pack the garments away, careful not to crease them.

Her anger had darted out like flame and scorched me. But her words meant little. This world of theirs, where a bundle of new clothes had the mysterious power to arouse fury, was too heavy for me to carry. I went back to him. He still sat there in his marble fixity. Mixed with my fear was another feeling, only later identified, new and unsettling; I was sorry for him.

He stirred and took me in his arms and put me on his knee and spoke softly: 'Don't worry your head about all this. She may be clever and think she's very grown-up but she's got a lot to learn about life. She's spent too much time with her nose in books. Life doesn't happen the way the books say it does, all neat and tidy. She'll come to her senses one day. Let her go. We'll manage without her'.

As far back as I could remember Lilian had been distant, controlled, purposeful, building an incomprehensible life across a widening gulf of time and attenuated feeling. She could not, for all I knew would not, express affection through that life-giving alphabet of childhood, contact and warmth. Father expressed my feelings exactly when he spoke of her as always buried in books, almost sheltering behind them, at the kitchen table, or kneeling on the floor in her narrow room, wedged between the bed and the wall and using the bed as a desk, piles of books littering the blankets.

What dreams I fashioned about the mystery of those books! If only I could divine the magic communication that passed between her eyes and those pages! In the silence of the night something would waken me and I would know at once what it was and be drawn to it, the shadow on the wall in her room cast by the gas mantle, a brooding presence separate from her and also part of her. I would get up from my palliasse and creep to her door and stand there, ignoring the cold linoleum chilling my bare feet, and watch, not moving, hardly breathing. What spells did she weave in the quivering yellow light? What was that potent shadow on the wall commanding her to do? What was she writing, writing, writing?

Would that I could get near her, would that I could understand.

After a while she would sense my presence and swing round and each time I hoped she would say: 'Come to me! And I'll show you the magic!'

Instead she would take off her round glasses with an impatient sweep of the hand and rub her tried-looking eyes, and say crossly: 'I can't study with you standing there watching me! Get back to bed. Go on!'

Still, that was contact of a kind. Remote she had always been, but she was *there*, part of the fabric of my small world. Now she would go out of the door weighed down by that monster suitcase and make her way for the last time down the cold stone stairs into the street, to remain out there in some other world, far away. So another bit of my world would break off and float away, never to be seen again, as when father's two brothers departed and took aunts and cousins with them. And Charlie!

I could not foresee the furtive meetings in the coming years, planned many days before, when Mary would take me by the hand, swear me to secrecy, and take me to visit Lilian in a smart flat far away across the city. For some days after each visit I would be sick with guilt, fearing father's intuition. Certainly, for me, those meetings were stiff, hurried, miserable affairs, audiences given grudgingly. For Mary, as I learned many years later, they did have a dark importance.

Meanwhile, tearfully watching her go, I steeled myself again to the thought that life would always be punctuated by departures, bits of me lost for ever, everything transient. I would travel from one void to the next. Yet even as I thought this I knew that somewhere within me I did not, would not, believe it. At the next moment, the next turning in the road, I would see all that I had lost, the things I had clung to and thought I would always have beside me, the people I had loved and was going to hold close to my heart for ever, come racing back to me.

15

Sisters' Flight

I must have sensed that night that other forces, alarming because hidden, were at work. That awareness must have troubled me even more than the enactments I did see, especially because all three, father on one side and Lilian and Mary on the other, though ranged in conflict, appeared to connive at the concealment.

One feature worried me particularly, though it would surface in my mind explicitly only when much older. Mary was out at her evening classes. Why did Lilian choose *that* night, knowing Mary would not be at home, to pack up and leave us, an act that must have been prepared some time before?

Mary, somewhat nearer to me in age – Lilian at twenty-eight seemed as distant in age as father – could have been a comfort to me simply by her presence. Even at that age I felt it inconceivable that she did not know of Lilian's intention to leave. Obviously my sisters had settled the timing between them, and for some reason, whether for Lilian's interest or Mary's or both, had decided that Mary should not be present. Why?

Since all three of them were united to exclude me from knowledge, there was no one to whom to express my worries, or appeal to share them, perhaps even explain them away. Battened down, they gnawed away at me within.

Many years later, Mary would reveal the background, and I would come face to face with the truth of what, as a child, I had partially seen. All the details of my sister's egoism and ruthlessness, clearly defined at last, would click into remembered places. Even with adult understanding doing its best to silence those memories, the pain would return as sharp as it had been long before.

The question remains, had I known it all *at the time* would I have been hurt the less? The answer must be yes. The unknown terrifies more than the known.

The adult wrestles with the logical, which usually means the superficial, and sees less and less of what lies beneath appearances. The child pierces straight through to the raw core of things, and suffers because he sees far more than he has experience to understand in its wholeness. He sees too much for comfort, 'Expert beyond experience'.

In my fashion I had perceived it all, the paths that Lilian and Mary had chosen of escape and safety and worldly gratification, and a muddled urge to avenge mother's suffering by hurting father.

Though they rated their sensitivity highly, proclaiming in proof their heartache on mother's behalf, the fact – obvious one would have thought – that their strategy entailed suffering for their little brother, perplexed and defenceless as he was, did not occur to them. I had put the raw facts together and reached a harsh verdict, and set it down in the books as a debt against them. In doing so I tore at my love for them as at a sacred thing, and was wounded still further.

I could not have put words to their behaviour. In my memory it remained incised as twisted and wrong; and, sadly as injury done to themselves as they strove to outstrip the Furies. I sorrowed for them too.

In their view, it seemed, the desirability of their goals justified any injury inflicted in pursuing them. For them too the end justified the means.

Both were naïve emotionally, at least on the evidence of their personal lives. When it came to manipulating people in their business affairs, however, it seems they were sensitive and shrewd.

Obsessed with escaping mother's fate, Lilian set herself to be hard and mercenary, to use men solely to advance her career. She would sell what she had to offer them discreetly, with calculation. Not of course an unusual scenario: some might say it was justified, or at least the more understandable, bearing in mind that in the Twenties and Thirties for women to enter the professions, let alone advance in them unaided, was rare. It must be admitted, however, that the crux of the matter is the road the emotions want to follow, and for many women Lilian's choice would have done unacceptable violence to precious feelings and beliefs.

Such a profit and loss account had no interest for Lilian. For her the need to call the tune was paramount. She must not repeat mother's mistakes.

Even so, was hers the only way? If she had been kinder, less ferociously insensitive where her professional interest was not involved, would she have forfeited one moment, one iota, of fulfilment? One may doubt it. She might well have gained. I saw her always as steeled and tight-lipped, with no sign of happiness in her, no free laughter, no joy, only fixity, demons in possession. And that grim aspect continued even after she left home, when she had begun to practise, and to prosper.

With what irony, with what precisions, do the Fates deal the cards? She was to die solitary, well off, her grudges unappeased.

Mary, too, longed for escape but also for safety. In some ways she was less single-mindedly mercenary. However, in her own fashion she was as detached as Lilian. And she too paid heavily.

She set higher store by emotional security, and thought she would find it with a man soft-hearted and caring and pliant, far removed, as she thought, from father's toughness and uncontrollability. In her most crucial relationship, in which she invested eight years of her springtime – from about seventeen to twenty-five – she discovered that, as so often with seemingly weak and dependent people, the man was strong and cool-headed enough where his own interests were at stake.

Both Lilian and Mary invested too much emotional capital in their opposition to father, whose influence naturally remained dominant, try as they might to escape; and this imbalance distorted their view of relationships and of the world. Self-doubt continued, defiance its obvious antidote. The secure person does not need such defiance. He presents himself for what he is and others are likely to accept him at his own confident valuation. Father did not intend to instil self-doubt into us, though he may have inadvertently transmitted his own. They misread him. They misread themselves.

Mary drew back the curtain during a reappraisal of what had been for her an exciting, careless time.

'D'you remember,' she asked, 'that I was out that night?'

'How could I not! I've thought about it often. Too often. I'd have found that whole business a lot less upsetting if you *had* been there.'

'I didn't *dare*, in case I couldn't keep it all in! We didn't know how much father knew, or suspected. About what we'd *both* been up to, I mean! You remember how intuitive he could be sometimes? We didn't know how he was going to take her going. Remember his terrible rages? I couldn't have kept stony-faced like Lily could! We didn't want a whole lot of things to come out! So we decided she'd go that night when I'd be out at my classes.'

'What *was* all this you had to keep secret?'

'You mean to say you never guessed?'

I guessed now. Memories returned. Whispers overheard, glimpses of meaning looks; perplexity, helplessness, knowing and not knowing.

'How could I have guessed? I was only about nine! Don't you remember? So she was pregnant, was that it?'

'You sound angry.' Her tone reproached me. 'You can't still be after all this time? We couldn't help ourselves! You must understand that surely?'

For Lilian to have had any tender attachments at all seemed bizarre as I had seen her, cold, controlled, detached, someone in whom calculation always came first.

Later however, in adolescence, it did cross my mind that Hieger, her employer and patron and later a principal client of her accountancy practice, might also be her lover.

'Of course he was!' Mary was astonished. 'Though I wouldn't use the word love! Not with a crude man like that whose mind never got as high as a woman's belly button. Anyway, why d'you think he did all that for her? She paid him for it with her body. As simple as that! Well, no, it wasn't that simple, not for him I mean. He wanted her badly. Needed her rather, I should say. But he was only one of them. Whether he knew he was sharing her I don't know. I don't think so, not at the beginning anyway. Later on, when she had him where she wanted him, it was different. He probably did know. But by then she didn't have to care. He couldn't take back what he'd given her, and he had to go on giving her what she wanted. Anyway, I'm not sorry for him. He did get what he wanted from her, as far as it went. So she was entitled to everything she got out of *him*. You look shocked?'

'Never mind,' I said roughly. 'Tell me the rest. I want to see the whole of it.'

'Try and understand how we felt, Lily and me. We used to cry together about the life mother had; how *she* got paid back for being nice and gentle and loving and long-suffering! From about the time I had my very first period, Lily kept on at me that that wasn't the way a woman should be. Oh no. *She* was using her body as well as her brains to get what she wanted. No man was going to get anything for nothing! *She* would always be in control! Men would pay through the nose, not only money I mean, or not the way you think. First of all to help her get qualified. That cost plenty, you know. And then money to set up her accountancy offices. And help in building up her practice, bringing new clients to her and so on, help in making useful contacts, and in moving into profitable deals on her own. She led them on till they were mad for it, till they would do anything she wanted. I admit I was a bit shocked myself sometimes, in the early days. Anyway it worked! She got what she wanted.'

Hieger was a man of many interests, property, cinemas, bookmaking, a shrewd wheeler-dealer who cheerfully sailed close to the wind. It was said that one of the sources of his wealth was the enhanced value of many of his properties which he rebuilt with the insurance compensation following fires. Such a man had useful contacts. For him to arrange for an abortion to be done discreetly in a private clinic was a simple, if expensive matter.

'Lily came to the office one lunch time and we went and bought some buns and milk and sat on a bench in George Square round the corner, near the drinking fountain where the meths drinkers sat, and she told me about it. Oh I'll never forget the look on her face!

A sort of glory! No, that's wrong, it was wonder at what she'd done. I'll tell you – I was always frightened of getting pregnant myself but at that moment, in my girlish way, I was proud of her. Though she'd never said it in so many words, I knew that she intended to fix Hieger that way. And now that she was pregnant she would never look back. She was going to get everything she wanted.'

The pregnancy had been confirmed only the day before. Lilian radiated a half-incredulous triumph, and a fevered intensity. The soldier going over the top.

'She said it must be Hieger's. It was only then I knew for certain there were others. You knew he was giving her all that time off work to go to college, and paying her college fees? Didn't you?'

'No, of course not. I knew nothing about any college. I remember her saying she qualified by studying at night and doing a correspondence course. I suppose she didn't dare let on at home she was going to college or father would have wanted to know where she was getting the money from. Ah yes, she said she often had to work into the small hours doing Hieger's books for him.'

'God, that's rich! It wasn't his *books* she was doing at night but something else! At one time he was even saying he wanted to marry her, didn't you know that?'

How could a child have known any of these things? To assume that he did, and that he knew them with an adult's understanding, must have been her naïve device to escape guilt.

'How was he going to marry her?' I asked stupidly. 'It seems he made himself out to be a proud family man?'

'Well you may ask! If the way had been that clear to marry her he might even have done it. Anyway he talked big about making a settlement on his wife and getting free. That kind of talk. Life is not very original, is it?'

Epitaph for herself.

My image of Mary in her teens was of a lovely, graceful girl, with translucent creamy skin and dark silky hair long enough for her to sit on. Eyes wide in innocence and candour, a warm-hearted sprite. She tripped through the world seeking an equal innocence. The kind of girl of whom people said: 'She'll fall in love once, and that'll be forever. The sort that sticks to her man through thick and thin!'

From mother's photographs, she too had looked like that as a girl.

I must have been eight or nine when Mary let slip that she was 'going out' with a rich Indian student. She was about seventeen then; certainly it was before Lilian left us. Something new and wondrous and totally absorbing made her glow from within. I was aware of waves of feeling, exciting but enigmatic, radiating from her. But the accompanying secretiveness weighed me down. There seemed to be so many things father must not know! And how terrible these things must be. Fear of discovery by father added to my stock of nightmares.

The word love rang like the voice of a golden bell, but a muffled one, to be heard in secret, coming from Mary's lips breathless with enravishment. This love, whatever it was, must be something important to fill her with such glory! But was it also to be feared if father must not know about it?

It seemed that her lover, Gil, was gentle and caring, but indolent. He would marry her, he said, when he had finished his studies. That, if it meant getting a degree, never happened. Year followed year, of happiness and luxury for her, of timeless *dolce far niente* for him.

How she explained her frequent absences, trips to the country in the Bentley, down-river on his boat, days at the races and in his flat, I dimly traced to her references to the many girl friends she stayed with – difficult for father to verify in those phoneless days – and the midnight whisperings with Lilian. I smelled the guilt, and would carry it vicariously, faithfully, through puberty and adolescence. That I was acting out lies to father, blindly taking her side against him, keeping him in ignorance of things he had a right to know, I understood well enough. I feared to ask why. I feared to tell.

When I was older, and Mary had left home, it was too late to make a clean breast of it to father. He probably knew, and understood why I had not spoken. Even in his sadness and disappointment, he never once stopped to tax me with my complicity against him.

In the eighth year the family in India foreclosed on Gil. Or so he said. 'Come home. Time for play is over. You must now take your place here and marry your betrothed.'

This was his first mention of a betrothal, arranged by his parents long ago, he said, without his consent. Mary pretended to take the news stoically. She decided that, as the woman 'in possession', she was strong enough to restore her position to what she had thought it had been, his bride to be. Endlessly they talked about how to 'rescue' him; she assumed, alas, that he wanted to be rescued. Like mother, she tried to save her man from himself.

About sixteen then, I sensed her heartache only in the abstract; her agony seemed to me overblown. I felt, and in my callow roughness probably said it too bluntly, that she had chosen, almost deliberately, to play a game that she was certain to lose: what was predictable must have been intended.

It was so obvious: a gilded and feckless fellow from a totally different culture, language, outlook, destined to return to a country where she could not hope to slot into a place of equality, let alone tranquillity. In the grand tradition he had picked on her for totally different fulfilments, necessarily transient. Like father, she had *chosen* to be defeated, and to carry the mark for the rest of her life.

Gil insisted that he would obey the summons home only to lay his hands on his inheritance, and so possess the wherewithal to marry her. But he would also try hard to make his family accept her as his bride; failing that he would come back and marry her.

Fearing to part from him, she pleaded with him to believe that his money was unimportant. She would be the willing sacrifice: 'I will work my fingers to the bone for you! We will manage. We will have each other!'

He had smiled sadly. Manly pride would not permit anything of the kind.

There came the classic farewell: 'I will send for you as soon as I can or come back to you. We shall be married come what may!'

His early letters were confident. He hoped to win the support of this or that influential relative. In time the tone changed; they were less and less specific. He would never give up the fight. One day he would come back and marry her. One day. The years passed. His letters ceased.

She never saw him again; she never married.

Lilian, at least by her own lights, played her cards better. As she had expected, Hieger, scared, ignored his previous talk of marrying her. Everything must be kept secret at any price. She knew then that he was at her mercy.

She imposed her conditions. He must personally arrange for an abortion in a private clinic, and make her a much bigger 'allowance', which must include establishing her immediately in a flat in one of the smart districts. He did everything she asked. Somehow she got hold of the receipt for his payment to the clinic. With that evidence, the threat she held over him was ruinous, and permanent. She would have other demands in future.

I said: 'So much for the talk about leaving home to be independent and to escape being dragged down by father! Somehow I must have seen through it, realised it was a smoke screen for something else, but not knowing what it could be, assumed it must be too terrifying to be told. No wonder I didn't believe in much after that time. With a flat of her own she could go into the clinic with no one around to ask where she was going. Afterwards she could operate more freely with other men. And of course a flat up west was a status symbol useful for business!'

'That's right. That was all part of the strategy. Hieger furnished the flat in real style. It was all expensive stuff, believe you me. Everything put in her name. The phone and all the other bills paid, everything.'

'And you too?'

'Me? No, he didn't pay for my abortion. Gil did. He was scared out of his wits his family would find out. I was scared too. It was one of those accidents. Anyway Lily got Hieger to make all the arrangements and write out the cheque to the clinic and get the receipt in his own name, which of course Lily took charge of.'

'The two of you! It's hard to believe.'

'Oh I don't know! Those were funny times, desperate times in a way. God knows how many times I've thought about it all these years. I don't *think* I was trying to trap Gil, I really don't. Sometimes I think it may have made him make up his mind the wrong way, who knows! Anyway, at least somebody benefited from it!'

'Who?'

'Lily of course. In that way, maybe in every way, she came off better than me. At least that's what I thought at the time.'

'What do you mean?'

'Well! With two clinic receipts in his name for abortions – they called them "curettages" but that wouldn't fool Hieger's wife or anybody else! Lily had him more than ever where she wanted him. How do you think she got the money to set herself up in style with offices and staff and everything? And got all those clients so quickly? *And* a finger in the pie in his big property deals? Stands to reason!'

'Very nice! Playing a wild game like that, no wonder she'd no time to care what happened to us small fry at home!'

That was a way of putting it. I know, even as I said it, that I was ignoring many things. I was reacting impulsively, in the heat of the emotions her account had resurrected. It was as impossible for me, as an adult, to see into my sisters' hearts all those years ago, as it had been for me as a child at the time. Oppressed, fearing for themselves, did they see in flight and opportunist calculation their only hope? Who was I to judge?

16

Pawn Ticket

Mother took a clean pillow case and gently eased into it the items to be pawned, smoothed it out and wrapped it in a sheet of newspaper. Everyone in the street knew when a woman was on her way to the pawnshop, for even though it happened so frequently – the demand was such that there was hardly a street in the Gorbals without at least one pawnshop in sight – and 'respectability' constrained one to conceal the deed, a common telepathy made everyone aware of it. Or perhaps it was the ritualistic manner of the attempt at concealment? There was a special pose of unconcern as one approached the pawnshop door, a pause at the window as if some item there had caught the attention, a shrug as if to say to any observer: 'Oh well, no harm in asking how much that cost!' and a quick entry. On the way there, the neat shape of the newspaper package was itself a give-away, confirmed by its absence when the woman emerged.

Mother threw her old grey shawl round her shoulders and tucked the parcel under it, not wholly concealing it, snatched up a battered shopping basket and put a string bag in it, and hurried out, still without a word.

Father stood for some minutes like a statue, heavy shouldered, lantern jawed, tight lips bloodless in the twilight. Collecting himself he moved to the long-sleeved vest – and washed vigorously, blowing hard as the icy water shocked his skin.

How often did he scourge himself?

Mother might get ten shillings from the pawnshop at the corner. She went along the street and bought potatoes, bread and margarine, broken kippers – sold off cheaply by the fishmonger – or herrings to fry with onions and potato fritters, flour, oatmeal, sugar, tea, milk, and candles in case pennies for the gas meter ran out again, and a ha'penny box of safety matches. In the next few days we would eat. If father was in work, luckily he usually was, she would hope to persuade him to bring his wages home without visiting the faro table that week, and the next week, and so on for as long as possible. She would give him eightpence for cigarettes, the price of twenty Woodbines or a small portion of rubbed tobacco with which to roll his own; something he hated doing for it offended his pride. In the next few weeks, putting by a few coins at a time in a hiding place she alone knew, she would get enough money together to redeem the treasures from the pawnshop. And back they would go into the trunk under the bed.

To be fair, father would not need much persuasion, his abstention a tribute to her loyalty, her love, her sacrifice. By coincidence it usually lasted just long enough to get those emergency reserve items out of pawn.

Whatever the blows that fell, both observed a fierce nicety of behaviour. They would not expose their bitterness – and father, especially, his disappointment with himself.

Had my sisters and I been closer in age we might have helped one another to understand the feelings father and mother kept battened down, and made fewer demands on them. A child's worried dependence clouds parents' vision, triggers ill-considered action. Discord and guilt grow. Father, when he seemed to exclude us, was doubtless trying to clear his mind the better to wrestle with his perplexities. Mother's unwillingness to show concern might have been her way of protecting us, lest the depth of her suffering hit us too hard.

If only they had been open with us! We knew, and did not know, what worried them. The child's intuition illuminates random patches, uncertainly understood; and in the darkness that remains his imaginings conjure images far more shocking than the reality. Allowed to share their worries, our love might have given them strength, and the burden of ill-digested experience we carried into adult life, there to distort our judgement too, would have been lighter.

As it was, their silence increased the uncertainty and wariness between us children; certainly between my sisters and me. Stretch out to them as I might across the gulf of age and experience, I could never reach them. And they, eagerly facing the adult world, did not try to reach me.

I did not abandon hope of understanding them. I would try to grow quickly out of childhood to be closer to them, faint yet pursuing. That the distance sometimes appeared to shorten proved, alas, a mirage. When I left school at fourteen Mary was twenty-one and Lilian thirty-two; she had been living away from home in her own flat for some years, a 'professional person' with a flourishing accountancy practice, a new woman. Mary had gone to live with Aunt Rachel and Uncle Salman.

We learnt to know when father, out all night, had been cleaned out at the gambling table. He brought home a paper bag of sugared buns still warm from the oven and breathing its magical aroma, bought with his last shilling at the bakery passed on his dawn walk home, only on 'skint' mornings! A pathetic effort, I realised in later years, to show his love for us, an antidote to guilt.

The buns, a rare treat in our house, were at first a delight, a sign of plenty. Then I found they signalled the opposite, lean times, even whole days without food, and they were like the ritual bitter herbs we ate at Passover.

Astonishingly in one who could be so sensitive, he seemed not to grasp that his morning bounty of buns, symbols of the riches he could *not* bring, had this effect on us, or perhaps he could not bear to, for he never failed to bring them.

One day he let slip that he sometimes had to 'borrow' that shilling from one of the men at the table. He said it ironically, as if he ridiculed his posturing self from afar, weakly defiant.

How could my father, so fiercely proud, court such humiliation? When I was about thirteen I once plucked up the courage to ask him. Why go on and on taking such punishment?

The grey-blue eyes darkened and he looked at me in sympathy, as a seer might regard a disciple not yet fully schooled to the higher understanding: 'It's hard to explain. All other ways are closed. I don't *know* what other way to go, maybe that's the way to put it.

One day I must win. Really win. Everybody does sooner or later. And then I'll be free to do what I want.'

I wished and wished I was strong enough, *knew enough*, to lift him up. He was groping in the dark. Sadly I glimpsed in him what he had been long ago, a man of vision, of soaring imagination, confidently aware of his powers, sincere, creative, courageous. Somewhere along the road, long before the fight in the umbrella shop, life had hit him hard. He was a beaten man and knew it, yet struggled on, aimlessly now and with lessening strength, to gainsay that knowledge.

I did not have the heart to ask: 'And what *is* it you want to do?'

Young as I was, I saw it would be futile. He knew that he had not given me an answer. To do so he would have had to rehearse too many blunders which, like so many pledges in the pawnshop, were now unredeemable.

The very young have no past to regret, and no stake in the present. The future is their glittering possession, an amorphous treasure waiting to take shape at their command. An effort of will is all that is needed. Nothing is impossible. Why was it that father, in my eyes all-powerful for so long, would not make that effort? Would I understand, one day, why he punished himself?

Meanwhile I wept for him. I had no power to do more.

He had always worked hard. He liked shaping materials with his hands, carving, turning, carpentry, making things work. As a small child, seeing him bend over something he was working on, a broken chair, a bicycle, a sewing machine, seeming to grasp its essence by being close to it, in a kind of devotion, I felt that he perceived the world not by words and logic but emotionally, by sense and feeling, touch and form and texture, the elemental relationships of things, a lonely innocent.

In a world made up of people like Hieger, such a soul is buffeted without mercy, draws in upon itself for frail shelter, treads the shadows.

Farfalla in tempesta,
Under rain in the night.

In the market place the Hiegers will always win. That is, as the world knows winning. They have no inner quest, or rather turn their backs on the one they were born with. They despise the innocent for persisting in his.

The innocent asks uncomfortable questions. He reminds people of the spiritual essence they prefer to forget. The Hiegers ride over him.

From early days I knew that father's moments of fulfilment were few. I doubt whether he enjoyed even the flush times when he went on a spending spree, when he seemed possessed by a sardonic frenzy, threw his winnings in the faces of the Furies: 'You see! This means nothing to me! The prize I seek is greater, much greater, than this!'

When he did have a biggish win, forty to fifty pounds perhaps, a fortune to us, he brought back no sugared buns that morning! He brought nothing. But later that day he would start spending. For mother a coat and hat and blouses and handkerchiefs; boots and stockings and underclothes for me, shoes and stockings and knickers and vests for Mary. Lilian, who for as far back as I could remember earned her own keep, got luxury items like lace handkerchiefs or a silk blouse. He would bring lengths of cloth and trimmings for mother to make additional clothes with, sheets, pillow cases, towels, a tablecloth. And much food; though with no refrigerator there were limits to what we could store. The first item was usually a huge chicken, a wondrous treat, which mother would cook with dreamily exciting stuffing, and with various additions in the ensuing days make it last for many meals. There would be real butter, large duck eggs, many jars of jam. The coalman would fill our coal bunker, a wooden bin behind the front door, to overflowing even if it was summer; coal at least would not go bad.

Only when he had done all this would he buy anything for himself, cloth and trimmings for a suit and overcoat, shoes, shirts, socks.

The only times mother raised her voice above her usual controlled tones were when he was about to sally forth to the shops with that possessed look in his eyes: 'Don't throw money away buying things for *me*! And don't spend it all *now*. Put some in the Post Office for the future! For the children, for things that might happen!'

She would look into his eyes with hope, then turn away, shoulders drooping. Both knew, I suspect, that to spend the money was for him the only way of saving it. Otherwise it would go back to the faro table.

Some did find its way back, indirectly, through the medium of the pawnshop. That was brought home to me later, when I was about seventeen, in a manner so traumatic, so unbelievable, that the shock remained with me for years.

I was then earning about thirty shillings a week, nearly a man's wage. I decided to realise an ambition, to own a decent suit. For a garment worker that meant a bespoke suit, a fine quality 'other' suit. I saved and saved for about a year, and at last had enough money, four pounds or so. In the garment workshops, especially the smaller ones, workers collaborated to make the occasional suit or coat or pair of trousers for one of their number or a member of his or her family, in their own time – working on these private jobs in the factory early in the morning or late in the evening – but using the boss's sewing machines, thread, gas to heat the press irons, electricity for light and power. You bought the cloth, lining material, canvas, buttons and other trimmings, got one of the tailors to measure you and cut the garment, and later fit you and make adjustments, and a machinist, a hand sewer, a buttonhole hand and a presser to do their parts, paying each a few coins previously agreed. Most bosses tolerated the practice provided the workers were not making a regular business out of it.

In this fashion I at last had a proper suit, of the best worsted, made to measure. A high-class suit of charcoal grey with a delicate white stripe the width of a thread, hand stitched edges, four-button cuffs with real buttonholes. Every penny of it earned with my own hands. I was in glory.

One day in early autumn, not long after I had got it, I came in from work tired but uplifted by pleasant anticipation; I was invited to a family gathering at Bernard's house that evening. There would be noisy, easy talk, the kitchen crowded out into the lobby, the heat intense, reddened faces blooming. Bernard's mother, dressed in shiny black with a fresh-looking white apron, rosy with pleasure in her guests' enjoyment, would dish out simple wholesome food, devotedly worked on that day – as a child I often sat in her ever-cosy kitchen watching her cook; there might be baked rolled herrings, potato latkas, thick slices of her ginger sponge cake. A friendly, homely evening. The like of it in our flat, dimly remembered, had been long, long ago.

I would wear my suit!

Our flat had its familiar air of desertion, cold and grey and damp, of life stilled. There were only the two of us now, father and me. Small as it was, the flat was too big for us – to say nothing of the cost – but he would not move to an even smaller one. He would never have admitted it but I fancy he secretly dreamed of a day when the four of us would be together again. More deeply still, in his heart he could not bear to leave the place where mother died.

There was no fire in the kitchen grate, not unexpected, but on this grey evening its absence, emphasised by dead ash spilt down the fire bars beside the oven door, made the atmosphere more than usually cheerless. I would feel better when I had heated the big copper cooking pot full of water on the gas ring, emptied it into the sink and had a good wash, put on a clean shirt and my new suit.

The tiny lobby was little bigger than two telephone kiosks put together. Facing the front door was a press, a cupboard in the wall, where we kept our few clothes, bits of household equipment, boots, a few tools. I decided to get my suit from it and take it into the kitchen with me so that I could put it on immediately after I had washed. In the semi-darkness I half-opened the door of the press and reached in for the suit. My fingers touched the wooden coat hanger. It swung freely. The suit was not there.

I felt I had expected this. Had I conjured up a piece of negative sympathetic magic, hoping to persuade the evil powers to stay their hand? But I was hit hard, very hard. I was astonished to find myself trembling, gripped by fear and rage, fear of what my rage might do if I let it command me. And then, as if a breaker rolled in from a dark sea, I felt thrown down and helpless.

I was roused by the sound of a key being turned in the front door beside me. Before I could move, it was pushed open and jammed me hard against the press. Father stood in the doorway, his stocky bulk almost shutting out the grey evening light from the stair window behind him. Face pale and drawn, he looked at me in a kind of wooden apprehension.

All the winds of the world screamed round me. But in the midst of the tumult I felt an awareness unlike anything experienced before. I was responding in a manner totally new, reasoning with myself in a counter-point that years later I would understand marked the beginnings of maturity. The expression on father's face, the lines at the mouth etched black and hard in the dimness, reached out to me, forced me away from my hurt and anger. I wanted to deny the appeal but my heart would not let me. Compassion hurt, yet it brought a small release from fury and self-pity. Other thoughts were admitted. I saw why I had half-expected this crisis. That morning, he had come home from a night at the gambling club bringing a bag of sweet buns.

He knew why I was standing there.

He said: 'I'm sorry.' It was the first time he had ever used those words to me.

He turned his face away quickly. But in the weak gleam from the stair window I caught the sheen of tears in his eyes.

Mine were damp too. In the midst of my racing anger I felt shame for him. To pawn his son's only suit – worked so hard for, saved and skimped for.

At Bernard's they would all be in their 'other' clothes. Of course it ought not to matter. Bernard would not ask himself: 'Why is he turning up in his shabby working clothes? Why doesn't he wear his other suit?' But to me it would matter. It would look like disrespect. I couldn't wear a notice on my chest saying: 'I didn't wear my other suit because my father's just pawned it!'

Not that it would have shocked anybody to say that. But you didn't flaunt your troubles. Everybody had plenty of their own.

I could not trust myself to speak. A single word, any word, might have released the violence bottled up inside me and God knows what I would have done. I doubt if I could have raised my hand to him, but I am sure I wanted to. I thought of Cain and Abel, but that was different. To strike your own father! Perhaps he blindly wanted me to. What deterred me, finally, was pity.

He brushed past me to the kitchen, half-turned, fumbled in a pocket, held out a small square of blue printed paper, the pawn ticket. I took it. He had some brown paper bags with him and went on into the kitchen and deposited them on the table.

Handing me the ticket was another clang of the doom bell, as if he said to me. 'You'll be able to get your suit back from pawn before I can.'

His dreams of winning streaks, even of little ones, were fading.

It would take me a good few months to save up the twenty-five shillings, plus interest, to redeem my suit.

A chair scraped on the bare floor planks in the kitchen. He sat there, back straight, hands clasped on the table, and stared in front of him. His sparse hair, once a vigorous ginger, now mainly silver, gleamed softly in the chill grey light that filtered through grimy window panes.

I remained there in the dark. If only I could walk away from all this! Now. For ever! Why not? What had happened belonged to a known pattern. It was one more blow in a long line. Was our family *so* different? Where were all those high principles of family life – love, loyalty, the cleaving together of parents with children, and children with each other? Or were they empty formalisms, products of habit, addiction to shibboleths, with no spiritual force? No, there must be more. Other families – Bernard's, Alec's, Meyer's, Phil's and the rest – seemed genuinely bonded together. Their members took thought for one another, willingly, unselfishly; they kept faith.

I thought back to when Lilian, and then Mary, had left home, and of how fiercely he had denounced their betrayal, how deeply he had been hurt. Why was obligation always from us to him? In pawning my suit had *he* not betrayed *me*? And was not his gambling addiction, even allowing that it sprang from pain within, a betrayal of us all?

Should I, could I, follow the example Lilian had set so long ago, and then Mary, and cut the invisible strings? I had never seriously asked myself this before. I did not dare answer it – yet.

I went into the kitchen. In silence I put water in the kettle and set it on the gas ring to boil, then made a pot of strong tea and placed a cup and saucer in front of him, put three lumps of sugar in the cup. I took from its brown paper bag the crusty loaf he had bought, cut a couple of slices and spread them with margarine from the quarter pound slab in another of the paper bags on the table, and put them before him on a small chipped plate with gold edging. Years ago there had been many more pieces of china with that gold decoration. Once upon a time, mother had told me, they had formed a magnificent tea service, part of her wedding portion. That plate and cup and saucer were all that was left of it.

On the cracked oil-cloth table cover I set out what he had bought, a pint of milk, bag of sugar lumps, bread, margarine, six eggs, a few herrings, about half-a-stone of potatoes, onions, a bar of soap ... pieces of my suit.

But this was not all surely? Some of my suit must still be in his pocket. Unless he had been back to the faro table in St Vincent Place already! Today was Monday, four days to go till pay day. If he were to gamble away the rest of my suit we faced a day or two of fasting after we had eaten what was on the table, and there would be no money for the gas meter even if we did have a spoon-ful of tea left. And on Thursday the factor would be knocking on the door for the rent. We could be put out on the street.

Why had he not told me that all that stood between us and hunger was my suit, our only pawnable asset? How could I have re-fused to let the suit go? Why did he have to take it without asking me?

A bizarre irony struck me. In pawning my suit and forcing me to make good his gambling losses he had in effect made me a partner. He had given me the right, in fact the duty whether I liked it or not, to say how money should be spent. I had no choice but to speak out. I tried to sound calm: 'Father, how much have you got left?'

He may have been expecting the question. His head jerked up

and the liquid stare searched through me. He seemed ruffled by this shift in our relationship, but perhaps a trifle relieved too. I was trying to share the load with him.

'A pound,' he muttered.

'You'd better give it to me. I'll go to the shops after work tomorrow. It's the only way.'

I added: 'And we've got the factor coming for the rent on Thursday and there's coal to be got.'

He did not reply.

I poured out the tea for him. He took the cup and picked one of the sugar lumps out of it in a teaspoon and took it between his teeth to suck the tea through it, piping hot as always. Then, still holding the cup to his lips, he reached down into his trouser pocket, brought out a pound note and put it on the table and went on drinking the tea. There was a crackling sound as he crunched the sugar lump. With the money out of his pocket, some tension had gone too.

I picked up the pound. This was what mother would have done, expect that she would not have had to ask for the money. And our plight would not have got this far. The iron reserve in the little trunk under the bed, grimly maintained, would have saved us.

I put the tea pot in front of him and covered it with the red and white woollen tea cosy I had watched mother knitting long ago. A memory returned, one of my earliest, of sitting at her feet near the brass kerb at the cooking range, looking up at those nimble fingers, the only sounds the fire's crackle and the needles' click. Everything bright and cosy and warm and tranquil. A golden time.

He sat there, elbows on the table, the empty cup held in both hands near his lips, stilled. Perhaps he too thought of times past; did he think of good times, or only of other bad ones, to be compared with this one only in degree?

I took the cup from him and re-filled it and put it down before him. I went to the sink and stripped to the waist and washed under the cold tap, teeth gritted hard. The luxury of washing in hot water from the cooper pot would have to await another day; the cold water was a fitting masochism. The tensions within me might explode any moment. The sooner I got out the better.

I put on a clean shirt, wetted my hair to flatten it, put on my tie, bought a week ago in Woolworth's for sixpence on the day my suit was finished, brushed my working jacket and put it on again.

He was looking at me in an unfamiliar way. It was an appeal but I could not read it. Or would not. To whom? Not to me surely. What could *I* do for him, expect, perhaps, forgive? That I could not do. Not now, not after this. Maybe it was an appeal to nobody in particular – to the Furies, to Destiny. For God's sake give me some luck!

Something in his look switched perception out of the present, into the interstices of time, where the blink of an eye seized a truth denied to ordinary vision. As in the theatre, when a change of lighting lifts part of the stage into dramatic focus and cancels all else, the table shifted and moved towards me with its cargo of tea and bread and margarine and sugar lumps, herrings and potatoes and the rest, and hung in a void, outlines edged thickly black as with a charcoal pencil, and I saw that it had become a still life painting, set at the edge of the world, the final darkness surrounding it. And father, in crumpled jacket and soiled shirt, stubbly face drawn in perplexity, those good square hands resting on either side of the gold-rimmed plate and saucer, part of it, a prisoner.

Pawning my suit was the end of a road, and he knew it. Many other things had gone to the pawnshop and remained there 'unredeemed'. Ironic word. He saw that too.

And that pawn ticket he had given me was a kind of farewell, a renunciation, a seal on the past and the future, for me the end of that infinite optimism of childhood and youth when all things were malleable, all mistakes could be put right.

Nothing, any more, would be redeemable.

'Have your tea, father,' I said, 'It's getting cold.'

He put knuckles to his eyes to rub away the damp, and lifted the cup to his lips, and began to suck the tea noisily through another lump of sugar.

I went out.

17

Siren Dance

News from the hospital coursed round the factory each morning. Annie was improving. She had relapsed. Complications had set in, gastric, intestinal, kidney, liver. She would be out in three weeks, she would be in for a long time. So the weeks had gone by. Today she had 'turned the corner', was more cheerful, though pale and thin and looking ten years older. Youthful resilience might pull her out of the battle. Not, however, as good as new. An ailing survivor.

I too had turned a corner. I suppose I had needed these weeks to order my mind, cast the account. The books could now be closed.

In a sense only. A line could not be drawn under everything. She was part of me; her place in my heart might change but it would never disappear. Its power would continue, unforeseeable and perhaps unalterable. I asked myself how I could have clung to the secret thought that there was unfinished business between us which would contrive, one day, to command us to its fulfilment. That illusion must have been necessary to me, and perhaps she knew it. Trying to exploit it she had erased it for ever. What remained was a longing, unidentifiable, persistent, the voice of a potent genie stalking in the shadows; a longing not for her but for the enrichment of feeling I had known with her.

These days, however, it was pushed into the background. Obsessively I traced and re-traced that inner colloquy in which I projected myself to Oxford, rehearsed dreams and plans. Now and then I would waken from it, perhaps when I turned on my heel to slam an iron into the oven to reheat, or stepped over to the water bucket on its wooden stand at the end of the table to soak my damp rag and wring it out; and find myself in a different world, empty, cold, featureless as interstellar space. No, not really empty, for there were other people, many, many others, journeying helplessly, solitarily, with no warmth flowing from one to another, no signals from the heart. And then the longing would return in full force, a fierce and desperate hunger that gripped the soul with fingers of steel.

A different obsession sometimes took over, especially after the day's report from the hospital. Shifting shapes and landscapes, gardens, fountains, phantasmas whispering, siren melodies tugging at the heart; mirages possessing me so completely that I would wake up from a morning's work not knowing what hours had passed. The sirens sang of a special state of being, misty yet effulgent, where magic reigned. Had I truly found it with Annie? The scenes would pass and repass before me. A time of golden light, of total understanding. 'Think each in each, immediately wise ...'

True or no, I had breathed its rarefied air, clear, astringent, as on a mountain top when the rays of sunlight sing to you. No wonder the memory brought pain.

In later years I would know how seldom life enwrapped you in such glory; and how persistent and intransigent the longing for that siren land could be, and by what Protean mischief it deceived you.

Enclosed in these repetitive thoughts, I shut out the enveloping thump and clatter of the factory, a hermit seclusion in whose creation we were skilled. But it was selective; a sensitive antenna remained active, so that when anyone approached the signal broke through to you at once. Some time during the morning after I had talked to Bernard's mother on the telephone, I sensed someone at my elbow. Driven as we were by the self-imposed pressure of piece working, one never stopped work unless for a crisis, an injury to someone, a fire. Continuing to move the iron quickly over the coat I was working on, shoulder and back muscles straining to hold the heavy block of hot metal in light contact with it, I shot a glance to my right. It was Bunty Birrell, Alec's cousin. Called the office girl, she sat in a glass-partitioned corner at the far end of the workroom, received the job tickets from the piece workers, tallied them and entered the figures in the daily ledger, did a little typing, answered the telephone, made tea for the boss and the master cutter.

She drew close and put her lips to my ear to make herself heard:

'Ah've go' a message for ye.' Little gusts of quick breath caressed my ear. 'Bernard Lipchinsky's just been on the phone. He says tae tell ye he'll meet ye the night as ye said, a' hawf-past eight a' the union offices in the Saltmarket. Did ah get tha' right?'

She was about seventeen, in the brilliance of her springtime, full-bosomed, wide hipped, with fresh, clear skin, the long slender Birrell nose, cool blue eyes. Fluffy fair hair parted in the centre over a high smooth forehead gave her regular features a wondering, questing aspect in repose. Botticelli could have given that face to his Venus. And the earthy symbolism fitted the rest of her. She wore a white cotton blouse, crisp and blooming, and a dark skirt in the newly fashionable flared style tight over her middle, that fetchingly emphasized the womanly span of her hips and their incurving sweep to the slender waist.

The long workroom was a place of patches of concentrated light shed by green shaded electric lamps hung low over pressing board or cutting table or sewing machine, each patch surrounded by dusty shadow. A lamp hung over the pressing board in front of me, but where I stood was in obscurity. Here, at one end of the thirty-foot table my back was to a blank brick wall, with which a short flank wall to my right made a secluded corner. Behind me against the main wall, an arm's length away, stood one of the low gas ovens that heated our eighteen-pound press irons, so placed that I could swivel on my heel and slam the iron I had been using, needing re-heating, into a slot in its front where it came to rest on a steel grid above a line of gas jets, then from an adjacent slot draw out a newly heated iron, which in a return swing I would bang down on the metal stand beside my pressing board. The jets burned all day even when slots were empty, and since this corner trapped their heat as well as that of the steam we produced and the radiant heat from the irons in use, I stood within a column of tropical air as if in an oven of my own. Even in cool weather some of us pressers worked stripped to the waist, as I did today; and sweat streamed down from armpit and neck and chest into the waistband of my trousers and the top of the short apron – made from a spare bit of cloth from the cutting table – we wore to protect the front of our trousers from fraying against the edge of the pressing board. By the end of the day every inch of clothing was sweat soaked, trouser knees caked with a deposit of expelled salt added to those of previous days.

I turned my head, and her face being still close my lips touched her cheek. She grinned happily and did not move away. In the high heat and humidity her body smell throbbed through me in waves as if I bathed in her enfolding flesh, and the glorious womanly chemistry went instantly to the senses and took possession. She smiled, quietly knowing. She put her lips to my ear again: 'Did ye no' hear me askin' ye? Did ah ge' the message right then?'

The message was different one now.

The idiom was familiar, and powerful. It belonged to the ancient tenement rituals of sexual teasing, patterned measures that could be savage, even frightening, but always mysteriously alluring, that started for all of us in pre-pubertal days, and slowly progressed, with knowledge and confidence, to experiment and finally to tenderness.

Teasing intrusion, thinly veiled in play in the tenement close, was serious and demanding. Budding and ripening, the blood racing, celebrants pounced on those a shade behind them in experience, paying tribute to the myths of sexuality in an antic tradition, roughly, crudely. Tribal rites. The day had to come, and more than once, when a boy ran the gauntlet of a group of nubile girls who plucked at him as they heaved him in mid air from one end of the close to the other, their exultant cries all but drowning his yells, first of fury, then mixed with growing excitation, overtaken at the last by orgiastic confusion as they triumphantly wiped hands on his gaping trousers; and similarly, but in some ways chastely, a girl with boys, till her shrieks brought grown-ups to her rescue, usually not before the boys had seen if not touched.

Preliminary skirmishing. Heat of new knowledge, new because outside the home and thus far more intoxicating than any experience within it. Preludes to teasing singly, confidently. And so, in due time, to the shrine at the ash-pits.

Her play now, in the mood of that ritual dance, threw out its maturer challenge.

The impetus taking her onwards, she added breathlessly: 'Bu' *ah'll* meet ye in the Saltmarket masel'! Any time! Ah dare ye tae!'

The word Saltmarket made the play totally unambiguous. Eager, simple, primitive, and in its way pure.

I looked across the wide table. Standing in his own patch of shadow, head bent, Alec stolidly worked away.

Her lips, moving from my ear, as if by chance brushed my cheek, and at the same moment her hip pushed hard against me. A minute or so before, I had taken from the oven an iron so hot that it nearly scorched my hand even through the iron-holder's six layers of heavily stitched cloth. Both hands were occupied, my right in moving the iron close above the damp rag, here and there letting it rest on a chosen patch with a hissing burst of steam as it made contact and almost instantly rendered it bone dry, then raising it and passing on, my left in smoothing and shifting the damp rag and the coat to prepare another patch for the iron; I must not allow it to rest on one spot for more than a second or it would burn through the thin cotton sheet and scorch the coat. Thus entrapped, the determined leverage of her hip, forced like a wedge between me and the table, half turned me to her.

Thinking about it afterwards, that hectic moment had a comic quality, though I was too flustered to appreciate it at the time, for with the fiercely hot iron needing swift and careful manoeuvre on the coat, apart from safe handling, I was at her mercy as completely as the boy being plucked in the close. I arched my body sideways a little away from her but the hard contact of her loins remained. Glancing to my right I saw that her blouse had a damp patch on the left where it had pressed against my sweat-damp skin, and the firm dark nipple showed.

'Ye cannae dae anythin'!' She laughed delightedly, cheeks pink and damp in the heat. The knowing look changed, touched now with a kind of gravity. The time had come, it said, for the play to move on.

I needed to put the iron down to rearrange the coat, but fearing to hurt her with it in this close contact I exclaimed: 'Watch what ye're doin'!' not thinking how droll the words were in the circumstances. But since she was the only one to hear it hardly mattered; they might even have added spice to her play. But in truth I was worried that the iron might burn her as I swung it over on to its steel stand on my right, for she stood in its path. Burns on the arm or hand, from getting in the way of a presser's iron, were common.

I pushed her aside with my right elbow, hastily but not too roughly I hoped, and brought the iron over and set it down. With surprising strength she resisted, moved hardly at all, simply leaned a little backwards to let it go past, maintaining her body's pressure. In the second or so that the iron was in its transit only inches in front of her, its radiant heat stinging face and arm like a fiery breath, she did not flinch.

'There!' she shouted in my ear, 'ye see?'

'Watch!' I shouted, alarmed, 'ye could've made me drop it!'

The words were out before I saw the other, slang, meaning. She laughed as she seized upon it: 'Och no! Tha'd never do! A great big feller like you's no gonnae drop 'is iron for nothin'! Whit wid a lassie do then? Come on, ah'm sayin' i' again – ah'm darin' ye?'

Matching her tone I said: 'The Saltmarket's no' a place fer a respectable lassie tae mee' a feller! Whit wid yer cousin Alec say if ah did mee' ye there?'

I was only half drawn in, but as I said the words I knew I moved further. I added: 'He'll no' like i' mind?'

'Och him!' she said. 'He'll no' say anythin'!'

She spoke confidentially now, joining me to her in complicity.

The play was part of you. It was always there, awaiting its time. It spoke to the willing heart if the moment was right. And what was happening now was a link in the chain of its endless regeneration, prompting us, drawing us in, poised to take us forward if we were both ready. That was not the wonder. With a fury of innocence not to be denied, with intuitive precision, she had *found* the moment.

Or with her power created it.

'Anyway', she said in my ear, 'Alec's go' a great opinion of ye. He says ye're gawn tae Oxford! Ah like clever fellers. There aren't too many o' them abou'!'

She added: 'An' that's why ah'm darin' ye like this. Ah'm no' afraid. Ah'm no' afraid o' anythin' tha' might happen. So there!'

I can be a match for you. I can be what you want. Don't doubt me.

Before I could answer she moved away a few inches. A shade anxiously she was looking towards the far end of the workroom. There, through the steam and dust, I saw a portly figure appear at the office door and look searchingly about him – Bompert, the boss. She said urgently in my ear: 'There 'e is wonderin' where ah am! Ah've go' tae go now. Don't yew forget ah'm darin' ye. The Saltmarket or anywhere else. Come on! Will ye see?'

Intent on rearranging the coat on the pressing board so that I could work on its other facing, I stretched out my right hand automatically, without looking, to lift the iron again, and touched her middle in passing.

Laughing she said: 'Ah'll take tha' for "Yes" then, eh?'

Her eyes were a wonderful china blue. I would have liked to see her smile like that all day, for ever.

And still I would not move quickly: 'I'm not staying long,' I said, meaning in Glasgow. 'So long as ye understand that?'

To my surprise I had spoken as if my doubts about Oxford were over. That made me hesitate. Before I could continue, she said quickly: 'Ah know! Alec's told me. He thinks maybe you shouldnae go. Ah don't know why he told me about i' at a'!'

She put her hand to her lips as if she had said too much.

Hurriedly she went on: 'Ah don't care. Ah want tae … Oh ah've go' tae go the now, the boss wants me there! Will ye see? Will ye?'

'Yes I will.'

18

Nether World

The union offices were on the third, top floor of a building that had fallen from grandeur, that had known the expansive days of the tobacco lords and other merchant venturers and traders to the West Indies and the Americas. You entered it by an ample doorway with fluted pilasters, a tri-glyphed lintel, and a timber canopy with classical pediment, supported by wrought iron brackets in a thistle and leaf design. Four stone steps, worn hollow, led up from the pavement. On either side was the dark cavern of a loading bay, in whose depths could faintly be discerned the raised platform, like the stage in a darkened theatre, the whole emitting a powerful stench of horse manure and nameless decaying matter. From within their impenetrable shadows, as I ascended the front steps, came little rustling sounds, masculine grunts, quick clear female voices chiding, comforting, hastening: 'C'mon if ye want it!' – 'There ye are, that's ma fine man!' – 'Och away wi ye! Ye've had yer shillin's worth o' me!'

The heavy panelled front door hung half-open, its great brass handle and knocker gleaming dully in the light from a gas mantle in a grimy glass globe high on the wall of the square vestibule. Beyond, this solitary point of light grudgingly revealed a spacious and lofty entrance hall with corniced ceiling, its timber floor knobbly from long wear, crowded with packing cases. In a far corner of it, as one advanced cautiously through the spectral obscurity, one came upon what must have been in its day a stylish staircase. A wide wooden balustrade, carved with foliage, much dented, topped iron railings thickly interwoven in floral clusters, vestiges of paint curling off. Broad wooden steps were partly covered with metal tread plates; these, burnished by much traffic, showed faint silvery gleams. On the wall that rose beside the stairs the last covering of some dark paint, its colour unidentifiable now, had almost disappeared among the many paler patches, presumably dirty white in daylight, where broken plaster had received minimal repair.

On the first floor were offices of tramp ship owners, and a customs agent whose brass plate announced that he was also honorary consul for one of the Baltic Republics. Outside his door were stacked several empty liquor crates. On the landing above, the gas jet had lost its gauze-thin mantle and the naked blue flame, weakly shining among the jagged remnants of a broken glass globe, cast a sepulchral light. Here were doors whose painted name boards, contemplated in these dismal surroundings, prompted questions much more than they gave information: South American Hotel Agency, Argentine–Scottish Friendship Institute, Mrs Parchment's Governesses Ltd. Rumours about the white slave trade to South America were persistent these days. Could there be any significance in the siting of these enterprises here, on the edge of dockland, in the territory of the night walkers?

From the top landing came no light at all; the gas tap, as I found when I got there, was turned off, probably because of a break in the thin pipe extending beyond it to the mantle, a common occurrence. In the meagre light from the blue flame behind me I mounted gingerly through the gloom, straining to see outlines, guided by the balustrade, encouraged by sounds from the union offices above, murmur of voices and the rhythmic rattle and slap of duplicating machine, and on the final steps by the rays of electric light escaping round an ill-fitting door. As in many buildings in the poorer commercial districts, the old gas lighting persisted on stairways long after electricity was wired in to the offices.

I found Bernard in a small bare room whose walls had once been distempered cream but were now darkened to a pale tan colour, with a grey stain round the narrow iron fireplace. No fire burned in it. On a slate coloured hearth stone stood a gas fire in a shiny black metal casing, unlit.

A thick grey overcoat round his shoulders, Bernard sat at a brown wooden desk much pitted with cigarette burns. I wondered idly about the burns, for he had never smoked and, naturally fastidious, he could be relied on to insist that visitors used the two metal ashtrays stamped: 'Smoke De Reszke' and bearing a begrimed image of the renowned singer in evening dress and cloak. The desk was either inherited from another union official or bought second hand in a 'disposal' auction – where the equipment of bankrupt businesses was sold off – in the Gallowgate nearby.

A green metal cabinet stood in one corner near him, and four brown bentwood chairs were ranged in a stiff rank against the wall opposite the desk. It was the first time I had seen him in his working quarters, and this aspect, orderly, austere – almost military, the coat flung round his shoulders like a campaign cloak of old – was an astringent reminder of how far he had travelled from the ecstatic visionary, disdaining lesser things, of two years ago. When I came in he was looking at some papers in an opened file, the only object on the desk besides the two tin ashtrays. He looked worried, greeted me with no change in expression, and signed to me to close the door. Then he snapped the file shut, stepped over to the cabinet, unlocked it with a key from a bunch he took from his trousers pocket, put the file on a shelf within and locked it. Facing me again, with a jerk of the head he motioned me to come round the desk to the window, the point furthest from the door.

'There's something I want to tell you,' he said quietly, 'but you've got to keep it to yourself, *absolutely* to yourself?'

I nodded.

'That file I was looking at. Government are putting to us arrangements for rapidly turning garment factories over to the making uniforms! Wanting union co-operation "in the event of an emergency", as they put it. Mealy-mouthed bastards! Trying to be jolly decent chaps to the unions. We're expected to do our bit to make things run smoothly when war comes. In the national interest. That's where things've got to. That's how near it is.'

Side by side we looked out at the black night.

'Yes,' he said. 'Fucking near. God curse them. What a hopeless world we're living in. And it's all been for nothing.'

Spain. The fight extended. But whose fight? The people who got it in the neck were always the same, the groundlings, people like us.

There was nothing to say.

He said: 'What about you? I know what this must mean to you. Oxford. Pulling yourself up out of this. Who knows how long any of us have got? It's why I'm telling you this, warning you in advance. When are you due to go?'

I did not answer immediately. For one thing I was disconcerted to find that he knew about Oxford. Ahead of me in much more than years, sophisticated, hardened by Spain, long committed to following his own line while I was only now beginning, I suppose I had naïvely hoped to take him by surprise with my news, note his reactions and chew them over. But his apocalyptic revelation pushed all that aside. It was a greater shock than it should have been. I had chosen not to see what was happening, believing it was pointless to think about it, unalterable anyway. Oddly, now, the thought of 'taking the King's shilling' came into my head, a potent echo. The uniform. Marching to war. Glory. War to end War.

That shilling bought *you*! What did *you* get?

And the woman's voice from the loading bay rang in my ears: 'Ye've had yer shillin's worth o' me.'

Down in the street a man in a dark overcoat and bowler hat emerged from a black doorway and walked quickly away into the deeper shadows. Almost immediately a female figure darted out of the same doorway, long skirt swinging, and strutted slowly along the pavement, looking behind her now and then. In the eerie, shut-down street other skirts swung and floated, or paused and turned idly about, in the yellow discs of light round the infrequent lamp posts.

Away to the south, over a tumbled expanse of roof tops outlined like black teeth against the glow in the sky beyond the Clyde, the orange flame flared high over Dixon's Blazes. For me it has always proclaimed the unfeeling sovereignty of the iron forces of the world. It was also a reminder of departure, the end of things. Charlie long ago. And my turn soon: if not to Oxford, then out into the void, dressed in the khaki our factory would soon be turning out?

Recent events in Europe had passed as a freak nightmare, its menace in innocence disbelieved. Miraculously, reprieve had come. Magic had worked. And now, standing here staring at the black window panes, the world came roaring back; newspaper headlines I had seen but not seen: the faltering negotiations with Russia, double-dealing in the international poker game, the party screaming that the imperialists did not want to stop the dictators in their course.

Stumbling towards the unthinkable. Flanders fields all over again?

'October,' I said. 'If I decide to go in the end.'

The Furies seemed to have plans of their own.

'What will happen to you?' I asked.

Watching his back still, he looked over his shoulder at the door. 'Let's go.'

Down the dark stairs he cantered confidently ahead of me. On the first floor landing, out of earshot of the people still at work in the union offices, he planted his elbows on the balustrade and looked down at the ghostly assembly of packing cases in the hallway.

Almost in a whisper he said: 'Even though you've seen it coming all along you can't believe it when it's staring you in the face. What am I going to do?' He shook his head, addressing an inner voice; a hint of something I was to divine presently.

'It's a strange feeling for me. I've been there before – or something like it. But when it comes – when, not if – it's certain to be different, worse and longer. A few days ago a comrade from the garment workers in France was here and he had a fine turn of phrase for it: "It will be *une guerre kilométrique*" – going on and on and on. What d'you think of that? That's what we've been born to live through. If we do.'

'Spain's getting on that way,' I said.

'Perhaps it *was*. But it's really over. Franco's rolling the whole thing up. And by God I want him to do it quickly now. The misery's gone on too long. And with the big war looming over the world, the *guerre kilométrique*, things in Spain will settle down; something not too good, not too bad.' He paused, and when he resumed his voice had an unexpected tenderness. 'And I can't wait for that to happen. I need to go back there.' He stopped abruptly, perhaps surprised at what he had allowed himself to say, then hurried on: 'I mean – well it's a long story. It'll keep.'

I was reminded of his telling me, in a few opaque words, of his escape from Spain: 'One day I'll tell you, when it's safe …' Safe for whom? I had assumed he meant the people in the apparatus over there who had helped him get out of the country. Something in his tone spoke of attachment, yearning: a distant flame, the sweet helper on the frontier, the waiting heart.

'And now,' he spat the words out with sudden ferocity, 'this fucking war's going to shut the gates one way or the other. God knows when I'll get there.'

In his evangelist day I was seldom aware of him taking girls out. Essentially a private person, he had kept his amours to himself, a defensiveness doubtless strengthened by his mother's match-making proclivities. Since his return, digesting Spain, drawn even further into himself, and in the last few months living away from the Gorbals, I knew nothing at all of women in his life.

At least *he* had someone waiting! Alas, far away, but someone.

In different ways the Furies had hit us both: sod's law, waiting to trip you up.

'Spain was a war of principle,' he said ruminatively. 'Or so we thought. And I went willingly. Even in a sense joyfully. This one's going to be infinitely worse, and it won't even have the excuse, the great shining cause, we thought justified us going there to shed blood. Like the Great War it'll be another case of supposedly clever and civilised people stumbling into savagery. And just as futile. Greed, arrogance, lust for power, stupidity; and the leaders – my God, what leaders! – pandering to people's lousiest instincts, driven mad with power. And the cynical game the Russians are playing's no better. But the hell of it is, once you're in it, people like us can't back away and pretend it's no business of ours, that it doesn't matter if we're defeated and taken over. As the pacifists want us to believe. This is our place, where for all its faults we're a damn sight freer than in a lot of other places – Spain, Russia, Germany, Italy.

We're stuck with the job of stopping this country getting trampled down and going the same way. You know how I feel about war? And it'll sound strange to you when I say this – it's strange to me too – but it's true. When you're in the thick of it, it is an intoxicating, passionate thing: it draws you in.'

'So you'll go?'

He turned away from the balustrade and faced me and the thin yellow gleam from the gas lamp in the hall below touched his broad face with timid highlights, and it seemed that he breasted the darkness and pushed it away from him, in a lonely affirmation that recalled his apocalyptic ardour in that last talk before he left for Spain. But there was also a steely desperation, the fighter with his back to the wall. The battle would have no victory, for this time there was no new dawn in prospect, only the hope of preserving a little light in the darkened world.

If you've got to go down, go down fighting.

'There's something else, isn't there?' he said. 'Haven't you seen the refugees coming in from Germany? The union's been doing something to help. Old men, women, children, degraded, bestialised, by those fucking bastards over there, Hitler and his gangsters. People from their concentration camps with numbers tattooed on their arms. Numbers! Not people any more. What sort of animals are those Nazis? We've got no choice.'

The ardour faded from his voice and he said sadly. 'Maybe bestiality's what the whole world is heading for? The rough edge of man's nature will be all that is left.'

He glanced up into the dark reaches of the stairway, then turned abruptly to lead the way down: 'Let's go. The others will be coming down any minute.'

On the entrance steps the damp wind crept between the ribs. He shrugged deeper into his coat and raised the wide collar up to his ears. I pulled my muffler higher under my chin.

A few yards to the right, in the cone of thin yellow gaslight from a street lamp, two women strutted back and forth, no doubt as much for warmth as display. As we stepped down on to the pavement they lunged towards us and took post one on either side of us

as if it were an assignation. The one who linked her arm in mine
was about twenty-five, with bleached hair falling in crimped waves
down to her shoulders, turned up nose and small pouting mouth;
she reeked of crude perfume and cigarette tobacco and also, as she
leaned close, of beer from her clothes, presumably from the breath
of her last client. The other was about thirty, with dimpled cheeks,
a pointed nose and full lips darkly rouged. Smooth black hair
curled inwards at the shoulders and a fringe, 'bangs', partly curtained deep-set eyes.

Mine said huskily, 'Come on an' enjoy wha' ah've go' fer ye!
Here ye are.' She pressed close and the pubic bone bored into me.

Her companion, in a chuckling whisper, said something in
Bernard's ear.

To my surprise he knew their names. 'Now listen to me Kirstie,
Jeanie,' he said good-naturedly. 'Don't waste your time. Anyway
I've got some business to discuss with my friend here.'

It crossed my mind that he might be a client; but it was just as
likely that he knew them from encounters like this as he came and
went.

Kirstie gave him back in practised style, half-mocking, half-
kindly: 'Och, yew're a right saint aren't ye now? Ye cannae kid *me*.
Yew know ye could do wi' a bi'! An' *ah* know ye could! Ye're a normal healthy feller! Come on an' ah'll gie ye yer pleasure dear. Ony
a shillin'!'

She made to reach under his coat and he gently pushed her hand
away.

'None of your tricks,' he humoured her. 'I mean what I say.'

'Och, away wi' ye, ye don't mean i'. Ah can see ye don't. Come
on, ye can have a free grope tae start wi'!'

She seized his hand and at the same time took hold of her skirt
below the knee and began to pull it up.

'None of that I told you!' he said in that gentle, coaxing voice.

In mock despair Jeanie exclaimed: 'Kirstie, they're sae pure!' She
turned to face me squarely, her back to the light from the lamp post
so that her front was visible to no one else: 'Here, ah'll gie ye a free
look.' Swiftly she gathered up her skirt to the waist. 'It's a' yours.

Wha'ever ye like, see? A shillin' that's a'. Come on then!'

Remembered afterwards, this nocturnal encounter, imposing a harsh yet magnetic counterpoint on his words on the stairs, had a bizarre, Inferno quality, questioning life to its limits, testing the spirit and the will.

Nether world of flesh and calculation; exquisite torment of proffered bliss one was doomed to refuse.

The shower room's callow and superstitious view of life was confused about whores. They excited primitive attraction one moment, revulsion the next. They were an irritant. They debased conventional attitudes to women, yet confirmed them too. They placed themselves in the twilight of society. They degraded a sacred essence by commerce. They were branded with guilt. But they exercised an arcane power, and were objects of appropriate awe. Supposed exemplars of finished excellence in the arts of the flesh, they threw out a teasing challenge to manhood; but, alas, life was so unfair that to accept it brought the high risk of getting a dose.

I could not have said which of these influences doomed me to refuse; probably none specifically. Inner tumult pulled me away.

'Listen,' I said, 'this isn't the way I want to get it, that's all. I'm sorry.'

I wondered if I had sounded priggish, unmanly. What matter! Those priestesses of the night must surely have heard every variation of excuse many times over.

It was her turn to be patient and kindly: 'Think of i' like this, dear. Ye'll ge' yer pleasure wi' nane o' the bother ye'd ge' efterwards frae one o' them stuck up respectable lasses! Nae tears, nae worries, nae naggin' ye fer promises tae marry them! Nae bother at a'! An' a' fer jist a shillin'. Aw come on!'

Kirstie snuggled up to Bernard: 'Ah know *yew* appreciate a wumman tha' understands whit ye want eh? Yew're fine an' strong an' randy. Come on show me whit ye can do!'

She turned her head to survey the street. Her tightened features, crudely limned in shades of darkness, spoke her anxiety: 'Shall I persevere? Is something better coming along?' It was about nine o'-clock, peak drinking time in the pubs. Not another man in sight. In a new tone, one of comradely seriousness, she appealed now to both of us:

'Ye can be *free men* wi' us! Ye can *say* anythin'. *Dae* anythin'. Whit yew want's on'y *natural*, ye see! An' ye'll get a' the understandin' ye want. An' when we've sa'isfied ye, an' ye're at peace wi' yersel' ye walk away an no' a soul in the wurrld's goin' tae know a single thing about i'.'

Oh world where the wish is law; siren land.

Seizing on our silence, she went on eagerly: 'Ah've go' a wonderful idea. If ye want a bi' o' comfort, there's a fine boardin' hoose near here. A big room wi' two double beds for five shillins. Nice an' cosy an' warm. An' dead secret ah promise. Ye can do wha'ever ye want wi' us there! An' ah mean tha', *anything!*' That's right isn't i' Jeanie?'

'Aye, anythin' at a'! A' the things ye've ever dreamt aboo' doin' wi' a wumman an' maybe never dared tae say! Come on let's go there, eh?'

Bernard's clipped soldierly tone returned, finishing it: 'We're not in that league. We'd sooner get it for love. No offence, Kirstie. Jeanie. You're good women and I like setting eyes on you when I come out of here. So we'll leave it at that.'

Kirstie shivered, accepted it, hugged him again, this time for warmth. 'All right, dear. But mind ye gie us a turn while ye're waitin' fer yer love! Ah know ye well enough! An' ah'll keep mind o'yer friend here as well. We'll be here when ye want us right enough.'

'That's real *serrvice* for ye!' Alec had said.

In silence we walked to the end of the street and turned north and went on into Argyle Street. In that long defile of dazzling light from shops and department stores, there was little traffic this late in the evening, but crowds of window shoppers moved slowly along and dreamily contemplated fumed oak sideboards and gate-leg dining tables, leatherette three-piece suites, bed-settees, radio-gramophones in tall mahogany cases with gothic bas-reliefs, suits in the Fifty Shilling Tailors – fulfilment on the never-never.

The scene was no different from any other night. Naïvely I wondered why. The nether world we had just left belonged to a distant, immutable universe. But in *this* day-to-day world as it lurched to war, surely the collective mind must concentrate? One should feel *something*, a tremor of fear, a closing down of perspectives, a postponement of hope? Why didn't they stop everything, as people did when the end of the world approached?

We crossed and entered another hinterland, of long narrow streets where we passed beneath cliffs of darkened office buildings, once more among shadows, but not as profound as in the Saltmarket, for in this better class business district lamp posts were closer together and lighting brighter. An electric sign and warmly glowing windows announced the presence of an upper-class restaurant; and at a nearby corner a little group of nightwalkers strutted and whirled, on faithful watch. Here was a different caste, fashionably dressed in fitted tweed coats with fur collars, toque hats, silk stockings, high Cuban heels.

'Five shillin' touches!' Alec called them, 'But ye'll get tae lie in a bed, an' she'll gie ye bacon an' eggs after, so it's probably wurrth it!'

As we came near, two of them, young, poised, debonair, halted and assessed us, hesitated, then turned away. Bernard with his trilby and smart coat and shiny leather portfolio would have met their standards, but I saw that my muffler and cloth cap and scruffy working clothes ruled me out. Off-balance as I was, I resented the rejection. It recalled Annie's long ago. She too had assessed me as a poor economic prospect and turned away.

Would I in the future become sentimental about Kirstie and Jeanie? Unpretentious, kind in their fashion, surely they must be the salt of the earth.

Bernard, head sunk at a slant in his coat collar, spoke in a low, troubled voice: 'Sooner or later they make you question your feeling, your integrity. I used to see whores simply as a social problem! Not a bit of it. It's a state of mind. We'll never understand it. Don't dare to perhaps. It would mean destroying too many illusions. Why do we feel shame for them sometimes? And for ourselves for wanting them? We have an idea of woman that's almost a religion on its own, and as unrealistic. We want her to be tender and caring. We

want constancy. We demand that a fuck should mean love, on *her*
part but not always the other way round! It had to be a man who
wrote:

> Man's love is of man's life a thing apart,
> 'Tis woman's whole existence.

'But come to think of it, it's in the woman's interest to say that too,
to make us feel guilty if *we* fuck without love. But we don't feel
guilty, not often anyway. We blame it on the Old Adam. At the
same time we don't like a woman to think of *herself* that way.'

Oh waiting heart on the frontier! Will *you* be constant?

'I'm not cut out for abstinence,' he went on. 'But I can't stomach
the idea of pretending I care for a woman simply to get her. That
would make me feel guilty. Sometimes when the pressure gets too
much I feel there's a lot in what Kirstie says. Take what she offers
and walk away free. Well, free in a sense.'

'The soldier's way of looking at it?' I said too quickly, and then
wondered if I had touched a sensitive nerve.

He wasn't put out: 'You're right up to a point. But it's more than
soldierly savagery. In war you feel your manhood's in jeopardy
more than life itself. That may sound absurd but it's true. Having a
woman gives you back a breath of your own proper existence. But
it's not only when you're a soldier. Day to day living brings you to
the same sort of breaking point, where you need a woman to give
you renewal.'

If only I could think of it in that fashion – a woman, any woman,
one supreme enfolding, one still moment of certainty! I thought of
Bunty, and Jeanie. Could I find the plentitude of content he spoke
of – however temporary – with either? If I needed to ask that question the answer must be 'No'. It wasn't so simple. With Bunty it
was fire kindling fire. That was something to be going on with. But
could one look there for renewal, removal of doubt? No, nothing
so exalted.

Without naming her, I told him.

He thought about it, and laughed, taken out of himself: 'Why are

you worrying? Why does it have to be genuine? And what is genuine? Take it while you can! You've had a bad time one way and
another. You deserve something from life at last. Don't punish
yourself. Enjoy her!'

'But you do care? I can see that.'

'Is it as plain as that?' he said heavily, obviously taken aback for
letting it be seen. 'All right then. There is someone in Spain. She
saved my life, but it's more than that, much more. And it's hard for
us. It's hard to keep in touch. And dangerous, I don't mind telling
you. I still can't be sure she's in the clear. I don't know how much
the party knows. Or the other side for that matter. She can't get out,
not yet. And I daren't show *my* face across the frontier. Not till the
shooting's stopped – and they've stopped settling scores. I'm going
to swear you to secrecy again.'

'I won't say anything.'

'You're right. I do care. And that's why – all right this is something else between ourselves – that's why I take Kirstie sometimes.
I suppose you guessed that too? Though she was discreet enough in
her way. I don't like doing it. And apart from anything else I'm
afraid of getting a dose. Not a pretty picture.'

'Maybe you'll get over there soon.'

'I don't know. I don't like to think what will happen if I don't.
There's a limit to constancy when you can't be together. And there's
something else, sad in its way, and ironic. Mother's constantly at
me, wanting to get me married off. This nice girl and that nice girl!
She'll probably have a go at you too. And how can I tell her? She
wouldn't make sense of it. Love? What's that got to do with anything! Perhaps love, like beauty, is in the heart of the beholder?
Nothing more. What a come-down to have to admit that! Like admitting we need faith. We don't know why, or even what it is, only
that we need it.'

Something had been nagging at the back of my mind. 'How did
you know about Oxford? I didn't mean you to find out from someone else.'

He took a moment to answer. Perhaps he indeed been hurt not to
have heard of it first from me.

'Annie told me. One of the machinist girls from your factory came into our office about her branch dues and told me what had happened. I went up to the Infirmary to see how she was. She said you'd told her.'

'Did she know how I came to tell her?'

'No. Why?'

There was a lot to tell him, for when she had gone away from me I had been too sick at heart to talk about it.

He said nothing for some minutes.

'So it was her in that close with Phil?'

'Yes.'

'Christ! Sometimes life goes out of its way to be cruel.'

'It would have been worse if you'd chosen to stop at a different close that night. I wouldn't have know about her and Phil at all.'

'Would it have made any difference *whose* child it was, if it wasn't yours? Besides, you didn't know she was pregnant. You backed away from her for other reasons altogether.'

'You're right. The pregnancy had nothing to do with it, except to sicken me afterwards, when I did know, and realised what she'd tried to do to me. No, the drawing back had started before, when I thought about her in the close with Phil. I doubted everything. Either she had become a different person, or I had never known her at all.'

His going to see her in the Infirmary surprised me. Certainly it could be explained as part of his role as a union official, caring for his flock, but it wasn't usual.

He said: 'All the same I have a feeling you're sorry you let her go like that?'

'No, I'm not. But I must admit I'm thankful I had no time to think about it. I had only just got the letter a few minutes before bumping into her like that, and it blinded me to so many things. It answered so many questions for me. I wasn't thinking at all. And so it saved me – just! I saw the trap only later, when she landed herself in hospital.'

He brooded over it. 'In the old party days her head was too much in the clouds to believe anything she said. But *she* believed in her visions – at the time! Beautiful women do. They think their visions will take them anywhere they want to go. At some point she decided she could get what she wanted not by being a heroine of the workers' movement, but by going after money – and maybe power too, who knows – by manipulating men. It's an old story! And she was impatient. Come to think of it she should have been more patient with you! Your news about Oxford must have been a shock, to discover that *you* are moving higher and she could have risen with you! Well. She had to come to earth some day, but she shouldn't have tried to save herself by trapping you. I suppose she was at her wit's end.'

He sighed. 'It's a sad business. I'm trying to persuade Bompert to keep her job open. God knows what will become of her. For a brilliant girl she was stupid, and arrogant and ruthless into the bargain, but she's been punished, hard. I can't help feeling sorry for her.'

I dared not agree with him. If I did I should have to go to her.

As if I had uttered the thought he said:

'Don't look back any more. The sooner you get another woman the better. Emotional ballast! We need that to keep us sane.'

'Listen,' he said, warmth returning to his voice. 'I haven't had a chance to say anything about Oxford. There's only one word for it – wonderful! Like a breath of fresh air! For you to have done that, you starting from here, from these conditions, competing against people with a far better start than you, shows what you're made of! It makes even me feel there's hope! Maybe, at last, life is making it up to you after all you've gone through. You deserve every bit of that and more. And look here, you mustn't have any more doubts. Of course you must go. In spite of what's happening. It's the hand of Fate. You've got no choice.'

'If there's war I suppose I won't be able to anyway. The choice will be taken out of my hands.'

He said: 'If I were you I'd go ahead as if the way *was* clear. I'm going to report this to head office. The union's got a small trust fund to help members going after higher education, if they've shown achievement, and by God you have! So I'll put up a case for you, to see if you can be given a grant. We'll see. Anyway, by hook or crook you must go. I've become a bit of a fatalist after Spain. War does that to you. It's all written! We used to say, "If it hasn't got your number on it don't worry!" Well, one did have *my* number on it – an inch or so to my right and I wouldn't be talking to you now. That must have been written too. So accept your destiny. Where it'll take you Christ only knows. You won't know the answer if you don't go! I'm sorry it's turned bitter for you – I mean the Annie business. You've got to get away – in every sense.'

19

Carry the Torch

In the close where Bernard now lived the flag stones were devotedly decorated with pipe-clay in an interwoven curly scroll design, the sharp edges of which showed that they had been washed that day. Further evidence was the smell of carbolic soap. There were no broken steps. The wall plaster, painted cream from ceiling to a little below half-way down and green the rest, was clean and uncracked. A door at the back of the close shut the ash-pits away, and no smell came from them.

Bernard's house was the first I had been in that had hot and cold running water, a bathroom and its very own lavatory. The tiny parlour had a linoleum square on the floor, imprinted with a Persian carpet pattern, and round it the bare planks were stained brown and polished. Heavy oak furniture thronged it – high-backed chairs with leatherette seats, a hexagonal table with bulbous turned legs, a horse hair sofa with a white antimacassar on its back rest. Brasswork shone on fenders and doors. The kitchen range smelled mustily of the day's black leading, and the flanged edges of oven doors and handles and hinges had been rubbed with emery paper to the high gleam of steel. Against the wall facing it was a plain wooden table with hinged flaps, spread with a fringed white cotton cloth. The air was heavy with scents of food and herbs, the warm exhalation of newly ironed laundry. An atmosphere of care.

We washed face and hands in the bathroom wash-basin, and went into the kitchen and stood at the table and waited for Bernard's father, who sat reading a book in a high-backed wooden arm chair in a corner near the fire, to take his seat first and say grace.

Of slight build, with long narrow features and a high forehead topped by a mop of snow white hair, he was elegantly turned out in a well-cut double breasted suit of pearl grey worsted with hand-stitched edges, and a wing collar with grey cravat held in a gold ring. At first sight he seemed boyishly slender, but a moment later one recognised the thinness of the very ill. He rose with obvious effort, levering himself up by gripping the elbow rests of the chair with quivering hands on which the blue veins stood out, stepped with care the few feet to the table and sat down heavily in the battered ladder-back chair at its head. Before he said the prayer he sat with eyes closed for some moments, as an ardent preacher composes himself to be a medium between God and the people. The words were uttered in a distant voice as from a crag in the wilderness, with tenderness and awe. He was not only the celebrant; he was part of the sacrament too. The sounds bubbled in his throat and his dark eyes watered. Bernard, opposite me on his father's left, studied him with concern.

When he had finished, Bernard placed a hand on his shoulder: 'Be careful, father. Be gentle with yourself. In any case you shouldn't have waited supper for us. You need your rest.'

His father regarded him tenderly and the wrinkles at the corners of his mouth deepened: 'What good will rest do me, I ask you? I'll die with my boots on when God wills. I'll leave it to Him. Don't worry.'

The voice was soft and resonant, gentle, almost a purr, but there was a rasping note of phlegm from deep in his chest, betraying his sickness. The hollow cheeks had little colour. His manner was alert but plainly he kept fatigue at bay only by an effort of the will.

Bernard looked down, determinedly composed, and began to spoon up the steaming cabbage soup.

Mr Lipchinsky turned to me: 'My son, I wanted to tell you myself what I think of your achievement. Bernard told me your news and I was over-joyed. A new world is opening up for you. It's a wonderful thing. You are young, you will drink in new knowledge! Only with knowledge can we change the destiny of Man, stop him blundering, let him reach out for his rightful fulfilment. Be sure to use your knowledge well. I am happy for you.'

From his inner breast pocket he brought out a folded sheaf of papers and laid it beside his plate and pressed the sheets down flat.

Caressingly, he ran his finger tips over the close lines of curly writing, then looked up and addressed me again: 'I have studied all my life. It takes so long, hours stolen from other things, so many years – yes, years! It wearies you to do it the way I did, in the moments that were left after work, at night while my wife lay sleeping. And those hard years have taken my strength. You, my boy, will race ahead and do it all so quickly. I envy you, I don't mind admitting it. Without this wonderful chance, you might have gone the way I did. That is why I am pleased for you.'

He put his hand to his chest and gave a little gasp. A cloud darkened his face, and his eyes assumed the wondering look of an injured child.

Gently, Bernard chided him: 'Come on now, father, you don't need to envy anybody. You've achieved a great deal, more than most, and done it in the face of tremendous difficulties. You're probably the greatest scholar in Kropotkin's ideas in the country, maybe in the world.'

His father shook his head as if to say: 'I know you want to reassure me, but alas I know better.' Turning to me he tapped the papers:

'I have been working on this for years. I am writing a book – the other things have been pamphlets, articles, little things – it will be a reassessment of Kropotkin's work, but also my own ideas for a way ahead, going far beyond him, towards universal populist reform. I shall call it *The Torch of Constructive Anarchy*. There is so much new thinking now, and I have so little time to keep up with it. Take Clarence Streit's *Federal Union*, for instance. Now there's an ambitious vision for you! A glorious one and no mistake. A federal union of the whole world! No one, no country would need to think of conquest any more. No need for rivalry, the curse that has always led to war. We would all be part of one another, think of it! We would settle disputes by democratic action. War would become unnecessary!'

Bernard said nothing but I was moved by the compassion in his face, and the bitterness. What a moment to be talking of utopian systems! His father seemed unaware of the shadows of war. He was living in the clouds, far from the Hobbesian brutishness of the real world, of Hitler, Stalin, Mussolini. To shed tears for him was too late, and to let him see them would be cruel. Loved and respected father, so ill that he was visibly wasting away, who had made his life forfeit trying to force an impossible dream to come true, a world peopled only by men and women of goodwill, who had painfully trudged towards it sustained by hope through all the years, and seen it remain as remote from fulfilment as when he had set out; and still, the flame burning low, he pressed on innocently towards the receding horizon.

Lacrimae rerum, the tears of things. Always awaiting you.

He began to cough, a deep, tormented struggle with his lungs that shook him through and through; and there was a rumbling up-surge of phlegm as if a monster thrashed about inside him. In the midst of his agony, even as he fought for breath, a look of embar-rassment came over his face, incongruous, pitiful. He wanted to hide his plight. He turned away from the table, pulled the handker-chief from his breast pocket and put it to his lips, apparently trying to hold the phlegm in his mouth, and with the other hand gripped the edge of the table and tried to get to his feet. Bernard was up in a moment, plainly alarmed that he might choke, needing to bring up spittle but stubbornly restraining its rise, and put a hand under his elbow to help up. Mrs Lipchinsky had also got to her feet, push-ing her chair back so quickly it crashed to the floor; she reached be-hind her and snatched up from the dresser a metal sputum jug with a hinged lid and came round the table with it and held it, opened, to his lips. He shook his head. Mouth pressed tight, half-risen, he indicated the door; he did not want to use the jug in our presence.

I wondered about this new nicety. To see him spit phlegm into the jug was nothing unusual. Bernard was familiar with the sight as a matter of course, as I was too, in and out of their home as I had been over the years. How could he have forgotten? And then I saw that these facts were irrelevant. This evening was different. And that difference came to me as a shock. In his eyes I had acquired a new significance, touched by the magic talisman of learning and enquiry, the imprint of that place, Oxford, I had not yet even set foot in, but which he chose to salute *through* me. And even though it was plain that all this was in *his* mind, a private piece of play-acting necessary for him, I felt there would be something incongruous, silly in fact, in seeming to accept this proxy role he had given me. To pretend to do so simply to humour him felt like cheating; and I was saddened that he seemed to want me to do that. He was urging me, willing me, to be the medium for a bizarre, pathetic, appeal. Through me he wanted to be seen as someone worthy of recognition in the world that Oxford symbolised for him. Scholar, thinker, seeker.

I imagined he had prepared himself with care. The effect sought was not so much in the details. His dress, the perfectly tailored suit for example, was hardly to the point, for it was the product of the humble craft that earned him his bread. He must have cut the cloth and sewn most of it himself. Nor was the gold cravat ring. None of these things in themselves, but the wholeness of the person he had worked so hard and suffered with such longing through all the years to be, the *savant*. That was the identity, the only one, he wanted me to see.

Above all he must not be the sick one. He must be seen as blazing the trail unfalteringly, the quest sustaining him, potent till the very end.

To have to use the sputum jug in front of me, or rather the world of learning he had made me represent, would spoil it all.

Somewhere within him, surely, he must be aware of the pretence? And the knowledge must hurt.

With a sad shake of the head, in which he managed a hint of jaunty defiance, he went out, holding on to her arm, and into the little bathroom. Through the half-open door we heard him battling with his lungs, the shuddering cough and the throaty dredging up of phlegm and the rasping spit, the gasp and rattle as he fought to drag breath through the mucal obstruction, the tired sighs between each convulsion. In a few minutes the contest subsided. We heard her speak soothingly, compassionately, urging him to lie down on the parlour sofa. His reply was gentle but determined: 'No, no, I have more to say to the young man. It is important. Let me be.'

Bernard put his spoon down and sat tensely listening. Sweat shone on his face.

I felt he must be thinking, as I was, of the progress of that condition. At a certain point, consumptives went down quickly.

And I thought of my father. Could I, even after all that had happened, steel myself to leave him?

He came in, ashen, shoulders hunched. He pushed her supporting arm away. The rasp of his breathing, laboured, tired, was pitiful to hear. The fight had weakened him. Again he shook his head, this time as if he grimly answered a secret question. The boxer, leaving his corner after surviving a knock-down near the end of a bout, shakes his head to clear his mind and focus it on the next round, and then the next. Can I stay on my feet? Can I finish this fight?

His wife, shorter than he, small-boned and neat, by comparison presented a vision of strength. She smiled to hide her anxiety.

Carefully he lowered himself down in the chair once more, slumped for a moment, then gathered himself upright, took a careful breath, testing himself for pain, thought about it, took another. Some of the taut brightness returned.

'There now,' she said, 'Don't talk so much, please.' She looked into his face with a burning brilliance, as if she would project into him all the energy she possessed.

He looked up at her, trustingly: tenderly: 'What is left for me if I cannot speak my thoughts?'

She went out and returned with the sputum jug, put it back in its place on the dresser, took a pencil and scribbled something on a printed form that lay beside it. The hospital must have instructed her to log these attacks, and the amount of phlegm deposited, measured on the graduations incised on the inside of the jug. She went to the sink, poured some carbolic solution into a pan, soaked a cloth in it, and draped it over the jug, presumably to trap the bacilli within till she could take the sample to the hospital.

It crossed my mind to say 'Speak your thoughts to posterity' – meaning, thinking of his book, 'They are important enough for that!' No, that would not do. It would reveal that we feared for him.

Bernard must have picked up the thought, or perhaps we were

on the same track. He spoke up eagerly: 'Father, I've got an idea. I want you to finish the book soon. I want to see it in print! You've been working on it so long, too long. Listen, take a few months off to work on it full time? Belloc's will take you back again, I'm sure. I think the union's educational trust fund would pay for the time off. I'll go into that. You deserve some help now after all you've done for the union over the years. What d'you say?'

He avoided my eye. The aim was clear – to lead his father to give up, without loss of face, bending low over the cutting table in the dust and heat of the workshop, heaving bolts of cloth from the racks behind him, on his feet all day except for the few hours he might spend crouched cross-legged on the table basting and sewing a coat for an important customer. The pretence of union support might serve. For all I knew it was not a pretence. In any case, as Bernard had often told me, living at home he could afford to support his parents, As for telling his father so confidently that he would get his job back, that was a white lie to conceal what both of us now knew. And I must support him in it. Belloc's high-class bespoke workshop would soon be turning out khaki uniforms with the rest of them. And they would have no need of his refined styling and craftsmanship.

Mr Lipchinsky leaned over his plate, deep in thought. As he did so, my eye was drawn to the handkerchief he had tucked back into his breast pocket, not neatly folded as it had been before but hurriedly bunched up. In one of its folds a streak of blood showed. His wife must have seen it at the same moment. She got up quietly, hurried out of the kitchen and came back with a neatly ironed handkerchief. Tenderly bending over him, without a word, she substituted it for the old one, and resumed her seat at the other end of the table.

So blood, too, was now commonplace? Till that moment I had not understood how ill he was.

Absently he touched the fresh handkerchief. He took a spoonful of the hot soup, laid the spoon down and sighed.

Half to himself timidly, he said: 'Maybe the time has come to take the risk? Do you really think I dare?'

The risk he referred to had nothing to do with getting his job back.

If he finished the book he would be offering himself to the judgement of the wide world. The recognition he craved might not come. But if you hid your light under a bushel you risked nothing; and you could always take refuge in what might have been.

How did one still the doubting voices within – as I was trying to do? That was one tenuous link between us. Young and green as I was, there could be no comparison between my doubts and his, except in fantasy. I could make no pretence of a high unselfish motive. All I had to spur me on was a vague vision of 'betterment'. There came into my mind some words in a report on me by a lecturer at the university whose extension classes I had attended: 'He has a lively and genuine intellectual curiosity.' There too, in a sense, Mr Lipchinsky's case and mine converged. His intellectual curiosity had been a burden all his life, and it had broken him. Wisely, sadly, he had warned me against that fate. But here we diverged. His sense of mission would not let him rest. I was driven by something far less explicable and, perhaps, infinitely less worthy. I was aware only of some unidentifiable power pushing me forward, sense of adventure, a desire to achieve. But achieve what? I had no idea.

Even if I did achieve that something, would it take me to anywhere I truly would have wanted to reach, could I have known in advance? Would it banish discontent?

But if Mr Lipchinsky could have answered it, long ago, would he have abandoned his quest? Probably not. His wife might have been listening to my thoughts. Or it might have been intuition, for in a tone of deep reflection, as if she too looked back along the years, she addressed Bernard and me:

'Men try to jump too far ahead of themselves sometimes. Me? I do not read books. But this I know. Whatever way a man wants to go, he needs a good wife to help him, to keep him steady. And when things are bad, it is good to weep together! Bernard, I am always saying this to you, you are in a good position now, you should be married! I can see you are not happy with yourself. And you also'– turning fully to me – 'you are going to Oxford, that is a credit to you, and I am happy for you. And I know you will study well and get a good position, and your father will be proud of you. You also should be thinking of a nice, steady girl to be a wife and support for you. Believe me I know what life is! Listen to me well.'

Perhaps she had a further, deeper motive, to deflect her husband from his melancholy thoughts as he searched along the road he had travelled, weighed the choices made along the way, and the one that now menacingly confronted him, and stir him to look to the future.

If so, she succeeded, for his face brightened and he gazed at her lovingly.

'Yes, you are right,' he said, and his tone suddenly lifted, became resonant, conveying an almost youthful resilience, 'It is true that we have wept together, yes, many times. But we have been joyful together too. Bernard, listen to your mother. Where would I have been without her at my right hand?'

The surge of energy faded. His voice wavered and he put his head in his hands, hiding tears.

Where indeed was he? Unable to answer, or afraid to. No matter, the tears had answered clearly enough.

And his wife, how could she be so calm, so strong? Where, I wondered, had *she* wanted to be? How often did she weigh the present against hopes of the past? Perhaps she never did. Perhaps she simply lived and asked no questions?

I didn't know how to live that. I wasn't sure I wanted to. One day I would wish I had.

Bernard sat quietly, seeming to ruminate as she talked on, as he had predicted, of this nice girl and that one. If only we would let her bring us together, carefully, respectably?

And then, to my astonishment he said: 'All right mother. As your say, there's no harm in meeting. Go ahead and arrange it. Let us see.'

She glowed as with inner sunlight. For her, as in some ways for her husband, the future held out its arms to you ready to be lived, to be fashioned into an improved version of the past. It must be welcomed confidently, without delay. She talked briskly, happily, about arrangements.

I wondered why Bernard had done it. At first I thought it was simply to comfort her, his father so ill and her world crumbling, as well as to assuage his own guilt perhaps, knowing that her concern about his future made her the more unhappy. But was there also a hint here that he might be hedging his bets? The *guerre kilométrique* might make the love in Spain forever unattainable. The guilt about taking Kirstie might be getting too heavy to bear, even though, as he said, it kept him sane. But for how long could it do so?

Yet how sincerely he had talked about the golden claim of the heart, the one sure, sustaining thing! Like the other principles that had failed him, was he preparing to abandon that one too? I couldn't follow him that far. Not yet.

I said to her: 'I must get to Oxford and see what happens first.'

There, I had said it, more to myself than to them.

For a moment, immaturely arrogantly, I had looked upon her match-making as an easy way out, where love was immaterial, and achievement, adventure, the spiritual journey, were irrelevant too. And I had shut the door on that road. It seemed to me that I had said something brave, momentous, decisive. I felt uplifted.

But I had answered not one single question of any importance. And unlike Bernard, if I had read him right, I had not even hedged any bets. Or if I had answered any, they were the wrong ones: the war would see to that, What I saw, dimly, as my goals would lose their meaning.

I knew it in my bones. Bernard, for himself, knew it too.

His father probably did see it, and that, unknowingly, must have deepened the despair against which he fought so valiantly. His mother, I am sure, could not. That, I suppose, was a blessing.

Gently, magically, Mr Lipchinsky did make me want to take up the torch he was about to relinquish. In the excitement of thinking about it, disquiet about going to Oxford was put aside. In a sense I had already begun that confrontation. The reality, with its aspects of the picaresque and the bizarre, calculation, opportunism, make-believe, tragedy, the light and shade of self discovery and discovery in others, I shall try to set out in a further volume.

GORBALS BOY AT OXFORD

Goodbye Gorbals

Talking to John Betjeman in his room at Blenheim Palace, I happened to mention that I had come up to Oxford from the Gorbals. Part of the palace was in use by departments of the British Council, still in wartime evacuation quarters. He was standing before one of the huge panels of biscuit-coloured plywood covering the walls of the little salon which, like most of the rooms put to office use, still carried this protection for delicate surfaces beneath. He had been chalking on it a complicated notation of change-ringing. Betjeman had a job at the Council as Administrator of the Arts and Science Division, to which he had come from being Press Attaché at the Embassy in Dublin. His present duties could not have been burdensome; to judge from the vast arrangement of chalk marks he had drawn on the board, he had spent most of the morning at it. He turned, the loose lower lip, drawn to the left as always, sagging further, and searched my face, plainly wondering what to say, which was unusual for him. Then, resuming the habitual mandarin drawl, half-eager, half blasé, said, 'You *must* tell me how the place struck you – I suppose "struck" is the word! Dear boy, did the architecture transform you?'

In pre-war days, for a Gorbals man to come up to Oxford was as unthinkable as to meet a raw bushman in a St James's club – something for which there were no stock responses. In any case, for a member of the boss class, someone from the Gorbals *was* in effect a bushman, the Gorbals itself as distant, as unknowable, as the Kalahari Desert. Betjeman, plainly unable to fit the phenomenon into any context he understood, had picked on a theme in which he did feel comfortable. Externals were his forte.

In one sense, his instinct was accurate, to probe for the first, aesthetic, impact of the place. At the time of this conversation of

GORBALS BOY AT OXFORD

Blenheim, a piquant convergence in itself, as he was quick to point out, my first arrival on my bike, though some six years behind me, was still fresh, not yet in perspective. *That* would take many years. I tried to re-create it for him, as I then understood it.

He was a good listener when he cared to suppress the urge to interject a bright sixth-form quip whenever one paused for breath. He stepped away from the wallboard, baggy beige clothes hanging sack-like, and sat down at his desk, swinging round to face me in the armchair at his side, forgetting to relinquish the chalk. Possessed as when he had stood with me contemplating the poetry of Keble, he raptly traced my words on some inner palimpsest of his own.

Despite what seemed arrogant posturing, and certainly a core of toughness, he had a timid, gentle streak, carefully protected. When I had finished he said, the sideways smile returning, 'You *must* write about it one day. There's so much more to that journey isn't there – like a second birth?'

I wheeled the bike out of our flat on the third, top floor of the Gorbals tenement, and leaned it against the iron stairhead railing. I turned and pulled the door shut, and was about to put the key in the lock when something made me step back and contemplate the battered old doorway, an eerie command to etch the image on my mind, its meaning for me through the years. It seemed that I saw it for the first time, the door hanging crooked in its frame, its dark brown paint chipped and scratched and flaked away by time and damp, yet still possessing a certain dignity, the slender flutings enclosing the six panels, the fine rings in relief on the brass knob-plate, the ringed boss on the brass knob itself, the keyhole plate scrolled at the top and waisted like a violin; all battered and begrimed, never touched with Brasso since that day, long ago, when mother died.

The finality of the moment, unbelievable, held me fast. Surely nothing was ever finished? One day another word, another deed, would be added to the account to change the judgement? Standing here on the cold stone landing, part of me fiercely wanted to write 'finis' under it all. Another voice told me I *must* not, could not. That was not for human hand to do.

Vengeance is mine, I will repay...

Indeed the place was already receding from me. I would carry the bike down the winding stone stairs and ride away, further than I had ever travelled, to take up the scholarship, For this journey there was no name, no measure. I thought of the times when, as a child, staring through the black window panes at night, I soared far away among the stars. This time the journey would be real. I would not return. I might stand here again physically, but I would never feel the spiritual breath of this place, palpably on my face, as I did now.

I checked that the straps closing the shiny black saddlebag of oiled canvas were buckled fast; and those securing the oilskin cape across it. The bag was packed tight with three changes of under-clothes, two khaki shirts, socks, trousers – I wore khaki shorts for the journey – and a thick woollen jersey with sleeves; nearly all from the army surplus stores. Food was in the outer pouches; a small loaf of black bread, three hard-boiled eggs, a slab of cheese, a bag of raisins, milk in a medicine bottle, tobacco tins containing tea, sugar, salt, matches, and Metafuel for the primus stove clamped under the cross bar. I could carry no more. A parcel containing a few clothes, all I could afford in the list sent by the college, with the only books I possessed – *Chambers's Dictionary*, Hegel's *Logic*, Fisher's *History of Europe*, the whole bought with the loan from Aunt Rachel – I had sent ahead by rail.

When Meyer the boxer joined the army, to escape the debt collectors' retribution, after he had knocked them out for beating up poor Mr Fredericks in the street, his father sold me his bike, fully equipped, for two pounds, which I was still paying off at a shilling a month; it had the new derailleur gear change, dropped handle-bars, and the luxury of dynamo lighting in place of conventional acetylene gas lamp. I was in good training, and looking forward to the test of doing a hundred miles a day. I would stay at Cyclists'

Touring Club bed-and-breakfast houses for ninepence a night.

Father had left for work at seven. We had parted in an atmosphere of apocalyptic phlegm, overlaying an uneasy, hesitant, stilted kindliness. The hooded figure of the wounded past stood beside us counselling forbearance, generosity if not forgiveness, at this close of an epoch. Years later I would see that the old epoch had begun to die long before, on the day I found he had pawned my suit. Oh that suit!

That parting in the cold grey kitchen, the imprisoned passion, the forlorn longing to recreate love and gentleness, still lacerates the spirit. Tumult roared within – the desire to erase the past, pity for him, remorse at leaving him, eagerness to take my chance away from him, the tingle of adventure, voices of doubt, foreboding. If only I could find the calm, the lucidity, to close the distance between us, spread out before him all that I felt about the present and the past and the future, smooth away all anger, all hurt, make him see that I had no choice but to go. I saw the disappointment in him, the defeat. I saw that he longed to understand and sympathise, to reach out to me, but that he could come only a fragment of the way. He knew why I was stricken dumb, but could not help me utter the truths that clamoured to be set free, perhaps because he too could not open his heart. We both had too much to say, and no words fitted.

I knew that for him the parting was cataclysmic. He did not see my going to Oxford as Bernard's father did, as a romantic, heroic quest, but prosaically as doing something 'to better myself'. In attempted stoicism – his only reply to Fate over the years – he did try to accept that I must follow my star, as he and others of his generation had done long ago when they had left *der heim* to seek fulfilment in the melting pot of another culture. For me, as it had been for him, 'it was written' – *es shtayt geshreeben* – it had to be. He could not have failed to see in my going a re-enactment, in reverse, of that day when as a young man he had set out to meet the unknown. He divined, I think more clearly than I did, that I too would journey to a world light years distant from these my roots, as he had done from his.

In the cold kitchen, in the grey morning light, as he stood ready to go to work, we faced each other at the end, in silence. As always he was neatly dressed, navy blue overcoat, blue serge suit, white collarless shirt and grey wollen muffler, grey felt hat with black silk band. His tools were in a small Gladstone bag on the cracked oilcloth table cover. He looked deep into my eyes and then at the floor; would the Almighty send a sign to stop me going? At last he held out his hand and gripped mine hard: 'Gey gesunterheyt' ('Go in health'). He picked up the bag, blue-grey eyes looking at nothing, turned, squaring his shoulders, and strode out.

Downstairs, I wheeled the bike over the broken flag stones in the close, absently avoiding the little heaps of putrescent rubbish and rat droppings. Out on the pavement I heaved it round to set it in the gutter pointing south, the near pedal propped on the pavement edge, and sat on the saddle, one foot on the raised pedal and pressed into the toe-clip ready to move off.

The coalman stood on his cart at the far end of the street, his powerful bass booming out, 'Caw-aw-aw-aw-aw!'; the organ-grinder and the tin-whistle man kept their judicious distances behind him, hoping for the odd penny wrapped in newspaper to come down from a window. Women hurried past – dodging with raised skirt-hems the litter of horse droppings, rotting fish heads and vegetable matter, vomit – on their way to shops, the Steamy, the pawn-shop, or to deliver washing 'taken in'. A few men slouched past aimlessly to congregate at the corners; it was too early for pubs. Some would make their way, later, to the offices of the *Evening Citizen* whose 'Situations Vacant' page would be displayed, for those who could not afford to buy the paper, in a wire-fronted case outside the back entrance in St Vincent Place across the Clyde; but that would not be till noon.

I sat and stared; something was hidden that I must uncover and take with me; some furtive spirit of that life, a talisman, a reference point from which to take my bearings wherever I went. It was there; of that I was certain. But it hid from me.

I dug my foot on the raised pedal and pushed away, head down, impatient now to be away on the open road and there, in the hypnotic rhythm of pedalling, lose myself in thoughts of what awaited at the other end.

In the afternoon, ten miles after the long climb up to Beattock Summit, two things happened, almost at the same moment, to force me off the bike; either, by itself, would have been enough. I got 'the knock', the sudden draining of energy from the legs; and the chain jumped off the gear train. The cure for the knock was food; for the chain, a spike to dig out a stone that must have lodged in a link. I looked about for shelter. I needed to put the stove, myself too, behind a windbreak. I must be quick; twilight was near, and I had twenty-five miles to cover to reach the bed-and-breakfast house. On these bleak approaches to the bald Cheviot hills, a keen south-west wind swept across the road; and there was not a tree or hedgerow or wall in sight. I spotted a layby a few hundred yards further on, littered with concrete blocks and pieces of timber. Stiff-legged, I wheeled the bike towards it, the jumped chain rattling angrily against the rear fork. I longed for a mug of scalding tea and a doorstep of bread and cheese. Luckily I had brought water from my last stop in a screwtop container – another ex-army item – for there was not a burn, or for that matter a house, any-where in sight. In this deserted land near the border, burns were hard to find.

I leaned the bike against a stack of timber, quickly assembled the primus and, in the lee of some concrete blocks, got it alight despite the wind, and put the billy can on to boil; then upended the bike and stood it on saddle and handlebars to deal with the chain. Another purchase from the army surplus stores was a clasp knife fitted with a long spike, presumably an all-purpose implement for life in the trenches; with it I gouged the stone out of the chain and re-threaded it into position in the gear train.

Absorbed, I had been dimly aware of the approaching rumble of a heavy vehicle. Hands oily from the chain, I stepped to the raised bank at the rear of the layby to rub my hands clean on the grass, my back to the road; there was a grating of brakes, the slam of a door and crack-crack of steel-shod boots on the road and a shout: 'Fuckin' hell! Whi' are *yew* doin' here?'

Meyer Melek shone in glory. There was something more than the ruddiness of the outdoor life, an added stature, a calm, an acceptance of power, and of acclaim. Meyer was lightweight champion of the Command. On his sleeve were corporal's stripes and the badge of P. T. instructor. About a dozen soldiers now clattered down on to the road from the tarpaulin-covered rear of the truck and drew near to him, their faces aglow with hero-worship. Only later did I learn how men at arms forgave a man almost anything, even being a Jew, if he was a physical star. The more aggressive the sport the more open their hearts – to, supremely, the boxer.

Meyer was in the Engineers. He was returning with his squad from a last field exercise before an overseas posting; he thought it would be to Singapore. Seeing him wistfully contemplating the bike, I told him that when he got out of the army he could have it back; meanwhile I would look after it well. We dared not say what was in our minds; the Fates probably had other plans. In the army, he said, everyone pretended it was still a peacetime world; but no one felt sure of anything any more. What had happened to the old imperial certainty you learnt at school, that used to hold everything solid?

He worried about his father's ill-health, and whether he could keep the little workshop going if things got worse and his brothers were called up.

I had last seen him on the day the 'menodge men', sent to exact retribution for his interference – after he had stopped them beating up Mr Fredericks for being behind in his debt repayments – had given him their ultimatum. The next morning he had gone up to Maryhill Barracks to escape them. Years later, that would strike me as another of the Fates' ironic tricks, for in a sense he had fled the lesser doom; the menodge men had threatened to do no more than finish his boxing career by damaging his hands – if, that is, he refused to join them. But he would not survive building the death railway for the Japanese. This was the last time I saw him.

In the gathering twilight, on the lonely, anonymous road that was taking us God alone knew where, on tangents far from the world we knew, we shook hands in silent tribute to the felicity of this ordained meeting, acknowledging the fears and doubts that dwarfed us.

> The glass is falling hour by hour,
> The glass will fall for ever ...

The others clambered raucously into the truck. Meyer stepped up into the cab next to the driver, and the heavy vehicle rumbled away on the empty road, heading south too. I watched its lights draw away, and disappear, then went back into the layby and gulped some tea and packed up; I mounted and rode hard after it, head down over the handlebars, trying to think of nothing.

Seeing him departing into the shadowy future, a fellow-exile, loneliness was diluted. We were voyagers together. The ambiguities of this encounter were those of life itself; they would persist, tantalisingly, in all I did, wherever I went. Meyer had never been as close to me as Bernard – Communist firebrand, returned disillusioned from the Spanish War – at least not in the same confiding, questing fashion. Meyer, like Alec who worked opposite me in the factory, did not examine life; he lived it. His sympathy and warmth, a gentleness that went hand in hand with his strength, were given sparingly, tokens of trust, regard, duty. Not overtly religious, his morality was fixed in the old rock of Moses, unquestioned. He was a man of simple, unambiguous values, who acted surely, unwaveringly, without reflection, come what may. Long ago in childhood these qualities must have drawn me to him, a natural alliance of sympathy, valued without thought. Many years later I would understand that his was the sureness I had always wanted to possess. Now, as he departed, I knew that I would carry his spiritual presence with me always, a steady point of light in moments of doubt. A premonition may have told me to mark that moment in my memory; I would honour him in my heart always.

Four days later, at about ten in the morning, I rode into Oxford in the middle of a cloudburst, the rain sheeting down in great wet curtains such as I would not see until, many years later in Pakistan, the monsoon rains fell down in masses from the sky. I had decided to spend the night at a Cyclists' Touring Club house a few miles short of Oxford, so that my first sight of the place would be in daylight. Coming in from the north, the Banbury Road was awash up to kerb height, my wheels swishing through the rushing brown waters. The screens of trees and shrubbery guarding the tall Victorian houses glistened wetly in brilliant greens and reddish browns, thin streams of water tumbling from leaf to leaf like myriad little waterfalls. The deluge must have driven every living soul indoors, leaving a perspective of broad, cambered road, ample pavements interrupted by wide driveways flanked by massive wooden gateposts topped with romantic wrought iron fantasies, a tree-sheltered world, settled, comfortable, ordered; an Elysian contrast with the world I had left behind. To the people in these tall, protected houses, I saw that my world would be not only unknown; it would be incredible. That was a shock to begin with.

The rain ceased and the grey skies lifted, and soon, instead of riding crouched within the sweating rain-cape, I sat up and flung the cape back and rode slowly, hands resting on the handlebars in the high position, and looked round at ease. In the Mitchell Library I had studied photographs of Oxford; but now, nearing the centre, a vision rose up out of the earth more powerful than any picture. In feeling totally foreign to the comfortable North Oxford of evergreens and tall brick houses, here was a world of citadels and power, with echoes of lawless times, the iron tread of men-at-arms, the embattled order of the church. So astounding was it, so awesome and yet so magnetic, that I forgot my immediate purpose, to present myself at the college, and rode on through the old precincts, winding through alleys and under blind college walls, beating the bounds of the grey monastic *mise-en-scène* again and again, tracing the map imprinted in memory. I knew that I was seeing it as I would never see it again, and that I must absorb this first impact in its completeness. Here was a world that flaunted mediaeval certainty, the caprice of secular riches and of clerical power, the tenacious retention of old categories, a secretive world of prejudices grimly maintained. Each turret, machicolation, mullion, buttress, each baronial portico, each fortress doorway that might easily have sheltered behind a portcullis, spoke of protected domains of flinty rule, of secret follies and public arrogance. This was not the blessedly illuminated world that Bernard's father dreamt I was joining, of simple savants dispensing gentleness and light and humanity, but a hard, jealous, defensive one.

Through half-closed eyes I saw grey-cowled figures, secure in grace, putting heretics to the torture or the stake.

Catching at the heart, however, there was also a delicate, fugitive beauty, a poetic spirit that this old jealous monasticism could neither contain, nor banish, silver voices trapped in the stone.

At last, in Radcliffe Square, that seemed to enclose the innermost spirit of the place, I stood and contemplated the combination of lumpy ostentation, dignity, simplicity, baroque detachment and coldness. I heard a gravelly voice near me, incongruously formal, trembling with pathos. It came from a stocky man, military-looking, with bristling grey moustache, dressed in a bright blue blazer and pale trousers and a white shirt with an orange bow tie, and a boater with an orange ribbon. He punctuated his worlds by tapping the ground with a thick malacca stick. He was, I would later discover, known as the Major, an official Oxford City guide. Addressing a middle-aged couple, he had the air of making an important pronouncement. Catching my glance, he beckoned me over with a wave of the stick, to include me in what he had to say: 'Always remember this, my friends. Going into the gun room and ending your troubles is the easy way. But it is *wrong*. The Bible says so. Don't do it, I beg of you. Pass it on.' He raised the boater and stumped away.

I would hear of his sad fate about a year later.

I thought of this sad coming together here, in this fortress of past certainties, dwarfed by rich indifference and gothic chill. Inexplicably, that gruff military voice, with its shattering exposure of inner pain, recalled the drum-like voice of the Clincher crying out, too, for a warmer, kindlier world. The gun room? What world did that man come from? That apart, in this setting of arrogance, over-ripeness, wintry power, those words were frighteningly fitting.

Standing here, I felt more of an outsider than I had ever dreamed possible. Where among these blind strongholds would I find a weak point, a sympathetic wicket gate, to enter and find my rightful place?

2

The Citadel Takes Over

In retrospect, John Betjeman may have been right after all. 'Dear boy, did the architecture transform you?' may not have been as absurd a question as I had thought.

Of all the influences at work in those first days and months, the physical must have been the most potent; the arrogant baroque and neo-gothic and what they stood for, proclaiming certainty, permitting no challenge, seized me, gauche and impatient spirit that I was, and threw bridle and harness upon me. Here was order, fixity, unquestioning and unquestioned. How wonderful to feel such confidence!

In these comfortable, complacent bourgeois streets, still those of a tight little country town – where not a fish-head or boiled-out meat bone lay in the gutter, where even the poor areas of Jericho and Paradise Square were 'respectable' by Gorbals standards – black-gowned figures inhabited every perspective. Wherever you went, power and tradition were inescapable, brushing aside the pretended languor and indifference of the privileged denizens, those who truly belonged. For the vast majority of them, I assumed, the ethos was not totally new as it was to me, but was received essentially as a continuation of school, richer perhaps, more theatrical and stylised, but essentially of the same order, irksome sometimes but only in the sense that the complex minuet of a large settled family might be. That, I reflected, must be why Oxford did not fall upon them with anything like the shock of a completely alien culture, a new way of life and thinking invading the spirit, as it did on me. Oxford must be their recent past writ large, a pattern of thought and manners already absorbed, a drill-manual to be put on a shelf, no longer referred to except as an instinctive refuge in time of crisis. Many affected to reject it altogether, a pretence that at first deceived me, and I wondered at the paradox – that we should be going in opposite directions, *they* appearing to scorn the codes of this place while I strove to acquire them! Later I would see that they were not truly in rebellion; and that it was only because they stood so solidly – if unknowingly – upon the beliefs of this place that they were secure enough to put on a show of disdain. I had no such certainty. I trod the unknown at every step, fearful of stumbling. For me the drill manual was something to absorb as quickly as possible – the insecure ardour of the *arriviste*.

I went into the grey monastic quad of the Bodleian, the Old School quad, and read the legend in gold above each doorway, Scola Mathematica, Scola Physica – the sovereign estates of the mind laid out as on a chart, once again a picture of certainty, the ways made distinct and clear. I climbed the wooden staircase, short flights ascending within a square dusty shaft, beside a wide wooden balustrade of ducal proportions, each broad tread worn down in two concave patches – I saw the uninterrupted procession marching up and down in file over the generations. In a little musty room I signed the register of Bodleian readers. Being told that I was now a member for life, the moment took on apocalyptic significance, like that in the factory, on my last day there before leaving for Oxford, when I shut off the main power switch in a final gesture, and felt that an epoch had slid away for ever. Here, with the register before me, was my first true step into the citadel, a person fully recognised. Here in a different sense I could say, with father, 'es shtayt geshreeben!' In the Gorbals I had had little sense of being a person in my own right – rather it was a fragile, secret identity, timidly guarded, whose signature was evanescent, written in the rain on the pavements on my way to the Mitchell Library, in the decaying rubbish carpeting the flag stones in close and pavement.

Here was a gentler contrast with my first impression of the citadel, when I had stood out there in Radcliffe Square beyond these grey walls, and the grandiose *mise-en-scène*, showy perpendicular and gross baroque, drying after the wild downpour, had glistened with the menace of old steel, and I had felt a shiver of fear contending with longing and hope. Here was my name inscribed for all time in the very heart of it! Its lances were raised; its sword points were lowered – provisionally.

It is hard to believe that I could have thought of the Bodleian in these momentous terms – perhaps I had given the Mitchell Library an equal sanctity? – and that I was callow enough to be shocked when others appeared to treat it with scant respect. There was Hamish, confirmed practical joker, who donned stage make-up and a false beard and, pretending serious research, persuaded a member of the Bodleian staff to bring him John Wilkes' *Essay on Woman* – a work so scandalous that it was on the restricted access list – and copied it out for *zamizdat* circulation among a select few:

> Awake my Fanny, leave all meaner things,
> This morn shall show what rapture swiving brings ...

I accepted a copy, on several sheets of smudged carbon, and for many weeks hid it in the lining of my trunk, expecting that at any moment, in some fateful fashion, the sin would proclaim itself.

In the smallest of day-to-day matters, there was a whole new alphabet to be learnt, the manners and controls of a totally different regime of living – you did not, for example, use certain Anglo-Saxon words with the unthinking freedom we did in the Gorbals. It seemed at first that every single response to life must always be muted, till I understood that the codes, though the form might be silken, could in Gladstonian fashion be ferocious: 'Suaviter in modo, fortiter in re.'

I realised, too, that I must not show surprise at the ways of this new world, for that made you vulnerable; I must quickly present myself in a new and permanently changed persona. That meant wearing a mask while I sloughed off the old skin – fearful always that the mask might slip. Sometimes, looking in the mirror, I could understand how Hoffman felt when his reflection was stolen – the 'I' that I had known was not here!

I had never, for instance, had a room of my own, where I could shut my door and read or write or dream, or have guests – that, too, a new experience – precisely as I chose. I could burn the light in my room at night as long as I liked with no fear of having to search for pennies for the meter. For the first few weeks this feeling of possessing sovereign territory was unnerving. I paced up and down restlessly, glorying in this new state, but at the same time feeling that I had lost whatever bearings I had ever had. With dismay, even shame, I regarded the bookshelves beside my writing table – a writing table all to myself! – empty except for my pitiful stock of three books, one of them a dictionary; I thought of other students' rooms with well-stocked shelves, ornaments, bric-a-brac, pieces of a well-found home life.

Pyjamas symbolised another dramatic change. I had never owned any; for years I had slept in my 'semmit', vernacular for undervest. When I first put on my newly-bought pyjamas I said to myself: 'What a waste of money – still, it is "the done thing"'! Similarly, following the guidance list thoughtfully sent me, I had bought a dressing-gown, an unbelievable luxury known only from films. What was it for, I wondered – after all, when you got out of bed you simply put on your clothes! Presumably you wore it when you went to have a bath or to the lavatory? In the Gorbals one used a chamber pot or, for 'Number twos', slipped on shirt and trousers and went out of the house to the shared lavatory on the stairhead. Slippers, too, were another enigmatic extravagance! As for baths, in the Gorbals the day of the domestic bathroom for the lower orders was not yet; you went to the public 'slipper baths' near the Steamy, the public wash-house, or made do with a hot shower after a swim; here there were baths of gentlemanly dimensions, long enough to lie in at full length, where you could soak for as long as you wished, whenever the caprice possessed you. Nearly everyone else here, amazingly, had a bath *every* day!

Nor could I get used to lying abed after five o'clock in the morning, my usual waking time in the busy season at the factory. For most of my first term I rose at that time and bathed and shaved and dressed, and read till breakfast time – until neighbours complained about the noise I made in the echoing ablutions, when I ran a bath or flushed the toilet and sometimes, forgetfully, strolled about whistling.

College life was in many ways burdensome, a teasing mixture of independent sovereignty and the constraints of community. One was surrounded by people with strange tastes and preferences, to adapt to or steer clear of; there were so many pitfalls to avoid, and always the nagging awareness that others seemed to navigate without any special care, but that my vigilance must never relax.

The greatest shock was the social discipline, ceremonial, tribal. The regularity of meals, for instance, was inexplicably irksome; in the Gorbals I ate – if there was food in the house – when I was hungry, and as often as not alone; here it was an undeviating ritual at long refectory tables and hard benches, that joined you to your neighbour in a formal compulsion of manner and speech, even in the passing of bread and salt. Above all, there was the burden of obligatory conversation – burden partly because I did not know the codes of what was acceptable, and because the talk seemed deliberately directionless yet mysteriously selective. Its purpose, slowly grasped – as Stevenson at the Institute of Experimental Psychology would put it – was to establish one's place in the pecking order, one's identity. There were unspoken limits, which took me some time to decode, as to what was permissible. Wrongly, I at first treated this wary table-talk as a joke – my tart remarks about its 'high level' must have been insufferable – until I realised, to some extent too late, how hurt the others were. It was hard to accept that the talk, stiffly conducted at the long tables, was intended, first and foremost, to show that you respected the code, and only secondly to establish your position within its terms. Above all you must be subservient to its subtle, intransigent values. In the Gorbals this purpose was unknown; our youthful talk, in the shower-room group at the baths for instance, aimed at clearing doubts about the puzzling and impatient world, always concrete; here, that purpose was treated as 'cocky', the presumptuous baring of the soul, better suited to the intimacy of late-night talk with trusted friends.

At every meal you were on show – 'on parade', as the army would put it – giving a good account of yourself. Here too, the others seemed so much better practised.

Perhaps the greatest revelation came from seeing my name up on the tally of rooms – a label on this new life. That, and the fact that wherever you went, people called you sir! I had never thought of myself as a 'sir' before. The others, some not yet used to daily shaving, yet addressed as 'sir' simply because they were students, took the mark of authority as their due. Seemingly, because they *expected* to be treated as important, in this and many other ways, so indeed they were! Why, I wondered, should striplings of seventeen or eighteen receive such respect from men old enough to be their fathers, even their grandfathers? There was something wrong in such a society. Each time I was 'sirred' – actually or figuratively – I felt I must look at myself afresh, as one does in a mirror at random, in case my image had changed unawares; but as time went on, secretly, ashamed, I welcomed such signs that I was 'fitting in', even though part of me despised them.

Another surprise was the ritual of sending notes – invitations to tea or some other social meeting – often on embossed gold-edged cards in creamy, parchment envelopes. Here was an unbelievable, courtly stiffness compared with the Gorbals where, if you wanted to see someone, you climbed up the tenement steps and 'chapped' on the door! In Oxford few people lived further than a short bicycle ride from almost any part of the college area, and there seemed no practical reason for the formality. When I first went to my pigeon hole and found a small square envelope, crested, containing a gold-edged card inviting me to tea at Somerville, I wondered: 'Why spend all this money to ask me to come in for a cup of tea?' And then: 'Must I reply in the same way? Probably yes – or she'll think I don't know how to behave!' The card itself, nearly as stiff as a piece of wood, must have cost as much as the tea! That, I would see as time went by, was not the point. Social discipline was the point, useful when you came to think of it; privacy and personal sovereignty went hand in hand, especially if, for reasons of finesse or caution, you wanted to keep the world at arm's length. After all, it was far easier to dissemble by correspondence than face to face!

Of course, being invited for tea meant more than a simple cup of tea, possibly in a chipped cup, as it would have done in the

Gorbals. There were cucumber sandwiches of wafer-thin bread – in winter, anchovy toast – and tea in fine china edged in gold, cream sandwich biscuits and rich fruit cake, almost a meal in itself; afternoon tea, as the genteel folk in Glasgow called it, that I had previously seen only from a distance, standing in the street with nose pressed against the windows of Crawford's tea rooms.

Those cards and little notes, messages of propriety – as well as 'sir' and the like – signalled two things that I learned slowly, too slowly: the importance of ceremony in this new life, and that I must behave as if I really was someone of importance! The others imposed that view of themselves – unthinkingly perhaps, but they did! – so why shouldn't I? But it was a lesson hard to remember.

More painful was the other lesson: that the polite niceties – 'Kelvinside', as we called such behaviour in the Gorbals – were a necessary stage between formal acquaintance and friendship, and that it was unwise, even dangerous, to confuse the two. In the Gorbals they were subtly, intuitively separated, a process that this upper-class politeness – with its refined and in some ways misleading usages – made much more difficult, at least for me; in the Gorbals, 'Kelvinside' was treated as hypocrisy, not to be trusted. Hard to stomach, too, was the thought that these public school folk sailed through it all without effort – the meretricious codes had been learnt long ago.

Less worrying, but startling for a time, was that the word 'work' meant something dramatically different here. Someone would say 'I must get back to my rooms, I have some work to do' – meaning some reading. For me, work and play had changed places. In the factory, work meant the back-breaking routine of lifting and banging and delicately manoeuvring the eighteen-pound press iron on the garments, so that heat and steam and pressure should fix the layers of cloth and canvas in permanent adhesion and shape, and regularly heaving the cooled iron in an arc at waist height from its steel rest-plate beside the pressing donkey over to the gas-fired heating ovens standing against the bare brick wall behind me, the actions endlessly renewed, my clothes soaked in sweat, the noise and steam, and the drumming of the powered sewing machines enclosing me totally – a hermetic life in hermetic toil. For the rest, in the hours of choice, 'play' – or rather escape – meant going to the Mitchell Library to read. Even though in time I, too, adopting some of the protective colouring of this place, would refer to reading books and essay writing as work, that would not be true, for I never felt it as a burden or a worry – perhaps because, as John Buyers of Glasgow University had said in a report on me, I enjoyed the intellectual chase, a chase of ideas, the lure of new horizons. In truth it was essentially the same quest, now, that drew me to teach myself to sail a dinghy, play tennis and squash, punt straight, dance the waltz and the foxtrot and tango – to explore the Aladdin's Cave that Oxford was, the riches so numerous, the choices exhilarating, where the major burden was choice itself.

'*And we shall all the pleasures prove ...*'

I learnt to lounge in Fuller's in the Cornmarket of a morning, to linger over coffee and talk – learning the paces and poses of the *boulevardier*, considering the girls, showing one's plumage, testing the signs that could lead to the intimate walk by the river or, later, the sylvan privacy, unchaperoned, of Wytham Woods. The life of the *flaneur* was sweet.

One day, alone for a moment in a girl's room in Lady Margaret Hall – she had gone to fetch a tea-pot from along the corridor – I saw that she had left her diary open, it seemed deliberately, and I saw my name and the words 'he is a glorious young animal!' When she returned I wondered if she read the blushes in my face. 'Glorious young animal' was a modish phrase among her smart set – a cant way of presenting the Lawrentian, earthy image so much talked about. That, for her, and for others like her, seemed to be how my Gorbals crudeness was interpreted! This, in its way, was a shock too, for I saw nothing glorious in my own vision of myself, such as it was. Still, she had written it approvingly. That must surely be good enough for me too – one area of my Gorbals persona that I need not hasten to change.

To enjoy its sweetness, I must have dimly realised, would conflict with what I thought was the most urgent task, to adopt the Oxford persona as I crudely understood it; but that obsession persisted.

3

Crossman: the Game and the Power

Richard Crossman was presiding over a study group on social mobility – upward of course! – a favourite hobby horse of Oxford progressives in those closing days of the Thirties. There were about twenty of us. Most of the others wore loose tweed jackets and flannel trousers – Oxford bags – in varying shades of grey or dark blue, white cotton shirts and college ties; a few wore silk shirts in pastel shades and loosely knotted ties of Shantung silk in glowing colours. I felt staidly overdressed in my grey worsted suit, my only one, bought in Burtons for fifty shillings immediately before leaving Glasgow; I had borrowed the money from Aunt Rachel, and repaid her, for this and other pre-departure loans, out of the first instalment of my scholarship money, received when I arrived in Oxford. As soon as I dared spend more money I would adopt the uniform of tweed jacket and bags.

The square oak panelled room was hung with shafts of moted sunlight. A distant, dreamy murmur, as of lethargic late season insects, gently reminded one of a world outside. Round the walls stood tall book cabinets of dark oak, their leather-bound contents guarded by grilles of thick brass wire. Windows with small leaded panes looked out on a quiet college garden, whose high wall of sand-coloured Cotswold stone was pitted and streaked with slate and iron, and curtained with creepers turning red; the boughs of a solitary pear tree, heavy with late fruit, slanted down, and a few rose bushes bravely held their colours high – blood red, gold, and delicate white – in the slanting autumn sunlight. In this unfamiliar quietude, an ambience that spoke of careful, unhurried measure, I reminded myself over and over again – as if I needed a Spartan corrective of opposites – of the world I had so recently left, the clangour and steam of the factory, the fierce pace of piece work, heaving and banging the eighteen-pound press iron from dark in the early morning to dark in the night, the hermetic greyness of the Gorbals.

Crossman was beautifully groomed, in silver grey suit and dove grey silk tie, in pointed contrast with his turnout when he addressed left-wing meetings at the Plain – shabby flannels, a tweed jacket with leather patched at the elbows, grey or dun shirt and red tie, straight grizzled hair in disarray – which he must have thought gave him a proletarian appearance.

He strained forward in a leather wing chair in a posture suggesting youthful eagerness, twinkled at us through thick-framed glasses. Suave, brilliant, he shot out provocative questions, intervened to sharpen concepts and pose alternative definitions, threw new topics into the discussion, playing us as a conductor played an orchestra. Suddenly, with a lift of the chin that signalled a shaft to the very heart of the matter, he demanded: 'Why do people work?'

Fresh from the Gorbals, I must have become unbearably galled by what I felt to be dilettante arrogance in him, and in the others. Despite total ignorance of life in the lower depths – what it was like to starve or go wet-shod in the rain – how could they talk of the proletarian condition with such total assurance? There was an added irony. Here was I, the one person among them who did know, who carried the marks in my heart and on my hands, and I did not know how to make them see any of it. There were no common points of reference; and words themselves were deficient. To have no money, for instance, no money at all, was to them inconceivable. How *could* they ask, so innocently, 'Why do people work?' I said, curtly: 'Because they'd starve if they didn't!'

Partly I *chose* to misunderstand him, partly I was too angry to look at his question calmly, aware that for them it was in truth academic. I wanted them to hear a note of protest, and pause, and think. Even as I spoke, I knew the words were futile. What I did not bargain for, ignorant of Oxford's capacity for meanness of spirit, was that, in the smoothest possible fashion, Crossman would first patronise me, snub me, and then seek revenge. Revenge? Against whom? A youngster in his first term, totally insignificant!

He stared at me, the smile lines at the side of his mouth fading; then, practised performer that he was, the smile returned. A gasp had gone through the room, and there was a stiffening, a sense of the others drawing away from me. I had committed a gaffe. From my lowly level, Crossman was an important figure, entitled at the very least to ritual respect. Behind the Wykehamist polish, the seemingly careless charm, resided a flinty *hauteur*, dangerous to challenge. Like other middle-class progressives he might pretend to treat you as if you were an equal, but you must not behave as if you really were. I had presumed. I had told him to come down to earth, no longer to look upon the workers as ideological concepts or as the raw materials with which to make his way in politics, but as real people, for whom the choices implied in his question seldom existed. Behind his unwillingness to do that lay moral laziness and hypocrisy, and these I had exposed; the full import of my words had probably been missed by the others in the room, but *he* had understood it very well, too well. My shaft had found its mark, and could not be forgiven.

In another fashion, that I could not possibly have understood so early in my time in this new world, I had been even more unwise. The others in that room were part of the new leftwards drift among the middle and upper classes. This new love affair with the virtuous sons of toil, often dismissed as slumming – or by hard-line Marxists as class guilt – was probably an intuitive recognition of a Hagelian wave of social change. Technology was about to extend choices and expectations down to the very base of the social pyramid, and mass opinion would become too powerful to be controlled by traditional loyalties. This was a time to join the masses – or appear to – and *maintain control by leading them*, while you had the chance. Earnestly copying cloth-cap attitudes, these defectors also shared, vicariously, the satisfaction felt by working-class socialists when members of the boss class were won over. Such converts must be treated gently, their blind spots pardoned, lest they retreat to the comfort of their own kind. For such people simply to recognise class injustice was surely all that was required of them? Their witness might convince others of the rightness of the workers' cause.

Crossman was such a defector. In making him lose face I had upset the others too.

Having begun as an ardent Platonist, Crossman was in those days still enough of a pure intellectual to enjoy playing with definitions; but of course they had to have social significance. It was in keeping with the spirit of the place. 'Get your concepts clear!' was a prime catch phrase in hall and common room. Here, for Crossman, was an endlessly absorbing intellectual game, to set us analysing fashionable abstractions: 'express the personality through work', 'distinguish between personal fulfilment and "class fulfilment" in the sense of Veblen's conspicuous expenditure', 'work is a means of moral uplift' – the Fabian credo of progress through commitment. The voices of Ruskin and Morris were still influential in Oxford.

Green as I was, such theorising seemed far above in the clouds. I was, in effect, accusing him of hypocrisy, of *pretending* to address important questions while in reality keeping them at a distance.

As for the others, their hurt was plain too. After all, it was 'in' to attend study groups of this kind. They trimmed to the *zeitgeist*, a sure instinct for some of them; on their return from the war they would go into politics. I wanted to expose their smug assumption that the divide between them and the workers could be bridged simply by passionate avowals of unity of interest. As Crossman would demonstrate in his later career, the game, and the power, was what such avowals meant to him, and by inference to others like him.

I must have sensed this disingenuous, repellent quality in the Oxford atmosphere quite early. At first I thought I must be mistaken. Might it be some esoteric joke? If not, how could decent people be so cynical? It would be some time before I understood, with shame, how naïve I had been.

Crossman, the smile hanging on his face like a mask, said: 'Of course you're absolutely right! But do tell us, take your father for instance, what made him choose *his* profession?'

'Profession? I don't know if you'd call it that. He learnt the bone- and wood-turning trade. I suppose *his* father just put him into it, like my father put me into a barber shop to be a soap boy.'

'A soap boy! How fascinating!' The face seemed to light up in genuinely friendly interest, the smile lines beside the mouth seeming to deepen; but behind the heavy spectacles I saw cool reckoning. 'Do tell us about it.'

I described the job; 'and then he put me to the pressing.'

'Pressing? You *must* tell us more. This is *so* interesting.'

I wanted to believe in the apparent warmth, but some genie told me to fear it. I was to learn, painfully, that '*so* interesting' was code for 'I am humouring you while I decide whether it suits me to put up with you any further.' In its many permutations the code would deceive me again and again. The time would come when I would read it effortlessly; and even, God forgive me, use it myself.

Stupidly, thinking they did want to know, I gave a detailed account. The group listened, politely simulating interest. Some may have been fascinated in spite of themselves, and yet, too disturbed by the picture I painted, they were impatient to move away from it. Crossman put his chin in his hands and leaned closer. I could feel the needle-sharp mind acutely focused, almost hear the scratch of pen on paper within, taking careful notes – grist to his political mill.

Somebody interjected: 'You're making it up! If you had left school at fourteen you couldn't have come up here at all. Pull the other one!'

Crossman was smiling broadly now, no longer wearing the frozen mask of affability. This new smile, I would learn, the bluff hand on the shoulder, indicated satisfaction at having settled something in his mind, some ploy or scheme he would use to his profit. I was of no further interest. 'I want to hear so much more,' he told me. 'Yours is such a remarkable achievement. And such a valuable object lesson for our study of social mobility!'

Addressing the group again, he repeated the question 'Why do people work', as though I had not spoken, but with cloyingly flattering references to my having come up here from the Gorbals. In the code he was saying to me 'Now, be a good fellow and don't bother me any more.'

To patronise you was one of Oxford's favourite ways of responding to someone who came, as I did, from a world whose truths were disturbing. I would suffer months of it, retrospectively burning with shame, until I learned to identify it promptly. With a pretence of interest and regard, and the appearance, of welcome, the newcomer was kept at a safe distance, encouraged to lower his guard, to delay his awakening to their indifference or antipathy.

The mandarins prided themselves on their sensibility, but sometimes their lack of it – worn so arrogantly that I wondered whether it was deliberate – appeared in grotesque style. One day an invitation came, gold-edged, embossed, to *conversazione* at Balliol 'to extend support' to Basque refugee children still being cared for in Britain by a committee of distinguished do-gooders. I looked at the card mystified. I had no contact with any such cause. From curiosity I sent my acceptance. When I arrived, the Master, A. D. Lindsay – later Lord Lindsay – whom I had never met before, wrung my hand, his ruddy smile emollient, clerical: '*So* helpful of you to come! Our friends from Spain *will* appreciate meeting someone like you with a similar background – you will understand each other so well.'

He led me round the room, a prize working-class exhibit, as if to declare: 'Who says we are out of touch with the workers?'

It was too late to retreat. I knew not a word of Spanish, and the 'children' – some looked older than me – spoke no English, which was perhaps a mercy. They huddled together defensively, regarding us with wonder, searching faces for some hint as to what role we expected of them. I stood sipping tea from a gold-rimmed bone china cup, feeling isolated both from these 'guests' on the one hand and the group of North Oxford notables on the other, and tried to smile at everyone. A strapping girl of about fifteen, with great sad eyes like darkened lamps, and high arched brows, was cajoled into playing a guitar, and some of her companions joined her in chanting a dreamy, meandering tune. Then a few younger children, shepherded round a grand piano, sang what sounded like a march. I noticed Lindsay glancing angrily out of the window. Some undergraduates were marching round the quad loudly singing 'Arriba España' and waving a Franco flag.

4

Buchenwald on the Tennis Court

Others who brought unwelcome truths were the refugees from Germany.

Reports about Nazi bestiality, the concentration camps, and the flow of refugees from Germany, were complacently dismissed. The Germans were civilised and cultured people, surely incapable of such deeds. The Brownshirts might just possibly do a few unpleasant things, but these were inevitable in changing times. After all, was not Hitler raising up his country and restoring its pride after its humiliation by Britain and France and America? His antics, of course, could be tiresome, but were not to be taken too seriously. At parties someone would slick his hair down over one eye, smear a patch of black on his upper lip from the coal in the grate, and strut about shouting in Teutonic tones: 'Vee must haf Lebensraum!' amid delighted laughter.

The word refugee had meant nothing to me till one harrowing night in the Gorbals, just before Bernard left to fight in Spain, when he had raged about the atrocities against Jews in Germany. One feature caused me particular revulsion; refugees who had been concentration camp prisoners had numbers tattooed on their arms. 'Think of it. Numbers, not people any more!' His words had etched themselves into my soul.

It had been a time of troubled self-enquiry for us both. Certainly that night was memorable. Bernard, my closest friend, went away to Spain. I agonised over whether to do the same. It was a time when the romantic gesture seemed natural. Despite the hideous facts about the Great War, we did not believe they could ever refer to *us* if we shouldered arms. Youth knows it is immortal. Bernard intended to strengthen his communist faith with blood; at least *he* had a cause to fight for! I had none. My passion to break out of the

Gorbals was all-consuming. Almost any cause would have done. It was a nice balance. If I had followed Bernard, if I had gone *any-where*, it would in a sense have been for the wrong reason. That, obscurely, I already knew. The same emotions, whether they were 'wrong' too I would never know, would make me shoot an arrow into the blue and enter the essay competition and, miraculously, win the Oxford scholarship. Inexplicably, my thoughts about es-cape – the unanswerable question, which was the 'true' escape – were linked with that apocalyptic discussion with Bernard before he went away, and therefore joined, also, to thoughts of tattooed refugees forever carrying the mark of their savage herdsmen, never to be free of them however far they fled; as, perhaps, I would never be free of the Gorbals. Ever afterwards the word refugee triggered the memory of that night when Bernard went away, and the Furies would decide which way I should go.

Thoughts of refugees also upset me for other reasons, properly understood much later. Anti-semitism in the Gorbals, though far from as violent and as publicly condoned as in our parents' coun-tries of origin, oppressed us always, burdened as we were by mem-ories, retailed to us as children by the elders, of relentless persecution – pervasive injustice and humiliation, pogroms, rapes, floggings. Many of us felt driven to flee the whole miserable tradi-tion, to cease to be Jews. This was not *spiritual* revolt in the reli-gious sense. Few of us understood the need for spiritual props, or indeed what they were. 'You work hard, you do the best you can with life – what else is there?' That was the mood of the age but we did not know it. There was certainly no thought of conversion, only a blind urge to shed an identity that burdened every step of our lives, or at least to bury it beneath some protective colouring, so that we might go our private ways like everybody else. A diffi-cult test would come later, with the birth of Israel. For me, coming to Oxford was part of the fantasy escape from being a Jew, yet hardly had I settled in here than reality made me question this too. The refugees I now increasingly heard about, and soon began to meet, were Jews, and in each I saw a disturbing image of the iden-tity I was trying to shed, and was assailed by guilt for wanting to do so. I was betraying them. Their very presence was a reproach.

My first meeting with a refugee took place, ironically I thought, at the tennis courts, in a tranquil setting of trees and rhododendrons, with the slow waters of the Cherwell, tinted green by the reflected foliage, beyond the boundary wire.

I came to be there – I had never wielded a tennis racket before – in the course of trying to solve a prime problem Oxford presented, namely, time. This was something I had never expected. I knew that I would have to break down the Gorbals persona and build anew, but not that it would cling so tenaciously. The use of time was crucial. There was so *much* time. In Glasgow I had longed to be free of the factory so that I could stay in the Mitchell Library, or in the Art Gallery making pencil copies of pictures, as long as I wished. Now that the whole of the day was mine it worried me to find that I lacked the experience, or the training, to use it properly. The nearest to the imposed discipline of the factory was going to lectures. When I first met my tutor I asked him what lectures I should attend. Too timid to ask outright, I wanted help in getting the best out of all this time.

He was astonished. 'My dear fellow, you must sort that out for yourself. You'll find the lectures listed. You can attend the lot if you want to – or none at all – so long as you present your essays promptly, and satisfy me that you have done the reading and the thinking expected of you.'

His response, letting me sink or swim, was probably sound, but at the time it felt brutal. I had hoped for the guidance I had lacked in those hungry hours and days and years in the Mitchell Library. They must have been the richest I would ever know; with help, how much richer might they have been?

Now that I could go to the Bodleian whenever I wished and read all day if I liked, the will to use all these empty hours was fickle. Wanting to reach out for so much, I fretted and fidgeted, and time trickled away.

Accustomed to the sharp-edged air blowing up the Clyde from the sea, in the sluggish, marshy climate of Oxford I found it hard to stay awake, especially in the afternoon, when even the hard wooden chairs in the Radcliffe Camera failed to keep you alert, and a half-hour could be spent staring unseeingly at one page of a book. No wonder the place was nearly deserted then. After lunch it seemed that the entire college streamed out of the gates in games kit. That must be the thing to do, to defeat torpor with hearty exercise. I must find a game I could learn quickly on my own. I bought the cheapest tennis racket I could find, a box of balls, white shorts and white tennis shoes. I decided not to risk buying a special white shirt and white socks. That might tempt providence; I might never learn to play properly. As I donned my new games clothes, the first I had ever owned, symbols of luxury and privilege, my Gorbals self nudged me, as he would again and again for a long time to come: 'Is it really *you* doing this?'

The hard courts, of a smooth green porous substance on which the white markings gleamed luminously, stretched in a long line, with the Cherwell on one side at the foot of a sloping bank of glossy green shrubbery, and a row of poplars on the other. At one end, the main entrance, was a squat brick building, the squash courts, and at the other a timber boat house half-buried in shrubbery and overhung by willows, its peeling green paint betraying slow dissolution in long sleepy summer days. On this November day there was no one on the tennis courts, but in an open gravelled space beside the squash court building a man was hitting a tennis ball against a side wall of it, maintaining a rally on his own. I had seen him at sherry parties, noticeable partly because he was older than the rest of us – he looked about forty – and because of a certain air of detachment, of being ill at ease, that chimed with my own sense of being a stranger within the gates. He was short and somewhat tubby, with sallow features, dark receding hair brushed flat straight back from the brow. Whenever I had seen him he had worn a grey flannel suit, to my experienced eye the work of a high-class bespoke tailor, with real button-holes at the cuffs. Today he was in white flannels with a knife-edge crease, crisp white shirt with short sleeves, grey socks and tennis shoes with thick soles. His smart tennis trousers diminished me somewhat, but the grey socks were consoling.

I walked across the court nearest him and stood by the wire

boundary fence pretending to contemplate the river below, and studied the precision and economy of movement as he made each stroke, the grace with which he swivelled and balanced his body to position himself for the return. As with all good players, the skill appeared effortless. Still, I could learn. However it would not do to go over there and try to copy him; in my rawness it would be silly, even embarrassing. I walked along the line of courts till I reached the furthest one, hung my jacket on a hook on the boundary fence, opened the box of balls and threw one high above my head as I had watched others do, and hit it over the net to the further court, hit another, and another, till I had sent over all six, then walked round to the far service line and hit them back again; and so, going back and forth over the over again, I began to get the feel of the racket, featherlight in my calloused palm, and to judge the arc of swing needed to aim the ball.

The strangeness of this new life had a way of striking home at unexpected moments. And now, at the service line again, ready to toss the ball in the air and swing the racket up, something made me halt and be still. I felt the shock of new vision, as when one breasts a mountain ridge and sees a newborn world in its completeness. It seemed that I was lifted up by the thin gleams of sunlight and floated with them as they slanted low through the sombre poplars. I felt the touch of the light breeze on the dark waters passing by. The enveloping quietude was not broken by the harp-like twang of the solitary player's racket or the thwack of tennis ball on brick, but joined and absorbed them. I looked about me, and would not have been surprised to find this sleepy insouciant world replaced with grimy Gorbals streets and black tenements, the roar of Dixon's Blazes beneath the plume of orange flame slanting from the chimney stack. Yes, it was true. I really was here. There was an astringent exultation, a mystic communication from the sinews and the soul, the first awareness, still to be accepted, that the days of heaving the eighteen-pound press iron were behind me.

I resumed my practice. When I was getting five out of six deliveries into the far service court, I felt there was hope.

A voice hailed me: 'Would you care for a game?'

I had forgotten the solitary player. He walked towards me, amiably swiping the air with his racket.

'I can't play!' I said. 'As you can see. In fact this is my first time on a court.'

'Oh, I don't know. Anyway, if you do not expect anyone to join you, we could have a knock-up? Werner Grenz,' he announced, with a stiffening of the back and a slight inclination of the head, and offered his hand.

He was obviously a little out of condition – I put this down to age – for he seemed short of breath when he ran for a ball; but this was not often, for he was so skilled in anticipation and moving into position that he usually seemed to *wait* for the ball to reach him, poised for the stroke, in exactly the right spot. I marvelled at his patience with my wild returns. After about half-an-hour, the light passing into autumn greyness, by tacit agreement we stopped, collected the balls, and strolled in meditative silence to where our jackets, and his white sweater, hung on hooks high on the netting. As he reached up for his sweater, I saw on his left forearm a line of thin blue marks. This was my first sight of Nazi tattooing, but I *knew*. I was hot from exertion, but a chill swept through me, the flesh contracting in goose pimples. An awed fascination made me ask: 'What are those numbers?'

He had begun to draw the sweater over his head, and his face was hidden. He must have answered the question many times. When his face emerged, the cordial expression had changed to blank fixity. 'My concentration camp number.' His eyes searched my face, seeming so say: 'How could you, a Jew, not know that?'

Bernard's words rang in my head: 'Think of it – number! Not people any more.'

Stupidly, I blurted out, 'Which one?'

Later, alone, I blushed at my question, as one might ask someone at a party: 'What college?'

'Buchenwald.'

In the stillness of the early evening we walked out of the courts without speaking, along quiet roads lined by detached brick houses set well back behind glistening evergreens and close-set board fencing. Tall sash windows on the raised ground floors, hung with gathered lace curtains, glowed yellow from table lamps with large drum-shaped parchment shades. From one house came the sound of a flute, pure, precise, detached, suggesting Vivaldi. In another someone picked out on a piano something of Bach. No cars passed. Now and then a creaking sound, as of metal dragged along the ground, slowly approached, and a student rode by on an old 'sit-up-and-beg' bicycle from whose handlebars a wicker basket hung, swaying from side to side with the effort of pushing the complaining chain round, gown swishing behind him.

Press and radio, as we learned in later years, had clouded or suppressed reports of the camps, but we did know the names of Buchenwald and Dachau; and while none of us knew with certainty what went on there, the fact that people were being herded into them like animals was horror enough. Dehumanisation as an instrument of state policy was yet to become familiar, but its practice, already sensed, lay heavy on the heart. Unimaginable, I yet tried to imagine what the camps were like, with little to go on except films and books about prisoners of war in the Great War – grey-faced people clutching a few belongings, the mud and the cold, stark huts, barbed wire, brutal guards.

Buchenwald. Now that I had made him say the word, I looked at the quiet tree-lined road, everything in it speaking of comfort, ordered living, secure horizons, and was filled with sadness. How could there be such serenity when Buchenwald existed? These house should burst open with grief – or at least show their awareness, their revulsion, by even one break in this composure! Why did the sky not open up and a great cry come down from on high?

Yet who was I to judge this world behind its lace curtains? I too was trying hard not to be touched.

Feeling inadequate, I said, 'You are the first I've met. I'm sorry.'

He nodded, looking straight ahead, and remained silent.

After a minute or so he began to talk, at first stiffly, grudgingly; and then, perhaps sensing how upset I was, more easily. A biochemist, he had been forced out of his research post at Berlin and sent to Buchenwald. He was in Oxford at the invitation of a committee for refugee scientists, but he had been waiting for two months and the expected offer of a post had not come.

I asked, 'How did you get out?'

Instead of answering, he asked, 'Where do you come from?'

'Glasgow.'

He shook his head, as if I had answered the wrong question: 'And your family? They are not surely from this country?'

An imperious quality in his voice nettled me. I countered with a question: 'How can you tell?'

Why did I resent his unerring perception that I was a Jew? And then I saw it, something that spoke from deep within him, or rather through him, mysterious, powerful, inescapable, buried far away in history, a demand that I honour an ancient bond.

How ironic that this voice should speak now, when I sought to shed the identity? Or was it rather the bond I wanted to disown? It was a bond in more than one sense; it had bound us together through the ages, from the days in Egypt and Babylon, assailed by prejudice and the self-doubt of many faiths. In our shower-room group in the Gorbals baths we often said: 'If the Jews weren't persecuted they'd be assimilated out of existence in no time! If only they [the persecutors] understood that, they'd have got rid of us long ago!'

However good his protective colouring, did some self-punishing impulse make the Jew reveal himself unawares, perhaps in defiance? If that impulse was working within *me* I must root it out. Perhaps the only cure was to destroy the sentiments that defined you as a Jew *to yourself*, the urge to treasure a secret identity, uphold traditions that attracted hate? Pride in being a Jew was dangerous luxury.

That was a way of putting it, suiting the embattled spirit. It settled nothing. It raised other demons. If it was too painful to be a Jew, and if I was an outsider not only in the Gorbals but here in Oxford too, where *could* I belong? 'Wait,' I told myself; 'it's too soon to say that – you haven't given this new life a chance!'

Werner seemed lost in thought; he may not have heard my question, or more probably, felt it was unimportant. At last he said, as if pursuing a thought aloud, 'My family in the days of the Kaiser were *Hofjuden*.' He looked at me closely, searching for an expected response. He raised his shoulders. 'And now this is where I am!'

'Talking to me, you mean?'

I was ashamed. How could I be so boorish?

Many years later, in some ways too late, I would see that my obsessive worries about belonging, about shedding Jewish identity, though in themselves important, were only symptoms of that oceanic disquiet natural to this phase between adolescence and maturity, especially at a place like Oxford. Ceaselessly you harrowed the spirit with questions about religion and final ends, closely related to concern with personal worth. You were driven by heightened sensibility to regard every detail of your response to the world, every shift in the response of others to *you*, as a comment on your own fledgling solidity. You felt vulnerable much of the time. In this extreme of self-regard I had been stung by something in his manner – the word *Hofjuden* meant nothing to me – suggesting that he was an aristocrat talking down to me.

A flush suffused his sallow features: 'You misunderstand me. I was thinking about the change in my circumstances. Our position, what we have contributed to our country, Germany – after all, we thought of it as our country – it is all gone for nothing, *finished*. As if it had never been. You see? That is it.'

'What are *Hofjuden*?'

'Ah – you do not know? I thought you would have – well, never mind. I will tell you. *Hofjuden* were Jews who were recognised by royal court. They had status. They were *Juden* – I mean Jews – who were what you would call here the upper class? I do not mean to be impolite. I simply state facts. Our family were bankers, merchants, important business people. In those old days of my grandfather some were in the army as officers. We moved at a certain level of society.'

He looked away, perhaps in delicacy.

I told him my parents had come from Lithuania.

'Ah yes, Litvaks!' He nodded to himself as in confirming a judgement.

It was easy to see what it was. There had been no *Hofjuden* where my family had come from. From Germany, he told me, few if any *Hofjuden* had emigrated; in those far-off days they had felt secure. Emigrant Jews were the poor. I was not of his class.

After a silence he said: 'Forgive me, when I referred to your family as Litvaks I meant no disparagement, you understand? In the old Pale of Settlement days things were bad for the Jews, but at least there was no *pretence*. The Jews there *knew* they had no secure place. They knew where they stood. In the old Germany we thought we did have a place. That is why for us shock is greater.'

His words, suavely dismissive now, sustaining his position, spurred me to look for weakness: 'How Jewish were you?'

Again I felt ashamed. Who was I to weigh the worth of *his* Jewishness – anyone's?

He drew in his breath sharply: 'We were not observant. We were, you know, three times a year Jews, Rosh Hashonoh and Yom Kippur Jews – that and Bar Mitzvah and so on. But we were openly *known* as Jews. We thought …' He shrugged. 'We thought of ourselves as really no different from people who were – what shall I say – who were known as Lutherans or Roman Catholics. Normal people! That was what we thought. It is hard to believe it now. Life was good. We felt secure. We belonged to a civilised, cultured society. How could that ever change? And then it was as though all that had been a dream. The old poison reappeared in full force. We had been blind. We thought it could not touch *us*!'

'Did all your family get out?'

He did not reply at once. 'What did you say? I am sorry, my thoughts slipped away.'

'Your family, where are they?'

'They are in the States now. My wife and children; my father and mother, uncles and families. Yes, thank God. We all got away, perhaps just in time. As for me, if the offer here does not materialise soon I shall go on to the States myself.'

Bitterness returned; here was another one who had only to make up his mind: 'I'll go …' and the money was there, ready to hand. Would I ever stop envying people who could do that? The thought slipped out: 'At least you've got the money to go where you want to.'

'Of course! That is to say, we *had*.' He looked at me narrowly. 'Let us say we were reasonably well off. Now it is different. Most of it has gone, partly with confiscation, or what amounts to that – forced sale of assets for a few pfennigs. The price of our lives. Partly in bribing people, to get out of Buchenwald, to get papers and so on. We did get some of it out but –' he shrugged '– not much.'

Not much? Here was yet another lesson in the bizarre values of this place. 'Not much', in Oxford language, would mean riches to me. If I heard someone say 'I haven't any money', he did not mean that he literally had not a single penny to his name – as I would if I said it – but that his allowance would not stretch to something he particularly wanted to do; a slight inconvenience, a matter of asking family or trustees for more cash, or waiting until he could draw on the next ample remittance.

I said: 'And what about all the others?'

He halted, scrutinised me again, then turned away: 'I know who you mean.' His thin lips drew tight. 'The people who cannot buy their way out. Yes, it is true. For them it is bad – very bad.'

I thought of Bernard talking about the *guerre kilométrique* that was so near, on that traumatic night on our way to his house, to the sad meal with his dying father who would still affirm that the humane world must soon come into its own, and that our simple task was to hasten that day. I had half-believed him, or rather I had wanted to. Here in the tranquillity of Oxford it was hard to imagine that the *guerre kilométrique* was imminent. If it did come, what fate awaited 'all the rest', the Jews in Germany who could not buy their way out?

It seemed that a cloud of guilt hung round Werner's shoulders and spread out to envelop me also. Was it his fault that *he* could buy his way out? Would I have done the same in his place? It was a hard question. I supposed I would. In a sense I *had*. With my scholarship I had bought my way out of the Gorbals. I had left 'all the rest' to their fate, as Werner had done. No, that was an absurd comparison. Even so, luckier than the people I had left behind, did

I go about as he did lamenting my ill-fortune? I hoped not. Then I remembered my self-pity of a few moments before. Who was I to sit in judgement on him?

As if speaking to himself, he said: 'Those others, they will not survive – most of them, I am sure of that.'

I dared not look at him.

No hint of the unthinkable, the Final Solution, was as yet even whispered. Reports of anti-Jewish atrocities in Germany, dismissed as mischievous Zionist fancies, were plausible enough to me; childhood memory, imprinted with stories of pogroms, had incised its lessons deeply. I could not have put a name to what was in store, but I *knew*.

Until this moment, despite the occasional reminder of Bernard's talk of the *guerre kilométrique*, thoughts of a coming war had troubled me little, kept at a distance, perhaps, as I savoured my new world to the full. In unthinking moments, however, walking in Christ Church Meadow, swishing through the fallen leaves, or in hall listening to carefree talk, the outer world would come close and say, 'Don't waste time – there's not much left.' Or leaning out of my windows in the stillness of the night, pondering upon the stars suspended in a sky of Prussian blue velvet, above a skyline easily imagined as mediaeval – low gables leaning together, irregular roof-lines huddled below unruly steeples – the enigmatic powers hovered near, brooding presences, ageless, savage, unrelenting from century to century, no longer romantically alluring as they had been long ago, when as a child I had sailed out to the galaxies and heard the sibylline music. There beyond the spellbound roofs lay an infernal horizon where the dogs of war moved steadily nearer. How many days were left? How many moments?

Werner was a messenger of the Fates, a lone symbolic figure projected across Europe, to herald the unthinkable. I knew it in my bones. Yet I could not, would not, hold the thought steadily and look at it.

I had been amazed to hear him talk of the old poison 'reappearing'. When had it ever gone away? In the Gorbals it had been with us always, contained – at least in its more violent forms – only by frail constraints, mild social disapproval, unease among Christian clergy, wary self-interest in some of the prejudiced, and in recent years the beginnings of organised defiance from Jewish youth. It needed only a beguiling stimulus, which Mosley looked like providing, to erupt in the savagery from which Werner had escaped. So that too was on its way.

When Bernard had talked of war just round the corner I had believed it intellectually, not in my stomach as I did now. I had needed little urging from him to take up the scholarship and behave as if war was not going to happen. How ironic were the Fates? They had plucked me out of the Gorbals, let me taste this bounteous life, and were now ready to snatch it away. I said to my soul: 'Be still. It is yours. Take it while you can.'

Once again I tried to imagine what awaited the Jews left behind in Germany. Thoughts went back to the old people in the Gorbals talking of programs *in der heim*; soldiers rampaging through a ghetto, mediaeval cruelty and ecstasy. Perhaps it had already begun? At a different level, how could I imagine what it was like to lose the security Werner had known – financial, social, and in freedom of choice – when I had never known it myself?

What *ought* I to feel? Thinking of that moment years later, my insensitivity appalled me. Detachment must have been my defence in the Gorbals, and it persisted. My years of Gorbals squalor and closed horizons, all my life so far, must have calloused the souls. I should have understood more, cared more. Petty feelings, like resentment at Werner's condescension, should not have ruled me. For that matter I may even have misunderstood him. Bitter at being here on sufferance, awaiting the favour of a faceless committee, his talk of *Hofjuden*, putting me to the proof of rank, may have been his way of presenting himself at what he took to be *my* level – a conventional Oxford undergraduate of a like social position! I had no idea I played the part so convincingly.

The deserted road skirted the grounds of the University Air Squadron. As we reached the gates the deep rumble of a powerful engine approached from within, and a long boat-shaped Bentley crunched the gravel round a clump of shrubbery and swept out.

The driver, about twenty, fair-haired, with a knobbly face, wore a dark grey flannel suit, a shirt with a cutaway collar, a tie of sponge-bag pattern in a massive Windsor knot, and a charcoal grey bowler low over his eyes, a turnout sometimes referred to as the undress uniform of the Brigade.

Werner asked, 'Do you know him – Fiorenza?'

I had heard the name, that of a wealthy Jewish family long settled in this country.

'I've seen the car about,' I said. 'I suppose that's why the face is familiar.'

I remembered something else about him, and without thinking how discordant a note it would strike, I said that I had seen him in the tails and pink facings of the Bollinger.

'Please? What is the Bollinger?'

I told him about the roistering dining club.

He nodded understandingly, even a shade wistfully. 'It is logical after all. You might say that Jews like him are the *Hofjuden* of this country. More English than the English – just as people used to say of *us*, disparagingly, that we were more German than the Germans.'

He was more open now. Something had changed between us. Fiorenza, and the attitudes he exemplified, had brought us closer. Werner must have regarded him with the poignant emotions with which a refugee French aristocrat of the *ancien régime* could have contemplated the insouciance of the English gentry. My own envy, though it sprang from totally different sentiments, must have been clear to him too. Our isolation and doubt, and guilt, were in origin so diverse, but we could share emotional bridges, and our burdens became lighter. In an unspoken compact, we could cautiously lower our defences.

When I knew him well, I would see the sensitivity and compassion beneath the appearance of arrogance. For the present, however, neither of us had any sympathy to spare for the world – and without the need of words we understood this of each other, and accepted it.

He said: 'People like that are putting on the same airs as we did in *our* mistaken sense of security. Look where *we* are now. That is where you too could be, one day.'

'I mean,' he added quickly, 'not you personally of course, but Jews like him who believe the insular English superiority belongs to them too.'

That ultra-Englishness contained a further irony, hidden from us; the model of the Englishman, proconsular, Arnoldian, was already a sunset vision, its reality deep in the past. He said: 'Members of our family, and others like us, served the Emperor – Iron Crosses, other honours. Germany was our country. Our culture. Nothing could touch us! The ghetto was far back in history – we did not look back to it, just as *they* do not.' He gestured to where the Bentley had disappeared from view.

With a wry grimace he told me that some of Fiorenza's relatives in the City were helping to fund the committee whose decision he was awaiting.

He turned to me, halted, and startled me by bursting out laughing. 'My God, I must stop this. As you English say, pull myself together, no? I tell you what I propose. Let us dine together tonight if you are free? We should look at the bright side, yes?'

The sudden change was a release. I was flattered, too, that this sophisticated, scholarly man should want my company.

'All right. I'd like that.'

Before we parted, he asked: 'You do not go to the University Jewish Society? I have not seen you at meetings? You should go.'

'Frankly, I've been avoiding that sort of contact.'

This was not the time to say that I wanted to stop being a Jew. I was not the only one – Hitler and history had pulled him back into that old identity, and now, paradoxically, he was forced to claim it fully once again, to draw on the compassion of *other* Jews, the historic bond.

He studied me again, deep sadness on the sallow features: 'I think I understand,' he said, 'how you feel about being Jewish, but believe me this is not the time to turn away; to be isolated is the last thing we should wish for at this historic time.'

Stupidly, I would not grasp his meaning. His reference to

Fiorenza still hurt. Despite his quick denial he *had* bracketed me with him, no doubt assuming that our attitudes were the same. Arrived here from the lower depths of the Gorbals, what could I have in common with the English *Hofjuden*?

I said: 'The Jewish problem will never go away. Why don't we simply stop being Jews and be done with it?'

'They will not let us! They hunger for the scapegoat of the past. There are such people even here in Oxford. I used to think that in the atmosphere of pure enquiry at a university there could be no prejudice. That was foolishness. Look at that student in Trinity with a swastika flag in his window, and his gramophone booming out the 'Horst Wessel Lied'. Such people will not let you forget your Jewishness – when it suits them. That way, believe me my friend, there is no way out.'

We had halted near the corner of Holywell, where he had rooms above a bespoke shoemaker whose window displayed a sheet of paper with pencilled outlines of the Prince of Wales's feet – apparently the good man did not qualify for the display of the three white feathers. Street lamps glowed, and dim yellow electric light shone in the tall sash windows behind the pillared portico of the Clarendon Building across the way, where the Broad opened wide opposite the Indian Institute and the Bridge of Sighs at the entrance to New College Lane. Bicycles rattled by on every side, some with carbide lamps hissing, the gas acrid in the nostrils, some with dynamo lamps, many with none, the riders' gowns fluttering like witches' cloaks among the glow-worm lights wavering and bobbing. From the far end of the Broad there approached a din of shouting and chanting and a cacophony of bicycle bells. Down past Trinity and Blackwell's, four abreast, rode a group of about twenty young men and women, sounding the bells on their handlebars in shrill chorus, and singing at the top of their voices the Zionist anthem, 'Hatikvah' – Hebrew for 'The hope' – to the melody of a Moldavian folk song: 'Cart and Ox'.

> As long as a Jewish soul
> still yearns in the innermost heart,

and eyes turn eastward
gazing towards Zion,
then our hope is not lost,
the hope of two thousand years,
– to be a free people in our land,
the land of Zion and Jerusalem.

In the middle of the front row two girls led the chanting, their clear silver voices carrying the song up into the sky triumphantly, joyously. Both radiated an energy, a womanly earthiness, that crackled through the dark air and touched my flesh like sparks of static electricity. One of them, buxom, long-legged, had glossy black hair cascading to her shoulders, and pale, finely-drawn olive features; she wore a white blouse embroidered down the front with red flowers and a skirt of claret-coloured velvet that billowed out above a dimpled knee as the pedal reached the top of its circle. The other girl was fair, with full rosy lips, high cheekbones and dazzling white teeth, small waist and wide hips, wearing a long flowing woollen dress in blue and white vertical stripes. Both wore scholar's gowns.

'I see you have good taste in women!' Werner chuckled, smacking his lips. 'Like me, but the less said about that the better. Still, a man must live, must he not? Those two are leading lights in the Jewish Society – the dark one is Rachel, and the other is Hannah. A word of advice: they are firebrands – prophetesses of a Jewish national home in Palestine. My God, what can one say about that? I cannot see any hope of a Jewish Palestine. And even if by a miracle it did happen, what are you and I going to do – you in a mood to discard your Jewishness, and as for me, I don't know what to say. Do I want to live in a totally Jewish milieu? I'm not sure I do.'

I said I would go with him to the Jewish Society. He grinned and slapped my shoulder. 'I will introduce you to those two. It will be interesting to see what develops. I think I can guess. They will not know what to make of you, but will be drawn like moths to a candle. But be careful. That kind could take you up, be amused for a time, and drop you and move on. Still, who knows?' He shrugged. '*Le coeur a ses raisons*, eh?' Then he added, slyly, 'Remember my friend, they are *Hofjuden*, the lot of them. You will learn a lot – maybe not all of it to your liking.'

5

G. D. H. Cole: Fabian Twilight

I never dared ask why I was invited, out of the blue, to join the Cole Group. Later, receiving other such unexpected invitations, and putting together scraps of gossip dropped from high tables and passed along the bush telegraph, I concluded that they must have indirectly resulted from my outburst at Richard Crossman's seminar. Suavely dismissed by him at the time, I had assumed it had been forgotten, but I was wrong. His pride had suffered. I was too inexperienced to know that Oxford luminaries did not feel safe on their Olympian heights but guarded their positions with a million bayonets. Stories about the incident had made the rounds of senior common rooms, undoubtedly spread by Crossman himself, a way of getting revenge in a typically tortuous manner. I had much to learn about Oxford gossip, addictive, obsessional, Byzantine, instrument of manoeuvre and war. That story of the rough young fellow from the Gorbals slums doubtless titillated cloistered superiority and its liking for condescending swordplay; it would be amusing to confront the strange creature – and take him down a peg! Crossman must have reasoned that if I ran true to form, others would lose face as he had done; and in their merciless response yet more bayonets would turn their points towards me. An elegant scheme.

G. D. H. Cole brought together selected people to his rooms, undergraduates and a few senior members of the University, like Patrick Gordon Walker, to discuss, as he put it, evolving socialist policy. In his gradualist idealism there were echoes of Bernard's father, though founded on a richer scholarship. We must emancipate the lower orders through betterment, refined social design to level people upwards, cultural uplift linked to spiritually rewarding work. More humane social principles would raise men and women to the full expression of the personality – a concept I found mystifying; no one paused to define it, and I was ashamed, at that early stage, to ask what they meant by it. What were 'humane' principles? What did expression mean, what *was* the personality, and how did you know when its expression was beneficial, to you or to others? Was all this vagueness deliberate – lest you pin anyone down? That labyrinthine discussion led nowhere. For the Cole Group, and in fairness other 'progressive' gatherings, expression of the personality was simply a comforting shibboleth. There were echoes of Keir Hardie, Paine, Rousseau. Even in his appearance Cole suggested the advanced élite of the turn of the century, Bloomsbury and South Place – well-tailored smooth tweeds, sharp boyish features and fresh complexion hinting at long breezy walks along ley lines, severity of thought, closeness to the lodestone of Nature.

One sensed, in the Group, the feeling that the creed must accommodate to a changed *zeitgeist* impatient with the old, gentle, persuasive posture of socialism; and that it must blunt the aggression of the new radicalism by moving towards it – or appearing to do so. Progressive Oxford still reeled from the shock of *The Road to Wigan Pier*. A visitor from another planet could well have assumed that Oxford had just received reports of the way of life of a little-known breed of person called workers, and that the information had yet to be understood, let alone digested.

I marvelled that *The Road to Wigan Pier*, to me naïve, had made such a stir. I could think of nothing in it that was not obvious, but when I said so in the Cole Group it was as if I had uttered a mortal heresy. I forgot that having lived all my life at the lowest level of the pyramid, lower than anywhere Orwell had been – or would have recognised as such if he had – I perceived its characteristics in my heart, not in my mind, with its subtleties of outlook and aspiration, far more clearly than the middle-class voyeur Orwell could. I should have been quicker to understand this at the time. If I had, I would not have been so arrogantly dismissive, so determined on the impossible task of making others see the workers' life truly, when there was no common language, no shared sensibility. Sadly, as the years passed, I would have to accept that my non-conforming vision, whether the effect of heritage or the imprint of the Gorbals or both made no matter, separated me emotionally from 'them' for ever. I could never truly join them, except in specific, personal – and alas often short-lived – felicities; and even these would owe their stimulus, at least for people on the other side of the divide, more to fascination with my differentness than true sympathy. The attempt to 'go native' was doomed from the start. That irony was hidden from me, or I might have fled Oxford there and then.

I had worshipped Cole on the printed page, and my first sight of him in the flesh was fittingly magical. His dark-panelled sitting room, dimly lit by parchment-shaded table lamps, and the leaping flames from heaped coals in a wide stone fireplace, was dominated by the enormous flared and curling horn of a gramophone – suggesting Thor's hunting horn – which rose up to within inches of the ceiling and cast an apocalyptic shadow upon the wall behind his head. Till I arrived in Oxford I had never met anyone who *owned* a gramophone. This one was of the highest class, using fibre stalks as needles, considered a mark of the fastidious mind. Cole sat beneath the horn, enveloped in a deep leather chair, peering over the arm of it, birdlike, a furtive smile on the small, slightly pouting mouth.

I noted the others' technique as they helped themselves to coffee from a silver pot on a wheeled mahogany server, in tiny cups of fine china with minute saucers, used silver tongs to pick sugar lumps from a fluted silver bowl, wedged a small round ginger biscuit between the cup and the steep side of the saucer, and sidled into the crowd. They did these things with automatic ease, but I had to watch and copy as I went, and was slow. Before coming to Oxford I had never tasted coffee, but as in many other untried things – drinking, smoking – I sheepishly followed the mode. Many months would pass before I found coffee palatable, or thought I did. I fancy I told myself it was necessary to enjoy such things – force myself to do so, come what may! – if I seriously meant to fit into this new world.

Nor had I mastered the social art of drinking and eating in mid-air, with no solid surface at hand on which to rest cup and saucer.

As I moved gingerly into the middle of the room, someone nudged me gently and I barely saved my coffee from spilling; Rachel said at my shoulder: 'How *amusing* to meet you here!'

Werner, true to his promise, had introduced me to her, and to Hannah, at the University Jewish Society. Girls in the university, outnumbered by the men eight to one, were in a buyers' market. These two, signalling to each other in their mysterious feminine code, must have decided that Rachel should sample me first; Hannah's turn would come. Rachel, in her mannered speech – hybrid of Garsington and Mayfair – had confided to me that I was sympathetic. As the next step in the genteel social measure, in a few days I was to go to tea with her, when she would be chaperoned.

The room having filled up, and with the waves of heat from the coal fire, the place was torrid, and her dark odour as she leaned close surged through me, making me breathless. These were child of nature days, new to me; girl undergraduates experimented with the persona of the Lawrentian woman, the earth mother, whose pure, demanding essence, the life force, rightly proclaimed itself in the potent message of her sweat.

The crowd pressing us together, the earthy chemistry took possession. If only I could go – somewhere, anywhere – and take her with me! Social punctilio, I reminded myself, demanded small talk – a skill I had never learned. Unsteadily I said, 'This is an odd place to find you.'

'Good Heavens why?'

I searched for a reply: 'You're not left-wing are you?' That sounded pompous; my attempt to recover was little better. 'The other day you were full of plans for capitalist enterprise, buying land in Palestine for settlers, setting up industries, investments and profit returns and so on. I thought...'

'Oh how sweet!' She leaned closer and the siren smell took all sense away; and she, perfectly aware of that, continued with complete composure, saying gently, half-coaxingly, though the words were irrelevant: 'One does have to make things pay, doesn't one? And the idea is joint ownership among us settlers. So we'll *all* be workers then, won't we?'

She smiled half to herself. And I nodded, nothing more needed. We both knew that the words had no purpose but to endorse this contact – every formality, as by a miracle, now stripped away. Signals had been exchanged. We would now move on as if we had known each other for ever. The smile, I knew also, was a reference to the chaperoned tea! That too was now irrelevant. We were content.

A movement in the room told us that the coffee overture was at an end. There was a scraping of chairs. She whispered: 'Let's sit on the floor.'

In the Gorbals, sitting on the floor was not respectable. Apart from gentility, since many tenement dwellers could not afford floor covering, if you sat on the rough planking you might get a nail or a splinter – a 'skelf' – in your bottom, to say nothing of making your clothes dirty. People here seemed deliberately to *choose* the floor as a sign of the free spirit, scoffing at 'stuffiness'. In any case they could afford not to worry about spoiling their clothes.

Cole talked about Fabianism. Cant phrases recurred – social betterment, dignity for the labouring man ... Change was in the air. How should Fabians respond? Crucially they must not be tempted, moved by compassion, to advocate social changes before the evils they were designed to cure had been fully understood, as well as the distant implications of the 'cures' themselves. An immediate need was to study the challenge presented by *The Road to Wigan Pier*. He turned to me: 'I hear you are from the Gorbals. That is highly interesting; a personal view from such a place would be most valuable. I imagine the conditions are comparable?'

Before I could answer, he went on: 'I wonder if you would care to tell us what you think of Orwell's message?'

Awe of the great man fought with hurt. Seeming to want to hear what I had to say, he was looking far beyond me. The intellectual steamroller moved urbanely, inexorably. I was being used in some way, unrelated to any insights I could offer. I had a feeling they were not desired. Unlike these people, Orwell at least had had the courage to acknowledge his ignorance and try to remedy it.

I said: 'I don't think he *has* any message – except, maybe, a warn-

ing that the do-gooders from the boss class should try to understand the workers before it's too late.'

Rachel drew her breath in sharply and I felt the ripple of excitement in her body.

Cole straightened his lean form in the deep chair, the ghost of a
smile flickering across the pursed lips. 'That is *most* interesting.
Now, do tell us – are the conditions Orwell describes, and the attitudes of the people, a fair representation of working-class life as
you knew it in the Gorbals?'

'What do you mean by fair?' Some of the people in his book are
a damn sight better off.'

He seemed to draw into himself, still considering me with that
youthful, open gaze. With a little shake of the head, he said, 'We
have a lot to learn from you. But it will take time. We speak, alas,
different languages.' He finished with a flicker of a smile.

Unlike Crossman, I felt he was sincere.

It was, surely, hard for these people. I thought of Bernard's father
exhorting me to carry the torch. Where in this comfortable, obscurantist preserve would I look for it? Even prophets like Cole were
in confusion, skilled though they were in concealing it.

The dusty abstractions were thrown back and forth yet again, a
dead language; Benthamite and Platonic formulae, élite condescension: 'we must take culture to the workers', Shakespeare in the val-
leys. To instil elevated aesthetic sensibility in the workers was a
moral imperative.

If Oxford undergraduates played football with unemployed
miners a blow was struck for uplift.

The role of prize exhibit, untutored savage from another world, at
first beguiling, even a little glamorous, was now spiritually lowering. Even among the tiny sprinkling of working-class students –
whom the genteel Glasgow parlance would have describe as 'respectable working class' – the Gorbals was regarded as the lowest
of the lower depths.

Werner, it was true, was becoming a friend. We met often for
knock-ups on the tennis court, and long talks over tea or dinner.

His cultivated company, opening up wide new horizons, was stimulating, but in the absence of shared childhood memories, as there had been with Bernard, an indefinable frontier remained closed; I could not talk from the heart. The link with Bernard did continue by letter, but that was no substitute. On paper, thoughts lost the fine touch the emotions needed. There was, however, a ray of hope; Bernard, moving fast up the union ladder, would soon be travelling south from time to time on union business, and we would meet.

As for my family, there had been little enough communication in the past, and now there was nothing to build on. I wrote to father and my sisters, Lilian and Mary, and Aunt Rachel, and got laconic messages back. In my sisters' letters, reading between the lines, I found a self-justifying resentment, the accusation – mystifying to me – that it was I who was guilty of severing the vital links, when in truth it was *they* who had done so long ago when I was a small child; they had gone off on their own after mother's death and left father to cope with me as best he could. Aunt Rachel, mother's sister, sent fragmentary news, of Uncle Salman's declining strength, of familiar hardships, bonds of a kind; there was warmth, but also concern for me, regret, fear. The worry was genuine, there was no doubt of that. I knew that it was doubly charged, as if she tried to give me what mother, dead long ago, could not. I read the letters again and again as I strode furiously across the Parks, and the wind threw tears cold against my face. Often, reading her carefully rounded copperplate English – learnt at night school long ago – I heard again the words she had uttered through tears when I first told her of the scholarship: 'If only your mother could have been spared to see you turn out like this! Her beautiful baby boy she had to leave so soon.' She worried – as Alec had done but for more profound reasons – seeing her sister's line broken in fragments, that the road I had taken would sever the heart's roots. She tried to extend to me the concern my mother would have shown. I knew that Uncle Salman, seen in the mind's eye forever crouched over his sewing in the little front room workshop, shared her feelings. I would not understand their fear for me till many years of stumbling and picking myself up again had gone by, long after they too were dead;

and all I could do in acknowledgment and homage, and futile gratitude, would be to stand at their graves and bare my soul to the wind.

Father's brief lines were full of a sombre perplexity only too familiar. Indirectly, however, they carried a special shock, for to my amazement I had difficulty deciphering the words. He wrote in Yiddish, and following the common practice used the Hebrew cursive script. As a child I had learned to read and write Hebrew and Yiddish fluently; now the knowledge was fading fast. Soon it would be irrecoverable. There indeed was a reminder, like a wind from the icy mountains, of how far I had fled. I was destroying all signs of the way I had come! How many more fierce ironies were in store? Here was Rachel, and so many more, rushing to recapture a fading Jewish identity, and here was I fleeing madly in the opposite direction.

It was a shock to see from such signs that a demon worked within me in secret, devious, implacable, destined always to get his own way.

Though outwardly gregarious, this new life was lonely. I longed to find one soul with whom I need not be defensive, or alert for pitfalls set by the code, to whom I could open my heart – or so I thought. Bernard had equated the doubt and loneliness of ordinary life with like feelings in the soldier: 'Having a woman gives you back a breath of your own true self.' He had meant much more than sex, as Alec had done in *his* stoic summing up on life: 'Ye go tae wurrk, ye eat a bit, fuck a bit! Whit else is there?' The two voices were not so far apart. As Bernard saw it, renewal through a woman was a Lawrentian key to everything else – to a spiritual balance, a necessary plenitude of feeling. The child of nature vogue, perhaps, had some sense to it after all? When I had come away from Glasgow I had left Bunty behind, Alec's cousin, passionate siren in the factory; she had begged me to let her come south to Oxford with me. She would work hard, care for me, simply to be at my side. No, I had told myself, it would be wrong to make her travel his road with me. How could she? How I had underrated her!

In any case, in the rigidly conventional conditions of Oxford at that time, life with her would have been made unworkable.

And now here beside me was Rachel, who was perhaps even more distant from me in outlook and personality than Bunty – rich, assured, fanatically pursuing a quest that was surely futile – a fantasy, a blind determination to make the Bible come true, against all the historic odds. Was I exchanging one doomed relationship for another? What had I in common with Zionism? Nothing, as Werner observed, but a heavy heart.

A measured, sonorous voice broke into my thoughts. Cole was addressing me again: 'You say we need to learn more about the workers. That observation contains a serious criticism, and you may be right. But tell us, how do you suggest we go about it, since you think that Orwell's effort falls short?'

Anxious to repair my inattention I spoke hastily – too hastily – and my words, encapsulating doubts about myself, the world, the road I was on, took me by surprise: 'That's what I thought I came here to Oxford to find out from people like you.'

I felt my cheeks flush in shame. He looked at me with a kind of wonder, of recognition, as if he remembered a time, long ago, when he had felt an equal disappointment. Softly he said: 'There is a profound irony in what you say. Our task is harder than yours. We need to see the workers as you can; but; you do it *without trying*, as naturally as breathing, encompassing innumerable truths, tiny but vital, at a glance. Alas we cannot. There are many things you could tell us, but you do not know how to – yet. The enlightenment you want from us – and will certainly get if I judge you correctly – conceptual, disciplined, is likely to destroy the freshness of your untutored vision, the unique quality you now possess.'

The openness staggered me, and I almost worshipped him afresh for it. Blinded by knowledge, philosophy, qualification, they saw too little because they knew, or 'saw', too much! They groped about in a fog of knowledge. If the road I was following would do no more than take *me* into that same fog, what was the point?

6

Rachel

Rachel exclaimed: 'My God these Oxford men are *so* juvenile.'

In her MG coupé we were bowling along a switchback Cotswold road towards her parents' country house. Her father had provided a suitable reason for her to go down for the weekend. He was a valued friend of her college. 'What is the use of having money,' she had observed, 'if you don't use it to get what you want?'

The house would be empty except for the servants. Her father was at their London house, her mother wintering in Nice, and her younger sister at school in Switzerland.

This was my first car journey. I was glad it was in the dark, the sense of magic, of freedom, of taking wing, heightened. She handled the sprightly car with relaxed skill, her exhilaration overflowing and possessing me too. We spoke little. Communion was emphasised, not broken, by thoughts that bubbled to the surface.

The early winter sunset had left behind a sky of hard grey steel. In a scattering of high cirrus the stars gleamed sullenly. Hills were dark shapes against the sky, dark against dark. We were alone on the clear road, the very infrequent oncoming vehicle visible miles ahead. Like a racing driver on a track she took a line straight through curves, and cornered by hugging the outer lip till she could aim the car to slice off the arc and resume her direct line on the other end of it, the bodywork swinging outwards at the turn as if it tried to leave the wheels to their tighter course, and yawing inwards again as we re-entered the straight, throwing us together in the cramped cabin, joined in breath and body. The only illumination came from our dipped lights reflected from the cambered road sliding towards us beneath the bonnet, and gleaming dully on bare brown hedges moving steadily past, and from two little green bulbs on the dashboards. Their eerie luminescence picked out in soft chairoscuro her finely rounded classical features, gleams in the curls cascading to her shoulders, tiny glints in her great eyes – Aphrodite in tender meditation, sailing through the night.

'What's wrong with them?' I asked.

I envied them for their sophistication, their poise, their worldly competence. They had accounts with tailors and bookmakers, drove cars, sailed yachts to the Baltic, flew planes, were much travelled, moved with ease in society. In this view of them I was being juvenile too; and I would blush in retrospect. Whether she noted this at the time – or had already sensed it and in her love forgiven it – I would never know.

The road reared up again and she changed down with a burst of engine revolutions – a racing change, she called it, that Geoffrey Fiorenza had taught her.

She murmured peevishly: 'They are so wrapped up in their pretty selves. They haven't a notion how to treat a woman.'

At the crest of the hill she moved briskly into top gear and flicked on the overdrive switch.

'They are so ...' She searched for the word, gave up, and rushed on. 'What do you think of this? I went to Geoffrey's rooms for tea and he showed me photos of racing cars till I wanted to scream! I popped into his bedroom and slipped my knickers off and came back and said I wanted to do a cartwheel. His sitting room's quite big, you know. Before he could answer I did one, and then I stood in front of him and asked him if he'd seen my ace of spades! You'll never guess what he did. He said, "Careful! You might break some of the Sèvres," and turned back to his blessed photograph album.'

I saw the flying thighs and upturned skirt hem descending, and my flesh grew hot; and then, green as I was, there came a prudish reaction. A Gorbals girl would not have expressed her pique in that outrageous fashion. She would have broken off with the man, 'respectably', and taken care to be seen with him no more. Rachel's set, smart, glossy, arrogant, was hard, and in its way cruel; it had little forbearance with the weak or the unsure. Beneath her abrasive impatience, however, there must surely be some sensitivity, some tenderness? As if answering me, I sensed within her another, gentler, sentiment, almost an appeal:

> Oh God where shall I find
> A soul to listen,
> Not to words but to my heart,
> And speak to my condition?

I wanted that too – I always had. I had thought I had found that soul in Annie – my first love, alas indelible – and how wrong I had been. Annie's desertion of me, for money, or the hope of it, had taught me something of worldliness. On that view, money was the key to everything, to choice, to the shaping of life. Rachel possessed that key. She could have virtually anything she wanted, *do* anything she wished with her life. Why, then, such savage discontent? I knew the answer. We both knew it – she from riches and I from poverty – and, with our differing prejudices, we fought against the knowledge. Annie was wrong: goods only got you part of the way, the rest was inside you. I had already set it out in the scholarship essay, but with the mind only, not in the language of the heart.

'What are you thinking about?' she asked.

Later, too late – oh that repeated story! – I would see how much I had underrated her, the sensibility, the courage. The reason she had told me of that incident in Fiorenza's rooms had almost passed me by. It was obvious enough – a contrast in sensibility. She saw in me, rightly or wrongly, a light that drew her – we saw it in each other:

'Think each in each, immediately wise ...'

Did I really possess such riches? I wanted to believe it.

'I was thinking about money,' I said, surprising myself. 'And whether one can be happy without it.' Then added, hastily, 'How stupid that sounds!'

'I wonder about it too. I feel one *should* be able to. But you said something a moment ago, so quietly all I heard was '... speak to my condition.'

I said the lines again. She repeated them and was silent. Then she said in a whisper: 'Never to explain – ask or be asked? How beautiful life would be – how free?'

It was too much to ask of life. Some part of you must be kept inviolate. With Annie I had given without reserve, and she had inflicted a wound that would never heal. And so, in fear, you invented excuses to avoid handing yourself over so completely ever again – myths and superstitions so transparent you were half ashamed of them, but potent none the less. 'Was love,' Bernard once asked, 'like beauty, no more than a dream in the soul of the beholder?' Love was an indulgence. Tread that path with care. In the commerce of the heart, as in so much else, I was ill-equipped to deal as an equal with these gilded people endowed as they were with unquenchable confidence, schooled to *expect* success in whatever they touched. And always, in the last resort, they had money to cushion a fall. Part of me knew that this was callow stuff. Sooner or later the heart would win, and throw me into the mêlée to take my chance.

Echoing my thoughts she murmured: 'One has to trust – sooner or later. There's no choice.'

We went through a village strung out along a single wide street, most of it in darkness or deep shadow, except for a cone of weak gaslight from a street lamp near each end, scattered glimmers from curtained cottage windows and, near the middle, a patch of intense yellow light from two oil-burning carriage lamps hanging from iron brackets on the doorposts of a half-timbered inn. A group of men, their trousers corded at the knees, leaned on bicycles and talked.

A mile or so beyond the village we slowed at a break in the grass verge, turned into it and rolled to a stop, facing ornate iron park gates flanked by massive cylindrical gateposts of rusticated stone. A few yards within, the lighted windows of a stone lodge shone warmly in the surrounding blackness. Someone within must have been watching for us, for hardly had Rachel drawn the handbrake lever up on its ratchet than the door opened and the black silhouette of a stocky man in gaiters appeared in the rectangle of yellow light. The man hurried towards the gates and heaved them open.

Wheels crunching and crackling on the gravel of a tree-lined estate road, we drove round the base of some rising ground for about a quarter of a mile; then the main headlights picked out a Palladian façade, with broad steps leading up to a portico above a sunken ground floor.

She left the engine running, and we mounted the steps and went through the wide front door. From behind us there floated up, in the crisp notes of night, the sounds of the car boot being opened and our bags lifted out, then the wheels rustling on the gravel once again as the car was driven round to the back of the house. She led the way up a broad wooden staircase that rose from the middle of a square entrance hall lined with dark linenfold panelling, along a corridor hung with William Morris paper – large panels of pastel blue foliage on a primrose ground. She half-opened a door and paused, hand on the doorknob. I glimpsed a four-poster bed from whose canopy hung silk curtains embroidered with tea roses. Silently, by the way she stood, the slight inclination of the head, an expression at once audacious and wary, she warned me that people were listening, watching. Though our purpose in the house must be perfectly obvious to the staff, we must follow a code. She nodded towards a door opposite hers: 'They'll put your bag in that guest room.'

Keeping straight faces we managed a smile of complicity, and turned away to our separate rooms. I took off my stiff fustian overcoat and dropped it on the settle at the foot of the bed, a narrower version of the one in her room. Our Gorbals flat could have been put into this room with space to spare. This was luxury I had seen only in films. The cream rugs on the polished wooden floor seemed ankle deep. Before a broad-paned window stood a curved dressing table draped in the same heavy silk that curtained the bed, on it a looking-glass triptych framed in gold. Beside a second window was a gilt writing table with slender fluted legs, covered in gold-tooled calf. Opposite the bed was a door; the room had its very own bathroom, with toilet *and* a bidet. Here was a life and a half.

The butler, white haired, had the compact figure and economy of movement that often indicates the neatness and precision learned in the Navy; gravely he served dinner, assisted by a pretty dark-haired girl of about sixteen in crisp white apron and frilled cap. I sat with Rachel at the end of a long mahogany table, beneath a chandelier whose crystal pendants cast rainbow gleams on silver and stiff white linen. A log fire crackled in a tall fireplace of green marble, a high brass fender before it, We talked little, our silences close.

She said softly: 'I am not a bit promiscuous. No, that's not what I meant to say. I mean this. If we ...' She sighed, then words came with a rush: 'I think I want to live with you.'

I was dismally provincial, for the words startled me. Intellectually, safely in the abstract, one was expected to show sympathy with the raffish goings-on of the smart set; you took part eagerly in coffee-table chatter about trial marriage, a modish theme among progressive women undergraduates. It all seemed so mature, so adventurous, but it was surely not 'me'. It was not, in the deeply incised Gorbals judgement, 'respectable'. Here it was, however, close beside me, not abstract but real, her dark-scented flesh breathing it and speaking it – romantic, and yet daunting. Shocking thoughts crowded in. The kind of behaviour that people of her set looked upon with jaded eye, in the Gorbals was anathema – though it happened!

Was there not a rule in the boss class: 'Never comment on a like-ness'? Immorality such as ours was to be this very night – here under a parental roof – would be unthinkable in the Gorbals, where lovers were expected to stand together at the rubbish heap at the back of the close. In the boss class, money shut people's mouths, made certain actions invisible, and many things smell sweeter than they were. Above all you sinned in comfort, in style – and in a fashion respectably.

But living together? In the Gorbals morality, Jewish influences were joined with the host culture – Calvinist fundamentalism linked to Dickensian calculation. The latter now pulled me up short. A girl's value in the marriage market was sharply diminished by a 'previous canter over the course', as the sardonic vernacular put it. For that reason if for no other she would – she *must* – cling to you, literally for dear life. And worse still, if she was 'knocked up', be she ever so smart and modern, all the fine talk of *trial* marriage would fly straight out of the window! In pure self-interest would she ever let you go free?

How lovely she was! In the light of the leaping flames she glowed from within like a goddess. She had come down to dinner in a clinging dress of black velvet. A rope of pearls was just long enough to hang below the curved décolletage. Now and then the lowest pearls slipped behind and were gripped between her breasts, and she freed them with a lift of the shoulders and flick of a forefinger in the cleavage. How heady to be here at her right hand, her consort in this her palace, and hear her say, confidently, with longing, words of blessing and joy and accolade: 'I want to live with you.'

Prosaic thoughts, churlish, selfish, intervened again – ashes in the mouth. Living together would entail abandoning Oxford. For one of her class that would be unimportant. For me, having reached Oxford by a million-to-one chance, how could I throw it all overboard now? There would be no other way; it would be impossible to support a woman on my scholarship money; I would have to get a job. And what was I fitted for? Only the pressing? How could I take a girl like her back to all that? Simplistic Gorbals verities asserted themselves, man the breadwinner, woman the homemaker. Doubtless that was why, in retrospect hard to believe, the idea that we might live on *her* money did not immediately occur to me. That would mean, despicably, being a kept man! Even if I did somehow stretch my scholarship stipend to support us both, what about the future, when I went down? So far, I had sailed along totally absorbed in books and lectures and friendship and talk, discovery and self-discovery – a marvellous licence, with no thought for a tomorrow that remained invisible beyond the horizon. When that final day did come, I would be back, literally without a penny, where I had started.

As if she had listened to my thoughts she broke in, spitting out the words in a fierce whisper: 'Don't – please – think about *money*. Money's irrelevant.' She raged at the world.

We left the dining-room and crossed the hall, shadowy now, lit from wall lamps at the top of the monumental wooden staircase, and by a gleam from the logs in the room we had left. The house was sinking into the night, the only sounds the muted voices and clatter of dishes and pots drifting up from the floor below. We went into a small room on the other side of the staircase, furnished in glowing mahogany, with heavy tapestry curtains. A brass standard lamp, silk shade depicting flamingoes feeding, stood in each corner. On a small sideboard near the door were two silver trays, one with decanters of whisky, brandy and sherry, and assorted glasses, and another with a glass coffee percolator on its diminutive spirit stove, tiny cups and saucers, cream jug and sugar bowl of fluted silver. We sat close together on a long leather sofa facing a fire whose logs gave off an unfamiliar scent, a mixture of resin and pine and lavender.

'There is so little time,' she murmured, 'almost no time at all.' She leaned her head on my shoulder. Despite the room's warmth, she shivered. 'There's something I must show you tomorrow.'

She added hurriedly: 'No, don't ask me now. It's – it's a sign of where we all are in the world.'

She got up and absently smoothed the dress over her hips and went to the little sideboard. She refilled our cups, half-turned and said timidly: 'I don't really drink. I feel like it tonight, though.'

I awoke, as I thought, within a dream. I was in the curtained alcove bed in our Gorbals kitchen, in the days when as a little child I shared it with father and mother. In a half-light full of shadows, the curtains were closing in on me, brushing my face. I turned my head to look out through a chink where two edges barely met, aware of the silvery shimmer of a winter dawn, expecting to see the rough kitchen table with its cracked oil-cloth cover, and beyond it the shallow earthenware sink, and above it the grimy window panes dimly showing the dark slate roofs of the tenement on the other side of Warwick Street. Instead, I saw a dressing table hung with close-pleated flowered silk down to the deep pile ivory carpet, with an array of silver-topped bottles on it, and beyond, through large window panes – clear but bearing the ghostly mark of the night's frost – a fairy tracery of branches picked out in white rime, just beginning to be touched by the delicate watercolour pink of the awakening sun. Rachel stirred beside me, shifted closer so that her face fitted into the hollow of my shoulder, murmured something, and slept on.

And so I lay in this magic bed of silk, pauper into prince, suspended in wonder, her breathing the distant suspiration of waves heard in a sea shell, her breast gently rising on my ribs and softly subsiding, a caress lovingly repeated; a still moment between two fragments of time, of revelation, of awareness. Life was taking yet another great leap into the unknown, as on the day, a century ago, when I ripped open that first letter from Oxford, or in the gleams of new certainty that came and went in this new life.

For the very first time it seemed, I tried to look emotion in the face – how juvenile that sounds – and yet it was probably true. Desire and sentiment had always masqueraded as one and the same. Now, sated from the night, I could attempt to see them apart. Love, happiness, commitment, attachment – where was their place in the ebb and flow of lust?

The natural vigour in the venial sin...

And where did calculation – the enemy of love I had always thought – have its place, as it seemed to have in other people? Here I was, so close to Rachel that her flesh was part of me, how could I think of her – of us – so coolly? Alec had said I must learn to be callous; was this what he meant? I was detached as I had never been with Annie, and that *must* be wrong. Love alone should be real – the world an enigmatic mirage.

What alchemy of the soul had taken me back to that kitchen bed – where mother had died – to re-affirm the indelible stamp of that other life? What *was* this message from the Kindly Ones?

I recalled another dawn long ago, when I had awakened with Annie in that broken Roman embrasure on Carbeth Muir, a silken moment too. Then I thought of the moment on the factory steps when she told me we were finished – in effect, that my 'prospects' were not good enough. I waited for the wound to hurt freshly once more, as it had done unfailingly before. Instead the vision receded, lost its sharpness. The pain was no more than a contrived memory. The time would come when even that would slide away and only mourning remain, to be transmuted in the end into simple regret.

And what of this, joined with her, flesh breathing with flesh in this silk-curtained bed – would this exaltation fall away in its turn? And others, each in a fashion also incomplete, follow after?

About a hundred yards from the house, at the base of the hillock we had skirted when we arrived, we entered a copse, the path twisting through shrubbery and spreading oaks. Rachel stepped confidently ahead, and soon we stood before an old stone door-way set into the rising turf, flanked by Doric columns supporting a classical pediment. We entered a bunker equipped as a last refuge from the irresistible devastation from the air that was talked about in the press as the dominant feature of the next war – the bomber would always get through – no place in town or country would be immune. Here were rooms with desks and type-writers, telephones and teleprinters; there were Spartan sleeping quarters, food stores, water from an underground spring, fuel supplies, a generator.

She said: 'Papa's main business will move down to the house when war comes. But he's hoping that if air raids don't get here too often the staff can work mostly *above* ground. The old stables at the back are being got ready for that. They'll live in the house and in cottages round about.'

The room was cold and still as a tomb. Beneath the harsh neon light, its infernal hues relentlessly flickering, her features were drained of colour; or was the cause within her? Forlornly she looked about, her lips moving as if she whispered a prayer. Perhaps a benign spirit, guardian of the earth that pressed down upon us here, would pronounce a reassuring spell?

Feverishly her words tumbled out: 'I don't *want* to believe this. You saw those black boxes – fireproof storage for the records papa's had photographed and brought down. That shows you where we really *are*? What's the use of dreaming any more? What future is there to plan for? Oh God in heaven, there *is* no time left. No time at all.'

The place was awesome in its cold stillness, its sense of anticipa-tion, its readiness for the last trump. There was nothing new in the message, only that there was no further retreat. Here under a green hill in the heart of England, in a meticulously planned business fortress waiting to outface the collapse of the known world, pretence crumpled. The savage promise of the times would *not* pass us by, or mercifully strike others instead.

'Let us be happy in each other,' she murmured. 'Let us imagine that time stands still. We might only have days, weeks, a few months at the most. What is there to lose? Nothing. Oxford? My God, at a time like this how can you even think about that?'

On the face of it she was right. But it was easy for her. For children of the boss class, Oxford was nothing more than a playtime interval, a place, or rather a state of mind, in which to drift in pleasurable experiment – a shadow play till you made up your mind to face the real world. For me? Were there any words to explain it? – a pilgrim's progress, though to what salvation I had no idea.

She raged at me, but tenderly. 'That's all for nothing *now*! Don't you see? And for heaven's sake don't worry about money. You're clever, you'll get a job. Papa will help when he's faced with it. Anyway, I've got money of my own. Dearest, there's so little time!'

Ah yes – to be a *kept man*? The respectability principle of the Gorbals, honoured even while necessity enforced its betrayal, stared at me pitilessly. Many men in the Gorbals, in bad times, had been just that; but no one dared criticise, for who knew where hardship would strike next? But in her class, being a kept man seemed neither uncommon nor particularly noteworthy; respectability was liberally interpreted; you did what you wanted to do – and your money *made* the rules fit.

Mean thoughts returned. What if the world did *not* crumble around us, and our idyll, confronting 'the long littleness of life', faded into nothing? Would *she* suffer as I would? Of course not; she would simply go back to papa and take up the pampered life as before. And I? What would I do, stranded – in some ways worse off than before?

I was humbled by these thoughts. I fancy she sensed them. There was no reproach, only sympathy, a kind of support. To *understand* was beyond her.

And so the insistent dialogue of lovers continued. Walking in the woods in the chill March air, or gazing into the log fire in the little sitting room, and later, back in Oxford on the windy towpath, we fought for answers – except that the fight was one-sided; for her there was simply the decision to be made and let the future look after itself, what was left of it. As for me, I fought with fear itself, without faith.

Marriage, of course, was not considered. After all, there was no need to, this was to be a trial marriage! It was *the* daring adventure. She mentioned marriage only in passing, as a distant possibility – 'something we could grow into'.

Again and again she wrestled with my financial fears, to her incomprehensible. One day she said: 'Listen, I am of age. I suppose I could settle something on you. I mean, to make you feel less dependent on me – and maybe to cope with emergencies? If it would make you feel better, I could get the lawyers to put it in some sort of trust?'

She said it from a good heart, but in sadness. Why could I not say, as she did, let's seize fulfilment while we can, and to hell with everything?

7

Philip Toynbee: the Soul-Mate Treatment

In spells of remission we would be happy for a few days; the lightning would strike once more, as likely as not from a clear sky.

On a blustery March afternoon we were on the river path leading to the Trout Inn at Godstow, a popular walk when work lay in the doldrums between lunch and tea. Strung out on the windy bank, dozens of couples walked close, or strode with hands linked and arms outstretched in confiding separation – exulting in love's conquest of the world. In warmer weather some might leave the path and wander to the far side of one of the fields that stretched away from the river; and there under a hedge, or the sand-coloured cobbled wall of ruined Godstow Abbey further along near the Trout, they would primly sit and commune.

We, too, floated along in our private world. Suddenly she broke the silence as if a dormant pain had burst into wakefulness and must be transferred at once. She struck at Werner, or appeared to; if it had not been for him, she said, 'I would never have got to know you at all.'

That, she implied, would have saved her much heartache.

I almost welcomed the chill bite of the wind that cut the face with the fine sting of a razor blade. It drove the steel grey water beside us into angry white-edged wavelets, with a crisp rustling sound like tearing paper. Beyond the river, on the distant edge of the empty steppe of Port Meadow, the sad poplars leaned down low. Was our case hopeless? Were our tempers so opposed that all effort at fusion must fail? If our coming together had been one of Destiny's false throws, perhaps our felicity was false too, not worth fighting to preserve? Or was this the dénouement Werner had warned me against: 'These *Hofjuden* can take you up, simply to satisfy their curiosity, and drop you – hard.'

I wanted to banish defeat from her mind. I told her of the day when I had seen her riding down the Broad with the others, in passion hurling 'Hatikvah' at the Trinity window where the swastika flag hung; and Werner, seeing I wanted her, brought us together.

The sun broke through in her again. She shook her hair in the wind, and murmured: 'Do you believe in Destiny?'

Oh that poignant question, asked all around us!

'We have to. For that matter, what brought Werner here?'

That might not be a happy way to put it, linking our happiness with that disaster for our people – for the world – which had brought Werner here. I had assumed that she knew he had been in Buchenwald. Amazingly she did not. On an impulse I decided to enlist sympathy for him. After all these months he was still waiting for the committee to decide whether he was to receive the research appointment. Werner was deeply European; to stay and work in England was important to him, a toehold in the culture. And now, giving up hope, he was making plans to join his family in America. Would her father intercede with the committee?

I did not understand that my impulse could be suspect, the selfish temptation to shift the course of someone else's life. I had still to learn that the Fates, in their refined irony, transmuted good intentions into the tragic, the grotesque.

She was moved, but I saw a shadow of something else, perhaps the guilt that fleetingly haunts the fortunate at such a moment.

Usually so quick, she did not reply at once, but walked on with head bent; then, speaking somewhat woodenly as if overcoming reservations, she said: 'All right. I'll speak to papa.'

She implied that her father would do what she asked. But her hesitation worried me.

She looked ahead along the path, eyes half-closed to the wind. Her manner changed suddenly, as if a blind was lifted, and her usual social gleam, the facile surface gloss, shone out. Coming towards us from the direction of Godstow was a tight little group, happily noisy, overflowing the narrow path on to the sparse grass at the side. Six girls, hair and scarves blowing, jostled round the tall saturnine figure of Philip Toynbee, in thick tweed jacket and flannels, dark hair standing on end in the wind, head intently inclined.

We were on the last stretch of the meandering path before Godstow, the Trout Inn a few hundred yards ahead on its spit of land beside the high arched bridge, and in front of it the weir, gate-like, that brought to mind the bridge on a willow-pattern plate, standing high and solitary in the swirling waters. A wooden farm gate stretched across the path before us, with a swinging wicket at its side nearest the water. Here part of the bank had fallen away taking a slice of the path with it, leaving a narrow ledge of wet and slippery earth that one crossed by gripping the post on which the wicket gate swung and taking a great step, almost a leap, across. The manoeuvre needed care, for with the collapse of the path the gate-post was unsteady in its few remaining inches of muddy earth at the water's edge. Philip and his companions came up as we passed through. Recognising me, his heavy features assumed the familiar rallying scrutiny, with just the hint of a smile – the commissar showing humanity. Perhaps to impress his girls, and possibly Rachel too, he launched into the aggressive banter then fashionable, whose aim was to 'wrong-foot' you into taking up an untenable position – in this instance political.

Philip could redeem a patrician flintiness with a convincing warmth and a highly developed sense of humour. When I had parried a few thrusts, he shook his head ruefully, more concerned not to lose face with the girls than with the substance, such as it was, of our exchange. 'Look,' he said, 'let's be serious. The proletariat is by nature politically conscious, and we've got to accept our responsibility in the fight against the fascists. If you don't come in now you'll be numbered among the class enemy when the time comes.'

'Did you say *we*? And *our* responsibility? Come off it, Philip, since when have *you* numbered yourself among the proletariat?'

Unusually for him, he was momentarily at loss. 'If only,' his expression seemed to say, 'I could *be* a proletarian for one moment, just to prove I mean all I say – the one attribute I lack?'

One of the girls, who wore heavy gold earrings in the form of the hammer and sickle, giggled at the notion of the proletarian Toynbee, then saw that she had struck a wrong note and hastily tried another: 'Oh Philip, do let's hurry. The crumpets and anchovy toast will be gone if we linger.'

Recovering, he looked at her in exaggerated horror: 'We mustn't miss that at any price, must we?'

He stood aside for them to stream past, and watched each girl point a foot and skip across the watery gap in the path and let the gate swing back for the next to follow. When they had all gone through he turned to me. 'All right, *touché*. But the point is this. We've entered a period of wars and revolutions – that's the Comintern analysis – and the logical place for a chap like you is in the Party. You've got a historical role in all this, don't forget. You and I must have a serious talk. I'm in Beaumont Street you know – do come in and see me. I must go now.'

Years later I would stand at the spot and see stretched before me along the path a straggling column of phantoms, weary *revenants* haunting their past. Each in a passion had faced the world hero-ically, and ardently striven to place a healing hand upon the future, and found that nothing of importance consented to be changed. I would see how truly, but with what poignantly twisted meaning, the words 'historic role' fitted them. That exchange with Philip, so symptomatic of the time, would return charged with its earnest-ness, its fervent but insecure hope, and in a mysterious way ritual-istic, as if we had uttered words written for us long before. It was hard to believe that anyone could have thought in Byronic images at such a time. We did feel that we were about to play roles in a world tragedy, the greatest ever known, but at the same time, con-fusedly, obstinately, even though we suspected that our entrances and exits were already written, we insisted that we could stand against the Fates and force them to yield – in *some* things at least – when the trumpets sounded.

When Philip and his party had gone, and we were plodding along the muddy path to the Trout, Rachel sniffed: 'How *dare* he hector you like that? Serious talk indeed!'

Philip had gone down about a year before, but he was still much in evidence. He had enjoyed power through the Party, and the thrill of continuing to do so, through friends still up as well as in his own right – apart from continuing a hectic emotional life – drew him back.

An especially magnetic facet of that power, where a Party mandarin was at the centre of a spider's web of manipulation, was control of the 'marking' – convert cultivation – of students thought worth 'bringing in' as Party jargon had it, as into a sacred community of the elect. A Party member, chosen for compatibility with an intended recruit – the target – would be ordered to make his acquaintance and try to become friends with him. The target would not know that he had been chosen. The 'marker' would pretend that the relationship was one of soul-mates, an idea that had a powerful appeal in a generation for which Pater's hard gemlike flame still held enchantment. Progress would be reported to a special committee, which would guide the marker through the changing subtleties of the Party line, and tell him how to overcome emotional or intellectual stumbling blocks. The Party leader, or one of the leadership group – sometimes called the Peckwater Gang because several of its members had rooms in the Christ Church quad of that name – would decide when the marker should reveal that he was a Party member; and, later, when the moment was ripe to invite the target – often with a baleful emotional ultimatum – to 'come in'.

If the marking had been skilful, an appeal to the target's sense of historic purpose, dizzyingly attractive to the romantic spirit in that tense time, could usually be relied upon to sweep away remaining doubts. Post-war revelations about the Cambridge traitors suggest, not surprisingly, that a similar soul-mate method was used to recruit them.

If the ultimatum failed, the target would be invited to a 'serious talk' with a leading member of the Party. Often this would be Philip, who enjoyed the role of spiritual guide; perhaps it helped to allay his own hunger for certainty.

The words 'a serious talk', with their overtones of familial concern, the strong hand of support on the shoulder, were intentionally misleading; they were code for 'We will *make* you see the light'. Sensing this, a nervous undergraduate worried about the state of his soul could find the prospect alarming as he made his way to Peckwater, blind to the grace of the façade, finding its patrician seclusion menacing, to face a Party mandarin, fluent and steely, sitting behind a green-baize table like an examining magistrate.

Philip gloried in personifying the Party's ethos of paternalism and menace. If, when the time came, it was in the Party's interest to send someone to the firing squad, he said, he would do so without hesitation. In him there was an irreconcilable conflict between the dreamer with his shifting visions of the quest for utopia, and the man of action hungry for simplistic belief on which the trumpets could confidently ring and the banners fly. Hence the attraction of Marxism's seeing elegance and symmetry. Being a revolutionary, for his upper-class coterie of the far left, was an élitist game in which, as when playing soldiers in the nursery, *they* must naturally be the commanders; and with total assurance they took it for granted that after the Revolution the top places would again be theirs. It was an assumption that made them more ruthless than many true proletarians.

To be fair, Philip had more sensitivity than many of them. That attribute, allied to a questioning tendency that Party discipline only temporarily held in check, would in the years to come lead him away from its narrow absolutism. Then, in sadness and some confusion, he would seek in vain a substitute for the old certainty – in founding a commune, for example – with which to regain the lost glory of spiritual leader.

In those passionate Oxford days, his could be a refreshing spirit. He could make you feel that in the next moment, with the very next word, you might change the world. He had come close to it in our exchange on the river path. We must cry *'no pasaran!'* to the fascists all over again. We must choose between nemesis if we sided with the forces of evil – in effect if we did nothing – and retribution from the Party when, after victory at the barricades, power was in its hands. That was not really a choice at all, a confusion that was not typical of him. Perhaps he had been distracted by the adoration of his band of admirers, but that too was unlike him. Franco *had* passed. Mussolini and Hitler *were* going from strength to strength. In country after country the Leninist 'revolutionary situation' which the party must bring about and then manipulate to obtain power – in Spain, Czechoslovakia, Greece – had been a mirage.

Rachel said, 'Philip is quite sweet in a *louche* sort of way. One simply can't *believe* he's as ruthless as he pretends.'

At the Trout we stood for a few minutes on the stone steps at the end of its promontory, the river at our feet noisy as a millrace. A short distance off, in a twelve-foot dinghy stopped near a submerged tree root, was Bill Challoner, another Party mandarin, son of a rich landowning house. I had recently taught myself to sail such a craft, renting it at the sailing club, and the thrill of the wind's power, the pulse of the elements felt in the vibrations of the sheet, was a spiritual revelation like the one on the tennis court. In our progress along the path I had watched him reaching smoothly up the river, and wondered idly how he would manage the return trip. Sailing up river on this stretch, the wind was usually astern, and took you here more or less on a straight course; but to get back down river demanded an athletic tacking back and forth hard into the wind, and you made distance in short zig-zags across the narrow channel.

Bill had brought the boat up with a fierce slapping of the sail. Now he braced himself across the stern seat and went about, and with a thwack the little sail filled, and he took the boat across, wavelets rapping on the timbers, to within a few feet of the opposite bank. He came up with what must have been only inches of depth to spare, went about smartly and tacked and sailed back again – and so, back and forth, shifting his weight from one side of the little boat to the other in precise timing for the turn, he went swinging away down river.

In our separate silences we turned away from the noisy rush of the waters and went into the Inn. The low-beamed parlour, hung with clammy river air, felt grey and cold. In the wide stone hearth a pile of resinous logs crackled and spat, and smoky flames rose, fell back, rose again, trying hard to dry the air. I went to the tap room window and ordered tea and hot crumpets. Rachel stood on the hearth stone and shook her hair loose, but did not stretch her hands to the fire, though her knuckles had been chilled blue through the red woollen mittens. There was a new, indefinable tension in her.

Dully she said, not looking at me, 'I'll get papa on the phone.'

In a mysterious association of ideas, as I stood contemplating the smoky flames, I had a vision of Alec, earthy, stoical, at his place at the other side of the pressing-table. What would he think of my life here – sailing on the river, the exchanges with Philip, Rachel immeasurable distances removed from Annie or Bunty, my stumbling efforts to unlock the codes of this place?

She returned and joined me on the hearth. Her father had been shocked to hear that the committee had kept the distinguished scientist waiting so long. He would speak to the chairman.

'Werner will get his appointment.'

She stood only inches away from the fire, and shivered. 'You wondered why I hesitated to speak to papa? Werner doesn't seem to be pining for his wife, does he? That's why. Never mind. I've done it for *you*.' She spoke with unfamiliar gloom, with a kind of resignation.

The change was baffling. Sophisticated, tough in a fashion, was she reverting to an ancestral type? I had a vision of mother from long ago, and heard her tired tones when father had come home skint and she must rush out to the pawnshop to rescue him. It was not a parallel at all, but in feeling it was close enough. Why had I been so insensitive?

In getting her father to intercede for Werner had she really gone against her principles? Or was this seeming resurgence of Mrs Grundy simply a woman's 'fancy idea', as Alec might have called it, a tactic in manipulation? With thoughts of permanence with *me*, did she hope to place contamination as far away as possible? Werner's infidelities, she was saying, cancelled his sufferings. He deserved no help, no sympathy.

Like everyone else around us she had always talked flippantly about morals. I had failed to sense the conventional prejudices strongly in place beneath. And now they had surfaced as feminine solidarity with a wronged woman.

How could I have foreseen all this? Yet I should have done. I had no excuse. I needed to find so many answers! Where, with whom, would I find them?

For the first time since I had left the Gorbals I longed for the pace of experience to slow down.

> Farfalla in tempesta,
> Under rain in the night …

I thought of *L'Education Sentimentale*. When would mine truly begin? I was a greenhorn, stumbling, falling, where others floated so confidently. Would I ever draw level with them?

A week or so later, Werner was bubbling over with his news. 'Can you believe it? I had just got my passage confirmed, and now the committee have written to say I have the appointment! And so now I must go into reverse and get my wife and children over here, which should not be hard because most people are going in the opposite direction! God knows if this is the right thing I'm doing.'

Fearfully, without knowing why, I echoed the question.

The day would come when I would curse myself for a blundering busybody. Time and events would have shifted, and perspectives with them, their significance hidden, but in retrospect painfully predictable. Waiting lists for Atlantic passages would lengthen. By the time Werner's wife and children embarked for Britain, war would have come. Werner would be interned in the Isle of Man as an enemy alien, and for that he cursed the whole world; how could they do that to *him*, a persecuted Jew from Buchenwald? While there, his wife and children would be killed in one of the early German hit-and-run raids. Shortly afterwards he would be released and return to Oxford for secret war work – but still, as he put it with a spark of his old irony, 'with them but not *of* them; the eternal fate of the Jew.'

I never dared tell him that I had meddled in his destiny – with goodwill as I had thought at the time, but in truth arrogantly. I should have consulted him first. Others had been punished in my stead, and their fate would haunt me in nightmares of blood.

Perhaps, after all, Rachel *had* been right? Someone must always suffer. Perhaps Werner was punished, if that was the right word, justly? These questions would never be answered. I would never silence the guilt. The sure touch that others possessed – as I thought – and which I so envied, would remain tantalizingly out of reach.

8

Ashenden's World

I was never given the soul-mate treatment. But I cannot be sure.
The Byzantine world of the Party was the one bit of Oxford life in
which I thought I knew my way. Bernard had illuminated the
Party's ways for me, but there was much he had left obscure, perhaps in self-preservation, especially the indistinct area where agitprop shaded away into secret work. The Party's intelligence was
good. When I first set foot in Oxford the mandarins were aware of
my links with the renegade Bernard; they must have concluded that
in some respects I knew too much. Their approach was therefore
more direct, invitations to front organization meetings for Spanish
refugees, to join study groups on Fascism – but never, significantly,
any effort to oppose Mosley's anti-semitism. Now and then one of
the mandarins buttonholed me. Why didn't I come in? With my
proletarian background, was I not better equipped for a leading
role than even some of them might be?

One encounter, seemingly without a hint of politics, took a
course that in wildest fantasy I would never have foreseen.

Bill Challoner was tall and slender, with sharp features, lank fair
hair drooping over a high forehead, and deep blue watchful eyes.
He was neither the demagogue nor the Marxist theoretician; indeed he appeared to have no interest in doctrine. Quiet-spoken, attractive, courteous, a person of long tranquil silences, of the apt
word at the chosen moment, his forte was deceptive charm. From
one of the older public schools he had come up to read modern languages, and was in his final year; he intended to follow an older
brother into the foreign service. Would his Party card be an obstacle there, I once asked him. He found the question amusing: 'Of
course not! The family's connections are quite sound.'

I met him occasionally at the sailing club, where I regularly took out a dinghy for a shilling. One day, when I was at the little wooden office at the moorings about to book a boat, he sauntered up. He was taking out his brand new fourteen-foot International for the first time – would I care to join him? I had never sailed this big-canvassed dinghy, designed for racing; indeed it was odd to see one here at all, for it was too fast for this narrow piece of Oxford water. Still, the invitation was a compliment; club members must have noted my fledgling ability with approval.

We strolled along the gently swaying raft beneath the leaning trees to its far end nearest the channel, and there the slim brown boat gleamed in the slanting sun of the waning day, the roped-down canvas glassy with newness. Bill stood aside to let me be first aboard; a little breathless I stepped on to the untrodden duckboard and felt the adhesion of new varnish under foot.

There was a momentary stab of envy. To buy this new boat and indulge a whim, Bill had spent more than I ever earned in the factory in a whole year.

We raised sail, the new cordage running grittily in spite of its wax, and shoved off from the raft. We swayed and drifted slowly in the brown shallows dappled with long splashes of sun low in a sky streaked with lavender. The mainsail flapped stiffly, then seemed to draw to itself the gently moving air and half-filled; the sleek shell rocked uncertainly, hesitated, went ahead and stayed and went ahead again, then as the canvas caught a stronger surge of air, moved confidently forward with a knock and chuckle of water, as if the craft were talking to the wind and the river. Away from the sheltering trees we skimmed over ripples dancing with gold. Dun-coloured banks and meadows of somber winter green drifted by; and so, dreaming, we were wafted up river. Near Godstow, seeing the lavender in the sky darkening to grey, we decided to start back immediately, for though the wind remained light, tacking in the narrow water, in an unfamiliar boat in full darkness, might bring us badly foul of the bank.

Remote from the world in the descending darkness, we set about tacking back and forth, alert to bring the sprightly craft up and about smartly, working together with precision, hardly speaking.

We beat back with only a few gentle groundings, when we mis-judged the boat's power and were too slow in bringing her up and round for the next in the long succession of acute zig-zags.

The sky had lost all light when we steered for the narrow chan-nel where the moorings lay, close to the lines of pollarded willows, their knobbed heads drooping meditatively in the obscurity. The night breeze freshening, we took in the mainsail, and with slack-ened jib she had enough way to bring us in steadily through ebony water flickering eerily with dulled reflections of distant lights. The line of masts at the moorings, ghostly in the darkness, slid into dim definition against gleams of paleness filtering between the trees. I took in the jib, and with our remaining way Bill brought her gently alongside the raft. We tied up, secured canvas and cordage and made all tidy and fast, retreating step by step, reluctantly, from the magical converse with the river.

Hungry, chilled by the clammy river air, we went back to his rooms for tea, talking little. Only as we neared his staircase did it occur to me that I had spent about two hours with a Party man-darin, and not a word of politics had been spoken. Then the spell of the river returned, and this passing curiosity faded.

His first-floor rooms, lofty, with floral plasterwork in white and gold in cornices and on walls, looked out over splendid lawns. We drew chintz-covered chairs close to the cracking coals in a tall fire-place of green marble. His scout, a tubby man in black alpaca jacket, with close-cropped white hair and the canny eyes of the old soldier, bustled in with a large brass-handled tray bearing a silver tea-pot, anchovy toast and fruit cake, the cups and saucers and plates embellished in gold leaf.

In the languid manner that suggested only a fleeting interest in the matter in hand, Bill mentioned an essay he had just written, on Goethe and the Romantic Movement. As it happened, I was in-tensely interested in the Romantics at this time, that explosion of creative thought so inadequately explained in reading and in lec-tures. We talked of French and German poetry. Surprisingly he knew that in addition to my main studies then – economics, politi-cal theory, philosophy, psychology – I had tutors in French and

German. It was not difficult to discover what a student was reading, and with which tutor, but it would take a little trouble. Someone in the Party had gone to that trouble. Why? It might have been routine. Or perhaps it was a subtle, charming nicety on Bill's part, to find an interest we had in common, so that conversation might be free of politics?

My French tutor was the eccentric Mademoiselle Fleury, who dressed *comme matelot* in flared navy blue trousers, zephyr and rope sandals, always with a Caporal drooping from her lips, the first avowed lesbian I had ever met. I read German poetry with the aged, charming Fraulein Wüschak, sometime governess in the Kaiser's family. Dressed in many layers of dusty velvet and gold brocade, she shared her Walton Street house with eighteen cats. Her manner, belying the cheery, rounded aspect of a good grandmother in a Grimms' fairy tale, was old-world and firm. If, struggling to say something in German, I took refuge in even a single word of English, she would not answer but prodded the air reprovingly with her cigarette in its long amber holder; I knew she would not relent – it was a matter of honour – until I conjured up enough German to fit. When I entered her dusty study, several cats squabbling fiercely about my ankles, she greeted me in the courtly fashion of a great lady in a gilded drawing room: 'Ah the young Herr Doctor!'; and I would think of the times when, as I stepped into the great arched reading room of the Mitchell Library in my ragged shorts or shabby working clothes, the staff murmured to one another 'Here comes the young professor.' Not much had changed.

With Mademoiselle Fleury that morning I had been struck by some lines in Ronsard's 'Sonnets pour Hèlàne', bittersweet barbed, that drove home a feeling I had recognised and resisted long before, a sense of the intransigent flux of life, unappeasable in the midst of sweetness – intimations of mortality, of transient triumph. I tried out the thought on Bill:

> Quand vous serez bien vieille, au soir, à la chandelle,
> Assise auprès du feu, dévidant et filant,

Direz, chantant mes vers, en vous émerveillant,
Ronsard me célébrait du temps que j'étais belle.

He thought about it: 'It's too late then isn't it? Don't you feel that
the blunt sentiments of "Gather ye rosebuds while ye may" are
much nearer the mark?'

He started and looked at his wrist-watch, and almost in a single
movement jumped to his feet, seized some papers from his desk,
and was at the door: 'My God, I should be reading my essay this
very minute! My dear chap, I do apologise. You *must* stay and finish the toast and so on, won't you?'

The door slammed. A moment later it swung open and he put his
head round. 'A friend of my brother's may pop in. Interesting chap.
Bit of a globe trotter. Make my apologies to him, will you? Oh, by
the way, he's obsessional about privacy so he'll sport my oak.'

The oak, an additional outer door to a set of rooms, usually
stood open, latched back against the stairhead wall; when closed –
sported – it was a 'Do not disturb' notice.

I turned back to the fire, picked up the shiny steel poker and
pushed it between the horizontal bars of the fire basket and raked
the coals and watched new flames, yellow streaked with grey and
blue, lick through the dull red interstices to the top. I thought about
'rosebuds ...', and looked round at the magnificence of Bill's state.
A walnut bookcase, diamond-glazed, held leather bound books
tooled in gold with the family crest. A row of silver beer mugs
gleamed on the mantelpiece. Walking sticks with handles of ivory
or silver protruded from a cylindrical stand of ebony struts bound
with broad silver hoops. A gun case peeped out from behind the
mahogany desk. On a sideboard a silver-mounted tantalus, with
crystal decanters of whisky, sherry and brandy, stood next to a
cigar box inlaid with silver. Here was no shortage of rosebuds.

Insistent at the back of my mind, there had been a question
about this encounter. Despite the charm and the shared interest,
and the avoidance of politics, had there been an ulterior motive
after all? Diffidently, I still thought of these leading figures as being
purposeful in all they did, every word and action aimed at a target.

Had I missed an inner meaning somewhere? Could this be a new, indirect approach? Rosebuds. Take what is on offer while you can. Pleasures of the flesh and the fleshpots. But where was the connection with the Party?

The speculation was not fanciful. The Party's conspiratorial ethos, familiar to *me* – and suspect – ever since Bernard's return from Spain, was meat and drink to the initiates in the university; for some of them, I felt, it was a prime attraction, joining them to a secret army of salvation. Certainly, Party mandarins were fond of speaking and acting in a style that echoed John Buchan and E. Philips Oppenheim. However, as we can now judge from parallels in Cambridge, it was not always play-acting.

I refilled my cup and cut a slice of the fruit cake, rich, glutinous, perfumed with brandy. There was a sound behind me. The door swung open, and I heard the solid click of the oak being shut. A dapper man in his thirties came in, nodded a greeting, turned and quietly closed the inner door. Lean-faced, tanned, with smooth fair hair, blue eyes, he moved with the relaxed poise of the good games player. He was dressed well but quietly in grey double-breasted suit of good cut, white shirt with fashionable semi-stiff collar, dark blue tie, shiny black shoes. In the university milieu, one might take him for one of the younger dons; in the commercial quarter of a city, a rising young bank official. In either setting you would pass him by without a second glance.

He introduced himself as Peter Pastern, the manner recalling Bernard's clipped soldierly style after Spain. Seated in the chair opposite, he helped himself to tea and toast. The tray, I now noticed, had been set for three.

'Heard about you,' he said. 'Come to think of it, I ran across a Glasgow chap in Spain you might know, name of Bernard Lipchinsky.'

'What were you doing there?' It seemed obvious that he had not been on the Republican side.

He did not answer but concentrated on cutting a large piece of cake and with a hand under it to catch falling crumbs, transferring it to his plate.

Settled into the deep chair, in the easy manner of someone bringing an old friend up to date with his doings, he talked of wanderings in India, Africa, the Middle East, apparently the patrician traveller; but there were hints of imperial *realpolitik*, of the interest of people in high places. Some quality, a magnetism, something supremely self-contained about him, recalled Jimmy Robinson at the socialist camp at Carbeth, charismatic veteran of the Wobblies, with his faith in salvation for the workers through bomb and gun. There was the same kindliness paradoxically joined to ruthlessness in pursuit of a cause, above all the same wonderful certainty that had drawn us young disciples across Carbeth Muir on those summer nights long ago – not so long ago! – to Jimmy's general store in the old bus body under the oak tree, to sit at his feet. Only the cause these two men fought for was different.

Deferentially, the green Candide, I waited for the chance to ask how he had come to meet Bernard, how he knew of my friendship with him, and of my Gorbals history. Skilfully, firmly, he seemed to anticipate the questions and blocked them in advance.

He refilled his cup, and sat back and looked at me appraisingly, blatantly so, wanting me to know it.

What he now proceeded to unfold, in careful stages, was so unexpected, so momentous, at once shocking and exhilarating, that I was torn away from all earlier thinking, and I knew I could never return – as when I had opened the scholarship letter from Oxford. Engraved on my memory I can hear his voice still.

The full intention did not strike home at once. He began with hints.

I keep a look-out, he said, for chaps with special talents for special work. Your Gorbals background makes *you* special. Here in Oxford you're crossing the class divide and you'll *never* make your way back. But you have brought with you a fund of rare knowledge, I should say understanding, about the other side, that could make you worth your weight in gold – in the *right job*. And the rewards are high. I happen to know people who could use you. But I must be sure. So we shall need to talk a lot more.

I tried to appear blasé, to hide shock. Among the possible meanings, one was clear, a vision magically made real – the first sign that my coming to Oxford might earn me a better living than I had left behind in the Gorbals; my achievement at last measurable! Here, thrown at my feet by a quirk of fortune, could be the answer to what was poisoning the hours with Rachel.

Were it not for her insistent entreaty to set up house with her, it would have been easy to continue to postpone all thought of what I would do for a living after Oxford. Absorbed in this new life, tasting freedom, all curiosity enjoying free rein at last, there was time enough, surely, two years at least? Sometimes I caught myself trying to copy the carefree attitudes of the others round me, and reminded myself that I lacked the cushioning *they* possessed – secure signposts, links to some vocation, the services, the law, the City, the landed interest. To the question: 'What are you going to do when you go down?' they could unhesitatingly say 'I am *going* to do ...' instead of the uncertain 'I *hope* to do ...' It was hard not to envy them.

In these last weeks, trying to cast my thoughts so far ahead had been depressing. Where should I begin, what aims should I have, what must I offer to an unknown market? In the Gorbals vocabulary, 'career' had only an ironic meaning, if it had one at all. Notions of a career had no place in the mission that Bernard's dying father had handed to me, to carry the torch of enlightenment. I was haunted by that last scene in the Lipchinskys' kitchen, the old man bravely sustaining hope, battling with disappointment, coughing blood. I was a fortuitous Hamlet wrestling with that blunted purpose, and now fearing it. I now *knew* that I lacked the certainty it demanded – as I had even then dimly suspected. I had been born with too many doubts. The more I read and pondered and talked far into the night, the more the unanswered questions taunted me:

> ... but evermore
> Came out by the same Door wherein I went.

There was a comic irony in this puzzlement over *what* to do. I did have a choice! In my simplicity that came as a shock; I remembered with shame my enraged response, a new arrival here, to Crossman's question, 'Why do people work?' – when I had said 'Because they'd starve if they didn't.' One day I would have to summon the courage to go to him and apologise. Oh yes, I knew so much more now. Nothing would ever be as black and white as I had hoped.

Pastern must surely know a lot about me to be able to say 'you're crossing the class divide'. I was not aware of doing that, except superficially. It seemed to me that I possessed only a provisional identity on this side of the divide – the boss class side – given me by this place. As Alec had foretold, I was here on sufferance, tolerable only if I steeled myself not to think about it. Pastern, in making that remark – airily, but with sympathy – had touched on a question that I shrank from thinking about, even in the most searching moments at dead of night: what *had* I come here for?

Leaving aside the fulfilment of fantasy, romantic dreaming, the lure of adventure, I really had no idea. To change into another person? Very well, what was the change to be, from the ragged, directionless Gorbals boy – to what? The questions 'who', 'what' were unanswerable, especially 'who'. Yet if I could not answer them I could answer nothing of importance. It would be years, too late perhaps, before I understood that 'who' was in truth the *only* important choice life asked you to make – if choice it was.

Yet surely the day must come when I did know *who* I wanted to be, and therefore *where* I wanted to go? Till then, whatever Pastern offered, why look at it too closely? Take it with both hands and be glad of it!

With remarkable appropriateness, that very morning had brought yet another revelation. A letter from Bernard had come. Bernard wrote few letters. The man of action preferred to send laconic signals. If he unburdened himself, it was in speech, forced out of him, settling accounts with himself – and then, like a soldier who has halted on the march, he shouldered his burdens once again and trudged on. Here, then, at a distance, being forced to write at length, the occasion must be momentous. Yes. His father was dying.

I was drawn back to that last meal in his house, while I was still not sure whether I dared take up the Oxford scholarship. Even then the saintly old man was sinking, coughing blood. Master cutter, aristocrat of the tailoring craft and paragon of the working-class intellectual, he had striven all his frail life for his faith – gentle anarchism. He was writing a great work on the subject, knowing them that he would never finish it. At the thought of my going to Oxford I remembered how his eyes had blazed in vicarious glory, for in me he saw *himself*, and what he might have been; and surely now, he silently said – appealing to me – I would take up the torch of human betterment that he must lay down?

'He keeps talking about you,' Bernard wrote. ' "What is he doing; where has he got to?" For God's sake, what does he expect of you? Of any of us? How can I tell him what's happening to the world? It hurts to see him dying in delusion, but if there was nothing I could tell him when he was strong, what can I say to him now? Well, he's had his run. He's done his best – I suppose. That's all there is to be said. My heart tells me that it's just as well he doesn't see what's coming; after all he's done, after all his hopes.

'Now listen to me. I don't want you to come back here for the funeral, d'you hear? You *must not* waste the time and money. Things are moving so fast, your time there may be short. Anyway funerals don't benefit the dead and I've seen plenty of death, as you know. All that talk of respect for the dead! I wonder what any of it means. What you didn't give them in life it's too late to think about. What the living get out of a funeral God alone knows – maybe settling scores with themselves? Maybe thanking their stars that *they* are still alive?

'I've got to come down to London soon. I'll come and see you.'

My first reaction was relief – and I would remember it forever with shame. I would never have to admit to the old man that I had failed him. Perhaps he already guessed, hence his anxious questions about me? Never again would I have to look upon that sadly slender figure, in the finely tailored clothes that those long spatulate fingers had sewn, the lofty brow crowned with bushy white hair, dreamy eyes probing straight through me to his distant vision. He was too gentle a soul ever to have reproached me, but I would have felt the hurt within him. I knew that I would think of him often in the years ahead, and guilt would return.

Bernard's harsh tone, hand in hand with his grief, shocked me at first. And then I understood. The desperation of the time scourged us both. Perhaps we *were* more sensitively attuned than others? We were not aware of that. In youthful imagination we saw ourselves, and our feelings, as symbolic of the age. We did feel the weight of the world on our shoulders. We knew each moment to be of epochal significance. We viewed everything *sub specie aeternitatis*. And Bernard, therefore, from within the ruins of *his* beliefs, could contemplate his father's life steadily only by traducing the faith that had blighted it, and which retained its meretricious hold even these his last days. And they might be the last days for all of us.

And then I did weep for the old man, for Bernard, for us all.

Had I been pretending all this time? No. I *had* tried to believe in the old man's gentle creed of perfectibility. Yet here I sat in this opulent room, the fruit of capitalist ruthlessness, and listened to Pastern's gospel with something like welcome in my heart, the relief of a tired wanderer seeing a sure landmark at last – devil take the hindmost, the voice of that Victorian bridge across the Clyde! I was telling myself that I no longer cared. How could I do that?

Bernard's desolate words burnt into me. Maybe there *was* nothing else? Maybe it mattered little if you tried to change *nothing*? If so, did choice matter? Yes it did; it must. But where? How? The answer would come. I must wait.

Pastern would not be pinned down. He needed more time. As he was in Oxford only briefly, would I dine with him that evening? We would meet in the lobby of the Clarendon Hotel. As I got up to go, he said 'I'll stay on for a few minutes – I must write Bill a note to say I'm sorry I missed him.'

Plainly he did not want to be seen leaving with me.

The Clarendon Hotel was a sedate place of mahogany and red carpet and dim yellow lighting, whose waiters, in shiny black suits recalled cartoons in old copies of *Punch*. I arrived punctually, but

seemingly too early. Pastern appeared at my side. I learned in subsequent meetings that he had a gift of materialising out of thin air.
'D'you mind if we don't dine here? I thought it might amuse you to
come to a club where I belong – we call it the Explorers. Limited
membership, simple but acceptable food, above all privacy!'

I wondered why he had not asked me to meet him there in the
first place – another secretive quirk?

We stopped at a doorway and pulled at an iron knob in the
brickwork, and far away in the depths a bell clanged and echoed.
Heavy footfalls thumped on stone steps within; a brass grill slid
back and was quickly shut. The door was opened by a large-faced
man of about forty in a dark suit, whose aspect suggested the ex-
boxer.

We went along a flag stoned corridor sombrely lit by electric candles on brackets high on the walls, hearing low voices from deep
within the building, up an austere stone staircase, and entered a
small square room with blackened beams, oak panelling, and buttoned leather benches against the walls. A shallow shelf running
round the room was lined with pewter beer mugs, each engraved
with copperplate initials, some with crests. Several square oak tables were laid, but I had a feeling that we were to have the room to
ourselves.

Pastern said: 'We've got hold of some audit ale. Care to join me?'

Idly I wondered how they had come by audit ale, only served, as
far as I knew, in college.

The ale was brought to me in a guest's tankard, the first time I
had ever drunk from silver. As the rim touched my lips, thin and
cold, the inner surface gleamed with an aloof, hermetic light. I
thought of the cracked enamel of the mug of tea that had been my
welcome at Jimmy Robinson's door under the oak tree at the socialist camp at any hour of the day or night – as uplifting as am-
brosia from the golden cup of Zeus himself. I had travelled a whole
world away, yet it seemed that I had not moved at all.

Yet I had. That evening brought further shocks, though at the
time they were muted – possibly by the potent audit ale, pungent,
faintly aromatic, dark as the river waters had been that afternoon.

Or perhaps the atmosphere of unreality, of miracles, that had attended my coming to Oxford, had lingered in my mind ever since, and taught me to be sparing of astonishment? I cannot remember being shaken – though I was when I thought about it later – when Pastern casually proposed that I should join the Communist Party and work within it, in secret, for the forces of law and order, in effect to become one of the Party's own favourite weapons, the 'underground member', in the fight against it! Ordinary decent men and women deserved to be protected against the poison in the body politic, and it was the duty – in fact a noble and historic vocation – of the honest man, men like us, privileged and with a sense of right and wrong, to do whatever was necessary to accomplish it. Some of the methods might appear dishonest, but used in a disciplined fashion for worthy aims, they were surely justified.

In the blink of an eye, unaware of the instant of transition, I had stepped through a magic mirror to find myself behind and beyond the façades of the known world where, between the shadows, was the ambiguous one of *Greenmantle* and *Ashenden*. I had been rubbing shoulders with it unawares. It seemed that it had been stalking me! And now, for its own mysterious reasons, it made itself known.

As he talked, I thought of Bernard in Spain, threading warily through that world of intrigue and double-meaning and danger, a vision I had accepted at the time but only in the abstract, something to be wondered at. It was a wonder no longer. It was the real world after all.

If I played my part well, Pastern said, the organisation he spoke for – not named, but linked in some way with government – would admit me into an élite body of men dedicated to defend the Englishman's liberties. When I went down, I would be found a job consistent with the 'underground' role; there would be travel, perhaps some glamour, good pay. Unfortunately my work would *always* be secret.

'Look,' he said, 'it's nearly end of Term and nothing much can be done during the vac. May I be frank? Money's tight with you I know. When you start with us next term, my budget allows me to advance you a hundred – in cash.'

He leaned back and watched it sink in.

I could live well on that hundred for a whole term and more. How easy things *could* be. My head was spinning with vision.

He leaned over. 'By the way, obviously you don't talk about any of this?' Unexpectedly he grinned: 'No one will believe you – and I can guarantee that you won't be madly popular with the authorities.' He shrugged. Enough of that side of it. Don't forget that hundred in cash.

Talk of betrayal made me think of Bernard's letter. I had betrayed his father's trust – whether through sloth or lack of faith made no matter – and that was bad enough. To join the Party and betray it for *money* was unbelievably worse. Apart from that sense of guilt, what retribution might come if I was unmasked! I felt the sweat of fear, sensing merciless forces closing in. Now, at last, I understood the fear that had stalked Bernard in Spain. This world of Pastern's gave off the rank smell of death.

I tried to steady my voice. 'When do you want to know?'

'I'll get in touch.' A hardness had crept into his voice. He rose: 'By the way, would you mind terribly if I asked you to find your way out? I have to make one or two telephone calls.'

I descended the monastic staircase, with a sense of invisible harness binding me to the room behind me. I heard the distant voices in the building but met no one, and was thankful.

I was desperate to talk to someone. Bernard was the only one I dared trust.

9

Beveridge: the Happiness Calculus

Sir William Beveridge held weekly court for selected students from various colleges. Though his hair, brushed flat and slanting across the forehead, was nearly white, with his fresh features, thin face and beaky nose, he contrived an air of youthfulness. With the same intention perhaps, and to offset the effect of a dark business suit, he often wore an informal striped shirt with attached collar, and an even more unconventional red tie. The tie, one suspected, was signal of solidarity with the forces of progress, a milder version of Crossman's sartorial slumming. Outwardly breezy, he was in essence the iron technocrat. He conducted the group's discussions in the manner of the commanding administrator he essentially was; he dealt with topics briskly like items on a packed agenda, speared each topic or problem with Mephistophelian glee, disposed of digressions or weak objections with a sharpshooter's panache – not that these were frequent, for the intellectual level was generally high – and with a final razor-sharp verdict tossed the item into an invisible 'Out' tray, and moved smartly on to the next.

As a reformer he was much more dynamic than G. D. H. Cole, but unlike Cole it was the administrative challenge of a social problem that was its prime attraction, justice less so; he had little patience with speculation about the long-term human effects of the solutions he favoured. Judging by his stock responses when such questions were raised, one suspected that he either did not understand them – unlikely for such a giant – or was no longer flexible enough to examine the received progressive wisdom. At bottom he was perhaps not truly a reforming spirit at all, but attracted far more by the virtuoso charm of achieving administrative excellence. He saw social problems with the eye of an engineer – as friction in the system. He lacked Cole's willingness to tailor policy to fit the imprecise philosophy of man. That was Cole's golden endearing quality; but alas it made it impossible for him to present simple solutions to anything, seeing too clearly that social mechanics alone could not address the complexities of human aspirations. That, of course, was far from being Cole's 'defect' alone – it was perplexity as old as man! The Thirties, however, was a tired epoch – people hungered for simple answers. So Cole had to decline as a prophet, as Laski would for similar reasons; and Beveridge's star would rise.

Beveridge must have had a premonition of his coming role as the high priest of welfare, for the subject figured large in our discussions. Green as I was, convinced still that a fine mind could always see clearly, it was hard to accept that he really did believe, with the early Fabians – as with Bentham – that happiness was *quantitative*, and could be created by bureaucratic fiat. Welfare was palpable and measurable; you produced it, and distributed it, as you produced and distributed shirts or shoes or bread.

One day, impatience overcoming awe, I asked him: 'If the system could be so easily organised to redistribute income, why do we have low incomes at all?'

Unusually for him, he paused to consider. I did not immediately realise that the pause was in part a rebuke; I had interrupted the élite game of social mechanics. He said: 'There are too many people with *low* marginal utility [the comparative value of their "product"], and too few with a *high* one!'

'You mean the "highs" will always have to hand over some of their earnings to the "lows" – a sort of charity? Why not organise society so that the "lows" produce more in value and so get paid more?'

'It is more complicated than that – levels of thrift and prudence, for example, enter into it. But, yes! You may be right – in the very long run. But that's like waiting for the Messiah! We must organise an efficient welfare system before it's too late.'

The boss class was fearful. The dam might break.

I was stung by his reference to prudence and thrift. Even now, as I write in 1987, suggestions that hardship among the lower orders results from their improvidence are made with caution, if at all.

Beveridge was speaking in academic shorthand, but the traditional sentiments of the boss class were there too, plainly shared by the others in the room. His words recalled the classic sneer in Glasgow at mention of better housing for the lower orders: 'If you gave them bathrooms they'd use the bath for keeping coal in!'

I persisted: 'Can't we *ever* level up?'

'I have my doubts.'

Surely, I wondered, even with massive transfers from 'highs' to 'lows', complete 'welfare as of right' could never pay for itself? The poor would always be less well provided for than the rich? The Poor Law principle of 'less eligibility' would remain. Beveridge seemed to think this would not be so. Not daring to put the question directly, I murmured under my breath: 'From each according to this ability, to each according to his need.'

J. P. R. Maud, later Lord Redcliffe Maud, then Dean of University College, sitting near me on the cushioned window seat, inclined his willowy form towards me and said smoothly, addressing me but facing Beveridge, 'I don't think Sir William is thinking of implementing Marxism by stealth, are you, Master?'

Maud was warning me to shut up, but I was too green to see it. He was right. Who was I to imagine that I could drive the great Sir William Beveridge into a corner?

'Of course not,' Beveridge retorted. 'That formula's impossible anyway. State welfare must pay its way.'

Tea was served in fluted Leeds china. Beyond Maud's head in the window seat, through the little square leaded panes, I saw the quad thronged with men returning from games, tired, slouching in mannered languor, their murmurings sleepy in the torpid air. Diffused sunlight bestowed on sleeping Cotswold stone a down of golden velvet. I wanted to correct this vision, cancel that insouciance which I could not share, inject reality, *my* reality. I tried to recall the factory, and feel the steam and the noise and the sweat – yes, and a fatigue quite different from that of the slouching games players in the quad. But I could not.

I looked round the panelled room, at the eager, lank-haired, well-nourished men in shining brown brogues and well-tailored tweeds and flannels, deferentially hanging on the great man's words. Beveridge caught my eye, and with a slight movement of the head beckoned me, at the same time disengaging himself from the courtiers. Pink face lit up by his thin, Cheshire Cat smile, but the hawk-like eyes watchful as ever, he took me aside, leaning towards me to exclude the others. 'I know how keen you are and it's a refreshing quality. But let me put the point beyond doubt. No one will get something for nothing – except in the "swings and roundabouts" sense. The aim is not to destroy inequality. That can't be done. Inequality will always be with us. It is, to put it bluntly, simply a more efficient method of *compelling* people to make wise provision for their own emergencies and for their future!'

Bernard was arriving that day on his promised visit. I felt as though the Gorbals, my old life, was coming to visit me, a meeting with my submerged self; and the prospect may have produced a recurrence of exile's fatigue, the strain of contending with the alien culture.

I wondered, with resentment, whether these smooth people round me, cosseted all their days, ever felt insecure? It was silly to be wounded by their settled attitudes and manners, their inability, or unwillingness, to meet me half-way. They might say, of course, 'Why should we? *You* came here to be with *us* – not the reverse!'

With Bernard I could share thoughts freely.

What would he think of Beveridge's dismissal of 'levelling up'? Bernard, I reminded myself, now the dedicated union official, must be fully committed to that gradualist route. Certainly the Party, typically vengeful towards an erstwhile leading member who had lost his faith, vilified him on that account as a reformist traitor to the working class.

No doubt he saw the irony of that – many ironies. In his Party days he had not scrupled to attack others in the same fashion. Beveridge's words, he would see, underlined a strange coming together. The Party and the boss class were united in opposing levelling up, the one for Machiavellian motives – the workers must not be allowed to believe they could get 'betterment' without bloodshed on the barricades – the other because of a different, ruthlessly realistic view of life itself; Beveridge would say the *only* honest one.

Beveridge breathed the optimistic but severely righteous middle-class air of the high Victorian epoch that had bred him. Born in Bengal into the proconsular tradition – his father had been a judge in the Indian Civil Service – he expressed inherited attitudes. You prescribed for the lower orders, as was your right and duty, but *your* team must remain on top! Life was necessarily hierarchical. Any other view was hopelessly impractical.

For old Mr Lipchinsky – Bernard's father – levelling up had been a visionary ideal, essential to his gentle Kropotkinian faith. For Bernard it lacked the revolutionary glamour of the faith he had lost; but until he could think of something better, it would have to suffice.

A different disturbance raged within me every hour of the day – thoughts of Pastern and his offer. A demon voice would not be silenced: 'Decide! Decide! Where's your courage?' Courage for what, to sell my soul? So Faust must have scourged himself to the brink. Zest for work and play vanished. Writing an essay took a whole day instead of a couple of hours. I read and re-read a page of a book for hours without absorbing a single word, sat up late and accomplished nothing, walked alone, endlessly, in the murmuring summer air by the green river; saw less of Rachel.

Pastern's proposal, that I should join the Party and work within it as a secret enemy, demanded a passion I did not possess; but what repelled me most about it was that I would have to feign beliefs, deceive people to win trust. When I thought about it, however, I had to ask myself: was I not doing exactly that here in Oxford, seeking acceptance by counterfeiting manners, attitudes, even values, that were not mine – walking among these people and yet not of their world? And never would be? Ah no! In such deception, if that was the right word, there was no hostile intent, as there was in Pastern's plan; the sole aim was to make *myself* understood, and in turn understand *them*.

These scruples, and others too, seem juvenile in retrospect, but they carried seeds of maturity. Pastern's offer of money, dizzying riches to me, stank of the corrupt values that repelled me in this place – boss class people poisoned by worldly ease, their arrogance founded on money. Yet that was the road I too would follow, if I agreed to work with him.

As for his threat, I tried to imagine how Meyer must have felt when the menodge men 'invited' him to join them, or else. What could Pastern do to me? Could he, as he had hinted, contrive a scandal that would get me sent down? Mrs Grundy's influence was still powerful, secretive and, of course, hypocritically selective. One felt it in the air. Reports ran through the junior common rooms with the speed of drums in the bush: Mr X had resigned his fellow-ship because packets of French letters were found in his rooms; Tony Y, brilliant student, had been sent down when his girlfriend's parents complained to his college that he was 'consorting with her immorally'. A few left-wingers, in transient rebellion against their class, murmured that his college might have taken a different view had his family been richer, or more elevated; preferably both. A case in point was Pippa, an aristocrat, who sat her Schools six-and-a-half months pregnant; her condition had been obvious, of course, for some time, but the story was put about that she concealed it so successfully that her college tutor remarked in hall, in seeming in-nocence, 'What strange clothes Pippa wears these days!' The van-dal excesses of the Bollinger would never have been tolerated if class and money had not given them protectors in high places.

I could look to no such natural allies here. Pastern could be re-lied on to invent a story the authorities would accept without ques-tion. He and his cohorts belonged to this system. They knew the ropes. I did not. I would be in a minority of one.

The summer term was well under way and still there was no sign, no word. Yet I sensed his presence. Any day, any moment, I ex-pected to turn a corner and meet him face to face, catch sight of him browsing in Blackwell's or strolling in Christ Church Meadow. Once, going into Fuller's tea shop in Cornmarket with Rachel, I glanced back and thought I saw the dapper form slide past the win-dow outside. At the sailing club, Bill Challoner greeted me affably and talked of many things – never politics! – but Pastern's name was not mentioned. Perhaps the whole affair had been a practical joke, and I would never hear of him again?

'You will,' Bernard said. 'He *always* means business. I wish I knew why he mentioned *me*.' He glanced round warily.

We were in a punt on the Cherwell, and had stopped in the Parks near the slender high-arched foot bridge. It was early evening, the river almost deserted. Slow water gleamed under slanting sun-beams in a vista of gently sloping green banks, tree-lined in the dis-tance. Frail curtains of sun-filled weeping willow hung low – scent of cherry and syringa. Distant voices and laughter and whispers floated down the stream. Sprites danced in the air. This world, surely contained no danger?

In the only other craft in sight, a punt some thirty yards away, a man in white flannels and long-sleeved white shirt lay on his back, his head propped up on the cushioned back-rest. His boater, with a dark blue ribbon, was tipped over his nose; an open book lay face down on his chest. He seemed to be asleep. The punt had been un-occupied when we moored. He must have been strolling on the bank and returned unnoticed. To my short sight, with so little of his face in view, he was no one I recognised.

Bernard studied the figure, then leaned over to me and whis-pered: 'Can you get this thing away from here quietly?'

I unhitched the leather strap from round the dug-in pole, swiv-elled the pole free and pushed away at right angles for a quick turn into the middle of the channel where the bottom was hard and one could pole strongly. He leaned back on his elbows on the buttoned cushion of brown moquette and watched me. The blue jowls wrin-kled: 'You've gone native, and no mistake!'

We drew in under the bank near the tennis courts where, it seemed years ago, I had first met Werner. Despite the lengthening shadows, the soft light now diffused, some courts were in use; the noise of play would be cover enough.

'Last time I saw him,' Bernard said, 'he had a moustache, but it's him all right. Still, it's worse *not* to know you're being tailed! What I don't understand' – he pushed out his lower lip – 'is that he's taken no trouble to conceal it. He *wants* us to know!'

Bernard's manner told me that he too needed to unburden.

Something had resurrected the deep bitterness he had brought back from Spain. I thought of that first talk soon after his return, on a cold morning in Castle Street with the pavements deep in half-melted snow, when by ironic chance we had sheltered from the sleet in a close a few yards from the Party offices. In the grey desperation of that Glasgow scene, the inferno of Spain possessed us both. Its tortured logic fitted. And now, even in this Elysian setting, unimaginable to me then, every word cut deep – deeper still, coming from a savage world beyond all understanding, all reason. You could not keep any of it at a distance, or turn away from it – the gratuitous cruelty of life, the seeming futility of care, defeat of the heart.

In Spain too, Pastern had trod the shadows; and in his own chosen time he had intervened. I began to see why he had mentioned Bernard to me. He wanted to emphasise his power – over us both.

The Republican intelligence network had taken note of Pastern's existence among the miscellany of foreign camp-followers, journalists, voyeurs, political busybodies, but could not decide whether he was simply another crank fishing in troubled water on his own account or, as Bernard concluded, a British agent. How had their paths crossed? Pastern had helped his escape!

Bernard still puzzled over that.

How Pastern knew he was on the run, Bernard never discovered, or so he said. Pastern's money accomplished many things. It found Bernard a hiding place, a little stone house – a herdsman's mountain shelter for the high pasture seasons – tucked away in wild country on the frontier. And it had found the girl to lead him there along ancient unmapped tracks, and hide him and feed him; and after many days in the cramped hut with him, waiting for another moonless night, to guide him across the heights into France. Pastern had been the unwitting catalyst. In those remote waiting days Bernard and the girl fell in love and were happy – despite the unceasing vigilance, the sense of implacable menace.

Night after night, awakening beside her in the pure crystal silence of the mountain, he weighed the temptation to stay – or to take her with him. They were held in a terrible balance. Pastern's money would protect him finitely. If he lingered beyond the allotted time he was doomed; that was certain. If she were caught with him she would die too. Go with him she *must* not; for that would reveal her part in his escape, and bring death to her whole family.

'*Et in Arcadia ego*' *spoke the skull.*

Why had Pastern, the dispassionate British agent, gone out of his way to save him, and at so much risk? In the confusion and fear and cruelty of the time, chance discovery, or more likely betrayal, were to be reckoned with at every step, their lives forfeit on the turn of a card, a jealous word, settlement of private scores. The only logical explanation was that Pastern, in the labyrinthine interests of the British secret service, was a fisher of disillusioned men.

Bernard muttered, 'I suppose Pastern's masters ordered him to fish *me* out – instead of other International Brigaders on the run – because a political officer was potentially more useful to them.'

If you agreed to serve them, I thought savagely, as Pastern wanted *me* to do? I could not bring myself to put the question.

Bernard must have sensed it. Abstractedly, he said, 'He got no promises out of me. Let's say I allowed him to hope! I'm not ashamed of that. I was fighting for my life.'

He dug a forefinger inside his shirt collar and scratched the bullet wound, moving the scar-tightened shoulder up and down, while he turned and once again scanned the green river and the leaning foliage. With his back turned to me, he spoke again, and the change in his voice shocked me even before I understood the words. 'A few weeks ago I got an unsigned note – I knew it was from him, don't ask me how; I just knew. All it said was: "There's been an accident. They got to her. I'm sorry." There was no need to tell me who "they" were. Even with the war lost, the Party looks far ahead. Retribution must be exacted *pour encourager les autres!* Pastern himself might have put them on to her, to silence her and destroy that piece of evidence. And maybe to pay *me* out for not being a good boy. I can't be sure. Pastern's lot know how to wait. I *know* how they work. The secret service is a world on its own – it goes on for ever. Some day, they think to themselves, I might be useful to them. That's the way they work.'

We sat in silence. Here on the long slow curve of the sleepy river in its garlands of jewelled foliage, there seemed no place for this dark side of life, only for gentleness, generosity of spirit, hope. I thought of the evening long ago, on the way to his house, when he had first hinted of the existence of that waiting heart on the frontier, his hopes of being with her one day, and with it the overhanging sense of doom awaiting its moment. Yet only an hour or so later, at the kitchen table, his mother innocently pleading with him once again to let her find a nice girl for him to marry, amazingly he had agreed. He had done it, he confided afterwards, to please her. At the time, I had said nothing. He was deceiving himself. Deep down, I now saw, he had been preparing for the worst, hedging his bets. That was a frightening thought. Was hope always so feeble?

Softly he said, his face still turned away, 'I've been lying awake at night chewing over my chances of getting back over there, and carrying a pistol again. Trouble is, without money for palm-greasing I'd be picked up right away. But if I did get through, by God I know who I'd go after! And when I'd paid them back, I wouldn't give a fuck what happened to me. That's all I want now – to get even!'

Without thinking, I said, 'Maybe *that's* why Pastern's reminding you – partly through me as well as sending you that note, If it *was* him – that he's still active, that he still wants to use you? He must know you're not with the Party now, but even in your union work I imagine you could still be of use to him? After all, the Party's active there too. So, if you wanted to get even with them – he might think – you could let him use you after all?'

'I've thought of that,' he said bluntly, closing the matter. He lay there, facing up-river the way we had come, and was silent. He spoke again. The world was folding up like a paper screen. Tidal waves of destruction would soon be hurling us about. How strange that we should still insist, in days like these, on planning for the future? 'Where the hell *is* the future – you tell *me*!'

The unsigned message had reached him about six weeks ago. I shivered. That was about the time I had met Pastern in Bill's rooms.

'You should have told me,' I said.

Bernard was silent for some minutes. Then he spoke in a dulled, distant voice: 'I wanted to hug the misery close. I couldn't have talked about it to anyone, not even you. And then father died a day or two after, providentially you might say. I suppose I hadn't enough mourning to spare. As you can see, I can't talk about it properly even now.'

He sighed heavily and turned round, pulling himself together, reverting to the crisp manner. 'In a way I'm glad the *guerre kilométrique* is nearly upon us. I'd say we have three months left, four at the most. We should have stopped the bastards long ago, before they got strong – instead of deluding ourselves with all that sanctimonious *agitprop* bullshit about peace and disarmament. I went for my medical at Maryhill Barracks the other day. I volunteered soon after we buried father – God rest him – but this Franco bullet did for me. They don't want any wounded soldiers! I'm listed as in a reserved occupation in time of war. Think of that! They're suddenly anxious to keep the workers happy!'

He half-smiled at the thought, shaking his head at the irony. 'As for you,' he went on, 'look on the bright side. With your bad eyes they'll grade you C_3 and you'll stay on here.'

His manner had become business-like, incongruously reminiscent of Beveridge. I felt parochial, diminished, far removed from events – from worldly assessments, practical responses. Bernard spoke, as always, from the epicentre of the storm. How remote from lofty Oxford talk in study group and tutorial, the presumption of a godlike view – so beguiling, so flattering to the ego, so misleading!

It occurred to me that for years I must have seen in him the older brother, who would have bridged the distance with father, helped me make sense of the world, whom I would have honoured and trusted and copied. I saw that the attributes I wanted to copy had become fewer over the years; there was one now, precious above all – *competence*, the sureness that moved at once from thought to action. That quality was not diminished by his present disillusion, the veering compass needle. Those were surely the occupational risks of *living*. If only some miraculous contagion would give it to me, then I would be *in* the world always, instead of waiting in the wings for certainty to come to me. That was the quality I had in truth come here to find, inspiration not of the mind but of the spirit. Knowledge was easy. Competence – or was it wisdom? – moved always out of reach, like the grapes of Tantalus. If this was the wrong place to seek it, where was the right one?

'*Where is the wisdom we have lost in knowledge?*'

'In some ways,' Bernard said, 'it doesn't matter *what* you do about Pastern. If you say "no" I doubt if he'll bother to carry out his threat, war being so close. As for doing what *he* wants, it may be unpleasant but not as bad as knocking your guts out in the factory! And you'll get paid a damn sight more for it. Give your conscience a rest, for Chrissake! These bastards in the Party don't deserve it; they'd have no mercy on *you* if it suited their book. You'll find some of it interesting. You'll make a bit of money, give yourself time to make up your mind what you want to do with your life. As for the girl, if you're worried about accepting her money, my guess is you don't really want her!'

He turned to look up-river again. 'I'm going to say some hard things. About this sense of mission of yours. You're over-sentimental; maybe it's the effect of being here. Oh yes, it's nice to think you're carrying a God-given torch of light. I know what that's worth – it's balls! It blinds you to simple things. Father belonged to the age of hope. It died a long time ago. All that's left for us to do is hold on, preserve what's left of the System and stop the mad men taking over. In Spain, when we were in the line, we used to say "Keep your head down while the shit's flying." People like us have got one job to do now and one only – to live through what's coming. If we don't, everything's pointless. It may be pointless anyway, but I don't want to believe it.'

There was a sad irony in the words 'People like us'. He still thought, as his father had done, that we were the elect, the gnostics, who saw more, saw further, than the rest. If that was true, then God help the world.

It was nearly dusk. We were about to move away when Werner's voice hailed me from beyond the shrubbery leading down from the courts. He emerged, spruce as ever in immaculate whites, racket and a box of tennis balls under his arm, followed by Hannah. Her fair hair streamed smoothly down, tightly framing her face, and rested, curled inwards in a scroll, on the shoulder-straps of the box-pleated tennis dress. The bloom on her full lips matched the glow on her cheeks. At her throat hung a gold Shield of David – then rarely seen in jewellery. As I introduced Bernard, they regarded him curiously, a shade disapprovingly. His blue serge business suit – here on the river! – betrayed him as someone who did not belong. Naïvely I was stung to say something to mark him out as no ordinary person. With vicarious pride, I said he had fought in Spain. Werner stiffened and looked about him uneasily.

'On which side?' he asked.

Bernard snapped; 'On the anti-fascist side, of course.' He tightened his lips and gave a sigh: 'How could a Jew do otherwise?' He pointed to the tattooed number on Werner's forearm. 'I see *you* have good reason not to like the fascists either – or the Nazis!'

He turned to Hannah and indicated the Shield of David. 'Yes, and you too? If the fascists get control here – and it's perfectly possible – *that*' – he pointed at Werner's arm again – 'is what will happen to *us*. And worse.'

I thought Hannah was about to make a frosty reply, then something in her softened. Her gaze fixed on his shoulder, the glow on her cheeks brightening, with a tremor in her voice, she said: 'You were wounded? I *am* sorry. All this shedding of blood. If only we could achieve things without it.'

Bernard, I sensed, was moved not so much by her words as the tone, the concern bridging the distance between them. A flush suffused his ruddy features. He reached out and touched the Shield of David, and said gravely: '*That* dream's going to demand blood – and plenty of it.'

I thought of the many times, as a child standing in the doorway of the Workers' Circle, the immigrants' social club in the Gorbals, when I had heard the sad, yearning talk of the Return, half-hopeful, half-despairing, not truly sustaining the stooped figures huddled round the bulbous coal stove, but a frail bond among historic exiles, and of the heroes – Herzl, Jabotinsky – dedicated to the achievement of the dream: 'Next year in Jerusalem', a distant light forever beckoning. And I remembered the sudden shrug, and a scornful voice saying 'Effsher koomt der Mesheeach!' ('Maybe the Messiah's on his way!') Even here, in a few élite outposts in North Oxford, the vision passed from dreamer to dreamer. A few years before, the Russians had proposed a Jewish autonomous region in remote Biro-Bidjan, though many cynics condemned the idea as a strategem to attract capital from Jews in the West. But a Jewish state in the ancient holy land itself? That was as distant as the sun.

Werner said, uncomfortably, 'Please, I am not a political person. I am a simple scientist, a guest in this country. I must not express a view.'

Bernard gave a harsh laugh. 'You have already expressed a view by *being* here – simply by having escaped from the concentration camps! And what about the others you left behind? They are silent. They depend on *us* – and that means you too – to express a view! And God knows we'll have to do a damn sight more than that by the look of it.'

Werner's eyes were blank as if in shock. He spoke in a flat voice. 'All I ever wanted was to do my scientific work and enjoy life. What is wrong with that? What can one individual do? Soon my wife and children will be here with me. This is a civilised country. Such things will not happen here.'

Hannah seemed deeply shaken, as if Bernard's unfamiliar, savage sentiments had struck her across the face. She appeared to draw away from Werner and yet to excuse him. Struggling to find words, her eyes filled with tears. Amazingly, for this usually collected girl, she made no attempt to hide them. Her words, when they came at last, emerged clumsily and seemed to astonish her: 'You batter us with light. I am not used to it.'

Cassis: Decadent World

Though the war had been so potently expected, the storm cloud steadily darkening the landscape, one part of my mind had refused to believe in its coming until it was upon us. And then, to my surprise, stiffening the spirit to take myself off to the war and, as I was convinced, to death, had been easier than I had thought.

In retrospect it is plain that I chose not to see *anything* clearly as the last peace time days slipped by – or rather I saw with only one part of the mind. We talked of the approaching war, indiscriminately condemned warmongers and appeasers, and tried to believe that the closed-in student life would continue unchanged for ever. Towards the end of the summer term, meeting Bill Challoner at the sailing club, he asked me if I was going to have any free time in the long vac? Free time – our whole life here was free time! Would I care to join him and a few friends at Cassis for a week or two? Nothing grand, just lazing about on the beach, that sort of thing: 'It's rather a select place. Interesting people, friends from the Nest and so forth – none of the bourgeois seaside holiday crowd.'

I had never heard of Cassis, nor of the Nest. The latter, I gathered later, was the kind of night spot where members of the Bollinger might go when out on a 'thrash' in London.

Seeing me hesitate, he added quickly: 'My dear chap, if you're a bit tight at the moment, do let me lend you a few quid. No, I insist! I'm quite sure you'll pay me back later. So that's settled then?'

I was flattered and a little confused. Was the invitation a final mark of acceptance? Had I truly crossed the class divide at last? Or was it yet another piece of patronising? This, surely, would be the acid test. As for being tight for money, I had put aside £12 to see me through the long vacation, if I was careful; but it would certainly not pay for this Cassis jaunt.

Rachel was going with her family to their mountain villa in the Haute Savoie, and I was to join her there in September. I could go on there from Cassis. It would all fit in neatly.

Cassis was then still essentially a fishing village, but it had been discovered, like Cyril Connolly's Trou sur Mer, and settled by a small number of sophisticated expatriates. It also had a floating population of moneyed drop-outs, identifiable by their garb of fashionable versions of local working-class clothes – espadrilles, rust-coloured trousers suggesting sails and the sea, fishermen's jerseys. Even in late August the place baked under a relentless sun in a sky of blue enamel, the rocks hot to the foot, the air hot to the lungs, the edges of buildings shimmering in the hard brassy light. There was a small harbour for a handful of high-prowed fishing boats, and fronting it a peeling Hôtel du Port and a few bars, open-fronted, their striped blue shades permanently drawn down. A bistro and a few shops – chandlers, ironmongers, domestic supplies, a baker – were scattered in the winding streets behind. In a tiny square was a little church in whose shade men played interminable, enigmatic *boule*. The sea, to my city eyes an unbelievable blue, glowing with a savage hardness, was fringed with tumbled white rocks. Above the village, on an escarpment that gleamed pink in the early morning sun, was a scattering of new-looking villas with walls of dazzling white and roofs of raw red terra-cotta.

By the standards of the foreign denizens, living was cheap. To me it was unimaginable indulgence, lotus-eaters' paradise. Was I truly here? Did the Gorbals exist? Here was a dreamlike progress – initiates moving in an endless minuet of pleasure, capricious tasting of many things, *dolce far niente*, ambience of sunlit grace and easy charm. As if bewitched in an enchanted demesne where the day and the night were as one, they mingled, drifted away together, returned and mingled differently and moved away again to some secret place, a secluded pool perhaps, among the scatter of white rocks to the side of the harbour. Pairings were seemingly ignored the next morning. I was too green to understand, at first, that some of the hectic, unreal, bewitched quality – an improbable, total detachment – in those around me came from hashish and cocaine.

I moved among them with leaden feet. To be fair I was being faithful to Rachel. Apart from that, a hardness about these knowing women repelled me. Avid for 'action' – the coterie word for love-making – their siren call was: 'Fling woo!' Come on and fling woo!' Undiscriminating, or so it seemed, they had no time for tenderness, slow-ripening familiarity, sharing visions by moonlight on the edge of the empty sea.

Above the village, overlooking the sea, one of Bill's friends owned the Villa Vallombrosa, with marble swimming pool and wide white terrace, set in a cool grove of pines. In the velvet darkness one night, about a dozen of us sat or reclined on the edge of the pool whose surface, now still as glass, shone with a ghostly reflection of the moon. The cicadas croaked in booming chorus. I was in the middle of the horse-shoe of bodies, in the hypnotic mood left over from a long day in the sun and in the sea. Someone to my right lit up a cigarette that had an unfamiliar, herbal aroma. He took several long draws in quick succession, then to my surprise passed it to his neighbour. She too drew on it several times and passed it on. As it came near, I had a moment of revulsion at the thought of accepting the cigarette, wet with saliva from several mouths. That apart, however, this was obviously no ordinary cigarette.

Drugs were not yet spoken of, or written about, openly. I had no idea what was in that cigarette. Ashamed to show my lack of sophistication I dared not ask. I may have guessed it was hashish. Even if I had known, I doubt if I would have had the courage to appear 'stuffy' and refuse. Despite the unpleasantness of sharing, it would be an interesting new experience.

The cigarette advanced slowly. The next recipient would be the girl on my right, who I had seen in the distance in previous days but never met till this evening – dark, petite, voluptuous, bobbed hair sticking out spikily, in red trousers and a blue zephyr rolled up high to bare her midriff for coolness. She held the cigarette, now much shortened, between thumb and forefinger, inhaled deeply with each draw, then pressed close, her sea-scented hair brushing my face, and put it to my lips, her other hand, fingers spread and vibrant, upon me. The smell of her hot brunette sweat was powerful, ecstatic. The dark world of her flesh sang in my head. I drew on the soggy cigarette; the acrid taste was disagreeable, but there was no other sensation. I took another draw, and the next instant the top of my head was being lifted off, not unpleasantly, and beginning to float away. In a moment all control would go and I would plunge into the unknown. She pushed the cigarette more firmly to my lips. 'Go on!' she hissed with a fine edge of desire. 'It'll *take* you!' Now panic struck. No more! I took the stub and passed it to the fellow on my left, and leaned back to move away from her. Suddenly her taut little form lunged and pushed me over completely, flat on the warm marble, then came down on me, her trousers sliding down over her hips.

The comic elements did not occur to me till much later – my naïveté, my panic. So this was going to be an orgy! Visions raced through the mind, forbidden, magnetic, challenging. Particularly repellent, to judge from the salacious anecdotes that went the rounds, was the virtually inevitable contact, however slight and fleeting, with male participants. If it could be only with women – ah, that would be wonderful!

Around us the somnolent talk had faded, and there was a quiet rustling and murmuring, the small private noises of people changing position close together.

'Not here,' I whispered. 'Let's go ...'

'Come on! We're nearly there!'

Roughly I rolled away and jumped to my feet and moved quickly to the steps leading down to the driveway and the road. The clamorous creak of the cicadas was suddenly thunderous, reverberating against the walls of the house and the hill behind. Stupidly I wondered why she had said nothing more. I glanced back. Her compact figure, now naked, had entwined itself with the couple who had been on my left. Her trousers floated in the pool.

Heated, angry with myself, I ran down the pale marble steps to the gravelled driveway and stood there for some moments, harsh self-questioning feeding ill-humour to white heat. I followed the winding incline to the road and looked down at the few lights on the quay. Long past midnight, the bars were closed. The village slept. I began to feel shame at my flight from that lovely, eager, siren flesh; my callow nicety. Incongruously I thought of the encounter, long ago, with the prostitutes Kirstie and Jeanie on the steps of Bernard's union offices in the Saltmarket, and my embarrassed reply to Jeanie: 'I don't want it that way.' No wonder Jeanie had been dumbfounded, as the girl up there had been – but momentarily only. Was I making a fuss about nothing? Did I protest too much?

Roused, restless, repentant, I was half-inclined to return to the villa. Would I be ridiculed? Then it occurred to me that, stupefied as they were up there no one would care, or even notice. That settled it. What would be the point?

I leaned on the low roadside retaining wall, the cliff falling away steeply, and contemplated the sleeping world below. The immediate deprivation, the bruised pride, faded, became trivial. A new awareness, still to be understood, asserted itself, as if I had completed a pilgrimage and returned surer, stronger. Never again would I look in wonder and envy at the doings of these people. As if in proof of this conclusion I asked myself – astonished that I did so – how much longer could I stomach their insouciant, aimless existence? I must leave this place.

The night was hot, the air heavy. There was no wind. The sea shimmered silvery under a great moon solidly shining like a newly minted half-crown piece hanging in the sky. The little harbour thrust its arms out black upon the gleaming water like the outspread claws of a crab, one curved inwards within the other. In the stillness the whole world brooded.

And then, startled, I felt a shift in the air, an inexplicable sense of something momentous impending. My eyes were drawn to a patch of rippling silver a few hundred yards off shore that seemed to have become somewhat darker than the rest of the gleaming water. The next instant the silver solidity of the calm water shattered. I thought I saw a long dark shape break the surface, labouring to rise, phosphorescence flickering round it. The hair on my neck stiffened. Seconds later a black shape became distinct, rose higher, and through the clear, silent night there came the noise of turbulent water, and then, in a few moments, the clank of metal. I had never seen a submarine before. Soon, from the blunt protuberance amid-ships, a dim patch of light appeared; there came the sound of boots clattering on metal, low staccato voices. I remembered that there was a naval base somewhere along this piece of coast.

Why were they surfacing in darkness? And so near land? The questions were irrelevant. The augury was beyond doubt.

I walked down into the village, the road ghostly under the moon. In the narrow streets every window was dark, not a soul about. I went along the narrow outer arm of the harbour to the furthest bol-lard and there, alone in the night between land and sea, questioned the black shape on the silver water.

Except for an occasional low-voiced exchange breaking the si-lence, between two dark figures on the conning tower, the subma-rine could have been a black cardboard silhouette set in the solid silver sea, with no cargo of death within it. How could horror look so peaceful, so gentle, as this shimmering seascape? Only an hour or so ago I had been in fear of – of what? – the trivial decadence at the villa.

I must have stood there a long time. The moon was setting. The silver faded from the sea. As its surface darkened the submarine merged with it till it was nothing more than a deeper shadow, per-ceived only because I knew of its presence. I turned away and walked through to the pension near the little church, my steps echoing in the silence, let myself in quietly with the great iron key borrowed from the concierge, and tip-toed up the rickety wooden stairs to my room. Before going to bed I packed my rucksack.

Next morning the concierge said I was wanted on the telephone. After the submarine the call was not a surprise. It was Rachel. Her father had decided, war being a matter of hours away now, that the family must all return to London at once; they were closing up the villa. She would leave that day. Was I leaving too? Yes, I would catch the bus to Marseilles after breakfast and get on the first train I could. 'Thank God,' she breathed, 'there's so little time.' We would meet in London; I could stay at their house in Kensington for a while if I liked. I said I would.

Her clear, loving, serious voice ringing in my ears, I went down to the quay. The submarine was still there, wallowing in a long slow swell, the grey metal of the casing, and of the gun on the forward platform, gleaming dully in the sun.

A few days before, in a fit of extravagance, I had bought a cheap straw hat against the sun, a poor man's Panama. It was the first article of attire I had ever bought that had only a fleeting practical purpose. Perhaps it affirmed a new vision of myself, my own creation, yet another step towards independence from the past? Alas, the new persona needed far more time than this in which to mature. And now, I told myself, looking at the submarine, time had run out altogether. Suddenly, uncontrollably, I wanted to proclaim something – anger, defiance, disgust at what was heppening, contempt for the world, a snarl at the meddling Fates. I went to the outermost ledge of rock, where I used to dive into a deep pool of clear water, a favourite place for sunworshippers, attested by the yellow patches on the white stone where splashes of sunburn oil had stained it. Further out than the projecting mole of the little harbour, it was as near as I could get to the submarine. I stood at the edge and hurled the hat as far out as I could. It floated through the torpid air, turning lazily round and round, and glided to a landing on the water not many yards away. Of course it was nowhere near the submarine, in fact a few hundred yards short. Still, I had made my proclamation.

The few early bathers, drying themselves or lazing on the rock, stared as if I had gone out of my mind. That was how I did feel. In a bitter fashion I was proud of it. A lone swimmer spotted the hat bobbing on the water, rescued it, and swam back to the rock with a skilful one-armed back-stroke, the hat held high: 'Is this your hat?'

'No,' I said, and walked away. Already somewhat ashamed, pride would not let me take the hat back. In any case, when would I ever need a gentleman's straw hat again?

In consigning it to the sea there may also have been a timid attempt at sympathetic magic, propitiating the elements, to let me return one day – fully armed, sure of myself. I knew, and did not know, that the imprint of those days and nights in Cassis would deepen over the years, for Cassis was my first true trial of strength with a sophisticated if decadent world. They illuminated so much that Oxford obscured – a whole universe of nuances, whispers of sensibility, awareness of self. I was too solemn, too fearful of commitment. Some truths were so self-evident that I failed to see them at all – *refused* to see them. I recoiled from awareness because it demanded instant response! Perhaps, in the Gorbals as a child, awareness *was* intolerable and I had taught myself to suppress it – and now, learning to be aware was frightening.

After Cassis, if there was still time, I might become freer, let myself go at last, see people in their own timid humanity, lives within lives, layer beneath layer, and warm to them; a slow ascent from the depths of doubt.

Some of those Cassis people would cross my path again and again. Many would not survive the war. One – brilliant, charming, rich, seemingly endowed with everything needed to make life fulfilling – would shoot himself. Deprivation was relative, a very personal thing, a state of mind. Perhaps their sensibility *had* been more complex, and more penetrating, than I had thought? In the light of what was in store, they may have been wise to snatch fulfilment, however shallow, from every single moment, each tinctured as it was with sad questioning. And that lovely girl by the pool – who was I to flee from her, least of all to judge her? Yes, Bill had been right after all: 'Gather ye rosebuds while ye may.' I too, convinced that I would not survive, looked upon my return journey to England as a farewell to myself.

I would see those jewelled Cassis days as caught forever in sunlit amber, the players continuing their life of magical make-believe, each hour and minute prolonged to the uttermost, in tenacious simplicity of mind and desire. And I would envy them.

I was never to revisit Cassis. If I had, the golden image would have shattered.

11

Phantom Soldiering: Oxford in War

In the misty autumn air, raindrops suspended in the darkening afternoon, muted echoes of my footsteps were thrown back from walls of low cloud pressing in upon the pollarded willows on either side of the water-fringed path. All other sounds were muted except for the rough drone of heavy aircraft passing overhead, invisible above the leaden cloud, that rhythmically rose and fell and battered the mind with its purpose; bombers drummed their way eastwards to Germany, the imagined sky full of their black shapes of blunted crosses, gravid with death.

Thoughts were muted too, not yet freed from the suspended animation of soldiering. Horizons remained drawn in close, the future conditional.

These lines of close-standing willows leaning over darkened water, their rounded heads blurred in the mist, my first view from the train bringing me back from the army, aptly symbolised the Oxford I remembered, marshy, torpid, drawn in upon itself – and the dim, uncertain world to which I was returning. This had seemed the right place to start, on a deserted perimeter where all was indistinct, to beat the bounds of my new world again; not truly mine but a simulacrum I had fashioned for myself.

Now and then the leaden air was mysteriously moved by a breath from afar, and thick curtains of mist drew aside to reveal spectral trees and hedgerows and clumps of reeds beyond the quiet water on either side of this narrow strip of earth. A few feet away, the dark waters moved with barely a ripple, and softly, with a whisper, lapped the land. Between the trees the path twisted and turned and drifted away among the shadows, seldom visible for more than a few yards ahead. Here and there its surface of beaten earth was worn through, and tree roots unexpectedly protruded and snaked across, iron hard to the unwary foot.

In the intervals between transits of bombers above, the ghostly silence wrapped itself round me like the blanket of clammy mist itself – appropriate too, and welcome, for I needed to understand the fact that I was here at all! The *guerre kilométrique* seemed set for eternity. Few of us had shared the contrived optimism of the short-lived popular song, 'We're going to hang out the washing on the Siegfried Line'. We knew that we would not come back from the war.

Facing life again was an unbelievable anti-climax. The wonder and elation were almost too much to contain – and above all guilt, for there were many people I knew who would not come back; Rachel's memory would return unbearably through the years – and at dead of night I would tread useless circles in my room, stand at the blank window and gaze out at the unfeeling stars, and curse myself for a fool and a coward.

And so I walked here and marvelled once again – but this time for quite different reasons – as I had on my very first arrival in Oxford, asking myself, 'What right have I to be here?'

Bernard's prediction that the army would reject me proved right, except for some delay. I had written to the authorities asking to be called up as soon as possible, and they had done so. There had seemed no point in waiting. Since death was near, I might as well get it over with. In its own good time the army gave me a ticket back to civvy street.

In the still of the night in barracks I had pleaded with the Fates: 'Make Hitler turn eastwards! It's our only chance!' At last, unbelievably, the news came over the radio in the smoke-filled NAAFI canteen in Catterick Camp, barely audible above the din of shouting at the bar and the darts board and the battering of boots on the plank floor, the yelling of orders for beans and chips and 'char'. A shiver ran down the spine – a sense of divine intervention, the momentary fear of an answered prayer.

What an irony – that salvation would come from a titanic clash between two tyrannies that, as oppressors of the Jews, had outdone even the Spanish Inquisition and the Roman proconsuls! No one else heard the announcement, or if they did, took note of it; even though the words, and the portent, boomed out of the sky with Delphian force. I could *hear* the iron thunder of those far-off guns, like the apocalyptic drum beats in the Eroica. I wanted to share the answered prayer. I called out: 'He's done it! It's Napoleon all over again. We can win now!' No one was listening.

Yes, I *had* intended to go down with the sinking world, sad, obscene, despicable. But what now? If I did survive, then maybe there would be enough of the old innocent world left too, to be worth living for? Pastern, after a silence so long that I had ceased to expect any further word, did keep his promise to make another appearance. I told him I would not spy for him. In any case I was going into the army. Unmoved, he became very thoughtful. He would not take my answer as final. As for the army, he had some contacts; it might be most useful if I went into Signals. Whether by coincidence or not, to the Signals I was sent.

Rachel volunteered for a women's auxiliary unit; after a time it became evident, from various small details, that she was on secret work. She never once hinted at its nature, and I resisted the temptation to press her with questions – only much later would I see this reserve, on both our parts, as evidence of trust and love and mutual respect, a solidity that I ought to have valued more, while there was still time. After some months she was posted away, I assumed abroad. She wrote lovingly, but cryptically, from an army forwarding address. And then – silence. Wartime Oxford accustomed you to that; people went through a black door, as into a magician's cupboard on the stage, and vanished. She had warned me that the time would come when no letters at all would be permitted, lest a chance clue disclosed too much.

I knew in my bones that this silence was final. Again and again in the years to come I would ask myself whether she would have gone, or so soon, if we had been living together. I think she *would* have gone, in the end; for her it was a personal fight against the forces of evil. On our last weekend at the family's country house, then beginning to fill with staff evacuated from London, she had talked sadly about our life of 'living and partly living'. Oh we could have had a golden time together, happiness greater and deeper than this to remember! In a little while who could tell where we would be?

We peered into the dark future. There might still be a chance. Oh there must be? We must hope for that – and never, ever, give up hope.

She intended the affirmation as a promise; her heart would compel it to come true. It sounded like a farewell.

The time came when she was listed as 'missing'. Specific facts would have given me nothing. I knew she was dead. The family were not unfriendly, simply correct. How much they knew of our poignant tug-of-war there was no hint. Recalling her fierce independence, I imagined they knew nothing. And so we could not even mourn together. What rights had I, having failed her? What mattered more was that I had been untrue to myself, or to what I *knew* of myself. All that remained was to curse my indecision, my self-doubt – or was it simply lack of courage? – for evermore.

Towards the end of the war I would receive a letter in her tiny, rounded hand, one of those wartime 'pre-mission' letters intended for onward transmission only if the writer did not return. Two sentences in particular would burn into my mind, and whenever I thought of them I would hear her voice in my head: 'You suffer because you are the man you are. I did not always know how to give you the understanding you need.'

Far away in the mist voices floated, snatches of disembodied talk, muffled one moment, clear the next, distant whispers, a trill of female laughter, an answering low chuckle, cadence of speech rising and falling, sometime companionably familiar as if heard through the winding corridors of a rambling old house. They grew stronger, wafted closer by some mystic surge of the floating masses of grey vapour, a timid counter-point to the undulating drone of the bombers overhead, then were lost again.

Sometimes the voices sounded so near that they seemed to be fragments of an inner colloquy of my own, or echoes of conversations from another, distant time.

Many times, in the army, I had reason to think of Bernard's bitter words on the river – 'deluding ourselves with all that sanctimonious *agitprop* bullshit about peace and disarmament'. Possibly my unit had been issued with older material, so that more favoured front-line formations could receive the best? That might have been why I was carrying a rifle stamped 'drill purpose only' and dated 1900? But why were we still trained in flag signalling, and in the use of primitive buzzer sets, suitable for trench communication, dating from the 1914–18 War? If this was the equipment of the war-mongering country which the Party had condemned for being armed to the teeth and bent on aggression, then God help us!

The nearest I came to battle – though whether it *was* battle I never discovered – was the night of the General Alarm. There was great talk of invasion. The orders were strict. The signal for a General Alarm would be whistles; when we heard them, whatever the hour of day or night, wherever we were – in camp or in the town – we must get to the barrack square 'at the double' in full battle order, with canvas bandoliers of ammunition draped about us, and await further orders. One Saturday night, idly whistling as I prepared for bed, I heard a shout from a nearby hut: 'Hey – shut that fuckin' whistling! I think that's the fuckin' General Alarm!' I stopped and listened. Unbelievably, through the thin night air there came the clear sounds of whistles, frenetically repeated, coming from all directions in the vast Catterick complex. From barrack huts on every hand came a cacophony of shouts and curses: 'Christ this is it! I can't fuckin' well believe it! All right lads, get crackin'! Jerry's on his way!'

Within seconds it seemed, by some miracle – untried soldiers that we were – we were assembled in ragged company formations on the dark barrack square. The coast was not far. It would not be long now before we trundled away in trucks and manned the cliff tops and the beaches with our massive firepower of superannuated rifles! And with any luck we would see Jerry off. There was a curious calm among us. There was no speculation; no bravado.

I cannot remember feeling fear, only impatience for something to happen. And to get it over and done with.

'… *half in love with easeful death.*'

All around us in the black night the whole world had broken into monstrous noise and movement. Trucks and guns rumbled all over the blind countryside. Despatch riders, their thin beam headlights ignoring the black-out orders, darted among the heavier traffic. Planes – ours or theirs? – droned up above. Far to the east, great coronas of light burgeoned and died down. Distant thuds were heard – could that be artillery? Something momentous must surely be going on.

Gaps in the ranks gradually filled as men dragged themselves in from a night out in the pubs and dance halls, and trudged on to the square pulling on their equipment.

We waited throughout the night, standing at ease at first, slowly subsiding to sit on packs or on the ground. Smoking was forbidden. In the first faint light of dawn, silence retuned. Some vehicles trundled back along the narrow roads, but not the great mass we had heard before. Orders came to return to quarters. The General Alarm was over. We went in silence, scraping boots on the ground, too tired for talk – or thought.

We were ordered to say nothing of that night. Was it the famous invasion attempt, talked of after the war, from which barges bearing dead Germans were said to have been seen floating in the shallows? The mystery was never lifted.

When it became clear that the military machine was going to extrude me back into 'civvy street', a puzzling depression set in, a sense of wasted time – but more particularly of wasted emotions.

There came a period, seemingly endless, of being posted back and forth across England – like a ball punted about a field simply to keep it in play – and I sank lower and lower into the depths of futility; I might as well be *anywhere*, or nowhere, and the next posting would be as meaningless as the last.

One day the feeling miraculously lifted, as by a healing touch. I arrived in an isolated holding depot in the Peak District, among jagged crags, fast running streams and tumbling, milky falls, reminiscent of the Highlands; perhaps the resemblance worsened my overcast state? I entered the quartermaster's stores, housed in an old dark barn dimly lit by a few dusty electric lamps, its high cross-beams giving the place an eerie, other-world atmosphere, and there in the shadows behind a counter, surrounded by shelving crammed with clothing and equipment, stood Alec.

I would discover that he too was being posted about with apparent aimlessness. Possibly because he was older than most of the current intake, the army seemed reluctant to let him go to a fighting unit; he chafed at being relegated to what some men would have welcomed as a series of cushy billets. Perhaps because of his obvious solidity he had been put in temporary charge of stores. We were all, it seemed, in temporary charge of something – ourselves too. That was war.

For the first few moments, however, we stood there among the dusty mountains of military paraphernalia and gaped at each other without speaking. Once again, no words fitted. He was, if anything, the more shaken, the result, as I was to learn in a moment, of seeing me in such gloom, and seemingly in worse case than he was. He was the first to speak, and the words burst out of him impulsively: 'Christ Almighty, fancy meetin' *yew* here! Yew being a' Oxford, ah thought they'd have put yew in a grand big job by now – orderin' the likes o' *me* abou'?'

I had after all, joined the boss class. How could it be that I too was being shunted about like this? People like him, he seemed to say, had no right to expect anything better. For me, matters should be different. Yet here I was – as he saw it – still an underdog.

The long bony features reddened. Ashamed, he plainly wondered how to make amends. I was more amazed than hurt. The Alec I had known, sensitive, stoical, looking life squarely in the face, was not given to petty spite. Perhaps he was changed too, as I was? The shifting horizons of war, especially the barrack-room culture of grudges and 'ticking' – kicking against the pricks of life – could so easily corrupt. He had let himself down.

He stood, head bent over the counter much as he used to stand over his pressing board across the table from me in the factory. Suddenly he turned on his heel and reached towards a section of shelving crammed with hundreds of pairs of thick grey woollen socks, pulled out a couple of pairs, turned and reached across the counter and thrust them into my hands. 'Here – ye'll need these some time.' Seeing my surprise he rushed on: 'Och, th'army'll no' miss them! Go on. Put them out o' sight.'

Supply and equipment rules being strict, he knew he faced a charge if discovered. His action was not strictly necessary and he probably knew it; I was not short of a pair of socks. But socks had come to his mind first, naturally enough; in our Gorbals life, next to boots and trousers, they were the most important items of clothing. And so the 'gift' of socks, and the risk he ran – though small – took us back to a shared life, joined us as no words could have done. His action conveyed something else. This sympathy, sad and warm and delicate, could not say everything – far from it. We both knew it. At the very heart of life the world had turned its back on sympathy. That was the tragedy of all of us. The primeval melting-pot was engulfing us all.

'Aye,' he murmured, 'this fuckin' war ...' Once again there were no words to fit.

Uttered with such rasping feeling, the curse joined us together even more, affirmed our shared sadness for the world, our defiance of the powers of evil that made it so – and lightened our hearts.

A few days later we both left the depot and went our separate, inscrutable ways. I would never see him again. The next I learned of him was some time after D-Day, when I read the posthumous citation.

The mist drew closer still, curtains of sodden grey cotton wool trailing wisps of vapour, the steamy breath of a giant. It was easy to feel a sense of other worldliness – imagined flicker of marsh gas, suspirations from the dark heart of the earth, myth and magic, sprites and Jack o'Lanterns, spectres of the past and the future flitting between two worlds here brought together.

Army life had drawn down the blinds of the mind; you were in the bowels of the machine. By a caprice of the Fates I *had* come back. And now I must learn to think in the future tense once again. How much of the chemistry of this place would I find as I had left it? How much of the previous 'me' had I brought back? What had been lost? What was new?

The sky was silent. The bombers had all flown on. I heard the voices, closer now. They faded as the mist closed down again. After a while, another movement of air lifted it again, and they were so near that I peered among the shadows, but there was no one. And then, from out of the trees ahead, a twist in the path brought three figures, two men and a girl. One was Bill Challoner, but so changed that in a busy street I might have walked past him unaware – the face drawn and thin, the dark blue eyes sunk deep into the sockets, as if he had retreated into timid old age and peered out from the empty shell of youth. A quiff of hair was pure white, contrasting disquietingly with the remaining fair hair, now dulled, thinner than I remembered it. His left leg was held stiffly as he walked, and he leaned on a thick stick. He wore a long khaki greatcoat over a blue double-breasted blazer and grey flannels, scarlet silk shirt and dark blue silk muffler.

If Bill looked as though he had the mark of death on his brow, the other man, Ivan – whom I had not met before – was the classic picture of vigorous, self-renewing youth, tall, dark, broad, ruddy-featured. The truth would prove to be the reverse. Bill would live on, permanently scarred – in mind as well as body – by his torment in a 'brewed up' tank. Ivan, I would learn, was doomed; he had Hodgkin's disease.

He must have been about eighteen. He was dressed in a long rac-coon coat, down to mid-calf, red corduroy trousers and fur-lined ankle boots, and a silk scarf, striped lengthwise red and blue, wound several times round his neck and hanging down below his waist. A bushy moustache gave him an old-fashioned appearance, recalling steel engravings of late Victorian and Edwardian men of fashion. He walked with a suggestion of a swagger; perhaps he compensated in this fashion, unawares, for the knowledge that his time was short.

The girl was Diana Gollancz, also met for the first time – daugh-ter of the firebrand left-wing publisher and founder of the Left Book Club. The immediate, arresting impression was of her in-tense, pre-Raphaelite pallor. Indeed intensity was the keynote, questing, indomitable, innocent – a self-wounding innocence. Rich

brown wavy hair tumbled on her shoulders and framed her paleness dramatically. She wore a dark blue cloak over chestnut cor-
duroys and a voluminous red sweater. Something about her looked
bohemian, an impression soon confirmed; she was at the Slade.
Oxford had lost its severe, aristocratic aloofness, and had become
a steamy, wayward, cosmopolitan colony of London, with the influences of Bloomsbury, Hampstead, Soho and Chelsea dominant.
C. E. M. Joad was to epitomise the change, dismissively, when he
referred to Oxford as 'the Latin Quarter of Cowley'.

Ivan, despite a certain defensive exhibitionism, was a gentle soul,
of great sweetness of character. He hid his knowledge of the sentence of death. Bill, who seemed to know him well, with characteristic nicety never once, by the slightest hint, drew attention to his
condition, or the bizarre background to his presence in Oxford. It
was Diana, when we became close, who told me the story, tears in
her eyes as she told it, and in mine as I heard it – after his death. It
was awesome, with an absurdity that made it the more terrible –
and to me amazing, for unlike my Gorbals experience, it had nothing to do with living at the very edge of survival, but with caprice,
prejudice, cosseted obstinacy.

Ivan had set his heart on going up to Oxford; no great ambition,
for most people he knew did so as a matter of course. His parents,
however, strict fundamentalists, apparently saw Oxford as the very
pit of iniquity. To go there would be to seek damnation. They must
not allow it. Living the life of a chronic invalid, he pined and
pleaded. At last, when he had been given at best a year or two to
live, his parents relented. Perhaps, knowing now that he would not
be able to taste Oxford to the full, they could let him go with a
lighter heart?

He tired quickly. He devoted what hours he could, and his ample
funds, to being a dilettante aesthete.

Diana had been drawn to him in mystic sympathy, compassionate tenderness, love that was forfeit from the start. She watched
over him, sat with him on the days when he lacked the energy to get
up, listened, followed his whims – *cared*.

Bill's voice was a shock. Remembered as deep and resonant – he had sung baritone in his college choral society – it was croaky, unsteady, the voice of a very old man. Seeing my concern, he grinned deprecatingly, as if to say 'I'm still alive, am I not? What more can one ask?' After the introductions he turned to me: 'I did hear that you were coming back. Must say I never expected to fetch up in *this* place again!'

Incongruously, those words must have triggered some remote connection in my mind, awaiting its cue. His part in the Pastern affair clicked into place. It was *he* who had been Pastern's spy in the university branch of the Party – well-camouflaged as a mandarin! When Bill had been about to go down at the end of that last summer term of peace, he must have suggested to Pastern that I was the right person to be infiltrated as a replacement. Many years later, meeting Pastern by chance in the Sind Club in Karachi, I taxed him with this interpretation. I hardly expected him to confirm it, but he did not deny it. As for Bill, though we became good friends as the years went by, he never once, even indirectly, referred to the episode.

Bill said, 'I suppose they've sent me here to convalesce in comfort.' Thoughtfully he added, 'I didn't want to come back here. The course I'm on is just an excuse.'

I would find that Oxford was full of service people on courses; if a course was ill-defined, or dismissed as of no importance as Bill had done, it must be secret! When he was not at the Radcliffe Infirmary for treatment, he divided his time between Bletchley Park, supposedly occupied by evacuated sections of the Foreign Office, and what he described as a briefing department at Woodstock; I learned later that the latter was a branch of Intelligence at Blenheim Palace.

'Remember those times sailing on the river?' He grinned feebly, gritting his teeth against the pain from his leg, banging the stick on the ground. 'Funny! I've still got a boat here. With this gammy leg I'm not as nifty as I was...'

He left the question in the air, waiting to see if I would recognise it and respond. In earlier days I might not have done. I said I would be glad to take him out in his boat.

'A boat!' Diana breathed. 'Oh I'd love to go sailing!'

Bill said I could use his boat whenever I liked.

Ivan, perhaps feeling the need to assert himself in riposte to our maturer attitudes, to him esoteric, struck a declamatory pose, and with music hall fruitiness, addressed the curtain of mist: 'How now mist! Avast there! I command you to listen to the music of the spheres.'

He bent his knees, pretending to sit, stretched his hands over an invisible keyboard, and struck imaginary chords. Diana smiled affectionately and nodded her head, pretending to follow the transcendental sounds.

Bill half-turned away and looked at me steadily. Alas *we* could not share that world any more. What did it matter? Who could smile now? What had been good enough for Dada, as a comment on this world, made just as much sense now – or as little.

Compared to Ivan and Diana we felt old, and were sad with the knowledge. Had *we* had enough time to be young? For our separate reasons we thought not. The differences between us, now, seemed insignificant.

Although I had not been in battle as he had, life in uniform had left a similar stamp on us both. We had returned to this place seasoned in inexplicable ways. We were rougher, earthier, surprised by fewer things. Strangest of all, it seemed that Bill saw *me* differently now. My Gorbals origin was now a bonus! What an irony! After all this time I had spent trying to suppress it, or excuse it – he now saw it, with envy, as an added seasoning of the soul. Before, if that had been said to me, I would have been angry, thinking I was being patronised; now, even if I was, I cared little. There probably was some truth in his impression of me after all. So we were drawn together, sharing a world that was already in the past. We were not as others. We knew what things were like before; at this distance simpler, clearer cut. We were already a generation with no links to the present; and there was no going back. Others would never see our vanished horizons as we could. We were now closer to each other than we could ever be to them – to people of Ivan's age – to anyone! And we had better *stay* close, for there were fewer of *us* with each day the war lasted.

In one sense at least – for what it was worth – I had crossed the social divide at last, as Pastern had said I would.

What *was* it worth?

12

Victor Gollancz: Ideals in Confusion

One of my dreams, when leaving the Gorbals, had been the glory of meeting some of the heroes I had humbly read about, who trod the high places of the world, and draw from them a new charge of pilgrim inspiration, a vision of the selfless road ahead. Of the three foremost, I had met Cole; for Laski I must wait and hope; but now, through Diana, I was making the acquaintance of Victor Gollancz.

It was as a prophet, in particular of worker enlightenment, that I had worshipped Victor Gollancz from afar – passionate trail-blazer, bringer of light, powerful champion of progressive thought. His founding of the Left Book Club had been a stroke of genius, epoch-making. With it he made *contemporary* thought, and discussion of great issues of the time, accessible to the lower levels of the social pyramid as they had never been before. The Everyman Library, previously the lifeline of the workers' education movement, had clung to the safe ground of the classics, and near-classics like T. H. Huxley, essentially a view of the past. Those orange limp covered Left Book Club Editions, with their stark, robust black lettering, were carried proudly at left-wing meetings and demonstrations, Workers' Educational Association classes and summer schools, a common recognition signal among 'progressives', badge of a new Enlightenment.

With these visions of him shining strongly in my mind, seeing him in his home setting was in many ways unsettling. The name of his country house in Berkshire, Brimpton Lodge, suggested riches, ample acres, a style of living violently inconsistent with my image of the egalitarian evangelist. To my eyes this Gollancz life was princely – perhaps not as much so as that of Rachel's family, but rich enough; there was, however, an important difference –

Rachel's father did not pretend to be anything other than what he was, a rich businessman.

Two features of Brimpton Lodge, a house of sombre aspect enfolded in oaks and beeches, with hummocky country surrounding it, seemed to cast similar shadows over my earlier vision of the man himself – in retrospect perhaps unfairly. In a gallery lined with books, otherwise a graceful setting for browsing and reflection, slips of white paper peeped out here and there on the shelves, in effect loan slips, giving title, the borrower, and the date removed from the shelf. Gollancz entertained a good deal at Brimpton Lodge, and many of the loan slips referred to books that guests had borrowed and taken with them when they departed. On the face of it the record-keeping was logical; still, this blatant evidence that the great man kept careful account of his benevolence smacked of ungraciousness – at best, he could have taken the trouble to be unobtrusive about it. In the grounds, near a mound partly concealed by trees, Diana led me down a flight of stone steps into a smaller version of the underground bunker at Rachel's country home. She watched my reactions, and I was sure that my feelings echoed hers. Why did this air-raid shelter disturb me so much more? Some prejudice, perhaps from the example of Bernard's father, still clung strongly. For a prophet to be self-centred was surely a contradiction – he did not go to great lengths to protect himself and his interests, least of all did he use riches to give himself an unfair advantage in that respect over the common man. As for that other, much more elaborate shelter, there was some excuse – it had been built by a capitalist who made no claims to highly developed social conscience as Gollancz so blatantly did; indeed Gollancz publicly brandished his social conscience as his *raison d'être!* Yet here was Gollancz revealed far differently, tough, egocentric, looking after number one.

I told myself to curb this naïveté, and not to be mean-spirited either. The Gorbals viewpoint was still too strong. I must stop looking at the world from the bottom of the pyramid.

Diana, though she had no interest whatever in politics or current affairs, could show an intuitive grasp of what was appropriate in public life, and she was sometimes ashamed – though loyally trying to hide the fact – of his more extravagant posturings. In all seriousness he could flaunt a prophetic grandeur, or perhaps it was simply uncontrolled showmanship, which would have been comic in less traumatic contexts: for instance, in the title of his pamphlet on the Nazi brutality to Jews, apostrophising not only Hitler but all other rulers – *Let My People Go* – words befitting a Moses, not a Gollancz.

She treated him with a mixture of reserve and wariness, as one might an unpredictable Caliban. Certainly, when the mood took him he seemed to enjoy playing the role, though it sat incongruously on that fastidious personality, eupeptic, urbane, the chubby features shining with facile amiability, quickly changeable. Crudely aggressive he certainly could be, with an unabashed appetite for power and influence, and an inclination to be a bully not always kept in check, certainly a dangerous man to cross. There any affinity with Caliban ended. Cultivated, responsive, with great sensibility, he could be delightful company.

He set great store by his friendship with Maisky, the Soviet Ambassador since the early Thirties, and would be downcast when it hit stormy waters, for Maisky would sometimes show displeasure at something Gollancz had said or done by failing to invite him to embassy events. When this happened, Gollancz feared that his exclusion would be permanent, and that his public position and influence would diminish in consequence. Seemingly he had not learned that support for Stalin did not earn anyone that prime privilege of friendship – freedom to criticise or hold divergent views. Perhaps he had dreamed of being the favoured Western counsellor to the Russian Bear, and would school him to behave like an old-fashioned Fabian socialist? I wondered how so perceptive a man could be so innocent. At dinner one might, in an aside to Ruth, his wife, Gollancz mentioned one such rap over the knuckles from Maisky, in tones that showed profound hurt. She may have shared my wonder, for she nodded absently, and made no comment. Diana caught my eye and shrugged.

I asked him, 'Why do you care?'

The little moustache bristled. He pushed his lips out in a pout. 'I will not tolerate people trying to control me. Besides, I do genuinely admire the Russians ...' There followed a startling paraphrase of Churchillian rhetoric about 'our noble allies' and the 'historic deeds of the valiant Red Army'. 'In any case,' he went on, 'I feel it to be my mission to be a bridge between the old democratic West and the new socialist order being built there in Russia. They are making a big mistake, turning away from me.'

I mentioned Stalin's sham-legal murders of his comrades, and his treaty with Hitler. Surely it was interest, not sentiment or principle, that was the essence of *realpolitik*? Was that not also true for the Party here – Stalin's fifth column? The Webbs and Bernard Shaw, and so many others, had hypnotised themselves into believing that Russia was a humane democracy instead of a despotism only differing in style from that of Czarist Russia. Surely *he* saw that?

The domed brow furrowed, and with the wintry vibrations the table was stilled. Had I gone too far? Then he seemed to shake himself, and a smile reached out across the table to me like a great warm handshake; he turned to his wife and winked: 'Not a bad *pilpul*! Yes! In fact a very good *pilpul*.'

In Yiddish tradition the word *pilpul* had many connotations. In the expressions 'pilpul-maker', for example, it could imply respect, say, for a scholar; but the word was more often used in gentle teasing, and sometimes, more harshly, to refer to an arid logic-chopper. It was obviously in the latter sense that Gollancz had used it in reference to me. Old enough to adopt the privilege of age towards me, the bully in him had taken over, and he had delivered what was meant to be a crushing rebuttal. After all I was very young, and poor, and he was an important public figure; he had me, he supposed, at his mercy. I decided to stand my ground; 'Sir, calling what I have said a *pilpul* does not diminish the force of it.'

To his credit, he professed delight at my refusal to be crushed. Part of him, at that time in his life at least, was drawn to someone who gave as good as he got. Grinning, he withdrew. I must not think he was dismissing what I had said. He was impressed and wanted to talk to me more fully later.

I had been stung by his introduction of the word *pilpul* for an-other reason too – not the word itself but the pointed introduction of an irrelevant Jewish context to the conversation. It exemplified a device I had often encountered among assimilated upper-class Anglo-Jews, English versions of Werner's *Hofjuden*. When with Jews they did not know well, wishing to oil the wheels of discussion or lesson tension, they would temporarily abandon the character of the standard Englishman of their class and throw into the discus-sion a traditional Jewish image or association or trick of speech, aiming to trigger thoughts of shared history and shared emotions and create enough sympathy for the needs of the moment – a cul-tural trick to gull you into lowering your guard. Gollancz had dredged up the word *pilpul* to show me that within the shell of the cultured upper-class Englishman he was at heart a Jew like me and therefore at one with me. In the act of crushing me he proclaimed that we were brothers. He knew very well that but for the chance of Diana bringing me to his house, he and I could never have met under the same roof – we were light years apart.

In the Gorbals, by contrast, for better or worse the cultural and religious linkages among Jews were real, natural, always present; there was no need to invent them for the convenience of the mo-ment. What angered me particularly, however was the condescen-sion in his use of the trick. Perhaps I was being too much of a purist? I was forgetting the lesson of Germany; the concentration camps did not distinguish between rich Jew and poor, religious or not.

Lost in thought, Gollancz repeated the word *pilpul* – 'a *pilpul*, yes, a very good *pilpul*'. He savoured it, pleased with himself. Then, good humour restored, he regaled the table with anecdotes about Maisky and the Embassy over the years. However, my *pilpul* must have continued to exercise him; after dinner he took me aside: 'The extreme Left does worry me. I sometimes feel we are all being manipulated by the Party.'

The remark was amazing in view of his long association with the Party in various contexts, in particular the Popular Front and the Left Book Club. Indeed, at one stage many people assumed that the Club *was* a Party front organisation. How could this cultured, worldly wise man, close to great affairs and the rough and tumble of politics, imagine that the Party would not manipulate him as it did everyone else? For a time he had towered in the political arena like a giant; did he dream that he, not the Party, was the stronger? When he opposed the Party, as he did over the Hitler–Stalin Pact, he had been shocked and deeply hurt when the Party and its fellow travellers – such as D. N. Pritt – attacked him. As for Pritt, the rich barrister, elected to Parliament for Labour but whose 'line' was so close to the Party's that a membership card would have made no difference, Gollancz had numbered him among his friends; so the fellow traveller attitude should have been familiar. As for the Party itself, over the years Gollancz had had many dealings with its principals, including Harry Pollitt the leader and Palme Dutt its steely theoretician. How could he not know that the Party would react as it did?

That he did *not* know, or behaved as if he did not, must have reflected the heady confusion of the time, when everything, events, attitudes, the positions taken up by people in public life, seemed the products of distorting mirrors, of desperation, a kaleidoscopic charade that would be unbelievable to who came after.

Sometimes he spoke as if he was the arbiter of rectitude in political and social attitudes – what he did or said must be judged by *his* standards alone. He was genuinely astonished, and bitter, at having been pilloried for donating to *Daily Worker* funds. Surely a cheque to the Party's paper, he seemed to imply, was as bland an action as supporting any other humane, gentle cause – like the lifeboats or Dr Barnardo's Homes? I asked what he would do if the red revolution came; would he expect to continue in his privileged position?

Thinking back, I must have sounded – on this occasion and on many others – insufferably cocky, too clever by half. Perhaps I was? More charitably, I was over-sensitive and simply reckless, stung as I had been so often by condescension and being patronised. Envious of highly placed people who could, misguidedly yet seemingly with ease, put their mark on affairs, too often I employed what gifts I had wrongly, tactlessly, to probe for their weak points.

What I said at such times may well have been intrinsically accurate – but that could only have made my behaviour all the harder to tolerate!

He stopped in his tracks and I thought he was about to say 'yes'. Obviously he had never asked himself the question. The words red revolution jolted him – too much like calling a spade a bloody shovel. In supporting the Party, enemy of his class and way life, he was certainly not alone in the phalanx of prominent fellow travellers – Dr Hewlett Johnson, the 'Red Dean' of Canterbury for instance, and John Strachey, that charming but muddled stormy petrel who had been a colleague of Mosley and would soon be a Minister in a Labour government. Like them, in politics at least, Gollancz seemed to cling to the child's conviction that all the nasty things happened to others; after the barricades he too would remain at the top of the heap. Or did he refuse to believe that the Party meant what it said when it talked of *red* revolution?

He stood quite still, head down, then collected himself and said, with a kind of bluster, 'I'm not a Communist! Where did you get that idea from?' He turned to his wife, his voice taking on an anxious note: 'D'you think that's how people see me?' Again she was non-committal. I said the impression he gave, as Pritt did, was that he was as close to the Party as made no matter.

In characteristic fashion he bounced back, turning away from the point. There would be no red revolution in this country. We did not need one because the basic job of class demolition had been accomplished here a long time ago. By the time the war was over we would be on course for socialism by parliamentary means.

If this prophet I had worshipped from afar could be so blind, what hope was there?

Still, his company remained magically stimulating. He presented himself as so enmeshed in the public affairs he commented upon that he spoke from *within* them – the image came to me of a ticker-tape commenting on itself. Publicist to his very marrow, he sniffed the changing wind of ideas shrewdly, if perhaps selectively, in tune with the wartime counterpoint of discussion and controversy, the shifting contemplation of present and future, dizzy juggling with nostrums – initiator and follower, critic and transitory disciple, ideological travelling man.

He discoursed on war aims. As an antidote to war-weariness the manipulators of opinion, himself one of them, had 'sold' people the idea that the war was a price paid for social betterment. Discussion of the nature of that reward would be a useful opiate for the masses! What was wrong with being Machiavellian in a good cause?

In this too he was in tune with the times. People now talked less about how the war was to be won, and far more – amazingly – about the benefits that *should* accrue from having fought it. How could we talk of benefits, I wondered?

Surely, I said, there was only *one* aim, to stop the killing and get rid of the fascists? No, he said firmly, that was not enough; the issues had changed. What kind of social order were we to have after the war? We must have better schooling, health care, conditions of living, better social morality – in short, progress towards socialism.

Do you really think, I asked, that we went to war to achieve socialism? He stood his ground; we have to give people a better life to repay them for their sacrifice.

How can you think of *repayment*? Unless, I said, the people at the top feel guilty about getting us into the war? Is it fair to trade on people's sadness and fear of the future simply to get support for you and the Labour Party?

I must have been very disrespectful. When I talked of 'the people at the top', he knew I included *him*, an important leader of opinion in the Thirties, who had helped to create the collective flight from robust action against Fascists and Nazis.

He was patient. I should be more realistic – meaning less naïve. This was the way the political game had to be played. The Tories were doing the same! One could do nothing without power. Rab Butler and his friends were cooking up a new deal for education – of course the Tories meant it to be a vote winner! If *they* were already bidding for the post-war vote why shouldn't Labour do so?

That said it all, the whole sad, unscrupulous story of politics – much in my mind at this time. Bernard had urged me to go into politics. He thought I had the mind and the passion for it. Here was the discouraging reality. To be in politics you had to join the power game and become as cynical and opportunist, and as ruthless, as the others. It was a Mephistophelian trap. Principle, where you started from, soon lost its force because, without power, it was futile. You told yourself that principle could be postponed, played down, to *get* power. In the manoeuvres and compromises along the way, principle imperceptibly became secondary, malleable to fit the game, even at times dispensable – until calculations about power, getting and holding it, excluded all else.

Gollancz expected the Labour Party to find him a seat in Parliament if he wanted one. Could the Labour chiefs, I wondered, having burned their fingers with such as Pritt, afford to have yet another fellow-traveller in the House? I dared not put the question; but he was quick to sense the thought and to forgive it, one of his many engaging qualities. A capricious gleam of sunlight broke through behind the round spectacle lenses, and he grinned boyishly, ruefully, the tooth-brush moustache quivering with mischief. 'After all,' he murmured, 'I *have* done a lot for the Labour cause.'

I doubt if he was convinced that life in House of Commons would suit him. He had flourished, soared with zest and euphoria, in the freebooting life on the fringes, the fast-moving sharpshooter, uncommitted, untrammelled by party discipline. He must have guessed that the answer might be as I expected, but he would be hurt when it came. There would be no offer of a constituency.

During these talks, Diana's pale, dreamy features contemplated an unknowable infinity. When we were alone she would say. 'The world – what's it got to do with *us*? What we are to each other is all that matters.'

How could that be enough? Confined within four walls and domesticity! Where would the wide world be then? I thought of father's fate. I began to understand, at last, what he had tried to tell me long ago, when I was about fourteen and already working in the factory: that his way forward had been blocked when mother had insisted on joining him in this country too soon, from *der heim*.

Her coming had burdened him before he had had a chance, as he put it, 'to do something with myself', to confront the world and taste victory. He blamed himself; he should have stood firm and let her wait. His better nature had betrayed him. The truth was, perhaps, that in letting her come he found a convenient excuse for failure? He had doubted his ability to carry the burdens of family life and still be truly himself, to use his powers to the full; and that doubt had crippled him.

Had he infected me with the same doubt? I knew in my bones that Diana's vision was right. It was there, in the heart, that life should be rooted. But I *would* not see it.

In years to come I would curse myself for a blindness that was close to arrogance. I would then understand – too late – what Peer Gynt meant, the battered seeker returning to his starting point: 'Fool that I was, my empire was *here*!'

But there would be no Solveig waiting for me.

It was not only Diana's vision of things. Others had tried to show it to me: Rachel, Bunty in her siren song in the factory, even perhaps Annie.

In Gollancz I sensed a frightening object lesson. He had conquered much more than I – starting from nothing – could ever hope to, but he had little feeling of triumph. Like the eyes of the Trolls in the Dovre Mountain – always seeing things awry – his vision too had turned away from the heart. Awareness of that neglect, the arid area beneath the flourishing surface, must have come to him in recent years, together with the perception that he lacked the power – or the will – to correct it. In that dispiriting knowledge, aware also, perhaps, that the inner conflict was blunting his touch, once so sure, he had fought doggedly on as before.

Mrs Gollancz, dark-haired and pale, reserved, outwardly serene, had something of Diana's dreamy quality. To my surprise, she invited me to see her collection of Leeds pottery. What, I wondered, went thought the mind of this well-intentioned woman, daughter of a rich house, to imagine that her luxury hobby would mean anything to a poor lad from the Gorbals? Diana, I knew, had told them where I came from. Much later, remembering this moment, I would think of John Betjeman, similarly at a loss for a point of contact with me. For Victor, too, the word Gorbals had meant little, simply a remote social fact. For her, it seemed, as for Diana, it must have had no meaning at all.

The very idea of collecting things struck me as strange. Apart from anything else, it meant that one already possessed a sufficiency of all the things one needed!

As she stood before the tall tan-coloured wooden cabinets containing the collection, the pieces gleaming in their still serenity on the shelves, I could almost see some quality in them stretch out to her in sympathy, like hands reaching out to a friend. Showing them, perhaps, may have been her unthinking way of testing young men for suitability, for sympathetic rapport – if they shared her feeling for those objects, they would do. I respected her, and so it was natural for me to admire them for her sake. There was surely more than this? We lingered there in the stillness of the afternoon; from a shelf here and there she took a piece and smoothed her fingertips over its flutings and the entwining of the handle, and murmured something about it – the words of little importance in themselves. They reached out and sought an answer, but not from me. Somewhere, from far away, she listened to other voices. Incongruously, with a little shiver of shock, I had a vision of Madame Ranevsky looking out of the window and surveying her cherry orchard, soon to be lost. Perhaps, after all some sympathy did flow between us? Much later I would understand. I must have sensed her premonition, or perhaps a perception slow in its maturing, of changes begun long before – that for her husband the soaring years were over.

The Rip van Winkle feeling was strong, here at the corner of The High and Turl Street. In place of Oxford's earlier sedate pace, the atmosphere of quiet detachment, as if the world began and ended here, there was a sense of volcanic action on the surface and purposeful scheming beneath – all with distant horizons in view. Unending streams of traffic, predominantly military, roared indifferently through. The narrow pavements over-flowed with service uniforms – Poles in tilted polygonal caps, Free French in képis,

Americans in what seemed the unmilitary garb of draped jackets and pale oyster shaded trousers, British in a variety of unfamiliar regimental and divisional flashes. Strangest of all were the bearded faces and raffishly shapeless khaki – the new, carefree identity of the commandos.

Gowns were few; one suspected that many were guiltily concealed. Students were in the main distinguishable because most of them looked absurdly young – even to me – little more than fresh-faced schoolboys. There seemed to be many more women in the streets than before, their numbers augmented by students from evacuated colleges, Westfield and the Slade, workers from the Cowley motor works, and from the ministries and other governmental or ancillary institutions like Chatham House and the British Council, housed in some of the colleges.

In place of the old ethos of unchallengeable confidence, mannered languor, display of foppish indifference – echoes of Oscar – there was intensity, immediacy, calculation; and over all a cloud of uncertainty.

The Oxford I had left for the army had changed little since that first morning long ago when I rode in on my bike from the Gorbals; it was then still enclosed in its *fin de siècle* dreams and hiding its confusion beneath many masks, listening to the shades of Wilde, Pater, Ruskin, Morris, Hardy, tilting at bourgeois values peevishly and selectively – one suspected somewhat enviously – straining to hear the pure voice of Nature, fearing science and the machine, praising muscle and sinew in lingering loyalty to the arts and crafts movement. The gibe 'arty-crafty' was in vogue, wistfully disowning a faded illusion. I had marvelled at the prevalence of Morris wallpapers and curtains full of freshness and light. In the Gorbals, if walls were covered at all – which was the 'respectable' thing – the paper was in traditional designs of flowered trellises printed in dark colours 'so as not to show the dirt'. In the more progressive North Oxford houses, simplicity, vegetable dyes, pastel shades, rough-textured materials – proclaiming hand-work – in curtains and furnishings and even clothes, were things of faith.

Nearly everyone's rooms had a Van Gogh or Cézanne print. In

the Glasgow Art Gallery where I used to make pencil or pastel copies of pictures, I had been under the spell of the Romantics, fascinated by their pastoral and sylvan scenes, and full of mystery. Here the innocence of the Impressionist, the stillness, the purity of colour, a new and magical openness, drew the mind deep into the heart of the world, where a long-locked door had been opened to let sunlight and joy and hope flood in. Seeing them everywhere, apparently as necessary as icons to the devout, I was misled. They did not express the feeling of the Thirties, but rather the sunset beliefs and hopes of progressive souls more than half-a-century before, when salvation might lie in retrieving lost links with Nature, and only a touch on the helm was needed to bring the world back on course to rediscover the Golden Age.

In my previous life here, standing on this spot beside the pale green wall of the Mitre Hotel, it was still possible to imagine that Bradley's untroubled world of Mr Verdant Green was not so far away – to whom it was said, not entirely in jest, that if he stood in the middle of The High and fired a pistol in any direction he could be fairly certain of not hitting anybody! Now, a tidal wave of people raged past. Going where? With what new thoughts? To what purpose? Ah yes – those questions were now urgent for me too.

In the world of the intellect also, this place had been living in the past, still fascinated, like the eighteenth and nineteenth centuries, by the shifting images of truth and illusion. The logical positivists, acclaimed as innovators in philosophy, wrestled with language, or rather the imprecise use of it – concerned with questions like 'When is a statement a non-statement?' Echoes were heard in the cant nonsense of sherry party talk, as always mordantly accurate in attacking scholarly conceits: 'Have you been to any interesting non-events lately?' or 'Ask me a non-question and I'll give you a non-answer!'

If distinguished and gifted people could not move beyond such trivial exercises, there must be crippling self-doubt in the contemporary culture greater than at any time since the later Middle Ages – a conclusion soon to be confirmed by the vogue acclaim given to the pretentious posturings of the existentialists.

An exception, far from generously recognised, was R. G. Collingwood in his luminous exposition of the proper business of philosophical enquiry, in lectures and in the Olympian sweep of his book *Speculum Mentis*. Its opening sentences I would remember in all the years to come: 'All thought exists for the sake of action. We try to understand ourselves and our world only in order that we may learn how to live.'

This down-to-earth, lucid statement, joining hands across the millennia with Socrates, must have been too challenging and too critical for the Oxford of that epoch. Though *Speculum Mentis* had been published fifteen years before, Collingwood was respected for an earlier work, something quite different, excellent within its scope but offering no such challenge to contemporary thinkers – *Roman Britain*.

Stevenson, at the Institute of Experimental Psychology, a refreshing person who transmitted his enthusiasms with the infectious zest of questing schoolboy, talked of the pecking order of hens, a line of thought hailed as providing revolutionary insight into the nature of society. Its attraction was demonstrated by its appearance in cant speech: 'Where is So-and-So in the pecking order?' What, I wondered, could differences of status in the animal kingdom tell us about Man that we did not already know? Ideas about the natural heirarchy among people, differing abilities and rank, qualities of leadership, interdependence, were as old as classical Greece. Pecking order theory *might* give comfort, I supposed, to people who were guilty about opposing egalitarianism – for if individual of other species were not equal within their groupings, why should we expect men and women to be?

Gollancz chided me for being 'too young to be an old conservative'. How *could* I be conservative, I reminded him, coming from where I did? He insisted in his judgement: I had obviously swung too far in the opposite direction. As a product of the Gorbals, he said, I was living proof of the need to correct inequality; how then could I question this article of socialist faith? I mentioned the day, at school, when I came top of the class – so intolerable to the others that it got me the worst beating of my life! Was it my fault if I was so far *unequal*? Should one attempt to 'correct' such an inequality? If you gave the less able person the same status or reward as the high performer, where was the incentive to excel? He refused to see the point; I was, he complained, confusing the issue.

Standing here, noting servicemen's badges of rank, and the bowler hats of senior civil servants, the pecking order was obvious and in full strength. It was not Stevenson's fault that people were so insecure, so burdened with historic anxiety, that they seized on scientific objectivity for solid ground to stand on. Solidity had gone. Among these restless crowds, a new, iconoclastic, opportunist view of life predominated, epitomised in the sardonic barrack-room maxim, 'any gravy train will do'.

A new, specifically wartime city – foreign in many senses – superimposed on the old one, hummed with the management of war. Tucked away in back alleys, or in specially erected huts on college playing fields, were organizations rumoured to be 'hush-hush', enclaves of barbed wire.

The aloof world of university licensed lodgings, in its old gentlemanly amplitude of two rooms per person, had shrunk. Hundreds of landladies had doubled and trebled their incomes by converting their houses to bed sitting-rooms. A new, cosy, stifling world of the bed-sitter had taken over; with narrow divan bed, sometimes the luxury of a wash-basin behind a curtain, wheezing gas fire with a little boiling ring to the side of it on a hinged bracket.

This usurping city also housed thousands of refugees of many origins, most of them comfortably off people who had no apparent purpose here but to avoid the London bombing. There was also a sub-world of miscellaneous misfits, exiles stranded in Britain by the war. An example was Domenico Altamura. Son of a rich South American landowning family, he had lived in Britain since childhood, gone to a leading public school, and war had come while he was trying, in leisurely fashion, to complete his education in Oxford. Family remittances reduced by the war, he supplemented them with his wages as a clerk in the Pickles and Sauces Section of the Ministry of Food. He had applied to join the RAF to train as a pilot, but for some obscure reason of diplomatic protocol had been refused entry to any of the services. Behind the patrician nonchalance, he was bitter at being denied the chance to fight for the only country he knew.

He was tall, broad-shouldered, with narrow hips and the balanced poise of the athlete. His long features had a Latin pallor. The black hair brushed back from the temples was unruly and sprang up in little horns; and when in full fig for a Bollinger rout in the old days, in long black cloak lined with flame-red silk, he was perfect for the Mephistophelian role. Laconic, correct, with a sardonic wit, one might imagine that he consciously played the classic upper-class Englishman, but that would have been unfair; he really was that Englishman, in upbringing, education, outlook. The touch of self-mockery marked the spirit of the man, a wry affirmation of his predicament – held by Destiny in a country whose ethos was his, that he was prepared to die for, but which denied him the privilege. Pickles and Sauces, he solemnly explained, were vital to the war effort. Because of meat rationing, the sandwiches that coal miners took down the mine usually contained meat loaf somewhat bland in taste, and in the obscurity often unrecognisable as meat – and so the tang of pickles or sauce reassured them and imparted greater zest for much-needed coal production! His work in Pickles and Sauces, therefore, was crucial for morale. The ironic style was part of his slow, tight-lipped, brooding charm. He was compelled to explain away – weakly, comically as he well knew – a status far below his aristocratic vision of himself. In his case, he thus insisted, there was clearly a fault in the pecking order.

There were deserters from the services. Hubert, of distinguished family, as an undergraduate had been a model of the Regency buck; from the army he had returned in a new avatar as aesthete and anarchist, and lived in a rotting old shed, rat-infested, on the canal bank near the slum area of Jericho. Dapper, with mockery in the cold blue eyes, the ruddy features showed early intimations of the brighter scarlet of the hardened toper. He composed poetry, played the flute, and wrote letters to the newspapers about the futility of war. He seemed to take no pains to conceal his fugitive position; obviously, money enabled him to live outside the system, or rather to make it 'work' his way. A deserter lacking money, and forced to get a job without appropriate documents, would put himself in someone's power. I never discovered how Hubert managed without a ration book for food and clothing coupons. One could eat tolerably – for about ninepence – at the subsidised British Restaurant in George Street without producing a ration book. To buy food in the shops, however, would mean dealing in the black economy. With aristocratic detachment, like Bakunin, Hubert saw no contradiction between anarchist principles and the use of wealth to live well by manipulating the system. I thought again of Jimmy Robinson, diehard anarchist, doing well by making the system 'pay', as he put it, while fighting it at the same time. Hubert, Jimmy, Gollancz – strange bedfellows!

Domenico and Hubert, as far as I knew, never met. Essentially from the same social class, the war had put them in different worlds; Hubert had defected to join the shadowy, bohemian one – the term 'drop-out' was not yet current – of those who by temperament or tradition were ranged against conventional society. Domenico, on a different fringe, supporting his straitened circumstances with aristocratic panache, stood unquestioningly for established values. Had he met Hubert and discovered he was a deserter, he would have seen it as his Englishman's duty to denounce him.

Possibly someone did denounce him; or he may have run his luck too far. One day, as I stood looking at the display of books in Blackwell's windows, he came up and prodded me in the ribs. Unusually, he wore a gown over the shabby army jacket. Ruddy features flushed, he bubbled over with excitement, part hilarious, part serious: 'Guess what! I've just been progged!' (caught in misdemeanour by the Proctors). The commonest reason was being discovered in an out-of-bounds pub. Being a deserter, in effect an outlaw, this was bizarre stroke of ill-fortune. On being challenged, he must have given his true name and college. He may have done so because, in liquor, he was off-guard, or it may have been an automatic expression of upper-class arrogance. More likely, tired of living in the shadows, he had unconsciously put himself in the way of being caught – accidentally on purpose? I wondered what to say;

form the eager look on his face he expected me to share his hysterical mood. It was customary to commiserate with someone for such bad luck – apart from being fined there could be considerable inconvenience – but I had for some time resented his mixture of boss class condescension and his charade of living as a deprived member of the working class. He lived in the lower depths *from choice*, not necessity. Being progged served him right! Still, it would have been unkind to say so. Before I could think of an acceptable remark, he waved a hand to dismiss me as a dullard, and rushed off up the Board, presumably in search of someone more responsive, his grown streaming defiantly behind him. Later I heard that he had disappeared from Oxford. Long afterwards I would see his name in the casualty lists and think of him sadly, with compassion, a rare, unfortunate soul – who had been, for reasons totally different from mine, equally lonely.

Domenico and Hubert represented two aimless groupings in suspense. Other, purposeful ones, were hard at work. In this frenetic city, so closely linked to the *realpolitik* of the war, one sensed the muffled clamour of people plotting to reshape the future to their designs, manipulating whatever forces they could – a microcosm of the world in apocalypse. Nothing was still. The worlds of political intrigue, personal manoeuvre, and fleeting passion interflowed. In tall Victorian houses among the North Oxford evergreens, in cramped bed-sitters in Walton Street, in college rooms, even in the streets and pubs, there was volatile talk, groups and pairs drawing aside from the stream, interchanging and reforming as in a classic dance – molten sympathy and scheming. Hectic, tumid excitement fed on instant intimacy and instant confidences, a hunger to fill each moment with the whole of life.

Some groups, especially those linked to governments in exile, plotted for advantage in their countries after the war; others, without nominal statehood, lobbied in the corridors of Allied power to turn promises or rhetoric into commitment. In a Zionist circle, a leading spirit was Walter Ettinghausen, a don at Queen's, a stocky figure with high bulging forehead; a man of charm, force of character, and sense of mission.

Walter Ettinghausen's confidence was strong; he may have had better grounds for it than most, possibly through contacts in the shadowy international bargaining. In the event, he would go to Palestine immediately after the war, and as Walter Eytan achieve high position in Israel, as Director-General of the Ministry for Foreign Affairs and Ambassador to France. The change of name, common among the first pathfinders, would perhaps be prompted in his case partly by the desire to shed the German associations of Ettinghausen – born in Munich in 1910, he went to St Paul's School and Oxford – partly by the compulsion to make a declamatory gesture. 'Eytan', a Hebrew word meaning strength or immovability, in this case would stand for 'indomitable, unconquerable', but with Old Testament overtones too, for instance in reference to the 'original strength' of the Patriarchs. In retrospect the choice of name, apart from offering intriguing insight into the man's vision of himself, and more to the point how he *wanted* to be seen – revealed a great deal about the ethos that possessed the builders of the new state.

Ettinghausen was a fine chess player, and it was chess that first drew me into the circle. I learned the game on my first landfall here, and was now rated a strong player. Chess, however, was not the circle's primary interest, which was to create a Jewish state in Palestine after the war. That, for most of us, remained fanciful, a mirage in the desert. Still, perhaps because so much else was in the melting pot, there was a feeling in the air, inexplicably, that history might decide, in this at least, to favour the dreamers.

In Ettinghausen's circle I met some of the group I had seen riding down the Broad singing *Hatikvah* long ago. Hannah, working at Bletchley Park – 'writing reports' was all she would say of her duties – was sometimes there, her willowy form elegantly turned out in finely tailored tweeds and sheer nylons, then as rare as peacocks' feathers. Her fair hair, once worn in long ringlets, was now cut short, and the curls nestled round the translucent features, emphasising their firm moulding and the pensive set of the lips – a Judith awaiting her heroic hour. Thoughts of Rachel drew us together.

I ran into Werner there, and that was something of a shock. Not having seen or heard from him for over two years, I had assumed that the break had been deliberate. He had vanished from Oxford from one day to the next, and no one knew, or would say, where he had gone. Only later did I hear that he had been interned. In those far off 'last days' – as I thought of them – people did simply slip quietly away. Even so, I had been hurt to find that he had left without a message of any kind. In fact, he said, he *had* written a few lines, which the authorities told him would be sent to me. If that note *was* written, it never reached me. Presumably, as an enemy alien, any message he wrote was suspect, and this one may have got no further than some confidential file. Absorbed with my imminent departure to the war – and, as I thought, to death – tracing him was beyond me. From the army, I wrote to him several times care of his Oxford research institute. Getting no reply, I said to myself: 'Put it down to experience!'– one of Bernard's favourite comments on life's disappointments.

He told me that he had written to me many times from the internment camp, and afterwards too – presumably when I was still in the army – and had been desolated by my silence.

Even in the Gorbals, I reflected, where the emotional language was familiar, signals had sometimes been hard to read – and to trust. In Oxford, learning a new code, I had often misread a comment or action as a slight and turned away, and discovered, sometimes too late to remedy, that people found me aloof, difficult to get to know. Now after another type of isolation in the army, I had to learn to read the signs anew. In time, I would conclude that Werner *had* written. Buchenwald and the rest had broken his patrician detachment. In the Isle of Man, he told me later, puzzling over my silence, reassessing me over and over again, he had reminded himself that I had always been dependable, never once asked him for anything; he could talk to me from the heart and I would say what I thought, holding nothing back. He had missed that solidity.

Which of us, I wondered, was the less mature *now* – which the smaller man? Many years senior, he should have been stronger, more thoughtful than this. It was time I ceased to assume that others were always the more mature – wiser in the world, more competent. Why did it not occur to him, for instance, that some mishap had befallen *me*? Back in Oxford, he could easily have found out that I was in the army – and speculated about my fate.

Slowly, in this strange, wary, buccaneering city, we moved towards a kind of trust once again.

As for our missing letters, it occurred to us that the answer might lie in his secret work and the accompanying surveillance upon him. He never did tell me what the work was. His correspondence, inwards and outwards, must have been intercepted, and some of it withheld. But why should *my* letters have been stopped? By an extraordinary chance I was to stumble on a possible answer. I met a girl who worked in one of the intelligence sections at Blenheim. In her bed-sitter one evening, as we sat in a tipsy huddle close to the wheezing gas fire, she murmured that she had seen my unusual name in an index of Communists. Her hand flew to her mouth in shock at what she had revealed, and quickly, as camouflage, she converted her guilt into concern for me: 'You *must* be careful! – though it's surely some silly mistake to have your name there at all. *You* don't talk like a Communist!'

Had there been a time when I *had* talked like one? Entry, I supposed, must date from the days when Bernard was a leading Party member – and I had been branded red by association. That, perhaps, made me an unsatisfactory person – a bad risk – for Werner to correspond with.

I would never be able to tell him this without revealing the source. I kept her secret.

Only at this chance meeting at Ettinghausen's did I learn that Werner's wife and children had been killed. 'I am not superstitious,' he said, 'at least I try not to be. It seemed the right decision, at the time, to stay on here. If I had gone to America when I intended, they would still be alive. Ah yes – if!' He raised his hands and let them fall back on his knees.

Werner was thinner now. The sleek black hair, brushed tightly back from the domed brow, had receded further; in the long, pointed features the mouth was tighter, the lines beside it deeper. I had to look carefully to discern the shadow of the once debonair *flâneur* I had first met, a lifetime away, in distant green days.

I wondered if he had thought back, in guilt, to the philandering that had so shocked Rachel. Astonishingly, he did know what she had thought about him. Gently kindly, she had begged him to mend his ways. As he told me of it, her voice spoke to me out of the darkness. Oh Rachel – sincere and forthright spirit, seeing all things simply! In this instance too she had spoken wisely, and in vain. Now, when Werner scourged himself for the fate of his wife and children, it was for his error of judgement, nothing more.

What of me? If I had listened to her, she too might still be alive.

He talked on, meditating on her words. 'What I was doing, she said, might bring a judgement on me. What a woman! She spoke from a good heart. But I am a scientist. I think logically. Did the German bombers *know* that I had been playing about with women and therefore decide to drop the bomb at precisely that moment?' He shrugged. 'Those little affairs had no world-shaking meaning! I *like* women! – flirting as you say? No it is more than flirting; a little diversion here and there – innocent pleasure! After it you go on your way with no harm done. What is it but a natural expression of the masculine personality – what Freud calls the libido? – a different motive entirely from marriage? Women are so insecure about such things. They refuse to understand!'

Half-bitterly, half-whistling in the dark, he referred to himself as a 'reconstituted' bachelor. Reconstituted was a wartime word everybody had had to learn – reconstituted dried eggs, dried milk, dried baby-food ... He pursued the role with slowly returning zest. His flat in St Giles, not far from the Lamb and Flag pub, became a convivial place, destined to live in my memory for many reasons, pleasure and friendship, and self-knowledge – not always pleasurable, especially in a grotesque experience, which I explain in its place later, when I would put myself in danger of killing a man or being killed, a hero for no good reason: and I would discover for myself that fear, as Bernard had said, did not strike at the moment of its genesis; you simply acted, did what you were impelled to do, and then the fear would surge home overwhelmingly, shocking reminder of brooding death, and return again and again over the years.

On most Saturday nights Werner threw a party that stretched well over into the Sunday. The flat was usually well-stocked with liquor and food, mainly from the black market, but it was understood that guests brought what food and drink they could; judging by the quantity and quality thus donated – good champagne, smoked salmon, fine chocolate, even caviare sometimes – most of it came from privileged sources, the services or diplomatic missions. This life, insouciant in spite of the *angst* of war – or perhaps because of it – suited him. After the war, he thought, he would probably stay on in Oxford; plenty of young women, sport, parties, convenient for the bright lights of London – why not?

'Even if the Zionist dream does come true,' he said, 'I am not the pioneer type; but it *will* not, that is sure! No one will give the Jews anything. Apart from that I am not cut out to be a conspirator either. In any case I must keep my nose clean, as they say. I have had blows enough to last me all my life. I do not want to be sent back to the Isle of Man as an unreliable alien.'

In this rough, jostling foreign city, unsettling reminders of *realpolitik* and its tireless scheming constantly appeared. I went to Chatham House with the idea of earning some extra money translating from German newspapers; abortively as it turned out because, worried about accuracy, and steeped as I was in the High German of the classics and Fraulein Wüschak's mandarin style, I was too slow at turning colloquial German into English. That glimpse behind the scenes of war, however, was disturbing. From here, though it was not the only source; government departments, and presumably the intelligence services, were provided with foreign press summaries. This output would influence policy analysis and strategic judgement – what the enemy wanted its people to know, or indirectly the world at large; what was being concealed and what the concealment itself indicated, and conversely, why certain things *were* selected to be know. What, on the other hand, should *we* feed into the great Byzantine shadow play? The end result? Redesigned strategy perhaps, adjusted tactics possibly, death and destruction none the less. Yet everything looked so harmless! In these dingy college rooms whose grimy leaded windows, crisscrossed with sticky tape against bomb blast, kept out more light than they let in, charming, cultivated people sat among piles of newsprint, drinking tea and reading the papers – as if at a marathon March Hare breakfast – pausing now and then to send reports over the wires or by courier. Similar people did likewise in Germany and in many other countries. What price the noble fourth estate, supposed instrument of enlightenment, used for deception, invasion of the mind, thought control!

The newspapers and magazines were fresh. Obviously most of the enemy material was flown in from neutral countries, but a macabre fantasy struck me – the war was being *co-operatively* organised between the obliging combatants – reminding me of the story featured in the 'Nicht wieder Kreig' exhibition in Glasgow, of the factory on the border between France and Germany that had supplied munitions to both sides in the First War; the inference being that the combatants co-operated to keep that supply line open for each other.

Someone tapped me on the shoulder: 'Contemplating the eternal verities eh?' Bill Challoner stood beside me on the narrow pavement, leaning on his heavy stick. His features were less drawn than when I had met him on the river path a few weeks before. The long khaki greatcoat was creased as though he had slept in it, but worn this time draped over the shoulders like a cloak. The badges of rank were gone from the epaulets, but little black holes showed where the major's crowns had been. The well-cut double-breasted suit of chalk-stripe clerical grey, to my experienced eye new, also betrayed itself as having been tailored for someone with influence, or money; the trousers had turn-ups, forbidden by the clothes rationing regulations – another sign of high status in the pecking order!

The man with him was somewhat older, in his thirties, also in civilian clothes, dark, dapper, keen-eyed, intense. He reminded me of Bernard in his pre-disillusion days. Introducing him, Bill called him Colonel, indicating – not only by the formal address but the tone of voice – that he was in some way of importance to him. Oxford seemed full of surprisingly young majors and half-colonels

– eager *apparatchiks*, able, ruthless, glorifying in virtuoso manoeuvre. I will call him Colonel James. Both of them looked flushed, and James was unsteady on his feet.

'We're just going to have tea.' Bill indicated the Mitre Hotel at our backs. 'Come and join us?'

James had the trick of regarding you with head inclined, scrutinising you warily beneath the lowered brow, partly concealing his expression. As we turned towards the Mitre, he seemed to stoop still further, lost his balance and would have fallen on his face if Bill had not caught him by the arm and hauled him erect. One of Bill's nicknames was Stone Head; he was one of those rare drinkers who showed little outward sign of the effects. He murmured to me that they had just come from a rather heavy lunch. It was getting on for five in the afternoon. He looked at me steadily, rubbing the side of his nose with a forefinger. I caught the warning and did not ask where. The world 'heavy' obviously referred to more than drink; he and James had been in attendance, as staff officers, at a high-level meeting.

In the low-ceilinged lounge, dark panelled, the broad sash windows, their sills at knee height, were tightly closed to exclude the noise of the High, as they had shut the world out for generations. The leather in the old brass-studded chairs was cracked with age, and perhaps wartime ill-use; the ceiling was yellow with old smoke. In the dimness of the late afternoon, a breath of sadness rose up from the red patterned carpet and squat oaken tables, a sense of faded, invaded dignity. The tubby white-haired waiter, in a shiny black suit, was much as I remembered him from the 'last days', as was the great tea tray with brass handles, but not its austere fare or furnishings – a square china pot of weak tea, thick cups and saucers instead of fine Wedgwood, a metal jug for milk, a chipped china rack with triangles of tired toast, a little dish with three small blobs of margarine and another with a few teaspoonfuls of thin jam. James, who had flown in the previous day from the fleshpots of Washington, inspected the tray and sighed.

He and Bill were obviously still borne up by the excitement of momentous discussions at lunch. I did not know at the time that the meeting – at a country house not far from Oxford – had concerned Operation Overlord, and the position of de Gaulle. Left to themselves they might have been tempted to exchange thoughts about it, which Bill must have been desperate to avoid for fear of being overheard; hence his decision to shepherd James about in the noise of the streets, where eavesdropping was less likely, until, sobered up, he could safely see him on his way. Having spotted me at the corner, Bill had watched me for some minutes, to be sure I was not waiting to meet someone; I could guess the rest. The pain in his bad leg had become unbearable from trudging about; at all costs he must sit down. He hit upon the idea of getting me to join them, in the hope that in the presence of a stranger James's training would assert itself and keep his tongue under control. As far as I could guess, the gamble succeeded, but only just.

Even so, James's efforts to control his tongue were pathetically obvious. Restlessly he glanced about the empty room, tugged at his lower lip, stared at Bill as though pleading for a safe cue. Though Bill looked the more composed, almost his normal self, they both talked excitedly, compulsively, as one might when a subject uppermost in the mind threatens to burst out, hoping that a torrent of extraneous talk would block the dangerous channel. As always, the forbidden subject must have exercised a powerful, spiteful magnetism. Not surprisingly it occurred to me – since here were two staff officers who, I guessed, were close to great affairs – that the secret concerned what everyone suspected was in train, the plan for an Allied 'return' to Europe. Whatever it was, their desperately irrelevant talk must have skirted the censored subject closely.

James, service aide to a ministerial committee dealing with de Gaulle, grumbled about the incessant difficulties created by the proud, spiky general.

'Why do you put up with him?' I asked. 'You people put him there! You can stop backing him if he's hampering the war effort'

'It's too late. Whether we like it or not, whatever he was before, he is now *the* Free French leader.'

Immediately after the fall of France, when it was crucial to find someone to personify France in exile and command its forces,

James had worked for a steering group in the anxious governmental discussions as to whom Britain should support for that role. It was vital that a clearly dominant leader should emerge quickly. In some ways, James mused tipsily, he himself had been a lucky man – in the right place at the historic moment; his canny, astute voice, at a time of such uncertainty, might have tipped the delicate balance in favour of de Gaulle. At one stage General Giraud seemed a possibility. Another was Admiral Darlan, the intransigent commander who had resisted British proposals, after the surrender on the mainland, that French naval units should be placed under British control. A powerful figure, the object of considerable French loyalty, it was feared that Darlan wanted to set up a new sovereign entity, based on French colonial territories, and break free of the Alliance. There was also a suspicion that he might use his control of still formidable French sea power to bargain with the Germans. Britain dared not risk such a 'third force' on its flanks. I remarked that at the time I myself had thought that this deadly danger clamoured for a classic Byzantine solution, assassination. Just as I was later to pray that Hitler might invade Russia, and wake to find the prayer answered, amazingly Darlan *was* assassinated. Yes, James casually said, it was no accident. There was no other way.

'Of course,' he went on enthusiastically, 'we were right to plump for de Gaulle' – meaning that *he* had been right.

'How can you tell if he *is* the right man,' I wondered aloud. 'The French people have no say in the matter? Obviously, whoever has the backing of the Allies will be the 'sitting tenant' when the war is over, and he will step straight into the Elysée Palace. The French will be saddled with de Gaulle for a long time, whether they like it or not. You people have made the choice for them.'

'But he's so obviously successful,' James began, then stopped, glancing at Bill, who looked away.

'How can he *not* be successful?' I persisted. 'There's no one to measure him against! You, a few strategically placed individuals, have fixed the nature of France after the war – you've determined the history of France, the history of Europe, for the next – what? – fifty years? He nodded excitedly, savouring the thought. The war had given him, fleetingly, a spell at the wheel of Destiny.

So this was how the world lurched through 'time and chance'? People like James and Bill, brilliant, artful schemers behind the scenes of an apocalyptic puppet show, ventriloquists speaking through the mouths of the seeming holders of power? Was the whole of life, the 'great sweep of history', as empty of principle as this – the world run by grown-up school prefects, descendants of Stalky & Co., with cleverness, power of persuasion, nudging the figureheads this way and that?

Bill had been studying me gravely. 'You should go into politics,' he said. 'You're too fundamental for the likes of us. *We* are just the operators behind the scenes! We enjoy the game, that's all. We have no principles really, except to keep the *status quo* – the game as we know it. We know the ropes. We're not interested in anything else.'

He was speaking, typically, with Machiavellian false modesty. He meant that he and James and their like would always be the true prime movers behind the scenes – *eminences grises*, who would implacably retain the decisive power.

Yes: they would always be the fixers, the cool-headed operators, the secretive network of power that I would never be permitted to join. They sensed, finely tuned as they were, that I was not cut out for the role. They and their circle *might* just conceivably allow me a minor one – even pay tribute, when it suited them, to my high principles – permitting me a small amount of influence, until the time came for me to be displaced, or neutralised, when I ceased to serve 'the game'.

Guessing my thoughts, he murmured, 'That's the way the world wags, old boy. The pecking order works in mysterious ways!'

He smiled to himself, and nodded thoughtfully.

13

Figures in a Brueghel Landscape

In vino veritas applies in behaviour as well as in speech. One summer night, so drunk that I had to cling to the nearest wall to stay upright, I left a party in Beaumont Street on my way to another in Museum Street. The night was balmy and still. A great round moon hung in the luminous sky; and in its light the simple domestic façades, flint-grey, with transomed doorways and window embrasures and glazing bars picked out in white, stood out in muted silvery splendour against the dark velvet background of the night. The street was deserted, or so it appeared, enclosed as I was in alcohol's special isolation. To me it was entirely normal to be moving along hand over hand against the walls, floating through this breathless world as Cocteau would portray Orpheus making his way through a silent Hades in his film *Orphée*. Nearing the corner where Beaumont Street gave way to the wide expanse of St Giles – the Giler – the rusticated stonework of the Ashmolean Museum's screen wall comfortingly rough to the touch, the grey pinnacles of the Martyrs' Memorial some fifty yards away receded and merged into the trees of St Mary Magdalen churchyard behind, seen now in miniature as from the wrong end of a telescope; and Balliol, on the other side of the Giler, squat and muddy in the moonlight, retreated swiftly too and was soon a mile away at least. I clung to the Ashmolean's corner stone, and with the crystal-clear logic of the very drunk, assessed my situation. Of one thing I was sure; I could not cross that immense open space of the Giler on my own two feet. And then, simplicity itself, the solution was obvious – I would crawl across on hands and knees.

In retrospect it is hard to believe that I ignored the cars going past. Some part of me must have dismissed them as irrelevant. Hands and body pressed against the rough stone, I subsided on to my knees and then, reassuringly solid on all fours, made my way over the wide pavement, across the cobble stones of the broad sunken gutter, and steadily – pleased with my cleverness – crawled across the broad roadway, from time to time surprised to see floating lights moving near, like large glow-worms – later realised to have been headlights – approach and float past me, first from my right going left, then from my left going away to my right. At last my hands felt the smooth round cobbles in the gutter on the far side, then the uneven flag stones of the upward incline towards Balliol doors, closed at this hour. Reaching the arched doorway, I pressed against the pitted stonework and climbed up on to my feet; and continued my progress, in the blissful floating manner of hand-over-hand against the walls, aware of nothing but the eerie joy of this primitive victory, and passed along the perimeter walls of Balliol and St John's, turned right through the tunnel entrance to Lamb and Flag passage to reach the old-world enclave of Museum Street and its single short row of narrow houses, unlit windows open to the soft summer air, and join in the sweet abandon of the night, bottles and glasses passing to and fro, talk and happiness flowing.

The next day at breakfast, casually mentioning the manner of my crossing the Giler, I met a shocked silence, and then: 'Good Heavens – what about the *cars*?' I was about to say that I could not remember any, and then I thought of those lights floating past my head.

Freud says, 'What was predictable, was intended', but it is an ancient truth. The drunken mind – or the overwrought one – releases the troubled spirit to cry havoc and trip you up. Perplexed as I was by sibylline warnings – 'you are on the wrong road, in the wrong place in the wrong epoch!' – perhaps I had asked myself, as father in bitterness must often have done, 'What does it matter if I do destroy myself?'

Yet that day had brought such a bright message, a victory I had told myself I must not expect – as I had also reminded myself when entering for the scholarship. I had sat the examination for the Economics and Political Science Diploma, and that morning I had gone to look at the results newly posted up in the Examination Schools. In the evening I had arranged to meet some of the other candidates – whatever the result – for a classic celebration, and drink the world away. On my way to the Schools I tried to stroll jauntily, to affect a happy indifference, but I must have looked as I felt, wooden, fearful. Again and again I said to myself, falling back upon the old Gorbals sympathetic magic, 'Expect the worst and you won't be disappointed!' How I wished I had not promised to join the revel that evening.

Nearing the Schools, some of the others, returning from their scrutiny of the lists, hailed me with the thumbs-up sign. Thinking they referred to their own results, I tried to look happy for them. At the great dark doors I paused, half-unwilling to go further; the shadowy, cavernous hall, emptied of the rows of examination desks, yawned its indifference. At last I went in. The stone floor chilled the still air. To the left, in deep shadow, on a neo-gothic screen of massive timber, hung the green baize notice board, and pinned on it were the Diploma results in tiny black handwriting. Perversely my eyes went first to the bottom of the sheet of paper, in case I was among those who had not 'satisfied the Examiners'. Slowly I read upwards through the names of those who *had*. My name was not there – anywhere! I turned away and stared again into the brooding shadows of the hall – glad that I stood there alone – and tried to tell myself that it did not matter. I had soared too high. The gods had spoken. What a sorry mistake to have come to Oxford!

No! Wait! Fury took hold of me, and in that instant I could have torn down the whole world. How could my name not be there? I must *exist*! I turned back to the board as if I would force my name to appear on the paper in letters of flame – Orpheus on Phlegethon. And then, as I stared, I felt cold sweat. In the dimness I had missed – how could I have done! – a few lines of crabbed writing at the very top of the paper, separated from those below by a blank space and a thick black line. Under a heading 'The following were judged worthy of Distinction', were three names; mine was there.

The breakfast table wondered, delicately, not in so many words but plainly enough, how strange it was, on a day of success, to go and put yourself in the way of death, accidentally on purpose. You were lucky this time – one day you won't be!

What I had done was out of character – or so I thought. What was that *alter ego* trying to tell me? Why did success unnerve me so?

The insouciant life here, especially in the first period, before going into the army, was so bewitching that sometimes, awakening in the night, it was hard to believe that I was the person for whom, so recently, the unrelenting burden of work in the noise and steam and squalor of the factory, from dark in the morning till dark at night, had been the natural order of things, and who now dispensed my hours as I pleased – sailing, tennis, squash, the theatre, concerts, parties, sometimes getting drunk; I had never had a drink in my life till I came to Oxford, except for the occasional sip of wine at religious ceremonies. What people here called 'work', reading, writing essays, was pleasure! I touched the hard calloused skin on the palms of my hands. It was true and not true:

> Which of us commands here,
> Within this husk of life?
> Which of us will arrive at any destination?
> But if all is conditional,
> Until the final trump,
> Does it matter?

Instinct made me an indefatigable joiner, participator, explorer of this new world – a flowering unimaginable in the Gorbals days. This appetite was natural enough in a very young man; there were, however, equivocal voices within. A black cloud hid behind the sun, fleetingly appearing and sliding away again, tantalising – reminder and warning. To live the *dolce far niente* existence, beguiled for ever by the Sirens, was surely not the real me? It must surely be a self-indulgent deviation from my true course – if I could only divine what that was. A bout of heightened pleasure would sometimes carry a sting of guilt in its tail – perhaps the residual influence of Calvin and Moses, the powerful mixture permeating the life of the Gorbals. More prosaically, perhaps, the feeling sprang from a sense of living on borrowed time. Unlike most other students here, I could never expect to live in the fashion again.

Sometimes a fog of unease and discontent descended, like the heaviness of the spirit on a 'morning after', but unattributable to any cause. This was a new unease, far more profound than the passing discomfitures of my first days here. Life then, apart from those initial shocks, had had the magical quality of a continuous, wondrous party. Like le Grand Meaulnes I had floated through an enchanted demesne, searching the light and shade of self-discovery and discovery in others, the hours sparkling and short, too short.

Disquiet flowed not only from disillusion, imperceptibly grow-ing. Certainly the distant gleam of Mr Lipchinsky's torch had all but disappeared. A more immediate reason for unease, and guilt, was loneliness. Thinking of it dispassionately, the idea was absurd. I knew dozens of people, to drink and talk with, join for squash or tennis; girls to take to the theatre or concerts or on the river. Yet it was true. I was lonely. Only on Benard's occasional visits did I speak in a shared idiom. Yes, Alec had been right!

In retrospect, guilt – or was it self-doubt? – showed itself in dra-matic, comic, frightening ways, pulling me up short for no obvious reason, awareness of brooding shadows, intimations of sibylline prophecies wafted away on the wind, to be understood only long afterwards, mostly too late.

At a party in Werner's flat, I took a mortal risk seemingly with a clear head, for I was not drunk, and the danger was plain; I did it, amazed at myself, unhesitatingly.

It was a large party, drawn from a wide spectrum, Bletchley Park and Blenheim, the Slade, university luminaries, service officers – in-cluding Bill Challoner and James – and fringe people, self-evacuees seemingly with no greater reason to live in Oxford than anywhere else. Diana and Hannah were there. Bernard was there too; on one of his trips south, he had taken a weekend off to visit me, and Werner, who had warmed to him after their first, somewhat combative meeting on the river bank, had asked me to bring him.

One of the fringe people was Julian, son of an old colonial trading family, a convivial character to be seen most days – depending on the hour – propping up the bar at the Randolph or the Playhouse. Tall, thin, angular, with sharp features drawn tight, sunken eyes glittering with intensity, signs of his condition perhaps; he was tubercular, but I did not know it at the time.

Rejected for military service, his surface roughness – probably cultivated – may have sprung from a sense of inadequacy, an unhappy protest at the unfairness of life; brothers and many relatives were in the services, and here he was letting the side down. With a thin moustache and a peremptory way of speaking, he may have hoped to be mistaken for the tight-lipped, dashing officer of his imagination, who just happened to be in civilian clothes. Not far beneath the surface lurked a meditative, solitary soul, attributes that may have helped to bring about the incident.

Another factor, perhaps the crucial one, must have been the undercurrent of homosexuality in this milieu; and it is hard to believe that in my innocence I was unaware of it. I had heard of homosexuality only as a distant, hidden phenomenon, living in the shadows somewhere, which a 'normal' man would be unlikely to encounter. I had had no reason, as far as I knew, to think about it till that evening, still less to speculate about who might be, as Proust put it concerning the Baron de Charlus, 'so'. It would be a long time before I realised how numerous they were, and how unconcernedly their sexual preference was looked upon by these boss class people. The subject hardly ever seemed to crop up in conversation. In fact it did, often, but I had been too green to perceive it – in remarks, for example, about mutual acquaintances and their 'difficult relationship' such as might be made about a fellow and his girl, puzzling because the reference was to two *men*. In the Gorbals, all I had known of homosexuals came from the usual gross stories, so hard to believe. How could love, inseparable from the magic of a woman's silken flesh, exist between men? Homosexuals were thought of as less than manly – the demotic use of the word 'pansy' conveying effeminacy, the opposite of aggressive, muscular, masculinity, the only proper kind. For a 'normal' man to be approached – made a pass at – by a pansy was a terrible affront to which the proper response must be violence, incontrovertible proof that he was not 'so'.

Werner's flat occupied the first floor of an old, rambling building. In its spacious drawing room a low latticed window looked out, through a screen of trees, to the wide expanse of St Giles. A large study opened off it, where, at a long oak refectory table, he would sit his guests when he gave one of his small dinner parties. On the other side of a dark hallway were two big bedrooms, a bathroom and a kitchen. The party flowed over the whole area, into corners, into the shadows of the hall. On the dining table in the study stood rank upon rank of bottles, a whole world of drink, added to as people arrived with their offerings until, space exhausted, new additions formed ranks on the floor below it. They would not stay down there long – these were days of *angst* and thirst. Large serving plates were piled with food, a gourmand's dream come true, denying austerity – smoked salmon, cold meats, cheeses, fruit, biscuits, fine chocolates straight from Washington. Werner, not a great drinker, moved hospitably among his guests refilling glasses.

The party had been in being for about an hour, and some of the early arrivals, going on to dinner, said their good-byes. With their departure, the initial throng, so dense that it was virtually a solid, heaving, clamorous mass, enclosed in a blue fog of cigarette smoke, had thinned into dispersed groups, opening up a clear view through the drawing room doorway to the rooms on the far side of the hall. I was on the edge of a group standing near the long window, which included Nevill Coghill and Maurice Bowra; the talk was about a production of *Salômé*. Bowra, next to me, his interest obviously fading, turned as if to go, brushing against me; seeming to lose his balance and to save himself he threw an arm round my hips: 'Dear boy – so sorry!' He righted himself rather slowly, looking at me fixedly, searchingly. I moved away to break the contact. He did not look drunk. I must have scrutinised him coldly, the wrong response presumably. He tried again: 'We've met? At Lindsay's, was it not?'

To be remembered by an important man was flattering, and I must have shown that I was pleased, but perhaps not in the right way, for he stood back, his broad face assuming a distant look of preoccupation, and with an indistinct murmur he turned on his heel and strode away.

I had had a couple of glasses of champagne, but I was far from drunk. As he turned away, his expression had been a mixture of annoyance and hurt. Puzzled, I watched him cross the hall and merge with the crowd in one of the rooms on the far side. What had I done to offend him? It was beyond me. As I stood, for the moment separate from Coghill and the others, speculating on the encounter, Bill Challoner came up, leaning unsteadily on his stick, glass in hand: 'Maurice must be hard up!' he muttered in my ear. 'I shouldn't have thought you were his type.' So that was it! Seeing my shock – and resentment – he added quickly: 'My dear chap it's nothing – really it isn't. It's par for the course!' Then with a tilt of the head he indicated Hannah and Diana at the door talking to Bernard; Hannah's willowy form leaned on the door frame, her hip curving out, breathtakingly defined in the straight grey skirt. 'In any case you're doing all right!' His wolfish grin was eloquent – there, surely, is living proof that you are not 'so'!

If Bill was right, and this *had* been a pass, was there something about me, an unconscious mannerism, that misled some people into thinking I was 'so'? Paradoxically, I was glad that I had *not* understood, for the ingrained Gorbals reaction would have been to knock the fellow down – a matter of honour; and where would that have landed me! Bill, in his kind, intuitive fashion, was comforting me – the pass was nothing to be upset about.

His words prompted a different worry, however, in its way much more important; I had failed once again to read the infernal code of this place. I cursed myself for a fool. I should have known – of course I should. What Bill had called 'par for the course', must happen to all of them, and some must welcome it. For all I knew, such passes had been made at me before and I simply had not noticed. Bill leaned close again: 'One doesn't mention these things. I'm doing so because you look a trifle puzzled.' He meant *upset* but was too nice to say so. 'He's not a bad sort actually. As a matter of fact, he's not my type either!'

These words, too, startled me, or at least the Gorbals part of me with its stereotype of the pansy as effeminate; for Bill fitted to perfection the standard image of the tough, masculine man. He was also very much the ladies' man. That term, I reflected, had its own germane ambiguities, implying, among other things, that some men were – in the 'wrong' sense – men's men! That too was par for the course. It was not done to notice it, least of all to comment upon it.

I saw Bowra emerge from the far room and look about him tight-lipped. Werner was moving through the hall dispensing champagne. Bowra went up to him, a rigid smile suddenly donned like a mask, spoke briefly, nodded a brisk farewell and hurried out of the front door. In a few moments, glancing out of the window, I saw him stride through the line of trees and cross St Giles.

What, I wondered, would have been the right way to deal with the pass? – that is, one that would not have led to the man's obvious ill-humour? Perhaps there *was* no such way? Something in Bill's manner, even his words 'par for the course', suggested that for most young men of his class such passes, and the related sexual experience, here in Oxford or previously at public school – or both – were accepted features of emotional development. For my Gorbals persona the idea was repellent, but that in itself meant nothing, except, perhaps, that there was something wrong with *me*. Well, I thought perplexedly, if that whole area of experience really was necessary phase in emotional development, I had no choice but to manage without it.

I reminded myself that I had only Bill's word that it *had* been a pass. Plainly he spoke from experience. His words did seem to fit. Of course, such passes must take many forms. How many times, here in Oxford, had I responded in the 'wrong' manner, misreading the code – *all* the codes? I thought of the many masculine acquaintanceships that had begun in seeming friendly fashion and then, inexplicably, had faded. Was this the reason? Slowly, over the years, I would understand. I had had no conditioning in what continentals sometimes called the English malaise, the sympathetic brother-hood in the boss class which, even if not sexually expressed, was a secure bonding of the spirit, an ineffable guide to 'belonging'. To achieve that special acceptance no brain power, no intellectual cu-riosity would help me. Like a wrongly scented animal in a herd, I would never belong.

Later in the evening, the crowd having thinned still further and many more bottles emptied, Hannah came up and gripped my wrist. She was deathly pale, not so much frightened as strung taut. 'You must do something! Julian's got a knife. He's hurt someone al-ready!' She pointed to the room beyond the hall, were Bowra had been.

The vibrant hum of party noises was stilled. The expectant si-lence was almost palpable. Moved by some hypnotic compulsion, I found myself walking across the room with only one thought in mind, a certainty in itself frightening – there was no way out of this. I would confront Julian and get that knife from him – *how* I had no idea. Behind this thought was a troubling question: why was it that not one of these people, now moving aside to let me pass, came to my side to help me? There were so many of them, more than enough – many times over – to overpower one man.

I was the chosen one in a tribal sacrifice, central character in a play of death, all the others frozen in their places in fascination. Why should it be me? What quality, what power, could I possibly have that any one of them did not possess? Perhaps the answer was absurdly prosaic – I was the least drunk. That was too simple, even if it had been true; Werner, for one, diligent host, had so far drunk nothing. Was it that among these people a primitive prudence ruled, which had made them single me out precisely because I was *not* one of them, the brotherhood? What would it matter if *my* blood was shed? Apart from that I was simple enough to be gulled into playing the hero.

All except Bernard. Suddenly he was at my side. I had noticed him refilling his glass steadily, and he swayed a little. He lurched against me. 'Come on, *we'll* sort him out.' He squared his broad shoulders. 'Seen it all before.'

There was a hint of comradely swagger, born of distant bugles: we'll face this together, whatever it is. The poignancy would return, in memory over the year, again and again.

No, I said to myself; he's in no state for a fight, not if Julian's got a knife. I could not, *must* not let him go into that room with me, or there would be disaster. 'No! Stay here.'

'It's all right,' he muttered again, 'done it all before.'

We were at the drawing room door. Werner stood rooted to the floor like the rest, champagne bottle in one hand, glass in the other – in retrospect a comic, pitiable sight. There was only one solution – I gave Bernard a heave with my shoulder and he toppled over and crumpled at Werner's feet.

Diana, standing near, suddenly clung to Werner, stared at me in terror and said in a strangled voice: 'Oh don't go in there – please!'

I crossed the hall to the open door of the facing room. Julian stood with his back pressed against the far wall, staring fixedly as if possessed; I wondered if he saw me. Round the room, people hugged the wall or cowered behind furniture. A man crouched in a corner, blood dripping from a gash on the back of his hand. As I entered, they edged towards the door and filtered out behind me. Someone whispered as he passed: 'Careful! He's got a commando knife!'

Julian's right hand was by his side, and from it, pointing to the floor, hung the long blade of a heavy knife, broadening towards an angular point. On one of its sloping edges a smear of something red and wet caught the light. He was about fifteen feet away. Cold fear streaked up the back of my neck, but curiously distant as if it was *someone else's* fear. I could not have turned back. I was driven by something already written. The whole world was shut out. Nothing existed but the infernal stare on Julian's face, a mask of sad fury, the dark blue veins bulging out on his neck; and that long blade. Oh God, make him stand still! I must get close, really close. What I would do then, I had only a vague idea.

A thought boomed in my mind like a drum beat. I must project tremendous calm and determination – overwhelm him with my confidence. Confidence? I had none. I felt only that I moved automatically, not with my own will, the slave of some power – God alone knew what or why. A man stood there with murder in his eyes. I must make him understand that I was not bluffing, that I *would* attack; and that he was going to drop that knife. I must go for that wrist. I must not look at the knife lest he be alerted. I tried to remember the army training in unarmed combat, disjointed visions of using the adversary's strength and weight in falls and locks and leverage – to throw, hurt, disable. These thoughts, it occurred to me afterwards, transmitted to him in the electric moments as I steadfastly approached, may have spoken to him more powerfully than words could have done, broken through into his secret world of doubts and demons, dragged him back to reckon with the world as it was.

I would leap for that wrist, trip him off his feet and get a knee on his neck. He was about my height, and quite strong – speed alone must save me. If he continued to stand still there against the wall, all might be well. If he once brought that knife into action, with that terrible blade the length of a small bayonet – God help me.

Slowly, taking short steps, I narrowed the distance, looking fixedly at him, trying to hold his eyes. Now I was ten feet away. He did not move, still stared glassily, but I saw the dark veins bulge on the hand holding the knife. I said, hoping my voice sounded steady, summoning all the menace I could, 'I am going to take that knife from you.' I softened my tone: 'It's better if *you* drop it. Come on, open those fingers and let it fall.' He said nothing. His expression did not change. I moved one more small pace. Another. Another. Five feet away. Now for it! He must have seen my eye flicker to the knife, for the blade rose and the point was levelled at me. I said: 'Drop the knife – *now*.' I tensed to jump. And then – I could not believe it – his fingers opened and the knife thudded to the floor. I leapt forward and kicked it away, facing him, poised for what might still need to be done. The mask of fury had gone. He looked at me in helpless appeal, open-mouthed, gasping with an awesome croaking sound – dreadful reminder of Bernard's father – then his spare form slide down the wall and he fell on his knees, and tears streamed down the lean cheeks; a paroxysm of tubercular coughing seized him, and his lips were wet with bloodstained phlegm.

Cold sweat drenched me. And now it was I who was rooted to the floor, all momentum spent. I stared down into a bottomless abyss of tragedy – beyond the power of all pity, all compassion, all sadness to assuage or cancel. I was sorry to have humbled him, but that was insignificant now. A wave of despair swept over me, not for him alone, for all of us. Gazing down at him, I looked beyond him into the Inferno, into the mind of Dante himself, the world as it really was. In torment, Julian had pulled the mask from himself and from the world too – while the others clung to theirs. That was the only difference between them. He had spoken, in his fashion, for us all.

The others drifted cautiously into the room – wild-eyed, apprehensive. They stared blankly, seemingly with no stir of feeling, at Julian's crumpled figure as he fought to breathe through the barrier of his own blood; they took refuge in the childlike innocence of the tipsy – but not in truth innocent! With their sure instinct for self-preservation they kept their distance in every sense. From behind them came sounds of curses and thumping feet, and Bernard forced his way through the stony ranks, halted and took it all in. He gave me a fierce look – partly in reproof for having excluded him, partly a signal that he was now taking over. This is none of *our* business – yours and mine – but if this lot won't stir a finger to clear up the mess, then *we* must do it!

He could have said that about many things!

His stocky bulk swung round and confronted them, and it seemed that I heard his voice from afar, on some remote barrack square, with the bitter rasp, the full-throated roar of the drill sergeant exercising 'power of command' on a squad of unhappy recruits: 'Come on you lot! Ye've gottae get this poor bugger to a hospital fuckin' quick! Jump to it! – if you don't want the police sticking their noses into everything!' That, he knew well enough, was the last thing any of them wanted. Somebody muttered that the Radcliffe Infirmary was only a stone's throw away. 'Now you're talking! All right – you, you and you, and you – take his arms and legs, and be fuckin' quick about it!'

Nothing was solid. As when a child shakes the doll's house and sends its contents flying, the world raged about me in fragments, re-fused, came to rest in new juxtaposition – people, perceptions, truths – and now it presented yet another face, cruel, calculating, unyielding. I must begin to comprehend it piece by piece, all over again.

I had stepped into a Brueghel painting, and incarnations of people's secret emotions and desires, delicate, savage, insatiable, crowded round me, pulled me this way and that, danced and jeered: 'Do not turn away from what you see! Accept us, acknowledge us, or we will kill you.'

There was shame to be digested, dangerous innocence – or was it deliberate blindness? – unmarked or ignored before.

I went into the deserted drawing room and sat in a corner, in a gilt armchair with back and seat embroidered with silken scenes of Arcadia. What of the unappetising behaviour of the others? One explanation came to mind, enshrined in a piece of barrack-room wisdom handed down through generations of old sweats: 'Always let someone *else* carry the can for you if anything goes wrong!' That was what they had done to me – these people with their superior boss class airs, their fine public school principles of what was done and what was not.

Perhaps I too should have backed away, as they had done? What then would have happened? Ah no, that was not the question to ask. 'Look after Number One!' the old sweats said: 'That's all you must think about.'

Bernard came in. We sat in silence. After a few minutes he sighed and said, 'How the hell did *you* get lumbered with this? You weren't even *in* that room when it all blew up.'

Much later I would see that there could have been no shortage of catalysts in the *louche* coming together of high and low, of innocence and experience, hard, twisted, predatory, careless in every sense. In many of these people, caught in the mesh of war secrets, the energy needed to keep dangerous knowledge battened down must have clamoured for release in some alternative way, seemingly less dangerous; and for everyone there was the *angst* of the hour. The forces that had exploded in Julian, or rather through him, had been 'par for the course' too.

A few of the remaining guests drifted in. Glasses were refilled. Assurance rose to the surface once again. There was an urge to forget, as when someone has committed a gaffe at a dinner party, and the talk moves on to erase its memory. The trauma, however, persisting beneath the surface, now and then broke through. Hannah, who had observed Bowra stalk out of the drawing-room and into the room opposite, had gathered that he had gone up to Julian, spoken briefly and turned away and briskly left. Another man – the one who had suffered the gashed hand – had then spoken to Julian, who had pushed him violently away. When and why the knife had made its appearance no one knew. The man with the bloody hand had slipped away. Hearing this, Werner sighed with relief.

Bill entered, unperturbed, genial, carrying a bottle of Veuve Cliquot. He handed me a fresh glass: 'Good man! Pity, though. Poor chap's in a bad way. Anyway, the whole thing's best forgotten.'

Bernard held up a glass for a refill. Now that the need for action and control was over, he had resumed the manner of the soldier in his cups.

Draining the glass almost in a gulp, he sucked breath between his teeth and said: 'I've seen a man shot out of hand for pulling a knife like that.'

Diana, her hair in disarray, still clung to Werner as to a lifeline. Perhaps in shock, she said to me, in a troubled, peevish tone: 'You shouldn't have got mixed up in it. Someone else should have …' She did not dare continue. 'Anyway, it wasn't your business!'

Werner said stiffly, plainly aware of the undertones, 'I am sorry. I feel responsible, as your host, but what could I do? As a foreigner I have to be so careful.'

Hannah said, 'I couldn't think of anyone else who could cope. Something had to be done quickly.'

Bernard said, carefully, 'It's not a nice thing to say in front of women, but when there are pansies about, some men get nervous about themselves.'

Hannah wrinkled her nose. 'Yes,' she murmured, 'It's true.'

I misjudged Diana, though I did not see it then. In her total detachment, a kind of nihilism, she had been right. None of it was my business; clearing up other people's messes was *their* affair – the people who belonged. I resented what I thought was her refusal to understand – that I had obeyed peremptory forces *within me*, that I had acted for the righteous cause as I saw it, come what may. I was wrong. She did understand. In the confusion of the moment her tumbled words were solely of distress for me, pleading that I should not foolishly go in the way of death. Those who stood back and chose their moment to act in their own interests, let *them* be the heroes of this world!

Yes, her assessment was right; but that in itself was not important. It was I who had been insensitive; I had not *tried* to understand her. Pride overruled sensibility. Stupidly hurt, I was to turn away from her, though at the time it would appear as the inevitable distancing of souls that had ceased to resonate together. Here was yet another piece of self-inflicted pain. I lost *her*, her sensibility, her innocent, uncompromising strength – a wondrous, caring heart.

A few years later, when we were together in London after her marriage to Prince Leowenstein, there would be bitter-sweet sympathy, mutual recognition of loss – too late.

14

Laski: the Still, Small Voice

I wrote to Harold Laski and asked if I might come to see him.

I could no longer postpone an answer to the question: what was to be my next move? Where *could* I go? What should I do? At last I had hit upon an idea. Laski must surely be the right man to talk to about it.

Over and over again my thoughts were drawn back to Alec's words before I left the factory. A recurrent nightmare must have been associated with them. I was trying to walk through a street flooded with some gluey substance, and each time I pulled one foot out to take a step forward the other sank deeper and pulled me back; then some power gripped me and turned me round to face the way I had come, where there was a gigantic creature too terrible to gaze upon, and so I turned away from it and was forcibly turned again, and each time the unseen power gripped me more and more tightly and the swamp held me fast – and I must continue this futile and terrifying struggle for ever. I would wake up shivering in fear.

Across the silences of the years Alec's words brought an acute sense of loss, as yet indefinable. What could I do about it? How? It seemed to be too late. I must follow this road wherever it led, whatever the chagrin and penalty. Did every move in life have a debit side?

Alec had tried to tell me that I was making a tragic mistake in pinning my faith in the things of the mind and letting the heart go unnourished; and that life would take its revenge. In so far as I heard him at all, I had shrugged aside the emotional resonances he delicately tried to convey – not to neglect the vital essences in relationships, awareness, the progress of the soul. I heard the words but not the music – a fault I would repeat again and again:

The words of a song fade in the wind.
The music speaks to the heart.

At that time the surface logic of Alec's words had been easy to reject, dizzy with success as I was, seeing nothing but a golden road opening out before me – all other things would surely look after themselves. More profoundly – the music beneath – he had questioned the wisdom of going away at all. The spiritual losses would outweigh the gains. I pretended to myself that I did not hear, but I think I did – at least a hint of it – and shrank away. The thought was intolerable. It would return in increasing strength as the years went by.

From the very beginning I must have assumed that I would never go back to the Gorbals. To do so would be a defeat. Now, as I posted the letter to Professor Laski, I asked myself: would I, given some magical time machine, translate myself back, as if I had never been away, stand again at my old place at the pressing table, resume the old life? Would I, if I could, cancel the Oxford experience altogether? The questions were absurd, but they were an acid test. I touched the calluses on my right hand, plates of hard flesh, once as tough as board and with as little feeling, on the inside pads of the fingers and on the palm – relics of the years I had invested gripping the thick twisted bar of rough metal that formed the handle of the eighteen-pound press iron, and only now beginning to soften and shrink. No. There could be no going back; not to that, not to *anything* in the Gorbals.

There was no weighing of pros and cons. My certainty had little to do with Alec's words, or so I thought. Perhaps, as in the dream, the primordial forces he conjured up were too terrifying to face – spiritual influences I had been too green even to try to understand. Dimly, now, I did begin to understand them. When Alec had spoken of them I had recoiled instinctively; now I did so consciously, with an after-taste of inexplicable bitterness, telling myself that in any case the questions came too late – they were irrelevant now. Time had moved on, the old choices were no longer there. I was changed, and if I did venture back, it would not be in truth a *return*, for I was not the person who had left; and those who remained I would see differently. The old picture – and I myself who had belonged to it – would have disappeared, overlaid as in a palimpsest:

> Fare forward, you who think that you are voyaging;
> You are not those who saw the harbour
> Receding, or those who will disembark …

I was not the same person for another reason, in its way just as crucial. In the Gorbals I had believed in absolutes, in black and white – there was one single thread to be found that would guide me through the labyrinth. That sureness was gone for ever. The ideals I had brought away with me may have been wildly unrealistic, but they had given me firm ground, of a kind. Because they had not fitted the new world I had found here, I had let them slip away, never to be recovered; to be replaced by – what? I wished I knew.

What I did know, or rather sensed, was that I *had* moved, profoundly, with hints of new forces at work – as one feels, on a late March morning much like any other, a new tincture in the air, not yet warm but astringent, impatient, the earth quick with new forms as yet unseen, long before the first crocus peeps above the ground. I was shifting to a new course, as yet only a whisper in the mind. I was going to strike out and fashion a new *weltanschauung* of my own – *how* I had no idea – leave behind the received wisdom I had found here, create a new 'cause' to replace the one I had lost. Dimly I saw that I must resume the quest where my scholarship essay had left off – saying 'No' to the question 'Has science increased human happiness?' – and go on to the bitter end wherever that might be. Writing to Laski was the first concrete step.

I had revisited the Gorbals once, and that encounter would last me for ever. Going up to the little flat I was shocked by the filth of the close and the stairs, and the melange of stenches from the flats on each landing, amazed that I had forgotten that this was their proper state. I had felt shame too, as if I stood exposed before my Oxford acquaintances. Why shame, I wondered, I who had flaunted these origins in their faces? Did I think I had risen above the inhabitants of these tenements? Or did I glimpse the shade of my former self here, unquiet spirit haunting the shadows, and fear to meet him face to face – yet powerless to turn my back on him?

Once again, confronting my beginnings, was I daunted by the vision of how far I must travel to escape them – and the thought that I never would?

Father was out at work. The flat looked a little tidier than I remembered it; but every object – the old kitchen table, the lopsided wooden ladderback chairs, the alcove bed beside the stove with its yellowing undersheet and the great 'perraneh' like a huge well-stuffed duvet filled with down feathers, a precious relic of mother's marriage portion brought all the way from *der heim*, flung back against the peeling wall – proclaimed that here was an embattled man living alone; a line was drawn between caring about the essentials of existence and neglecting appearances. The place smelt of damp and decayed food, in a grey twilight even on this summer day, the windows as grimy as I remembered them, the unlit stove still streaked with grease; there were rat droppings in a dark corner. Father's shirt and other washing hung on a string stretched above the long shallow earthenware sink.

He greeted me in somewhat puzzled fashion, stolidly, with perfunctory warmth, wary curiosity. He seemed taken aback by something unfamiliar in my bearing, but especially by my speech: 'Voossfer redstoo azay?' ('Why are you talking life that?'). I did not know what he meant at first. Unconsciously I had dropped the Gorbals twang and now spoke a version of standard English – what the vernacular called 'hoity-toity' speech. I resolved, for the remainder of my stay, to try to revert to the old way of speaking. Alas, it would be as unconvincing here as my acquired diction was in Oxford.

Observing me during long silences, he seemed surprised that I had returned at all. To his way of thinking, once a son had left home he had shaken its dust off his feet for ever. As on that last morning when I had left to ride to Oxford, when we had stood facing one another tongue-tied, he in hat and coat ready to go to work, no words fitted the immense questions that hung in the air between us. He sat across the kitchen table from me, shirt sleeves rolled up, elbows resting on the cracked oil cloth, holding a cup of tea in both hands, the grey-blue eyes looking at me and yet at something far away. They were damp. My new presence filled him with unfathomable perplexities. I felt his love trying to reach me, mysteriously thwarted. He wanted to speak to me, at last, on level terms, to guide me in the next stage of my life – something he had had little stomach for in the past, perhaps because his own guilt intruded. Now, similarly, he must have thought, punishing himself, 'Who am I to tell my son how to run his life, seeing what I have done with mine?' The silences lengthened. Foolishly I tried to fill them with talk of my life in Oxford, and saw an impatience, a sense of despair, cloud the long solemn features, in which I saw, as behind a curtain, a still youthful soul, furtive, anxious, unproven, but in his fashion still undefeated. For him, as always, talk had to be *sub specie aeternitatis* whatever the cost in pain – that or nothing. In any case, these visions I tried to bring him – hoping to involve him vicariously – came too late. The world I described with the uncertain eagerness of youth was to him not only a foreign land, unknowable, but, more to the point, contained no hint of that better life that was the only reason for a son to leave home. 'Vossgoot kimmt? Vee kanness a bessernlayben verdeenen – mit kayn trade in hant?' ('What good will come of it? How will it earn you a better living – with no trade in your hand?').

He said it from concern, not to hurt. Still, he struck unerringly at doubts of my own.

Lilian and Mary, living in middle-class comfort north of the river, had even less interest in seeing me. I was a reminder of their dereliction; I brought guilt. Stupidly I tried to tell them that the past was forgotten, that we should now think only of the future. Such sentiments, I realised too late, they interpreted as an accusation – to 'forget' the past must mean that it needed to be forgiven. I touched raw nerves. I hurt their pride. Yet to have said nothing about the past would have implied that I too felt guilty about it. That would be unfair; the deeds were *theirs*, not mine, and any guilt must be theirs too. If I offered forgiveness they should accept it with a good heart. Discordant voices spoke out of the unappeased past. With shock I realised that I still looked at my sisters with the eyes of the small child. They were still the great ones moving my small world volcanically. I still addressed them with the humility, the apprehension, proper to long ago, when each word, each fresh sound or gesture, could presage yet another trauma. I still waited for them to put my world together again – knowing they would not. Incongruous, too, was a comic element; here was I, the young brother, a pauper, offering *them* a bounty, a pardon.

When I was older I would see their inflated pride as infantile, and wish that I had been mature enough to regard it with detachment, and refuse to let it sting. And *my* juvenile pride – now asserting itself far beyond its proper time – made the impasse complete.

'*... it is a stiff-necked people.*'

In the years since they had left home, trust and love, the wholesome flow of feeling from a young boy to older sisters – the more crucial because mother had died so young – had bled away. The only common ground lay in the past, and that divided us. So also did subsequent events in their lives, as yet unknown to me, which I would hear about from Mary, in sad confession, after Lilian's death – dark relationships, shifts and compromises, as they strove to 'better themselves'. Conversation was artificial; we searched for safe topics. They expressed surprise that I had sought them out at all; each asked, before many minutes had passed: 'Have you come for money?' – not in the kindly sense of an older, prosperous sister offering a brother a helping hand, but challengingly, as if daring me to say yes. That hurt. The idea of holding out my hand for alms had simply not occurred to me. Certainly, a little extra money would have been of help, and to be fair, had I asked in so many words, I believe they would have given me some; but their tone, perhaps intentionally – knowing me as they did – made certain that I would not ask.

They were frankly sceptical, woundingly so, when I said that I had come, this time enriched by experience, solely to renew contact with my own flesh and blood, hoping for friendship at the very least – to join hands as adults journeying through the world. Perhaps their suspicion came from their guilt – making them as distrustful of me as they knew *they* had earned distrust. They could not believe that I wanted to come near to them for *themselves* alone – there had to be another, suspect, reason.

Their prickly suspicion held a monumental pathos; they were not happy behind their fortification, and it hurt me to see it. They could not, would not, believe that a warm-hearted word was all I asked, that I sought acceptance as rightfully close to them – a lowering of defences, a sharing of identity.

Instead, there was nothing but a halting exchange of trivia. There were tentative enquiries about father – why wait for *me* to come from afar, in order to ask after him, when he lived no further than the other side of they Clyde? About *my* life they wanted to know nothing – there was no money in what I was doing, either now or in prospect. For them, as for father but for different reasons, I presented too many uncomfortable questions.

The greatest shock came when I met the shower-room group at the swimming baths, people I had met regularly through the adolescent years. At first tongue-tied, aloof, embarrassed, they were finally resentful. Plainly they wished I had not come. Dimly I sensed that my presence, as with father and my sisters, prompted them to look at their lives afresh, and that upset them, the more so because they could not understand why. *They* were certain of what that pattern had to be, and if not content with it they were at least determined to pursue it as they found it – as I had *not*. They hotly rejected such questioning, and blamed their discomfort on me. In retaliation they launched their own barbs at me. They taunted me for my 'proper' speech – 'Whi' are ye talkin' doon tae us for?' They needed to pay me back for having made my escape and even more for returning – as they saw it – to proclaim superiority. I had shown contempt for their life, and for their valuation of themselves. In revenge, they had to reject me.

On the face of it they had some excuse; what they saw could not be denied – though their interpretation was pitifully wrong and no explanation would change it. I *was* no longer one of them. My

clothes for instance, sports jacket and shirt and flannels and tie –
poor by Oxford standards – were conspicuously middle-class in the
Gorbals of shoddy cloth, mufflers and cloth caps. They snarled at
me for talking Kelvinside. Above all, I saw different horizons –
which they interpreted as being offensively superior. The switch in
my life's course was to them enigmatic; indefinably it must be a step
up, and envy increased their fury. Yet, to do them justice, deep
down at a more mature level, they were suspicious of their *own*
stock responses, and their sense of injury mystified them; and so,
shaken, tight-lipped, not so much in malice as in frustration, they
would talk to me no more. In the streets and closes of the Gorbals
I was shunned as a leper.

Unawares, I may have increased their uneasiness, and hence their
resentment, by letting signs of my own doubts slip out – insecurity
at having broken away from the Gorbals, fear of being sucked back
into the old, wounding life. Looking round me in the familiar
streets and tenements – familiar but now unknown – I was dismayed to see that even with my new intellectual confidence and sophistication, I could not confront the past calmly – not yet. My old
foundations were destroyed and I had still to find new ones to stand
on. I had too little faith. I may even have hoped, a greater error still,
that the past was finished with, that it would trouble me no more;
that I could erase it – even, in fantasy, rewrite it. It would take me
many years to look at it with even the beginnings of detachment.

The responses from father and sisters, chilling and sad though
they were, were not unexpected – our wounded history had to play
itself out to the end. The rebuff from my old friends hit me so hard
because, stupidly, I was unprepared. Once again Alec was proved
right. I should have expected it; I should have been more *aware*.
Perhaps, secretly, childishly, I had dreamed of being greeted as the
returning hero. Remembering their cool scepticism at the first news
of my scholarship I should have known better. That settled it. I
must turn away, now, for ever. I must try my luck where there were
no reminders of the past – no spectres of doubt, where that unquiet
shade, my *alter ego* from the Gorbals, could at last be at peace.

In writing to Laski I was making a start on his new course. My idea was to probe to the heart of an unseen, potentially sinister, Machiavellian factor in government, the little-understood phenomenon of pressure groups, how they worked, influenced opinion, changed attitudes and, above all, political decisions behind the democratic façade; and a newer one, related to it, whose political importance for the future was then unnoticed, the use by caucuses and powerful business interests of the new techniques of attitude measurement or sampling – later to be called, misleadingly, opinion polls – to influence or even 'create' opinion. I wanted to persuade the great man to back the project and let me do the study under his aegis.

To do the work, and write a book on it, I would have to get a research grant, but that would not be difficult with Laski's support.

Laski, third of the socialist heroes I had worshipped from the Gorbals, bestrode, uniquely, the heights of learning and politics. Professor of Political Science in London University, he was in the front rank of the Labour Party leadership and for a time its spiritual and intellectual figurehead.

I was drawn to him for many reasons, most of them indefinable at the time. I think I saw in him a new standard to model myself upon, and in doing so fulfil secret visions of myself. I needed a new figure to occupy the vacant niche where long ago I had placed Einstein. Here was a Jewish firebrand of international distinction as scholar, writer, dealer in the political market place. When he spoke, people listened. What better star to follow?

I had so far seen him only at meetings and lectures, superficially an unimpressive figure, thin, narrow-chested, with a high square forehead under receding dark hair parted in the middle, sallow urchin features with deep lines beside the mouth, thin-framed spectacles with small round lenses, and a narrow moustache which – strange for a Jew to wear at that time – was not unlike Hitler's. In odd contrast with his gruff voice and ramrod bearing was a certain impishness, reflecting his delight in the ideas that bubbled forth in his talk in a coruscating stream. There was assurance verging on arrogance, an American forthrightness then alien to the English milieu, product perhaps of his Harvard years, a bluntness and accent later to be dubbed mid-Atlantic. These attributes, together with his natural bounce and vigour of expression, set him apart from the highly conventional English academics of that time and perhaps repelled some of them. In compensation he had great charm and warmth, the roughness perhaps a surface relic of youthful assertiveness that had out lived its season. When fairly launched into a subject, especially in a formal lecture in his favourite field, French political thought, these disquieting elements faded; and words and cadences flowed elegantly, engaging the imagination like themes in a romantic symphony – something not always present, alas, in his writing, which tended to be involuted and tantalisingly diffuse, defects of his supreme quality, a widely sweeping, impatient mind.

In recent years his star had been in the ascendant – leaving Cole behind – as intellectual leader of the socialist movement as a whole, with Gollancz its brilliant if erratic publicist. In time, however, Laski's highly individual mixture of Continental radicalism, Marxism, and traditional English socialism rooted in Chartism, together with a streak of carefree impracticality, would alarm Labour Party managers as storing up electoral danger in that tense, war-weary time, just as Gollancz's maverick quality was to lead to *his* political eclipse.

The poetic cast of Laski's mind was especially attractive; some of his images would remain with me in all the years ahead. Writing on liberty, arguing that its attainment was an inborn duty, he said that in order to divine its proper use one must 'listen to the still, small voice within you'. The image was not original. Poe, among others, had used it; and in Laski's usage it expressed the world view of the Philosophes. Still, it was an engaging one, despite its naïve assumption that clear sight, and goodwill, resided eternally in the noble savage within us – if we would only set him free. Laski, I suspected, found such imagery irresistible for aesthetic even more than philosophical reasons. Nevertheless, it was sincere, expressing his faith in the perfectibility of Man through reason – which he saw as inseparable from democracy, though how he squared the latter conclusion with his leaning to Marxist *étatisme* was not clear. At all events here he was, nearly half-way through the twentieth century, proclaiming his affinity with the extreme radicalism of the Age of Reason. Not surprisingly the Labour Party of stolid Major Clement Attlee and bluff Ernest Bevin found it hard to live with a Laski who could write thus lyrically of the spirit of the Philosophes: '[together with] faith in the boundless power of reason … it is a trust in intuition, a belief that the sentiment within most truly reveals the reality without, which enables us to insist not only upon the natural goodness of man, but also to make the discoveries of reason square with our own desires.'

Such a passage transported me back to crisp Sunday mornings at the speakers' pitch on Glasgow Green, when I stood in ragged shorts and shirt and wet boots looking up at the long lean features of the Clincher, his certificate of sanity rustling in the breeze from the Clyde, bellowing forth his gospel of Burnsian simplicity and innate human goodness; and to saintly Mr Lipchinsky with *his* version of the perfectibility of man; and even to Bernard himself in his days of Marxist dogma. I had come all this way and nothing had changed – except the language.

If the still small voice always guided man's natural goodness correctly, all human affairs would be perfect! When I met him and expressed these doubts, I would find that behind his charm was a juggernaut ready to crush dissent. Like Mr Lipchinsky, he had reached a point in his life where reassessment would feel like sacrilege. I suspect he knew – listening to his own still, small voice – that to talk of the purpose of liberty in this fashion was too facile, almost banal, not addressing the question but avoiding it.

However, this visionary side of him pointed to an engaging sensitivity and innocence, qualities I had assumed would be foreign to a mind so powerful and, as I would discover, so ruthless. Here was yet another romantic held fast in the lofty optimism of the Enlightenment, seeing nothing inconsistent in trying to marry Tom Paine's libertarianism with Marxist state discipline, another dreamer who had outlived his time.

In one short sentence of my letter I had stated the scope of my proposed study, and I was struck by the charm of his replying at once, in his own hand, to invite the unknown student to come for a talk. It would emerge that he had satisfied himself about me by enquiries through the academic network.

At such times of accolade – as when I was 'judged worthy of distinction' – I felt a twinge of regret, of spiritual loneliness, and wished that there had been someone of my own blood, father, sisters, Aunt Rachel or Uncle Salman, who could have shared fulfilment with me.

Making my way from Paddington to his house near Olympia I lost my way, London being unknown territory, and found myself near Broadcasting House instead of much further west. It was the morning after a night of bombing, and as I trudged through streets littered with debris – long shards of plate glass, mangled metal, piled-up broken timber and lumps of stone and brickwork – I saw, towering above an enormous crater filled with the remains of a house, the jagged outline of a shattered party wall which, as I looked, trembled as if it would thunder down at any moment; on it, some thirty feet up, in what must have been a recessed clothes cupboard, a woman's green frilly dress, still on its hanger, swung gently in the breeze. Where was the woman who owned it? Was she under that heap of rubble? I retraced my steps to where I could contemplate again the confident modernism of Broadcasting House, rounded like the superstructure of a great ship, and thought of that early, desperately sanguine motto of radio: 'Nation shall speak peace unto nation'. When would that ever be true? And what was I doing, going to talk to Laski about democracy and the subtle springs and levers of power, in the midst of Armageddon? In a sense Armageddon was with us all the time – all you had were remissions, pauses for breath and hope. All you could do was pretend that each breathing space might endure long enough to see you through your own life.

In a grey Victorian house, the interior scented with furniture polish and the faint acrid aroma of horsehair upholstery, Laski greeted me in a lofty, airy study. He was dressed in a grey suit and, surprisingly, boots. The last time I had seen boots worn with a suit was in the Gorbals; and as he sat down opposite me in a high-backed armchair, legs stretched forward and feet resting on a low stool, the soles of these great boots faced me like huge shields, seeming to loom too large, all but eclipsing him as in a photograph taken at too close range. The shield image, I would discover, was apt.

Early in that first meeting he made an extraordinary Freudian slip. It was evident that he liked to underline his closeness to the Labour leaders in the coalition Cabinet, and one method was to show that he was 'in the know'. Over coffee, before we got down to serious discussion, he gaily remarked *à propos* the night's bombing that 'a few hours ago' a huge bomb had landed close to where Churchill was holding a late-night meeting. Had Churchill been in any danger, I asked? He gave his characteristic rasp of a laugh: 'Not him! *He* was safe and sound in a bunker three storeys above ground!' I said, 'You mean *below* ground?' He looked at me in perplexity: 'What did I say?' I told him. He frowned, out of countenance, then laughed again: 'Good gracious, of course I don't wish him out of the way – *not yet*!'

The little moustache lifted as he smiled in complicity; then he changed the subject.

He began to talk about my proposed study, especially the political implications. I had a twinge of foreboding. It would, he said, attack the workings of government, and of parties, probably quite damagingly. I said that was precisely what I hoped to do. As if on cue, he launched into a series of leading questions, a Socratic dialogue: 'Do you not agree that ...' and 'If so, then ...?' He was trying to drive me into a corner, but what corner? In my innocence I thought he was simply testing my conviction, and my competence to carry out the study. Thinking only of defending my idea, and shining in this elegant disputation, it did not occur to me that he might be trying to talk me out of doing the study altogether. I told myself that he *must* be interested in my ideas about it, otherwise, surely, why would he bother to arrange this meeting? After about an hour he looked at his watch. 'I'm giving a lecture at the Senate House at twelve. Come along, we can talk in the taxi.' The lecture would be on French political thought after the Revolution. We would need to meet again, he said. We fixed another day for me to visit him.

The taxi – this was to be my very first experience of one – must have been already booked, for in a few minutes a bell sounded far away in the bowels of the house. On the outer step, the cabbie touched his cap to the great man, greeted him with the friendly formality of an old retainer – 'Morning, professor' – and with some ceremony led the way down the few yards of path to hold the cab door open. The vehicle had an old-fashioned cabriolet body, the driver's compartment open – apart from windscreen and roof – where he sat, as in horse-drawn days, with a piece of black tarpaulin over his knees against the weather.

As we bumped along on the old springs, Laski said, thoughtfully, 'It is a mistake to think we've got democracy in this country. In theory we have but it's really an electoral oligarchy! We need to widen the true franchise – but that's for the distant future.' By 'we' he meant the socialist movement, in particular the Labour Party as its 'conformist' vanguard. All the same, he added, we shall have to use the system *as it is*, with all its falsifications – the thing *you* are worried about for example, your pressure groups and opinion sampling, all the tricks of opinion management. In fact they might actually help us to get our hands on power. Power first – improvement afterwards!

Where had I heard that before, or something very much like it? Yes, from Bernard when he came back from Spain, having abandoned the dogma of 'abolish or nothing' and instead determined to make do, to use the system as it stood.

Laski's words should have warned me. Despite his earlier show of scepticism, in that moment of frankness he revealed that he saw the future very much as I did but without alarm, indeed with something like virtuoso glee – the death of hustings, the supremacy of marketing techniques in political life, unashamedly selective, finely tuned to 'consumer profiles'. He not only recognised the 'falsifications' of democracy that I wanted to correct, but was content to leave them untouched. Sensing imminent electoral victory for Labour, he saw himself making use of them soon, and doing so ruthlessly. The parallel with Kerensky occurred to me, far from exact but near enough; he dreamed of himself as that impossible hybrid, a Leninist Kerensky.

He may have realised the slip, for he veered away. 'We need,' he said, 'to get closer to the working class! Some of my good students go to work in he East End to get to understand the workers. You too, I should say, need to learn how the workers tick! I could help you get some social work in the East End if you life.'

I had forgotten to tell him that I came from the Gorbals. That showed how far I had travelled. Here was strange reversal. Long ago it was I who had told Crossman that *he* should learn something about the workers; and now – how could it be? – here was Laski telling *me* to do so! Luckily, at that moment, the taxi passed through the tall gates of the Senate House and swung to a halt in the forecourt; otherwise I might have told him about the Gorbals – and too bluntly. When, at out next meeting, I did tell him, he would remember his words and grin in salute. Quizzically, drawing in the thin lips under the symbolic moustache, he would say, echoing Bernard, 'You *have* done a good job on yourself – no one would have thought it!' And I would wonder if there was a hint of the envy I had seen on Crossman's face.

In the main entrance hall, Cyclopean, stark, mechanistic – reminding me of the approach to the machine hall in Fritz Lang's futuristic film *Metropolis* – his foot on the bottom step of the great staircase leading to the Macmillan Hall where he was to lecture, he abruptly turned: 'Say, d'you know where I can have a cock here?' It took me a couple of seconds to decode the question; he wanted to go to the lavatory. Why ask *me*? Here he was on his own territory; he knew I had never set foot in the place before. However, I owed the great man respect; I turned towards the long reception desk nearby, intending to ask one of the uniformed staff. He stopped me, saying gruffly 'The hell with it, I'll manage without,' and with springy step led the way upstairs. Once in the Hall, he courteously led me to a seat in the front row, mounted the dais, and without any notes, delivered an entrancing, evocative, exquisitely phrased discourse, full of gentle poetry. There was not a sign of the Leninist Kerensky.

Bernard said, 'You are barking up the wrong tree with Laski. *He* won't help you with this pressure group idea of yours. It's obvious. He doesn't want to be seen to be spreading doubts about the machine, especially *now* – with the Labour Party girding up its loins for a victory election, and to become, at last, a governmental party. He's just stringing you along! He can see you're full of ideas, perhaps like *he* was when he was young, and he wants to keep you hanging around so that he can pick your brains when he wants to. That's the way a "had been" thinks!'

Once again we chewed over the future. The switch from revolutionary soldier to toiler in the trade union vineyard had been good for his soul as far as it went; but now he dreamed again of shifting the world, this time through legitimate radicalism, in Parliament. Sniffing the wind, he predicted a Labour victory. Now a national figure in the union, close to Labour Party inner circles, he had been offered a constituency. Why didn't I take that road too? A swift 'demob election' was on the cards. The party managers, privately, were not speaking of victory, but at the very least aimed to fill the opposition benches with new talent. 'You're the kind of material they're looking for! Constituencies are going begging. I could put a word in for you. As things are, I think you'd get one.'

He would bet money on us both getting in. Time, however, was critical. There was going to be a governmental scheme for service people overseas seeking adoption as parliamentary candidates to be flown back to this country to face constituency selection committees. Now, therefore, before that flood began, was the moment to act.

He echoed Laski's reckoning. Old loyalties were giving way to new calculation. It would not be *principle* that would turn the country upside down, but an automatic revulsion against an old élite drained of the confidence of fifty years before, and now seen as inept, dull-witted, palsied – typified by the spectre of Neville Chamberlain.

Bernard was tougher now than he had ever been. He had acquired a manipulative streak I would never posses. That old, steady look of his, the eyes gleaming like dark cherries, had become contemplative, magisterial, charismatic; he could wait, temporise, scheme, calmly contrive compromises as stepping stones to the ideal. I knew I could not equal these attributes – not yet, if ever. The route he suggested demanded a pragmatism, an opportunism, a pretence of certainty as a means of manipulating people, which I could not stomach. Not yet. I must find myself first. *He* did not need to; in essence he was what he had always been. His trials and dangers and heartaches had tempered him, the basic substance was unchanged. For that I had always admired him, and envied him. I had no such solidity: all within me seemed freshly minted, with no history, as if I were my own new creation – as in some ways I was. Each new step demanded new questioning, new assurance to be bred within. I was certain of one thing only; I would try to create a new world through writing. How, in what form, I did not know as yet; I knew only that I would continue the quest begun long ago in the scholarship essay. For as far into the future as I could see, that would be my pilgrimage.

As for Laski, it was hard to accept Bernard's verdict. However, he had had many opportunities to assess Laski, and far more experience of the world; and I respected his judgement. I must wait and see.

I could not wait for long. Now, more than ever, I felt the burden of travelling alone. Foolishly, I had sometimes tried to explain this thought to people here; you felt stronger if you knew that a home hearth existed *somewhere*, even if you visited it only in spirit; its *existence* was the crucial thing – a fixed point of support awaiting you always, for you to conjure up in the imagination at moments of doubt, and draw comfort from the knowledge. Without it you were always vulnerable, like a commander with no reserves to fall back on. They listened politely, resisting insight; most of them affected to despise family links: 'You're jolly lucky not to have a family to tie you down!' In truth they were deeply dependent, evidenced by their unease at the subject being broached at all – yet another topic it was not done to talk about. It was too near the heart.

Ken Tynan would sum this up, and the Oxford experience too, with characteristic incisiveness and astuteness, quite early in his time here, in his days of stick-like thinness, the purple suit flapping on him as on a skeleton, his sunken cheeks and lips stretched tight over jutting teeth reminding me, incongruously, of the Clincher's cadaverous features: 'There's nothing to be got from this place of any value, except maybe a few contacts. Oxford's only use is to give you a stage to strut on and promote yourself! And that's what I'm good at!'

Tynan understood himself well. Happily, shrewdly, he used money and contacts to promote himself; and would have been amazed, like everyone else, were the strategy thought worthy of curiosity or comment. This too, as Bill would have said, was 'par for the course'.

Sometimes the grapes were sour.

Certainly I envied them their home base and ready-made network of people who could open doors; and berated myself for doing so. Envy was poisonous, I told myself – and anyway changed nothing, except to lower the spirit. But it was hard to be free of it; and perhaps that was why, trying to avoid the poison, I seemed to make friends more easily with other *déraciné* people like Werner and Domenico. If true, it was only part of the reason; sharing isolation was in itself a source of warmth – of a kind.

Tynan was not all display and calculation. Hidden away in his unique mixture of banality, tinsel brilliance and showmanship, was a mysterious, startling insight, revealing itself in the telling comment, apt as an arresting newspaper caption but containing much more – at its best a profound personal concern, shyly displayed and then hidden once again beneath the raucous and the superficial. At a sherry party, *à propos* of nothing, he said to me: 'Trouble with you is that you're after the old master stakes and nothing else will do. I'm too impatient for that.'

He said it with a mixture of wonder and sadness, almost of commiseration, ostensibly for me – but might it have been for himself too? I could not be sure.

If Laski did fail me, I would find a desk job – not too demanding – and write. It so happened that I had been offered a job at the British Council, part of which was then accommodated in Oriel.

That would be a curious alignment – a Gorbals boy purveying British culture! Why not? I could probably do it as well as anyone else, probably better than someone like John Betjeman, with his aristocratic acerbities and addiction to undergraduate satire of the British way of life.

Another irony had struck, momentous and terrible, that I would never understand, whose tragic overtones – sounding far back in time – I would never wholly digest. Father had given up gambling!

He had come to the decision – how I would never know, for he stubbornly refused to discuss it – shortly after my first, disappointing, return visit to the Gorbals. If only he had done it all those years ago when mother was alive! It was as if, with my going away again – this time, he was sure, never again to own the place as home – the last relic of his past life, wounded and wounding, had gone too, and nothing remained for his gambling to destroy.

As a result, he saved money in the Post Office, lived comfortably, probably more so than he could remember, apart from those brief spells when he had been flush after a win at the Faro table. At last he had forsaken the scene of mother's death, and discarded the mattress, on trestles in the kitchen alcove, on which she had died. He had moved to a small flat in the slightly more respectable quarter of the Gorbals near the Talmud Torah in Turriff Street, where he had a bedroom separate from the kitchen, a bathroom and separate lavatory. There, in his practical fashion, he looked after himself well, read a great deal, played solo whist in the Workers' Circle, spent hours chewing over the world with friends. He had several suits, smoked Balkan Sobranie cigarettes in a long amber holder with a gold band. Still, it could not be a happy finale to *his* pilgrimage. Guilt certainly persisted. His world, his life, he tacitly acknowledged, was past rearrangement. No further battle was worth fighting; but at last he was *free*. It was a Pyrrhic victory thus to be left, at the end, alone on the field. The freedom he had won must have been sour in the mouth.

As for my life, he had ceased trying to understand what I was doing with it. He thought me foolish to have challenged this new world single-handed. Having made that clear, he would not speak of it again. In effect he said, trying not to be too harsh, make your own mistakes, as I made mine, and take the consequences.

Separated in our widely different orbits, by some magical shift we had become comrades, on better terms than we had ever been. Here was yet another change that had come about at the wrong time, too late to be of serious use – or comfort – to either of us. Perhaps nothing ever happened at the 'right' time – whatever that was? No! Surely nothing could ever be totally too late? Yes. Some things were.

The fires of the past burned fiercely still. Accusations, claims and counter-claims, gyrated like demons of the Inferno, unappeased. None could be spoken of out loud. Yet there were questions I longed to ask. How long had he known that mother had cancer? Even allowing that he did not know, in those obscurantist days, that it was cancer, he must have had *some* idea that she was seriously ill. Why could he not steel himself to give up gambling then, knowing that the grief and hardship it brought must hasten her end? As for Lilian and Mary, would they have chosen to flee for safety if, seeing the rifts growing, he had stifled his pride and tried to heal them?

The enigmas were poisonously interwoven. It was surely too late to confront them? If only I could hear *his* reasoned account, his verdict. Sometimes, Vicariously, I felt his guilt festering within *me* Perhaps I carried with me, unrecognised, a memory of fearful efforts as a child, seeing him suffer, to share his inscrutable burden. Alas, to press him for answers would now be cruel, and futile – and in any case the truth would come too late. Or could truth ever come too late?

I could not bring myself to do it.

One day, facing each other at his kitchen table, covered with new oil-cloth in a fresh red check pattern, drinking 'Russian tea' – black tea in a glass, sucked through a lump of sugar – he said, 'Remember that fight in the umbrella shop – you were only a little boy then?'

Oh yes I remembered all right – and even now could shudder at the immediacy of that volcanic, ferocious scene – my little world fallen in fragments, father covered in blood, the shop furniture and stock shattered as the three brothers clashed in fury – two united against him.

'Yes,' he said, 'I see you do. I want you to promise me something. If you ever run into them or anyone connected with them, "Zogg azay: mit letsten ottom finsterniss woonshich" ("Tell them this: with my last breath I will curse them with darkness").'

He said it quite calmly, the grey blue eyes solemn, clear, unflinching.

In the context, the dreadful statement included Lilian and Mary.

What could I say? Our new-found comradeship was fragile. Certain topics remained, in sunken menace like an old minefield, too dangerous to approach. In him there could be no forgiveness. Within the family, blood must always be thicker than water; that was paramount. However badly you behaved, punishment must not hit you too cruelly. No sin or omission of his could have merited what his brother had done to him – above all throwing him out of the partnership in the shop – and what Lilian and Mary had done. He was saying, in effect, '*If* I had done anything wrong, what they did went too far!' This was the nearest he could come to accepting responsibility for *part* – part only – of all that had happened. What had mother done to *him*, I wondered, to merit the retribution of his gambling?

It was all too late.

All right, father, I will tell them.

I never did meet the uncles. As for Lilian and Mary, I did not tell them. But I owe it to him, even this late in the day, to set down these words of his without judgement. They have to be proclaimed as he wanted them to be; I still believe, as he deserved them to be – right or wrong! – a last trumpet blast of defiance. To me, inevitably, he must remain a hero, solitary, for all I know totally misunderstood, who communed honestly with his own transcendental voices, who fought the chimera fearlessly and stubbornly – and lost. Or did he really lose?

That trumpet blast would continue to ring out down the year.

Guilt at having left father on his own returned often. I told myself that there had been no other way. It was not true; there *had* been. There always was. Could I have chosen to stay? Lilian and Mary had had that choice too; their decision to go, bitter for me as a little boy, must have hit father unimaginably harder. He had never, by the slightest hint, reproached me for going, as he had blamed *them*. Not explicitly, but in his own quiet way, he made it plain that I must not take their guilt on to my shoulders. My case was quite different. In his eyes I had done what any young man of spirit could be expected to do – what he himself had done. And though pride would never permit him to say that he was lonely, his expression said – with an imaginary shrug of stoic acceptance – 'Es shtayt geshreeben'.

Lilian and Mary prospered. Their coolness continued. What harm had I done them? None that I could think of. Perhaps, in leaving father, I had underlined *their* desertion, for the tradition said that daughters did not leave home to seek their fortune. Paradoxically, even my failure to ask for their help gnawed at them. My buoyant independence, even in poverty, they could explain only by madness. Or something even more frightening, unworldliness, for that questioned the values they clung to, the fulfilment for which they had cheerfully sacrificed me. Imprisoned within their fortifications, they remained troubled. That, in part, was *their* punishment.

Lilian had become a pillar of charitable effort in Glasgow. Was that her way of expressing remorse – intercession for the soul before the Seat of judgement? Or was it simply one more manoeuvre in the interests of business?

Their detachment hurt. I tried to see my behaviour from their point of view. Did they feel they must keep my unworldliness at arm's length, lest by association it damaged their standing among the worldly? That was not wholly their fault. They were victims of their milieu. One day, Lilian having asked me to visit her at her office – she would 'fit me in for a few minutes' – I arrived just as she was showing out a client, a gross, middle-aged version of the assertive Phil Emet who had got Annie into trouble. With scarcely concealed unwillingness she introduced us – he was in the *shmat-tah* business, the rag trade. Her feelings must have transmitted themselves to him, for with an aggressive leer he said: 'An Oxford student, eh! I'm proud of you – but d'you know what's worrying *me*? I've got money coming out of my ears, now what d'you say to that?' He was putting me down with a vengeance, according to his lights. Why, I wondered, did people like him feel so defensive?

Stung, I answered him: 'Am I supposed to feel sorry for you?' He was startled, and the anger burst out: '*You* – feel sorry for *me*!'

'*You* said you were worried – I didn't!'

He was shorter than me, and overweight, but looked quite strong; for an instant, seeing the blood rush to his face, it looked as if he might lash out at me. I thought of the time, all those years ago in the school playground, when I got a beating for challenging another little boy for calling me a 'sheeny' – and here I was facing a like hatred – again for the crime of being different from the herd; this time from a Jew. Nothing had changed.

When he had gone, Lilian said, pale with fury, eyes red and damp behind the thick round lenses, 'That was an important client. He didn't mean any harm. I will have to grovel to excuse your behaviour. You had better not come here again.'

Mary moved to London. Years later, when I too was living there, she would ring me up one day: 'I've just realised, thinking about what the Nazis did to the Jews – that some of *our* relatives over there must have been among them! I didn't think of it before. Do you want to come over and talk about it? I can offer you some good Scotch.'

I should not have replied in the way I did, but this innocence so late in the day – about terrible things now common knowledge – carried another, intolerable implication, that she chose to be equally innocent about the events of our own past. Bitterness overflowed. Before I knew it the words were out: 'There are a lot of things you didn't think about at the right time.'

I was ashamed. After all, she was holding out a hand to me; and I was being self-righteous, in some ways like father, sticking implacably to principle. Yet I longed for true feeling; no superficial substitute would do. Instead she was trying, in her fashion, to put a lid on the past with weak sentiment, or rather to pretend that neither of us remembered what had happened. What would it have cost her, or Lilian, after all this time, at least to acknowledge the possibility – as father had done for his own deeds – that their leaving home might have caused me suffering, and express remorse? 'I felt I had to. I didn't *realise* what it would mean to you' – as perhaps they hadn't! That would have been *something*. But no; she too could not bring herself to utter it – not a single word of doubt or regret.

15

Winners and Losers

Bernard was right about Laski. To be fair, Laski's opposition to my idea was a proof of his clear-sightedness. He was not being obscurantist, simply Machiavellian. Implicitly he admitted that he shared my view of the forces I wanted to expose and how they were likely to change society. But that was bleak comfort.

He stonewalled beautifully – full of charm and sparkle and warmth. Almost in the same breath he maintained that the work I wanted to do was not necessary 'at the present time', and that in any case it had all been done before. Superficially the first statement contradicted the second – though of course 'not necessary' was code for politically inconvenient. The second statement could not possibly have been true. The pioneer work of Mass Observation, for example, though it contained clear and dramatic pointers to the future, was only two years old when it was suspended for the duration of the war. True, the psychological and statistical principles were known – at least to specialists – on which would be based the massive post-war expansion, into almost every corner of life, of attitude measurement, opinion sampling, 'consumer profiling' for product design and sales promotion, including the selling of politicians and programmes; but their probable use and consequences, especially their social impact, had still to be examined and understood.

He would not admit to political reasons for opposing my project, but the signals for me to drop it were plain. I pretended not to see them. What possible harm could my work do?

'Harm?' He repeated the word with a touch of pique. The round spectacles glinted as he shook his head. 'None at all. You wouldn't dig up anything we don't know already. As for what you say about "bending" opinion – creating bias – what's wrong with that? What politician in his right mind wants to cut out *bias* among the electorate – that is, bias in his favour? Bias in itself is not unfair! An "unfair" bias is one that doesn't suit your book, that's all. What do you expect from the electors – the pure light of reason? Come off it. We are working in a good radical cause – and if we can bend the bias in our favour, so what? It's a tough old world my boy, and you'd better get used to it.'

I murmured: 'The end justifies the means – do we ever escape from that?'

He learned back with a chuckle, the great boots, and gave a sly smile at the ceiling as if to say, 'What do you want? It's the way of the world.' Then he resumed the mien of the serious sevant: 'Now look here. I'm going to give you some good advice. There is a lot in what you say – if there weren't, I wouldn't still be talking with you! Bright young men love to tilt at received opinion – we've all done it in our time. But don't go too far or you'll make an awful lot of enemies. In the real world – and politics is part of it whether you like it or not, though I often wonder about it myself – it's called rocking the boat. And that makes a lot of folk uncomfortable and they don't like it, believe me. They could make life hard for you.'

In itself, it was good advice, but it was hard to conceal bitterness. He was simply protecting his own position, as he saw it, or rather political life in general, for him and for others. In fact, had he given me his support, it would probably have made no difference to *his* political future; but neither of us could know it. His political importance was about to end. Naïve as I was, I expected honest opposition – instead of sheltering, as he did, behind specious objections.

That phrase rocking the boat, was to haunt me in all the years ahead – in business and institutional affairs, in international life; it encapsulated the most wounding lesson I would learn since leaving the Gorbals, that the questioning mind is seldom welcome anywhere. Was mine less welcome than most? Was I too impatient, or did I blunder because, as Bill had hinted, I did not 'know the ropes' – how to manoeuvre and persuade by guile and finesse? There would always be some people to be upset, guarding special interests, inertia, or simply the desire for a quiet life – and some would strike back with feline stealth and ferocity. Many years later, when I was in Budapest as vice-chairman of an international congress, a charming Rumanian official representative – doubtless anxious to avoid suspicion of being influenced by my Western views – would express this disquiet to me with outstanding frankness: 'Monsieur, je suis *ineducable*!'

I admired his honesty.

Laski remained friendliness itself. 'I enjoy talking with you. Please come whenever you want. My door will always be open to you – and I will help you, as I said, if you want to do some social work.'

Social work stank of condescension, or wrong-headedness in diverse guises, pompous, opportunist, fey, self-deluding. I thought of the Glasgow do-gooders with their 'fresh air fortnights' for tenement children as a cure for deprivation. The voyeur, the troubled mind, seemed drawn magnetically to the lower depths where, under various concealments, it sought balm for inner conflicts – like Maugham's missionary in *Rain*, concealing shackled lusts with good works among the heathen – or solace for upper-class guilt, or freedom to experiment in safety with other people's lives. This was still the epoch of smart primitivism among some of the upper-class *avant garde*. Affecting to see the poor as the salt of the earth, they could not get close enough to them – that is, safely so! It was partly a self-indulgent conceit, partly a sincere, if confused, rebellion against suspect values.

Perhaps some upper-class people condescended with a clear conscience, a version of *noblesse oblige*? How could a Gorbals boy presume to counterfeit that?

If I had had time – that is, money – Laski's refusal would not have been a blow. I could have dispensed with backers and, like other people here, gone ahead with the work at my own expense. I thought of Rachel – if only! – and guilt washed over me. How could I think of her in this selfish way? I thought of her often, but not for this reason. Yes, I had to admit it, the thought was there: *if* I had sunk my pride and gone to live with her and accepted her money, she would be living still, and there would have been no shortage of funding now. I could have followed any path I pleased, and not been forced, as I was now, to abandon the project and get the first serious job I could – one more 'might have been' of life.

As to Rachel, Bernard had probably been right in that too – if I had really wanted her, as he had remarked, I would not have been afraid to accept her money. That was a bitter thought. How true was love if pride could thwart it?

Looking round, there were reasons in plenty to count one's blessings. Richard, a partially-sighted student, had come to Oxford from a school for the blind, and was reading law. I got to know him through a friend of his, Vincent, also virtually blind and from that school, who lived in the same house as I did for a term; I often helped them with set questions by reading a 'crib' to them. By chance I also knew Richard through his sister Betty. Richard was tall and sturdy, ruddy-faced, with a shock of reddish hair; he had a keen and sensitive mind, and much natural charm. With a prodigious memory, and a feel for the law, a good career awaited him, he said, as a solicitor. I could not know what 'partial sight' meant, but from hints they unintentionally gave, and the way they moved about a room and handled objects, feeling their surfaces and outlines to understand them, I got the impression that all they saw was a grayish blur of light and dark. I was amazed, and sometimes alarmed, by the way these two men lived their lives with dash and confidence; it was wrong, I knew, to admire them for seemingly making light of their disability, for what else could they do? After dinner Vincent would light up a cigarette, operating the lighter near his nose to feel the heat of the flame; he always knew, presumably by a change in the feel or temperature of the cigarette, when it was time to reach for the ash-tray and knock the ash off. Walking in the street, I marvelled that they guided their progress by the echoes of their footsteps – their shoes steel-tipped on heel and toe – sensing gaps in pavements and between houses, even the width of a crossing and the proximity of vehicles and people. They did everything with an ease of usage, an expansive reaching out to the world – seemingly not hermetically locked in inner darkness as the sighted person supposed; but who could tell? They did their best! And I would say to myself: 'Dear God. who am I to think that I am disadvantaged?'

Betty had rosebud lips, gentle brown eyes and a wonderful glow in her cheeks – innocent, tender, with not a trace of the flippant arrogance of the smart set. Our close friendship was platonic; it could have gone beyond that, and perhaps it should have done. We swam in the river beside the great sweep of Port Meadow. When the river path was deserted, seeing the spires and domes of the city far in the distance, beyond fields and marching willows and sentinel poplars, we could imagine ourselves in one of those romantic paintings of northern Italy showing rural simplicity in the foreground and the enigmatic city on the horizon, an Arcadian interregnum of our very own. Afterwards we lay on our backs in the grass under the walls of ruined Godstow Abbey and watched the clouds slide past in the wide sky, talked and were silent, and talked without words through our silences.

After the turbulence and tragedy of Rachel, the egocentricities of Diana, Hannah's unpredictable switches between Amazonian assurance and fragile dependence, I may have been drawn to Betty as a peaceful contrast – but even if true as a motive, that thought took nothing from the bright gleam of her spirit, her grace, her dancing heart.

Once, staying on in Oxford after Betty had gone home, I did not see her for a few weeks. On her return I sensed a sinister stillness in her, as if part of her normally vibrant self was frozen, closed-off and silent. After a while I asked 'How is Richard?' She went pale. Gently she said: 'So you didn't hear?' Richard had gone up to London and fallen under a Tube train as it came into a station and been killed. Our tears mingled, and we were silent for a very long time.

Richard had been anxious about his approaching Schools. Betty said he had no need to be; his tutors had been confident that he would do well.

On a dark evening a year or so later, Betty stepped off the pavement to cross St Giles; the exact sequence of events I never discovered, but according to one account, as she threaded her way among parked cars filling the ill-lit space between the pavement and the line of trees fringing the wide thoroughfare, a car suddenly reversed towards her and she, trying to avoid it on a cobbled patch slippery from recent rain, must have missed her footing and was thrown against another car, hitting her head on it. She was taken to hospital in a coma, and remained enclosed in it, beyond reach, for many months. She never awoke.

The circumstances seemed so bizarre, so improbable, that I looked beyond them and wondered what force had been at work, what fate, which she, half-aware, welcomed?

After going down she had taken a job in Oxford, so that she could stay on and be near Richard, feeling her responsibility as an older sister. In the past year she had let slip a sense that she had failed him.

Had I failed *her*, given too little, *demanded* too little, shared less than I should done? How many moments had there been in her heart, poised between joy and emptiness, when she had hoped for a step closer from me, in commitment, in revelation – and that vital movement had not come?

For many days I moved automatically, senses numbed. I too could willingly have stretched out a hand to welcome the darkness. Recovering, it seemed that mourning too – or rather misery – could hide self-indulgence. Who had the right to judge, theorise, be detached – pre-empt the Fates? Had father done so, contemplating mother's death? No – that thought too was forbidden. And yet, pacing my room at night, fists clenched, fingernails sometimes drawing blood in the palm, I told myself again and again that things could have been so different – if only! If only I had returned her love without restraint, fortified her with sensitivity – and myself too.

When would I cease to wait for certainty, delay movement till the turning world compelled me, so often too late? How many years, how many lives, dared one let slip:

> ... what a dusty answer gets the soul
> When hot for certainty in this our life?

16

Whispers in the Enchanted Forest

Only now, on my first morning on the staff of the British Council, seated in my office in Oriel looking out through leaded panes on a quiet grey stone inner quad, did my transition from the factory seem at last complete. The room had a huge desk – at least it seemed so to me, about six feet long – with two telephones on it, a side-table, bookshelves, several chairs. And I was actually being paid to sit here at my ease, to read letters from romantic-sounding outposts abroad – from cultural attachés, Council representatives – organise supplies, and dictate replies. How could this compare with heaving that eighteen-pound press iron in the steam and clatter and sweat of the factory, the hectic pace of piece work, the corrosive fatigue? Here was civilisation, clean hands, a sense of a place in the world!

I looked back on the years between with a sense of unreality, ineffable, fugitive – whispers in an enchanted forest. Despite the early shocks – the timid arrival at the citadel gates from the lower depths, self-doubt, the brief stage of being patronised as a freak – the first period here had had the feeling of being at a continuous, magical party. I had floated in miraculous freedom through a gilded world, a wondrous minuet of rank and privilege beyond anything I had imagined in the Gorbals, discovery and self-discovery, glory in ease of achievement, the days sparkling and short, too short. The second period, after the army, had been magical in a different style: a *revenant*, partly worldly-wise, partly disillusioned, I was at last beginning to select experience instead of submitting to it blindly, to observe with detachment this turbulent wartime city, aware of apocalyptic change, the Fates stirring the crucible in the sky, myself hurled about within it.

That day of reassessment, when I stood at the corner of the High and the Turl and tried to see where I was and where I should go, *could* go, seemed another age. Certainly I had not got from Oxford what I had come for. For one thing, my romantic vision of it – from the Gorbals – as the home of the pure, gentle savant, tolerant, worshipping wisdom and sweetness and light whatever the cost, had been ridiculously false. Behind the shallow refinement it could be as ferocious as the Gorbals, in some ways more so, for the Gorbals did not pretend to be other than what it was! And where had Oxford's old, slow, confident pace been heading? That perspective was fading in sunset mists of Empire, effortless superiority, the *hubris* of 'Gentlemen v. Player'. Yet who was I to criticise it? Was it sour grapes again, seeing that I had arrived too late to join the Gentlemen, their day already fading? Still, they *had* been certain of where they were going, and surely confidence was all that mattered? I thought again of the red sandstone crenellated railway bridge sprawling wide-legged over the Clyde, a declamatory voice of Victorian certainty dominating the speakers' pitch at Glasgow Green where Bernard and the Clincher had once proclaimed their contrasting hopes for man. That assured voice had been heard here too. Stupidly, I had hoped to be infected by that certainty. With it I would surely know *where* to go? I had failed to hear the hollow note within it. Now, even the pretence had gone. They confident pace, the Galsworthian 'sniffing' at other standards, had withdrawn into the shadows, to wither in North Oxford.

The dream of finding a philospher's stone to cure man's ills had been childish – though old Mr Lipchinsky had believed it. Certainly the torch he had passed on to me was now extinguished, and with it the foolish fancy that I would unlock all doors, all secrets, all relationships, life itself, simply by being brainy. In any case, which doors did I now want to open? I was not sure. Still, I had proved myself intellectually, but I had paid for it; I had scaled magic heights and found obscurantism, absence of hope, a world infinitely darker than I had ever imagined possible from where I had stood in the Gorbals. Yet here I was, with the British Council, committed to project the complacent boss class view – the word 'establishment' was not yet current – of where we all stood. Aside from

Lord Beaverbrook's obsessional jibes about the Council's élitism, its lack of realism in sending Morris dancers and Elizabethan lute players to portray Britain in foreign lands, one could fairly say that the Council projected the British way of life as seem from the top, seemingly unaffected by the surge of history – the sunset of Imperial Britain was as yet only whispered. That the Council worked under the aegis of the Foreign Office gave credence of this view. To do my job at the Council, even in my junior position, I felt I must believe in the establishment view – if not believe, then at least be at peace with it. Amazingly, I found that easier than I had feared.

Was it mere opportunism? After all, the Council was giving me a living! Or had I lost my bearings altogether? I was learning a simple, obvious truth – not obvious then – that nothing in life was all bad. Many progressives in the Council, shocked by the horrors of Nazism and Fascism, found grim consolation in the thought that the British way of life, even though unfortunately capitalist, was not so bad after all. Others, more or less apolitical, such as John Betjeman and Louis MacNeice, would sometimes appear uneasy at certain aspects of it. This ambivalence was neatly expressed when a colleague at the Council, later to achieve distinction as a poet, sent me a copy of his first slim volume of verse with a note: 'This is to get you into trouble with the secret police!' A characteristic irony, for the poems were far from subversive; the reference, I think, was rather to what he *could* have written but had suppressed. In the general feeling of shifting sands, the sentiment was understandable.

The knowledge that I was not alone in my insecurity was not comforting – if anything it was disturbing, for everyone else seemed to deal with it more competently. They retreated from innocence into a wary, opportunist view of life, concealed beneath an urbane rapprochement with the system. A typical example would be Akkie Shonfield – Akkie was short for Akiba – who would become Sir Andrew Shonfield, Director of Chatham House. Akkie had been conventionally progressive, certain that the system could be made over; all that was needed was a new social morality. While he was still up he had registered to do a B.Litt. degree, setting down as the subject of his dissertation, appropriately enough, 'Marx's theory of social morality'. One evening, when he was back on home leave from Alexander's staff, he was with a group of us at a performance of *The Ascent of F6*. We were chatting about the scene in the play in which the climbers inveigh against the use of pitons and other 'artificial' aids by the rival teams attacking the mountain – they were not playing the game. I remarked upon its nostalgia for an age in which you won through by your personal gifts and virtues and commitment alone – the death of the Romantic faith. Akkie said, 'No – it's all about the Oedipus complex!' This view was odd, for though his comment might fit other parts of the play, it was wide of the mark for this one. Akkie was bright but inclined to follow fashion; he was now possessed, like many progressives, by a new, inward-looking philosophy – life was no longer to be explained in terms of 'systems' and boss class manipulation, but by the new Freudian cant. What you must now try to shift was not the world, but *the way you looked at it*. Epitomising this shift, Akkie would come back from the war after distinguished service and become a leader-writer on the *Financial Times*.

Joining the Council kept me in Oxford at a time when I would have preferred to shake its dust off for good. The occupying force, the colonising city of individual and institutional evacuees, began to drift back to London. Occupied colleges would soon reclaim their buildings. The departments of the British Council in Oriel would move out to Blenheim Palace in the wake of the departed intelligence organisation. Here was another unforeseen, unforgettable, dream-like stage on the road from the Gorbals, to walk through the ducal park at lunchtime, look out from my office window over its calm, aristocratic greenery to the John Churchill obelisk, and hear, through the vibrating wall of my room on a gleaming summer afternoon, transcendental Bach on the chapel organ. In this Arcadian quiet of glistening green, profusion of scents, *mise-en-scène* of baroque opulence and confidence, we were separated by epochal distances from the collapse of worlds. Yet we knew it was all very close, just across the horizon. It was surely wrong to be here? This glittering ambience was too good to last, and rightly so, too insulated, yet spilling over with questioning about the future. Exemplifying the unreality, the detachment, a few yards away down the stately corridor John Betjeman passed the hours chalking intricate notations of change-ringing courses on the plywood wall-coverings!

Soon – it could not be soon enough for me – the Council would home back to London and take me with it. London must be my next citadel.

I would then be married; and realise, after a little time – again too late – the wisdom of John Buyers, my tutor at Glasgow University extension classes, in a letter to me, newly arrived in Oxford: 'Many students make the mistake of forming relationships at university on intellectual grounds alone; the necessary emotional substance is often absent ...' But that is a story for another time.

VE Day would come and go with a huge bonfire at the Martyrs' Memorial, and sudden orgiastic couplings on the pavements in the indifferent night, as a huge crowd seethed in mindless release along the length of the Giler, the contents of the apocalyptic crucible, a boiling mass of lost, directionless bodies, defiant, exulting in forgetful release, with nothing in view, faintly nostalgic for the stilled, provisional life that had been the war, when the future need not be faced.

In the light of the leaping orange flames, with little groups of free-booting foragers breaking through the mass of exulting bodies with freshly purloined fuel – tables from pubs, pieces of fencing, empty barrels, bedsteads – Domenico climbed to the topmost step of the Memorial in his black cloak lined with scarlet, and in the infernal fiery light stretched out his hands, saturnine features livid now, in a hectic but solemn benediction, his sojourn here at last over; then he jumped down and was lost in the crowd. I never saw him again. Whether he regained his unknown homeland I never heard. Over the years, rumours would filter back, attributing to him various avatars – playboy, aristocratic mercenary, professional gambler. He was cast by fortune as a dedicated misfit, though in his fashion made for higher things – in the ranks of the Gentlemen – if the world had not been out of joint. In him was another loser – for no very good reason – saddened at the passing of the only world he could call his own; in comparison with which all else, not meeting his patrician standards, was unworthy.

Still, if Domenico could not realise the aspirations he had inherited, he at least *knew* what they were! What was I left with? If I had been born with any goals, I had no idea what they were – or so I thought. As far as I could see I possessed intellectual equipment but very little else – certainly no conscious compulsion as to where and how to employ it. At my back was a vacuum. Unlike most others here, my background contained nothing that I was driven to preserve. At least I did not then think so. Later I would realise that my passion to shore up crumbling tradition under attack by 'progress', to oppose the shedding of values proven by time, must have begun then, perhaps even earlier, in the Gorbals.

What other assets did I possess? Laski had remarked that I had a talent for scepticism. I could analyse with the rigour of Occam's Razor. Was that what Destiny had in store for me, to stand out against received opinion all my life, and suffer the combined fates of Cassandra and Sisyphus? What a future!

I could make dreams explicit. I would write a novel. It would remain hidden, but parts of its essence would speak again and again in other work. Before I started writing I chose the title – *A Parcel of Their Fortunes*, from *Antony and Cleopatra*:

> Men's judgements are
> A parcel of their fortunes, and things outward
> Do draw the inward quality after them,
> To suffer all alike.

That title, though I did not know it then, would contain the *leitmotiv* of all I would write and do in the future, a consistency of vision I never realised I possessed until now, as I write these words.

The journey from the Gorbals had not ended after all. It would continue at every moment – not always with a backward glance, for in a sense I would, at last, take the place *with me*, with all its ghosts.

GORBALS VOICES, SIREN SONGS

In homage to the Zealots
and for
Roland Saul and Miranda Rachel
who will carry the silken thread

Enigmatic Marriage

Of Kay there remains an echo of a tender, perplexed, courageous spirit – a companion through the labyrinth, but one who held a different thread from mine. Passionate, witty, seemingly a free spirit, with her I was happy to forget, for a time, the differences between our respective worlds – she was middle class and not Jewish. I met her at a party at Westfield College, then in wartime evacuation quarters in Oxford, and the attraction was immediate, so powerful that I did not take seriously her compulsion to make slighting remarks about my Jewishness, which I at first blindly ignored, masked as they were as witticisms, thinking, if thought was the right word, that one so warm and humane could not possibly *mean* them. In love, or passion, it was easy to find excuses for many things; and in the unreal, tense, crucible atmosphere of Oxford at that time, it seemed natural to make allowances for weaknesses, and trust that in time, when things were once more normal, they would pass. Normal? That was a dream too, never to be realised. And so passion ruled, and marriage a magnetic compulsion in its train.

Later it was plain that she did mean these comments; and, amazingly, that she did not understand that they gave me pain. After all these years our marriage remains an enigma. That Kay was not Jewish is in some ways beside the point, which is that I did not want to recognise her compulsion for what it was. Something made me not *want* to see, I who thought I saw so much. A sequence in Cocteau's film: *Le testament d'Orphée* illustrates the illusion with profound artistry; the hero walks along with eyes wide open, seemingly unmoved by the fantastic creatures and events around him – and then one realises that he only *appears* to have his eyes open; they are closed, but each eyelid is painted over with the image of a wide-open eye. I too, in this at least – and probably in other things

– preferred to walk with eyes seemingly wide open, but in truth closed.

But why? Remembering the suffering at school in the Gorbals simply for being a Jew, beaten, bullied, vilified; and the fights when all patience was spent – usually getting a 'tanning' because I was not strong enough and had weak eyes, and all around me the stink of prejudice – there seems at this distance only one answer, bizarre, unbelievable. In all the years, when as adolescents and youths we talked and debated under the hot showers at the Gorbals swimming baths trying to unravel the world and ourselves, we told each other that the only way out was to cease to be Jews. Being a Jew was too painful. The historic suffering must end. When the miraculous scholarship took me to Oxford, I was in full flight from Jewish identity. Not that I thought of marriage at that early stage, but at the back of my mind there must have been an idea of assuming the protective colouring of the non-Jewish culture; and what more radical way of doing so than by 'marrying out' – anathema to the orthodox Jewish tradition that bore me – or, slightly less extreme, finding a Jewish girl who would join me in letting the Jewish identity fade away? Yet how could I have *chosen* to take the anti-Semitic virus into my bed? What masochism had me in its grip? Even in the Gorbals there was refuse, to some extent, behind the closed door of the tenement flat. Perhaps I needed to prove to myself that flight was impossible? No – all theorising in vain, an exercise in *esprit de l'escalier*.

At first I tried to condone this behaviour in Kay, treat it as a harmless idiosyncrasy, humour her, while I marvelled that I tolerated it at all. Had I imagined that after the Gorbals I was desensitised? Nor was her animus superficial, immature, something that would wear itself out; its strength became clear when she showed me, with signs of emotional excitement, a treasured possession, a Nazi armband. Caught in shock, I could find no words. She must have noticed my distress, and for once made no show of dismissing the incident as unimportant – overborne not only by *my* petrified reaction, but by her awareness, too late, that in showing me how carefully she had preserved the armband she proclaimed its significance for *her*. In silence she put the dreadful symbol away, once again in safe keeping, among her mementoes.

Yet our passionate affinity had seemed enough. How could Kay, warm, sensitive, aglow with enlightenment and humanity, flaunt this prejudice to *me*: and at this time, so soon after the press photographs showing British soldiers using bulldozers to clear mounds of Jewish bodies in the liberated Nazi camps – nose and mouth covered to shut out the stench of death and putrefaction – the reports of gas chambers and incinerators, the Nuremberg trials? And yet some part of her innocence must have been genuine. I would think of it years later when Hannah Arendt wrote of 'the banality of evil' in reference to Nazi bestiality – the ordinariness of it, performed by ordinary people – implying that evil did not need specifically evil people to do it, for prejudice could lead otherwise decent, ordinary people to do, or to think, terrible things, driven by a seemingly inescapable 'logic of the situation'. Kay, I think, genuinely believed that she 'meant no harm' in condemning what she considered the Jewishness of my appearance, manner, thoughts; she was simply stating the obvious. Her astonishment, when I objected in distress, was that of the little boy I had fought in the school playground for calling me a 'Sheeny', who said, amazed at my fury: 'Bu' ye *are* a Sheeny!' He too saw no harm in stating the obvious. That boy in later years – or such as he – may well have marched with Mosley's Blackshirts, in innocence and provocation, along Gorbals Street.

As for the source of Kay's animus, speculation is as futile now as it would have been at the time. Even so, the dark question remains: feeling as she did about Jews, why did she marry *me*?

John Buyers at Glasgow University, my tutor in the evening classes there, had written to me long before, while I was at Oxford, with Delphic foreknowledge: 'Many students make the mistake of forming close relationships on intellectual affinity alone – that is not enough.' I ignored the classic warning. Perhaps Kay knew its truth – or sensed it – and also chose to ignore it.

Escape from being a Jew was of course an immature idea. Identity was in the marrow, in the veins. I refused to believe it. Flight from it was to seek a special anaesthesia of the spirit, an erasure of sensibility, a kind of death. No wonder the traditional Jew, if a son or daughter married out, said Kaddish, the mourner's prayer. I would understand that in later years, when I had begun the road back.

For the return journey I would have to learn a special understanding all over again – and learn it differently. In ritual or observance almost every word, every symbol, would be deeply interfused, and are so still, with bitter-sweet memories of childhood days when I clung to mother's long black apron – even now my fingers remember the feel of the shiny, worn cotton, warmed by her body, wrestling with the darkness of life, with shadows that prefigured the menace of the future; sadness that would not be put to rest. I still remember father telling me, his voice full of pride mixed with sorrow, how at the first Seder of Passover feast after my birth, when I was only a few weeks old, he laid me on a pillow beside the table, so that I should absorb the atmosphere – the food scents, the brilliant starlight of the candles, the prayers and chanting, the family united in dedication. Slowly I would learn to placate memory, allow it come and go, lessen its grasp.

I would hear father's deep, musical voice, even long after his death, intone the visitation of the plagues on Egypt – or in the synagogue make the prophetic affirmation: 'Shimah yeessrawayl, Adownoy elowhaynoo, Adownoy echod' ('Hear O Israel, the Lord is our God, the Lord is One.') And turbulent feelings about him returned, bringing back the bewilderment I felt as a child at the gulf between faith and action; for father did *know* what the words stood for, and he did believe – yet still he could not quell the chimera within him.

The road back would begin almost imperceptibly, following a long period of aimlessness, and an oppressive isolation of the spirit – a pang at the centre of consciousness like a persistent toothache – banished temporarily by transient passions, or frenetic absorption in work, or in writing that I now see lacked conviction, only to return in strength at moments of silence or inattention, as in the darkest hour of the night. When the movement back did begin, or rather when I became aware of it, I would pretend to ignore its significance

– seemingly trivial steps, making friends anew among Jews, going in curiosity to Yiddish plays. To acknowledge it was to confess, in fury, to monumental folly in the past – above all else the tragic irony of my parting from Rachel; I saw that it had been her ardent Jewishness, not her wealth, that had sapped at our relationship, and that I had feared, unawares, that through her I would be shackled to the Jewish identity for ever. And yet, hidden in the future, I was set on that very course. The refusal to see clearly, really my immaturity, had destroyed our chances of felicity, and in the end destroyed *her*. There too, our passion had provided no answer. We had come together at the wrong time. Here again, dust in the mouth, was the old classic lesson, the futility of fighting against a Fate already at work within – an inner self, a hidden fifth column dedicated to negate the will. As father would have said, 'Ess shtayt geshreeben!' ('It is written!')

Can a marriage be an attempt at sympathetic magic, to force one along a road that contradicted all the inherited influences, like Salvador Dali's 'bending of blood'?

At the ceremony itself, in the dingy grey of the Oxford Registry Office, even at that last moment I might have heeded the atmosphere of ill-omen. Perhaps in presentiment, I had informed no one related to me, not father, who would have been still more deeply cast down, nor my sisters Mary and Lilian, whose flight from home after mother's death had left few links between us. I knew that these were not the true reasons. I was a defector, troubled by what I was doing, and I had set myself to attempt this 'bending of blood' alone, shutting out the troubled voices from the past. If only the will and the mind would always go hand in hand, there would be fewer 'dusty answers'.

The marriage would prove short-lived, for about two years in Oxford and a similar period in London. Nothing held me to Oxford but my job with the British Council, in the evacuated offices now moved from Oriel College to Blenheim Palace. When the Council moved back to London we moved too. Thinking about the marriage only a few years after its end, it seemed that it had happened to someone else.

2

Miss Lawson's Voices

Miss Lawson's house in St John Street, my last lodgings in Oxford as a bachelor, was instinct with sympathetic magic from other generations, poignant, tragic, a palimpsest of many lives and much spent hope, held fast in time. Looking back, it mirrored much of my future.

Here is a morning – *any* morning – in that house. Coming down the steep wooden stairs from my bedroom, thinking of breakfast, I heard Miss Lawson talking excitedly in the ground floor corridor immediately below, her voice genteel, fruity, in tone and manner inexplicably youthful. Another quality in it, a measure, a punctilio, suggesting a bygone age, aptly conveyed the essence of the place – of her, and her life.

On the strip of old red stair carpet, thick dust shimmered like hoar frost. In the tiny entrance hall, a huge oaken hallstand, carrying a permanent burden of coats, Inverness capes, gowns, trilby hats, tweed caps, mortar boards, the whole covered with the tufted grey dust of years, jutted out from the wall like a dark cliff. Beside it, the red carpet had worn away in patches, and the web of light brown backing fibres showed through. All was sombre, brown, grey, black, dingy red, fitfully brightened by gleams of morning sunlight filtering through the little panes of coloured glass in the front door. At the stair foot the wooden newel post marked a frontier between the lodgers' territory and Miss Lawson's twilight world at the rear of the house; here, at whatever hour we came down in the morning, she would be waiting to hear what her 'young gentlemen' wished for breakfast.

As I stepped off the bottom stair she had her back to me, evidently facing someone who stood in the shadow of the staircase. She half-turned to me and said in her customary bright tones, engagingly formal as always: 'Do excuse me, Sir, I will be with you directly. I am just having a word with Mr Mordaunt.'

The name Mordaunt, often on her lips, belonged to one of many familiars.

From force of habit I glanced past her into the patch of obscurity between her world and ours, and saw no one, nor did I expect to. We were used to hearing these one-sided 'conversations' of hers – or rather they were one-sided to *us*. To her they were not, judging by her animated replies to the invisible visitor – or visitors – of the moment. Mordaunt was one of the long line of young gentlemen who had spent their allotted time in this house many years before; she was vague about dates, but it could have been twenty-five years before – or even more.

There was a second group of disembodied interlocutors, imprisoned in her past, with whom her relationship – her true one of long ago – must have been less formal than the term 'young gentleman' conveyed. She addressed most of these by Christian name; but there was another ingredient, proclaimed by a delicate, affecting element in her voice, the harmonic of intimacy, as she reached across to them over the chasm of time, in pleading or tenderness or reproach, passionate, touching the heart. Hearing it, a shiver chilled the spine, for every one of these exchanges had the ring of the *present*; I had to remind myself that it was all in the distant past. Yet not all of it, for it seemed that her own part of the 'conversations' contained a gloss, a correction, what she *should* have said at the time – a gnawing *esprit de l'escalier* – emotions of the restless present.

In the callousness of youth, Derek and I tried to look upon this performance as a comic sideshow of life, a harmless addiction of her lonely state. Derek had been living in the house for a year or so when I moved in; we would be almost the last of Miss Lawson's young gentlemen. The house, magisterial, undeviating in the discipline of a former time, swept our flippancy aside; it insisted on serious questions. What was hidden, what unresolved, far back in her history, which now Miss Lawson strove to reshape, to say the 'right' words, make the 'right' choices, in these moments 'magicked' out of the past, to reap felicity at last? The questions troubled us, for we feared the answers; they must surely bring warnings for our own lives too – perhaps too late to be heeded – of shadows already cast across our paths.

In years Miss Lawson was not very old, probably about sixty, but to our eyes antediluvian; her world, locked in her youth, was beyond our understanding, mysterious, formal – and plainly, in its own correct fashion, exquisitely cruel. Yet despite the echoes that came to us, of disappointments, wrong turnings, polite deceits, per-plexities, betrayals, those distant days shone within her, their brightness sustained with a spellbound logic that disdained the reckonings of time – engaging, poignant, awesome.

About five feet tall, with ramrod back and girlish figure, her slightness of build was emphasised by the black satin dress – never changed – that fell in deep folds straight to her ankles, fastened close under her chin with a large cameo brooch in a scrolled frame of old, dull gold. In her finely sculptured features the cheeks flamed with a bright red sheen like the fire that kindles in the face in a crisp March wind. The blue eyes changed tone with her moods; some-times they were contemplative pools of deep cerulean, sometimes, in laughter, they darted with glints of pale sapphire. I saw in her, fleetingly, the breathtakingly beautiful girl she had been, the grace and poise and floating freshness of the nymph, new in the world, threading sunbeams.

Miss Lawson truly inhabited her youth. Its days lived and breathed for her as though they had never gone. Why did she defy time like this? In the rude impatience of youth, that thought dis-turbed us – sibylline warnings we feared to read.

Mordaunt, obviously, had held a special place in her life of long ago. She had pointed out to me one day, with a vibrant shift of voice, a faded sepia photograph, in a heavy silver frame, on the sit-ting room mantelpiece. A young man in old-fashioned tropical whites and pith helmet posted on the steps of a bungalow; on the timbered verandah behind him a dark-skinned man in long robe and tarboosh stood to attention. The photograph was old. That young colonial officer – probably on his first posting – by now might even have finished his proconsular career and returned to dignified retirement in the Home Counties; but never in all these years, it seemed, had he come back to this house to take away a trunk that stood in the corner of the room, or a gown, stiff with age and dust, bearing his name on a linen tab, that hung among the other garments on the hallstand.

'Sitting room' was a misnomer; the floor was covered with the deposits of decades, and one would have had to scramble across mounds of furniture and paraphernalia even to move from door to window – horsehair sofas, plush mahogany chairs, a Victorian conversation piece with S-shaped back-rest, two upright pianos with gilt candle-holders on their front panels, little hexagonal tables with tasselled covers, whatnots crowded with bric-a-brac, games equipment, trunks, rolled up rugs, pictures, hundreds of books in scallop-edged book-shelves or stacked against the walls or in loose piles on the furniture – smells of the long static years. In a tiny clearing in the middle, at a square oak table, I ate breakfast and the occasional supper, an intruder in that sleeping past.

In years to come we would understand why the riddle of Miss Lawson stirred our uncertainties so – about maturity, understanding the world, values. The days of youth, progressing with the immutability of the sun, overflowing with power and renewal and choice – at least potentially, ready to be possessed – seemed quick with a kind of immortality, singing of a journey without end, towards the Grail. Miss Lawson, who had held youth in suspense for a lifetime, showed us the price to be paid. Her tenacious claim upon the past, her refusal to acknowledge the present or the future, was *her* immortality, but in truth it was a death – and still she defied it.

Why did we go on living there, amid the squalor and sadness? In spite of it all, the old greystone house breathed a spirit almost serene, a sense of living outside time. In our comings and goings we seemed to leave no mark, as if we were insubstantial – the house and its world solid, inviolate. We did not hang our own coats on that hallstand, sensibly, because of the layers of dust, but in truth we chose to leave the ghosts in peace. We ceased to notice the chaos. Miss Lawson spread about her a paradoxical certainty, a dignity, an endearing correctness, above all an atmosphere of unswerving discipline. This is how life must be; you smiled through to the end. In all the years afterwards, whenever I thought of that house, and of her, lines of a wartime popular song, '*Keep smiling through*', tugged at the heart. She did smile through, almost to the end.

For us, living for the moment as we thought – a time that did not 'count' – till London should claim us, these digs had decisive attractions; they were cheap, and in the very heart of things, almost literally a stone's throw from the bar of the Randolph, the Playhouse, the Gloucester Arms. We clung to a conceit of the time, that life was a string of temporary halting places from one avatar to the next – so this bivouac served us well enough.

We were caught in an Oxford in whose life we fitted less and less as the place strove to transform itself, now peace had come, from the frenetic wartime melting-pot – the 'Latin Quarter of Cowley', as Joad had dubbed it – that I had found on my return from the army, back to its previous boss class persona of composed superiority and detachment.

For a more profound reason, not realised at the time, Miss Lawson's dusty limbo was an appropriate halting place. In some ways like her, and perhaps as innocently, we tried to delay time while we digested the forced pace of maturing – mine more so than Derek's, I imagine, for in bridging the gulf between the Gorbals and Oxford I had fitted in a whole new life I still did not properly possess. Until we had done so we could not turn our backs on Oxford and travel on; and each shift was a rebirth. Some illusions would never be wholly discarded – dreams of reading the secrets of life, of changing the world.

The day would come when Miss Lawson began to speak, simply, seriously, of little people who streamed out from under the skirting-boards and ran chattering about her feet, holding her in discussion that distracted her from household affairs. For some time previously, the one-sided 'conversations' had not been heard. Had she at last acknowledge that the invisible visitors, Mordaunt and the rest – resurrected with such overflowing fidelity – were

creatures of her own magic? Had she ceased her re-enactments of
the past, and dismissed the actors too? And had they, rebelling, insisted on returning in this different form? Why were they now 'little'? Belonging to the past, seen in distant perspective, she might at
last have decided that they *had* been 'small' – not worth the anguish
of attachment! What had brought this revelation? What defences
had fallen?

By then I had moved away to London, and I heard it all from
Derek, who had stayed on in the house for a year or so after I left.
When he moved to a flat of his own, he visited her regularly.

She referred to her little familiars as her 'television people', astonishing because television sets were then still rare, and she did
not possess one. She could have known of television only from her
infrequent gossip with neighbours. So, in bizarre fashion, the
world of the present, shunned for so long, forced itself upon her.
What more apocalyptic sign could it have chosen – little people
peering out at you through that new glass window? 'A new world
has come! The past is over.'

Paradoxically, she seemed to have conjured her television people
to defend her past and keep its characters alive, but with *her* towering above them, in command. That brave effort was her final
one; from then on, she declined fast.

Why was the spell of that house, unsettling yet compassionate,
so powerful? When you entered from the street, though the dust
filled your lungs, the whole place, grey, patient, waiting, enfolded
you in old steady understanding. The dirt was not that of poverty –
who better than I to know that? – but of indifference. Having asked
me if I would like a chop for supper, Miss Lawson would throw a
fine angora shawl over her thin shoulders and rush out to the
butcher in Little Clarendon Street, and proudly show me the meat
in its fresh wet redness, turning it over delicately with fingers
almost black with wrinkled grime. I would tell myself that with
luck the heat of the grill on her rusty old gas cooker would disinfect
the meat, and say: 'How splendid!' Seeing her long narrow features
light up in joy, I would add: 'You *will* have some yourself, won't
you?' 'Oh no, Sir, it must be for you. At your age you need

the nourishment, the very best.' The voice was eager, breathless, trusting.

The television people had the final victory – and Miss Lawson was at last defeated, but only in the small details of life. Derek helped to get her into a home for the infirm. Once out of her house she did not last long. Some years later, on impulse I walked past the house. Would I sense the old aura? Part of me did not want to see it in its new one, of the present. Miss Lawson could exist only with every old thing in place – the worn carpet, the dusty garments on that hallstand, Mordaunt on the mantelpiece, voices of her world. What did happen to all those things – no, not *things*, people? They must all have crept away, with her, into the poignant past, there to remain, holding on to life as it should have been. The house looked smart and clean; more significantly, however, like all the others in that tight little street, it now projected an air of impatience with the slow pace of life, of brisk attention to the matter in hand. There was not a whiff of that old, arrested, correct world of Miss Lawson's – her world of faith and honour.

But her voice did return – and would do so again and again, faithful as ever, over the years.

3

The Gale of the World

Derek was stocky, bespectacled, fresh-faced, a perpetually surprised look on his square features, as if the world had moved out of reach at the very moment when he thought he had at last caught up with it. His clothes were crumpled as though he slept in them – chestnut-coloured tweed jacket, elbows patched with leather, dark blue corduroy trousers, grubby checked shirt, stained college tie knotted carelessly off-centre, his pockets bulging with books and papers. The round black spectacles had been repaired at the bridge with sticking plaster, and rested askew on the pointed nose. His careless appearance only superficially confounded the conventional middle-class stamp – an affirmation of independence, of integrity, the perpetual quest.

Not that his appearance was especially noticeable in the prevailing confusion, as it would have been in the Oxford of the 'last days'. As military personnel, foreign and British, melted away from what had been a centre of the management of war, the streets had filled with demobilised servicemen, impatient, world-weary, sporting redundant military clothing, often with a theatrical swagger, cocking a snook at the machine of war and statecraft that had drawn them in and now disgorged them – greatcoats and British warms worn with college scarves wound in multiple rolls under the chin, baggy fatigue trousers and crested blazers, desert boots, flying boots, sheepskin jackets, duffle coats. The display proclaimed rejection, opportunist detachment, disgust with betrayal by the broken world, mimicking the chaos of Europe with cold detachment – Céline and *je m'en foutisme*. It was not a true nihilism but perplexity, a demand to know what values still stood secure, what identity would fit the unimaginable future – *angst* and disgust. Among these slouching figures, wary, defiant – some of them parodying, as a coterie joke, the stock image of the hardened old sweat – Kenneth Tynan's purple suit, blindingly luminescent on his cadaverous frame, sounded a trumpet blast of confidence and arrogance, matching his manner: 'Here I come, a star, watch me soar!' Tynan, outwardly at least, showed none of the interfused uncertainty – and many people did give way in his path. In that atmosphere of negation, scepticism, burlesque, Derek's modestly bohemian presentation of himself was almost conventional.

He was always in a hurry, rushing to a concert, exhibition, play, a talk by some notable visitor to the university. His cultural hunger – hunger was the only word for it – was catholic and insatiable, from theatre to Japanese art, music to anthropology, pottery to the dance. He was driven to live more lives than he had. He had been born with a heart murmur, hence his rejection for military service; and he knew that his life must be shorter than the allotted span – but not by *how much*. He must count each day as a mercy, but he never showed it, except in that hunger.

His soul was gentle, too gentle – at the opposite extreme from the juggernaut self-promotion of Kenneth Tynan. If Derek ever felt that the grapes were sour – certainly he never showed that he did – he might have meditated on how much someone with only modest endowment could achieve if he had 'brass neck', which Tynan possessed in plenty, and he himself not at all. Tynan, fresh from school among so many veterans – both of Oxford and the war – and remarkable for his confidence and vigour, was helped of course by money. He was helped, also, by the 'trimmer' phenomenon among the majority – in a climate of uncertainty it is safer to follow an apparent trend than run the risk of being left behind. His self-promotion, therefore, based as it was on shrewdness in manipulation, was helped by the uncertainty of others. He once remarked, with evident satisfaction on the toothy lips: 'Oxford's only use is to give you a stage to strut on and promote yourself. And that's what I'm good at!' His mental horizon, compared with Derek's, was narrow. He had little true curiosity, and beneath the native astuteness his understanding was shallow. Derek's broadly flowing interest was profound, with no other aim than spiritual, recalling Bernard's saintly father, the Kropotkin scholar, for whom the highest attainment was to be the pursuer of enlightenment. For Derek, 'Beauty is truth, truth beauty ...' expressed a deeply held faith – and the quest was important above all else.

The first impression of him was of warmth; and with it an eager innocence, challenging but engaging. Always, however, one sensed a shadow within; how much of it grew from knowledge of his heart condition I never knew. The innocence was the man himself. That apart, his hunger for reassurance was an afterthought, a sop to the wary emotions, a quality that many women found irresistible, making them want to mother him. That was not always welcome, for in his unassuming way he was robust: 'Being mothered is all very well as far as it goes,' he would remark with the thin-lipped smile, 'that is, if you're not in a hurry to get to first base!'

Having failed his medical for the services, he had stayed up to finish reading history, and then remained, joining the throng that found Oxford as good a place as any in which to sit out the war. Its dilettante life suited him, though he occasionally longed for something to happen to force him out of it; he knew well enough that living on the fringe of the university brought an insidious corruption, the illusion that you could enjoy forever the student attitude to life, in which, as in childhood, nothing is indelible:

> sweet dalliance with life,
> Uncommitted, conditional,
> Singing of experiment and promise

choosing not to see that the authentic essence was far behind, in its true place in time, out of reach. There were many in Oxford who had succumbed. Who could say they were wrong? For Derek the ambiguities would sometimes strike home cruelly, and he would feel diminished.

He did have some excuse for staying on; Oxford had become his only home, or rather it was more home than anywhere else. He spoke little of his family. I gathered that his father, a distinguished lawyer, had remarried, and that in the new home Derek felt he had no place. I wondered how I would have felt if my father had married again; doubtless it would have compounded the trauma of mother's death – unless the stepmother had been miraculously generous-hearted and wise. For reasons he never discussed, Derek had preferred to stay away. It was simpler, he said, to stay put in Oxford. Many years would pass before he broke away, and followed most of the others we had known who had hastened away to the dream-city of fulfilment, London, in hope of political glory or creative acclaim. By then it would in a sense be too late for him – the 'right' move at the wrong time.

Oxford was my only home too. Not long after mother died, when I was six, my sisters Lilian and Mary, much older than me, left to 'better themselves', leaving me to the bleak care of father, loving but remote, and the Gorbals tenement flat was home only in the formal sense. Miss Lawson's house, therefore, was home as much as anywhere could be.

Derek's father came on the occasional visit. I was struck by the similarities, not only in appearance – the older man was also stocky, bespectacled, fresh-faced, with the same small neat mouth – but in a certain visionary detachment, a straining towards some private mirage. He too, as Derek was destined to do, appeared to have reached a goal at the wrong time – at first sight a trivial one, but to him obviously of great emotional importance. For years, with much thought and experiment, he had sought the answer to a traveller's problem – how to keep a cake of soap dry in the sponge bag. Hundreds of thousands of people, perhaps millions, would flock to buy the device. At last he found an answer, and called his invention, echoing Archimedes, the Euroikon. He showed me one of the small batch he had had made in the hope of finding a backer to manufacture and market it. It was a circular box of green mottled plastic about four inches in diameter and three inches deep, with a screw-on lid. Within, screwed to the bottom and the lid, in effect a false bottom and false lid, was a perforated disc or platform whose edges snugly fitted the concave sides of the box; whichever way up the container lay, the cake of soap would shed its slimy dampness through the perforated discs, and remain dry between them. Alas it seemed that he had hit upon the clever idea too late. As postwar austerity faded, and hotels became generous with soap, the traveller was less concerned about protecting his own piece of soap. So far the Euroikon had not found a commercial backer.

For Derek's sake I felt his father's disappointment. Had his years been wasted in other respects too – his official career was obviously successful? In one sense logic had carried *me* a long way, but in another it had left me at my beginnings. For logic hurt less only because it told you so little – because it *touched* you not at all. 'Be objective' was Bernard's favourite maxim, but the true guides for action surely lay far beneath, subtle, fugitive – dreams and fulfilments with meaning only for the self within. I longed for sensibility to be quicker, to sense the unspoken, the feelings that words concealed – where Miss Lawson had lost her way.

I wondered if I could help with the Euroikon. What did I know of the world of business? Unawares, I had assumed the student conceit that the true intellectual shunned business and its unworthy concerns – our minds were on higher things. Still, business should not be difficult if you put your mind to it. I looked at the Euroikon as a customer in a shop would. The green mottled plastic looked 'mere'. Its bulk was off-putting; it did not easily fit the hand. The design could be amended to attract shopkeepers to display it, and customers to pick it up, the crucial step in selling. The gnomic name Euroikon should be changed to something more in tune with daily life.

I thought of taking the Euroikon to Pilchard, whom I had met at one of Werner's larger parties. He called himself an ideas developer, a business midwife: 'Dear boy, bring me a good idea, and you can depend on it I know who to team up with and turn it into money!' He certainly looked prosperous, whether from business success or inherited riches was not clear; florid, about fifty, always with a rose in his button hole, seldom without a long Churchillian cigar, image of the *bon viveur*. His palatial flat near Eaton Square glittered with gold leaf. Like Werner he was a compulsive party giver, but while Werner's parties had an atmosphere of grace, of unhurried *bonhomie*, Pilchard's had an obsessional pace, a sense of pressure, of effort sharply focused, of no time to waste. It was exhilarating, at first, to be translated in one leap to the higher slopes of industry, finance, politics – what was a Gorbals boy doing up there? The sensation soon faded, as a similar one had done in Oxford; and I warned myself, once again, that I had much to learn before I could play in that league. For one thing, I hated myself for pretending that I *was* of their world – which I had never done at Oxford, where I had insisted on being the Gorbals proletarian: 'Take me as I am!' That had been a puerile challenge, and I had been lucky to find people – Bill, James, and the rest – who saw beyond it and found agreeable qualities beneath, and became friends, thereby encouraging me to stop rubbing people's noses in the Gorbals. Still, I could not abandon the challenge altogether. The Gorbals was my truest identity. Without it I would be nothing – Hoffman without his reflection.

Marriage to Kay would finally drive that lesson home, and prove that however far I fled, or thought I did, I would never lose my Gorbals 'reflection'. I must change it, add to it – be warmer, less defensive – stand straight within myself, make peace with it at last, the sooner the better. I would still remain, however, and probably for ever, an intruder in the Establishment, the outsider who saw most of the game – sometimes too much – a dangerous gift that I must not flaunt but use with care, and even conceal at times.

I had an open invitation to Pilchard's parties. When Council work took me to London, I could ring up and propose myself. He, meticulous in maintaining his contacts, would telephone me if I had not been in touch for a month or so. I had sometimes thought I might meet Bill there, but never did. Bill, in his debonair fashion, was a 'fixer' too, but at a higher level. In the wartime crucible of Oxford, where he had returned for his mysterious work dose to the high councils of power, he had made it plain that he would always be near the centre – *of* the Establishment, unquestionably. That was his special magic and he knew it – steady of eye, unhurried, sure of action and word, a competence of class that no talent of mine, no effort, would ever equal; and he knew that too, though to his genial credit he never rubbed it in. Certainly, Pilchard was not *of* the Establishment as comfortably as Bill was; Pilchard was an 'operator', a *franc tireur* on the margins, and I would meet many of him in the frenetic post-war kaleidoscope of London.

One day, lunching with Bill at his club, I mentioned Pilchard. With a glance at nearby tables, he leaned towards me and said very quietly: 'He certainly knows a lot of people.' That dismissed Pilchard. 'But' – he thought about his next words – 'be careful.'

I was still too green, he gently implied, to know my way in that Byzantine world; in any case I lacked his inherited cushioning of money and friends, the protective network of the Establishment, were I to 'come unstuck'. The true, inner Establishment, he subtly emphasised, always looked after its own, and I certainly would not qualify for that protection – perhaps in the future, who could say, but not yet. These were warnings he had uttered before, in the wartime days.

Keynes's gibe, after the previous war, came to mind: 'The hard-faced men who had done well out of the war.' As if he had caught the thought he said: 'There's nothing sinister I'm sure! but these chaps have been playing the game a long time – and sometimes they play rough.'

Belying his easy manner, Bill's choice of words was never random. Even so, 'sinister' sounded too strong a word; but it would be futile – and tactless – to ask why he used it. Pointless also, for I was still too excited by metropolitan glitter to be warned off any part of it. I knew that the excitement would pass. I would learn to be selective. Meanwhile, whether Pilchard's activities as a fixer went beyond purely business wheeling and dealing did not interest me; nor, except for the occasional passing thought, why he included *me*, with no influence whatever, in his invitation list.

In those tremulous days of the new peace, when earth's foundations were still shifting from the shocks of Armageddon, the most likely explanation for Bill's use of 'sinister' would have been obvious had I been more politically aware. The British Council, indirectly, was a vantage point from which to interpret long-term trends in Foreign Office thinking; indeed it was essential for the Council's leadership to do that, for the Foreign Office was the

Council's paymaster, and determined not only the Council's regional and country budgets, but also the spending strategy within a country, between one university and another, between technical or 'cultural' institutions – patterns of possible influence. Perhaps significantly, a number of senior officers from the services – among them General Sir Ronald Adam, former Adjutant-General to the Forces – moved through the highest positions in the Council. Foreign political analysts could well have sought, through someone in the Council, a view of that policy formation and interpretation, if only to confirm assessments reached in other ways.

My work in the Council's Arts and Sciences Division was at first largely concerned with supplying learned journals to universities and similar institutions in China and the Far East, and later in Eastern Europe and Greece, finding runs of back numbers to replace stocks destroyed in the war, or to build up new faculty libraries. In those years immediately after the war, the Council – founded in 1934 – still laboured under the consequences of having been rapidly put together, and lacked a properly defined staff career structure and 'establishment'; at one stage I was asked to adapt Estacode – the Civil Service staff regulations – to Council conditions. The Council had no systematic intake of staff – people were recruited *ad hoc* for particular jobs, sometimes directly by heads of specialist departments. We were certainly a very mixed crowd, an ex-policeman, senior naval and army officers, various ex- teachers, ex-dons – and myself an ex-garment presser; nearly everyone was an 'ex' of some other vocation, necessarily so in the circumstances. There was a sprinkling of more obvious cultural affinity – cultural in the artistic sense – Alan Ross, Gavin Ewart, John Betjeman – and in overseas posts Ronald Bottrall and, briefly, Louis MacNeice. The Council as a whole was learning how to conduct a new, difficult, historic mission, to project a changed moral identity for Britain, in a new age whose essence and challenges were as yet not understood, and old ideas of personal, as well as national, mission and dedication had to be thought out afresh. It is not easy to judge, even now, how well the task was understood at that time within the Council itself; outside, it was hardly understood at all, to judge by the fierce criticism the Council attracted, notably from the Beaverbrook press; and Ernest Bevin, as Foreign Secretary the Council's overlord and supposed protector, once said in his self-consciously cloth-cap style: 'Teaching English in foreign countries to get "influence" is like pouring good money into a bucket full of holes! What do they do with the English we're teaching them – emigrate to America! Or to this country if they can't, and take our lads' jobs away!'

In my junior position I was never present at the highest level of meetings; but I often went to medium-level ones in attendance on senior officials, and to briefing meetings with overseas staff. It was also the practice for these staff – on leave or on a business visit – to make the round of the officers dealing with their region, and so, meeting a great many of them, and reading reports and correspondence that passed across my desk touching on Foreign Office opinion, on shifts of power and policy overseas and Foreign Office responses to them, and on the thoughts and comments of overseas Council staff at post, there emerged a fascinating picture of a world in traumatic change, and of how the holders of power in Britain – both of the left and the right – grappled with the altered terms of *realpolitik*. There were visions of distant peoples – of shifting balances under new political dispensations – old philosophies, traditions, values, adjusting to a shaken world. Council gossip too, reflecting the often squally exchanges with the Foreign Office, added piquant insights into the making of policy.

Here was a heady flow of new impressions, potent in a fashion quite different from those of Oxford; the feeling of being linked to Hegelian surges of history – previously sensed only remotely in the lower depths of the Gorbals, if at all.

Derek showed no enthusiasm when I suggested taking the Euroikon to Pilchard. He was troubled, not by scepticism about its commercial prospects, in which he had no interest, but by bitterness on his father's behalf, a conflict of love, sympathy, pity. He said: 'If *you* don't mind wasting your time on it, go ahead.'

When I telephoned Pilchard to say I had something to show him, he quickly interrupted: 'Not another word, old boy – never know who's listening. Come along and talk …!'

Unwrapping the Euroikon, I had the feeling that he had expected something much more precious – a secret so momentous that it could only be whispered. There was the faintest lift of bushy eyebrows, a pursing of the lips instantly banished. He turned the Euroikon over in his podgy hands. Something about his mien, the way his bulging waistcoat sagged, dampened hope.

At test he said: 'Tell you what. I'll show this to some good friends of mine – if they think they can sell a million of these things, we're on to something! Anything less than that simply isn't on.'

A few weeks later he telephoned: 'Sorry. I did try! Don't be discouraged, old boy. Always happy to listen – information's the thing! There's money there!'

Derek was neither surprised nor sorry: 'When I think of father, the mind he has, and what he could have done with his life – and this is how his years have gone! Do we all take the wrong turning – whether we act on impulse or take our time about it?'

For his own life I think he knew the answer – knew and did not know, or dared not. Seeing his life's shadow shortening before him, he may have thought, or rather felt: 'Why aim at *anything* – whatever I choose will be stunted! Let Fate decide.' Even at his most convivial, he kept himself apart, hovered tentatively, pursued the dilettante life-waited.

We talked of talent, the old student obsession. His was the pithy, ironic turn of phrase. Where could he sell that? He waited. As I had seen so often in this favoured world of Oxford, if you could afford to wait, what you wanted, or something near it, would come your way – and so it happened with him. How close it was to what he wanted I would never discover. Perhaps he himself did not know. The *Oxford Mail* took him on as a reporter. He settled down to become an Oxford character. Years would pass, frenetically gregarious, knowing 'everybody' but always uninvolved – like the young man in Henry James's *Figure in the Carpet*, moving in an empty circle, waiting.

He was not a heavy drinker, but he was a connoisseur of beer, and he must often have drunk more than was good for that murmur in the heart, for he put on weight. Pub life was necessary to him, partly for the same reasons as in Fleet Street, for gossip – the journalist's inspiration – the companionship of the shifting battle-field, partly the attractions of particular pubs, the theatrical milieu of the Gloucester Arms a few steps from the Playhouse stage door, and the cosy literary one of the 'Vicky' Arms near the Radcliffe Infirmary.

For more than ten years after I moved to London we continued to meet often; sometimes he would come up several times in a single week – for the theatre, the opera, to sell review copies of books to a shop near Holborn. One day he telephoned to say he had something tremendously important to discuss. We met in the evening at the Stag's Head behind Broadcasting House. We went out on to the pavement, glass in hand, to escape the clamour of the packed saloon. He had a look of excitement mixed with concern; I thought at once of his heart. Had surgery been suggested – risky but with hope of cure? Yes, it was surgery of a kind. He had been offered not a cure but a threat – which had come, with exquisite irony, disguised as a golden prize. *The Times* had offered him a job, which meant, of course, moving to London.

Should he take the prize or stay in Oxford? I did not know that his heart condition was worsening; but I should have guessed, for it was unlike him to show fear. And so, at first, I misread his doubts. Did he fear to exchange his established position in Oxford for the uncertainties of Fleet Street? Oxford was his own manageable world, where he had status, a personal niche; he could write on topics he enjoyed, air his wide interests – books, the theatre, music, opera, art. We did not openly speak of his health, but the shadow was with us, especially the assumption we shared but did not dare discuss – he would probably live longer if he stayed put. In Oxford he could jump on his compact Moulton bicycle and go to an assignment easily and quickly, with little stress; he could work at a familiar, manageable pace. London was vast, fast-moving, by contrast a jungle – a struggle in every way. Ten years earlier he might have mastered it – but could he do it now? I dared not put the question, for if it had to be asked at all, the answer must surely be no.

Then I remembered him writing to me some months before: 'A colleague has recently left for the *Times*, which leaves me feeling restless,' and his characteristically poignant image: 'I still get scorched by the dying embers of Fleet Street ambitions.' How could I speak against that?

It seemed right to say, 'Stay on in Oxford'. Part of him, wanted me to say that. Something stopped me; I thought of the time, in the 'last days' before war came, when I had meddled in Werner's life, with a disastrous result. Werner had bought himself out of Buchenwald – and sent his family to America – and had been waiting in Oxford for a committee for refugee scientists to find him a promised research appointment. Months passed, the appointment did not come, and he became increasingly cast down; he hated the thought of deserting the Old World. At last, despairing, he booked passage to America to join his wife and children. And I, for the best of reasons as I thought, asked Rachel if she would persuade her father to use his influence with the Committee. I did not ask Werner first, in case my intervention failed. Werner got the appointment, put his plans into reverse and booked passages for his wife and children to join him in England. By the time they embarked, war had come; soon after their arrival, before they even reached Oxford, they were killed in an air raid. Oh yes, my intentions had been good, at least on the surface. Underneath, however, had there been something else, self-indulgent, unforgiveable – the lure of power over the lives of others?

In spite of his fears, plainly Derek dearly wanted to take the *Times* job – that classic leap from the provinces to Fleet Street, and straight to the very pinnacle, *The Times*. Why should he not taste victory, however short? But London, I was sure, would kill him – and I think he knew that, or he would not have sought my advice. What would I do, he asked, in his place? He wanted me to join in his debate with himself, between desire and prudence – life itself hanging on the outcome. He demanded the truth. Had I the right to utter it, to confirm his fears? If I did, his remaining days – even if he stayed in Oxford – would be the darker. Who was I to play the arbiter – I who had agonised so long about accepting the

Oxford scholarship and was not certain, even now, that I had decided wisely? How cruel of the Fates to send fulfilment so late in the day!

No – I could not – must not. This time I would be impartial – only later would I see that to conceal the truth he asked for was *not* being impartial. I set out the case for and against, trying to lay no stress either way. My guilt must have shown in my face, in my voice. He had looked to me, trusted friend, to come down on one side or the other. What irony – I who could not bear to hear my own fearful voices! I think of that moment to this day, when so much that might have helped him – insight, instinct, prescience – remained unspoken. If I had said 'Stay where you are – where you are safe,' I think I could have persuaded him. But I cannot be sure.

As we stood there, I remembered another night, in the early London days, standing on this very spot outside the Stag, when Louis MacNeice swayed out of the saloon bar and stood in the doorway looking up and down the quiet street, meditatively mouthing words to himself. He caught my eye – we had met at the British Council – and swung near, and said in his flat, dark, gritty voice: 'Where's the *bearing*? That's the big question, eh?' He looked away, murmuring to himself once more: 'Where's the *bearing*?', turned on his heel as if about to return to the bar, then swung round again, grinned, and edged away into the night.

'Where's the bearing?' A verdict on the *zeitgeist*. Perhaps on himself. And certainly on me – on us.

Caught up in that memory, I must have murmured the words. How I wished I knew the answer: 'Where's the bearing?' Derek started; he had gone pale, the thin lips tight. Fear hung on his features. I was drawing away, refusing to help. Searching my face with that quick, darting glance behind the lopsided glasses, he must have seen the truth, and that I feared to speak it. It was at that instant, I think, that he made up his mind to accept the *Times* offer. He stepped to the edge of the wide pavement, raised his glass and made the gesture of a toast to the empty night air, apostrophising London itself: 'Hail! We who are about to die salute you!'

He was not even slightly drunk; he knew what he said. He would have his time in London – a curtailed portion. At that moment, I think, he knew it well. We never spoke of it again.

And so he went to *The Times;* and I found him a small flat in Fitzjohn's Avenue in Hampstead. Despite the hectic conviviality of the new life, seemingly enjoying the tang of metropolitan sophistication, and London's higher pace, he remained solitary in himself, as in Oxford. I sensed that he was husbanding his strength – a tragic paradox; he had come to London to taste life more fully, and now he must reach out to it sparingly.

Slowly, over about two years, a crucial change in him must have come about, but the evidence seemed to show itself suddenly. In retrospect it was not sudden; preoccupied, I had not seen it. He spent more and more of any spare time in his flat, listening to music, studying his collection of Japanese prints, reading, now and then darting out for a pint or two at the Holly Bush in Hampstead village. Perhaps the changes had begun even before the move to London – the current within him already slackening.

Sometimes I called for him and we walked up to the Holly Bush together, up the long steep hill of Fitzjohn's Avenue. On one of those sorties, as he puffed up the hill, I was struck by his unusual shortness of breath. Before I could say anything, he got out a few words which, though spoken in his usual jesting manner – yet only half-jesting – should have warned me: 'This pull up the hill is getting too much for me!'

The tempo of London, and its vastness – after Oxford's narrow compass and leisurely pace, where people moved in small orbits, easily met or visited on impulse – deterred spontaneity; and we met less frequently. Late in the December of his second year, I telephoned and invited him for dinner on New Year's Eve; his voice sounded faint, but I put that down to the bad telephone line. Yes, he would have liked to come but he thought he shouldn't, for he would not be able to stay to see the new year in: 'You see, I get *so* tired these days!' I should not have pressed him to come; I should have gone to see him at once. 'Oh, come on!' At last he agreed. We saw the new year in and drank to it, but he was unusually subdued, the face drawn and tired, a somnambulist putting on a brave effort to seem awake. A few months later, getting no reply when I telephoned his flat, I tried to get him at *The Times*. A colleague said that Derek had gone into the New End Hospital in Hampstead 'for a check up'. He did not know the reason. I went to the hospital at once. He was wired up to various monitoring devices, the heart beats zig-zagging on a little green screen placed high on the wall beside his bed, out of his line of sight. He had a higher colour than usual, with a glaze on his cheeks like that on a fresh red apple. Several times he said that he was glad to be having a rest. I visited him as often as I could. We talked widely as usual; he seemed to be regaining his old zest. One day a burly ward sister, stolid, flat-faced, with the dogged aspect of a worried drill sergeant, interrupted and told him sharply: 'You mustn't get so excited! After all, this is a terminal cardiac ward!'

The word 'terminal' was chilling. I dared not look him in the eye; and he, face set and lips tight, looked down at the bowl of oranges and grapes I had brought. I was hurt for him, and saddened – how cruel to speak to him in that fashion! Should I go to higher authority in the hospital and protest? No, the resulting row might make things even more unpleasant for him. I said nothing. A few days later, he was dead.

The funeral was at Golders Green Crematorium – if there was anything worse than a friend's death, it was to attend his cremation. Why burn the thread that joined earth and life? What was wrong with the logic of 'dust unto dust'? I remembered Bernard's words when his father died: 'What the living get out of a funeral God alone knows.'

Friends from Fleet Street and from his Oxford years trooped up Hoop Lane and into the windy asphalt courtyard, some already flushed from stops at a bar, or long pulls at pocket flasks. Curiously, there was a collective sigh of relief as the guardians shepherded us into the cold, efficient atmosphere of the room of farewell. How brisk it all was! A snatch of Brahms sounded out from a speaker, and the coffin disappeared into the wall and the little wooden doors, like a serving hatch, shut fast upon it. I wanted to cry out: 'Send him on his way slowly – slowly, for God's sake!'

'Where's the bearing?' Did he ever have a chance to know it?

In the cold courtyard again, treading almost furtively, an uneasy chorus, excused their haste to depart, took breathless options on the future, and faded away.

MacNeice was right. Nobody knew where 'the bearing' was. Yet in all the years, I had thought that a fortunate few – among such as these – *did* know. And that if I got close enough to them, I would know too.

In more than one sense the new peace seemed to be a continuation of wartime under another name, with the dominant feeling that we were still in the toils of an apocalyptic time, when everything was still being thrown about, and no direction was secure. From an unexpected quarter a phrase had struck me, a lapidary statement, that aptly – and tragically – put a label on the whole turbulent epoch since the beginning of the war, precisely conveying the sense of driving insecurity in the shifting world. Though it had been uttered in defiance, referring to the war years, it was equally true for their aftermath. General Mihailovic, leader of the Chetniks, once acclaimed by the Allies as a hero, then attacked for opportunism and equivocal loyalties, and executed by Marshal Tito in the settling of scores after the war, had used it to sum up the epoch: 'the gale of the world'. At his show trial, Mihailovic had sardonically thrown his own verdict in the faces of his prosecutors: 'I was caught in the gale of the world.'

That image cut deeply into the mind, like the mark of a chisel in stone. I pictured the gale breaking the world into fragments – and people too – as a storm hurls slates off roofs, and shakes trees bare of leaves, levels crops and carries the ears of corn away, all whirled about in the unending apocalyptic wind – and people fighting for a moment of peace and silence, and above all certainty, in the slightest lull, but not expecting permanence; until the wind strengthened again and the fragments rose up to darken the sky once more, to scatter and fall in a totally different pattern.

This mental picture was constantly brought home by the physical – skeletal bombed buildings quivering in the wind, jagged gable walls like great broken teeth outlined against the sky, gaps on every hand where bombs had destroyed totally, the empty ground over-grown, as by an afterthought of the Fates, with colourful wild flowers and shrubs – Deadly Nightshade abounding. It was still smart to wear items of military uniform, not only because of short-ages but seemingly to express nostalgia for the timeless limbo of the war years, contempt for the result, a robust independence of mind. It was smarter still to proclaim American contacts with a Brooks Brothers suit or shirt – the tired Old World tapping into the sup-posed certainties of the New. One sensed a feeling that all land-marks – of purpose, values, design of life – had vanished in the crucible of the war, and that people snatched at shadows, insisting that they were certainties, lest they be left with nothing – and that was so for ideas, and for relationships too. Not that pre-war per-spectives had been dependable either, but pre-war was another world, now seen as having possessed an amplitude churlishly un-dervalued at the time, its days painful to remember because of what had been lost, and because of guilt for having had too little faith. Though those 'last days' had worn down the nerves with anxiety and perplexity, in retrospect, by a strange guileful magic, people talked of them as having been rock solid.

The insecure *zeitgeist* seemed natural in the grey austerity of these years of unfamiliar peace, little changed from the shifts and chances of wartime, in which so much energy was spent pursuing immediate certainties – finding flats and furniture, managing with rationing, better still evading it – the stuff of so much eager chatter. A similar urgency appeared to have infected personal relations – where cer-tainties, even if insecurely glimpsed, must be instantly grasped in the passing moment, for the *next* moment might not happen!

An incident at a party at Anne's flat epitomised that sense of con-tinuing turbulence, emotional pressure, egotism, anxiety. In the Gorbals I would not have given it a second thought, for there the passions were close to the surface, the future bleak like the present, and all things had to be fought for and held fast lest they slip away, and so you were careful, controlled, circumspect – until disappointment, fear, or anxiety boiled over. In the Gorbals the gale of the world was always with you; here, among these refined, middle-class people, this comfortable fringe of the establishment, I was surprised – though I should not have been – to find it in full strength, and therefore behaved, I think, foolishly. In the new, uncertain mores of the time, my behaviour was probably no more out of place than anybody else's, but I was shaken by the incident for reasons I could not fathom, and especially by my own, unnecessary, part in it.

Certainly most people appeared to behave as if the gale of the world was set to last for ever, as if the *je m'en foutisme* of the 'last days' would remain the egotistic inspiration of the present and the future. For me, the feeling was not new, but I had hoped to escape it at last here in London, taking cautious steps into the middle-class milieu whose certainty I had so envied at Oxford. It seemed that I was too late. They too groped for certainty.

My attempt to join them was not conscious, but part of the same search for solid ground that had made me try to shed the Gorbals identity in Oxford. I did have some excuse – I had nowhere else to go. Apart from my old friend Bernard, whom I saw on his frequent trips to London on union business, and the occasional terse signal from father – in his Yiddish script that I had almost forgotten how to read – my Gorbals links were broken. This middle-class life, through Kay and her friends and my own acquaintances from Oxford and the British Council, was now the only one I knew. Bernard had once remarked, watching me poling a punt on the river in Oxford, that I had already 'gone native'. His comment went deeper; he was telling me that it was a mistake to try to assume the protective colouring of the boss class: 'Be what you really are and to hell with what people think.'

My Gorbals self, granite hard against all attempts at assimilation, seemed to agree:

Emerkoff: Tell me, what is the "Gyntian" self?
Peer: The world that's here inside my head;
                         That makes me "me" and no one else,
                         No more than God could be the Devil.

The old inner dialogue settled nothing; I could not go back to be the person I had been, for he did not exist, or so I thought. As for presenting my true 'Gyntian self' to the world, it would be years before I could be sure what that was. Meanwhile, to assimilate was to hide in the crowd – cowardly but a temptation hard to resist, later to be regretted. Unconsciously I had learnt a few basic disciplines, not much more than middle-class table manners and other fragments of etiquette, as well as some of the habits of speech – but that was treacherous ground, for the talk of this milieu, its tricks of imagery and usage, drew upon middle-class upbringing and schooling which I manifestly did not possess – and to appear to counterfeit it would be absurd. I hovered on the edge, troubled neophyte.

Anne had been a friend of Kay's at Oxford, more than a friend, a heroine who moved, enviably, on the slopes of Parnassus. Her pale, pensive face and willowy figure, the glistening brown hair cascading to her shoulders, reminded me of the darkly glowing, Pallas Athene aspect of Hannah – lovely, fearless Hannah I had admired in the Oxford days, now gone to build up a kibbutz in the new State of Israel. Chic, clever, downright in manner, Anne was an adept of the terse, pithy remark that summed up a world of meaning, sometimes disconcertingly, and she would often – presumably aware of this effect – interpolate a tinkling laugh to soften the impact. On going down from Oxford, she had sailed into the BBC to become a producer in the Features and Drama Department under Lawrence Gilliam.

For some time, Kay told me, Anne had been living with Michael – later to become a distinguished journalist. In those days, the state of 'living with', previously a matter one spoke of in a whisper, was still mentioned with a barely suppressed *frisson* of wonder; for to show it would reveal a deplorable lack of sophistication. Kay and I met them occasionally, at the BBC pub, the Stag's Head, or in one of the little restaurants in the vicinity, where the BBC had taken over so many buildings that the quarter had the atmosphere of a Broadcasting House colony. To us, their 'arrangement' displayed a settled solidity – they could have been any married couple.

We arrived at the party very late. Kay could never be punctual;

even the polite fifteen-minute 'guest lateness' was beyond her. Once, having arranged to meet friends for an early supper at the Players' Theatre and then to see the performance with them, I was ashamed to arrive with her long after supper was over, and the curtain about to go up, a record in delay even for her – effectively souring the whole evening. Our companions, a charming and cultured doctor and his wife, were not only Jewish but friends of *mine*, which may have prompted that special display of Freudian aggression on her part. Sometimes, when we were expected as guests some distance away, and I paced about fretting while she implacably let time slip by, ensuring that we would be unforgivably late, I wondered whether my vexation, and concern for those being kept waiting, gave her a needed satisfaction.

Anne's flat was in a mock-Tudor house in Hampstead, half-way up the steep hill of Arkwright Road. At the gate giving on to the little paved pathway through the front garden, the roar of voices told us the party was well into its peak. At the open door on the first floor landing, Anne waited for us. Perhaps, knowing Kay, she had shrewdly guessed how late we would be.

Anne had the gift of making you believe that your arrival was the most important event of her day – doubtless a useful attribute in a producer. Behind her a blue fog of cigarette smoke enveloped the crowd. Pitching her voice above the hubbub, she leaned towards me: 'There's someone you simply must meet.' Turning, she reached into the crush as into a store room, and drew out by the sleeve a tall, ruddy featured, owlishly breezy man. 'You two come from the same background,' she said, adding her tinkling laugh. 'You will have so much to say to each other.'

Her words brought to mind A. D. Lindsay's greeting at the Oxford tea party for the refugee Basque children: 'Our friends from Spain *will* appreciate meeting someone like you with a similar background – you will understand each other so well.' Newly arrived in Oxford, I had resented the ignorance and indifference behind that automatic expression of what he plainly thought was the 'right' sentiment. I had wanted to say to him, but dared not: 'Don't try so hard! You don't *mean* it.'

Reggie Smith, also a producer at the BBC, was married to the novelist Olivia Manning. She was to draw him with exquisite accuracy, and some bitterness, as Guy in her series of novels, *The Balkan Trilogy* – schoolboy innocence, unthinking cruelty, shallow enthusiasms, superficially generous-spirited and outgoing but essentially egoistical, a mixture of coldness and an insatiable need for warmth.

Reggie seemed as nonplussed as I was. Tweedy, untidy, some indefinable quality about him spoke of the grammar school, not public school – I had learnt a few of the 'herd signals' in Oxford. To many boss-class people, grammar school stood for working class without distinction; therefore Reggie and I were brothers. We regarded one another with polite curiosity. The Gorbals would have classified him as Kelvinside, a whole world removed from my tenement. Bernard had met him, when Reggie, following the contemporary literary fascination with the working class, had been doing research for a radio programme, and summed him up with characteristic acerbity: 'totally confused, the sort that thinks you can make the class war superfluous through culture'.

Olivia, in a brown silk dress of paisley pattern, neat and composed, sat solitary in a nearby corner, in an oasis of stillness of her own, as if the crowd did not exist, but alert to every word and movement around her. In personality she was almost the opposite of Reggie, as a film negative shows light where the positive is dark and *vice versa*. Where he was superficially ebullient she appeared quiescent – a misleading impression; and where he was inwardly cold and defensive, her banked-up fires burned close to the surface. I once asked her, a shade mischievously perhaps, what she thought of Reggie's work at the BBC: 'He must be good at it,' she replied indifferently, throwing the words away, taking a meaning I had not intended; and then, deciding to seize the point, added, 'But I don't think I understand it.' Going further, she explained that, despite the abundant literary talent in the BBC's Features Department, in trying to picture the changing world it fell between two stools – not powerful enough to be listened to as drama proper, and too superficial to be taken as serious social interpretation. She cared deeply that Reggie did not do himself justice – that was a polite way of putting it; her regret was that he *could not*, that he chose to be less than fully aware. As she was to portray him in the trilogy, part of his charm was in his power to switch on enthusiasm for the 'causes' of the moment – inevitably half-understood. At heart he was too remote to be warm. Thus she summed up her life with him.

Reggie recovered from Anne's introduction before I did; with a quick, boyish smile, he said: 'The Gorbals! That must have been a fascinating place to grow up in!'

I was tempted to say: 'Do you know what you are saying – do you *really* know?' What good would that do? Moon-faced, pathetically eager to hit the right note, he knew that it was beyond him.

Late in the evening, when the crowd had thinned, something made the room go still. The air quivered as in the moment before thunder. At the far end of the room near the door, Michael stood, dark, slim, dapper, shoulders hunched in tension, and Anne faced him, an arm's reach away – the air between them charged, the sparks almost visible. In twos and threes, people stood in arrested silence, gestures frozen as in a Paul Delvaux conversation piece, inner turbulence exposed. In instinctive disengagement they had drawn away to the fringes of the room, leaving a clear space around the two.

Anne, her pale, dark-framed face inclined, had the determined expression of a schoolmistress dealing with a recalcitrant pupil. Michael said something quietly, indistinctly heard from where I stood, the words forced through clenched teeth. Judging by his tone he was remonstrating with her, civilised, subdued. Anne's voice rang out hard and clear, making the matter plain to the world: 'No, Michael. You are *not* sleeping here tonight!'

Michael, with the intense, brittle politeness of one controlling extreme anger, again spoke quietly. Anne repeated: 'You are *not* sleeping here tonight!' – implacable, assured, in command.

Later I would ask myself why the scene had shocked me so. In the Gorbals, the public 'marital' quarrel was common, on tenement landings, in closes, in the street, infinitely worse than this. Men and women came to blows. Women were struck and fell down the stone stairs of tenements. Men bled from whatever weapon came to a woman's hand – kitchen knife, kettle, copper pan. This was a long way, surely, from the Gorbals – or was it?

Everyone stared expectantly at the two. I thought: someone must stop this. No one made a move. Impulsively, foolishly, I tried to help.

Anne turned away. Michael stood with head bent, features leaden. I went up to him, beginning to regret the intervention almost at once, not thinking far enough ahead, only that someone must help him leave with dignity. I said: 'Come back with us! You can stay the night at our place.' He shook his head.

At that instant I could still have retreated. It was none of my business. Had he hesitated a fraction longer, I think I *would* have retreated, and been glad of it; but as that thought crossed my mind he gave a shrug and nodded, and the chance of escape had gone. He turned his back on the room and went with us to the door, and trod heavily down the stairs behind us into the street.

It was nearly midnight. Without speaking we trudged up the hill to Fitzjohn's Avenue and on to Hampstead Underground station to catch the last train for Golders Green. Stonily separate, we sat on a bench on the deserted platform. The dingy tiled walls and dirty white concave roof, meagrely lit by patches of weak yellow light, drained away all hope. I searched for something to say, to slacken tension, but the very idea of beginning a diversionary conversation about something else – about anything! – was absurd, and to make any reference at all to what had happened was out of the question too; I did not know him well enough. There was no way forward and no way back.

Kay said nothing. She seemed to have distanced herself from what I had done.

At last an almost empty train rumbled out of the tunnel. Mutely we boarded it and sat, together but separate, for the few minutes' journey through the deep Hampstead tunnel to where the line came out into the open air and approached Golders Green between grassy banks, now silver-grey under the moon – always a moment of happy release, but not this time. We trod the dead defile of Hoop

Lane between the twin silences of the Crematorium on our right and the Cemetery on the left, whose dark leaning trees and ranks of angular shapes stretched away in mystery behind the tall railings – we mourned together, our silences weighing us down. I was impatient for the night to end as we trudged up the last incline to the Central Square of the Garden Suburb, the mood far from lightened by the gloomy mass of St Jude's Church that faced our flat, the vast expanse of Nordic roof overhanging its low walls like a black glacier poised for cataclysmic descent.

Kay showed Michael the spare room and he disappeared into it at once. Next morning, after a monosyllabic breakfast, he departed.

It was some years before I saw him again – a shock of a different kind. I had gone into the Stag's Head, and had not noticed him in the dense crowd of chattering evening drinkers; suddenly he was at my elbow, and asking me, in polite curiosity, 'Have we met?'

Yes, I said, and started to explain; I was in mid-sentence when he made a half-turn away from me without a word, stared straight ahead, and continued with his drink as if I did not exist. I moved away. Was this pantomime calculated rudeness, or had he in truth forgotten that we had met before, and in embarrassment at the reminder of our last meeting could think of no other way of ending the encounter? I would never find out. I said to myself, as Bernard did: 'Put it down to experience!' The gale of the world had thrown everybody, and everything, off course, and nothing would be in its expected place, ever again.

4

Cocteau and Poetic Realism

Jean Cocteau came up to me. 'May I invite you to see a film that is "not very proper"?'

We were in the foyer of a small viewing cinema in Biarritz, the morning after the opening of the Festival du Film Maudit – *maudit*, in the context, meant 'damned but worthy' – held under Cocteau's patronage. He was accompanied, as always, by a group of dapper young courtiers.

Shorter than average and spare of figure, with greyish features long and pointed, wavy grey hair brushed upwards to stand almost erect from the brow, he held himself poised like a dancer, grey jacket draped as a cloak on pointed shoulders. In spite of this general aspect of greyness, when he spoke a brilliance illuminated his features as if the thoughts themselves were incandescent, as they often were. Words resonated with the easy authority of the Master, subtle, powerful, beyond challenge – rightfully spoken from on high. Cocteau was wholly conscious of his greatness, and coolly, aristocratically, accepted as his due the star treatment he received. Even so, within that sense of power, there was gentleness and charm.

He could, however, display a fury that was also magisterial, serenely controlled, with the fine cutting edge of a razor – as I explain later.

In his question, the slight emphasis on *convenable* should not have puzzled me; but I was too slow in decoding it – I might have been quicker had I known more about Cocteau, but plainly his meaning was clear to others who stood near. The black and white film consisted of homosexual fantasies, not explicit by today's standards but impressionistic, cleverly and economically presented; the themes were power and submission, and imminent, not actual,

ecstasy. After the screening, Cocteau turned to me: 'Tell me frankly
– what did you think of the little film?'

In awe of the great man, I dared not say it was boring and distasteful. I said: 'I couldn't see what point was being made. If it was
meant to convey deep emotions in that kind of experience, I don't
think it succeeded – at least for me.'

He nodded, indicating that the response was what he had expected, and said, in a manner that contrived to be both combative
and smooth, letting me off lightly: 'I too do not think it a master-
piece – but it is a *beginning*, that of a new wave of poetic realism.
You will see!' He turned away, contemplating something far off,
beyond the heads of the courtiers, then faced me again: 'You are
right. Impressionism, though for the poet fascinating, by itself is
certainly not enough. The poet must point the way – yes, your
word 'point' is fitting in another sense! – fearlessly, without equiv-
ocation.'

He stood still, meditating as if quite alone, right hand on hip, the
draped jacket all but slipping off that shoulder, then added: 'You
will see me deliver a statement with "point" later this very morning, if you will be at the beach at midday. I shall express a judgement upon the reception given to your group at the opening
yesterday. Au revoir!' He strode away, the courtiers falling into step
around him.

Already impressed by his precision with words, I wondered why
he had said 'see'.

The title 'Festival du Film Maudit' had some slight artistic justification, but for the Biarritz city fathers the Festival's true purpose
was tourist promotion. The device of the film festival was being
widely copied on the Continent in those years of economic repair
after the war, considered particularly suitable because of its essentials of gala atmosphere, the allure of stars in the flesh – and much
other display of flesh – and over it all a worthy label, that of culture. The war had been fought for culture, had it not: you cannot
have too much culture. Let us not trouble ourselves with whether
the cinema qualifies as culture! If it pulls in the clients, we are content. The film industry was content too; festivals stirred public

interest, encouraged self-promotion by producers, directors, and actors, assisted by press coverage of inspired 'happenings' and the presence of distinguished or notorious people, and the creation of an international following of film addicts who would assist the promotion, for whom there was a new French word – or new to me – *cinéastes*.

I was at the Festival in a sense by chance. Derek and a few friends had organised a British 'delegation' of about a dozen, large enough to qualify for cheap travel; the Festival authorities would find us lodging. While Derek and perhaps two or three others of the group might have qualified as *cinéastes*, for the rest of us, going on the delegation was a way of getting an inexpensive holiday away from austerity in Britain, and the chance of enjoying things virtually un-known – plenty of butter, rich pastries, steaks, chocolate, cheap wine.

For me there was another motive, secret, private; I wanted to see whether I would recapture, in Biarritz, the revelation that had come on that other journey abroad – my only one – to Cassis in the very last days of peace. Bill had introduced me to Cassis, then a haven for expatriate boss-class drop-outs; in memory, it had re-tained its original magic, bitter-sweet as so many profound experi-ences were, the needed catharsis of being 'taken out of oneself', never to be the same again – as the 'lost domain' had done for le Grand Meaulnes, an experience attainable only by an arcane spell at one lucky conjuncture of the stars, once in a lifetime. The heart, however, obstinate as always, did not accept that the 'lost domain' was lost for ever; now, alas, I was beginning to see how naïve I had been in hoping to rediscover it here. Biarritz was very much of this world. In place of the romantic fantasy life of Cassis, it breathed toughness, embattled patrician indifference, business calculation.

We had arrived early the previous morning, after a sleepless night on hard wooden benches on the long train journey to the Côte d'Argent, finding the little town, glistening white among neat flowerbeds and scattered palms, hardly more awake than we were. Offices were not yet open, so we could not make our arrival known officially and find the promised lodging – desperate as we were to lay our heads down somewhere. There was nothing for it but to search for the beach – or indeed anywhere – where we could collapse for a few hours, till the time of the opening of the Festival in the late morning. We bought warm rolls and coffee at a workmen's bar near the station and then, eyes and head aching in the harsh morning sunlight, stumbled through empty, shuttered streets, drawn by instinct to a boulder-strewn stretch of beach below a fringe of leaning palms – there to lie down, indifferent to pebbles digging into back and hip, and, despite the crash of incoming breakers, fall asleep at once.

Mid-morning roused me, the brazen sun now high in a sky of hard blue enamel, with the noise of chirping children and voluble family groups descending upon the beach. Limbs ached, eyes were sticky from sleep. The others stirred too. We climbed to our feet; it was nearly time for the official opening of the Festival. Unshaven, in wrinkled, grubby flannels and open-necked shirt and gym shoes, clothes glued to the skin with sweat from the roasting sun, there was grim reassurance in seeing that the others looked as weary and bedraggled as I felt. We shrugged rucksacks on again, trudged up the incline from the beach and found a little square where an old iron fountain slept in the sun; we splashed tepid water on our faces, dried as best we could on handkerchiefs, and drove ourselves on to present ourselves – far from presentable though we felt – at the ceremony.

Of course we should have given more thought, in simple politeness, to our disreputable appearance. Travelling in carefree student mood, though most of us were students no longer, we were in that make-believe state of mind that saw the rest of the world as taking their cues from us – therefore 'they' must care as little about appearances as we did. Had I been on my own, the remnants of Gorbals respectability would have imposed discipline. Light-headed with fatigue, feeling the support of a crowd, responsibility faded, the temptation to flout convention was irresistible. Later in our stay, I would join others of our party in jeering at a notice outside the Casino warning that entry would be refused to anyone not wearing a tie – marvelling that the others were in effect ridiculing their own class. I had still not fathomed how the boss class decided when to lampoon itself and when not – part of the code I had never wholly cracked in Oxford.

The little we knew of Biarritz should have warned us, the pre-war image of a tight little patrician backwater where royal personages and miscellaneous nobility, with the help of the Continental version of Galsworthian snobbery, set the tone. Perhaps we had assumed that the war had changed it all, and that the privileged minuet was ended? Yet some instinct must have told us that this was not so; and therefore it was with shaky laughter, the iconoclastic mood possessing us, that we progressed, bleary eyed, swaying with exhaustion, rucksacks bumping on our backs, along a main thoroughfare gleaming with expensive shops, to the pavilion. There, at a flower-decked entrance, a stream of well-dressed guests, moving at ceremonial pace, arrived for the reception. Entering, in sudden contrast to the harsh sunlight outside, the interior seemed at first dark, then, as the eyes accustomed themselves, sprang out in a magnificence of red and gold, of floral plasterwork on ceiling and frieze, crystal chandeliers. It became plain, too, that these beautifully dressed people were edging away from contact with us. I looked down at my clothes, and at the rest of our party, and saw that we had made a bad mistake. But there was no time to think about it – even if thought could have changed anything – for a phalanx of men in morning coats, some wearing chains of office, advanced upon us holding up their hands to block our further progress: 'No, no! You may not enter! This is an official reception!'

'We *are* official! We are the British delegation!'

Uproar exploded. The morning coats attempted to wave us away, politely at first, then in increasing frustration and anger. We refused to retreat. They tried to herd us into limbo in a corner of the entrance foyer as if we were presumptuous peasants, while continuing to welcome, with as much ceremony as they could muster in the confusion, the 'acceptables' – formally dressed, the women elaborately coiffured, in swirling, sparkling dresses, adequately *décolletée*. Something else completed the official discomfiture; flash-bulbs flared as press photographers triumphantly captured a scene of the collapse of worlds – the morning coats holding the line in bewilderment against our raffish advance, and the amazement and affront displayed by the 'acceptables', as if the Duc de Guermantes and his friends, at the portals of the Jockey Club, found themselves jostled by stable lads presuming to enter as their equals.

We must have behaved badly. Exhaustion, frayed nerves, doubtless played their part; but our fury had been ignited by the contempt with which they had attempted to dismiss us – and the realisation that we had brought it on ourselves. There was also a serious practical worry. Even if we had had time to bathe and spruce and change into the spare clothes in our rucksacks, we could not possibly have equalled the elegance of the 'acceptables'; consequently, if the authorities persisted in excluding us, they would certainly withhold the promised free lodging as well. If that happened, to stay on in Biarritz at my own expense would be out of the question; and that would also be true, I suspected, for some of our party. There were visions of an ignominious retreat to the train that night, and another punishing sojourn on those pitiless wooden benches. We stood our ground – the morning coats stood theirs. The inglorious encounter, with shouting and jostling, and protests hurled back and forth, prolonged itself. I wondered how long it would be before the gendarmes appeared.

Suddenly a new voice sliced through everything like a fine steel blade: 'Who closes the door to these gallant young people – seekers of the poetic spring? They must be admitted *immediately*! I, Cocteau, insist upon it.'

The phalanx divided like the sea before the rod of Moses. Cocteau made an impressive stage entrance from somewhere in the rear of the foyer, spitting out the word 'commerçants!' in impatience and contempt.

The very air changed, as if the coffered ceiling had been drawn back to admit the purity of sun and sky. The morning coats showed their dismay as he strode towards us smiling, hands outstretched: 'English friends! Forgive the misunderstanding – it is of no consequence! You are my guests – come, follow me. We will take part in the proceedings together!'

Both in this serene dismissal of convention, and in the 'comment' he was to make the following morning on the beach, Cocteau had a greater sense of the changed world than did the city fathers, who seemed to hope that Biarritz would continue comfortably into the future in the exclusive aristocratic mould of the past – though the very presence of the film festival perhaps pointed to a difference of view among them. To be fair, that past, though fading, still survived, as the bizarre encounters with the Duke of Windsor and King Farouk would show.

For Cocteau also, self-interest must have played a part. His 'poetic reality' needed support and patronage not only from the rich and the well established – where he already had a strong base – but from the younger generation, restless, impatient with the past, but who yet longed for the enchantment of the ancient mysteries, for which the only language was poetry. To them he spoke naturally – he whose eager mind was itself youthful. He needed this new following for another reason too, a hint of which he let slip one day; acclaim from among the 'poetry of youth' might not by itself be decisive with the Immortals of the Academy, but it would help! Hidden in the future, only six years away, was the day when he would present himself, with a sword whose hilt he had designed in the form of a profile of his *Orphée*, to join them. The 'commerçants' must not place obstacles in his way. If the price of reaching out to the impatient new generation was to breach the old proprieties, so be it.

A few minutes before midday on that morning of the little film 'pas convenable', I went down to the beach wondering how he would make his poetic point. Word of the event had been efficiently spread. On the curving slope overlooking the stretch of pebble and sand where family groups engaged in the minuet of the *heure de la plage*, a crowd jostled for vantage points, craning to see something taking place at the water's edge towards the right where, in contrast with the breakers crashing between the great boulders to the left, the sea rolled on to the shore in long, quiet, swishing wavelets. True to Cocteau's astute sense of management, an assembly of press photographers was in position. At the water's edge, incongruous in the hard, brassy sunlight, a group of black-clad figures faced the crowd – Cocteau and about a dozen of his courtiers – all in immaculate 'smoking', in bizarre contrast with the conventional *costume de la plage* worn by everybody else. As the cameras clicked, Cocteau's slim, boyish form bent down, removed shoes and socks, and rolled his black braided trousers to the knee; the courtiers did the same. Then the group spread out, arms linked as in a chorus line, the Master in the centre, turned and advanced into the wavelets till the water came up to mid-calf, turned about and high-stepped out of the water and bowed to the wondering assembly, reversed and entered the water again, turned and high-stepped out and bowed low once more, turned and entered the sea for a third time and, emerging, bowed to the delighted cameramen. 'This is my answer,' Cocteau proclaimed, 'to the myopic arrogance displayed yesterday! The poetic spirit makes its own laws!'

His intervention the previous day, well publicised, had changed our fortunes and our image; officialdom began to treat the delegation with a certain cautious correctness if not, as yet, generosity. There would be a few disagreeable moments, however – and one especially that made me wonder, desperately, how far Cocteau's charismatic power would protect us. After the inaugural ceremony we were driven to a school on the outskirts of the town, whose dormitories were to be our sleeping quarters, the school being closed for the summer vacation. We contemplated the grim building with dismay; we had hoped for something better, perhaps a modest pension – if such existed in the magnificence of Biarritz. The squat building in old grey stone, its shutters tightly closed, sweltered in the hard southern sun; it looked as though it had stood sealed for weeks. An official unlocked a great brass padlock and pushed open the sombre grey door. A cloud of heavy warm air, baked almost solid, bearing innumerable black flies, hit us in the face, together with a stench like that of a hundred urinals. We were thrown back almost physically, and despite our fatigue in no mood to enter, but honour demanded it – we must at least see what was offered. In the airless dormitory, clouds of fleas enveloped my legs; we had stepped into a reservoir of teeming insect life. The stink from the adjacent lavatories was so overpowering that we fled downstairs and out into the pitiless sun of the courtyard: 'Good Lord! We'd be better off sleeping on the beach!' Certainly I had seen worse in the Gorbals – but coming here was supposed to be pleasure!

Had the authorities, I wondered, selected this accommodation for us *before* our dishevelled arrival at the inaugural ceremony, and before Cocteau came to our rescue? That question was now critical.

'We will go,' I told the officials, 'and ask M. Cocteau for his opinion of the lodging provided for the British delegation.'

They looked at one another in ill humour. Their superiors would not relish yet another intervention from the Master. Cocteau had remarked that he would publicly disassociate himself from the Festival if the British delegation – or for that matter any other – failed to be treated with 'proper generosity of spirit'.

In sour silence they shepherded us into the vehicles again. I asked that we be taken to see Cocteau immediately. 'Wait', was the tight-lipped reply. Back at the Festival offices, there was much telephoning, and judging from the officials' deferential tone, they were speaking to highly placed personages: 'Very well, Monsieur – if you will order accordingly ...' By the end of the afternoon a miracle, had come to pass. We were installed in the *grand luxe* of the Palais Hotel, then virtually empty. That evening, after sumptuous room service, and having soaked away two days of sweat and fatigue in a bathroom of princely proportions and appointments, I went down to a truly palatial restaurant to feast in what was for me unparalleled magnificence, my first taste of what would later be called jet-set living, a setting I had seen only in Hollywood operettas – vast as a tennis court, ranks of tables in gleaming linen starched stiff as board, with serviettes standing like glistening white sculptures, flowers in cut glass vases, crystal chandeliers scattering shafts of rainbow light, platoons of crisply uniformed waiters. Tall window doors opened on to a white terrace with classical stone balustrade, completing an empty *mise-en-scène*, real enough but speaking of lost enchantment, waiting for champagne corks to pop, an unseen orchestra to strike up and prompt the players – if they should ever return.

Sitting there commanding limitless luxury, it was hard to believe that the *guerre kilométrique* was such a short time behind us – VE Day seemed to have come and gone only yesterday – and that for legions of its victims it was not yet over, and would never be; there were still Displaced Persons' camps not far beyond the horizon. 'Displaced' – what an inglorious euphemism for having had one's world destroyed! After Armageddon, how could this old pantomime of privilege continue as if nothing had changed? What would Bernard's father have said, could he have been conjured here from the grave – convinced, as he had told me in the 'last days', that a purer world, for which he had worked with such hope, was at hand? A familiar feeling returned, as when I was translated to Oxford from the Gorbals – the sense of living in a waking dream, everything real enough, and so desirable, but it *had* to be a mirage! For me to be in such splendour was surely 'against nature', therefore it could not be true. At any moment these coruscating chandeliers would fade, the stiff white linen wither, the smells of the Gorbals tenement take possession once more.

What of the people who only a few hours ago had spurned us as presumptuous peasants, and now installed us here to live as princes? What values moved them? What had changed? We were still what we had been that morning! And the 'commerçants' were what they had always been. They had been moved only trivially, in tactics not in feeling; the lesson they had chosen to accept from Cocteau was that to behave with at least the appearance of humanity was no more than good business sense! In years to come I would see many such examples, in many contexts, in many countries, and I would remind myself yet again not to be astonished – or even to notice – or if I did, try not to be disturbed. It was all 'par for the course'.

When, many years later, I saw Marcel Ophuls' documentary film *Le Chagrin et la Pitié*, steely analysis of the less worthy attitudes in France during the Occupation – blatant nastiness, gratuitous betrayal of neighbours and friends, fascist manipulation and self-interest, zeal in hunting down Jews to hand over to the Germans, and other forms of ingratiation, revelations that provoked revealing fury when shown on French television – this scene would return. I would remember that some of the interviews in that film were shot not so very far from this place, and shame would come, for in accepting the bounty of these people, though it had not been generosity but self-interest on their part – even to be there at all – I partly condoned that behaviour; for surely the attitudes and motives portrayed in that film were still alive then, so soon after the Germans' departure? Had I known, at the time, what *Le Chagrin et la Pitié* would reveal, would I have had the courage not to go there at all?

I would wonder, too, whether Ophuls would have captured similar attitudes in Britain had there been an occupation?

On that evening at the Palais, however, in that empty splendour, thinking no further than the moment, our party ate and drank in triumph, and raised glasses to the Master. There was a wonderful exhilaration in defeating the system.

Cocteau said that film was a means of bringing many people to 'dream together'. It might not always be the *same* dream for every person, but that must remain the poet's purpose; and the extent to which the dreams did converge was a measure of his creative power. That image, of participants dreaming a dream together, was apt for this film festival, and presumably for most. Directors, stars and starlets and aspirants moved in an elaborate fantasy sequence – dances of display, little dramas of self-promotion, sumptuously staged receptions, parties at night clubs and villas, episodes from films re-enacted live; borne up on a limitless current of champagne; the 'performers' floated along, and dreamed together – and in some degree their dream enveloped us also. In this collective suspension of disbelief, actors and actresses were of course adept – fascinating to watch in their chameleon changes of persona. A few, however, were so locked in their most recent professional roles that they continued to enact them automatically, and I wondered how deeply the true self was hidden – or if it had withered. An example was Dennis Price, who had appeared with Alec Guinness in the recently acclaimed film *Kind Hearts and Coronets*, and now, as he went about

Biarritz, seemed still to be occupying the stock persona of scion of a noble house that he had portrayed in it. I was wrong; it was not a pretence but the man himself, or rather it was the contrived patrician shell inhabited by some actors, often of pre-war breed, who were so much in sympathy with the aristocracy as to behave as if they were rightful members of it. In an earlier royal epoch, Dennis would have been the most constant of courtiers.

He showed this trait in his reaction to an incident, comic and poignant, involving the Duke and Duchess of Windsor.

One evening he suggested I go with him to the Casino. I had no intention of gambling at the tables, for father's example would last me for ever; but I had seen the inside of a casino only in films – in settings for romance, drama, style – and I must have wanted to see one in reality at least once. Being in Biarritz, the only boss-class gambling resort I had heard of apart from Monte Carlo, this was obviously the place. I had brought a tie in my rucksack, and so I could appear in minimally acceptable rig – light jacket and grey flannel trousers, shirt and tie, black shoes. As we approached, a small crowd loitered at the pillared entrance, seemingly intent on something taking place in the little ante-lobby. Threading through them, I was ahead of Dennis, and had glanced back to answer a remark of his, when a man's weight fell hard against my right shoulder and I hit the side wall and went down to the stone floor with my 'assailant' on top of me. Someone seized him and lifted him off me, and I heard a murmur of excitement in the little group through which we had passed. As I picked myself up, and saw him being hauled to his feet like a great sagging puppet, I remembered seeing him, staggering and obviously very drunk, on my way in – red face, pointed nose and tight little mouth, shiny grey hair brushed close to the head, trim build emphasised by a well-cut dinner suit. Standing now unsteadily, a wilting figure in the grip of the big man who had lifted him off me, he said something to a slim, almost angular woman, elegantly dressed and wearing many jewels, who stood a few feet away from him, further inside the foyer; she had the look of someone impatient to move away.

Dennis whispered in my ear: 'Heavens! It's Windsor!'

The Duke was now going through a bizarre burlesque; knees wobbling and head askew, he leaned forward towards the Duchess – now also recognised from press pictures – his arm raised and waving a limp hand at her and saying over and over again in the monotone of the very drunk, slurring the words: 'Take it easy baby! Take it easy …!'

It might have been a key 'code phrase', dredged up in stupor from an old, private comedy of their own – now offered up, as a child might, to charm away disapproval. It seemed not to work. She stood stiffly, the square features frozen – a mother whose small son is behaving badly in front of strangers. With a slight lift of the chin she made a signal to the bodyguard, who had been joined by a man wearing a chauffeur's peaked cap, to take the embarrassing presence away. The Duke made a half-hearted show of not wanting to go; evidently this was not the first time he had had to comply with that command. For a few moments more, obviously relishing his performance, he continued: 'Take it easy baby – don' forget, take it easy …' The men lifted him, with hands under the armpits, causing his head to loll grotesquely between his uplifted shoulders, and carried him, legs dangling, out of the foyer through the entranced spectators, to a black limousine that had drawn up at the portico steps, and placed him, inert now, in the grey-upholstered rear compartment.

Dennis said, indicating the woman who stood beside the Duchess, also glittering with jewels, 'she's with Mrs Vanderbilt I see,' in the tones of a solicitous family friend musing on the portent of its members' comings and goings.

When the limousine had glided away, the two women exchanged a glance – a public glance, affirming that nothing unusual had happened – and moved in stately progress into the interior. Perhaps, from their point of view, nothing unusual *had* happened!

Dennis, totally absorbed, watched the receding figures. Each measured step, flash of jewels, shimmering fall of long gown, proclaimed calculation, affirmed the opposite of movement – a determined fixity. He must have felt that a comment was expected of him, a justification: 'Poor things – chasing the sun all the time!'

Life, he wanted me to know, was hard on the Windsors. Their mission was the transcendent pursuit of perfection – to be shining paragons for us all. Life had set them too high a standard; they had fallen short, and a terrible judgement had been visited on them – and so they chased the sun, paragons only for themselves alone; and that was hard. We must feel sorry for them.

For me the episode held sadness, and bitterness, but not for their sakes. Life dealt out the cards so unfairly – what had these people to complain about, or Dennis on their behalf? I remembered those hours, long ago, at the feet of Jimmy Robinson, the veteran anarchist, round the brazier under his oak tree near the socialist camp, and his talk of 'the great day' when the workers would mount machine-guns at the banks and the stock exchanges, 'to get rid of the parasites!' At last I understood his passion, and Bernard's too, going off to Spain to fight for *his* creed while it still possessed him. How shallow my awareness had been! Their passion was futile. You never did get rid of the people on top, and you never would, for if that had been possible, surely at some time over the long centuries men would have found the way – and done it once and for all? No. Like the many heads of the Hydra, as fast as you destroyed them, others replaced them faster still. In time, passion faded; and even Jimmy Robinson, clever entrepreneur that he had become, had in effect joined the parasites, though he had claimed to be still fighting them. That claim had disturbed me even then, and I had wanted to question him about it, and been too timid to do so; I was only a boy, drunk with the charisma of that grizzled but still sanguine adventurer. To question him would have been useless. He would have denied that he had joined 'them', and claimed that he was simply using the System against itself! After all, it was only human nature to get what you could out of it, while the System lasted; and stealing from 'them' was not stealing *really*, for 'they' had stolen it first! 'So wags the world ...'

Equally, there would always be people like Dennis to be uplifted by the magic they saw in such as this Duke and Duchess, and feel blessed to breathe the same air as they. The magic, and his response, were part of the System too – and necessary to it.

COCTEAU AND POETIC REALISM

Dennis's compassion was obviously genuine. Why did it anger me? These people surely merited none. They were the bleak answer to the dream, remembered from childhood, of what it would be like to have *everything*, total volition. Who has not dreamed it? With riches you could achieve everything you longed for, and in doing so you would surely atone, in some degree, for the unfairness of possessing the riches. What had these two achieved with their good fortune? They chased the sun.

I was angry with myself – sour grapes diminished one. Yet surely I could have used their riches, their limitless freedom, so much better than they? What did 'better' mean? To write, throw light upon a dark world, make it a better place? No, that would not do; it was simply the old envy, still undigested, that I had felt towards the golden people at Oxford to whom so many doors had 'rightfully' opened with so little effort. None of *them* had thought himself lucky! They had all nourished unfulfilled claims against life. These Windsors were no different, only infinitely richer – and they too must have their unfulfilled claims against life.

Was there another world, if only one could find it, hidden among the shadows of this one, where generosity of spirit alone ruled, that set purer standards, where envy and doubt, egotism, meanness, had no place? It was another of childhood's questionings, when I had tried to make sense of mother's death and father's destructive obsessions. I must have recognised even then, with the small child's fearful fascination, that it was not one question but many, addressed to the heart of life – too awesome to wrestle with. Dimly, I must have seen that even limitless opportunity was not enough; you had to choose what you did with it, and that was hard, for what you chose must be worthy – whatever that meant. What did you base the choice on? Father must have made a choice – whether it was a worthy one or not I had no idea, but I hoped it was – and it had proved unattainable, or perhaps he did not see it clearly enough, and therefore was doomed to fail. Why, I had asked the Almighty again and again, did he do that? I remembered, at the age of about twelve, staring up at the stars through the black windows, waiting for an answer. I had still to learn that it would never come.

Perhaps the Almighty had already answered it long ago, in the ashes of the past: 'the race is not to the swift, nor the battle to the strong ... but time and chance happeneth to them all.' No – that surely was no answer. It made the enigma even more frightening. It left you without hope. If all was 'time and chance' why bother even to make a choice? There was no test of good or bad! No wonder father had lost his way, and mother had been crushed. If faith had not helped *them*, what could it do for me?

Who was I to scoff at Dennis – or condemn the Windsors? Did it matter what *anybody* did or thought?

Another object lesson came a couple of nights later, this time with barely concealed ferocity – but also with a comic element. With befitting irony it unfolded at the screening of a film called *Ossessione*. By some fancy of the festival organisers, very long films were often put on at midnight – perhaps to test the endurance of the *cinéastes*, or provide diversion for night-owls when other pleasures palled. Derek and I arrived at the door of the viewing theatre just before the film was due to begin. I slipped in ahead of him, and as he followed me, the house lights were switched off; there was some delay in the projectionist switching on his machine, during which the place was in total darkness. I saw Derek outlined for a moment in the rectangle of the door, against the dim light of the little lobby beyond, and then he moved into the darkness, confident that he knew the seat layout well enough to make his way by instinct alone. The next moment I heard a confused mixture of exclamations and a scuffle – and an official at the door cried out in shocked tones, 'He has fallen upon the king!'

Derek had tripped over a pair of legs stretched straight out into the aisle, and fallen on top of some bulky individual sitting in an end seat, landing head first in the space between two rows. The man had planted himself sideways in his seat and stuck his legs out where they must trip anyone trying to pass. From my seat in the row behind, I saw shadowy figures grab Derek and haul him to his feet. I stood up as the house lights were switched on again, and there, confronting Derek, was the bloated form of King Farouk, wedged into a seat far too small for him. His pale, fleshy face was set in mingled fear and fury; his hand reached into a bulge inside his jacket. Farouk, a familiar figure in Biarritz, was said to go about armed. Several large men held Derek prisoner, while another frisked him. Derek angrily wrenched himself out of their grasp, but they closed in tightly round him, a human wall, preventing him from moving away, and awaited the king's command.

A group of sober-suited men were often seen with him, no doubt partly as protection, but mainly, one heard, as personal gambling opponents.

In the crimson half-light the scattered audience sat frozen, necks craned to the source of excitement, but in a moment turned back to face the screen, the *frisson* over. Officials had suddenly gathered round the king, and I heard the word 'gendarmes' whispered; hearing this, Farouk waved a hand irritably, staring all the time at Derek, who had turned very white. I said: 'Let him go – it was not his fault!' The royal scrutiny, in that square pale face, was unpleasant. At last, his experienced eye presumably deciding that Derek was no assassin, the venom in his face faded slowly, but not completely. He brought his hand out of his jacket and let it rest on his rounded belly. He made a sign to the men holding Derek prisoner – an upward movement of the chin reminiscent of the Duchess's command for the removal of the Duke. They edged apart slightly, sufficient to free Derek, who continued to stand facing the king, staring him out. Then with a theatrical gesture, but one that left no doubt of its menace, Farouk tapped the hard bulge in his jacket, and muttered: '*Va t'en!*'

Officials fussed round the king, scattering apologies. Derek pushed his way through them to join me; his normally fresh features blanched. He was breathing very hard, and shivering, though the air was thick with enclosed heat. He held a finger on his wrist taking his pulse. When he leaned over to whisper, he was trembling, furious with himself for being so shaken – perhaps anxious at the physical effects too.

'Not quite the thing for the old heart muscles, I must say! Not a word of apology either – just: "*Va t'en!*" His own bloody fault, sticking his legs out for the peasants to fall over.' He leaned back in the seat, and his breathing became less laboured. 'The king can do no wrong, eh! If that's what royalty's like, Dennis Price can have the lot!'

Ossessione began. The airless theatre became hotter and hotter, filled with mosquitoes attacking hard. In futile effort to hold them off, Derek puffed at a pipe, and I smoked cigarette after cigarette. With nearly everyone smoking, the atmosphere thickened by the minute. Derek fell asleep from time to time, and snored gently. Occasionally Farouk looked back at us. Was it force of habit, keeping a weather eye open; did he ask himself whether, after all, Derek *was* an assassin?

When an hour or so had gone by, I saw that his seat was empty, and those of his companions too. The hours of night were for gambling, for him as they had been for my father. What motive linked them? Father had always claimed that he gambled only in hope of the freedom that money could give him, freedom to realise himself. Farouk was immensely rich – what freedom did *he* hope to win? Or was the thrill of risk an end in itself? Yet who could compare the risk for these two, father and the king? No – it was something else – they were shutting out the world.

Farouk would not evade the caprice of the Fates. He would not fall to an assassin's bullet or knife. In a restaurant in the Via Cassia in Rome, dining with a pretty woman, he would choke on his food. A Beretta pistol would be found in his pocket. Reading of the manner of his death, I would feel sad, not for him, but because it struck a note of nihilism in the fullest sense – *nihil*, nothing – *his* life, father's, mine, all of us.

Yet surely it was a conceit to think that life should have 'point'? No wonder Cocteau had raised an eyebrow at the word. Like justice, fairness, playing the game, point was a man-made idea – a mirage. Most people seemed untroubled by 'point' – Bill, Ken Tynan, Pilchard – maybe they were the wise ones?

I too did not stay to the end of *Ossessione* that night. After a couple of hours I left the stifling heat and the relentless mosquitoes. Derek was quietly asleep, still recovering – as he later confessed – from the heart tremors brought on by the royal encounter. Outside, the warm air was scented with the velvet suspirations of the night, and freshened by a soft zephyr off the sea. Flickers of phosphorescence in the shallows, seen through the line of palms on the rim of the promenade above the beach, appeared to dance between their slanting trunks. In the hard moonlight, the softly rippled water, that seemed motionless, shone as with a coverlet of silver; and all around the silvery gleam was repeated in the white stonework of villas whose outlines quivered in the refraction of the warm air, appearing to lean together, exchanging whispers, behind their screens of foliage.

I walked up the road that led out of the town and rose above the southern curve of the little scimitar-shaped bay. The deep croak of cicadas pounded the air like the beating of a thousand cracked drums. Down below, most cafés and bars were dark, and hotel terraces had dimmed their lights; the street lamps, lines of jewels on a dark tapestry, marked out the pattern of the sleeping town. I leaned on the low retaining wall on the seaward side of the road and looked down on the still, silvery world, the tidy beach, the neat flowerbeds in the square above it, the houses well-kept, avenues and pavements and façades immaculate, the whole speaking of solidity, of people well provided for – and marvelled yet again that no sign of Armageddon remained. Behind me, along the road fringed with substantial villas, expensive cars gleamed in shadowed driveways. Even the low wall beside the road was free of cracks as though newly built. All looked settled. The past had been tidied away. True, the main armies had not clashed as far south as this, but surely one should sense *some* small sign of the regime of war – vapours of deprivation, fear, anxiety, the sweat of stress?

I walked on. At the corner of a tree-lined avenue that struck away inland, something made me pause. Set back amid palms and oleanders was a building at first sight much like the other opulent villas, but some quality, even in the indistinctness of the moonlit *chiaroscuro*, demanded attention. The gates stood open; a few paces within stood a large wooden sign lettered in gold – a Russian Orthodox Church. Pausing in the shadows, I wondered why I was startled to find it here – or rather moved, disturbed. Here, Russian gentry had first of all chosen privileged places of ease, and later had come here fleeing red revolution – as *my* people, earlier, had fled from *them*, from the savagery they had supported. What powers of survival the boss class possessed! In the hard moonlight the building looked in mint condition. I studied the sign again; the crisp look of the gold lettering spoke of care and rich endowment. The place had the indefinable atmosphere of regular use. Many feet trod this gravel driveway.

So, despite the war, the exiles' way of life had not withered entirely. Something of the former aristocratic chic of this town was preserved, not only as a moneyed pleasure resort, but a haven of continuity.

I returned to the wall and looked down again. Thoughts of another moonlit seascape returned, my last night in Cassis, when I had stood at just such a wall and looked down on the dark crab-like arms of the little fishing harbour, another great silver disc of moon hanging in a clear velvet sky, and had seen the calm silver surface of the water beyond the harbour break open and a black submarine rise up – a signal that the *guerre kilométrique* was only hours away, and that the expatriates' dream world was about to die. Biarritz was also a place of make-believe, but infinitely less innocent; this place was contemptuous of simplicity – and now, to feed its survival, it had formed an uneasy alliance of discordant worlds, Cocteau's domain of razor-edged fantasy, the cinema industry, with few exceptions feeding on its own banalities, the old aristocracy living out its indifferent days of 'Take it easy, baby!' – and the 'commerçants', who somehow survived through any apocalypse.

Cassis, for all its disillusion, had nourished gentleness, a tiny flame of hope in the 'last days'. Here there was none. The decadence of this place was virtually an industry, aggressive, steely, calculating, with a grotesque, childish quality – the Duke's 'Take it easy, baby!', and Farouk's peevish '*Va t'en!*'

Why did places acquire personal significance – milestones along the road? I could not have said why Biarritz would do so, as Cassis had done, but I knew that it would mark a movement in awareness, too late perhaps; life was *not* malleable – that illusion of childhood and youth! – and all action, all thought, all caprice, was in some way indelible. I knew as I stood there, that something – a murmur in the unknown forest, a faint trumpet note from afar, some event, some signal felt in the pulse long before it sounded – was about to incise this upon the spirit. To this place I had brought a slender gleaning of experience, and even that only partly digested, the callousing effect of existence itself, venturing to contemplate life, if not with tolerance, with wry acceptance. As a recipe for living it would not do – for Candide, as Bernard roughly put it, 'always led with his chin!' I had clung to the role with perverse satisfaction.

That must end. Everyone else *belonged*, somewhere, somehow – seemingly untroubled, like Dennis Price, by any desire to look beneath appearances, the opposite of Matthew Arnold's vision of enrichment:

Who saw life steadily, and saw it whole

But that was hard. Was the blindness – or elective indifference – of such as Dennis Price the only way to belong, to make life liveable? Could one not compromise, decide to see only *some* of life – and not be troubled by the rest? If so, how did one select which to see – think about, worry about, make adjustments to – and which not? Perhaps that was the crucial question.

A signal *was* on its way. Next morning I opened a telegram from Bernard: 'Your father very ill. I thought you should know.'

5

Looking for Yesterday's Day

That it was Bernard, and not my sister Lilian, who had sent the telegram was significant, and sad, but not surprising. In spite of her rift with father over leaving home – or perhaps because of it – she had behaved over the years as if she had exclusive rights over him, appearing to resent such contacts with him as I had. He was hers alone, her prisoner, in her debt because of his failures, answerable to her because of his unyielding principles – as in condemning her for leaving home, and for leading Mary to do so later – and his responsibility, as she saw it, for mother's death. He was also 'hers' in another sense; being well-off, she had the monopoly of helping him – when she chose. She might have treated me in the same way, had I accepted the vassal role. My guilt was twofold: I had escaped in a cleaner fashion than she had – far from a wounding one, even with some acclaim – and seemingly with father's approval, an aspect that had hurt her more than anything else; and I had never asked her for money. Once, when I telephoned her after a long silence, simply to enquire after her, she broke in harshly: 'Are you ringing up to ask for money?' When in surprise I said 'No', she sounded disappointed and sceptical. That I should telephone her with no selfish motive was too unexpected to be credible – perhaps no one ever did. It was *she* who was the prisoner.

Bernard kept in touch with the elderly and the sick – not solely because of his union work, but because he had a good heart. 'It's like it was in Spain,' he once remarked: 'men get hit and fall out of the line, and if you take your eye off them for a minute, they're done for!'

On the surface, Lilian's relations with father had never recovered from the blow she had inflicted, after mother died, by leaving home to 'better herself' – a meaningless phrase to me as a small boy.

Father had forbade all contact with her, but I discovered years later that in secret he did see her from time to time – especially in his gambling days when skint, but also, on flimsy excuses, at other times too; tenderness drew him, and perhaps a desire – which he himself might not have admitted – to glory in the sight of his self-made businesswoman of a daughter, a wondrous thing, for in his tradition a daughter left home only to get married. He might have tried to see in her the bold first-born son he wished he had had, and imagine how different life would have been. Sometimes, however, it was she who sought *him* out, and 'forcibly', as she put it, gave him money. Evidently he had stuck to his pride as long as he could. He probably divined that in seeking him out at those times money was an excuse, concealed even from herself. She needed to remain joined to him; and through him to our line and our blood. That thought must have burned into him like acid – if only she had shown that care, that awareness, years before! How different everything in our home could have been!

That chapter of concealment, bitterness, remorse, misplaced pride, furtive meetings, tarnished 'loans', must have begun when I was still a ragged youngster at home. Later, when Mary followed Lilian's example and left home, I was forbidden to see *her* too. Yet he made it his business to see Mary in secret also, until she moved to London, but never – as far as I know – to receive money from her. Again it was pride that made him conceal these meetings, and the fact that tenderness and concern had gained the upper hand with him – in both instances he would have justified the concealment in the name of principle; the old rules must be seen to be upheld.

Thinking of all this when older, when I did understand the words 'better herself', Lilian's reasons for bitterness were even more puzzling. She was caught in a knot of guilt and pride and hatred – and an attachment that should have been sweet but instead hurt. She had other reasons for bitterness; passionate woman that she was, she had been detached enough to use her relationships with men to make her way in business, but that self-knowledge was wounding too. Guilt for what she had done, and – more to the point – what those actions had done to *her*, must have bitten deeper and deeper year by year. Like father – she was very like him – she knew herself too well for comfort. In the milieu in which she moved, hard, materialistic – its values those of W. C. Fields's injunction, 'Never give a sucker an even break!' – she must have tailored her attitudes correctly, for she prospered, the only test her world respected. Her acceptance of these standards must have done violence to a deeply submerged sense of purity, and for that treason to herself the whole world must pay – father by being enchained to her, Mary by being condescended to and dismissed for being too 'soft' and tempering ambition with tenderness, an unforgiveable weakness. But why must I pay? I must have deepened her guilt, for she could never forget that I, a child when she left home, had no power to save myself – and now, keeping my distance, I showed her that I too could never forget.

Years later, when Mary was very ill, Lilian would not come to London to see her; and when Mary died, would have nothing to do with settling her affairs, or even with arranging the funeral. These matters would be left to me, presumably a way of making *me* pay after all! – thoughts and feelings and motives that defy disentanglement even now.

When I followed my own star and went to Oxford, I turned my back on her values, and that was unbearable – for I showed contempt for her world, and for her achievements; that criticism struck at the heart of her life. I would meet the same attitude among business people many times in later years; anyone who chose to follow learning or the arts deviated from their world view, and must be treated with aggression. 'What are you doing with all this study?' she asked with scorn on my first return visit to Glasgow. 'Are you going to be a *schnorrer* all your life?' That gibe – *schnorrer* meant beggar – might have had some basis had I ever asked her for anything. Perhaps, indeed, my failure to do so had hurt her pride, unacceptable arrogance on my part? But *schnorrer* had another shade of meaning – incompetent, someone who could not cope with life – and that, in her world, was the ultimate anathema. To have a *schnorrer* for a brother was a terrible indignity – a skeleton to be kept locked away.

LOOKING FOR YESTERDAY'S DAY

To be fair, she may have reasoned, in her cold business way, that my choosing to escape from the Gorbals, and to live in exile, was not her concern, and hence it was not her responsibility to be a source of information about father; that was for me to attend to. Alas, in such a history of sadness, remorse, criticism, self-punishment, 'reason' could do nothing; we were all in the wrong, the degrees of wrong immaterial – and none must sit in judgement.

When father, astonishingly, gave up gambling – not long after I left for Oxford – I searched for an explanation. Did he feel, with me gone, that there was nothing left of the family for him to destroy, and so gambling had no further purpose to perform? He knew that the true purpose was self-destruction. That may have been part of the answer; at the time I knew nothing of Lilian's meetings with him. When I did know, other things fell into place. Some part of his essentially masterful spirit, in particular his fierce independence, must have reasserted itself. That accomplished, and free of the burden of gambling, he could live in modest comfort, and above all independence, on his skilled earnings, and reject her money – in his eyes indelibly tainted.

By the time I reached Glasgow, father's condition had improved a little, and he was out of immediate danger; he would survive a year more, still smoking in spite of severe bronchial trouble. He had become ever more isolated over the years, and was now very much alone, but concealed the fact as well as he could. Many of his generation, his *lansleit* – people from his district in *der heim* – were dying off, and with them the world he had known was disappearing fast. There was a steady drift of Jewish families from the slum tenements of the Gorbals to 'better' neighbourhoods like Giffnock and Langside. He talked of politics still, very well-informed and of, people he had known who had stood with him at Gorbals Cross of a Sunday morning or at the Workers' Circle and talked about making the world a better place. 'At least they tried – we all tried, in our different ways!' A sparkle of youthful memory lit the grey-blue eyes. He fitted another Balkan Sobranie cigarette into the gold-banded amber holder – that holder that meant so much to him, talisman that affirmed his aristocratic vision of himself! And how many times, over all those years, had it lain in the pawnshop – and how often had he gone hungry to pay the interest payments on the 'pledge', against the day when he could reclaim it? 'Talking our hearts out – but where did it get us in the end? *A nechtigen togg*!' – literally, 'a yesterday's day', futility.

He looked me up and down and I thought he was about to add something about *me* in similar vein, but he changed the subject. He said nothing about the family – I think he understood, though he never spoke of *my* side of that past, how painful the subject was for me too; but he could not stop himself making an occasional harsh reference to the betrayal by his brothers-in-law, mother's brothers – he called them 'brothers' out of kindness to mother – their beating him up in the umbrella shop he owned jointly with them, the fight I had witnessed in terror as a small child, when they had accused him of what *they* had done, dipping into the till, and then closed the business and decamped to America with his share of the proceeds. The partnership had been the nearest he had come to his dream of 'independence'; its end still gnawed at his pride, at his sense of right and wrong. What good would it have done to tell him, now, what I wished I had been old enough, and confident enough, to tell him long ago – for I had seen it, frighteningly, even as a child – that he had an unreal perception of the human condition? His way, when wronged, was not to plan revenge, but to flare up in anger, and then trust, like a child, in 'making up'. The world was tougher, crueller, than he ever realised.

When his time did come, I learned of it too late; Bernard happened to be out of Glasgow at the time. Again, Lilian's silence did not surprise me, though it hurt. It was 'par for the course'. Nothing more needed to be added to the burden of the past – it had all been put there in full measure long ago.

I found the fresh grave on a little bare knoll, whence the rough ground fell away to the drystone wall that bounded the cemetery. Far below, a group of old grey granite houses among glistening evergreens marked a once-genteel suburb, now absorbed into a northern spread of the city. I looked for that other windy patch of hillside, remembered from years before when I was six, where I had stood among the grown-ups, giants against the grey sky, weeping round mother's open grave, the coffin newly lowered, hearing the hollow thud of clods of earth striking it, puzzled that I could not weep too. It *was* there, not far away, but isolated no longer. I did weep now, and wondered whether release of emotion would always come too late. Who was I weeping for – him, mother, myself, all of us, and for our foredoomed history?

Bernard said: 'You've got to stop punishing yourself, for God's sake! No one can run their life to suit other people's ideas – looking over your shoulder all the time.'

That was the nearest he would ever come to a judgement – a delicacy we both observed for the other's affairs.

We were having a cup of tea in Crawford's tea rooms, near the Central Station – I used to stand on the pavement outside in ragged shorts and watch fine ladies with hats piled up with feathers, and gentlemen with thick gold watch-chains across their waistcoats, go in to 'take' afternoon tea, and wonder whether I would ever do so. Now that I could, it seemed absurd that I should ever have envied them. Bernard now looked heavier – he was getting on for forty – but still sturdy, the ruddy features and shining dark eyes gleaming with awareness and dash, but now more watchful. The sideways tilt of the head seemed more pronounced – pulled down by the scar where the battlefield doctor had dug the Franco bullet out of his neck – as if he strained to listen to far-off voices. That, in a sense, was true. Since that moment on the river in Oxford in the 'last days', he had never talked of the girl he had loved in Spain, whom he had intended to rejoin as soon as it was safe – but that was not to be; she was murdered for helping him escape across the frontier. Whenever I met him I had a vision of her, as I imagined her, that is, for I had never seen her face – if he had possessed a photograph of her he had not shown it to me; I saw her as dark and glowing, with broad brow and clear, steadfast gaze, a look of courage and concern, staking all on *her* vision of life – as she had proved. What would his life have been if he could have gone back to her? He must have sensed these thoughts of mine, and perhaps his words about not living one's life 'to suit other people's ideas' had been a backward glance of his own.

I wondered whether his mother had ever guessed at the attachment, sad at how drenched he was with grief, and loneliness, at its end. I could hear her say to him: 'A man must have a wife to look after him, and give him children to his name!' She grieved for herself too, now that she was alone. In her tradition, grandchildren would have confirmed her image – and that of her dead husband and all their forebears – lengthened their shadows across the world. As the years passed, her gentle efforts to '*redda shiddach*' – arrange a betrothal – for him to a nice '*Yiddisher maydel*' gradually diminished, but did not stop. She still timidly talked in this way, whenever she thought he might be receptive.

He said, in one of his few references to my marriage, 'I know why you did it, and I am sorry if – well, what's the use of talking? I suppose you didn't tell him?' – meaning my father. I shook my head. He went on: 'If things had worked out differently for me, I would have brought her back here, of course – there would have been no other way. It would have been very hard, especially now, with mother left on her own – for of course she would have had to live with us!' At the word 'us', he drew his breath in sharply. 'You never get free! There's never a clear road through, to anywhere! For mother there *is* a clear road – and only one – laid down in tablets of stone. And I marvel at that – perhaps it's women; they always do see things in simpler terms than we do.'

He was silent, then added softly, half to himself: 'You have to do what's right for *you* – if you can find out what it is!'

He looked about him – at the world so far removed from us, prim matrons from out of town leaning over three-tiered display dishes set in the middle of each table, bearing tea cakes and scones and coconut 'snowballs', discussing shopping, office girls gossiping in their illicit tea-break – the trivia of life tumbling away indifferently like the waters of a burn rattling over rocks. With a tired shrug he turned towards me again, lips tight: 'Yes – I would have done it. It would have been right for *me*.'

He protests too much, I thought sadly. Had I been as sure, before marrying Kay, that it was 'right' for *me*? Had I thought at all?

I think he sensed how I felt; and perhaps he tried, troubled as he was, to give me strength too.

He leaned across the table to speak quietly against the tumult: 'You worry too much about being Jewish. That was part of it, wasn't it? Wanting to break away from it all – from what we are and where we come from, and for you the family trouble too – everything. But it's nothing special! We're not alone in that – you and I! Look at the fellows we grew up with.' He mentioned some who had married out, and I thought of my cousin Simon, Aunt Rachel's son – and as he came to mind, it struck me that I had never thought of him as a similar 'case'; and now that Bernard had mentioned the others, I wondered what self-deception had made me blind to Simon's example, so close? True, Simon was so much older as to be almost a whole generation away, but that was not the point; plainly I had shut the memory away because I did not want to be reminded of the futility of escape. Simon had married 'out' soon after qualifying as a doctor and setting up in practice. I was still in shorts when he left Glasgow. He had left suddenly, for reasons that I puzzled about at the time, but I guessed that they concerned things I must not ask about – and that Aunt Rachel plainly retreated from.

I remembered him as pale and handsome with a very high forehead – he was going bald in his mid-twenties – reserved, seemingly old and wise. He had long slender fingers, always scrubbed white, the fingernails rounded and gleaming – a young surgeon's hands, the cleanest I had ever seen in the Gorbals. Seeing them, I longed for a life with clean hands too. Soon after he qualified he grew a pencil-thin moustache, fashionable at that time, making him look even older, a man of substance, someone you had to respect. He was the first person I had known – as far as a little boy could *know* anyone as important as a doctor! – who had a car of his own. I wondered why he never took Aunt Rachel or Uncle Salman out in it, until one day he let slip, perhaps thinking that I would not grasp the significance, 'It wouldn't look good.' I puzzled over the words. If you took your parents out in your car, *what* 'wouldn't look good'? How could such a wise man be ashamed of being seen out in his car with his father and mother? They had literally slaved for him, in rags, lived in one small damp room – which was bedroom, sitting-room, kitchen, all in one – behind Uncle Salman's tiny clothes repair shop in Gorbals Street, to pay for his long years of medical study. How proud they had been when he qualified! He had fulfilled one of the immigrants' golden dreams, that a child would move upwards into what they saw as the Establishment, a vicarious status later lampooned among Jewish families who had moved away from the Gorbals, in bitter jokes about the longings of the ghetto: 'My son the doctor!' – or lawyer, dentist, accountant.

Simon's marrying out could have been of small interest to me as a little boy. Only many years later did I understand what a traumatic impact it must have had on Aunt Rachel and Uncle Salman, and the resulting ostracism – the Jewish world of Glasgow was a small one – that led him to flee Glasgow finally. Uncle Salman did not live long after that, and Aunt Rachel, already small in stature – I was nearly as tall as she when I was about ten – shrank into herself and walked with bowed head. In place of her exultant pride in him she did not speak of him at all. The tears were hidden. I never saw Simon again. In later years I heard whispers of him, often through Bernard, who knew so much about so many people. Simon's marriage ended in divorce. He was last heard of in the south of England, working as medical officer in a mental hospital. He died in his early fifties, alone.

Now, thinking of what he had done, I saw the parallels with my own flight, but the differences too. By contrast, he had an assured, comfortable, settled future ahead of him in every sense; he had only to follow the lines marked out for him. He must have known, long before his marriage, that it would force him into exile; and so, in a sense he *chose* it; for me, through a fancy of the Fates – the scholarship – exile chose *me*. Simon knew what he was doing. In the old days, as youths chewing over 'life' in the shower-room of the Gorbals Baths, we saw Jewish girls as upholders of the old traditions; thoughts of marrying one of them brought visions of wearing the shackles of Jewish identity for evermore. When in the company of a Jewish girl, whatever her protestations of modernity, one knew that the ancient values were there within her, strong, ever-watchful; and one sensed that atavism would have its way. Her very deportment, traditional turns of speech, the stamp of upbringing stretching far back in time, turned one's thoughts guiltily inwards, forced one to monitor one's behaviour by those very values – and yet one shrank from them at the same time. A *shiksah*, gentile girl, we thought in our innocence, was not thus restricted; with her one would feel freer, the curbs of the ghetto fallen away. Plausibly we manufactured our own 'modern' excuses; but cruder voices among us dismissed them as the hypocrisy – unconscious perhaps – they really were. 'Freer' meant only one thing! After all, the nice Jewish girl was no fool; she was well-schooled in what she must demand of her 'respectable' future, and what was in store for her if she let herself be beguiled by our smooth talk of freedom. By the standards of the Gorbals ghetto, you brought a 'nice' girl home to meet your family. A nice girl was one who stuck to the rules.

What would have happened to Simon if he had not taken the *shiksah* road? Following the classic pattern, Aunt Rachel would have arranged a betrothal, probably through a '*shadchan*' or match maker, with a girl from a 'better off' family outside the Gorbals – for as a newly qualified doctor, in those days, the mark of middle-class eligibility was already upon him, his value in the marriage market high. A sizeable *nadaan* or dowry from the bride's family would have been agreed, probably a fully furnished house, a car, and capital to start up in practice – or buy an existing one – and live well from the start. On marriage he would have moved away to Kelvinside or a similar 'better off' neighbourhood, to a way of life which, though nominally linked, through family and synagogue membership, to the continuing Yiddish culture of the Gorbals, was quietly disowning it. Synagogue membership had two levels. The upper one – referred to by the poor Jews as the *geveereem* or rich ones – proclaimed status by paying a much higher annual rent for a numbered seat with its private locker beneath it for prayer books, *tallis* or prayer shawl, and other paraphernalia, often with the seatholder's name ornately engraved on a large brass plate. The others paid a much lower fee, and sat wherever they could find

room on a bench. The *geveereem* often chose to continue membership of synagogues in the Gorbals long after they had moved away
to 'classier' areas of the city. At services they usually received a degree of respect from the lower level comparable to that of peasants
to their betters; they sat on boards of management and gave large
donations to synagogue funds, notably on major festivals when it
was the custom to auction the privilege of earning the *Mitzvah*, or
good deed, of carrying the scroll of the *Torah*. That was a harmless
enough piece of ostentatious expenditure, benefiting the synagogue's funds; but as a small child it worried me – surely God
would be neither pleased nor placated by such rough display of
wealth designed to win a 'front of the house' conjuring of His
name? To be fair, without this largesse as well as more formal funding from the *geveereem* there would have been fewer, and certainly
simpler, places of worship in the ghetto. Some purists said at the
time, as many do still, that poorer places of worship, even small
congregations coming together for the purpose in people's homes –
harking back to an earlier epoch – would be better, that is, purer.

Simon could have counted on a comfortable career, doing what
he wanted, and a steady rise into his own rightful place in the growing Jewish middle class. Why did he turn his back on all that?
Unexpectedly, father summed it up for me on my last visit, when
for some reason – perhaps he knew it would be our last meeting –
he talked at length, and from the heart, surveying our history as a
family, full of detail and poignancy, one of the few occasions he
ever did. Simon, the impatient, clever young man making his way,
could not bear to be burdened by Aunt Rachel's reminders of the
sacrifices that she and Uncle Salman made for him. 'They made
him too soft,' father said, 'and too selfish. They would have given
him *anything* – even the sky, the sun! And all their talk: "We did
this for you – we did that for you" – and so on, day after day, it
sickened him, because he *thought* they were saying, "You *owe* us
for all that, and we want something back from you!" It wasn't true!
No parent ever wants anything back! And *they* didn't. I know that.
They wanted to see him do well, and have a good life, that's all. But
he was too clever, too full of himself to understand a simple thing

like that. And so he turned away. Who can tell what to do for the best? They did the opposite of what I did with Lilian and Mary – I was too strict with them; and Rochke was too soft with Simon. What does it matter? The result was the same!'

He laughed without humour. Tears were in his eyes.

I wept too. It was not as clear-cut as he had said, but the essence was true; he *had* cared, and, caring deeply, had seen nothing clearly, failed to see that at bottom he had not given enough of *himself*. Detachment had bred detachment.

However, what he had described was common enough. As a child I often heard older people lament that their children were ashamed of their parents, and in their haste to seize the seeming freedom that beckoned from outside the ghetto could not wait to turn their backs upon them; and I heard them say, and was shocked: '*Kinder zollmen hobm – Steiner*!' 'Better have stones than children.'

Bernard said: 'You can't reason it all away – not any more. It's inside us. It's all round us. We want to destroy where we came from – what gave us breath. There's irony for you. I used to think of myself as a creator, as father did – and you too. And now look at us!'

We were in a complex labyrinth, of heritage, desires, illusion, dead ends – and no thread was secure. As for him, after Maria's murder the deepest wound was disillusion. The two together had quenched some of the old fire. He still wanted to make men over, and the world with them, but there was no way forward. For the present, the union road suited his sympathetic heart, doing good, as he put it, 'by seeing to the plumbing' as distinct from tearing down and rebuilding; but it was easy to see that that was not enough. He did want to change the world – the classic urge to leave his mark. In another avatar he might have been an aggressive entrepreneur, bold, innovative, ruthless, untrammelled by frontiers of any kind. As it was, there was no way to the heights – neither emotionally, nor in the world.

Long ago, in the closing months of the war, I had urged him to try for Parliament in the coming 'demob election'. Bernard had it in him to be a political star of the first magnitude; with his incisive mind, clear grasp of affairs, vision, magical oratory, he might have equalled, in his fashion, the brilliance of Rufus Isaacs nearly two generations before – whose name I had heard as a child in the Gorbals, uttered by the elders in pride and awe, drawing comfort and strength from it, a Jewish hero who had risen to the top in the host culture.

'I've thought of that,' he had said. 'But my record in Spain's against me. They don't want an ex-CP hard-liner like me on the Labour ticket! They had enough trouble with Pritt.'

Pritt, a rich barrister, had been elected to Parliament for Labour, but his 'line' was so close to the Communist Party's that he could well have been an 'underground' member of it. He was expelled from the Labour Party after supporting the Comintern line about Stalin's pact with Hitler.

Whether Bernard *had* been kept out, or simply decided not to try, I was never sure. If he had been kept out, it was as well that he was kept out, for he saw himself too clearly, at last, to compromise in what he called 'the big game' of politics. 'I am too close to all that hugger-mugger as it is! And I find most of it sickening, the fancy footwork, the deals, the choosing of platforms not because you believe in them but because you think they'll pull in the votes. The old way – what you call the "rabble-rousing" way-suited me, direct action, getting the class war on to the streets! But that's all over for me. Sometimes I wish it weren't.'

In the early autumn dusk we walked down to the Clyde, making for his office. At the Jamaica Street bridge we turned east to go along Clyde Street, the riverside way that I remembered as always busy with trade, lined with warehouses and workshops, now stilled. Here I had stood as a child and watched small vessels come up the shallows, their hinged masts lowered to pass under bridges, to tie up at Custom House Quay. A little further upstream, some of us climbed barefoot down an iron ladder on the blackened stone blocks of an old quay face, to reach the bank at low tide and search for useful 'lost things' in the mud – and returned, slimy black from head to toe, with lumps of coal, bottles, broken chairs. A few lucky ones found riches, a sovereign, a half-crown, an ivory handled walking stick, even a gold watch. Standing on the edge of the quay, watching the slack water drift past, I sometimes saw stalwart young men with red, healthy faces, boss-class students from the university – my first understanding of what boss-class meant, a breed so different from us – sweep past in rowing eights, and I had wondered what these fellows, so strong and confident and happy, thought about *us*, if at all. Probably that sight of us, from their perches in those gleaming light brown racing shells, was the closest view of Gorbals life they ever had.

Father, I remembered now, in one of his flush times, had taken me on a boating lake in a park and shown me how to manage the oars, position the blades for the stroke, feather them on the return. He handled the boat with vigour and smooth skill.

'Where did you learn, father?'

'In the army, back in *der heim*. Our training barracks was beside a lake, so they made us take boats out and learn – a few fellows got drowned because they fell in and couldn't swim, but that was' – he shrugged – 'normal.'

As a conscript in the artillery, he had had to learn about horses, and to ride. The training was harsh, often brutal.

'They made us learn to mount a horse in different ways – one way was to jump on to his back from behind. If you were frightened and hesitated, the horse knew it and kicked back, and that was terrible if his hoof got you here' – he pointed to his groin. 'And the officers and NCOs laughed. To cure you of your fear, they had a wooden horse with a pointed tail that stuck out behind, and you had to jump high, with legs apart, to avoid that tail. In a way it was worse than the real horse, for if you jumped just a little too low, that tail was *certain* to get you here.' Again he pointed to his groin. We sat facing each other in the boat, rocking gently in the middle of the peaceful boating lake, tree-fringed, little clouds sailing above, the green waters rippling with sunbeams, far from any imaginable horror. That memory was both happy and sad – happy that he talked to me, and reached out to me, and we were close; sad because, in trying to reach out to him and share *his* memories, I must have sensed – without understanding – the young man's bitterness when he saw the world change, from the first imagined brightness, full of hope, to cruel reality.

He looked away, remembering. 'Many of us – we were young, you see – didn't think too much about all that. It was not all bad. But it *could* be. If you were too frightened to jump on to the wooden horse you could be flogged, and sometimes they flogged a man with a leather whip studded with brass nails. And so you jumped! Oh yes, you jumped! And sometimes, when that wooden tail got a man in this place' – he pointed downwards again – 'he was never the same again. And one of the officers might say to another, speaking loudly, meaning us to hear: "Good! That will be one lot of little Jewish scum *less* in the future!" '

Abruptly he stopped and looked at me uneasily.

I must have been about ten or eleven. I had little idea what 'never the same again' was supposed to mean, or the officer's comment; but I had conjured up a vivid mental picture of that wooden horse and the pointed tail, imagining what it would feel like to be hit by it as I jumped, and I felt pain in my own groin, sympathetic with that of those frightened young soldiers, and my eyes were wet with tears for them.

'Did you get hurt, father?'

His blue-grey eyes were focused far away. He turned to look at me, reaching for the question, closing his lips tightly and sighing; 'Frightened? I suppose I was but I jumped all the same – and I was lucky. When you're young and strong you don't care much. All I thought about was to get it over and done with.'

'Father, was that why you went away – I mean to come here?'

'To answer that, my son, is not easy. You are too young, and yet I must try to explain. When you are young – not so young as you, but a young man – you can live through almost anything, but to be a Jew in the Russian army – well, anywhere in Russia – was to be less than a piece of *dreck*! They told you that to your face! And they laughed, and sometimes they made *you* laugh with them, and if you did not obey that order they flogged you for that too. I wanted to be – it's hard to explain – I wanted to be "who I was". I didn't know who that was, but I knew that I must go somewhere else to find out.

Yes – that's what you've got to do, find out *who* you are, and then *be* that person – and nothing else. But if you don't know – ah well – then it's hard to live at all. And let me tell you – it's even harder when you *do* know.'

That was the voice I remembered, and always would – sombre, sincere, regretful, but strong, vibrant with courage. What was it that made one select certain scenes to remember and not others, particular words, statements, fragments of unfinished thought, to engrave on the heart? At that moment, alone with father in that little tub of a boat that was our private world for a single rented hour, under a blue sky far from the Gorbals, his words linked my vaulting imagination with his own fiery youth – and the blood raced in my head with happiness. There was turmoil too, and fear, and an enigmatic excitement mixed with compassion – visions of plunging horses, brass-nailed whips crashing on to a man's white flesh while others mocked him, and then, separate from it all, father sitting in a boat on another lake – far beyond the horizon of time and place – on another, very different day, in another age. And then everything was swept aside and only those melancholy words, trimmed off the skein of his life, would echo for evermore: 'I wanted to be who I was.'

Though I had stood by father's grave that morning, trying to say farewell, I had the feeling that he was still near, the broadshouldered figure brooding, watching the world with longing yet separated from it – as he must often have stood near the gambling table when, skint, he could no longer take part in the play, but only watch what befell others. He had been a living ghost for years, haunting his past. I heard his measured, slightly gruff voice as if he were just behind me looking over my shoulder; and I knew that I would hear it, in the still moments of life, in all the years to come – trying to pass on to me something indefinable: '*Rachmeelke*!' – the diminutive of my Hebrew name, Yerachmeell, meaning: 'May the Lord have mercy on you' – '*Rachmeelke Rachmeelke! Zai stolz; gai mit gawldene gedenken. Chob gornisht zu gebn. Shver lebn in der welt. Zai gezoont*' – 'Be proud in yourself; go on your way with golden thoughts. I have nothing to give you. It is hard to live in the world. Be in good health.' The word 'nothing', in the context, meant, 'You've got everything I had to give.' It was a farewell of long ago, when I was about to leave to cycle to Oxford. There had been an echo of it at our very last meeting – summing up his life, hard on himself as always, forthright to the end.

I felt cheated by fate – like a child who has put something aside to enjoy later, and then, returning to claim it, finds it gone. Now, incongruously, I remembered a dream, and the awakening, where such a thing had happened. I was about five or six; in the dream, in fact, a dream within a dream, I was given a saucer containing slices of pickled cucumber, a great luxury, but something told me not to eat them there and then, but to save the fulfilment for the next day, and so I put the saucer under my pillow and went back to sleep. Next morning I woke – really awoke! – and reached under the pillow for the saucer. It was not there – and all that day, and many days after, I went about feeling that the World had cheated me, that I should not have trusted it, that I should have taken what was offered while I had the chance; for there was a spiteful Fate forever stalking you, waiting, for just such a show of innocence to seize upon. That feeling now returned; for I saw that in another fashion too I had been cheated, or cheated myself – and was ashamed and saddened to admit it, even secretly. I saw that I had nursed a juvenile fantasy in which I would ride home one day in triumph and say to father: 'Never mind the past! Here is your crown at last. Receive it from *my* hand!' So much in life always happened too late. He had slipped away, and that day could never come. Which was the greater, my sorrow for his passing, or regret for myself? I must have had an intimation, at that moment of candour with myself, of a truth that would return and inflict its wound again and again. I had completely failed to understand what he had wanted from me, what I should have tried to give him, the only things that mattered. What I owed him had nothing whatever to do with the sound of trumpets – that was childish, and selfish – but with simpler things: integrity, loyalty, care, however poor the offering. To have thought otherwise had been vanity, unwillingness even to see the *lacrimae rerum*, the tears of things, let alone respond to them – or rather slowness in doing so, unsure as always. Here was bitter knowledge. Now I knew, but too late, that anything I achieved would be as ashes in the mouth.

I looked at the Clyde sliding by in oily brown ripples, the decayed warehouses and offices, the enveloping dirt and greyness. They were all receding. Something else had changed, awesome, disturbing, yet unexpectedly comforting. With father gone, this place – this of all places! – would never again claim me in the way it had done through all the years. It had lost its arcane power to draw me back to my beginnings, as the migrant bird swings back by the stars to claim its starting point once more. From now on, I could make this place *appear* real only by recreating him – see him lingering in the shadows, a sad, meditative presence, unreachable as he had always been.

I myself was 'changed – I now had a visitor's sense of displacement. My true self was encased in the body of a stranger, at whose side I walked step by step, watching that self respond to surroundings now only mistily familiar, belonging no longer to *my* past but to the past of a little boy who had known these pavements so well – and walked them in loneliness and fear and perplexity, in sorrow and hunger and cold, and in coldness of the spirit, long ago. I now realised that I had only half-known him. And sometimes feared to know him.

Bernard said nothing, respecting my silence, no doubt divining its content. Stepping out beside me, sturdy, four-square, with the old hint of soldierly gait, he seemed the person he had always been, but there was a difference in him too, disturbing, hard to pin down. It was autumn, and had not Bernard always said, 'We change with the seasons'? It certainly felt like a time of change – but the word 'change' seemed too puny to fit, when everything, the earth we walked on, the very bones and marrow of the universe we had known as boys here, had shifted, and *nothing* could now be brought to life again – the visions that had beckoned to us so brightly then. Nothing would ever remotely resemble anything we had known before.

For Bernard to change was unthinkable. It was I, surely, not he, who retreated before the tide, changed course, tacked and ran before the wind – or so I had thought. And yet he had changed. To me he had always been fixed, solid, knowing himself, and the path he must follow, with God-given commitment, the faculty that had first drawn me to him all those years before. It had nothing to do with politics or causes or party but *himself*; he answered a clear voice within. Perhaps that view of him had been a mirage too, the quality of certainty in others which I had pursued in vain as an outsider in Oxford, that I would always envy wherever I found it, a solidity that strode through life undeflected by 'time and chance'.

Bernard said, looking straight ahead, 'My father was a loser in many ways. He was a good man, but it seems to me now that mother got little out of life – there we go again, their world and ours! How can we see it with their eyes? She didn't understand anything he did, not a thing. Perhaps he couldn't give her any more children after me – I'm not sure; but loyal though she always was, she did let slip a sign sometimes – little things, she could never *say* anything of that kind! – that he was never very potent after they left *der heim*. I didn't realise until recently that that was why – apart from tradition and so on – she so desperately wanted me to get married and give her grandchildren; and still does, though she's probably a bit old now to get as much satisfaction out of it as she would have done before.'

Why, of all times, should he talk of this now? In touching sympathy with me, on this day of my farewell to father and my childhood world, he was moved to re-perceive his own life too.

We left the river and struck through back streets, an ill-lit world of old warehouses and merchant offices, weaving our way through familiar but faded vistas, like old sepia photographs in which the blurred outlines beckon and yet recede, concealing unfathomable lives. Nearing the Saltmarket, the sky leaden, dusk was changing to night. Among the shadowed archways and loading bays – convenient niches of darkness – the Sirens swirled in flared New Look skirts, legs wide apart, announcing themselves more blatantly than I remembered, but also, astonishingly, in an atmosphere of childlike fantasy: perhaps there *was* something in Bernard's idea of the changing season needing to be marked by a different mood? As in a sentimental burlesque they swung up and down the deserted pavements, among the piles of decaying fruit and vegetables and discarded cartons and packaging, dancing to unheard music, moved by what capricious *jeu d'esprit* – dark, peeling façades leaning over them. Little had changed since that other evening, a lifetime away, when I had called for him at his office and gone with him for that last, sad meal with his father before I left for Oxford, and we had come downstairs to find the two priestesses of the night, Kirstie and Jeanie, waiting on the pavement outside – innocent and gentle within the rough portrayal of themselves and their trade.

It was on that night, in his office, that he had first spoken of the *guerre kilométrique* that was on its way, and I had understood why his links with Kirstie and Jeanie were necessary and intense.

He said now: 'D'you remember Kirstie and Jeanie? Well, you won't believe it but mother *knew*! Not in detail of course, but she knew – just as she knew about Maria in Spain – that is, *someone* in Spain. And she knew when Maria was dead – sensed it in me.' He drew a deep breath, and let it out through his teeth: 'She never said anything, but she mourned for me, almost as a man says Kaddish for a son or daughter that has strayed away and married out, though of course I hadn't – but she sensed that it was serious and that I had fully intended to marry Maria. And that did wound her deeply. But to be fair she mourned, also, because I had been hit hard. And she tried, in spite of her principles, to share the grief with me.'

We seldom talked about our private lives; a tacitly agreed forbearance. Now and then, especially at a bad time for one of us, something might be said, a hint for intuition to feed upon – unless, more often on my side I think, there was a need to unload. Delicately, with sympathy more than confession, we shared one another's ups and downs.

I asked: 'What happened to them?'

He stopped and faced me, emphasising the importance, to him: 'You could say, I suppose, that the war was good for both of them

– all those servicemen! Especially American sailors coming up the Clyde. Well, what do you expect? They both made money, and what's more, they looked after it. How they didn't get the pox or the clap is a miracle. They were good women and I think I loved them both a bit in my own way – and I admit I miss them. I miss them a lot – after all I knew them a long time, my own private – what can I call them?' – he shook his head in puzzlement – 'comrades I suppose, close as only women can be – we understood one another.' He turned away and we walked on. 'Kirstie married an American naval NCO and went over there after the war, and now has two children. Kirstie! It's hard to believe. I hear from her now and then. Jeanie I've lost touch with, though I hear of her from Kirstie. She bought herself a boarding house down the Ayrshire coast and married a local chap there. So they both escaped from the Gorbals, each in her own way. Kirstie misses "her ain Glasgow folk" – the old, old story.'

He too wished he could wind the thread back to where he had begun, the classic wish to wave a wand and be once more the person one had been, but armed with what one now knew! Even if I could, did I really want to be, once again, the timorous, doom-struck little boy who haunted my memory?

I said, taking up the thought left hanging in the air: 'I don't know about you, but even if I did want a *shiddach* with a Yiddisher girl, what *shadchan* would consider me a good proposition now?'

'You've always under-rated yourself. You and I have always been outsiders. For us the straight, ordinary road simply doesn't exist. We are *not* ordinary fellows, content to be judged by ordinary standards. For us – and you'd better accept it – that option is not there. You can only be what you *are* – and take your chance.'

That sounded like father's words. Behind them, however, was a worrying note of doubt. Battered and thrown off course though he was, I had never expected to hear *that*.

He said: 'Remember Hannah? I want to tell you about it.'

I had assumed that they had had an affair after she and I had drifted apart towards the end of the Oxford days. Physically, I re-gretted the parting, thinking of her, for a time, obsessively, that straight, vibrant figure – Diana the Huntress in the glow of youth. Perhaps her closeness to Rachel – reported missing, presumed dead – had doomed our relations from the start. Hannah had a toughness even more daunting than Rachel's; taut as a drawn bow-string, undeviating in her passionate certainty, her self-imposed mission to build the Jewish National Home in the Holy Land – Israel was then not yet born – while I was still set in the opposite direction, away from the Jewish identity altogether. Had Rachel lived, and had I been less unsure and stiff-necked, I might well have taken that committed road – another 'if.'

He said: 'Remember that day on the river bank in Oxford, when we met her with Werner, and I touched that gold *Mawgain Dawveed* – shield of David – hanging from a chain at her neck and said that blood would need to be shed for what it stood for? That hit her hard. It's strange with some women; blood, even the idea of it, can shock them, and yet stir them too. I found that in Spain, sometimes not a pleasant sight. She too was stirred – I could see it – and I had a feeling that it needed only an instant, a tremor – as we used to say in Spain, the fall of a leaf – and we could be together, she and I. Not *then*! Oh no. I was in no state for that – it wasn't too long after I'd heard about Maria's murder – but *some* time. You know how you get that feeling with a woman?'

After VE Day, Hannah wrote to him, and they met in London, at her flat in Hill Street. She had completed her preparations to go to Palestine, but had been advised to delay until Britain slackened its blockade of Jewish refugee ships. And so, waiting, she took him – that was the only word for it – 'stretched out a hand in her bossclass certainty,' and coolly took him.

'I hadn't expected it to happen quite in that down-to-earth way – just like that, I must say! In some ways it put me in mind of Kirstie – except that Kirstie was more homely, warmer – yes, very much warmer.' He sighed and was silent.

'That was how it felt,' he resumed. 'Detached! But it hardly mattered. I wasn't caring about the future. I wasn't going to get over Maria – *ever*. I knew that. In fact I told her about Maria. I was really telling her that whatever happened, *she* could only be second best; it sounds cruel but, even though it suited me to have her at the time – something in me resented her reaching out peremptorily like that – not moving towards me at all. Strangely enough, she didn't mind what I told her. That shook me a bit. And then I saw. For her, I too was secondary – my only role was to help her fulfil *her* mission. She wanted me as a bed-mate and as comrade in arms – as cold as that. I had to laugh sometimes. It was strange to be with a woman so much in need of taking control. That was not for *me*, and never could be, and she should have realised it. I let it drift on.'

At times he was half-persuaded. It was a solution of a kind, an escape from a double isolation – the loss of Maria, and the extinction of political hopes. There was also the thrill of the unknown quest, like the elation of going to fight in Spain had been; but something was missing. Going to Spain he had had no doubts what the goal was, or rather what he wanted it to be. In Hannah's mission he had many.

'Palestine meant many things to many people, so many strands of hope and ambition. For me, the Jewish homeland would simply be another capitalist state – as Israel has become. I would join hands with people whose views were the same as those of the bosses I was fighting here. The *political* need for Israel was clear enough. What an irony of history! – when Hitler was slaughtering the Jews, he didn't foresee that he was creating the best possible case for the creation of Israel. After centuries of the Jews being the victims of *everyone* who wanted to work off his bitterness at life, the creation of a Jewish state wielding legitimate power would be a historic achievement of tremendous moral force, and Jews would walk erect after two thousand years. But it wasn't for that reason that Russia and America supported the idea: it was cynical *realpolitik* – Russia to destroy Britain's leverage in the Middle East and get in there herself, and America to create a Jewish client state there, at the mercy of her own political expediency. It's a nasty old world – you get nothing for nothing. For the Jews it was a whole collection of dilemmas, and still is. And I couldn't see any place for me there, certainly not as Hannah's male concubine.'

It seemed that I saw him more clearly than ever before. Beneath the logic and the enlightened talk, tradition reasserted itself, and his personality, blurred for so long, sharpened again. Rejection of the role Hannah wanted to impose, to him a subservient identity, was only to be expected. He would go where he alone was master – that or nothing. Hannah, facing life with the assurance of a rich, emancipated woman, determined to bend it her way, could not compromise either; she could not – or would not – see that the role she offered offended him. I saw, now, the road he would go. He had swung all the way back; he would settle for nothing less than the traditional verities, a 'good' Jewish wife and a 'good' Jewish home. He would hold out, keep his principles pure. Purity on *his* terms! And in the meantime, as Kirstie and Jeanie had done, their successors would sustain him in his vision of himself.

Hannah had gone on alone. He parted from her, not with the heartache of a lover but the detached goodwill of a friend. 'It was like saying goodbye to a comrade going up the line! She was a good sort in some ways, but there was some quality missing, something womanly. Tenderness? Care? I can't put a word to it – something beyond the physical. I don't want a comrade for a wife; I want a woman, a full-hearted woman.'

Around us, among the shadows between the discs of yellow light thrown by the widely separated lamp-posts, the girls stamped their heels and pirouetted, their parted legs stiff as stilts, springing from one foot to the other, wild, demonic, conjuring magic, possessed. But their possession had purpose too. It was early evening, and they were fresh, and hungry, and this old trysting place must be given life. They must infuse the gathering night air with eagerness and gaiety, stir the wayward pulses and draw them near. They moved into the discs of light and out again, darting in laughter, calling softly to the dark male outlines flitting past the end of the street, beyond the line of warehouses. Men hurrying home glanced aside, were struck by the dance, hesitated – and some lingered, looked at watches, turned and approached and were magically spirited away, into an archway, or a patch of blackness in the angle of a wall. So another business night got under way, and the shadowed archways and loading bays sounded with brief murmuring and movement, as they had always done until after the pubs closed.

A pretty dark-haired girl, with large innocent eyes and dazzling white teeth, approached, swinging and turning in a twirl of feet like a skater spinning on the front curves of the blades. Pausing, she addressed Bernard in friendly tones: 'Evenin' Colonel! Are ye gonnae gie's a go the night?'

He smiled at her: 'Ah'm busy, hen. Not just now.'

She wagged a finger with an air of mock motherly concern – incongruous since she was about half his age – and, tossing her hair back, whirled away.

He chuckled with little humour: 'For some reason they've started calling me Colonel! They all know my name. They're like children inventing nicknames, and always with the sharp edge of truth. Maggie teases me like the rest of them, using my age and manner, especially my age – they pretend to see me as a working-class Colonel Blimp, more or less past it! And I'm not forty yet! How's that for stirring me up?'

Over the years, Bernard's affinity with the sirens of the night must have disturbed me more than I had thought. I had often caught myself disapproving, ashamed that I clung to residues of the old days of adolescent wonder and coarseness and ignorance under the hot showers at Gorbals Baths; when as youths we secretly feared the seemingly insatiable sexuality of these 'hairies', their arcane power, the awesome magnetism of their flaunted flesh, and in the instant of desire condemned them for causing it, never imagining they could be objects of affection. They diabolically awakened our flesh, willing us to fulfil upon *them* – if only we dared! – fantasies of sexual fury. They had freely chosen this role – we ignored the goad of poverty – forsworn the classic womanly splendour of care and tenderness, the 'normal' emotions. Bewildered as we were by our lust, their very presence, their predatory detachment, proclaimed that our desire was inconsequent – at their whim to quench in a moment – and we hated them for possessing a power that made our potency seem trivial, the quality we treasured – and feared – most. For that blow to our nascent manhood they were forever guilty, and merited no gentleness.

I was shocked that these prejudices reasserted themselves so freshly, as if they were still in control. Surely I knew better now? I thought I did, but I could not have said why, only that I saw Bernard's predicament with a sympathy I had not felt long ago, when I had looked upon his relations with Kirstie and Jeanie as of no consequence, a harmless diversion – not serious. Now I knew that they *had* been – more serious than perhaps he himself had realised. At that time they had been a solution of sorts – involving no ties, no commitment. Now, he felt caught, isolated, with no room left for manoeuvre – as the 'Colonel' gibe brought home to him.

He said softly, watching Maggie and the others, 'I have lost too much ground, and it's impossible to catch up. I want a young, womanly, fiery girl, like Maria – but Jewish. But young Jewish girls have been married off long ago. Even if I found one, how do I get to know a young girl, really know her, open the door and let her in, speak to her across all that chasm of time, when the language of the heart, and its chemistry, is no longer shared, and never can be?'

I remembered what he had said that night long ago, when we had met Kirstie and Jeanie – at a time when he still clung to the hope of rejoining Maria: 'Sometimes I take Kirstie – not a pretty picture.'

That sardonic summing up of himself did not square with his assertion, today, that he had loved them; the word 'take' meant detachment, taking relief when the need was great and then going on his way, at best a tentative experiment with the emotions, with no communication. He had never before even hinted that there *had* been more than that – almost in spite of himself. And now, those words of his – loving them in his fashion – sounded like an excuse. That too was unlike him.

We looked down the street. The dance had stopped. The girls had resumed the hip-swinging, professional saunter. From the busy street beyond, a few more dark figures hurried along the refuse-laden pavements towards them; here and there a girl swung away from the patterned, stiff-legged patrol – after whispered agreement with a companion – and fell into step with one of them, leaned

6

You were the Lucky One

Mary too had not been informed of Father's death at the time – or so she said. I was inclined to believe it; though closer to Lilian in age, Mary had also come to be treated as less than equal.

As far as I knew, she never visited his grave.

Mary, unlike Lilian, had never studied for a professional qualification – at the age when Lilian had done so, Mary had been deep in *dolce far niente* years with Gil, the rich, indolent student who had never told her about the arranged marriage awaiting him on his return to Rajasthan. Had she studied at night school, as Lilian had for a time, Mary might even have outshone Lilian, for she was cleverer, and certainly more imaginative. However, within the limited scope for women in the Thirties, she had done reasonably well, in advertising and then in shipping companies. She belonged to a women's club, went on group holidays abroad, but otherwise seemed to lead a solitary life in her flat near Clapham Common, where as far as I knew she lived alone for the rest of her days – never ceasing to mourn Gil.

Our infrequent meetings were in a restaurant: a Kosher one, such as Folman's in Soho, or the Kedassia in New Oxford Street, not for Kosher's sake but because traditional dishes of *der heim* revived memories of mother's cooking – gefillte fish, latkas, baked herring, cholent. Mary never admitted regretting her exile, for to do so would have meant disowning the entire sorry sidetracking of those eight years with Gil – and the deep hurt of their end.

However, opening *any* door to memory was perhaps a mistake, Like father, she would not let old wounds heal, as if to do so would endanger something fragile and precious – would break faith. When I urged her to forget, she would explode in fury, and contrive to block all other topics of conversation so that, inevitably, the past would be chewed over yet again. Each time I was saddened, still more, to see what had happened to the bright, slender sprite of long ago, the eager innocence ground out of her by time and chance. She had become fat, smoked incessantly and had a heavy, phlegm-laden cough – oh golden Mary of my childhood, where have you gone?

When, after I had returned from saying goodbye to father at his grave, I next saw her in London, she launched into the familiar ré-sumé of bitter recollection, a catalogue of accusations, emotional debts. Over the years I had often made the mistake of trying to per-suade her to take a view of his life as I fancied he himself saw it. This was no 'holier than thou' pose on my part, an accusation she threw at me, but rather thinking aloud – and trying to lead her to share my thoughts; after all, as I reminded her sometimes, *she* had no monopoly of grievances. I often asked myself, but with little comfort, how I would have acted in his place. The answers were always blurred; his burdens, his ill-luck, his mistakes – what else could I call them? – darkened the imagination. Sometimes, most discouraging of all, I told myself that he and I were in some ways alike! He too, as Bernard had said of Candide, 'led with his chin'. Talking in this vein to Mary, all I achieved was to send her fury to white heat, instantly transferred from father to me.

One particular episode in the past burned within her as if it had occurred only the day before; and she returned to it nearly every time we met. She must have been sixteen, and I about eight. We were alone in the flat one hot summer day – Lilian and father were out. We sat at the rough plank kitchen table, she with her long silky brown hair, shot with gleams of bronze – so long that she could sit on it – uncombed, hanging about her face and shoulders like a crumpled brown curtain. Father had told her to comb and brush her hair and plait it – which she usually did, in two long thick plaits tied at the ends with bows of pale blue ribbon; she must do her hair, he had said, after she had tidied up generally and washed some clothes. Instead, day-dreaming, she sat beside me letting time go by, drawing pictures with a stub of pencil in the margins of an old newspaper, telling me stories, holding me entranced while I leaned against her, drawn to the mysterious grown-up smell of her body that, reminding me of mother, sometimes brought tears to my eyes – inexplicably, frighteningly. On the cracked oil-cloth cover was an accumulation of dirty dishes, food in pieces of paper – bread, butter, cheese, a bowl with three eggs; on a chair beside the table lay shirts, underwear and socks waiting to be washed.

The fire had gone out in the coal range; the fire cage was full to overflowing with ash and cinders, and needed to be emptied. Its metalwork, bespattered with streaks of fat mixed with old ash, had gone for weeks without being cleaned and buffed with emery cloth, which mother used to do every day. Next to it on the right, the curtained alcove bed was unmade, with its great duvet of goose down – the *perraneh* – rolled back, exposing crumpled, yellowing sheets and the thin flock mattress striped black and grey, and the edges of planks resting on the brown stained wooden trestles. Against the wall immediately behind her, between the range and the sink, stood a bucket of refuse full to the brim with peelings of potatoes, turnips, carrots and onions, fish heads and other food scraps; in the hot, airless atmosphere of the little kitchen we had become accustomed to the acrid smell of the rotting contents, on whose surfaces dozens of black flies crawled. She had neglected to empty it into the ash-pits – the rubbish dumps downstairs, in the back yard of the close – for some days; this time father had specifically told her not to forget.

All was peaceful. Fascinated, I watched the point of the pencil move over the paper and a cat with a bushy tail emerge – at school she used to win prizes for drawing. I heard a step on the staircase outside the front door. Mary, absorbed, did not hear it, and there was no time to warn her; in any case the harm was done and nothing could now change it. The next moment father was opening the outer door; in one characteristic movement he put the heavy key in the lock, turned it and swung the door against the wall, letting it bang shut behind him. It was only a short step from there to the kitchen, and father had stridden in before Mary could make a move. Seeing the evidence of sloth and disobedience, the blue-grey eyes became cold as ice, and he drew his right hand across his chest to give her a 'back-hander'. She had been tilting her chair back –

something he had severely forbidden, for she had broken another kitchen chair in that fashion recently; it stood in the corner, its back legs askew, awaiting repair, and we were now a chair short. With a cry she raised an arm to ward off the blow and leaned back still further. Whether his hand did reach her, I am not sure; her abrupt movement must have tilted the chair too far and she fell backwards, her flailing legs knocking the table over, and everything on it, all the crockery and the food, crashed and scattered on to the cracked linoleum that partially covered the floor timbers. She landed flat on her back on her upturned chair, and with fiendish accuracy her head was buried in the rubbish bucket, which her fall overturned on to her, its damp and putrescent contents spread all over her hair and face and neck and clothes.

I remember father's jaw muscles, tightening as he bit back his fury, an awesome sign we had reason to know well. He bent down and lifted her to her feet. Her hair was covered with lumps of slimy refuse, yellow and brown and grey, to which the flies, momentarily scared off in a black flurry, immediately attached themselves again, among the sickly white flecks that were maggots. Mary, pale with shame and defensive fury, in tears, begged forgiveness; in silence he set her at the sink and told her to stand still there, saying he was going out to buy kindling and coal to re-light the fire so that he could heat water with which to wash her hair. He told me, spitting the words from tightened lips, to clear up as much of the mess on the floor as I could, and was gone.

Mary bent over the sink, pulling pieces of the sticky mess from face and hair and clothes, and through the tears telling me to say nothing – nothing at all. I nodded glumly. Even at that age I must have understood that no words *could* be said! I did not know what to do with most of the debris on the floor, for the kitchen table was too heavy for me to lift. Food that was still well wrapped in paper I put away on shelves in the cupboard next to the sink; the three eggs were broken, and I scraped up the watery patches of yellow with some of the newspaper Mary had used for drawing. In a few minutes father was back, carrying a brown paper bag of coal – some medium-sized lumps mixed with dross – and a small bundle of kindling; the latter would normally have been an unthinkable extravagance, for he usually kept a stock of kindling beside the range, chopped from pieces of discarded wood he had brought from work or picked up in the street. That stock had been used up, and though a few pieces of timber stood by the range ready for chopping with the little axe he kept there, in this emergency he had decided to forgo thrift. He put the coal and kindling on the floor, turned on his heel and set the table on its legs again, and told me to put on it the fallen crockery – most of it in pieces – and he would see whether he could glue any of it together; and then to take the coal shovel and collect as much of the spilled refuse as I could and put it back into the bucket.

He knelt before the range, spread a piece of newspaper beside him, and shovelled on to it the accumulation of ash and cinders. At the bottom of the empty fire cage he put a layer of blackened clinkers in which there remained some 'goodness', and on that base he built a criss-cross pattern of sticks interspersed with twists of paper, topped it with small lumps of coal hacked from a larger piece with the axe, then made a paper spill and lit the bottom layer, and putting his lips close to the bars blew up the flames. The kindling soon caught and began to crackle and spit with flame, which took hold of the top coals; he put some larger pieces over them, and blew the flames up again. The little room grew hotter still, and all the smells increased – of food, putrescence, sweat, damp – and floated in the heavy air almost palpably. He stood for a moment before the closed window, and I guessed his thoughts – to open it would bring in yet more flies to attack Mary's hair, and the sticky brown fly-catcher paper hanging from the ceiling, already black with a covering of dead flies, would not trap any more; and he probably had no money to spare for a new one. He shrugged and turned away, leaving the window closed. He filled a large black pot with water, and put it on the fire to heat. Mary stood by the sink, shoulders drooping in shame and misery, shaking her head to shift the persistent flies from her hair. While the water heated, he turned his attention to the debris on the floor, first of all the food. Some of it, which had spilt from its paper wrappings on to the linoleum, he threw into the rubbish bucket – with a wry grimace, for it was a sin to waste food; I knew he must be asking himself how he was going to get money to replace it.

The water heated, father plugged the shallow brown earthenware sink and emptied the pot into it, filled the pot again and put it on to the fire to heat, then added cold water to the sink to make its contents lukewarm, rolled up his sleeves, put a towel round his waist to protect his trousers, and gently bent Mary's head low while he gathered the gluey strands of hair in his hands and dipped as much as he could into the water at one time, pulling off the putrid mess in lumps. Then he soaped his hands with a bar of strong-smelling carbolic soap, and began a vigorous kneading of her hair – rinsing and kneading, over and over again.

I must have guessed that his silence hurt her more than any blow from his hand might have done. She sobbed excuses, promises of better behaviour. In her hurt pride she begged to be left alone to put all to rights by herself – even though the extent of the disaster had shocked her into helplessness. Yet, in spite of herself, she leaned against him, moved by his calm concern, longing to be overwhelmed in this fashion always, cared for by his strong hands. His love must have come to her bitter-sweet.

I must also have sensed that he could not bring himself to say anything to her. Years later, when I was about fourteen, speaking of that day, he said: 'There was so much I wanted to say – not just being angry – but about smashed hopes, smashed like the dishes on the floor, but my heart was dry, and there was nothing left worth saying.'

The sticky mess seemed to take hours to remove. While successive pots of water heated, he helped me gather wreckage from the floor; and Mary stood by the sink, her matted hair still beset by flies, and scratched her head hard.

The rubbish bucket refilled, I carried it down the three flights of stone stairs to the back close to empty it in the ashpits, and back again for it to be filled with more wreckage. It seemed that I carried that bucket up and down for hours. Father examined the broken crockery bit by bit to see what could be fitted together and glued and saved, and what must be put aside for me to carry away. With a gloomy shake of the head he pushed aside piece after piece till most of the broken items were condemned; there were few whole dishes or cups and saucers and plates left. He picked up one piece and held it in his broad palm; it was a curved sliver of pale white china with a gold line along it, fragment of a soup ladle, last of a gold-decorated serving set, remnant of her dowry, that mother had brought from *der heim*. He stared at it and I saw his eyes glisten wet, then with a suppressed cry he hurled it at the range, and it shattered into dozens of tiny specks of white. He bent his head and held his face in his hands. Mary, watching him, scratched her head with even greater frenzy, as if she could erase all that had happened – this day, and in all the time before.

He drew the back of his hand across his eyes to wipe the tears away, turned to the sink, and again attacked her hair. At last it looked as though he had cleaned all the dirt out of it. Still without speaking, he made her sit down in front of the fire, on one of the two solid chairs, and rubbed her hair with a towel, combed it and held the long wet strands as close to the fire as he dared, running his fingers gently through them to feed the heat to every filament, till all were dry. Then, leaving her sitting there staring at the fire, still scratching, he went to the press in the little lobby and reached up to a shelf where he kept some of mother's clothes, and came in again carrying a silk blouse that I remembered she had worn on the day she had returned from her last visit to the hospital carrying a brass jam-making pan that she had been told to use as a mirror. I had wondered, even at the age of six, why she had been told to do this, and only after her death did father tell me: it was to prevent her seeing how yellow her features had become. The blouse was still folded in the creases mother had given it when she had last ironed it and put it away among her remaining pawnable treasures. He wrapped it in a piece of clean newspaper and went out.

I went to the window and reached up to one of the lower panes and rubbed a patch clear, and saw him go into the pawnshop across the street. The blouse must have been valuable, for he came back in a little while with many brown paper bags – of rice, potatoes, onions, fresh herrings, bread, butter, eggs, fat, and set about cooking a wonderful meal of rice and herring baked in the oven – and, still in silence, he set it before us, making us eat before he did, for there were only two plates left. Mary looked at the food, hesitated, then turned away, saying she was not hungry, but he nudged her gently: 'Eat! You need it for your health.'

And so she ate, tears flowing.

Despite father washing her hair in that strong-smelling carbolic soap, about a week later her scalp erupted in painful red sores, perhaps the result of her violent scratching. Father took her to the Royal Infirmary; they cut off most of her hair, and shaved some areas, to get at the infection. There followed weeks of treatment with ointments and a blue liquid. She went about with a kerchief hiding her devastated head, pale, saying little, often bursting into floods of tears. Ever afterwards, her hair would grow no longer than to the base of her neck. She never forgave him for the loss of that wonderful curtain of hair.

To me, at eight years old, that day's upset was not especially noteworthy – there were many. When I was grown-up I saw that it must have been crucial. For her, many powerful currents of feeling had come together, their pressure irresistible, years of resentment, self-doubt, anger that nothing could be changed, conflict between pity for father and love for him. An unmanageable crisis had wounded her, at that time of flowering, in a way that she could not – perhaps dared not – ever put into words.

I asked her, many years later, what she thought father *should* have done? After all, the things he had told her to do that day *did* need to be done! There was no answer except – an answer of a kind – an outburst of anger at *me*.

Why at me? The reason emerged on another occasion, when I said to her in all innocence: 'Can we ever get free of all this guilt, hatred, self-punishment for the past? The past is round our necks. We're crippled because of it!'

She snatched the long cigarette holder from her lips and spat the words out: 'I don't know what you're talking about. You can take your high-falutin' Oxford talk somewhere else. *He* hurt us – Lilian and me – like he hurt mother, because he didn't *care*! And there's no forgiving and no forgetting. It's all right for you. You were lucky! You were the favourite – and anyway you were too young to feel the hurt as we did.'

That stunned me, and I must have shown it, for she stared challengingly, daring me to dispute her words. I tried to see behind that square figure in the flowered silk dress, the pale heavy features and small snub nose – searching for the slim, eager girl of that earlier time, who I had looked up to in wonder and love, a child's goddess.

She said, suddenly reverting to the Glasgow twang: 'Och ye don't understand! You were just a wee boy then – the things he did meant nothin' tae yew! But they did tae us – don't ye see? Why don't ye say something?'

This was Lilian's technique too, to talk to me as if it was all back in time and I was still the little brother to whom 'these things meant nothin" – so that I would be provoked and give them a cue to justify themselves all over again. I was not going to rise to that one, not any more. Father's death, inexplicably, had steadied me. I never had complained and I never would. Perhaps my silence made their guilt harder to bear – which might have explained why they preferred not to see me at all? But father was gone; and yet he remained powerful even in death, a solemn question mark, a warning. Still, nothing could now alter what he had done, or what they had done in fighting him through the years. The past must be buried – or it would kill the future too. Even that thought was arrogance:

> That which is hath been long ago,
> And that which is to be hath already been ...

As for me being the lucky one, if they could believe *that*, then nothing made any sense – or they had hearts of stone, and they deserved all the bad luck they got. No – I must not say that. Still, they did protest too much. Calling me the lucky one, they made *me* in some way guilty. For them, no one must be innocent, for that made *their* guilt indelible! And as for escape, they had tried that long ago

– and now they knew, too late, that there was no escape.

Why not admit, even secretly to ourselves, that we could have *tried* to help him and didn't? I thought, but could not be sure, that as a little boy I *had* sensed that he needed help, and wished I could fight by his side, but did not know how. Yes, father did lash out at us, between spells of sweetness, unreasonably, mistakenly, blindly – never, however, with malice, but trying to salvage something from chaos. For me at the time, that was beyond understanding, but it should not have been beyond theirs; and certainly not *now*.

I could see now why that day of the rubbish bucket *had* been crucial for them both. Father had hoped, stubbornly, that Mary, softer than Lilian, sympathetic – more like mother – would stay on and hold the home together. Years later, walking one Sunday morning on the Broomielaw, he indirectly told me that he had lived for that: 'I could never marry again. In spite of everything I've said about your mother, there could never be another woman for me. Life is like that.'

Mary must have sensed this; she must also have known that Lilian was planning to leave home, and that father could not prevent it. Mary did not see why she should stay at home to carry the burden for her smart, tough, older sister. On that day, and in many other instances of neglect, she was stating clearly – though perhaps unawares – that he must not put that burden on her: 'I didn't see why Lilian should get off scot free! Why should my life be ruined because of his mistakes?'

She would ruin her life in *her* way!

On that day, therefore, it must have seemed to him that she threw his hopes in his face, and yet his fury and pain had turned to tenderness and care, as it always did. She had been wounded too – his very tenderness in the aftermath mortified her; and the loss of her hair, with all it signified, struck a blow from which she never recovered, leaving a sense of futility – every action must prove ill-chosen and self-wounding. Flight, even if it gave only transitory release, would be no worse than what she would leave behind.

Now, with him gone, the only true escape, through forgiving and understanding, remained stubbornly closed – and bitterness must focus on me, for I had been, in a sense, the cause. Had I not been there, a small child needing care, her guilt would have been infinitely less; and so I had to be the legitimate target of her fury. I was 'the lucky one' because I had had no responsibility. That was intolerable.

For father, of course, flight had been impossible. Wherever he might have wanted to go he would have had to take me with him. And so, cornered, he fought his forlorn battle through to the end. For that tenacity, too – every day of it an accusation levelled at her and Lilian – they could never forgive him.

7

Freedom in a Borrowed Hat

Father's sayings often returned to me, his voice resonating in the cloister of the mind – lessons of his journeying, promptings of old wounds, tapping the wisdom of earlier generations; temper of Ecclesiastes. His words were always apposite to some concern of mine, and perhaps that was why, unawares, I called them to mind. That apart, they provided an arresting and often poignant insight into father's view of the world, his way of digesting experience, steadily adding depth and detail to my image of him. One that came to me again and again was: 'Never try to explain something you've done, some mistake, something that goes against what people call "respectable". Always remember that other people will have already seen it and made up their minds about you and what you've done; and *nothing* you say – nothing! – will change that. Only your behaviour in the future can change their judgement of you – and I mean *judgement*! Suppose you've gone out with a hole in your sock – it shows above the heel of your shoe. Once they've seen it – and you can be sure *somebody* always does! – you can make excuses till you're blue in the face; you can say you were in a hurry and that it was the first sock that came to hand, that the hole was not there when you went out, and so on. The best of reasons! It won't help you. In fact your excuses will make matters worse. People will have decided that you are the kind of person who goes round with holes in his socks, that you don't care whether you look respectable or not – which they will very likely take as an insult to *them*; worse still, that you can't afford to buy a pair. And, what's more, they'll think the worse of you for making excuses at all – because the man who is sure of himself does not make excuses! Far better to keep quiet and go on your way, and they will respect you for showing them that you are strong in yourself and that *their* opinion will not change you.'

At first hearing, when I was about fourteen, I had understood it only in its surface logic, not as a profound comment on life and attitudes and manners, and certainly not as opening a window into the man himself, permitting a fuller, more rounded perception, a discovery of him that would be added to over the years, refinements to a portrait never to be completed – of a courageous man, tough yet sensitive, very aware, who had insisted upon an unrelenting dialogue with himself, testing experience, and himself – perhaps too self-regarding, too hard on himself, as he was on the world. I marvelled that while living so much of his life with his back to the wall, existence in itself so often a triumph, digesting failed hopes, picking himself up and fighting on, he still could stand back and question the nature of living, setting himself apart in a necessary, hermetic isolation, insisting on his own exacting standards. But I mourned the high courage so often made futile by innocence – which I think he secretly admitted – by failure of judgement, especially of people, and failure of realism too, as in his refusal to compromise. I would forever think of him as recognising no measure of success or failure but his own – dreamer within a dream.

I wondered whether his demon possessed me too. After his death I felt a great loneliness, though I had seen him so little, truly seen him. I listened for his measured voice at my shoulder, a familiar in my own waking dream, like his a dream of perfectibility permitting no rest, as he had allowed himself none, whose pursuit did not bear examination. Not a comfortable inheritance.

Like the rest of his *dicta*, this one about the hole in the sock had many levels of meaning, but there was one that I must have absorbed, fearfully, even as a child – that the world made no sense. Life conformed to no logic. How could a hole in your sock make you a worse person? Where was the sense in people who thought like that?

He said: 'Remember that the sock is just an example. It could be anything, what you say, what you do, the way you live your life. But you *are* right – and also wrong. The people who think like that have the power to make *your* life easier or harder. You conform – or you suffer.'

'Is that right?' I asked again and again. 'should people have that power?'

'There's no "should" about it,' he said patiently. 'You mean: "Is it fair?" But who said life was supposed to be fair? Even the Almighty never said that! You can only say to yourself: "Do people behave like that?" And if the answer is yes, and it certainly *is*, then *you* must watch your step. If you don't conform, then you will suffer – there's nothing else to be said! I should know, for when I was young I thought I could stand out against the whole world for what I thought was right – and I was foolish, as young people are. So, believe me, I *know*, for I suffered plenty.'

'Father, why is the world like this?'

He put his broad hands on his knees and looked at me and through me, the blue-grey eyes softening, and smiled – but I knew it was not with happiness. 'If I knew that, I would be a very rich man, a very powerful man in the world.'

Then he told me another story. A little boy saw a bird fall from a tree and lie still on the ground. When he went to pick it up, it was dead. He went to the Rabbi, a wise-looking man with a long white beard: 'Tell me, Rebbe, that poor little bird did no one any harm, why did he have to die?' The Rabbi stroked his beard for many minutes: 'My son, there could be many reasons; perhaps the little bird was lazy and fell off the branch and died hitting the ground. Perhaps he had eaten too much. Perhaps a sudden wind blew him off. Or maybe the Almighty in His wisdom had a special reason to end his little life, perhaps ...' – and on and on he mused. The little boy listened respectfully till the Rabbi paused, then nodded, looking very worried: 'Yes, Rebbe, I see. You don't know either! Why did you not tell me sooner that there is no answer to the important questions?' And he went home sadly. 'What the Rabbi should have said,' father added, 'is this: "Who are we to ask for answers?" '

Another time, he said: 'Only the rich man can afford to look poor! He does not have to care what other people think of him. Riches bring power.'

Whether he ever talked to Lilian and Mary in this vein I never knew. I was too distant from them in those years, and in the early days I was too little to understand. That apart, such talk needed sympathy, and with Lilian and Mary burning with the conviction of father's guilt for mother's death – and therefore living in an armed truce with him – there was little sympathy. I am not even sure, as I write now, how honest they were in that judgement of him; it might have been a convenient excuse for mutinous behaviour. Father had no patience with rebellion: in his tradition, the father's word was law; compliance must be immediate, without reservation.

One evening when I was about twelve – Lilian and Mary were no longer living at home – I sat at the kitchen table tinkering with a crystal set that father had brought home from one of his jobs – presumably discarded in favour of the new valve-driven 'wirelesses'. The set worked well, and I had already spent many hours with the black bakelite head phones pressed to my ears, listening to crisp, 'correct' English voices telling stories from Savoy Hill, and dance bands measuring out gaiety in waltzes and foxtrots and quick steps. I decided to explore the insides of it. Like father, I was drawn to taking things apart to understand them, and putting them together again. The set was housed in a handsome cube-shaped case of polished light brown wood, held together by brass screws with broad flat shiny heads. Father sat by the coal range reading a paper and half-watching me, and I should have been warned by a certain restiveness in him. I had unscrewed the brass hinge holding the lid to the main box, and I was beginning to attack one of the brass screws on the lid itself when he said quietly, too quietly – which should also have alerted me: 'Don't take it to pieces. It is a good box.'

I must have forgotten that, from necessity, he always hoarded 'useful' objects for a rainy day, and that this handsome, solidly made wooden box doubtless had its place in his thrifty calculations. Without looking up, intent on fitting screwdriver to the screw head, I said: 'It's all right. I'll put it together again.'

The next moment he had sprung from the chair, seized the lid from my hands and smashed it on the edge of the table, the splinters flying all over the floor. His face was blanched as if he had become a ghost. I waited, every muscle contracted in fear, for him to tell me to take my glasses off, which he always did when about to slap my face. All he said was, the voice constrained in fury, crackling like brown paper: 'There you are! That shows you I don't want it for myself. You can do what you like with it.'

With each word the fury drained away from his voice, till at the end it was a dry whisper.

I looked at the broken pieces on the floor. The box was useless now. Glancing up, I saw him, broad-shouldered figure in blue shirt and braces, half turned away, wipe tears from his eyes – and was shaken with amazement and fear. What had I done, I asked myself – it must be something terrible, to have made my strong father cry. I wanted to tell him that he had made it impossible for me to put the box back together again, but I did not dare; besides, he knew it. He had said so. He had destroyed the box so that *no one* should have it; and the use he had had in mind for it was frustrated too. That must have been the first time I saw how shaken he was by the storms within him. He had wanted me to know that his reason for thwarting me was not a selfish one, but that his anxiety had been to preserve it for *us*, for the needs of the home – the intention had been good, but thinking back a few years later I saw that he must have been seized by shame at this evidence of the shifts he was driven to, the scrimping and saving, dependence on what other people discarded; and fury had blotted out words and reason. In violence he chastised *himself*. In the anti-climax of his action, its cathartic effect completed, he was full of remorse for striking terror into me, and for the destructive impulse uncontrolled; and tears had come because, with mother's healing hand gone, he was bereft of remedy. She had known, even in the worst of days, how to help him at these times, and lessen the emotional damage he could inflict.

Many years later, when in my writing I tried to make sense of the world, of people and manners, ideas and prejudices, as he had tried to do, it occurred to me that in part I was interpreting *him*, permitting *his* questioning mind, his scepticism, his divergent voice and images, to speak through me. Conversely, I tried to roll back time and speak to him as I often wished I could have spoken before – as if he could still hear me, the familiar that hovered behind my shoulder – and translate the contemporary world to him, as he had tried to do for me. As I wrote, I could imagine that I spoke to him. If I made *him* understand, I was on the right lines.

His sardonic presence was evident, for instance, in an Imaginary Conversation I wrote for radio: 'Socrates and Marx talk it over.' The two shades – Socrates played by Arthur Young and Marx by Leonard Sachs – encounter one another at Piccadilly Circus, observing a crowd that has gathered to celebrate the return of the winged statue to its pedestal after its banishment during the War. They reflect upon Man's fading will to pursue the great ideals. Socrates continues to proclaim his faith, though not too confidently, in the ultimate victory of truth and the pure vision, Marx to hope for one big push, a once for all fever of the will – as Jimmy Robinson had dreamed – to bring freedom; but when Socrates presses him to define freedom he shuffles and blusters. Father's shade understood well enough why, *faute de mieux*, I favoured Socrates – even though that concept of freedom was also suspect. The pursuit of truth, father murmured in my ear, was always a safer bet, but not everyone could stomach truth; in any case, he pointed out sadly, the crowd at Piccadilly Circus was interested in immediate, fleshly fulfilment, not in the higher symbolism of the winged god.

He was more in sympathy with a story I wrote for radio: *A Ticket for the Dog*, about a countryman and his dog in a railway compartment, the two in communion, the man in alert but relaxed contemplation, weaving a counterpoised pattern of life joined with past and future, the dog in an equal posture of stillness and attention. The wholeness is suddenly broken; the ticket collector slides back the compartment door with a crash, sees only a man and a dog, and demands the missing ticket.

In that countryman I portrayed someone whose like I had met, not often for he is rare, and seen in him gifts – or a discipline, a faith, qualities of acceptance, of wholeness and inner balance, that lifted his life far above the shifting sands of conventional strivings, towards the freehold of the self. The story had nothing to do with the sentimentalism of the Lawrentian school; I made the man a countryman because that figure, his contemplative posture in life, necessarily self-contained, fitted the virtues of balance I wanted to convey. The idea was suggested by an actual incident on a train; I had envied the man, and longed to find that secret key, and possess that freehold too. How I wished that father could have possessed it, earned a little contentment with himself. Distanced from him now, I began to understand him as he had longed to be understood, to feel that I could place myself at his side at last – transcending time and dust – *his* herald, *his* champion, and through him my own.

If only the emotions and the will worked hand in hand, how much less of life we would waste! Why had it taken me so many years to break free, so that I could make my way back and be close to him – and succeed only when he was dead?

He was much in my mind in the months before the hearing of my divorce petition, and even more on the day itself; and I wished he could have been with me, for he would have had some sardonic comment to make on the earthbound comedy of it all. He would have had to digest the shock of learning of the marriage itself, but apart from that the very idea of divorce would have plunged him into deep inner conflict. Life, he had often said, was 'indelible'; you could never behave as though some event had not happened: 'You don't get rid of a house you have lived in even if you burn it down! It is part of you for ever.'

His comments echoed in my mind as I lived through what I learned was the standard pre-divorce trauma, stretched on the rack of sleepless nights – the weighing of guilt, repetition of excuse and counter-excuse, conning every sign, every setback, since the first days of hope, asking myself whether *any* action I took, in any context, would ever be right. Why, for that matter, should the decision of a court change anything? Why should the law have any say at all in such a private matter? Since there were no children, questions of property or maintenance or custody did not arise. Kay being young, the law would see her, my lawyer said, as well able to support herself. Guilt, however, did appear to be relevant, a thought that endowed the whole undertaking with unreality. In those days, guilt or innocence were still crucial from the start – not, however, in the sense of whether I was right or wrong to have married Kay, or perhaps whether I had injured her by doing so; nor indeed whether I had injured *myself*.

When father had said to me 'Zai stolz' ('Be proud in yourself'), perhaps he realised that my fears and doubts in childhood, formed so much by him, had made me readier than I should have been to look for the beam in my own eye. Mr Giles, my lawyer, a paragon of patience and kindness, must have understood. I needed to be reassured that guilt did not always point one way – to me! Guilt, I was slow to learn, should be considered only when strictly necessary! Nevertheless, I must provide no opening for guilt to be attached to me, however unfairly – a point that would arise unexpectedly almost on the very threshold of the court.

Strange that there still remained a presumption that the man was more likely to be 'guilty' than the woman. The ethos of the time still saw woman as the 'weaker vessel', a stereotype that, surprisingly, remains strong even today. The woman did not originate action, but was the recipient of it. Action began with the man, and she, the soft, tender, responding spirit, was more likely – despite millennia of experience – to be sinned against than sinning. Even as I write, despite the march of feminism – perhaps even because of it – the myth of 'Woman as Victim' still informs our culture.

Mr Giles, wise, polished man of the world, had obviously pondered these quirks of prejudice. He would have agreed with Bill's comment, on this as on so much else: 'It's par for the course,' not worth the powder and shot of worrying about, and in any case it was too late; of course guilt in the 'pure' sense was in the end irrelevant to whether a marriage could continue or not, but the courts still had to go through the motions of caring about it! In such things, I could see, I was obviously a case of retarded development, but he would never, by even the slightest sign, have hinted at such a thing. I must not mind, he implied, but I needed to be steered through a disagreeable public performance, touching tender nerve-endings. It had to be done, and the game must be played by the rules. Mr Giles had seen so much. He went about the arrangements with the obvious wisdom, awareness of human nature, unruffled attention to detail, care to guard against the minutest possible pitfall, of the veteran *metteur-en-scène*. This last quality showed itself neatly in a seemingly tiny matter, for which I was quite unprepared – the question of a hat.

The day had arrived. We were in the ante-room of the court, a high, bleak brown-panelled chamber, waiting for my case to be called. We were next to 'go on', and I was lost in thoughts of what my performance would be like. I woke to find Mr Giles looking me up and down.

'By the way,' he whispered – there were a dozen or so others awaiting their turn – 'forgive me asking. You are Jewish, aren't you?'

'Yes.'

His brow clouded over and he drew his lips back, momentarily disconcerted, and I wondered what on earth had gone wrong, for clearly something *had*. 'You do wear a hat – I mean when you go to synagogue?'

The question, I saw later, probed deeply without appearing to do so. My mind still full of what I would say to the judge, I had no idea what he was driving at. 'I don't go to synagogue.' Then I added: 'In fact I don't possess a hat.'

'Oh,' he said. He looked worried, casting about for an answer to some new difficulty, turning the brim of his softly gleaming grey Homburg. 'The right impression is so important. One never knows what the judge may think. It's too late to go and get you a hat, or I would do so willingly. We'll be called any moment. Will you please take mine?'

I took the hat. Everything must be just so. The judge must see me as a thoroughly observant Jew – a *froomer Yeed* – careful, above all respectable, the 'right sort', one who stuck to the rules. Yet how could that be, for here I was married to a *Shiksah*! Still, the judge might not know that Kay was not Jewish – I had no idea how detailed was the information put before him; and so he might not grasp that irony. He might not even *care*, so long as certain conventions were observed. But the irony worried *me* – why? Later, much later, I saw that this performance disturbed me for other, deeper reasons; unawares, I was taking the first step in another full circle, to return to *being* the Jew that Mr Giles visualised. He might even have sensed that I was making this shift; and his question, and the business with the hat, were his response. In retrospect, I was grateful for this intuition; the hat was important to me too, though at the time I could not have said why.

As for the strategy of it, Mr Giles was of course right. He had to be. If I went into that court feeling that I had no identity, no loyalty, that the rules of the game meant little to me, something would be betrayed in my face, in my demeanour – the wrong impression.

Thinking of this after the performance, I heard father say: 'The world fears the one who does not conform. It's a dangerous thing to be. They say to themselves: "Does he know some secret we do not? We must see to it that he does not gain by it." '

There had been irony of a different kind, posing painful questions, many weeks earlier. Mr Giles dropped a bombshell. I must disclose adultery, even for the years of separation. So guilt did enter into it after all. But why – or rather how? Kay had been in Canada, as far as I knew, for several years – relationships I had had while waiting for the mystic seven years to elapse surely had no place in weighing the merits of an undefended case?

'Sorry,' he said. 'If you don't disclose, you can be in serious trouble with the court.'

'I can't do it.'

'Why not?'

'It's not fair on these women.' From his expression, he must have found me unbelievably naïve. 'Besides,' I added, 'I can't see why the court should want to know about them – in an undefended case like this.'

'The court treats it as privileged information,' he said patiently, studying me. Plainly, I needed help to quieten my conscience. Gently, he added: 'If you won't disclose, I can't act for you.'

And so, feeling like a traitor, the blackguard who kissed and told, I gave him the names, weighing each, though I did not mean to – what each might have meant, and what I had intended her to mean at the time. Each name took shape and turned and faced me, in a roseate half light, on a tufted rug in front of a gas-fire, or on a window seat looking out on to the moonlit Heath – why was it always *after* love-making? – and I was dreaming, not wishing to wake up, and wondering, half-ashamed, what had happened to the moment of total understanding a few minutes before, when time and circumstance did not exist. What had I found in her – or her, or her – or hoped to find, and she in me? There was no answer. Had we truly found the magic key? Why had we let it slip away? And why had it all come down to nothing more than this, becalmed here on a late October afternoon, in an office with hard-faced law books lining the walls, and beyond the windows red and brown autumn leaves blowing on the lawns of Lincoln's Inn, and imperturbable Mr Giles bent over his desk writing names on a sheet of stiff grey legal paper.

It seemed that I had put two phases of life in the wrong order. Instead of progressing from wild oats to undying love, I had done the reverse – first Annie and then Rachel, and now this roll-call! Surely I was too old for wild oats?

When the hearing began, I think I was so tense – with fear and, yes, a kind of revulsion – that for the few minutes it lasted I must have been in a protective day-dream, distancing myself from it all. Then the unthinkable happened, for I heard Mr Giles say something about 'exercise of discretion'. I think I had hoped that the catalogue would not be mentioned at all. Now, here it was – and I stood shivering, gripping the Homburg hat, wondering what on earth I was supposed to say about those names. I waited for a cue from Mr Giles, but none came. Instead, he seemed to be saying to the judge, gently, carefully, as an elderly gentleman of the old school might talk of a young nephew in a scrape – here was a young man in normal vigour of life in a difficult time … who hoped for the understanding of the court … The judge, a small compact man, wearing gold-rimmed glasses, leaned over his desk studying a paper in a folder before him. When he spoke, he seemed to make a public declaration rather than to refer to my case in particular. He appeared to dismiss Mr Giles's kindly plea. This was behaviour verging on the promiscuous. As such it must be deplored! I dared not breathe. So it was all for nothing? What was I going to do now? Then I realised he was speaking again – one short sentence, of which I heard only a few words: 'in the exercise of my discretion ... decree nisi ...'

The conventions had been affirmed to be right, and maintained strongly in their place. And from that position of unwavering rectitude, I had been shown mercy. Who was I to complain?

Making our way down the stairs towards the street, Mr Giles said: 'Care for a dish of tea?'

We walked in silence to a tea shop at the foot of Chancery Lane. Inside, he murmured: 'Mind if I have my hat back?'

Startled, I handed it to him. We talked of other things.

We parted on the doorstep half-an-hour later. He shook my hand, and the faintest glimmer of a smile crossed his face. As I went along Fleet Street, I might have been walking in a deserted field, my steps light as air – and I wondered why I felt such a sense of release, for in truth nothing tangible had happened. I was still the same. But I had a feeling, still to be made conscious, that I had shed something other than the marriage, passed through another door entirely, and was on the threshold of a world where I had been a stranger for a very long time, and never thought to re-enter. I walked all the way back from Fleet Street, up Kingsway and through Bloomsbury and across Regent's Park, unaware of distance or time, and ran up the stairs to my new flat on the first floor above the fur shop, as if to a tower in the clouds. It seemed that I had been a prisoner for years, and now the doors and windows were flung open, and freedom – if that was what it was – flooded in, astringent, challenging.

The comedy of the hat ran through my mind again and again, like a film sequence wound back and re-played. Mr Giles could not possibly have foreseen its significance for me – and I myself did not perceive it in all its strange colourings till much later. In making that public affirmation of the Jewishness this marriage was meant to cancel for ever, I consented, in all seriousness as it turned out, to become a Jew again – and did so wearing a Gentile's hat.

8

What *is* God up to?

Why did I wait several years, until shortly before the divorce hearing, to move away from the Hampstead Garden Suburb where Kay and I had lived for most of the marriage? I am still not sure of the answer. The events were so close in time that they *must* have been perversely linked. Staying on in that flat had been a waste of years, the will and the mind at odds. Was there a mysterious element that I had to find and understand, once and for all, before I could move away – which enchained me to trace and re-trace the lost years of the marriage? If so, had I found it in the end? *Were* those years lost – and what was loss and what was gain? One speaks of 'circumstances conspiring', a euphemism for Fate, or a pretence that what had happened was chance alone, and that the will had played no part in it. Perhaps I simply lacked the certainty to break with the past, not solely with the Kay period but with that tug-of-war with my Jewishness in which she had had her place, but whose beginnings were far back in the Gorbals – like the invalid who, cured of a chronic ailment at last, cannot bear its absence?

Even today if I visit the Hampstead Garden Suburb – which I seldom have reason to do – every road and landmark, every pathway across the Heath, has the imprint of Kay and her family. Our flat in the Central Square looked across to Henrietta Barnett School, *her* school till she went up to Oxford. Her parents had a house about two hundred yards away, round the corner in Hampstead Way near the Heath Extension, until she went to Canada a few years before the divorce, and they moved to Bournemouth. Did I wait for them all to leave the scene before I could do so? In retrospect a different explanation occurred to me, not reassuring. It was a stage – there would be others – when I pretended to halt time. It would wait for me while I plunged into writing in the free hours after the office, turned inwards, forgot the world, let things happen; a dangerous state of mind, for I would surface many months later, a piece of writing completed it is true, but with an uneasy feeling that I had allowed the world to drift past me too far and too fast, that I had let myself down.

On my first morning in the new flat in St John's Wood High Street, I awoke feeling that I had come home to a palace that had long been awaiting me in the imagination, a purifying place that was solely mine – the very first. It was as yet Spartan, large echoing spaces in which pieces of basic furniture stood isolated. In the lofty bedroom, with its stately latticed bow window about eight feet wide, uncurtained and hung for the moment with sheets of brown paper that rustled in movements of air from an ill-adjusted casement, and long low window seat, the only contents were a double divan bed, a bulky black telephone on the bare floorboards, and an old hinged tapestry screen that stood in the middle of a vast emptiness between the end of the bed and the far wall, and served for the time being as clothes horse – a surreal, disorientated grouping. The rooms were in a straight line. The bedroom faced the street, and from it a tiny lobby led to the sitting room, its floorboards bare too; from it, three broad wooden steps led down, through a wide archway, to the kitchen-dining area, and beyond the kitchen was another lobby, leading to a minute bathroom, where I had installed a heated towel rail, and an infra-red heater on the wall above the bath. Hot water came from an Ascot gas-fired boiler. Throughout the kitchen-dining-room, bathroom and connecting lobby, white floor tiles reflected light from the tall sash windows and threw it on to the newly painted white walls. All was agleam. Compared with our Gorbals flat, which could have fitted easily into the bedroom alone, here was luxury. Everything, even the old furniture, sang of a fresh beginning.

If I had been determined to find a total physical break with the past, the flat was as near as I could have got to fresh bricks and mortar. Not only was it a new conversion – a floor of a three-storey Victorian house – but I was its first occupant. Everything was new, layout and partitioning, plaster and paint, wallpaper, equipment, a blank sheet on which to write the future. All was open, crisp, airy – fresh resinous smells of timber, of newly-dried plaster and paint; breath of a new birth. Here was a place that was linked to no one. The few pieces of furniture were mine alone – some of it new, but even the second-hand pieces affirmed only an earlier, unidentifiable time with no claims on memory – the bed and screen, a few odd chairs, long low black-enamelled coffee table, beech-wood studio couch with cushions in grey and black hopsack, oak writing-desk, a small set of white wooden bookshelves and a large book stack, about seven feet high by six wide, that I had newly built with slotted angle-iron, painted white, and placed against the kitchen unit to screen it from the sitting room.

There was one welcome feature in common with the Gorbals flat; the street outside was vibrant with life. In the Central Square of the Suburb, with its bare lawns of poor grass fringed with gloomy privet, brooded over by the dark Nordic bulk of St Jude's, one looked out of the window and saw hardly a soul pass, especially depressing on a grey day in autumn or winter. St John's Wood High Street had not yet taken on the anonymous metropolitan ambience of boutiques and 'atmosphere' restaurants, which would happen in a few years' time; it still had the unique personality of a village street, or perhaps a small town street, full of the bustle of local comings and goings. Across from my bow window was a dog-grooming shop with the sign 'shampoodle'. Nearby, appropriately, was a pastry shop with little polished tables on a raised platform in the rear, where people of the quarter, many of whom in dress and manners suggested Sadler's in Vienna, met for coffee and tea and gossip. In dramatic contrast, further up the street was an unpretentious eating place, whose long bare tables and hissing tea urn gave it the atmosphere of a railway refreshment room, which served excellent fish and chips and steak and kidney pie. A shop with the name Quirk over it sold hand-made chocolates and fine cigars. There was a hairdresser, a wine shop, two chemists, fruit and provision shops, a butcher, a fishmonger, an old-fashioned drapers' with a faded blue-grey shop front, once presumably royal blue, in whose tall dingy windows hung blouses, skirts and dresses, children's clothes, cards of knitting and darning wool, men's shirts and ties; an art materials shop, a newsagent, two pubs. Diagonally across the street to the south were leafy gardens, really a small grove, part of the old burial ground of St John's Wood church; the trees were said to be all that remained of the original wood of the Knights of St John that gave the district its name. There, on warm weekend days, I would sit and read in a peaceful arbour where trees and shrubbery muffled the noise of traffic, then far less heavy than now, passing the long grey brick wall of Lord's Cricket Ground in Wellington Road.

When I explored the streets of the neighbourhood, beating the bounds of my new parish, I discovered two synagogues within a few hundred yards of the High Street, but I cannot remember being aware of their existence when I decided to take the flat. One was Orthodox, the other Liberal; the most obvious differences, from a layman's point of view, were that the Orthodox continued the traditional segregation of women worshippers, and used more Hebrew in the ritual. I had no conscious intention of visiting either, especially as I had forgotten most of my Hebrew, in which I had once been fluent; however a piece of paper pinned to a board outside one of them, the Liberal, was to trigger my return journey.

In the weeks after moving in, as I put the place in order, fitted curtain rails and curtains, put down floor covering, made a wardrobe cupboard in the bedroom, in an alcove between the old chimneybreast and the outer wall, I had a feeling of being physically on the move, as in a train leaving a station. Each task completed, the flat took me further away from the past, and in particular from the marriage – scenes from which returned at intervals, fleetingly, in minute definition, like photographs magically enlarged in one's hand and thrown upon a screen. I must have conjured them for a final understanding, to see the marriage beyond all doubt, in every inward detail, before I sent it from me for ever, or rather to its place in a distant archive of the heart. In those instants of close vision, incidents came to mind in retrospect incredible; and the pain was fresh.

Kay, especially when we were with our friends, or rather *her* friends that I thought were mine too, was so troubled by my 'differentness' that she was impelled to distance herself from it and at the same time explain it away, as one explains away an embarrassing mannerism in a child; she did so by attributing it to my being Jewish, in a sense explaining *me* away! Though she made the comments with a habitual tincture of sardonic humour, the aim was serious – as it had to be, I later realised, if she was to live at peace with that Nazi arm-band, treasured so faithfully. I saw now that my response to being 'explained away' had been foolish, and base. In private I had often ignored the offending remark – as when, looking at a photograph of me, she said tartly that I looked 'too Jewish'; or I brushed it aside with some facetious sally, inwardly hurt. When her friends were present, taking their cue from her, I pretended to share the ready amusement, persuading myself that to shrug the barb away would cancel the poison. I saw now that Kay's words had borne no conscious malice; she could not help herself. She acted in her proper character, as the person she was. 'Jewishness', however she defined it to herself, did worry her very much. To call that a 'fault' was beside the point; I should have been mature enough to understand it for what it was long before – and see it as permanent. For her part, she must have persuaded herself that these unwelcome attributes of mine were superficial, separable from the rest of me, and that I could be persuaded, or teased, into shedding them. How could I have been so craven, who had had the spirit to confront so much else in my life without flinching, to shrink from behaving in *my* true character as she did in hers? Why did I not insist – as she rightly did for herself – that I be accepted as the person *I* truly was?

If only I had heeded father's advice and been *stolz*! Plainly I had been far from ready for that. I would have had to ask myself too many uncomfortable questions: why I pretended not to mind being politely 'put down' for my Jewishness, for being *me* – for that matter, why I was among them at all! I should have turned and walked away, at the very start, from such captious treatment, as Alec would not have hesitated to do in comparable circumstances, he who had seen *his* identity so clearly. Instead I had been false to myself, imagined that I could be the person I truly was *without* my 'differentness' – that alloy of subtle elements, the movement of the earth in many generations, upbringing, the Gordian knot of influences that was the Gorbals, and another essence, call it spirit, emotional inheritance, what did the name matter? What part of that alloy was my Jewishness I did not know, but even that was irrelevant; it was interfused with me in every sense, and in refusing to see that, I aided and abetted Kay in *her* prejudice. It was hard to face that truth. Its poison would not go away.

Bits of the Gorbals were forgotten, truths it had taught me, which would have made life easier, or less likely to hurt, if I had taken them to heart. They returned in unexpected form and caught me unawares. Since in the Gorbals everyone I knew lived on the insecure margin between sufficiency and starvation, no one possessed anything worth coveting, or even noticing – and so, as Karl Marx pointed out, referring to the proletarian, the only thing of value a person possessed was himself. You had to value him for his qualities – there being nothing else – and that 'value', the proper respect for himself alone, was his due. Bernard reminded me of this one day after an incident in the new flat that I should not have allowed to upset me. Foolishly, I had forgotten, or chosen not to notice, that this new world did judge you by your possessions. I should have been prepared for people to come to my flat as guests and cost out its contents, and presumably the flat itself, and in effect put a price ticket on *me*. It should not have been a shock, but it was.

One Sunday afternoon I invited a few people in for tea. Apart from Bernard they were merely acquaintances, recently met in a world into which I had stumbled by chance, that of the charity committee; having accepted hospitality in various houses, I now opened my own door, a timid flat-warming for a new beginning.

One of the young women, Naomi, about twenty-five, voluptuous, with high brunette colouring and brilliant dark eyes, sat erect on the studio couch and looked about her in unconcealed appraisal, like a house agent valuing a property. Chin probing the air, deep-set eyes beamed like hooded searchlights, she focused hard on each item – the new cotton curtains with blue and white lozenge grid of flowers, the Old Master prints, the rush matting, a large globe lampshade of red raffia – and, as her gaze swung round the room, nodded to herself, lips tightening.

Call it insensitivity, boorishness – I had certainly swallowed much worse over the years, but this time I knew I could not. What new certainty had come? I interrupted her examination of the room: 'Have you noticed that some people, on their first visit to a house, quite openly look round and cost out everything in it?'

Wide-eyed, she said: 'Don't *you*? I do it all the time.'

'So I see! No, I don't. The value of what people own is of no interest to me. Either I like them or I don't. But tell me, having valued your host's possessions – and by inference *him* too – does the result affect your attitude to him?'

'Well it might …' The point went home. She glanced down at her hands, broad, stubby, empty of rings: 'I never thought about it that way. It's – it's just a habit.'

Bernard stayed on after the others had gone, and we sat in the darkening room looking out over the roofs, watching the sky change from cool autumn blue to dove grey. 'I heard what you said to her.' He shook his head. 'All the same, she's not alone! Everybody does it. She's just not clever enough to conceal it.'

'Or too arrogant to want to.'

He shrugged. 'Maybe – but who is she anyway? Let it wash over you. To hell with them!'

'I've taken enough.'

He laughed. 'We used to say in Spain, battlefield humour: "It's a brave man that says that – wait till the next load of shit comes flying, and get your head down quick!" '

The sitting-room faced east. The early evening light of the turning year weakened, and the slanting sun was reflected into the room from the windows of the redbrick school in Barrow Hill Road at the back, and rays of reddish yellow lit fainter gleams on the china scattered on the black coffee table. Here, at the rear of the building, all was quiet. Bernard sat in a white wicker chair looking towards the window, and the reflected beams of fire, dimmed as they returned to us, slanted upon him too. He wore a soft white shirt and red tie, fine grey worsted suit, the broad shoulders jutting angularly, square features lean and ruddy and alert, still the soldier – and still, as he would have put it, soldiering on.

He said: 'Don't get this out of perspective. This lot are no different from the *Goyeem*. I should know! I negotiate with both. The bosses, Jews or non-Jews, are all materialists – every one of them! And remember, these people are not the ones we used to know in the Gorbals, who were one generation away from *der heim*. This lot are middle-class! Unlike *us* in the old Gorbals days, they *know* where their next meal is coming from! So for us – for you and me – it's hard to stomach them. We can't help comparing this world with the Gorbals, where there was no point in costing people out – none of us possessed anything worth putting a price on.'

The reflected sunbeams touching him must have taken my eye to something unfamiliar; and then I saw for the first time, here and there on the dark head, white hairs. Surely we were still the same *people* we were in the Gorbals long ago? I felt no different! Yet even to say that was to say goodbye to our youth. Not long ago our past had not been remote; to the young the past was bound up with the present, and only the present was real – and the future very nearly so. A hard black line had been drawn across the sky.

He looked at the reddened windows of the school. 'You think you are moving *back* by mixing with this lot! There's no "back" to go to. Just look at them.' He gestured to the teacups and plates of biscuits, scattered on the low table in the casual displacement of people talking among themselves. 'It is a different world. They are the second, or maybe third, generation away from the East End where the first lot landed from *der heim*! A million miles away from the world we knew in the Gorbals! Nothing is the same – nothing. They don't *know* what it was like to live in a stinking tenement with rats running around the ash pits and under the floor boards, when people were just *people* – that was all they had, themselves! And you were happy enough to get a *cup* of tea when you visited anybody, never mind a saucer with it! And you valued a person for what he was – you *had* to. These people don't want to know about that! We're talking to them from far, far away – from a world they will never see, whose values they do not want to understand.'

He told me of an exchange with one of the other young women – Esther, petite, restless with imprisoned energy, with a habit of moving her right hand as she talked so that the numerous gold charms on a bracelet sounded a crisp rattle. She looked about her with a brittle challenge. For her the world moved too slowly.

'She asked me what I "did". When I said "Union officer", she looked startled and said, "That's unusual, I didn't know …" – and stopped, not knowing what to say. "Didn't know what?" I asked. I wasn't going to let her off lightly. Flustered, she said: "I've never met a Jewish boy who worked for a union." So I asked her what sort of people she did know. "Oh, people in business, barristers, accountants, and so on." Then she tried to get her own back: "If you're working for the workers, you can't be very well paid?" "And who do *you* work for?" I asked. "I don't work for anybody. I've got a dress business." "And who gave you the money to start it? Your father?" "Of course, what's so strange about that?" "Nothing – unfortunately!" I said. "Nothing at all." '

The fiery light had gone from the school windows. Soft grey dusk spread into the room. I switched on the great red raffia centre light and a table lamp with a slender, turned wooden base, the first item I had bought with my scholarship money in Oxford. I put a bottle of gin on the coffee table between us, with two small bottles of tonic water, and glasses; we poured our own. He studied his glass, gently swirling the contents, and murmured, 'Yes – this too – we *have* come a long way! None of *this* in the old days, eh? A mouthful of Kiddush wine on *Yomtov* if you were lucky, and if you weren't you didn't miss it!'

He gestured to the teacups again. 'This lot *are* no better, and no worse than anybody else. They embody the good old Victorian middle-class values as their parents and grandparents found them here – Galsworthy, Trollope, and the rest – where it's important to know what people are worth in money terms; and whom you mix with is important, for you must keep clear of your inferiors lest you get re-infected and slide back to where you started from. And you must flaunt these middle-class values too, for that tells the world that you have arrived; and that's another reason why they don't want to be reminded of the past – the past that you and I belong to – because their certainty is too new, too vulnerable.'

I raised my glass: '*Lachayyeem*!' – your health.

'*Lachayyeem*!'

We sat in silence, a lonely rearguard long separated from the main force, waiting for a sign – and watched the last light fade from the sky.

He said, 'Paradoxically, even their pretences of *Yeedishkeit* are hard to stomach.' He gave a short laugh. 'That's rich isn't it – me talking of *Yeedishkeit*! As to finding the old bearings again, where are they? Not with this lot! You and I didn't value the old traditions at the time. We scoffed at them with our wonderful juvenile logic – but now that they are gone, we see that they *were* bearings of a kind – even little things like the *Shabbos Goy* to light the gas on Friday night, or walking to the synagogue on Shabbos, could bring to mind old, powerful values, that is, if you *wanted* to be reminded. How many of them even bother to park the car a little distance away, so as to be seen arriving on foot? So what on earth do these people amount to? Who are they?'

There was no answer – or rather we had already arrived at it, but by separate ways. As he had often said of late, these things – the irrational, magical landmarks – remained close to the heart. Walking to synagogue was, of course, irrational, but that was not the point, which was the bearing of witness to eternal verities, so that the compass needle should swing back to the true course – with which such observances were linked, or should be. Bernard had been pulled away from them, firstly by his father – the extreme rationalism of the Kropotkinian anarchist, for whom religion, as a moral code and no more, could be replaced by 'right thinking'; but also by his own early Marxism. Yet here was the old internal tug-of-war resurgent – between reason and the thirsty heart. Logic was no help.

'I doubt if you and I can ever go back to being *froom*' – religious. 'How *can* we, after what's happened to the Jews in Europe? How could God allow that to happen? – God the Almighty, the all pow-erful, the all merciful? Was He punishing them as He did Sodom and Gomorrah? What about the millions of Gentiles that Stalin slaughtered? God must have done that too! As for faith, I don't know what it is any more, or rather what it's supposed to be. I *used* to, but I don't now.'

'I haven't thought of these things for years.'

'Oh yes, you have. I've seen it in things you've said.'

'Maybe I have without knowing it. I've been thinking that I want to write about all this – why decent behaviour and faith are so far apart.'

He said, 'Remember how we used to say when we were young-sters – If only people would *live* by the morality of religion, most of the unhappiness in the world would go? There are a few people left who try to do that – and for the Jews that means the humanity of the *Talmud* and the Rabbinic commentaries, but it's a losing battle. Maybe there's still a chance – with people thinking of the Bomb and Doomsday – to frighten them into a return to right principles and the decent life. I doubt it. But there's no harm in trying.'

I would remember his words many years later, when Father Tom Corbishley, the eminent Jesuit, and I wrote a manifesto appealing for religious leadership, in all the faiths, to be refocused upon the specific in personal behaviour. That manifesto was the theme of a conference at Church House, Westminster – which, alas, Tom Corbishley did not live to attend – inspired by an address I gave to an informal group of members of the United Nations Association and the Council of Christians and Jews. At a preliminary meeting leading up to the conference, a distinguished clergyman, uncom-fortable with the thesis, protested: 'It's not up to us to tell people it's wrong to steal – they know that already!' Yes – the higher general-ities were less disturbing.

'Don't kid yourself, though,' Bernard said. 'That idea has been tried and fizzled out in futility – remember Dr Buchman and the Oxford Group before the War? Besides, the clergy don't want it either; *not* for them the old thunder from the pulpit. That puts them on the spot individually! They prefer to stick to the higher platitudes – it's safer.'

I refilled his glass. 'Thank God you and I haven't any children. What a mess to hand on to them.'

'Amen to that. Unless that old villain the Life Force plays a trick on us! Oh yes, it's a hellish world all right – talk about Dante's *Inferno*. D'you remember those pictures in the papers of the liberated concentration camps and British soldiers shifting huge piles of dead bodies with bulldozers? That seems only yesterday – and now there's the beginning of a campaign to persuade the world that the massacre of the Jews, the gas chambers, the death trains and all the other bestialities didn't happen, and that the whole thing was a slander invented by the Jews for their own ends! What *is* God up to?'

9

Time Machine in Grosvenor Square

When the marriage foundered, many 'friends' faded away like morning mist. That was 'par for the course' too. Bernard, Bill, Werner, and the rest of my own friends, remained solid; in fact Werner came closer than he had been while the marriage lasted. I had sensed that it troubled him, but he was too correct to put his feelings into words. In action, however, he did show it, for I saw less of him during the Kay years – and that too I had been slow to understand. He was too busy with his scientific work, the management of his considerable financial interests and his amours. When we did meet, though the old warmth remained, there was also an elusive constraint. After the divorce, however, his relief was plain. Mysteriously in sympathy, he too felt freer. He became less busy, and I saw him often in London.

'My friend,' he said, 'you had your reasons, and I could say little at the time. I knew you were unhappy, and at a loss what to do – and it was hard to be silent. I can see you are still blaming yourself. That is dangerous. I am so much older than you. I do know.'

I heard Rachel's voice railing against his infidelity to his wife, conjuring the Furies to punish him, and I thought of the retribution – who could say it was not? – in the death of his wife and children. He had shown no guilt at the time. Sorrow, yes, but no more; a toughness that made me think of Alec's steely confrontation of life. Here was the first sign that Werner *had* blamed himself, and did so still.

'They say that time brings a consoling perspective, but' – he pressed thin lips together – 'it takes longer than I can stomach. As for you – you are young still – I am sure it will be quicker!'

I thought about 'quicker'. How could you compare one person's trauma with another's? What *was* a consoling perspective? When his wife and children were killed, he had been about the age I was now, yet after all these years that perspective had still not come to him; why should I be luckier? His words sounded like a bromide. But they were not; rather a lament for himself, for the age he now was, for the too-swift race of time. This also was unlike him. The man I knew had never shown self-pity. What else had changed in him?

Now, in spite of his words, he talked about my marriage – the unanswerable questions it posed. He did so, however, with an unexpected force, as if some other prompting lay beneath. 'Marrying out is not easy for *us* to contemplate, who have seen what prejudice can do – and how deeply rooted it is, even among the most humane and cultured. I have been thinking about Eliot and Jew hatred – a compassionate man one would say, cultured, civilised? And yet he can write poison like this:

> The rats are underneath the piles.
> The Jew is underneath the lot.

It is rumoured that Ezra Pound, bitterly anti-Jewish as you know, persuaded Eliot to moderate or suppress even worse than that! But that was only in what Eliot *published*! It could not change him as a *man* – he must still feel that "The Jew is underneath the lot" – and as you know there is more of it in his work, images of the Jew identified with mud and slime and general malignity. Culture and civilisation do not count for much where the dark gods reign! Can we wonder that Rosenberg and the rest of them in Germany were subhuman where Jews were concerned?'

For how many years had he wanted to say this to me? How inexplicable my marriage must have been, how wounding.

Perhaps sensing my thoughts, he had gone silent. Slowly the pale features relaxed. Almost visibly he hauled himself back from the depths, and the old, urbane, insouciant manner surfaced again: 'Enough of that! Think of yourself as a reconstituted bachelor and start to enjoy life. You will marry again. I am sure of that. You are young – unlike me! You will marry a Jewish girl, of that I am also certain. As for me, I doubt if I will marry again. It is too late. Commitment frightens me now.'

Mention of his age, especially the sad tone of it, startled me. I remembered the cruel gibes of youth in the Gorbals – when a man began to lament his age he was 'giving up'. For me, Werner was as he had always been. Until this moment I had felt that I too was still the age I was when I first rode into Oxford on my bike in that autumn deluge long ago. Could it be nearly twenty years since we had first met, strangers to that world, he from Buchenwald and I from the Gorbals, at the tennis courts by the river, a day fresh in my mind for ever as the first breath of freedom – the crisp rustle of autumn leaves, rounded clouds like bulging spinnakers scudding across the broken sky of bleached blue and taking my old world with them, a new life written across it? Werner looked much as I remembered him then, poised like a dancer, the long sallow features smooth and taut except for the lines, deeper now, slanting from nose to the sides of the mouth, and the dark brown hair turning to steel grey, now further back on the crown of the head.

How could *he* talk longingly of commitment – which had seemed to have no place in such a life, rich, free of the treadmill of earning a living, free to do exactly as he pleased? Perhaps I had taken that debonair, unconcerned exterior too much at face value? What had changed – in him? – in me?

Partly it *was* age. Unawares, we had outgrown the cynicism of the time, a *zeitgeist* that saw commitment, or behaviour that suggested it, as dull, old hat, naïve – a reaction from the war and the hollowness that had preceded it, a retreat from faith and its symbols. For that matter the world was still gripped in the nihilism of post-1918. When a young poet stood at Piccadilly Circus in the pose of a busker and went through the motions of 'playing' a stringless violin, many people thought he made a significant statement, as if thirty years had not elapsed since the tumultuous eruption of Dada in Paris. Topsy-turvy solipsism was in the air, shortly to be a modish theme of the Sixties: 'Be! Do your own thing! – the world will be better off' – meaning 'Let someone else run life – we haven't time for that!', a bizarre inversion of Villiers de l'Isle

Adam's 'Living! We'll leave that to the servants', three-quarters of a century before.

I had seldom been aware of the age distance between us, but now I saw him in his proper generation; and age was suddenly important, for him and for me. His words about commitment were a comment upon desire too, and on fulfilment that still eluded him. In his privileged early life, he had had little interest in the world apart from the intellectual chase of science, dilettante pleasures, and the passing delights he could easily buy. He had tasted the egotistic life to the full. His was the old European analytical scepticism, tinctured with optimism, of the Enlightenment. Buchenwald and the rest had added bitterness which, usually hidden, burned relentlessly within. Now something new drove him – he who had grown up with no knowledge of being 'driven', a feeling beyond all logic, a hunger to serve something other than himself. He needed a compelling purpose, a cause, to take him along the next stage of living.

Mention of commitment had startled me for another reason. I began to understand his guilt, his sense of wasted time, for I was guilty too – for letting the *zeitgeist* drive *me*, an excuse for neglect, for sporting with the Bohemian life, following the example of people who could well afford to waste time, as I could not – turning away from the world until I felt well-armed enough to confront it. Now, an awakened Rip van Winkle, I looked for old, recognisable things, deeply set in the earth – solid places, like the sprinter's starting-blocks, from which to leap forward once again. I thought of John Buyers writing to me long ago in his wise, cautionary way, of 'the progress of the soul' as the prime task of life, the measure against which all desire and action must be judged. What progress had *my* soul made since I had left the Gorbals?

I did not know it, but there *was* a cause awaiting its hour, a seed of long ago when, as a little boy, I had stood at the high black windows looking out into the night sky, and soared away over the roof-tops into the cool logic of the stars, and vowed that I would transmute that breathless wonder into new light for the whole world, a new view of life – *how*, I had no idea; I waited for a sign.

It came, to be fully understood later, in the scholarship essay where, replying to the question, 'Has science increased human happiness?' I had answered 'No'. Now, as I looked across at Werner and wondered what *his* commitment was going to be, I did not know that mine was already formed, that I would take up that 'No' where I had left the insight incomplete – or thought I had – and elaborate it, show that the technological or consumerist life, unguided by spirituality or a sense of the necessary wholeness of living, destroyed the ethical capital inherited from the past, and brought loneliness, futility, the opposite of fulfilment.

Unawares, I *was* on the move. I would find a way. Through work in the Third World, writing, international debate – *inter alia*, as an invited participant in the UN Conference on the Strategies of Development – I would propose a new understanding of what 'fulfilment' and 'quality of life', ambiguous terms misleadingly used to give people hope, should mean. A paper of mine challenging current development policies as destructive, *Perspectives of Fulfilment*, would find its way round the world. Searching for European object lessons – to show where we had *been* and how we had lost our bearings – I would find one in the mountains of Calabria and go and live there, in an Italo-Albanese community whose first language was Albanian, descendants of Albanians under Skanderbeg who had fled across the Ionian Sea from the Turks in the fifteenth century. Enclosed by physical isolation, language, religion – the *rito Greco* – its perspectives were rooted several generations back in time, in the nineteenth century's belief in the untarnished benefit of indiscriminate Progress. From this intimate experience would come my book: *The Net and the Quest*, and the BBC film: *S. Giorgio's Bitter Fruits*. There would be much more, a flux of commitment. Many years would pass, however, before I traced its inspiration to those Gorbals dreams, to the mind of the ragged boy trudging to the Mitchell Library after sixteen hours of hard graft in the factory, to that 'No' – to a purpose that refused to be denied.

Werner was silent. Did he too wonder where his uncommitted years had gone? What had *I* to show for mine? Where was all that original energy that had driven me away from the Gorbals?

The novel, *A Parcel of their Fortunes*, a surrealist journey, had been a near miss; a British publisher wanted to bring it out jointly with an American house, but that prospect gradually faded, and in the end my own interest in the book faded too. I had written two more, and was working on another. As for earning my living, I had had little idea of career in the conventional sense; work was only to pay for writing time.

One day, when the marriage was in its death throes, the British Council proposed to post me to Calcutta to help open a new office there; perhaps I should have gone, but the prospect of coping with the final trauma of the marriage while living in the confined world of an expatriate community was too daunting. I did not go. Some time later, after one of the Council's periodic budgetary battles with the Government – via its paymaster the Foreign Office – many posts at headquarters, including mine, were axed. The Council, however, was helpful, and through its good offices the North Atlantic Treaty Organisation offered me the appointment of Head of Conference Section in Paris. Again I was deterred, wrongly I am now convinced; I thought it better to stay in London till I got a divorce and found peace of mind. Had I foreseen that this process, as the law then stood, would be as lengthy as it proved, I would have accepted the NATO appointment; apart from its essential interest in that crucial time in the Cold War, it would have been valuable preparation for the international line I was destined to follow.

Instead I took stop-gap jobs. After a period as editor at the Institute of Management, finding I could write easily to order, I moved into public relations, mainly for the agricultural industry – a varied role that included writing speeches for leading figures in it, and interpreting the Byzantine thinking of people in high places. There were fascinating and disturbing insights behind the scenes of government, politics, business, opinion-making in general and the workings of pressure groups in particular. Moving in that predatory jungle was a new education in cynicism, in the difference between the public and private faces of people and the interests they fought for – where statements of intention, avowals of principle, were assumed to be disingenuous as a matter of course, and often intended both to cloud the true aim and provide an escape route through a verbal quibble in case of need, where the only criterion for adopting a manoeuvre was the probability of success – once again: 'the end justified the means'. Yet I was part of it, and tasted virtuoso pleasure, for a time, in using the required skills well. Now and then I caught an unsettling image of myself – weighing words, their timing and presentation, to fit a particular policy, and pretending, too easily, that the aim was public-spirited – I was a mercenary in a war devoid of morality. A story went round the advertising agencies, perhaps revealing a twinge of conscience, that nicely summed up the mercenary's position – sycophantic compliance, and robust pride in the sure deployment of his persuasive art. The creative director of an advertising agency was entertaining a prospective client in the agency bar. After many drinks, the latter suddenly asked: 'What time is it?' The creative director saw his opportunity: 'What time would you like it to be?'

I was to write about the craft of the mercenaries, and the influence they exert upon society, in my book *The New High Priesthood*, on which I comment later.

I often thought of those far-off Sunday mornings at the speakers' pitch at the gates of Glasgow Green beside the Clyde – what was the hope that drew us there? – where Bernard and the Clincher and the other evangelists shouted out their gospels of redemption. Despite hunger and cold, how dear all values had then seemed! Standing there in my rags and looking across a meadow to the red sandstone railway bridge sprawled across the river, its bombastic turrets and crenellations proclaiming overweening confidence in power, the 'devil take the hindmost' stance of high Victorianism, it epitomised all the indifference in the world, and I said to myself: 'One day I will break its grip.' Yet here I was sustaining it.

I thought of Harold Laski, when I asked him to support my proposed study of pressure groups, cynically steering me away from it with the excuse that everything was already known about them. It was not true, and he knew it – as he knew that I was powerless, then, to challenge him. The truth was that the Labour Party, like any other operator on society, *needed* pressure groups in the power game, and it was not in his interests, high in Labour's leadership as he then was, to have these instruments of policy examined too closely – their concealed influence, often dubious methods, and potentially malign power to 'bend' opinion. He was not alone in seeing their political importance. I had been naïve to expect him to admit it.

Now, ironically, I would have been well-placed to make that study from the inside. The skills and calculations were familiar day by day. As a very minor example of the tricks of the trade, I knew that certain letters to the press on particular issues of the day were 'inspired', drafted and sent out to sympathisers for them to sign and post, supposedly spontaneous utterances from the grass roots – for the simple reason that I had written them myself. But it was too late. The right time for me to have done the exposé would have been at the moment of inspiration all those years before, soon after the war.

Laski, charming and warm, presented himself as the opposite of ruthless and self-seeking – the plain man's egg-head, honest, broken. Others in the power game, however, proclaimed their Machiavellianism with pride, and perhaps achieved more, or what *they* valued more, by doing so. One was Sir James Turner, created Lord Netherthorpe. After being President of the National Farmers' Union for many years, he went on to high places in industry and the City. He was a big man, with a jutting jaw, an arrogant turn of the thin lower lip, gravelly Yorkshire voice, eyes sharp and appraising under a high forehead. Capable of much heavyweight charm, he brandished his ruthlessness, a gladiator challenging all comers. One day, when we had discussed a speech I was to write for him, he told me a story, ostensibly to illustrate the egocentricity of farmers, but it was also an exquisite depiction of his own outlook. A farmer asked a neighbour how he intended to vote in an impending General Election. Well, said the other, what I always say is, you've got to take the broad view – that's it, the broad view! So, whatever the issue is, I say to myself: How is it going to affect *me*? Sir James grinned; 'Nothing like saying what you mean, eh?'

As I picked up my papers and got up to go, he leaned back in the high leather chair behind the massive mahogany desk, and added: 'Don't you dare put that in the speech, mind! People might get the wrong idea!' He was smiling, but the familiar pugnacious edge to his voice was there too. 'Frankly,' he went on, 'I don't give a damn if you do – but don't anyway!'

For a time this life of manipulation and persuasion was stimulating – the thrill of playing the tricks of the trade, analysing the reactions of other interests and deciding on a 'correct' response, pride in professionalism. The truth, however, nagged at me – I was only a shadow behind the principal actors, treading the wings. I remembered Bill's words, after the momentous meeting about Operation Overlord and de Gaulle, which he and Colonel James had attended as staff officers: 'We are the operators behind the scenes! We enjoy the game.' Perhaps he really did prefer to pull strings in the shadows? Continuing that role after the war, moving cleverly on the fringe of affairs, bringing the powerful together, 'arranging things', as he put it, he seemed to have more direct influence than those distant words of his had suggested. That was *his* golden métier. For me, the role of 'mover and shaker' in the background was not enough; it held me in an existential vacuum. I must find an escape. Werner, aware of a similar emptiness in himself but for different reasons, had seen it in me too.

We talked of commitment in a double sense – to some *one* and to some *thing*, the images superimposed. Werner said, musingly, 'I should not admit this, but I cannot remember what it is like to be committed, really committed, to *one* woman – that is all so long ago. And now I shall never know it again.'

Either way, to a person or a cause, you could not surrender too much of yourself – if you did you were lost. You had to keep a private self inviolate. But what was 'too much?' – and surely such calculation destroyed the fragrance of life?

'You *are* romantic!' he said teasingly, the high forehead furrowing. 'Who can talk of "fragrance" as a litmus test of life? As if life owed you happiness!'

Yet in all tradition, all poetry, the dreams of men and women, felicity *could* be found, somewhere at the end of the rainbow. If not, what was life but existence – with no purpose, no prizes? Perhaps Alec had been right after all, the wisdom of the Gorbals that I had forgotten. Life owed you nothing, and gave you nothing. Life was the enemy – you *fought* it to get a crust to eat, to live at all. You compelled it at the sword's point – nothing would be given willingly. Each gain was a victory, though always a compromise, a minimum extracted from the unrelenting enemy; and it was a transient victory too, for you had to fight on to retain it! You 'made do' whatever happened: 'Ye wurrk a bi', eat a bi', fuck a bi', sleep a bi' – whi' else is there?' Fragrance! That was not for the likes of us.

'Aye – and even if ye *know* ye're losin', ye go on fightin'. Ma feyther used tae say: "If ye've gottae go doon, ye go doon fightin'!" Ay, ye've gottae have *something*' tae fight for, or ye're no'a man!'

Werner in his own fashion seemed to echo Alec, and that was bizarre; for Alec, seeing Werner's style of life, would have said in disbelief: 'What's *he* got tae bellyache abou'? He's got so much he doesn't know he's livin'!' You had to be near the dangerous edge of existence to feel life's essence, not cushioned, not secure, but in the ringing clash of battle. The less you needed to fight, the less you felt the astringent tang of life stirring the soul. For Alec, even my own modest state would have been affluence – the flat itself, enough money to buy clothes when needed, never driven by hunger! In the Gorbals I would have thought so too – so much had I changed.

Werner said: 'I am growing tired of Oxford – even of the scientific work there, and if it were not for the plentiful supply of young women …' He gave a little shrug. 'They are of course enjoyable, but the younger they are the more boring they are – between the good times in bed!'

He laughed, repeating 'the younger they are', shaking his head: 'I meant, of course, "the older *I* am!" ' He sighed. 'What drives it home is that feeling of impatience – you must have known it? – when the moment of pleasure is over and the knowledge returns that the girl is essentially boring – ravishing in her alluring moments, but boring, and you long for the next time of ecstasy to cancel the tedium. And you are guilty for thinking those thoughts.

Well, that may be part of it, but there are other feelings, more pro-found – and that may be age too, sad but true. I feel empty. There is no other word for it. Perhaps it has taken me all these years to di-gest everything that has happened, and now, looking outwards again, girls are not enough. I need a cause to fight for! Would you believe it! *Me* wanting a cause?'

We were sitting over an early evening drink in his flat near Grosvenor Square, his *pied-à-terre* in London. Small compared with his Oxford place, it spoke richly of Mayfair, silks and bro-cades, gilt mirrors and chairs, rosewood. There was a bedroom with canopied bed, an adjoining bathroom with marble floor and what looked like gold fittings, a sitting room with a tall gilt mirror over the marble fireplace, pale Chinese carpet, blue velvet curtains, silken chaise-longue with gilded frame. The kitchen was dominated by a refrigerator six feet high. In the mahogany panelled entrance hall, an alcove was equipped as a tiny office – desk and typewriter, teleprinter, tape deck with earphones and foot-pedal for transcrip-tion, steel filing-cabinet with combination lock. As with Bernard, I had never enquired into his affairs, nor he into mine. Over the years, however, I had gathered that in addition to his scientific work he managed the very considerable family finances, including negotiations for German compensation.

The telephone rang. He did not pick up the white handset on the little marquetry table beside his chair, but went out to the hall, let-ting the door swing to behind him, and I heard him pick up the phone on the secretary's desk. He spoke in German. Evidently the call was from New York, and concerned exchange dealings; Geneva was mentioned. There were long silences while he listened. At last he gave instructions for movement of funds and put the phone down.

The sitting-room windows were at a corner of the building, and from where I sat, looking down the street towards Grosvenor Square, had it been daylight I could have seen some of its greenery, but now this was visible only as a patch of deeper darkness against the buildings beyond, through which glinted the passing headlights of the evening rush hour. Thinking of Werner swinging vast sums across the world, amazed that I felt no *frisson* of envy or exclusion, I was taken back to the days when I had had an office in that very square, to me the heartland of the boss class, a few hundred yards from where I now sat, and had marvelled at the incongruity of my being there at all – at the wild caprice of time and chance. When the Council had moved me to London from Oxford, I was given a room in a bare aristocratic house in Grosvenor Square; like many others in the quarter it had been requisitioned by the government during the war, and occupied at one stage, judging by the presence of a flagpole over the front door, by an *émigré* embassy. With several other houses in the quarter, it had been allotted to the Council pending the building of its new headquarters in Davies Street. The entrance hall was paved in chequerboard marble, and many ceilings had fine floral plaster work. In the dark servants' hall in the basement, a row of bells showed the names of the rooms from which summons once came; my room was labelled 'small study', presumably to distinguish it from another room, which could have taken a full-size billiards table with plenty of space to spare, identified as 'library'. Sitting at my desk I reflected, as I had often done at Blenheim Palace when I had a room there, that but for the war I would never have set foot in such a place – and what did it mean to me that I now could? I was not sure of the answer; but I was amazed that there was so little of the resentment, the wish that I did truly belong to that setting, that I had felt long before, in Oxford for instance, when fresh from the Gorbals. Overhearing Werner on the telephone, calmly speaking of huge numbers of dollars, I had felt only a casual professional interest in what the moves signified. Where had the passion gone?

In those Grosvenor Square days, walking through the patrician portals to go upstairs to my room, I sometimes wondered, in fantasy, how the 'rightful' occupants would have responded, suddenly materialising in front of me – the house translated, in *Time Machine* fashion, back to its pre-war life? Doubtless they would have coldly dismissed me to the servants' entrance down the area steps outside, and fanned my hatred afresh. I thought of a day long ago in Glasgow when I was about fifteen; laid off at the factory, I had been going round the big shops in the city centre looking for work – 'Please, I'll do anything, carry parcels, polish the floors, copy letters or invoices, check stock – I'm good at figures – anything! Please?' The answers, kindly as a rule, had been much the same: 'Sorry, laddie, we don't need a smart boy today.' Hungry, desperate, I had just come out of a high-class ladies' dress shop in Buchanan Street and was standing at the pavement edge outside it, wondering where to go next, when a large grey Rolls glided silently towards me. The frilled grey side-curtains of the rear compartment were drawn slantingly apart as in the windows of a house, and gathered at each side by grey ribbons tied in neat bows; behind them a fur-coated woman sat very erect, smoothing gloves over her hands. I was determined to show my bitterness; I would not move, though my boots projected over the edge of the kerbstone and the car's wheels were certain to strike me as it came in close. I muttered under my breath, 'Capitalist bastards!' The chauffeur, a man in his forties with a heavy 'Old Bill' moustache, and a row of Great War medal ribbons on his dove-grey uniform coat, braked sharply while the car was still at an angle to the kerb, and stared at me, glancing down at my torn boots, and waited a few seconds for me to move out of harm's way. He must have intuited why I stood fast, for he leaned out of his window and said: 'Whit d'ye expect *me* tae dae aboot it? Ah'm jist earnin' ma livin'! So for Christ's sake *move* – an' le' me do that!' Yes – the old class hatred had gone deep, and yet it had faded, betrayal of Alec and his granite hard vision, and the others in the Gorbals for whom hatred of the bosses was pure and necessary, as mine had been. Where would I find an equal conviction again?

That house, with several others adjoining it, was gone, and in their place a red brick block of flats had arisen, pastiche of Georgian and Queen Anne. In a sense, however, the old house was still there, returned to its former boss-class identity, the new occupants reaffirming the old dominance. Had my view of them really changed? I still resented that unquestioning confidence born of money, but not as before. Now, I simply noted it and considered the person beneath. Nor did Werner's wealth disturb me as it had when

I first met him in those days of raw response in Oxford, when his attitude of *de haut en bas*, moderated since, had been hard to bear. What shift had I made? I did not know. Had the fine edge of sensitivity gone? I hoped not. How could one live and have no strong feelings about anything? At least if you hated something, the surge of passion was reward of a kind. Was it simply age – the weariness that Werner lamented – or could it be, at last, wisdom? Oh let it be wisdom!

Werner said: 'some of these things I do are very interesting. Managing money requires a judgement that I prefer not to delegate; but luckily some of my scientific work *can* be, otherwise I would give it up'

I wondered whether he had used the word 'interesting' as Continentals often did, to mean profitable! Here was a strange mixture of qualities, of scientist and international financier; the 'pure' savant had to be on the side of the angels, the money man was not – could not be. Good and evil could never be far apart. That flicker of old romantic imagery gave me *some* comfort – so sensibility had not died within me! Perhaps my heart was still in the right place after all.

He said: 'What I am about to say may surprise you, in view of my indifference to Israel in the past, but I am thinking of seeking commitment in that direction. I cannot be more specific. That might be unwise.'

I could not see the fastidious Werner as a rough and ready *kibbutznik*! Was he thinking of a scientific role there? Something in his tone suggested a greater influence. Why had his announcement come as so little of a surprise?

When he spoke again, there was a tremor in his voice. 'Your marriage showed me that the battle is far from over – Kay is a decent, cultured woman, and yet the virus is strong in her; and in so many others like her, the common run of decent people! Israel is a challenge to conscience, everybody's conscience – Jew and non-Jew – and the world finds that unbearable. Nazi sentiment shows itself again in Germany, and many Germans oppose the payment of compensation to Jews. No. The virus will not die. The white-washing of the Nazi period has already begun, and it will grow – or shall I say the sweetening of it, trivialising its horrors with *kitsch*. Even the bestialities of the camps, the great slaughter, is being denied, and that will grow too. Deeds for which no words seem fitting *now*, will receive the anodyne treatment, even, God help us, romantic – like that given to the conveniently distant savagery of Rome and Babylon and so much else. Music and poetry and literature will de-sensitise the residual revulsion! And you and I will wonder how *anyone* could bring himself to do that – and what is worse, how the world could be so calloused as to welcome it. And the greater the artist the greater the crime will be! When I hear "Va pensiero" in *Nabucco*, beautiful though the music is, my heart is torn – and I wonder whether Verdi ever tried to imagine what it felt like to be a Hebrew slave in Babylon, and whether *he* would have felt like singing if he had been one of them! I know *I* never felt inclined to sing in Buchenwald. And so the wheel will turn, and Jews will fight for survival over and over again.'

The Six Day War was hidden in the future. Only then would his apocalyptic words strike fully home. For the moment they were too dark – hope was foolish, doomed to disappointment, best rejected. I wanted to swing back to the simple faith of Bernard's father – 'The world *must* get better, it stands to reason! Man must surely learn from experience!' – which had seemed too innocent even then, in the simplistic Gorbals days. Yet even as I thought this, I knew that this time my flight to the past was not genuine – I was seeking excuses to be stoic, to shrink from intensity of feeling about anything, a last resistance. Bill had recently teased me for being no longer as spontaneous, as quickly stirred by events or encounters, as in the past: 'stop being the poor man's Buddha!' He was right. Determined to find tranquillity after the divorce, I had taken detachment too far.

I sidestepped Werner's words. 'Would you ever want to live there – that is, permanently?'

'I do not think so – but then I never dreamed that I would want to live outside Germany! History changes you.'

'You think it could come to that?'

He shook his head slowly. 'Who knows. The last refuge – and the last battle, like Masada? The end of the road. It could happen.'

'Last refuge' suggested, also, a place where you had to declare yourself, who you *really* were – what Ben Gurion seemed to have had in mind in his historic declaration about the Law of Return, that a Jew's right to settle in Israel was 'inherent in his very Jewishness': in other words, a Jew was someone who *knew himself as a Jew*. That question, 'Who is a Jew?' contained many ironies; in the days of *der heim* that test was unnecessary. My forebears, and all the rest, were clamped into that tortured identity; and for it to be otherwise was unimaginable. Now, that question had to be voiced, as Ben Gurion had voiced it by implication, because many Jews were not sure of the answer. Was I sure? After my long turning away, I had to say 'Yes' – but only because there was nowhere else to go – no other identity would fit. For me, as for Werner and Bernard, the past was too strong to be denied. I was – what I was, and could never be anything else. But I must still prove it to myself. Did Werner need to do so?

I said: 'If only we could live without asking ourselves who we are. Because Israel *exists* we have to declare ourselves – either towards it or turn away. That's a heavy responsibility. I feel, sometimes, that we have seen too much for one lifetime.'

'You are right. One lifetime is not enough. We are *centuries* old!' He went over to the corner window and stood looking out at the dark sky, and spoke without turning round. 'Past generations grasp us tightly and carry us forward. Wonders happen and we feel we knew them long ago. And what we do know now was prefigured long ago. Our Jewishness is an implacable inheritance. One thing is sure – the past enchains us. We cannot escape it.'

10

The Leaders Fall Behind

With Bill, facetiousness was usually a mask for purpose. When he telephoned me one morning – we had already arranged to meet for dinner that evening – and suggested a pub crawl in Bohemia afterwards, he plainly had an ulterior motive; pub crawls did not fit his patrician stamp. He gave no clue, however, and I knew not to ask – he would tell me when he was ready. He had two immediate reasons for telephoning me. He wanted to meet for dinner early so that we would have more time for the expedition; there was also the matter of dress. 'I suppose I need not remind you to change into your oldest weekend clothes – we mustn't stand out as philistines, must we? Though come to think of it, I suppose that advice is superfluous – you being a card-carrying Bohemian yourself!'

That quip was double-edged. He knew that I had no sympathy with the Bohemian mystique, an attitude probably determined long ago in the Gorbals, as I explain later; or rather – as his 'card-carrying' shaft hinted – I was ambivalent. Long ago, as he knew, youthful curiosity had drawn me to Bohemia, in wartime Oxford and afterwards in London – a romantic vision of a company of free spirits, to my naïve eyes super-sophisticates, who held the key to the Lost Domain. If I could only get close enough I might find the key too! That vision belonged to long ago. Bill had sometimes suggested, in a kindly enough fashion, that my present antipathy was the splenetic reaction of the disillusioned dreamer.

Bill knew Bohemia well enough himself, though how that squared with his dedication to the symbiotic worlds of power and business was hard to fathom – except that he was tirelessly inquisitive, intent on precise knowledge, so that he would always be well-equipped to exploit new twists in opportunity. He once remarked, in his careful way, 'It's good to know one's way around – wherever it might be! You never know when it might be useful.' One of his interests was property development; and in central London, in those grey post-war years, there were many bombed and run-down buildings awaiting the right financial climate, and a clear enough view of the future, for such as he to move in and make a killing.

'Bohemia's like Cassis was in the old days,' he once remarked, 'only rougher! They say that if you haven't done your stint there, your education is incomplete.'

The reference to weekend clothes was an ironic nudge in the ribs – for who was I, from the Gorbals slums, to go slumming? It was also a wistful backward glance to the tweed jacket and flannels of pre-war Oxford, when 'weekend clothes' were the student uniform, and to the wartime days when much of metropolitan Bohemia had migrated to Oxford for the duration. It occurred to me that Bill had recently taken to looking *back* – out of character for one so disciplined, so sure of his path through life. I had no such nostalgia for any of my past; I might mourn it, wish it had been different, but had no wish to bring it back. Perhaps, for Bill, it was not Oxford, or any of the past, but something closer to the heart – youth itself. So soon? He had just turned forty.

As for the purpose of the pub crawl, he obviously wanted help of some kind – perhaps it was information, and there might still be habitués there I knew, who could supply it. How many faces would I recognise now – or would know *me*? It was more than ten years since I had 'done my stint' there.

When we met that evening, at Scott's, he wore a soft green Norfolk jacket with leather elbows, crumpled beige cavalry twill trousers, brown brogues with scuffed toe caps, khaki shirt and blue silk cravat. Even if I had not known that he had his clothes made in Savile Row, to my garment-factory eyes – but perhaps not to others – his clothes were obviously hand-tailored, with the worn look that good cloth and good workmanship can carry off with an air. I was wearing an old brown tweed jacket that I had bought for fifty shillings in Montagu Burton's shop in Oxford when I had first gone up, dark grey flannels, suede shoes, an old blue check shirt and a tie. There must have been a sentimental bond with that jacket, for despite its lumpy shoulders and poor fit, and the fact that I could now afford to throw it away, it was so hard-wearing that I found excuses to keep it. He must have picked up my thoughts about the evident quality of his clothes: 'Well – you may be right – but we are not applying for permanent membership, are we? We are sympathetic spirits passing through!'

Over dinner he did not mention the purpose of our pub crawl. At one point, the conversation touching on the Bohemian life, I remarked: 'Bohemia is a state of mind.' He gave me one of his searching glances from under the thick fair eyebrows: 'Later this evening, we'll see how right you are.'

Mention of Bohemia always conjured up the sad, threadbare sentimentality of *La Bohème*, and my perplexity, on first encountering the opera as a ragged boy in Glasgow, at the powerful romantic magnetism of the life it portrayed – hunger, squalor, the cruel fate of hope and trust and tenderness – and the naïve mythology of 'genius in a garret', lauded by people who had never known starvation. In me, who *had* known it, that popular fixation inspired anger and revulsion. Now, more tolerant, I thought I understood the power of the Bohemian fantasy: Bohemia was an Abbey of Thelema where *any* behaviour, or nearly any, was accepted, a licence to which 'creativity', or even sympathy with it, admitted you; without it the artistic spirit could not flourish.

Bill said: 'I suppose one could convert Shaw – "He who can does …" and so forth, into: "He who *can* be creative goes away and does it; he who *can't* stays on in Bohemia!" '

He was right about Cassis, as we had seen it in 1939; it certainly had licence, but it had no time for the pretence of creativity, nor for the hypocrisy about the artistic virtue of poverty. Its denizens unashamedly chose the *louche* existence for self-indulgent reasons alone, in comfort or within easy reach of it.

I first heard *La Bohème* in snatches, when I was about fifteen, appropriately enough shivering in the snow and slush of a Glasgow pavement, my boots letting in water, blowing into my hands for warmth, outside a gramophone shop in Hope Street on my way to the Mitchell Library. Ownership of gramophones was still largely

confined to the comfortably off, though they were beginning to appear, and wireless sets too, in some Gorbals houses on the 'never-
never'. Many such shops in the centre of the city kept a
gramophone playing near the street door, to draw custom – a solid-
looking wooden box about the size of a modern micro-wave oven,
often embellished with carvings of flowers or gothic architectural
motifs or angular art deco symbols, with two little doors in the
front panel that opened to let the sound free, replacing the old
wide-mouthed horn perched beside the turntable. The music was
not always 'serious' – 'In a Monastery Garden', 'Love's Old Sweet
Song', and John McCormack the poor man's highbrow singer, and
the gritty voice of Harry Lauder that seemed to personify the
homely, humane, Rabbie Burns dreaming of that turbulent Red
Clydeside epoch. I never heard Harry Lauder proclaim 'a man's a
man for a' that', but it seemed as if he did, and I was repelled by the
hollowness of it. How could people be comforted by such facile
sentiment? When your feet were cold and wet from poverty, such
words could be no more than a bromide, almost insulting. They
made me angry, whenever I heard them, though part of me wanted
to believe in them as everybody else seemed to do.

Doubtless because that gramophone shop aimed at the better
class clientèle of the city's West End, presumed to be the upper
reaches of culture, opera was included in the free programme,
mainly of the lighter sort. Many years later those few minutes of
possession, out there on the pavement, would return whenever I
heard Bohemia glamorised, or any other example of suffering trivialised and sweetened, such as Werner had in mind when he said
'the greater the artist the greater the crime ...'

At that time, I had started going to see performances by the Carl
Rosa Opera Company at the Theatre Royal, standing for threepence in the topmost gods – or rather to *hear* them, for I was too
short-sighted to see much in the way of detail of movement and expression in the colourfully dressed figures on the stage far away
below. I was carried away on clouds of European Romanticism, as
I had soared up into the stars from the tenement window as a little
boy. What first drew me to opera? It may have been the snatches of

music from that gramophone shop, but more likely it was father. He knew nothing about music, but he had a feeling for it. When I was about five he made me a wooden instrument like a recorder with a clear, honeyed tone, on which I taught myself to play by ear. I played to mother as she lay in bed during what I must have sensed were her last months – though she did not lie there for long at a time, getting up several times a day, until close to the end, to move about the kitchen on her mysterious tasks, in obvious pain, stopping every few minutes to lean on the table or the sink and gasp for breath, a hand pressing against her side – and I wished I were strong enough, and understood enough, to take the pain from her sunken features, restore them to the fullness and glow that I saw in the photograph of her that stood on the narrow shelf over the stove. It was a large sepia picture, pasted on to a piece of stiff cardboard decorated with little transfers of white flowers; there she was, the young mother holding her first born, my older sister Lilian as a small baby, a chubby bundle in a mass of white lace, herself in a tight-waisted velvet dress with a little frill under the chin, in happiness and pride and youthful confidence. Sometimes, as she moved about the kitchen in those fragile days, she leaned on a chair and glanced up at the picture, and suddenly, remembering my presence, put her apron to her eyes to hide the tears. One day, she stood looking at the picture for a long time, then tottered and seemed about to fall and I ran to her and reached up to her waist and tried to support her. She leaned on the table with both hands, and I heard the rough breathing, betokening effort, and I burst into tears without knowing why. She put a hand on my head, and the hand trembled, and she said: 'Vayn nisht, mein kind – vayn nisht. Gott toot – vosservillt' ('Don't cry, my child – don't cry. God does – what he wants to do.') Then she sent me into the tiny lobby – two or three steps away – to fetch a shirt of father's that needed washing. When I returned, the photograph had gone.

Father came in soon afterwards, and his eyes seemed to go at once to where the photograph had been, and his jaw stiffened, and the blue-grey eyes deepened in hue. Mother stood at the sink, soaking the shirt and beginning to rub it with a cake of hard soap – Oh so slowly! Gently, without speaking, he took her hands out of the water that was dark now and lumpy with soap bubbles, and dried them on a towel and led her the few steps to the curtained bed in the kitchen alcove, she leaning on him but half in protest, saying in a whisper, 'Vay iz meer – chbeen zo shvach' ('Woe is me – I am so weak') and made her lie down without undressing, only removing her shoes, and covered her with the *perraneh*. He took off his jacket and hung it on the back of one of the ladderback kitchen chairs, and heated some soup she had made from a quarter of chicken he had brought home that morning, and poured it into a small china bowl, dipped a spoon in it and put the edge of the spoon to his lips to make sure the soup was not too hot; he put the bowl down on the kitchen table and broke up a slice of black bread into little pieces and dropped them into the soup, pushing them down into it with the spoon to soak them properly, and went to the bed and propped her up a little, then took the bowl and sat on the edge of the trestle and fed her, blowing a little on each spoonful before putting it to her lips. When she had consumed the contents of the bowl, he arranged the pillows again to make her comfortable and drew the curtains of the bed to keep the light from her eyes, turned to me and put a finger to his lips so that I should be quiet, and went to the sink and rubbed the shirt in the soapy water and rinsed it several times and wrung it out, the muscles on his pale forearms bulging and rippling as he did so, and hung the shirt over the back of another chair in front of the stove, placing sheets of newspaper under it to catch the drips. He made a pot of tea and sat down at the unsteady kitchen table, elbows on the torn oil-cloth cover, and sipped the milkless tea that gleamed reddish brown in the tall glass, sucking it through a lump of sugar held between his teeth – and seemed to stare at the leaping flames licking at the bars of the fire basket and the wisps of steam beginning to rise from the wet shirt; but in retrospect he must have contemplated the past that was portrayed so affectingly in that missing photograph, and what its sudden absence signalled. It seemed only minutes later that she moaned and called out weakly from behind the curtains; she was going to be sick. He leapt up, the chair overturning, and seized the basin – in which the shirt had been washed – from the sink, but before he could reach her with it, she had leaned from the bed, pushing the curtain away with her hand so as not to soil it, and the yellowish vomit pattered down on the cracked brown linoleum. He took a handkerchief from his trouser pocket and wiped her mouth, holding her quivering body in his arms and whispering to her. I took the shovel from the coal bucket that stood beside the stove and scooped the vomit from the floor on to an old newspaper, wiped the linoleum clean with more newspaper, and took the bitter-smelling bundle down the three flights of cold stone stairs to throw it on to one of the overflowing brick rubbish bins – the ashpits – in the yard at the back of the close. When I came back, he was giving her a spoonful of thick white liquid from a medicine bottle that stood high on the mantelshelf close to where the photograph had been.

Before father's entry, in the few seconds when I had been out of the kitchen to fetch his shirt, mother must have snatched the photograph down and put it under her pillow, the nearest hiding place; later, arranging the pillow for her, father found it and stood looking at it, his square figure seeming to me to grow and spread and overshadow the little room, my whole world, and I wished and wished that this giant would stretch out those strong arms and remake the world and put all to rights as it should be, and mother would rise from that bed healthy and strong and happy as in that picture, and all would be sweet. He moved to put the photograph back on the mantel shelf. Her thin, tired voice stopped him: 'Nayn! Varfessaveck' ('No! Throw it away'). Softly he replied: 'Nayn – zeeverren glookliche toggen – glookliche!' ('No – they were lucky days – lucky!') He went to the drawer in the kitchen dresser and took out a large brown envelope in which he kept the few family documents, his and mother's aliens' registration cards, family birth certificates, the rent book, and put the photograph in it and returned it to the drawer, and let his hand rest on the edge of that open drawer for many moments. I remember looking at that hand, at about the level of my eyes, and the feeling I had about it, broad with strong fingers, and with such wonderful skill to fashion things – as I had seen him turning and smoothing the shaft of the wooden recorder, pencilling the playing holes and drilling them precisely – and the sudden terror that came to me, for in his silence, his fixity, as if time had stopped within him, he was telling me, unbelievably, that strong as he was, this god of mine, my father, could change nothing.

Ever since that time, whenever I hear a recorder played, I think of the days when I sat beside the alcove bed in the kitchen where she lay, suppressing my fear at the sight of her yellowing face, and played traditional songs she loved, puzzled by the tears in her eyes as I did so – 'Rozshenkah-lach mit mand-lenn' ('Raisins and Almonds') or 'A Breev-eh-leh der Mama' ('A Little Letter from Mama') – and she reached out a hand on which dark blue veins stood out like thick string dyed the colour of ink, the knuckles on her slender fingers enlarged from years of work, to stroke my head. When I was six, not long before mother's death, father sent me to have violin lessons. True, he stopped them when he was skint from gambling, and most of the pawnable items in the house had gone to the pawnshop across the street; but later, when he did have money, and I pleaded to be allowed to resume them, he would not do it, in bitterness and isolation after mother's death.

About the time of *La Bohème* at the gramophone shop, years later, in one of the bright periods when he was flush with winnings at the Faro table, he took me once to the opera in the Theatre Royal – on that evening we sat in the stalls – and raised my pocket money from a penny a week to sixpence! I was then earning twelve shillings a week in the factory and handed him all my wages, and sixpence was riches enough. In the interval – while I munched a bar of chocolate, having to suck some of it out of a hole in one of my front teeth that sometimes ached maddeningly, and he smoked a cigarette in his amber holder – he said that he was sorry he had *had* to stop the violin lessons in those distant days, and that he hoped, somehow, to make it up to me; and I wondered, but dared not say so, how he was going to do that if this wounding see-saw of affluence and destitution continued.

Father had the gift of suddenly putting aside a black mood, like shutting a door, and making an occasion splendid, and so that evening remained memorable. From the stalls, the gilt and red plush and rococo decor had far more magic than when seen from the far gods above; all around us were grand people – many in evening dress, the ladies with jewels gleaming in hair and décolletage – and I had thoughts only for this great occasion.

Coming away from the theatre that evening, I said I wished I could hear more opera. He fished out a pound note and gave it to me as if it were a scrap of paper, though in those days a pound note was large and crisp and impressive, nearly as big as a fifty pound note today, and worth much more; a whole pound! He made me promise not to spend it on anything but the opera; and so I went to a whole season of the Carl Rosa, up in the gods.

As for the aching tooth, the constant pain did interfere with concentration at the Mitchell Library, and at the opera too. One day one of the shower-room group remarked, 'God! You could push a match stick through that great big hole in your tooth!' I was ashamed; no one had ever told me to brush my teeth. At last I mentioned the pain to father, and he told me to go to the Dental Hospital. There, poor people were dealt with by students. Without anaesthetic, they pulled out *two* front teeth – decay had attacked the adjacent one. I walked along Sauchiehall Street afterwards feeling that my jaw was broken, holding a large piece of cotton wool to my bleeding mouth and crying out loud with the pain.

The music of *La Bohème* having taken special hold of me, I read the libretto in the Mitchell Library, and as much as I could find about Murger and his world, and the people he knew who lived on black coffee and little else in romantic Paris, and was saddened and perplexed by the opera's alloy of sordidness and sentimentality. Sordidness I knew very well; in the Gorbals you lived and slept with it, breathed it in the air, wore it on your back, but there was no such cheap emotion attached to it. Above all it was not *chosen*, as it was in Bohemia; it was an old, familiar enemy, bitter, unrelenting, that had you by the throat, and you fought it to the finish. In London's Bohemia, this wonderment returned. Could Dylan Thomas really mean it when he proclaimed 'sordidness – that's the thing!' Or was he playing out, for the benefit of the gallery, a secret comedy of his own? Were they all playing a Murger-esque charade, a comforting conceit, placing a mask of heroics, even glamour, on a way of life adopted for other, suspect reasons? Did the appeal for sympathy conceal a device to gull the philistine – anyone who had the aspect either of unearned affluence or of having a steady job – into buying a round of drinks, in effect making him pay a tax to support the dedicated suffering of the garret? A favourite trick, when the philistine ordered a drink for himself, or himself and a friend, was to pretend that the order included the Bohemians standing near, who chorused 'and a pint of brown for me!' or 'and a pint of bitter for me!' If he repudiated these additional orders he was accused of impugning the honour of the deserving artists, who of course claimed that they genuinely believed he *had* intended to buy them drinks. Usually he was shamed into giving way, and paid up. On one of my early visits, the trick was played on me. Furious, telling myself that I had not escaped from the Gorbals in order to subsidise people who lived the squalid life from choice, not necessity, I stood my ground and refused to pay. The scene that followed was unpleasant. Who was I – unprintable insults – to suggest that these men of honour, toilers in the fields of beauty and truth, would stoop to trick me out of my filthy pennies? At one point I wondered if I would have to fight my way out.

Dylan Thomas laughed at such tricks. His methods were more direct, even in a sense a little more honest – and seemingly always successful; he was a master of the fast touch. I never heard of anyone getting their money back from him; and even to imagine the possibility was absurd. He lamented the passing of private patronage; in some form or other, it was essential to the creative life. The wonder of it was that he succeeded, after a fashion, in living as though it did still exist– at least for him.

Often, those who defended the 'genius in the garret' myth were the very outsiders who were pressed or cajoled into contributing to its support; they did so partly in compassion for the elective poverty they witnessed, partly in pleasure at sharing the ethos of a fancied Café Momus – patrons of art on the cheap. For me, such sympathy was impossible, especially for those denizens who were from the boss class, to whom other choices were easily available; they could at any time retreat into their families, into a conventional way of making a living, if they wished. How could they live this life if they had an alternative?

Over coffee, Bill told me the purpose of the evening's expedition. It would not have startled me as violently as it did but for coincidences so disturbing – or perhaps I was too unprepared – that for a moment I could not believe what he said; there must be other circumstances, other motives, not revealed?

Coincidences are not important in themselves, but in what we attribute to them; we are shaken only when they stir dormant emotions, guilt, broken faith, fear of the future – questions addressed to the Id. What he told me shattered a tranquillity that had recently come to me, still fragile, soothing the spirit after the divorce, enabling me to coast along, writing, thinking about what to do next. I owed this felicity to a new relationship, tender, peaceful, almost marital – except that certain areas of life were separate – with Nancy, a close friend of Bill's wife, Millicent. This evening, Bill said, we were to search for Tom, whom I had known long ago at Oxford but had not seen for many years, a cousin of Millicent's – Nancy's alcoholic ex-husband!

In the last year or two, Millicent had been increasingly worried about Tom. He had taken to disappearing into Bohemia for a week or two at a stretch; and now he had not surfaced for over a month. The family did not want to bring the authorities into the affair if it could be avoided. As a first step she had begged Bill to see what he could do.

He said 'There isn't much I *can* do. I'm not callous – but if the fellow wants to go to the devil, that's *his* affair. *How* he does it, it seems to me, doesn't matter a damn!'

Bill and Millicent had been married for about ten years. They had two children; and life had settled into a classic pattern, to me oddly detached. Millicent was happiest in the country; she came up to London occasionally from their house in Wiltshire for a few days' shopping. Bill stayed in town during the week, when not abroad on business, at their flat in South Street, and joined her in the country most weekends. Millicent retained the careless elegance of their early days together, still detectable behind the angular charm of the busy young county matron – smooth round face, small mouth and fine straight nose, blue eyes, mousy hair in a page boy cut, clothes of soft pastel shades. Beneath the downright manner was an engaging quickness, the sparkle of the bright schoolgirl, but deeper still was the wary self-sufficiency, the intent, shrewd scrutiny, of the traditional country person. She had been just old enough, in the last year of the war, to join the ATS, drive ambulances and supply trucks, and become a proficient motor mechanic. Some of the pre-war Mayfair culture lingered in tricks of speech. When accepting an invitation she would say, 'That would be *amusing*!' with the emphasis on the second syllable; or when about to visit someone she might say she would 'crash along' to see them – reach-me-downs from the flapper generation of mother and aunts. A friend who had just given birth was referred to as having 'pupped', or 'dropped'; and the period was still the 'curse'. The quality I most admired in her was a competence that accepted all burdens and problems and upsets with composure as they came, not the stiff upper lip of pre-war convention but something millennially older, womanly, earthy. Every trial was 'coped with', confronted, disposed of – or, if it had to be endured, put in its proper place and allowed for, in the normal turning of the earth. I could not imagine Millicent as passionate, in any sense; all life was in some way expected, as the seasons were, or the caprices and appetites of men and women and animals, likely at any moment to present unsettling versions of old problems, curious, intriguing, but never permitted to impede the main stream of living, a needful care for order and duty.

Equally, it was difficult to imagine Bill himself as passionate. It would be in character, I sometimes thought, if tucked away in a corner of his secretive way of life he maintained a hide-away flat – a 'drum' in the jargon – there to enjoy a turbulent separate life in the grand tradition; for which his weekly isolation in London provided ideal opportunity. Bill's detachment was so convincing, however, that I tended to dismiss the thought. He was dedicated to a mission of his own, the deployment of his talents in the broad market place, in subtle, potent 'arrangements', making money certainly but also notching up points on his egocentric score board, satisfying his private standard of success.

I usually saw Millicent when she was in London. She found a friend to make up a foursome with me, and we often dined in one of the less expensive restaurants then springing up in that area to serve the growing office population – and chosen, I suspected, to fit *my* budget, for I insisted on 'going Dutch' for my half of the foursome. The friend might be a divorcée, or single, or 'at a loose end' – one of Millicent's conveniently vague terms, not to be closely examined. Sometimes we ate in their flat, an old-fashioned place that had come down to Bill from an uncle, full of heavy mahogany and chintz, with a huge gas fire in each room. Since Millicent used it so little, and liked its vintage cosiness, she had made few changes. There we feasted on cold meats and cheese and fruit and French bread, and settled down for what Millicent called a relaxed evening, code for consuming a great deal of wine.

A few weeks after my divorce hearing, Bill and Millicent decided, touchingly, that we celebrate the event in just such an evening at their flat. The 'loose end' was Nancy. I cannot remember the moment, that evening, when certainty began; it seemed to have been there from the very beginning – a pattern prepared for us long ago. What it did for us we would probably never know, only that it was important; of that we were certain too. That Bill and Millicent might have consciously played the part of catalysts did not occur to me till much later, but even if they had, we had been ready for it to be so. It was not a purely physical affair, and I never ceased to marvel at the power that drew us; though I think we both suspected, but never spoke about it, that it could not 'work' for ever.

Nancy had divorced Tom a couple of years before. There had been no children – 'mercifully!' she sighed; and I did sometimes wonder about that sigh. She was twenty-nine, petite, with smooth fair hair parted in the middle, and the long narrow, meditative face of a Renaissance Madonna. That appearance of seriousness was balanced by a quick, ironic sense of humour – but that too was on the surface. At heart she was of the same practical, country mould as Millicent.

Although we were together several evenings and nights a week, and sometimes most of a weekend when she was not in the country, we remained rooted in separate worlds, from which we escaped each time to a private one of our own making, the only one that mattered. Her world, like Bill's and Millicent's was the moneyed one of country landowners with City interests; mine was now not easily definable, a heterogeneous collection of acquaintances, no more than that, in business, politics, the fringes of Chelsea and Hampstead. We clung to our separate sovereignties. There were moments, however, when we were on the edge of deciding to live together for reasons of simple convenience, to be free of minor irritations – finding that certain things were always in the 'wrong' flat, clothes, gramophone records, items of food or drink; she lived in South Audley Street, round the corner from Bill and Millicent. Without discussion we drew back. The idea of 'living together' – in those days one still thought of it in quotation marks – went too far towards the enchainment of the married state; and the mark of the divorce, for each of us, still weighed heavily. We compromised; some of her clothes, toiletries, miscellaneous personal items, were left at my flat and some of mine at hers, so that we could decide on the spur of the moment to spend the night in either, depending on where we happened to be, or our mood, at the end of an evening together.

The question: 'Is it love?' seemed juvenile. I am sure we both asked the question – never, however, out loud. The crucial fear – knowing the corrosion of day-to-day living as we did – was that our felicity would not survive it; and so we shrank from that test – except, unrealistically, for the occasional few days spent wholly together. We protected ourselves as best we could; which may be why my most poignant memory of our time together is its timelessness – its true gift a stopping of the clock, which neither of us admitted or spoke about.

That I should have considered living with her at all is strange for a different reason – fear that prejudice, lurking beneath the surface, would destroy us. True, Nancy showed not the slightest sign of Kay's feeling about Jews – not even that tell-tale one: 'Some of my best friends are Jews!' She had that apparent indifference towards religion that concealed a relaxed, true attachment, often found in the English upper class, which appeared to treat religion as a necessary convenience, seemingly social rather than spiritual, seldom taken too seriously. She might ask a question purely for information, prompted perhaps by a reference in a film or play or book – what *kosher* meant, for example, or why Jewish boy babies were circumcised – and as I replied I had no impression that the matter moved her in any way at all. The conversation would drift on naturally, with no tension. Perhaps, unawares, I myself avoided any closer reference to Jewishness; and perhaps Nancy did too. We left well alone.

Bill, with customary realism, had seen things differently. When my first meeting with Nancy was still hidden in the future – though perhaps already in preparation – he remarked: 'You must get that marriage out of your system! You need a good woman to get you started again!' By 'good' he meant undemanding, compliant, uncomplicated. Oh that word 'uncomplicated'! – fashionable shibboleth of the day. It was always the *other* person in a relationship who must be uncomplicated – lovers especially. They must be stoical, unquestioning, their humours easy to read, incurious about what lay beneath the surface of things, for whom life was spread out like a large-scale map, the road unmistakeable. Above all they must be untouched by the anxiety of the time.

By getting 'started again', he meant unfreezing the emotions, a charming image – reminding me of Munchausen's tale of a voyage to Novaya Zembla, where the winter air was so cold that people's *words* froze the moment they were uttered, so that no sound was heard, till the spring thaw brought a cacophony of words spoken long before, no longer relevant. Bill spoke as if he himself longed for a return of adolescent innocence, with its lavish outpouring of sentiment, frozen long ago.

Nancy, steeped in what she called 'old-fashioned values', professed to find such thoughts indelicate for a woman, and in any case 'not a practical attitude to life' – a remark that uncovered an innocence that sought serene, rightful satisfaction, comfortable habit, fulfilment and honest reward. Her need to move close, the flame of desire burning evenly, was simple-hearted and tender; and desire was the only certainty that remained, to be satisfied decently, with someone she could cleave to in full security. I said to myself: What fool would hold out for more? Perhaps life *should* be like this, not felicity, but rather contentment without ecstasy, a modest sufficiency predictable from one day to the next? Was *this* the golden mean? Was the time for seeking the topmost heights long past, the modest satisfactions of the middle slopes all that was left?

What was wrong with that? It seemed to be the one sure bearing I had found.

And now, as Bill spoke about the search for Tom, it seemed that I did not possess it after all – that an unsleeping Nemesis was about to strike. Had Nancy had a hand in this? Had *she* decided to 'rescue' Tom, and try to reach out to him once again – and, irony of ironies, do so through *me*? Yet I had been with her the night before, and there had been no hint, no change in her, to suggest any such thought. As far as I knew – not from her, for she never talked of Tom, but from Millicent and Bill – there had been no contact between them since their divorce. Had Bill delayed telling me about the search for Tom till this very evening so that I would have no time to question Nancy? I was not sure that I would have done so, but Bill would certainly have thought of the possibility and provided against it.

There was no need to voice my suspicions. He said: 'Listen – I give you my word. Nancy knows nothing – repeat nothing – of this. She had all she could stand of Tom long ago! Nobody's fault! Just one of those things.'

He had not mentioned it to me before because during that week – Millicent had broached the 'Tom problem' the previous weekend – he had been in Rome on business.

I said: 'But why *me*? You must see the irony of it?'

A faint smile of calculation crossed his face, and he pressed his lips together, as one who tells himself to be patient: 'You and

Nancy – we do care about that – we wouldn't dream of upsetting it. This business of Tom is separate – *totally* separate – and believe me I don't like being mixed up in it at all, not one bit.'

There were practical reasons for asking me to accompany him: 'You and I knew him at Oxford, in fact you saw him quite a bit at one time, playing squash and so forth; little things like that might help if we do run into him.' For such a delicate matter, he could not think of anyone else who would be sympathetic enough.

Tom had been one of the golden people at Oxford, beheld with wonder from my very first days there; seemingly possessed of every gift for a fulfilling life, plenty of money, a fine physique, well-connected, apparently limitless opportunity before him, and yet, as I discovered, consumed by unappeasable discontent. He had been drinking steadily even before he came up, and by his second year he was a heavy drinker. Following an élite fashion among moneyed aesthetes, he published, privately, a slim volume of poems on thick hand-made paper – *Eyes of Adonis*. Some of the poems were little more than doggerel, and he was hurt to find that he could not even *give* the little books away. At a sherry party in his rooms to cele-brate publication, guests were handed copies with their first glass. I left at the same time as Bill, then a communist mandarin I knew only slightly. Below us on the broad wooden staircase, a departing guest tossed his copy of *Eyes of Adonis* on to the bottom step, on top of others dropped there by people who had left earlier; lying there in disarray, the thick creamy-yellow paper, 'parchment edged', unruly by design, peeped from between the covers of dark blue board and eerily emphasised their forlorn state. If these people did not like Tom's verse, I said to myself, surely they might have had the decency to carry their copies back to their own rooms and dispose of them out of sight? What spite, what meanness of spirit, ruled here – in this citadel of the higher humanity? Bill said, in tones intended to be heard by those descending behind us, 'Some people care more about cultural snobbery than they do about their manners.'

I bent down and gathered up some of the little books, and put them under my coat, and he took the rest; and so we smuggled them away, hoping that Tom would not discover what had happened. Later, however, I heard that someone had passed the word back up the stairs to make sure that Tom did know.

An event of a different kind, which I think was oracular for Tom as it was for me, stood out above all else whenever I thought of him. It brought out a sensitivity in him that he normally kept tightly battened down, permitted to escape only when transmuted into a Puckish sense of humour that sat oddly on the broad, muscular frame, square face with bulbous red nose and full sensual mouth. Late one winter afternoon we played squash, at courts set amid playing fields a considerable distance from any other building. When we finished, and went to open the door in the back wall of the court, we found that the semi-circular metal handle, which swivelled into a slot in the door to make it flush during play, was jammed fast in the slot, and we could not swivel it out again to open the door. We had nothing in our shorts pockets with which to prise the handle free – a key or knife or other pointed piece of metal. Usually I carried a pocket knife, but on that day I had left it in my jacket on the bench in the entrance lobby on the other side of this very door. The unbelievable truth struck home – we were prisoners. Hot from playing, the cold air cooled the sweat on the skin and we shivered. Tom startled me by bursting into hysterical laughter and falling against the wall, holding his sides at the grotesque comedy of it – though in fact our plight was serious. There was no way of summoning help. Isolated as the courts were, no one would hear our shouts, and at this late hour it was unlikely that anyone else would use the courts that evening. It had been a particularly cold November day, and there was certain to be frost that night; wearing only shirt and shorts – soaked with sweat and impossible to dry out – with not a scrap of warm clothing within reach, we would be in a bad state if we had to spend the night in this suddenly hostile place.

To my surprise, a similar hysteria seized me, impossible to control, and in wild laughter I too fell against the wall and slid down on to the wooden floor. Here we were in this vast room with no way out, whose dazzling flat white surfaces and absence of shadows charged it with menace, other-worldly, with no windows except the skylights high above our heads jet black against the night, and total silence beyond the walls, containing no projections – not even a door handle! – featureless except for the court lines and the darker shaded lower part of the front wall and the wide gaping cavity of the gallery above the back wall, with nothing to show where we were in time or place, for that matter no proof of *who* we were, and no communication with the outside world, indeed – in the wintry silence – no evidence that there *was* one. We were encased in a Kafkaesque *anywhere* – or nowhere; and it was getting steadily colder, the coldness of nowhere.

Later, puzzling over that bout of hysterical laughter, I understood. Suddenly facing that impassable door, both of us, in a jolt of fantasy, were for an instant *relieved* to have shut out the world – and the knowledge that we *were* relieved, itself shocking, overwhelmed us. For me, fresh from the Gorbals, this new world was too powerful, too complex, too inscrutable to master, poorly armed as I was. I had yet to understand that mastery was not the point, for if 'advantages' were all one needed to win that battle, why was Tom, who from my point of view possessed them all, also in flight from it? Even in those early Oxford days I must have begun to see, unwillingly, that unhappiness had nothing to do with lack of 'advantages' – a truth that I had hitherto rejected through prejudice, the old simplistic responses I had brought with me from the Gorbals. If that old wisdom was not to be relied upon, where was the true road? Was it, after all, mother's stoic quietism? 'Lach tsoom draydl' ('Laugh as the wheel turns'). Or father's desperate turning and turning in the toils of chance? Or a fresh understanding altogether, still to be discovered? If fulfilment was not to be found through tangible things, where was it? Could it really be within? Did I have to remake myself? If so, into what? – a question as limitless and menacing as time itself, filled with sibylline murmurings, like this empty, freezing room, from which we had for the moment excluded time.

In retrospect, we had both recoiled from a glimpse of unbearable truth, different for each of us only in detail. Tom was not, after all, the charmed spirit I had thought; his perplexities were real in spite of his 'advantages' – life *was* spiritual after all. That truth was intolerable for him too. In the Gorbals Baths, in the discussion group under the hot showers, that view had been dismissed as boss-class mystification, invented to 'keep the workers down' – language of Jimmy Robinson the old anarchist, and even of Bernard in his fiery Marxist days.

That view had been satisfying, for it justified all discontent, freed one from all personal responsibility; but it would serve no longer. A new, upsetting awareness demanded admittance. To shut it out, I must have sensed – and I think Tom did too – was a kind of death. The world – the one that mattered, that of spiritual cause and effect – which Tom tried to exclude with drink, and which awaited us implacably on the other side of that door, already ruled within us, inescapable. We could distort its image, try to ignore it, but that would be pretence, nothing more. From that truth, childish laughter had been our refuge.

Suddenly we stopped laughing; perhaps the creeping frost in our limbs brought us to our senses. I got up from the floor, and Tom straightened up from the wall, and we faced the door in fury. Brute strength would not serve, for it was a very solid door, and it opened inwards. To break it down would have needed an axe. The place was now very cold indeed; fingers of frozen steel pierced the ribs, and breath drifted up before our faces in little grey clouds. Tom pulled the collar of his thin shirt tight round his neck to snatch a morsel of warmth, and shrank his head down between his shoulders, shivering audibly. 'God – I need a drink.' He muttered. 'I need a drink badly. What the hell are we going to do?'

I looked up at the wooden rail of the gallery above the door, and saw a way – the only way. It *must* work. Tom was much stronger than me; if he stood on my shoulders he could reach up to that rail and easily pull himself up and over, and run down the gallery stairs and open the door from the other side. I braced my back against the door and clasped my hands in front of me to give him a step up, and got him on to my shoulders, praying that he would reach the rail at first stretch, for I knew I could support him for a few seconds only.

'Got it!' he shouted; and breathless from the cold I echoed his gasps of triumph as he heaved himself up, using the friction of his rubber soles on the wall, and then over, and landed with a hollow thud on the wooden floor of the gallery. I stood away from the door as I heard him thumping down the stairs. My joints were stiff with cold, but the pulse raced now. The next moment he wrenched the handle round and hurled the door open. I leaped out into the little lobby, to the bench where we had thrown our clothes. We struggled into sweaters and jackets, and threw our arms back and forth across the chest to beat a little warmth into our bodies. From my jacket pocket I took the old army knife, 1914–18 issue, that I had bought in the army surplus stores in the Gallowgate in Glasgow. Its thick steel spike, about four inches long, could easily have prised the jammed door handle from its slot. Usually I carried it with me. Why had I left it in my jacket out here today of all days? Had I re-membered, unawares, that the handle on this door was defective, for we had had a little trouble with it before, and left the knife be-hind accidentally on purpose? – an example of what mother used to chide father for, sometimes in jest, more often in sad earnest: 'Shafft sich tsooriss fer gornisht – nisht genoog in der layben?' ('You make worry for yourself for nothing – isn't there enough in life as it is?').

After the harsh, unwinking light in our prison, the darkness out-side, though colder, was comforting. We got on our bikes and rode along unlit paths between rows of leaning willows, through cur-tains of ghostly mist floating in from the river, straining towards the distant lines of yellow street lights where the demons might not follow. 'Let's go back to my rooms,' Tom said, 'and we'll drown all that in good mulled claret.'

Before a great crackling fire, with a slender, white, cone-shaped enamelled jug of wine on the hearth, and plates piled high with an-chovy toast, the demons receded – but not far. Astir near the sur-face, there they would remain. The adventure appealed to Tom's taste for black humour, but his jokes were laboured, whistling in the dark. I wished we knew one another well enough to talk – *really* talk. For that, a special trust was needed, in which all the masks could be dropped, and there was no one, in Oxford, I knew well enough for that.

As for 'sharing', the Buchmanite concept of mutual airing of the soul, then still possessing some following in Oxford, I had found the mixture of boss-class amiability, evangelical bromides, and strong whiff of homosexuality, repellent.

Tom's drinking worsened from then on, whether influenced by that experience I never knew, imprisoning him more firmly. In consequence, I think, I saw less of him, and after he went down I did not see him at all until, some months after VE Day, I met him in Savile Row; I was walking away from one of the Council's scattered departments, and he was coming down the steps of a white-fronted house occupied by his tailor. He had had a 'good war', most of it in Cairo. He seemed much as he had always been, but heavier, redder in the face, the short thick nose broader than I remembered, the cheeks beginning to sag. We adjourned to Symond's Hotel – now gone – in South Molton Lane, whose quiet basement bar reminded me of a theatrical set of the perpetual cocktail hour of the late Twenties. Its shadowy, dated appeal of dove-grey luxury and art-deco innocence, and its club-like quiet and tolerance – no one cared how long you sat over your drink – was more congenial than the jostling pubs of the neighbourhood. There was also a suggestion of mystery about the upper floors of what must have been a very small hotel, reached by a mahogany staircase that rose up into the shadows to the left of the narrow street door, beside the steps leading down to the bar. In those days that still clung to remnants of an older propriety – Mrs Grundy was not yet quite dead – its air of naughtiness and faded comfort conjured thoughts of the hotel in *Mrs Warren's Profession*. Bill, when I mentioned it one day, agreed that it probably *was* a variation on that theme, and since he immediately steered away from the subject, I assumed that he spoke from experience.

Tom talked nostalgically of the Oxford days, and that was surprising, for he had always complained of being bored, and had gone down without bothering to take Schools. I asked what he was going to 'do', but remembered that for him it was an unreal question; he had no need to 'do' anything. He said: 'Oh, I suppose I shall write some more verse – I might start a literary magazine.' He shrugged, head drooping like that of a questing bloodhound: 'There's plenty of time.'

I had to get back to the office; and he was going to meet someone for a drink at Claridge's, a few yards away across Brook Street. We went up the short flight of steps and stood on the narrow pavement in South Molton Lane. He shifted uneasily, prolonging the moment. 'Let's meet for dinner some time?' he said. We exchanged phone numbers. It was a particularly fresh day in late September, and perhaps, after the years in the Middle East, he was not ready for the bite of English weather; he shivered. That must have triggered a memory. I said: 'Remember when we got trapped in the squash court?'

'Could I ever forget! There was something about it – the brooding presence of a minatory spirit! But *what* the message was I never discovered. Anyway, nothing much went right after that.'

He fell silent; his expression seemed to say: 'Don't ask why – I only wanted you to know.' Life owed him so much, and refused to pay up.

The old envy returned. Oh to have his volition – rich, free to do exactly as he pleased! I too had not fully understood that message from the minatory spirit – if I ever would. It struck me, then, that the whole Kay experience had been a defiance of it – not understanding who I was, reaching out for values that would never fit me, making failure certain.

I felt sorry for him. To the casual glance here was a conventional member of his class, discreetly but expensively turned out, all the disciplines in full control, except for one tell-tale sign. He had acquired a fashion of speaking in which he struggled to articulate each word with precision, that I later came to expect from the addictive drinker – from Maurice Richardson, for instance, good-hearted Maurice, who mouthed each word with care lest control should slip – signalling perplexity, praying for rescue.

I met Tom for dinner a few times, pleasantly enough superficially, but always with a depressing feeling that he himself was bolted and barred – as if I stood outside a house calling to someone far away in its interior, who sometimes came to a window and peeped at me from behind a curtain and retreated again, fearing communication.

Intervals between meetings lengthened, and then we lost touch, as happens easily in the whirl of London unless the will to the contrary is strong. After nearly ten years of silence, I met him in the Savoy, on my way into lunch with a group from Benson's the advertising agency. He stopped me and said his name, for I was about to walk past, not recognising him. I hoped I did not show my dismay at his appearance – eyes sunk deep and shadowed, the broad face bloated, red-blotched, the skin dry. His hand felt like soggy rubber. There was time only for a greeting, promises to meet, exchange of new telephone numbers. In the low, apathetic tones of his voice, desolation spoke.

As we parted it was he, this time, who referred to the squash court – shy reminder of an enduring link of a kind, belonging to another, distant world where hope had still been valid.

That meeting, some two years past, must have been fairly soon after Nancy divorced him – and long before I knew her. Had I known of the recent divorce, I would have made more of an effort, in sympathy, to meet him again; my own divorce was in the offing and I knew what it was like to be trapped, as he must still have been, on the obsessional roundabout of living and re-living old pain. As it was, he did not get in touch with me, nor I with him. I knew that I should, and was guilty, but I did nothing about it.

Sipping his coffee, Bill regarded me with that shrewd, intuitive look of his. He might have been listening to these thoughts: 'You mustn't feel guilty about him. There's so little one can do for a chap like that. He had his choices – and all the chances!'

He seemed intent on thoughts of his own, adding: 'There but for the grace of God, eh? Anyway, *you're* not likely to take that route out – nor, I think, am I. That's something, I suppose!'

An unfamiliar note in his voice, despondent, flat, startled me. I had never expected to hear him show the slightest doubt about the race he had run – confident, robust, successful, knowing so many of the answers. He had tried to disguise the tone by pretending to speak musingly, lightly; but Bill, or rather the Bill I thought I knew, had always chosen his words, and their presentation, carefully. True, in recent years he had seemed to be less guarded with me, but that was relative too – the Bill I knew never dropped his guard completely.

He said: 'How bizarre this "Tom problem" must seem to you? And I suppose unfair! – considering where you started from, and where he did! You've journeyed further than he ever will – or any of us.'

Even to go this far was out of character. The word 'journeyed' referred to things he had always avoided talking about, personal development, the progress of the soul. What doubts had the 'Tom problem' released, what soul searching, what unaccustomed casting of accounts? The suddenness of the change was itself disturbing. Perhaps it had not been sudden, but I had been blind to earlier signs of it? His note of disillusion prompted questions of my own; I had not realised how much his example had influenced me, the certainty he had always shown, if in truth it *had* been! In retrospect these thoughts are naïve, but they were dismaying then – as if I had been running behind the leaders in a race and they suddenly 'faded' and fell back behind me, putting me in the lead, and now I had no one to pace myself against. By some magic the evening's expedition had become powerfully symbolic. Beneath the quest for Tom we were seized by thoughts of lost horizons. In Bill too, I now saw, the outer and the inner selves were in discord. His remark about my 'journey' was thus exquisitely ironic, for he seemed to be looking back, not forward, to what paths, what fulfilments, he *should* have found – wistfully toying with alternatives long out of reach in the past, while I now moved in the opposite direction, not willingly, or even knowingly, but inevitably.

Unlike them, I had no ready-made choices. If mine were forced upon me, they were not choices at all. Bill, Tom, and the rest were born to certainty; and when that birthright let them down, disillusion was devastating. I saw that Bill's words – 'he had his choices', referring to Tom – could equally apply to himself. What were *his* regrets? His tone changed, and we talked of other things. The evening had much more in store.

We left Scott's about nine, the first dove-grey tints of dusk appearing in a clear summer sky, and walked along Shaftesbury Avenue to start our search in the Dean Street pubs. Apart from visits to restaurants in the locality for business lunches and dinners – the Étoile, Kettners, Au Savarin, the Acropolis, the White Tower – it was many years since I had spent any time in Bohemia, some of it in sorties from Oxford during the war and immediately after. Considered as a physical rather than a mental territory – not counting its comfortable outposts in Hampstead and Chelsea – Bohemia meant Soho and Fitzrovia, the latter a name that Tambimuttu – 'Tambi' – claimed to have given to the quarter of pubs and restaurants and run-down houses and flats that stretched north of Oxford Street from Soho, on the line of Rathbone Place and Charlotte Street and Fitzroy Square. Tambi was a 'wide boy' of Bohemia. He had arrived in England before the War from Ceylon, his only assets an alleged princely origin, and a marvellous ability to 'connect' when it suited him; with these he lived for many years in London, founded *Poetry London*, gave a number of poets their first appearance in print, and acquired a certain literary importance. Because of *Poetry London*, links with the publishers Nicholson and Watson, and the aura of influence he shrewdly hung about his shoulders, he was courted by writers and their friends, and by the unique demimonde attracted to the flame of creation.

Long ago, Bill told me, Tom had cultivated Tambi in the hope of getting his poems published in *Poetry London*, but without success. That may not have been a literary verdict on Tambi's part but the result of his disorganised ways; he might simply have lost Tom's poems – his pockets normally bulged with manuscripts – or absent-mindedly thrown them away, or *worse*. He told me one day, relishing the joke, that finding himself in *extremis* in a pub lavatory that had run out of toilet paper – a deficiency common in those days, for which it was wise to be prepared – he had searched his pockets for a spare piece of paper and, finding none, had used someone's poems instead. He would not tell me whose, pretending discretion;

the real reason, almost certainly, was that he did not know.

Tambi would have known where to find Tom; he knew where to find *anyone* who might one day be useful – and who more so than a man with money! Tambi had dropped out of sight long ago. Rumour had it that his picaresque career had veered to New York. Bill had heard that he was back in London, though whether his old haunts knew him again, he was not sure.

Bohemia's population as a whole had changed. 'Where has everyone gone?' Maclaren-Ross complained. Some had had enough of the Bohemian life and, in Bernard's words, 'gone straight'. Success in the creative market had lured some away, to revert, in time, to the conventional life previously tilted against. The superficially free-wheeling mood of the immediate post-war years – product not of elation but perplexity, when wartime stiffening had dropped away – had faded long ago, and with it the backward glance to romantic Thirties-style Marxist attachment. The wartime vogue for the iconoclastic treatment of service life and the accompanying class discordances, in which Maclaren-Ross, for one, had achieved acclaim, had run its course. Younger blood had invaded the Café Momus, impatient with past imagery, who had not known the war directly, nor the surreal yet cosy half-world of the Home Front where fire-watching and other fringe sources of freebooting income supported the Bohemian life, a resistance movement surviving, not unhappily, in the interstices of the Great Machine – precursor of later 'counter-culture'.

Faces that I did recognise were weathered like those of statues altered by the abrasion of time – not time alone, but the wear and tear of the Murger-esque life. They called to mind the scene in Proust where the narrator, entering a once familiar drawing room after many years of absence from society, imagines that the faces he sees, indistinctly recognised, are not real but masks, imperfect likenesses of the 'true' faces preserved in memory. Looking closely, he realises that the 'masks' really are the faces he once knew, worn and changed by time, which he likens to the rising waters of life, soon to engulf them.

As we continued from pub to pub – sometimes making a quick

survey from the doorway, more often going in and having a beer, to tune in to the flow of talk, not sure what we hoped to hear, a hint, a familiar name, a clue – the search began to assume an unreal, self-indulgent character, the original purpose overlaid by demonic visions – gleaming tresses of the Sirens, features serene, haloed in gold, their appeal still unbearably magnetic, but now the visions were admixed with contrition, regret for past mistakes, failed choices of love, plaintive cry of the might-have-been: '*O toi que j'eusse aimée!*' Only the shimmering legs and jutting hips of the street girls, and the obstacle course of rubbish and dustbins on the narrow pavements were unambiguous – the whole conveying the feeling of a surreal *mise-en-scéne*, stage properties and actors fixed in their places in expectant stillness, waiting for an unknown play to begin. Across this littered stage we picked our way, in truth looking for ghosts of ourselves. In the pubs, so many faces were too young. Too young? Was that why Tom might have decided to 'pack it in' – to retreat before this wave of youth for whom hope was not yet dimmed?

Bill was becoming more and more caustic about our mission. During dinner he had talked about Cyril Connolly's essential melancholy, and had quoted from *The Unquiet Grave*, fitting his own mood: 'Morning tears return ... Approaching forty ...' Bill was *over* forty, but only just. Still, he had said it – there remained, now, only the downward slope. Surely not? That *he* could mourn his past was too strange for belief. Except for that brewed-up tank in the desert, he had had a fair wind all the way. Yet the demons continued their clamour within, that was clear; and unfulfilled dreams waited their call to tread the stage. He had been right – it *was* unfair.

He said, in a burst of vehemence and strange irrationality, 'If I knew what in God's name I really was looking for, I wouldn't be wasting my time wandering about here!'

In one pub after another, getting into conversation with some of the older-looking faces, we casually mentioned Tom's name; had they by any chance run into him? Withdrawn stares and evasive answers told us that our Bohemian 'act' was not convincing.

Automatic suspicion closed the ranks against us; we reminded them of the common enemy, lackeys of 'them', the philistines, the Machine.

Late in the evening, entering yet another crowded pub – we had long since ceased to distinguish one from another – in the cloud of cigarette smoke a large-shouldered man lumbered past us; as he went, something about his appearance suggested Tom, but I was rather tipsy by now, and by the time the thought registered, he was out of the door. Bill did not think it was he, but we followed. Out in the street, the broad shoulders and bent head were disappearing into an archway. I called out 'Tom!', but the man did not look round. The archway led into a tunnel-like old cart-way paved with large rounded cobble stones, whose glossy convexities gleamed like dark wavelets in the moonbeams entering the tunnel at the far end, where it gave on to a long narrow yard flanked by shabby brick walls. Our man had gone to relieve himself against the blank back wall of a house. We lingered at the entrance, to get a better view when he returned. Half-way along the tunnel, a man and a girl stood pressed together – a prostitute and a client, was my first thought. Something about her, however, apparent even in the obscurity, did not fit – an air of innocence, and the small suitcase on the ground beside her, rounded, feminine, presumably hers. I had the impression of a girl of about eighteen, of medium height, with long fair hair hanging straight down to the middle of her back, in tight skirt and short leather jacket. Her companion leaned against the tunnel wall, stocky, with a straggly black beard, in shirt and trousers and open raincoat. She spoke to him in an audible whisper, the barrel roof of the tunnel amplifying a North of England voice slurred from drink and rough with cigarette huskiness: 'Can't we go to your place and do it – not here? It's not as nice! And I've got nowhere to sleep tonight anyway.'

Her words, half-beguiling, half-calculating, took me back in time, more than twenty years, to that night in the Gorbals tenement close when Annie's voice had come to me from the blackness at the far end beside the rubbish heaps, where she stood with Phil – who would discard her, as she had discarded me in favour of his 'better prospects'; and to the day, a few weeks after, when she waylaid me outside the Baths, in 'trouble' – though I did not know it at the time – and tried to persuade me to go with her, to entrap me. That girl, too, was trying to escape from her beginnings, making a bargain of a kind, as Annie had done with Phil and been defeated, and broken by Nemesis – and why should she fare any better? Not much had changed. Why did Annie return to me now – a cry from a remote valley of the mind? Figures and scenes from the past pursued and entwined and fled apart again, perception refracted by time and experience, unappeased – the wrong things desired, or the right ones at the wrong time, and nothing was ever for the best. You grieved for the wounds that mere existence inflicted. *Lacrimae rerum.*

'Here are the tears of things, mortality touches the heart.'

We stood on the edge of the pavement, a decent distance away. The narrow street was empty. The full moon sent slanting lines of shadow, cast by protruding window sills and door lintels, across solid Victorian façades, the brickwork stippled with flecks of light and shade like hewn rock. Here and there, on an upper floor, a boarded-up window showed a lonely crack of light – signal from a once-magical bed-sitter world that had proclaimed romance in other days, now fighting for survival against the march of property developers. From far away, carried on the soft night breeze, came the sound of a brawl – perhaps a pub landlord was making a clearance, preparing for closing time. This was the moment when people rushed to other pubs, across a 'licensing frontier' where closing time was half-an-hour later, to hold reality at bay a little longer. There were many kinds of mortality – the future drew close too soon, tantalising with choices one no longer possessed, visions of perfection that had faded; and the present was drawn away behind you into the past as in the wake of a ship, too quickly, and you could not delay it for a single moment.

Heavy, unsteady footfalls echoed in the tunnel; our man shambled out, a hand on the wall to keep his balance. It was not Tom.

Behind us, the couple were silent now. We crossed the street and stood in the doorway of a boarded-up shop, and lit cigarettes. The hard moonlight endowed the drab houses, square and blunt-edged, many with broken and boarded windows, with a silvery, soaring elegance. The life of this world drained away, leaving a sense of relief, but the many questions were postponed, not cancelled. Its symbolisms were too disturbing – visions belonging to a life now out of reach, desires long out of their season. Far away down Charlotte Street, dark figures, like wispy Victorian silhouettes, wavered along the pavements, taking the unfulfilled evening with them. The futility of our search, now obvious, weighed heavily; and I wondered why I had connived at the charade, superficially innocent though it had been. Moved by an ill-defined sympathy, we had not paused to question its purpose; and now there was an admixture of guilt; concern for Tom, we now saw, had been secondary. We stood there in silence for many minutes, each waiting for the other to begin.

Bill proclaimed to the night air, in half-comic solemnity, Cyril Connolly's valedictory flourish in the final issue of *Horizon*: 'It is closing time in the gardens of the West …'

It was all very well for Connolly to say that, I said, whose birthright had admitted *him* to those gardens; he at least had had *his* playtime there! I was instantly ashamed of my words. Connolly could never resist shooting off the elegant, loaded image, containing many levels of association. Taken superficially, these were often ridiculed by his enemies, and because in his dandyish indolence he found 'pedestrian' exposition tedious, he left himself open to dismissal as a witty lightweight. Here, however, he had made an acute, Spenglerian comment upon the contemporary rejection of cultural tradition, the nihilism polluting so many fields of life, soon to become a badge of conformity in the swinging Sixties. Connolly had a surer sensitivity to the long, slow, deeper movement of the *zeitgeist* than many cared to admit. For Bill, however, as for Connolly, the sadness was also uniquely personal.

Cyril Connolly's lamentations for the past, and rejection of the present, were much in Bill's thoughts – perhaps because Connolly expressed with accuracy and elegance a reluctance to compromise with a brutish, iconoclastic face of the post-war world. Connolly, it is true, was vulnerable to criticism for infelicities of behaviour, gross hedonism, egoism, waywardness – often adduced from motives of envy, to spoil recognition of his gifts. He saw many things too clearly for comfort, and to his enduring credit he was an unwilling trimmer. He posed an infuriating challenge for those who could not resist joining in, and adding to, the spiritual dilution of the time.

Bill waved his cigarette in an arc to encompass the whole array of gleaming, crumbling façades around us: 'All this stands for so much in me that I regret. I have allowed so much pleasure to pass me by.' He gestured towards the archway: 'Take that girl for instance. Delicious – fresh, eager, and a little *louche*! Don't look so surprised – I'm not as fastidious as you may suppose! Not that I would prefer to take her in exactly those conditions! – and not solely physically either but in the perfume of romance – but it's the *spontaneity* of taking her, to reach out without a second's thought, something I've never dared to do. Discipline has been too strong. Or perhaps I have simply been deficient in passion all along?'

The quick click of feminine heels resounded sharply in the tunnel, and the man's slower, heavier steps. The two emerged, he with an arm about her slender waist, the other hand carrying the little suitcase. She leaned into him, clingingly. They went briskly to the corner and turned away towards Tottenham Court Road.

'Maybe it's age,' he continued. 'For instance, I know I am a trifle drunk, and *that's* something new – in the old days I could drink *anybody* under the table! One hopes it is *not* age, declining libido and so on! But the only other possible explanation, that I never *have* had enough passion, is even more depressing. I have always been the calculating sort, fearing to be out of control. Discipline holds one together. In other ways I've done pretty well – but I dare not ask myself what it's all worth. Because I know the answer. I have sheered away from so much in life, too often from the sweetest pleasure of all – to take a new woman when I feel like it and hang the consequences.'

'The old, old story: "Sweet pleasures of the unintended moment!" '

'That's it! Remember that day all those years ago, when we sailed my new fourteen-footer up to Godstow, and I talked about

"gather ye rosebuds"? – I must have had an inkling of this deficiency of mine. Because "gather ye rosebuds" – in this sense anyway – was precisely what I felt, inexplicably, I was *not* doing – or
not enough. And now I *know* I wasn't, and it's probably too late to
change. You need a special certainty to be spontaneous, and I have
never possessed it, and I envy those who do. There are so many
wild cards in the pack, so many tantalising choices! But whenever
I have had to choose, for instance, between pleasure and power
– and money means power – I have chosen power. And yet,
possessing it, I ought to have been enjoying myself all this time. But
when I am honest with myself, I know that I seldom do – or not
enough.'

'Who does?'

'Oh, I don't know! When the pleasure's there for the taking and
you hold back, then it is worrying – when you catch yourself thinking "Will it be worth it?" or, worse, "Can I spare the time?" or,
worse still, "Will it be as ravishing as I want it to be?" – remembering past disappointments, the tedium of pandering to her fancies,
the trivialities that pass for conversation! That *is* age! And when you
baulk at details that never bothered you before, the *organisation* for
example. Booking into a hotel, and those humiliating precautions
against being spotted, or the petty nuisances of keeping a separate
flat for the purpose, never entirely free of discovery by that method
either. And all the time you *know* – and this certainly is age – that it
cannot possibly repeat the pure ecstasy of long ago. When you're
young, these dispiriting thoughts simply don't occur to you.'

Here was a new, unsettling candour, bearing a cargo of dangerous confidences. I had been mistaken in so much! Had the evening's
expedition been an unconscious preparation for this? He was
surely overdoing the self-scourging, indulging in a charade of his
own? Still, the feelings were obviously *there* – and demanded to be
shared with someone he could trust. The lament also expressed a
poignant sympathy with me, as if to say: 'I am not the paragon you
thought. We all have feet of clay – in some part of us at least. It's par
for the course.'

We strolled along and talked, hardly noticing the streets emptying of traffic and people, the pub doors finally closed, and the warm murmurs of a summer night – descending from open windows overhead, and the night echoes coming into their own. We must have talked for a very long time, for waiters from late-closing restaurants were putting out their dustbins on the pavement when we decided to call it a night. In Fitzroy Square we hailed a taxi; my flat being nearer than his, he gave me a lift home before going south. As I got out he said: 'I don't imagine we could have done anything for Tom even if we had found him – not seriously, that is. He can't face reality – he's the complete opposite of you, for instance. You have the guts to reach out and take hold of life as it really is, and take your chances! I've always envied you that.'

I stood in the quiet street and let the night sink in. In the church gardens across the street, the hard moon picked out leaves and branches of burnished silver, stilled as if fashioned of *papier mâché*. Yes, he must have been a bit drunk, for the candour had gone deep. His last words were astonishing, and saddening too. Envy *me*? Did anyone ever see *anybody* clearly?

I never did see Tom again. Later I heard the rest of the story, and where he had been in those periods when he had supposedly disappeared into Bohemia. Maintaining his flat in Belgravia, he had taken another in Islington, and there, in secret, had set up house with a beautiful West African girl. She looked after him, suffered his drinking and his furies, tried to dispel his melancholy. Not long after the night of our search for him, he went into hospital with liver failure and other complications – the final phase.

As we came away from the funeral, Bill said in a quiet aside: 'What is there to say? He never gave himself a chance from the start.'

Nancy, when we were alone, said: 'It sounds frightful, but to be honest I feel nothing. He broke my heart. He could have done anything he wanted – *anything*! I didn't understand, at first, how weak he was. He needed a mother, not a wife.'

After a silence, she sighed, and in fury she railed against the world. 'There are just no words to fit. It sounds so silly to say "Life isn't fair." But it's true.'

11

The End of Guilt

It should have occurred to me sooner that Tom's death must change my relationship with Nancy. It was, as I realised later, an especially crucial time for me, on the point of breaking away into international work – seeking dedication, looking inwards more than I should have done at such a juncture. There was no excuse; I was not sufficiently aware.

After their divorce some three years before, Tom had drawn into himself, and mixed little in their former social set. I must have assumed that she had sailed free of him completely, and no emotional linkages with him remained. That was naïve, with so much evidence of my own to the contrary. I had not seen Kay for a much longer time, yet the mark she had left was indelible; that, and the persistent presence of my Gorbals *alter ego*, should have told me that all passion, of whatever kind, imprinted the soul for ever. What mattered was not the persistent pain of old wounds, mistakes, defeats, but whether one could move beyond them – and that was hard. I should have known how to help Nancy do that.

Certainly some quality in our life together *had* altered. In retrospect, I could not be sure that the changes did flow, even partly, from Tom's death; they might have been already in train from other, unrelated influences. Perhaps our relationship had grown too comfortable, and the sensibility to tend it carefully had blunted? Neither of us had ever wanted to look beyond the present, and as that 'present' lengthened – we had been together about a year – nudging us at last to consider our future, both of us, for different reasons, had hesitated – and that hesitation itself may have been the poison. Its signs must have been there for some time, but I had chosen not to see them.

Tom's death hit us all hard. Perhaps Millicent, in urging that search for him, had been driven by a premonition. For Bill and me, more or less of an age with him, it stirred thoughts that were grim enough – what might be in store for *us*! For me, it revived wartime feelings, when, having asked to be called up as soon as possible, certain that I would be killed, inexplicably I had come out of the war machine alive – and ever since, a shadow had come close from time to time and tapped me on the shoulder, reminding me that the death I had escaped was waiting to steal upon me, any day, out of a clear blue sky. That, I preferred to think, was what had befallen Tom, struck down so young. There was, however, another way of looking at it, which we shrank from putting into words – but Millicent, I knew, brooded on it. Drinking obsessionally against all warnings, he had committed suicide. That was too near the bone for any of us. Besides, it smacked of sitting in judgement on him, and who were we to do that? If his death had been foredoomed, the manner of it hardly mattered.

Its immediate effect upon Nancy was not obvious. Decent, considerate, a certain nicety had always prevented her from talking to me about him. There were moments, now, when some inner tension forced his name to the surface – but she revealed little of her feelings, and soon switched the conversation to safer ground. Perhaps I should have encouraged her to talk about him; but some blinkered perversity prevented me; this was *our* world, hers and mine, a haven to be protected. I may also have feared that if we discussed her life with him, we would be led to examine where *we* were headed! On the surface, our life together flowed on unchanged. One day, she said something that startled me, a hint that she may have blamed herself, in leaving Tom, for his early death, in particular by her toughness, as he had seen it, in insisting upon the divorce. Surely, I said, she had acted in self-preservation? He had brought disaster on *himself*! He had been close to alcoholism when I knew him at Oxford, and well aware of the harm he was doing to himself – he had been warned by his doctor – but he had continued determinedly down that road. Did she really think she could have saved him? That question startled her.

'I didn't see myself ever trying to *save* him!' She put both hands to her temples and smoothed the hair away from the high, rounded forehead. 'Anyway, hard drinking's not exactly unknown in our family. People manage somehow. I didn't see further than that. And he was *such* fun in the beginning! I suppose he *was* drinking a little less at that time. And afterwards, when he was drinking more and more, I didn't see anything to do except grin and bear it. If I thought at all about *why* he was doing it, it seemed as though he'd never grown up – and I did feel desperate sometimes.'

That moment was crucial because of what was about to be revealed, and that is perhaps why I remember her appearance, then, so well. She sat erect on the window seat, trimly, with the look of a pensive schoolgirl, an impression emphasised by her dress – correct, austere but charming; it was a fitted dress of dark blue with a long front panel of white, from neck to hem, shaped and buttoned down the side, with short, cuffed sleeves. She looked down at her folded hands in her lap, pink and slender and graceful. Absently she added: 'And maybe I did ask myself: "How could I ever risk having children by him?" '

She gave a little gasp and her fingers flew to her lips; shaken by the admission. Curiously enough, the possibility of her having a family had never before been mentioned. Now that it *had* emerged, and in that fashion, I should have thought about it a great deal, but I put it aside.

Of course she had continued to love him from afar. A frayed mooring rope had survived. Little signs emerged from now on, unintended. She lingered over memories of places they had visited in their years together, and things done together – riding, for instance, which they had both loved; Tom had been a graceful horseman, and I remembered from the Oxford days that it was only in the saddle that he had ever seemed complete, fully himself. The hope that one day the link would become strong and rich again was not conscious; rather it was a vague longing, never acknowledged. It held her emotions in a traumatic suspense, impeding new movement – which was why *our* relationship, in which we pretended that only the present 'counted', had seemed to suit us so well. As it lengthened, assuming a settled character, the self-deception must have gnawed at us. In truth our relationship, did we but admit it, meant much more than that, but we dared not say it. Tom's death had done more than shatter the pretence; it had revived the bitterness of wasted years and forced her – forced us both – to see that the relationship *as it stood* could sustain us no more. We could stand still no longer. There must be further commitment – or nothing.

The signs of wear and tear were slight, hints pieced together long afterwards, shifts in mood or tone of voice or caprice; often they were not so much in what was said or done as in what was omitted. Looking back, in the weeks and months after Tom died there crept into our hitherto easy, unquestioning life together a tincture of restlessness, an unidentifiable discontent.

Trying to understand it, I remembered Bill's blunt realism shortly before I met Nancy for the first time at their flat: 'You must get that marriage out of your system! You need a good woman to get you started again!' When the chemistry with Nancy 'worked' I had been glad enough to let it take me where it would, to silence the warning voices, forget the unpaid debts – the flight from Jewishness, the search for belonging, for dedication. There was, however, guilt, for Bill's words, suggesting that Nancy and I, no longer innocent and starry-eyed, could legitimately 'use' each other in a mutual therapy, were not wholly convincing. Doubtless Millicent had talked to her in similar fashion. So, using each other, we were both guilty – each absolving the other! That was not convincing either. The old morality, woman the weaker vessel, pulled me back; if there was guilt, mine must be the greater.

Guilt apart, I should have realised that a relationship from which we each took what we could – if that was all it was – must sooner of later turn and rend itself; I should have been prepared, but was not. Secretly, we both hoped, childishly, that if we did nothing 'it would come out all right'. The modish talk of 'therapy' was a convenient euphemism for doing what was agreeable. Under that cloak I had counted on Nancy being there for as long as I wanted her to be – 'sauce for the gander but not the goose'. I was possessed by the old, old view of woman – father's view – as being by nature more deeply committed by her emotions than man, and rightly so,

not permitted to be dispassionate, to stand back and measure, calculate, be in control.

Though the strains of the relationship were beginning to tear at
the nerves, and we did try to evade or cushion them, we could not
bring ourselves to discuss our feelings, and what we each wanted
from life, with the surgical logic of adolescence – which might at
least have lessened stress, and made us more aware. Adult pride
would not allow it. I owe it to Nancy – if not to myself – to put it
all as fairly as I can. If we did 'use' each other, it was not with meanness of spirit. There *was* mutual care, and love, and tenderness, but
the ground on which we stood was never secure enough. Perhaps,
in spite of my care, I had betrayed my fears that Jewish sensitivities
would get in the way once again; though I observed the same
silence about Kay, as she did about Tom, some hint may have
escaped. Equally, she might have drawn back from closer commitment because of fears and prejudices of her own, unspecific, but at
bottom of the same nature.

Certainly the pretence of 'living for the day' wore thinner and
thinner, and despite her denials she did worry about the future. I
cannot be sure that she had *never* made any reference, however
obliquely, to marriage; if she had, I must have ignored or evaded it,
and that must have hurt her – and confirmed that our days together
were numbered. Once, not long after Tom died, when we were
staying with Bill and Millicent in the country, by chance I overheard a snatch of conversation between the two women. It was one
of those long, still, dreamy summer afternoons, with puff-balls of
high cirrus hanging in a hard blue sky, and sounds drifting clear
and velvety from afar. We had played tennis doubles on an old,
springy grass court behind the kitchen garden; and after a time
Millicent and Nancy had gone off to start tea on the little terrace
outside the drawing-room. Bill's old leg wound had left him with a
barely perceptible limp; however, he had once been a very good
player, and even now, confined to what *he* called 'a gentle game', he
was still formidable, but he tired quickly. We stopped and strolled
back, along a screen of poplars, to join them. Coming near – his
hearing must have been sharper than mine – he halted and made as

if to draw my attention to something in the foliage above, but I had already heard Nancy mention my name. Before I could turn back, I heard Millicent say: 'Darling, if you mean to have babies, you haven't got *masses* of time left!' Nancy said: 'I don't want to think about that – it's blissful as it is. I don't want *anything* to change, but …'

We were screened from them by part of the kitchen garden wall, but they might have heard our steps on the gravel path, for the talk stopped abruptly, the moment of alerted silence masked by a tinkle of teacups. Nancy's 'but …' had been eloquent; the present relationship could survive only if it remained unchanged, and that was now impossible. Our time in the still backwater was at an end. I think I could have stayed in it a great deal longer, but I cannot be sure. Nancy's fear for her own limited time, as those overheard words made plain, was decisive.

She had never made the slightest mention of having children; from then on, the thought slipped out in many oblique ways, usually concealed by a negative. Speaking of a friend's problems with her children she said: '*How* can she stand them! The joys of motherhood! I can't *imagine* myself having children.'

Once, after Tom's death – and near the end of our time together, though I did not know it – she said: 'Remember me saying, after the funeral: "I feel nothing"? It wasn't true. I was *trying* to feel nothing. I felt as though he had gone away and taken part of me with him – as if part of *me* didn't belong to me any more.'

I did not understand this fully at the time. She was telling me that for her the therapy had not worked. She was still not free, but must now go on her way.

Yet it was hard to make any move. I noticed that she was eating less, and complaining of listlessness; the family doctor said she was a little anaemic, and suggested a change of air, perhaps a long cruise. A few weeks later, she told me that an uncle had invited her to stay on his cattle ranch in Canada – there would be riding, open air life, above all a change of scene; it would put her to rights again, and she would be back in a couple of months. After a pause, she said shyly: 'Would you come with me? I'm sure Uncle Roderick would love to have you. And don't worry about the fare and every-thing. It's all right! Really it is!'

'I would like to go if I could, but I couldn't allow you to keep me afterwards while I found another job.'

'Oh, I wouldn't mind a bit. You know that! Still, we could call it a loan if you liked?'

I think she really did want me to go with her – something might be made to 'work' after all. In my confusion of the moment I thought she might be making the gesture in simple decency, to soften the break – knowing that I must refuse. It is hard to be sure even now.

I thought of Rachel, long ago, wanting to 'keep' me, and my im-mature refusal. Was I making the same myopic misjudgement yet again? This would be no ordinary trip, of that I was sure. It would be a way, first of all, of postponing the parting, with a vague hope of finding permanence, somehow, along the way – before our link-ages weakened finally. She must have read my thoughts, and bent her head in acquiescence: 'I know how you feel. I'll come back soon – I really will.'

We wept together on the day she left. We dared not say it was over. There might still be a tomorrow – one day.

Deserted Battlefield

Nancy had shown me that almost any relationship could 'work', in a fashion, if one made few enough demands on it. In the end, 'few enough' was insufficient – and she had said so, in effect, by leaving. I had said so too, by letting her go. We must both have known, but suppressed the knowledge, that to talk of a tomorrow was a kindly bromide to make our parting seem a trifling thing. All that was lacking was confirmation of finality. Fear of finality could be worse than the event itself. In a few months it came. Nancy telephoned one night from Winnipeg: 'I wanted to speak to you and tell you ...' She was breathless with emotion, whether it was undiluted happiness or simple nerves it was hard to tell; I did sense, however, a relaxation in her voice, as if a fear had been lifted, and I remembered, in our days together, that she had never sounded as free as this. What I had taken to be easy-going acceptance had been careful restraint, avoiding sharp edges – detachment. I had believed, it seemed, what it had suited me to believe.

'Oh, I'm glad I've said it to you – a letter can be simply beastly! I feel I can *talk* to you – oh I do hope I always will ... Jamie's a cousin. He's a widower. And I'll be a stepmother! But I'll have at least one of my own, who knows maybe two ... It's such a different world here, but I suppose I'll get used to it ... Oh please, please understand! I don't want us to stop being friends ...'

With finality came a strange, aching freedom – release from illusion and hope. It also brought, however, a bitter, astringent, restless quality – a note of warning: 'You must move away from this dead point, or die.'

The worst part of being alone was learning to resist the impulse to turn and share a thought with her, a natural sweetness in our days together, unconsidered till now. I spent many weekends, and many evenings while daylight lasted, walking the quiet roads of St John's Wood, between rows of tall narrow stucco houses behind screens of foliage dipping over leaning walls, that recalled the complacent affluence of North Oxford – chewing over the years, *all* the years since the Gorbals, ranging back and forth, looking for a pattern; but there was none, only movement. I felt an unfamiliar burden of empty time on my shoulders. What had I done with all this echoing vacuum of time before? What had I to show for it? On the face of it, nothing. That was surely unjust – there *must* be more. Why did I look back and see nothing – all the accounts cast, one side against another cancelled, a blank sheet remaining? No! Look again. The past had receded once more, or I had moved on without knowing it, and that expanse of emptiness behind me was a reminder that time was winding away fast, not waiting for me – as if it ever had! – and that I was now free, as I had never felt before, to put my mark on it. A giant hand had hurled me forward across that chasm of time, as the scholarship essay had blasted me out of the Gorbals and flung me to Oxford long ago. When had this latest charge of gunpowder been set? Was it during the time with Nancy in the quiet backwater off the main stream – or had its preparation begun in the years before, touched off by her leaving me? What did it matter *when*? It was enough to know that the standstill years – as I now saw they had been – were over.

The only question was – where to now? Standing alone in the weighty silence she had left behind, it seemed to have been answered.

One of mother's oft-repeated sayings returned: 'Laybn is der besten rebbeh. Herr tsoo! Fershtay vosser zogt. Lach tsoom draydl' ('Life is the best teacher. Listen well. Understand what he says. Laugh as the wheel turns.') I *had* listened, and at last I understood, and now many things clamoured to be written down – or be completed. I did not know it, but I was about to begin a long-delayed sequel to the scholarship essay, in fact a series of books to enlarge its simple, unitary vision of man's proper path through life. Perhaps I had needed Nancy to help me unlock a reluctant progress of the soul – an awesome resumption of awareness, like hearing the creak of old ice loosening its grip in the spring, breaking the accumulated silences of the mountains. There was a stoic reminder, too, which mother had tried to give me – too young to understand at the age of five or six – that life's pace was pitiless, and unless you learned to recognise its shifts and stay in step it would grind you into the dust and pass on without you. Even so, granted that life was the best teacher, I wished it would stop driving me from one false turning to another, as it seemed to have done in those standstill years! Ah, but how could you know a turning was 'false' until you reached the end of the journey – it might have taught you something you could not have learned in any other way?

The present silence, the insistent emptiness where Nancy had once stood, would have to be the spur I needed. Months before, I had started another book, but I had done little more than draft the outline and some fifty pages. In it, and in several that were to follow, a principal theme would be that people were losing the holistic view of life inherited from earlier generations, and that it was urgent to restore it. I took up the typescript again, certain that I would now finish the book, *The New High Priesthood*. It would show how the persuasion machine – advertising, PR, press and broadcasting, the design of products and their presentation, the 'marketing message' – was now the major influence in moulding people's beliefs, and instilled a shallow, infantile view of life. The most important damage that resulted, personal and social, was the weakening of inherited convictions about life's purpose – as expressed in the great religions – in favour of the supposed needs of business. In the age-old battle between the two, the interests of business must always win, because business now had at its disposal methods of persuasion infinitely more alluring and powerful than those of religion and the inherited culture. The only hope was that democracy would act quickly to shift the balance in favour of the transcendental values. I wrote later, in my paper *Perspectives of Fulfilment*,

'Implicit in each culture is a vision of human fulfilment, a set of standards of a desired personal identity which it exists to uphold.

Cultures get out of phase [when discordant influences impede performance of this task] when under attack, for example by new technologies ... The ideal identity then becomes indistinct, and the resulting emotional insecurity produces social breakdown, political reaction, conflict.'

I was to see examples of this breakdown, in its cruder forms, in the Third World, but the signs in the developed countries were no less alarming.

That ideal of identity, and the moral conventions that grew up to uphold it, I called the 'ethical capital' bequeathed by the past; this the new High Priesthood subtly destroyed, substituting trivial, transitory values – the annual model change for example – attacking the very idea of permanence. Democratic government itself was trivialised, shortly to be exquisitely demonstrated in the campaign to elect Ronald Reagan as Governor of California, a classic example of selling politicians like breakfast cereals or toiletries. The gale of the world had shifted from the battlefield to the high street and the home.

The New High Priesthood, published in 1967, was probably ahead of its time. Although aspects of its subject matter have been written about since, it is fair to say that none of the social evils discussed in the book has been effectively attacked by any government. Meanwhile society *has* developed along the lines I predicted in it. Perhaps the Siren voices of consumerism are too powerful for politicians to challenge? That they *are* so powerful is of course the heart of the matter.

So dedication had come – but I did not know it till much later. All I felt at the time was the compulsion of it, like the enchainment to the Mitchell Library in the Gorbals days. I did not understand how deep its roots were. One evening, walking in St John's Wood Road opposite the main gates of Lord's Cricket Ground, my eyes were drawn to a fly-sheet on a notice board outside a white classical portico. The building, I was surprised to see, was the St John's Wood Liberal Synagogue – surprised, for I must have passed it often, and because of its classical features it had not occurred to me that it was a place of Jewish prayer; Hellenist influence was unusual, as far as I knew, in synagogue architecture. The announcement on the fly-sheet was mysteriously moving – a lecture on the Dead Sea Scrolls. Recent talk of them had fired the imagination, the distant past reaching out to pluck the sleeve of the present; for me the touch was direct, compelling. The words Dead Sea had always fascinated me with their paradox, for since childhood I had thought of the word 'sea' as symbolic of *life*, whose turbulence I imagined reaching out from the piled up waters of Genesis to find a new home on the land. And now I felt a romantic aptness that on the banks of that 'dead' sea, these inspired writings, concerning faith and morals in all their universality – the ethical capital I myself was writing about! – had lain in hiding, enriching civilisation, wielding power from within the rock of Qumran. I stood there for a long time, transfixed by the words 'Dead Sea Scrolls', a shaft of truth tightening the heart – like the first breathless moment on a mountain top, all life spread out below, the shock of complete vision uplifting in the rarefied air.

The speaker would be an Israeli general and archaelogist. The idea of an Israeli general, too, was the stuff of romantic dreams, at last realised, bridging the millennia from the days of *The Sons of Light*, far from the conventional picture, until recent days, of the downtrodden Jew of the ghetto. The combination of the man of battles with the man of learning also fitted my early imagery of Biblical times, formed during long hours of Torah learning on the hard benches of the *cheder* or religion school, the Talmud Torah in Turriff Street in the Gorbals – swords and banners of Bar Kochba. These thoughts buzzing in my head, I decided to go to the lecture, to be held in a hall adjoining the Reform Synagogue at Alyth Gardens, near the flat where I had lived with Kay. I had no idea that this was to be the first step of my return.

Here I digress to explain the names of three main segments of Jewish observance, Orthodox, Reform, and Liberal, not always clear even to some Jews. Liberal and Reform, though for historical reasons separate, can be placed under the heading of Progressive. Between Progressive and Orthodox, the key doctrinal difference may be stated as follows: to the Orthodox, the revelation on Sinai is absolute and unchangeable, to the Progressive it is continuous. In Progressive synagogues there is greater use of English – or other language of the host culture – and less of Hebrew, non-segregation of women, and somewhat shorter services on the great Holy Days and at other times in the religious calendar.

In retrospect it was the thought of a silken thread of revelation leading all the way back to the Dead Sea Scrolls and the Zealots, constant over the millennia, that drew me back, not a matter specifically of doctrine but the awareness of an identity shared with the Zealots – and the feeling that their discipline, their understanding of the unity of every aspect of life, awakened a sympathetic resonance in me, the same holistic view that I had instinctively expressed in the scholarship essay – and which I was now committed to write about for many years to come.

On my way to the lecture a few nights later, the thought that I might one day attend a service must have crossed my mind, for it occurred to me, with a twinge of guilt, that I could not remember when I had last been in a synagogue – and not only guilt, but almost childlike apprehension, realising that I had forgotten all I had once known about the detail of behaviour at a service. If I ever did go to one, surely others present, secure within *their* identity as Jews, would spot me at once for what I was, a lapsed Jew? Looking back, how naïve of me to worry, in those latter days, that anyone would notice, or care! How fixed I still was in the thinking of the Gorbals days, when older ghetto Jews would certainly have noticed, and cared very much; even so, some of them would have stretched out a hand to help the lost stranger – inadvertently driving home his shame. When *had* I last been in a synagogue? It must have been more than twenty years before, in the Gorbals, not long before I learnt that I had won the scholarship to Oxford, when I had gone with father to say *Yawrtsayt* or remembrance prayers for mother – an awesome moment for us both, in different ways. We were alone, the last forlorn contingent of our family, desperately united but with no words to fit our feelings. I was near to him and far away, struck by the divergence between his obvious faith and the oppressed waywardness of his life, for which atonement was now impossible, or at best too late. This impression was especially strong when he came to the words: 'the memory of the righteous is as a blessing' – the act of remembrance confers grace on the doer. That statement appeared to assume – and I felt guilty even to think of questioning it – that in life the dead person had been righteous! Certainly it seemed right to think that mother was – but who was I to know?

As he uttered the words he wept. Did he really regard her as righteous – and had he thought so always, while she lived, or only now? All that evening and most of the next day, with the twenty-four hour *Yawrtsayt* candle burning in its thick glass tumbler on the high mantelshelf above the black coal range, giving the little kitchen, in its greyness, an eerie, other-worldly atmosphere, he sat at the kitchen table with its cracked oil-cloth cover, shirt sleeves rolled up above the elbow, shirt neck open, the dark grey straps of his braces hanging down from his trousers waistband, and drank many glasses of 'Russian tea' – lemon tea sucked through a lump of sugar – and talked about her. He did not talk directly to me but seemed to address *himself*, letting his thoughts spill out. On that day he did not go to work, nor to the gambling club. I realised, sitting there facing him, that despite my dear childhood memories of mother, I did not know, *really know*, much about her. Yes, I did want to know if 'righteous' fitted her. Why, when it was all too late? Suddenly, for no reason that I knew, each word, consigned to memory, had to have a trustworthy meaning, as a little child needs to be sure of each step he takes. The words 'memory of the righteous' gave everyone the benefit of the doubt, and now I saw that father too, in his tenacious analytical fashion, was aware of that doubt, and perhaps blamed himself for it more than he should have done. I could only guess at the guilt for which he had already punished himself, day after day, so grievously. Young as I was, I could see that the obsessional gambling was symptomatic of insoluble conflicts. Beneath it all he had kept his faith strong, in his own fashion.

Now, walking up the quiet road to the meeting hall, mysteriously aware that this really was the first step of return, I wished that he could have been at my side – wondering, even as the thought crossed my mind, that I could still mourn the absence of that support, flimsy enough as it would have been, and in any case too late in the day.

With some surprise, echoes of former cynicism still strong, it struck me that, as with father, faith had never left me but only appeared to do so. Disgust, fury, perplexity, had driven it underground. Listening to the Israeli general, awareness of that silken thread was unnerving – as well as the feeling of inevitability in my very presence there, as if the brown bentwood chair I sat on, in this brown-panelled hall adjoining an unknown synagogue, had been waiting for me all these years. Where had I been? Why did I sit here knowing that the mark of the fugitive was on my brow?

That meeting did lead to a certain opening of doors as months went by, though in a detached, social fashion. As in a dream I took a path that had been there all the time but I had passed it by unseeingly. I found myself attending charity committees – that strange growth of social networks that had replaced the old gatherings of the ghetto poor leaning together for comfort, such as the Workers' Circle in the Gorbals. It was a world whose manners, speech, associations of ideas, were as foreign as Oxford had been on my first landfall. As at Oxford but for different reasons, I knew that I had the wrong scent for this herd, and that its members knew it! For one thing this milieu, again like Oxford, was affluent, in class terms as far removed from the Gorbals as Kelvinside in Glasgow or, in London, as distant as the slums of the East End were from Bishop's Avenue in Hampstead. Above all, unlike them, I looked back, in spite of myself, to the culture of *der heim* as it had been lived in the Gorbals, my only link with common ground – and that set me apart, for it was too far back in time. Foolishly, I did not at once realise that the odds were against my finding what I sought among them. I was making the mistake, once again, that Alec had wryly pointed to when I was leaving for Oxford: 'Ye're playin' out o'yer league!'

As in Oxford, I was slow to read the code correctly. One evening, at the end of a charity committee meeting in a house off the Finchley Road near Golders Green, I was in the front hall about to leave, and two young women nearby were also putting on their coats; I remembered that one of them lived not far from me, and on impulse asked her if I might have a lift in her car. I had no ulterior motive; it was thoughtless self-indulgence, for there was a bus stop a few hundred yards away, and the bus would have taken me to within sight of St John's Wood High Street. I had forgotten that I was not in the Gorbals, where no one had owned a car and it was therefore no dishonour to be without one! Here, it seemed, it was. Everyone came in a car, either their own or one belonging to the family. The girl nodded agreement, but with a Galsworthian sniff that told me I had made a mistake. Not to have a car of my own was bad enough, but it was simply not done to advertise the deficiency – almost a dereliction of manhood.

As for the religious quest, progress was even more tentative. As a child I could read and write Hebrew with ease, and was so well-grounded in the ritual that performance was automatic. Now, I had forgotten nearly everything; I was left with a few words of some common Hebrew prayers, such as the blessings over wine and bread. This meant – or so I persuaded myself – that Orthodox services presented too many technical difficulties; it would be simpler to take the first steps of return in one of the Progressive synagogues. Even here I hesitated; what seemed to me their genteel atmosphere was a world away from the buzz and bustle and density I remembered in the Gorbals – the homely traditionalism, and the white-bearded rabbi thundering from the pulpit. Bernard, however, had told me that many things had changed in the Gorbals too, and that the mood of congregations reflected them. Thunder from the pulpit was no longer welcomed anywhere.

I should have foreseen that the latter-day Jewish world of the metropolis, especially the affluent sector I had stumbled into, would have little in common with the ghetto of memory, to which part of me, at least in imagination, longed to return – and which I had chosen to believe had remained as I had left it, not yet fragmented, secularised, assimilated. Here, signs of dereliction were everywhere.

Observance of the dietary laws was fading fast. The *shabbos Goy* was almost extinct – the Gentile invited into a Jewish house to light the fire, or the gas for cooking, on Friday evening and on the eve of major days of observance. Folk memories of *der heim* were recalled less and less; the younger generation found them distasteful, preferring to forget where they had all come from. The time to recall memory would come when most of the first generation, guardians of the living memory, were dead. The third and fourth generations, however, the young adults of the Eighties, would be drawn back to those memories, and even go on organised visits to the countries of the Jewish slaughter, to inspect the silent stones of the old, speechless, ghetto-land.

I went to Friday evening services and sat timidly in the furthest seat at the rear, trying not to be noticed, as father had done on days when he felt, as he put it, not 'good' enough – testimony to *his* faith. I told myself that the technicalities were not crucial – *must* not be – but it was hard to shake off the shame of having forgotten what a boy of thirteen, the age of *Bar Mitzvah*, was expected to know for ever. Slowly, fragments of the old knowledge did surface; I began to recognise Hebrew words by their individual shapes, as one learns to recognise shorthand outlines, and the meanings hesitantly followed after. Such primitive knowledge was not really enough, but it would have to serve.

On a recent stay in London, Bernard had suggested I go with him to a meeting in the East End in celebration of Yiddish writers, an area of Jewish culture he had never talked about before. Was Bernard turning full circle too, homing back to old Jewish visions? Some of his iconoclasm, the hard scepticism, would remain, ignoring inconsistencies as his father had done, in whom humanism and the anarchy of Kropotkin had lived side by side with Jewish identity.

I noticed something different about him, an excitement bubbling close beneath the surface, reminding me of the days, a lifetime away, when I had seen him uplifted by thoughts of Maria in Spain. I did not question him; he would tell me in his own good time. Beneath the excitement, however, was a tiredness – whether physical or mental was not clear – that I could not be sure I had noticed before, but now it was unmistakable; the old neck wound still hurt sometimes, and on those particular days he felt 'more pulled down'. The broad face, once ruddy and shining with vigour and ardour, was dulled as by a perpetual five o'clock shadow, deeply lined about the mouth, the cheeks beginning to sag; but the gleaming dark brown eyes, now somewhat narrowed, retained their sharp, searching glance, and in his step there was still that trace of soldierly swagger.

Entering the low, dark hall, I stepped straight back in time, into the smoke-begrimed meeting room of the Workers' Circle in the Gorbals; here were the same old men hunched into high-collared overcoats, Homburg hats, shiny with years of wear, set low over their ears, white faces sagging with age, cigarettes drooping from lips, coughing with the same old gurgle of suffering lungs. Another shock came – the entire proceedings were to be in Yiddish; it was being spoken all around us. I had not heard Yiddish since my last talk with father, and even then, because I had been away from the Gorbals for so long, it had been a strain to remain 'tuned' to it. I strained to adjust memory, searched for the sympathetic resonance, and amazingly it came; it must have been lying in readiness, quite near the surface. Bernard seemed to have no such difficulty, which was to be expected – living with his mother, and closer, because of his work, to the equivalent older generation in Glasgow.

Listening hard to snatches of conversation, I began to see these men differently – they were still the people of the Workers' Circle, but a sad change had come to them through the years. The eager congregation I remembered from childhood had looked *forward* with hope; the *Shoah* – Hitler's massacre of the Jews – was hidden beyond the horizon, though not far off. Now, their dreaming had turned *backwards* on itself, reached to the far off days when they were young, when the future was still unsullied. In coming here to honour the writers of that epoch, who had explored and explained that past – which was then their *present* – not always with joy, they tried to set themselves once again within those distant days of innocence, recapture their dreams of inevitable redemption, of the 'rightness' of destiny – if only for a brief, illusory moment. The eerie light of the dingy hall emphasised the melancholy character of this unreal coming together – the future they had struggled towards had betrayed them.

A tiny incident showed the bitterness beneath the surface, yet with a tincture of harsh, ageless wit, sharp, childlike, simple.

Under the low ceiling about a hundred chairs were ranked close together; and Bernard and I had managed to find seats in the back row, all the others being taken, near the battered brown swing doors that creaked and banged as newcomers surged in, and finding no seats, shuffled about discontentedly. The proceedings began. The chairman called for silence: 'Shoosh, please, gentlemen! Shoosh.' A clear space behind us filled with yet more arrivals, loud in complaint at having to remain standing, doubtless tiring for their white-haired years. In the corner nearest the door was a stack, about five feet high, of wooden trestle tables, their hinged legs and metal supports folded flat beneath them; presumably the hall was used at other times as a communal dining and reading room – glass-fronted bookshelves, and a rack of newspapers stood in a far corner. The chairman rose to introduce the speakers who sat with him at a table covered with a crisp white cloth; he struggled to make himself heard above the noise at the back of the hall, where some of the new arrivals had hit upon the idea of dragging some of the tables down and setting them in lower stacks on the floor to form benches to sit on. There followed crash after crash as each table hit the floor, and then a huge clatter as they were piled afresh by these old, determined, impatient hands, to make benches about a foot high, the whole cacophony battering down on our heads in thunderous reverberations from the low ceiling and hard cement walls. From all sides came renewed hisses of 'Shoosh! Shoosh!' but to no effect. At last, from near at hand someone shouted angrily: 'Can't you show respect!' There came a gruff retort from one of the jostling newcomers: '*You* can talk about respect! You've *got* a seat!'

A shrewd enough comment on life, it summed up many things, above all the unyielding, bitter realism of these veterans who had fought their way through, and in their turn had been left behind –

in every sense. There were a few laughs around us, a salute to a maverick independence. And then the laugh cut itself off, for there was here a reminder, too, that the cold wind of chaos, as ever, was too close for comfort.

Bernard smiled in admiration at the rebellious old men jostling for space on the tables behind us, his face almost sunny, as it had been in the old days of certainty, a surge of kindness almost paternal, as if they were his children – as in a sense some of them were, for with his union concerns he now combined care for elderly workers. I too felt compassion, followed by guilt, for it struck me that I was looking at them as an outsider, too coolly, with no indulgence, my sympathy intellectual, not emotional as Bernard's was; and I wished it were. So this was where *my* pilgrimage had taken me, the final dead end – here too I found no link, as Alec in the factory had foretold, warning me against going to Oxford: 'Ye'll have thrown away the wurrld ye knew ... And if ye try tae find yer way back it'll be too late, because *yew'll* 'ave changed as well – an' there'll be nowhere tae go back *tae*.'

Bernard must have sensed these thoughts, and understood. As we walked away from the meeting, he said: 'You shouldn't let it get you down – stop being a perfectionist. You've got to compromise. We're none of us where we wanted to be! One can't wait for ever.'

The word 'perfectionist' was startling. I had tried many paths – that was true – blindly, with no sure guide, only Siren songs.

We walked on in silence. Then he said, with a quick grunt of a laugh, at once suppressed: 'I've got something to tell *you*!'

I felt I already knew, and was amazed to find within me a furtive envy, but also happiness for him. He too had travelled far, and been cheated of so much.

In a taut voice he said, looking straight ahead: 'Life seems to be a matter of surrendering dreams! – one after another. Rearguard actions, fighting every inch of the way, giving up one objective after another, until you're finally cornered. After Maria was killed I couldn't think of *any* other woman, not in that way. And so it had to be Jeanie and Kirstie and the rest – what did it matter? Of course mother knew, she always did. She brought it all out into the open

629

one day. "You're forty-five! You can't throw your life away like this. I'm not going to last much longer – you know that." And so on and so on. Well, life chooses its own moments to shove your back against the wall, doesn't it? Apart from work, what had I got? A whole area of my life was shut away! Uninvolved, uncommitted, and strangely enough there *was* a feeling gnawing at me inside – demanding release, engagement, what did the words matter? And mother saw that. I said to myself: *Do something* – you can't hang around like this for ever! I knew what I had been doing all this time – unbelievable! I had been waiting – yes, waiting.' He paused, and said in almost a whisper: 'hoping against hope that another, what shall I say – *completeness* – as it had been with Maria, would drop from Heaven! Stupidity! That only happens when you're very young, as I was when I found Maria. Love! – when you look at it calmly, is really ridiculous after all ...'

I was saddened. Who was he deceiving? Bernard the realist, his feet planted so firmly – where was he now?

And so he had let his mother *redda shiddach* – arrange a match. It was with a cousin of poor Meyer's, who I had met on the Beattock Summit road when I was cycling for the first time to Oxford, and he was about to go on a Singapore posting, never to return. There was something warming in this link with him, with brave, unquestioning Meyer, who had fought the 'frighteners' sent to beat up old Mr Fredericks for not paying the weekly 'shilling and three-ha'pence' to the menodge, and had fled to the Army to escape them. So the thread of our old life was not completely broken after all. Hilda was about thirty – 'a serious girl', Bernard's mother called her, 'who knows how to keep a good Jewish home and look after a man.'

Bernard said she was a decent sort: 'We get on pretty well. It's time I handed in my chips.'

I was happy for him. Some fragment of the unfairness of life had been cancelled.

I had no idea that another such sign was about to touch *me*.

Jacqueline helped me to put order into my kaleidoscopic scattering of visions. She brought a shining innocence and resolve to our marriage – not serene but fiery; and the fire was necessary. The shift of forces that I had felt within me at last took control. I wrote a great deal, went far across the world in every sense – perspectives of fulfilment.

Though she is Jewish, in marrying her I did not go 'back' – that, I at last saw, was impossible; and like Bernard surrendering his objectives, I gave that one up – though dreams and visions, still tenacious, would return. There was no 'back' left. When I took her to see the Gorbals, by that time little more than a collection of dark grey ruins awaiting the bulldozers, it looked as foreign and as horrifying as a deserted battlefield. True enough! It was she who suggested that I look at that place with a fresh eye; consider how it made me, where it took me – and takes me still.

Here, self-enquiry has taken me deeper than I ever imagined, to show me that nothing, no perception, no vision, be the light however powerful and the images hard-edged and seemingly unambiguous, will ever answer the questions that possessed me when I left the Gorbals to cycle to Oxford long ago. Yet the ineluctable pursuit remains in command, intransigent as always, and of course no settlement, no halting place will ever be found. And Gorbals works upon the spirit implacably – how could it be otherwise? – still kneading the original clay, continuing its questioning, the Sphinx constantly changing the terms of the riddle, never to be solved. The temptation grows – more dangerous than all the others – to create my own, and usurp her sovereignty once and for all.